STEVE

S0-CMS-033

BARNES & NOBLE

Word Speller and Divider

A guide to correct spelling and word division

BARNES
& NOBLE
B O O K S
NEW YORK

Copyright © 1996 by Market House Books Ltd

This edition published by Barnes & Noble, Inc.,
by arrangement with Market House Books Ltd

All rights reserved. No part of this book may be
reproduced in any manner whatsoever without
written permission of the Publisher.

1997 Barnes & Noble Books

ISBN 1-5661-9775-9

Compiled and typeset by
Market House Books Ltd, Aylesbury, UK

Printed and bound in the United States of America

97 98 99 00 01 M 9 8 7 6 5 4 3 2 1

RRDC

A GUIDE TO THIS BOOK

The *Barnes & Noble Word Speller and Divider* consists of a spelling list together with a short section listing the rules of spelling and punctuation. The spelling list contains normal vocabulary words and some trademarks. It does not include names of people or places except when these are used as common nouns (e.g. **Camembert**) or form part of a two-word compound noun (e.g. **Alzheimer's disease**.) In general, two-word compounds (e.g. phrasal nouns and verbs) are listed only if either or both elements of the compound do not appear separately in the spelling list or to emphasize the distinction between a two-word compound and its hyphenated derivative (e.g. **air conditioning**; **air-conditioned**).

Centered dots within a word show the acceptable points for dividing a word at the end of a typeset line. These divisions are phonetic rather than etymological, i.e. they correspond to syllabification breaks (e.g. **cof•fin**, **di•ges•tion**). Syllabification breaks that are not acceptable points for word division are not shown. For example, **contra•band** cannot be broken after the first syllable (*con-*).

A few words that are spelled the same way have completely different senses according to which syllable is stressed. Such words have two entries in the *Speller and Divider*, with a stress mark preceding the stressed syllable, e.g. **'de•sert** (barren region); **de•'sert** (abandon).

Inflections are included after a listed word if they are irregular; rules for forming inflections are given in the **SPELLING RULES** at the end of this book. Irregular inflections include noun plurals, e.g.

    bu•reau (*pl* •**reaus** *or* •**reaux**),

present participles and past tenses of verbs, e.g.

    bug (**bug•ging, bugged**),

and comparative and superlative forms of adjectives, e.g.

    bur•ly (•**lier**, •**liest**).

Variant spellings and variant forms of words are given, with the most common variant as the main entry word; the less common variants are given in the form of references to this word, e.g.

blath•er (*or* **bleth•**)
bleth•er *variant of* **blather**

British spellings (including inflections) are treated as variants, e.g.

co•lor (*Brit* **•lour**)
bev•el (**•el•ing**, **•eled**; *Brit* **•el•ling**, **•elled**)

When giving inflections and variants, only the syllable(s) that differ from the main entry word are shown. The variant spellings *-ise* and *-isation* for the many verbs and nouns ending in *-ize* and *-ization* are not given because the spellings *-ize* and *-ization* are preferred in both American and British English. Some exceptions to this rule are listed in the **SPELLING RULES (Spelling Problems)**.

Short definitions (glosses) distinguish sets of words that have similar spellings, or that have different senses according to whether they have an initial capital or lower-case letter. When these words are separated from each other alphabetically, cross-references to other words in the set are also given. For example:

can•non artillery; *cf* **canon**
can•on priest; decree; *cf* **cannon**

Chi•nook American Indian
chi•nook wind

its of it
it's it is

Glosses are also given for a few British words when these differ from the American form of the word, e.g.

bur•gle (*Brit*) burglarize

Some words are used as only one part of speech (e.g. noun, adjective, or verb) while others can function as nouns and/or verbs and adjectives. For example, **mug** can be used both as a noun and a verb. Parts of speech are not given unless they are irregular. Therefore **mug** appears as:

mug (**mug•ging**, **mugged**),

indicating that the noun mug has a regular plural form but the verb inflections are irregular. If a word has two or more irregular inflected forms parts of speech are provided for all irregular forms. Thus **dainty** appears as:

dain•ty (*n, pl* •**ties**; *adj* •**tier**, •**ti•est**)

Parts of speech are also given for nouns or adjectives (single words or hyphenated compounds) formed from two-word phrasal verbs or nouns, to avoid confusion with the two-word form, e.g.

break-in (*n*) – derived from the verb **break in**
inner-city (*adj*) – derived from the noun **inner city**

The *Speller and Divider* includes entries for common misspellings, with the correct spellings indicated. Such entries do not have centered dots for syllabification breaks and they are preceded by an asterisk to alert the reader that the spelling is wrong, e.g.

*hankerchief *incorrect spelling of* **handkerchief**
hand•ker•chief (*NOT* hankerchief)

Abbreviations used in the Speller and Divider

adj adjective	*masc* masculine
adv adverb	*n* noun
Brit British	*pl* plural
cf compare	*sing* singular
fem feminine	*vb* verb

A

aard•vark
aback
aba•cus (*pl* •cuses
  or •ci)
aba•lo•ne
aban•don
aban•doned
aban•don•ment
abase
abase•ment
abash
abashed
abate
abate•ment
ab•at•toir
ab•ba•tial
ab•bess
ab•bey
ab•bot
ab•bre•vi•ate
ab•bre•via•tion
ab•bre•via•tor
abcess incorrect
  spelling of abscess
ab•di•cate
ab•di•ca•tion
ab•di•ca•tor
ab•do•men
ab•domi•nal
ab•duct
ab•duc•tion
ab•duc•tor
abed
ab•er•rance (*or*
  •ran•cy)
ab•er•rant

ab•er•ra•tion
abet (abet•ting,
  abet•ted)
abet•ment
abet•tor (*or* •ter)
abey•ance
abey•ant
ab•hor (•hor•ring,
  •horred)
ab•hor•rence
ab•hor•rent
ab•hor•rer
abid•ance
abide (abid•ing,
  abode *or* abid•ed)
abid•er
abid•ing
abid•ing•ly
abil•ity (*pl* •ities)
abio•sis
abiot•ic
ab•ject
ab•jec•tion
ab•ju•ra•tion
ab•jure renounce;
  cf adjure
ab•jur•er
ablaze
able
able-bodied
ab•lu•tion
ab•lu•tion•ary
ably
ab•ne•gate
ab•ne•ga•tion
ab•ne•ga•tor

ab•nor•mal
ab•nor•mal•ity (*pl*
  •ities)
ab•nor•mal•ly
aboard
abode
abol•ish
abol•ish•er
abol•ish•ment
abo•li•tion
abo•li•tion•ary
abo•li•tion•ism
abo•li•tion•ist
abomi•nable
abomi•nably
abomi•nate
abomi•na•tion
abomi•na•tor
abo•rigi•nal
abo•rigi•ne
abort
ahor•ti•fa•cient
abor•tion
abor•tion•ist
abor•tive
abound
about
about-face (*Brit*
  about-turn)
above
above•board
ab•ra•ca•dab•ra
abra•dant
abrade
abrad•er
abra•sion

abra•sive
ab•re•ac•tion
abreast
abridg•able (*Brit also* abridge•)
abridge
abridg•er
abridg•ment (*Brit also* abridge•)
abroad
ab•ro•gate
ab•ro•ga•tion
ab•ro•ga•tor
ab•rupt
ab•rupt•ly
ab•rup•tion
ab•rupt•ness
ab•scess (*NOT* abcess)
ab•scis•sa (*pl* •sas *or* •sae)
ab•scond
ab•scond•er
ab•seil
ab•sence
ab•sent
ab•sen•tee
ab•sen•tee•ism
ab•sent•er
ab•sent•ly
absent-minded
absent-minded•ly
absent-minded•ness
ab•sinthe (*or* •sinth)
ab•so•lute
ab•so•lute•ly
ab•so•lu•tion
ab•so•lut•ism

ab•solv•able
ab•solve
ab•solv•er
ab•sorb take into or permeate; *cf* adsorb
ab•sorb•abil•ity
ab•sorb•able
ab•sorb•en•cy
ab•sorb•ent
ab•sorb•er
ab•sorb•ing
ab•sorp•tion
ab•sorp•tive
ab•stain
ab•stain•er
ab•ste•mi•ous
ab•sten•tion
ab•sti•nence
ab•sti•nent
ab•stract
ab•stract•ed
ab•stract•ed•ly
ab•strac•tion
ab•strac•tive
ab•struse
ab•struse•ness
ab•surd
ab•surd•ity (*or* •ness; *pl* •ities *or* •nesses)
abun•dance
abun•dant
abuse
abus•er
abu•sive
abu•sive•ness
abut (abut•ting, abut•ted)

abys•mal
abys•mal•ly
abyss
abys•sal
Ab•ys•sin•ian
aca•cia
aca•deme
aca•demia
aca•dem•ic
aca•dem•ical•ly
acad•emi•cian
acad•emy (*pl* •emies)
acan•thus (*pl* •thuses *or* •thi)
ac•cede
ac•ced•ence
ac•ced•er
ac•cel•er•able
ac•cel•er•ant
ac•cel•er•ate
ac•cel•era•tion
ac•cel•era•tive (*or* •tory)
ac•cel•era•tor
ac•cent
ac•cen•tual
ac•cen•tu•ate
ac•cen•tua•tion
ac•cept
ac•cept•abil•ity (*or* •able•ness)
ac•cept•able
ac•cept•ably
ac•cept•ance
ac•cept•ant
ac•cep•ter (*or* •tor)
ac•cess
ac•ces•sa•ry (*pl*

•ries) *variant spelling of* accessory
ac•ces•sibil•ity
ac•ces•sible
ac•ces•sibly
ac•ces•sion
ac•ces•sion•al
ac•ces•so•ry (*or* •sa•ry; *pl* •ries)
ac•ci•dent
ac•ci•den•tal
ac•ci•den•tal•ly
ac•claim
ac•cla•ma•tion
ac•clama•tory
ac•cli•mat•able (*or* •ma•tiz•able)
ac•cli•ma•tion (*or* •ma•ti•za•tion)
ac•cli•mate (*or* •ma•tize)
ac•cli•ma•tiz•er
ac•cliv•ity (*pl* •ities)
ac•co•lade
ac•com•mo•date (*NOT* accomodate)
ac•com•mo•dat•ing
ac•com•mo•dat• ing•ly
ac•com•mo•da•tion
ac•com•mo•da•tive
accomodate incorrect spelling of accommodate
ac•com•pa•ni•ment
ac•com•pa•nist

ac•com•pa•ny (•nies, •ny•ing, •nied)
ac•com•plice
ac•com•plish
ac•com•plish•able
ac•com•plish•er
ac•com•plish•ment
ac•cord
ac•cord•able
ac•cord•ance
ac•cord•ant
ac•cord•er
ac•cord•ing
ac•cord•ing•ly
ac•cor•di•on
ac•cor•di•on•ist
ac•cost
ac•count
ac•count•abil•ity
ac•count•able
ac•count•ably
ac•count•an•cy
ac•count•ant
ac•count•ing
ac•cou•ter (*Brit* •tre)
ac•cou•ter•ment (*Brit* •tre•)
ac•cred•it
ac•credi•ta•tion
ac•crete
ac•cre•tion
ac•cre•tive (*or* ac•cre•tion•ary)
ac•cru•al (*or* •ment)
ac•crue (•cru•ing, •crued)

ac•cu•mu•lable
ac•cu•mu•late
ac•cu•mu•la•tion
ac•cu•mu•la•tive
ac•cu•mu•la•tor
ac•cu•ra•cy (*pl* •cies)
ac•cu•rate
ac•cu•rate•ly
ac•curs•ed
ac•cus•al
ac•cu•sa•tion
ac•cu•sa•tive
ac•cu•sa•to•rial (*or* •tory)
ac•cuse
ac•cused
ac•cus•er
ac•cus•ing•ly
ac•cus•tom
ac•cus•tomed
ace
acen•tric
ac•er•bate
acer•bic
acer•bity (*pl* •bities)
aces•cence (*or* •cen•cy)
ac•et•al•de•hyde
ac•etate
acetic acid
aceti•fi•ca•tion
aceti•fy (•fies, •fy•ing, •fied)
ac•etone
acety•lene
ache
ach•ing•ly

achiev•able
achieve
achieve•ment
achiev•er
ach•ro•mat
ach•ro•mat•ic
achro•ma•tism (or •tic•ity)
achro•ma•tize
a•chro•mic
acid
acid-fast
acid-forming
acid•ic
acidi•fi•able
acidi•fi•ca•tion
acidi•fi•er
acidi•fy (•fies, •fy•ing, •fied)
acid•ity (pl •ities)
acid•ness
aci•do•sis
aci•dot•ic
acidu•late
acidu•la•tion
acidu•lous (or •lent)
ack-ack
ac•knowl•edge
ac•knowl•edge•able
ac•knowl•edg•er
ac•knowl•edg•ment (Brit also •edge•)
acme peak
acne skin disease
aco•lyte
aco•nite (or •ni•tum)
acorn

acous•tic (or •ti•cal)
acous•ti•cal•ly
acous•tics
ac•quaint
ac•quaint•ance
ac•quaint•ance•ship
ac•quaint•ed
ac•qui•esce
ac•qui•es•cence
ac•qui•es•cent
ac•quir•able
ac•quire
ac•quire•ment
ac•quir•er
ac•qui•si•tion
ac•quisi•tive
ac•quisi•tive•ness
ac•quit (•quit•ting, •quit•ted)
ac•quit•tal
ac•quit•tance
ac•quit•ter
acre
acre•age
ac•rid
acrid•ity (or •ness)
ac•ri•mo•ni•ous
ac•ri•mo•ny (pl •nies)
ac•ro•bat
ac•ro•bat•ic
ac•ro•bati•cal•ly
ac•ro•bat•ics
ac•ro•nym
ac•ro•nym•ic (or acrony•mous)
ac•ro•pho•bia

ac•ro•pho•bic
acropo•lis
across
across-the-board
acros•tic
acros•ti•cal•ly
acryl•ic
act
act•able
act•ing
ac•tin•ium
ac•tion
ac•tion•able
action-packed
ac•ti•vate
ac•ti•va•tion
ac•ti•va•tor
ac•tive
ac•tive•ly
ac•tive•ness
ac•tiv•ism
ac•tiv•ist
ac•tiv•ity (pl •ities)
ac•tor
ac•tress
ac•tual
ac•tu•al•ity (pl •ities)
ac•tu•ali•za•tion
ac•tu•al•ize
ac•tu•al•ly
ac•tu•ari•al
ac•tu•ary (pl •aries)
ac•tu•ate
ac•tua•tion
ac•tua•tor
acu•ity
acu•men

acu•punc•ture
acute
acute•ly
acute•ness
ad•age
ada•gio (*pl* •gios)
ada•mant
adapt
adapt•abil•ity (*or* •able•ness)
adapt•able
adapt•ably
ad•ap•ta•tion
adapt•er (*or* •or)
adap•tive
add
ad•den•dum (*pl* •da)
ad•der snake
add•er calculator
ad•dict
ad•dic•tion
ad•dic•tive
ad•di•tion
ad•di•tion•al
ad•di•tion•al•ly
ad•di•tive
ad•dle
ad•dress
ad•dressee
ad•dress•er (*or* •dres•sor)
ad•duce
ad•duce•able (*or* •duc•ible)
ad•enoi•dal
ad•enoids
adept
ad•equa•cy

ad•equate
ad•here
ad•her•ence
ad•her•ent
ad•he•sion
ad•he•sive
ad•he•sive•ness
ad hoc
adieu (*pl* adieus *or* adieux)
adi•pose
adi•pos•ity
ad•ja•cen•cy
ad•ja•cent
ad•jec•ti•val
ad•jec•tive
ad•join
ad•join•ing
ad•journ
ad•journ•ment
ad•judge
ad•ju•di•cate
ad•ju•di•ca•tion
ad•ju•di•ca•tive
ad•ju•di•ca•tor
ad•junct
ad•junc•tive
ad•ju•ra•tion
ad•jure appeal to solemnly; *cf* abjure
ad•jur•er (*or* •ju•ror)
ad•just
ad•just•able
ad•just•ment
ad•ju•tan•cy
ad•ju•tant
ad lib (*adv*)

ad-lib (*vb*; -libbing, -libbed)
ad•min•is•ter
ad•min•is•trable
ad•min•is•trate
ad•min•is•tra•tion
ad•min•is•tra•tive
ad•min•is•tra•tor
ad•mi•ra•ble
ad•mi•ra•bly
ad•mi•ral
ad•mi•ral•ty (*pl* •ties)
ad•mi•ra•tion
ad•mire
ad•mirer
ad•mir•ing•ly
ad•mis•sibil•ity (*or* •sible•ness)
ad•mis•sible
ad•mis•sion
ad•mis•sive
ad•mit (•mit•ting, •mit•ted)
ad•mit•tance
ad•mit•ted•ly
ad•mix
ad•mix•ture
ad•mon•ish
ad•mon•ish•er
ad•mon•ish•ment
ad•mo•ni•tion
ad•moni•tory
ad nau•seam
ado
ado•be
ado•les•cence
ado•les•cent
adopt

adopt•able

adopt•ed

adop•tee

adopt•er

adop•tion

adop•tive

ador•able

ador•ably

ado•ra•tion

adore

ador•er

adorn

adorn•ment

ad•re•nal

adrena•line

adrift

adroit

adroit•ness

ad•sorb
    accumulate on a
    surface; cf absorb

ad•sorb•abil•ity

ad•sorb•able

ad•sor•bent

ad•sorp•tion

adu•late

adu•la•tion

adu•la•tor

adu•la•tory

adult

adul•ter•ant

adul•ter•ate

adul•tera•tion

adul•ter•ator

adul•ter•er (fem
    •ess)

adul•ter•ous

adul•tery (pl
    •teries)

adult•hood

ad•um•brate

ad•um•bra•tion

ad•vance

ad•vanced

ad•vance•ment

ad•van•tage

ad•van•ta•geous

ad•van•ta•geous•
    ness

ad•vent

ad•ven•ti•tious

ad•ven•tive

ad•ven•ture

ad•ven•tur•er (fem
    •ess)

ad•ven•tur•ism

ad•ven•tur•ist

ad•ven•tur•ous

ad•verb

ad•ver•bial

ad•ver•sary (pl
    •saries)

ad•verse

ad•ver•sity (pl
    •sities)

ad•vert•ence (or
    •en•cy)

ad•vert•ent•ly

ad•ver•tise (NOT
    advertize)

ad•ver•tise•ment

ad•ver•tis•er

ad•ver•tis•ing

*advertize
    incorrect spelling
    of advertise

ad•vice

ad•vis•abil•ity

ad•vis•able

ad•vise

ad•vised

ad•vis•ed•ly

ad•vise•ment

ad•vis•er (or
    •vi•sor)

ad•vi•so•ry

ad•vo•ca•cy (pl
    •cies)

ad•vo•cate

ad•vo•ca•tion

ad•vo•ca•tory

adz (or adze)

aegis (or egis)

aeon Brit spelling
    of eon

aer•ate

aera•tion

aera•tor

aer•ial relating to
    air; cf ariel

aeri•al•ist

aerie variant
    spelling of eyrie

aeri•fi•ca•tion

aeri•fy (•fies,
    •fy•ing, •fied)

aero

aero•bal•lis•tics

aero•bat•ics

aer•obe

aero•bic

aero•bics

aero•drome Brit
    spelling of
    airdrome

aero•dy•nam•ic

aero•dy•nami•cal•ly

aero•dy•nam•ics

aero•foil *Brit spelling of* airfoil

aero•mechan•ic

aero•mechani•cal

aero•mechan•ics

aero•naut

aero•nau•ti•cal (*or* aero•nau•tic)

aero•naut•ics

aero•plane *Brit spelling of* airplane

aero•sol

aero•space

aero•sphere

aero•ther•mo•dy•nam•ic

aero•ther•mo•dy•nam•ics

aes•thete (*or* es•)

aes•thet•ic (*or* es•)

aes•theti•cal•ly (*or* es•)

aes•the•ti•cian (*or* es•)

aes•theti•cism (*or* es•)

aes•thet•ics (*or* es•)

aes•ti•vate *variant spelling of* estivate

aes•ti•va•tion *variant spelling of* estivation

aether *variant spelling of* ether

(hypothetical medium)

aeti•ol•ogy *Brit spelling of* etiology

afar

af•fabil•ity

af•fable

af•fably

af•fair

af•fect have an effect on; *cf* effect (*vb*)

af•fec•ta•tion

af•fect•ed

af•fect•ed•ly

af•fect•ed•ness

af•fect•ing

af•fect•ing•ly

af•fec•tion

af•fec•tion•ate

af•fec•tive

af•fer•ent conducting inward; *cf* efferent

af•fi•da•vit

af•fili•ate

af•filia•tion

af•fini•tive

af•fin•ity (*pl* •ities)

af•firm

af•firm•able

af•fir•ma•tion

af•firma•tive

af•firm•er (*or* •ant)

af•fix

af•fix•ture

af•flict

af•flic•tion

af•flic•tive

af•flu•ence

af•flu•ent

af•ford

af•for•est

af•for•esta•tion

af•fray

af•fright

af•front

Af•ghan hound; people

af•ghan shawl

afi•cio•na•do (*pl* •dos)

afield

afire

aflame

afloat

aflut•ter

afoot

afore•men•tioned

afore•said

afore•thought

afraid

afresh

Af•ri•can

Afro-American

Afro-Caribbean

aft

af•ter

after•birth

after•burner

after•burning

after•care

after•deck

after•effect

after•glow

after•heat

after•image

after•life
after•math
after•noon
after•shave
after•shock
after•taste
after•thought
after•ward (*Brit* •wards)
after•word
again
against
agape
agar (*or* agar-agar)
ag•ate
aga•ve
age (ag•ing, aged)
aged (*adj, n*)
age•ing *Brit spelling of* aging
age•ism
age•ist
age•less
agen•cy (*pl* •cies)
agen•da (*or* •dum; *pl* •das *or* •dums)
agent
agent pro•vo•ca•teur (*pl* agents pro•vo•ca•teurs)
age-old
ag•glom•er•ate
ag•glom•era•tion
ag•glu•ti•nabil•ity
ag•glu•ti•nable
ag•glu•ti•nant
ag•glu•ti•nate
ag•glu•ti•na•tion
ag•glu•ti•na•tive

ag•gran•dize
ag•gran•dize•ment
ag•gran•diz•er
ag•gra•vate
ag•gra•va•tion
ag•gre•gate
ag•gre•ga•tion
ag•gres•sion
ag•gres•sive
ag•gres•sor
ag•grieve
ag•griev•ed•ly
aghast
ag•ile
agil•ity
ag•ing (*Brit* age•)
agi•tate
agi•ta•tion
agi•ta•tor
aglit•ter
aglow
ag•nos•tic
ag•nos•ti•cism
ago
agog
ago•nize
ago•niz•ing•ly
ago•ny (*pl* •nies)
ago•ra•pho•bia
ago•ra•pho•bic
agrar•ian
agrari•an•ism
agree (agree•ing, agreed)
agree•able
agree•able•ness
agree•ably
agreed
agree•ment

ag•ri•busi•ness
ag•ri•cul•tur•al
ag•ri•cul•ture
ag•ri•cul•tur•ist (*or* •tur•al•ist)
ag•ro•nom•ic (*or* •nomi•cal)
ag•ro•nom•ics
agrono•mist
agrono•my
aground
ah
aha
ahead
ahoy
aid help
aide assistant
aide-de-camp (*pl* aides-)
aide-mémoire (*pl* aides-)
aid•er
AIDS (or Aids)
aikido
ail
ailan•thus (*pl* •thuses)
ailer•on
ail•ing
ail•ment
ailu•ro•phobe
ailu•ro•phobia
aim
aim•less
aim•less•ness
air atmosphere; tune; ventilate; *cf* e'er; ere; heir
air•borne

air•brick
air•brush
air•burst
air-conditioned
air con•di•tion•er
air con•di•tion•ing
air-cool
air•craft (*pl* •craft)
air•crew
air•drome (*Brit* aero•)
air•drop (•drop•ping, •dropped)
air-dry (-dries, -drying, -dried)
air•field
air•flow
air•foil (*Brit* aero•)
airi•ly
airi•ness
air•ing
air•less
air•less•ness
air•lift
air•line
air•lin•er
air•lock
air•mail
air•man (*pl* •men)
air•plane (*Brit* aero•)
air•port
air•ship
air•sick
air•sick•ness
air•space
air•speed
air•stream

air•strip
air•tight
air-to-air
air•waves
air•way
air•worthi•ness
air•worthy
airy (airi•er, airi•est) breezy; light; *cf* eyrie
aisle passageway; *cf* isle
aitch
aitch•bone
ajar
akim•bo
akin
al•ba•core
ala•bas•ter
à la carte
alack
alac•ri•tous
alac•rity
ala•meda
alarm
alarmed
alarm•ing
alarm•ing•ly
alarm•ism
alarm•ist
alas
Al•ba•nian
al•ba•tross
al•be•it
al•bi•nism
al•bi•no (*pl* •nos)
al•bum
al•bu•men white of egg; *cf* albumin

al•bu•menize
al•bu•min a protein; *cf* albumen
al•bu•mi•nous
al•chem•ic (*or* •chemi•cal, •chem•is•tic)
al•che•mist
al•che•my (*pl* •mies)
al•co•hol
al•co•hol•ic
al•co•hol•ism
al•cove
al•de•hyde
al•der
ale
alea•to•ry
alert
alert•ness
alexia
al•fal•fa
al•fres•co
al•ga (*pl* algae)
al•gal
al•gar•ro•ba (*or* •ga•ro•ba)
al•ge•bra
al•ge•bra•ic (*or* •brai•cal)
al•ge•brai•cal•ly
al•ge•bra•ist
al•gi•cide
al•gid
al•golo•gist
al•gol•ogy
Al•gon•quian (*or* •kian)

Al•gon•quin (*or* •kin; *pl* •quins, •quin *or* •kins, •kin)
al•go•rithm
al•go•rith•mic
ali•as (*pl* •ases)
ali•bi (*pl* •bis)
al•ien
al•ien•abil•ity
al•ien•able
al•ien•ate
al•iena•tion
al•iena•tor
al•ien•ism
al•ien•ist
alight (alight•ing, alight•ed *or* alit)
align
align•ment
alike
ali•ment
ali•men•ta•ry
ali•men•ta•tion
ali•mo•ny
alive
al•ka•li (*pl* •lis *or* •lies)
al•kal•ic
al•ka•li•fy (•fies, •fy•ing, •fied)
al•ka•line
al•ka•lin•ity
al•ka•loid
all
al•lay
*alledge incorrect spelling of allege
al•le•ga•tion

al•lege (*NOT* alledge)
al•leged
al•leg•ed•ly
al•le•giance
al•le•gori•cal (*or* •gor•ic)
al•le•gori•cal•ly
al•le•go•rist
al•le•gori•za•tion
al•le•go•rize
al•le•go•ry (*pl* •ries)
al•le•gro (*pl* •gros)
al•le•luia (*or* hal•le•lu•jah)
al•ler•gen
al•ler•gen•ic
al•ler•gic
al•ler•gist
al•ler•gy (*pl* •gies)
al•le•vi•ate
al•le•via•tion
al•le•via•tive
al•le•via•tor
al•ley narrow lane; *cf* ally
alley•way
al•li•ance
al•lied
al•lies *pl of* ally
al•li•ga•tor
all-important
all-inclusive
al•lit•e•rate
al•lit•era•tion
al•lit•era•tive
al•lo•cate
al•lo•ca•tion

al•lo•path (*or* •lopa•thist)
al•lo•path•ic
al•lo•pathi•cal•ly
al•lopa•thy
al•lot (•lot•ting, •lot•ted)
al•lot•ment
al•lot•tee
all-out (*adj*)
all-over
al•low
al•low•able
al•low•ance
al•low•ed•ly
al•loy
all-purpose
all-round (*adj*)
all-rounder
all•spice
all-star (*adj*)
all-time (*adj*)
all together all at the same time; *cf* altogether
al•lude refer; *cf* elude; illude
al•lure
al•lure•ment
al•lur•er
al•lur•ing
al•lu•sion reference; *cf* illusion
al•lu•sive suggestive; *cf* elusive; illusive
al•lu•sive•ness
al•lu•vial

al•lu•vium (*pl* •viums *or* •via) soil; *cf* eluvium

ally (*vb* allies, ally•ing, allied; *n*, *pl* allies) friend; *cf* alley

al•ma•nac

al•mighti•ness

al•mighty

al•mond

al•mon•er

al•most

alms

aloe (*pl* aloes) plant

aloes purgative drug

aloft

alone

along

along•shore

along•side

aloof

aloof•ness

alo•pecia

aloud

alp

al•paca

alpen•stock

al•pha

al•pha•bet

al•pha•beti•cal (*or* •bet•ic)

al•pha•beti•cal•ly

al•pha•beti•za•tion

al•pha•bet•ize

al•pha•bet•iz•er

al•pha•nu•mer•ic (*or* al•pha•mer•ic)

al•pha•nu•meri•cal•ly (*or* al•pha•meri•cal•ly)

Al•pine of the Alps

al•pine of mountains

al•ready

al•right *variant spelling of* all right, *regarded by some as nonstandard*

Al•sa•tian

also

also-ran

al•tar table in church; *cf* alter

altar•piece

al•ter to change; *cf* altar

al•ter•abil•ity

al•ter•able

al•tera•tion

al•ter•cate

al•ter•ca•tion

al•ter ego

al•ter•nant

al•ter•nate

al•ter•nate•ly

al•ter•na•tion

al•ter•na•tive

al•ter•na•tive•ly

al•ter•na•tor

al•though

al•time•ter

al•tim•etry

al•ti•tude

al•ti•tu•di•nal

alto (*pl* altos)

al•to•geth•er entirely; *cf* all together

al•tru•ism

al•tru•ist

al•tru•is•tic

al•tru•is•ti•cal•ly

alum

alu•mi•na

alu•min•ium *Brit spelling of* aluminum

alu•mi•nize

alu•mi•nous

alu•mi•num (*Brit* •min•ium)

alum•nus (*fem* •na; *pl* •ni, *fem* •nae)

al•ways

alys•sum

Alzheimer's dis•ease

amal•gam (*NOT* amalgum)

amal•gam•ate

amal•gama•tion

amalgum incorrect spelling of amalgam

amanu•en•sis (*pl* •ses)

ama•ranth

ama•ryl•lis

amass

amass•er

ama•teur

ama•teur•ish

ama•teur•ism
ama•tory (*or* •to•ri•al)
amaze
amaze•ment
amaz•ing
amaz•ing•ly
Ama•zon
Ama•zo•nian
am•bas•sa•dor
am•bas•sa•dor•ial
am•bas•sa•dor•ship
am•bas•sa•dress
am•ber
amber•gris
am•bi•dex•ter•ity (*or* •dex•trous•ness)
am•bi•dex•trous
am•bi•ence (*or* •ance)
am•bi•ent
am•bi•gu•ity (*pl* •ities)
am•bigu•ous
am•bigu•ous•ness
am•bit
am•bi•tion
am•bi•tious
am•biva•lence (*or* •len•cy)
am•biva•lent
am•ble
am•bler
am•bro•sia
am•bro•sial (*or* •sian)
am•bu•lance
am•bu•lant

am•bu•late
am•bu•la•tion
am•bu•la•tory
am•bush
ame•ba (*or* amoe•; *pl* •bas *or* •bae)
am•ebia•sis (*or* •oebia•)
ame•bic (*or* amoe•)
ame•boid (*or* amoe•)
ame•lio•rate
ame•lio•ra•tion
ame•lio•ra•tive
ame•lio•ra•tor
amen
ame•nabil•ity (*or* •nable•ness)
ame•nable
ame•nably
amend change; *cf* emend
amend•able
amend•er
amend•ment
amends
amen•ity (*pl* •ities)
amen•or•rhea (*Brit* •rhoea)
Ameri•can
Ameri•ca•na
Ameri•can•ism
Ameri•cani•za•tion
Ameri•can•ize
Am•er•in•dian
am•ethyst
ami•abil•ity (*or* •able•ness)
ami•able

ami•ably
ami•cabil•ity (*or* •cable•ness)
ami•cable
ami•cably
amid
amidst
ami•no acid
amir *variant spelling of* emir
amirate *variant spelling of* emirate
amiss
am•ity (*pl* •ities)
am•mo•nia
am•mo•ni•ac
am•mo•nia•cal
am•moni•fi•ca•tion
am•moni•fy (•fies, •fy•ing, •fied)
am•mo•nite
am•mo•nium
am•mu•ni•tion
am•ne•sia
am•ne•si•ac (*or* am•ne•sic)
am•nes•ty (*n, pl* •ties; *vb* •ties, •ty•ing, •tied)
am•nio•cen•tesis
am•ni•on (*pl* •ni•ons *or* •nia)
am•ni•ot•ic
amoe•ba *variant spelling of* ameba
am•oebia•sis *variant spelling of* amebiasis

amoe•bic *variant spelling of* amebic

amoe•boid *variant spelling of* ameboid

amok (*or* amuck)

among (*or* amongst)

amor•al *morally neutral; cf* immoral

amo•ral•ity

amor•al•ly

amo•rous

amo•rous•ness

amor•phism

amor•phous

amor•tiz•able

amor•ti•za•tion

amor•tize

amor•tize•ment

amount

amour

amp

am•per•age

am•pere

am•per•sand

am•pheta•mine

am•phib•ian

am•phibi•ous

am•phi•thea•ter (*Brit* •tre)

am•pho•ra (*pl* •rae *or* •ras)

am•ple

am•pli•fi•able

am•pli•fi•ca•tion

am•pli•fi•er

am•pli•fy (•fies, •fy•ing, •fied)

am•pli•tude

am•ply

am•pule (*Brit* •poule)

am•pu•tate

am•pu•ta•tion

am•pu•tee

amuck *variant spelling of* amok

amu•let

amuse

amuse•ment

amus•ing

amus•ing•ly

amy•la•ceous

amy•loid

an

ana•bio•sis

ana•bol•ic

anabo•lism

anabo•lite

anach•ro•nism

anach•ro•nis•tic

anach•ro•nis•ti•cal•ly

ana•con•da

anad•ro•mous *migrating up river; cf* catadromous

anaemia *Brit spelling of* anemia

anaemic *Brit spelling of* anemic

an•aer•obe

an•aero•bic

an•aes•the•sia *Brit spelling of* anesthesia

an•aes•thet•ic *Brit spelling of* anesthetic

an•aes•thet•ics (*Brit*) anesthesi•ology

anaes•the•tist (*Brit*) anesthesi•ologist

anaes•the•ti•za•tion *Brit spelling of* anesthetization

anaes•the•tize *Brit spelling of* anesthetize

ana•gram

ana•gram•mat•ic

ana•gram•ma•tize

anal

analagous incorrect spelling of analogous

an•al•gesia (*or* •gia)

an•alge•sic

anal•ly

ana•log *variant spelling of* analogue

ana•logi•cal (*or* •log•ic)

analo•gize

analo•gous (*NOT* analagous)

ana•logue (*or* •log)

anal•ogy (*pl* •ogies)

analy•sand

analy•sis (*pl* •ses)
ana•lyst analyser;
cf annalist
ana•lyt•ic (*or* •lyti•cal)
ana•lyti•cal•ly
ana•lyze (*Brit* •lyse)
ana•lyz•er (*Brit* •lys•)
ana•pest (*or* •paest)
ana•phy•lac•tic
ana•phy•lax•is
an•ar•chic (*or* •chi•cal)
an•ar•chi•cal•ly
an•ar•chism
an•ar•chist
an•ar•chis•tic
an•ar•chy
an•as•tig•mat
an•as•tig•mat•ic
anas•to•mose
anas•to•mo•sis (*pl* •ses)
anath•ema (*pl* •emas)
anath•ema•ti•za•tion
anath•ema•tize
ana•tomi•cal (*or* •tom•ic)
ana•tomi•cal•ly
anato•mist
anato•mi•za•tion
anato•mize
anato•miz•er
anato•my (*pl* •mies)

an•ces•tor
an•ces•tral
an•ces•tress
an•ces•try (*pl* •tries)
an•chor
an•chor•age
an•cho•rite (*fem* •ress)
anchor•man (*fem* •woman)
an•chovy (*pl* •chovies *or* •chovy)
an•cient
an•cil•lary (*pl* •laries)
and
an•dan•te
and•iron
an•dro•gen
an•dro•gen•ic
an•drog•enous
producing only
male offspring
an•drogy•nous
having male and
female
characteristics
an•drogy•ny
an•droid
an•ec•dot•age
an•ec•do•tal
an•ec•dote
an•ec•dot•ist
anemia (*Brit* anaemia)
anemic (*Brit* anaemic)

an•emom•eter
an•emo•met•ric
an•emom•etry
anemo•ne (*NOT* anenome)
an•er•oid
an•es•the•sia (*Brit* •aes•)
an•es•thesi•olo•gist
doctor
specializing in
anesthesiology; *cf*
anesthetist
an•es•thesi•ology
an•es•thet•ic (*Brit* •aes•)
an•es•the•tist
person qualified
to administer
anesthetics, not
necessarily a
doctor; *cf*
anesthesiologist
anes•the•ti•za•tion
(*Brit* anaes•)
anes•the•tize (*Brit* anaes•)
aneu•rysm (*or* •rism)
aneu•rys•mal (*or* •ris•mal, •rys•mat•ic, •ris•mat•ic)
anew
an•gel
an•gel•ic (*or* •geli•cal)
an•gel•ica
an•gel•ol•ogy

An•ge•lus
an•ger
an•gi•na
an•gi•nal
an•gi•na pec•to•ris
an•gle
an•gler
An•gli•can
An•gli•can•ism
  Church denomi-
  nation
An•gli•cism
  English idiom
an•gli•ci•za•tion
an•gli•cize
an•gling
Anglo-American
Anglo-Catholic
Anglo-Catholicism
Anglo-Irish
An•glo•ma•nia
An•glo•phile (*or*
  •phil)
An•glo•phil•ia
An•glo•phil•i•ac (*or*
  •phil•ic)
An•glo•phobe
An•glo•pho•bia
Anglo-Saxon
an•go•ra
an•gos•tu•ra
an•gri•ly
an•gry (•gri•er,
  •gri•est)
angst
an•guish
an•gu•lar
an•gu•lar•ity (*pl*
  •ities)

an•gu•late
an•gu•la•tion
an•hy•drous
ani•ma
ani•mad•ver•sion
ani•mad•vert
ani•mal
ani•mal•cu•lar
ani•mal•cule (*or*
  •cu•lum; *pl* •cules
  or •cu•la*)
ani•mal•ism
ani•mal•ist
ani•mal•ity
ani•mali•za•tion
ani•mal•ize
ani•mate
ani•ma•tion
ani•ma•tor (*or*
  •mat•er)
ani•mism
ani•mist
ani•mis•tic
ani•mos•ity (*pl*
  •ities)
ani•mus
an•ion
ani•on•ic
an•ise
ani•seed
ani•sette
an•kle
ankle•bone
an•klet
an•ky•lo•saur
an•ky•lose
an•ky•lo•sis
an•nal
an•nal•ist compiler

of annals; *cf*
  analyst
an•nal•is•tic
an•nals
an•neal
an•nex (*vb*)
an•nex (*n; Brit*
  •nexe)
an•nexa•tion
an•nexe *Brit*
  spelling of annex
  (*n*)
an•ni•hil•able
an•ni•hi•late
an•ni•hi•la•tion
an•ni•hi•la•tor
an•ni•ver•sa•ry (*pl*
  •saries)
anno Domi•ni
an•no•tate
an•no•ta•tion
an•no•ta•tive
an•no•ta•tor
an•nounce
an•nounce•ment
an•nounc•er
an•noy
an•noy•ance
an•nual
an•nual•ly
an•nui•tant
an•nu•ity (*pl* •ities)
an•nul (•nul•ling,
  •nulled)
an•nu•lar
an•nu•late
an•nu•la•tion
an•nul•lable
an•nul•ment

an•nu•lus (*pl* •nuli
  or •nu•luses)
an•nun•ci•ate
  announce; *cf*
  enunciate
an•nun•cia•tion
an•nun•cia•tive (*or*
  •tory)
an•nun•cia•tor
an•ode
an•od•ic
ano•dize
ano•dyne
anoint
anoint•er
anoint•ment
anoma•lis•tic
anoma•lis•ti•cal•ly
anoma•lous
anoma•ly (*pl* •lies)
ano•mie
anon
ano•nym•ity
anony•mous
ano•rak
ano•rexia ner•vo•sa
ano•rex•ic
an•oth•er
an•oxia
an•ox•ic
an•ser•ine (*or* •ous)
an•swer
an•swer•able
ant
ant•acid
an•tago•nism
an•tago•nist
an•tago•nis•tic

an•tago•nis•ti•
  cal•ly
an•tago•niz•able
an•tago•ni•za•tion
an•tago•nize
Ant•arc•tic
ante (an•tes,
  an•te•ing, an•ted
  or an•teed) stake
  in poker; advance
  payment; *cf* anti
ant•eater
ante•cede
ante•ced•ence
ante•ced•ent
an•te•ced•ents
ante•date
ante•di•lu•vian
ante•lope
ante•na•tal
an•ten•na (*pl* •nae)
  insect feeler
an•ten•na (*pl* •nas)
  radio or TV
  device
ante•penult
ante•penul•ti•mate
ante•ri•or
ante•room
ante•ver•sion
an•thel•min•tic (*or*
  •thic)
an•them
an•ther
an•tho•logi•cal
an•tholo•gist
an•tholo•gize
an•thol•ogy (*pl*
  •ogies)

an•thra•cite
an•thrax (*pl*
  •thra•ces)
an•thro•po•cen•tric
an•thro•po•cen•
  trism
an•thro•po•gen•esis
  (*or* •geny)
an•thro•po•genet•ic
  (*or* •gen•ic)
an•thro•poid
an•thro•po•logi•cal
an•thro•polo•gist
an•thro•pol•ogy
an•thro•po•met•ric
  (*or* •ri•cal)
an•thro•pome•trist
an•thro•pom•etry
an•thro•po•mor•
  phic
an•thro•po•mor•
  phism
an•thro•po•mor•
  phist
an•thro•po•mor•
  phize
an•thro•po•mor•
  pho•sis
an•thro•po•mor•
  phous
an•thro•po•phag•
  ous
an•thro•popha•gus
  (*pl* •pophagi)
an•thro•popha•gy
anti opposed to; *cf*
  ante
anti•abor•tion
anti•air•craft

anti•bac•te•rial
an•ti•bal•lis•tic
anti•bi•ot•ic
anti•body (*pl*
•bodies)
an•tic
an•tici•pant
an•tici•pate
an•tici•pa•tion
an•tici•pa•tor
an•tici•pa•to•ri•ly
an•tici•pa•tory
anti•cleri•cal
anti•cli•mac•tic
anti•cli•mac•ti•
cal•ly
anti•cli•max
anti•clock•wise
(*Brit*) counter
clockwise
anti•co•agu•lant
anti•con•vul•sant
anti•cy•clone
anti•cy•clon•ic
anti•de•pres•sant
anti•dote
anti•freeze
anti•gen
anti•gen•ic
anti•geni•cal•ly
anti•he•ro (*pl*
•roes)
anti•his•ta•mine
anti-imperi•al•ism
anti-imperi•al•ist
anti-inflamma•tory
anti-inflationary
anti•knock
anti•log

anti•loga•rithm
anti•ma•cas•sar
anti•mag•net•ic
anti•ma•lar•ial
anti•mat•ter
anti•mis•sile
anti•mo•nial
anti•mo•nic
anti•mo•nous
anti•mo•ny
chemical element;
cf antinomy
anti•na•tion•al•ist
anti•na•tion•al•
is•tic
anti•nom•ic
anti•nomi•cal•ly
an•tino•my (*pl*
•mies) paradox; *cf*
antimony
anti•nu•clear
anti•oxi•dant
anti•par•al•lel
anti•par•ticle
anti•pas•to (*pl*
•pasti)
anti•pa•thet•ic (*or*
•ical)
anti•pa•theti•cal•ly
an•tipa•thy (*pl*
•thies)
anti•per•son•nel
anti•per•spi•rant
anti•phon
an•tipho•nal
an•tipho•nal•ly
an•tipho•ny (*pl*
•nies)
an•tipo•dal

anti•pode
an•tipo•dean
an•tipo•des
anti•py•resis
anti•py•ret•ic
anti•quar•ian
anti•quary (*pl*
•quaries)
anti•quate
anti•quat•ed
anti•qua•ted•ness
an•tique
an•tiq•uity (*pl*
•uities)
anti•racism
anti•racist
anti•repub•li•can
anti•revo•lu•
tion•ary
an•tir•rhi•num
anti-Semite
anti-Semitic
anti-Semitism
anti•scp•sis
anti•sep•tic
anti•sep•ti•cal•ly
anti•serum (*pl*
•serums *or* •sera)
anti•so•cial
anti•spas•mod•ic
anti•stat•ic
anti•sub•ma•rine
anti•tank
an•tith•esis (*pl*
•ses)
anti•theti•cal (*or*
•thet•ic)
anti•theti•cal•ly
anti•tox•ic

anti•tox•in
anti•ven•in
anti•vi•ral
anti•vivi•sec•tion
anti•vivi•sec•tion•ist
ant•ler
ant•lered
ant•like
an•to•nym
an•tony•mous
anus
an•vil
anxi•ety (*pl* •eties)
anx•ious
anx•ious•ness
any
any•body
any•how
any•one
any•place
any•thing
any•way
any•where
any•wise
A one (*or* A-one)
aor•ta (*pl* •tas *or*
  •tae)
aor•tic (*or* •tal)
apace
Apache (*pl*
  Apaches *or*
  Apache)
  American Indian
apache gangster
apart
apart•heid
apart•ment
apa•thet•ic

apa•theti•cal•ly
apa•thy
ape
ape•like
ape•man (*pl* •men)
aperi•ent
apé•ri•tif drink
  before meal
ape•ri•tive laxative
ap•er•ture
apex (*pl* apexes *or*
  api•ces)
apha•sia
apha•sic
aphid
aphis (*pl* aphi•des)
apho•nia (*or*
  aphony)
aphon•ic
apho•rism
apho•rist
apho•ris•tic
apho•rize
aph•ro•di•sia
aph•ro•disi•ac
apian
api•ar•ian
apia•rist
api•ary (*pl* •aries)
  beehive; *cf* aviary
api•cal
api•ces *pl of* apex
api•cul•ture
api•cul•tur•ist
apiece
ap•ish
ap•ish•ness
aplen•ty

aplomb
apoca•lypse
apoca•lyp•tic
apoca•lyp•ti•cal•ly
Apoc•ry•pha
apoc•ry•phal
apoc•ry•phal•ly
apo•dal (*or* •dous)
apo•gee
apo•liti•cal
apo•liti•cal•ly
apolo•get•ic
apolo•geti•cal•ly
apo•lo•gia
apolo•gist
apolo•gize
apolo•giz•er
apol•ogy (*pl* •ogies)
apo•plec•tic
apo•plexy
apos•ta•sy (*pl*
  •sies)
apos•tate
apos•ta•tize
a pos•teri•ori
apos•tle
apos•to•late
ap•os•tol•ic
apos•tro•phe
apo•stroph•ic
apos•tro•phize
apoth•ecary (*pl*
  •ecaries)
apoth•eo•sis (*pl*
  •ses)
apoth•eo•size
ap•pall (*Brit* •pal;
  •pall•ing, •palled)
ap•pal•ling•ly

Ap•pa•la•chian
Ap•pa•loo•sa
ap•pa•rat•us (*pl*
  •rat•us *or*
  •rat•uses)
ap•par•el (•el•ing,
  •eled; *Brit* •el•ling,
  •elled)
ap•par•ent
ap•par•ent•ly
ap•pa•ri•tion
ap•peal
ap•peal•able
ap•peal•er
ap•peal•ing
ap•peal•ing•ly
ap•pear
ap•pear•ance
ap•peas•able
ap•pease
ap•peas•er
ap•pease•ment
ap•pel•lant
ap•pel•late
ap•pel•la•tion
ap•pel•la•tive
ap•pend
ap•pend•age
ap•pen•dant
ap•pen•dec•to•my
  (*Brit also*
  ap•pen•di•cec•to•
  my; *pl* •mies)
ap•pen•di•ci•tis
ap•pen•dicu•lar
ap•pen•dix (*pl*
  •dixes *or* •di•ces)
ap•per•tain
ap•pe•tence (*or*

•ten•cy; *pl* •tences
  or •ten•cies)
ap•pe•tite
ap•pe•tiz•er
ap•pe•tiz•ing
ap•plaud
ap•plaud•er
ap•plause
ap•ple
apple•cart
apple•jack
apple•sauce
ap•pli•ance
ap•plic•abil•ity
ap•pli•cable
ap•pli•cant
ap•pli•ca•tion
ap•plica•tive
ap•pli•ca•tor
ap•pli•ca•tory
ap•plied
ap•pli•er
ap•ply (•plies,
  •ply•ing, •plied)
ap•point
ap•poin•tee
ap•point•ment
ap•poin•tor
ap•por•tion
ap•por•tion•able
ap•por•tion•er
ap•por•tion•ment
ap•pose
ap•po•site apt; *cf*
  opposite
ap•po•si•tion
ap•prais•able
ap•prais•al (*or*
  •praise•ment)

ap•praise assess; *cf*
  apprise
ap•prais•er
ap•prais•ing•ly
ap•prais•ive
ap•pre•ci•able
ap•pre•ci•ate
ap•pre•cia•tion
ap•pre•cia•tive (*or*
  •tory)
ap•pre•cia•tive•
  ness
ap•pre•hend
ap•pre•hen•sibil•ity
ap•pre•hen•sible
ap•pre•hen•sion
ap•pre•hen•sive
ap•pre•hen•sive•ly
ap•pre•hen•sive•
  ness
ap•pren•tice
ap•pren•tice•ship
ap•prise inform; *cf*
  appraise
ap•proach
ap•proach•abil•ity
  (*or* •able•ness)
ap•proach•able
ap•pro•ba•tion
ap•pro•ba•tive (*or*
  •tory)
ap•pro•pri•able
ap•pro•pri•ate
ap•pro•pri•ate•ly
ap•pro•pria•tion
ap•pro•pria•tor
ap•prov•al
ap•prove
ap•proxi•mate

ap•proxi•mate•ly
ap•proxi•ma•tion
ap•pur•te•nance
ap•pur•te•nant
après-ski
apri•cot
April
a prio•ri
apron
ap•ro•pos
apse
apt
ap•ti•tude
apt•ness
aqua•cul•ture
cultivation of
marine
organisms; *cf*
aquiculture
aqua•lung
aqua•marine
aqua•naut
aqua•plane
aquar•ium (*pl*
aquar•iums *or*
aquaria)
aquat•ic
aquat•ics
aqua•tint
aque•duct
aque•ous
aqui•cul•ture
hydroponics; *cf*
aquaculture
aqui•fer
aqui•legia
aqui•line
Arab
ara•besque

Ara•bian
Ara•bic
ar•able
arach•nid spider
arach•noid
membrane
covering brain
ar•bi•ter
ar•bi•trable
ar•bi•trage
ar•bi•tral
ar•bi•trari•ly
ar•bi•trari•ness
ar•bi•trary
ar•bi•trate
ar•bi•tra•tion
ar•bi•tra•tor
ar•bor rotating
shaft
ar•bor (*Brit* •bour)
tree-lined shelter
ar•bor•eal
ar•bo•res•cence
ar•bo•res•cent
ar•bo•retum (*pl*
•tums *or* •ta)
ar•bori•cul•ture
ar•bour *Brit*
spelling of **arbor**
(shelter)
ar•bu•tus (*pl*
•tuses)
arc part of curve;
cf **ark**
ar•cade
ar•cane
arch
archae(o)• *Brit*
spelling of words

beginning with
arche(o)•
ar•cha•ic
ar•chai•cal•ly
ar•cha•ism
arch•angel
arch•angelic
arch•bishop
arch•bishop•ric
arch•deacon
arch•deacon•ry (*pl*
•ries)
arch•dioc•esan
arch•dio•cese
arch•ducal
arch•duchess
arch•duchy (*pl*
•duchies)
arch•duke
arched
arch•en•emy (*pl*
•emies)
ar•cheo•logi•cal
(*Brit* •chaeo•)
ar•cheo•logi•cal•ly
(*Brit* •chaeo•)
ar•che•olo•gist
(*Brit* •chae•)
ar•che•ol•ogy (*Brit*
•chae•)
arch•er
ar•chery
ar•che•typ•al (*or*
•typi•cal)
ar•che•typ•al•ly (*or*
•typi•cal•ly)
ar•che•type
arch•fiend

archi•pelag•ic (*or* •pe•lagian)
archi•pela•go (*pl* •gos *or* •goes)
archi•tect
archi•tec•ton•ic
archi•tec•ton•ics
archi•tec•tur•al
archi•tec•tur•al•ly
archi•tec•ture
archi•trave
ar•chiv•al
ar•chive
archi•vist
arch•ness
arch•way
Arc•tic of North Pole region
arc•tic very cold
ar•den•cy
ar•dent
ar•dor (*Brit* •dour)
ar•du•ous
ar•du•ous•ness
are
area
arena
areo•la (*pl* •lae *or* •las)
areo•lar (*or* •late)
Ar•gen•tine of Argentina
ar•gen•tine of silver
ar•gon
ar•got
ar•gu•able
ar•gu•ably

ar•gue (•gu•ing, •gued)
ar•gu•er
ar•gu•ment
ar•gu•men•ta•tion
ar•gu•men•ta•tive
ar•gu•men•ta•tive• ness
aria
Arian follower of Arianism; *cf* Aryan
Ari•an•ism heretical doctrine
arid
arid•ity (*or* ar•id•ness)
ari•el gazelle; *cf* aerial
aright
arise (aris•ing, arose, aris•en)
ar•is•toc•ra•cy (*pl* •cies)
aris•to•crat
aris•to•crat•ic
aris•to•crati•cal•ly
a'rith•me•tic (*n*)
arith•'met•ic (*or* •meti•cal; *adj*)
arith•meti•cal•ly
arith•meti•cian
ark Noah's boat; *cf* arc
arm
ar•ma•da
ar•ma•dil•lo (*pl* •los)
ar•ma•ment

ar•ma•ture
arm•band
arm•chair
armed
arm•ful
arm•hole
arm•ing
ar•mi•stice
arm•let
ar•mor (*Brit* •mour)
ar•mored (*Brit* •moured)
ar•mor•er (*Brit* •mourer)
ar•mory (*Brit* •moury; *pl* •mories, *Brit* •mouries)
arm•pit
arm•rest
arms
army (*pl* armies)
aro•ma
aroma•thera•pist
aroma•thera•py
aro•mat•ic
aro•mati•cal•ly
aro•ma•tic•ity
arose
around
arous•al
arouse
arous•er
ar•peg•gio (*pl* •gios)
ar•raign
ar•range
ar•range•able

ar•range•ment
ar•rang•er
ar•rant
ar•ras hanging
  tapestry; *cf* **arris**
ar•ray
ar•ray•al
ar•rears
ar•rest
ar•rest•able
ar•rest•er
ar•rest•ing
ar•rest•ing•ly
ar•rhyth•mia
ar•ris (*pl* •ris or
  •rises) sharp edge;
  cf **arras**
ar•ri•val
ar•rive
ar•riv•er
ar•ri•viste
ar•ro•gance
ar•ro•gant
ar•ro•gate
ar•ro•ga•tion
ar•row
arrow•head
arrow•root
arrow•wood
arro•yo
ar•senal
ar•senate
ar•senic
ar•seni•cal
ar•seni•ous (*or*
  •sen•ous)
ar•son
art
ar•te•fact (*or* •ti•)

ar•te•rial
ar•te•ri•ole
ar•te•rio•sclero•sis
ar•te•rio•sclerot•ic
ar•te•rio•venous
ar•te•ri•tis
ar•tery (*pl* •teries)
ar•te•sian
art•ful
art•ful•ly
art•ful•ness
ar•thrit•ic
ar•thri•tis
arthro•pod
ar•thropo•dal (*or*
  •dan, •dous)
ar•ti•choke
ar•ti•cle
ar•ticu•lar
ar•ticu•late
ar•ticu•lat•ed
ar•ticu•late•ly
ar•ticu•late•ness
  (*or* •la•cy)
ar•ticu•la•tion
ar•ticu•la•tor
ar•ti•fact *variant
  spelling of* **artefact**
ar•ti•fice
ar•tifi•cer
ar•ti•fi•cial
ar•tifi•ci•al•ly
ar•tifi•ci•al•ity
ar•til•lery
ar•til•lery•man (*pl*
  •men)
arti•ness
ar•ti•san

art•ist person
  skilled in art, etc.
ar•tiste entertainer
ar•tis•tic
ar•tis•ti•cal•ly
art•ist•ry
art•less
art•less•ness
art nou•veau
art•work
arty (arti•er,
  arti•est)
arum
Aryan (*or* Arian)
  non-Jewish
  Caucasian; *cf*
  Arian
as
as•bes•tos (*or* •tus)
as•bes•to•sis
as•ca•ria•sis
as•cend
as•cend•ancy (*or*
  •ency, •ance,
  •ence)
as•cend•ant (*or*
  •ent)
as•cend•er
as•cen•sion
as•cent upward
  movement; *cf*
  assent
as•cer•tain
as•cer•tain•able
as•cer•tain•ment
as•cet•ic
as•ceti•cal•ly
as•ceti•cism
ascor•bic acid

as•crib•able
as•cribe
as•crip•tion (or ad•scrip•)
asep•sis
asep•tic
asexu•al
asexu•al•ity
asexu•al•ly
ash
ashamed
asham•ed•ly
ash•can
ash•en
Ash•ke•na•zi (pl •zim)
ashore
*ashphalt incorrect spelling of asphalt
ash•ram
ash•tray
ashy (ashi•er, ashi•est)
Asian
Asi•at•ic
aside
asl•nine
asi•nin•ity
ask
ask•er
askew
aslant
asleep
aso•cial
asp
as•para•gus
as•pect
as•pen
as•per•ity (pl •ities)

as•perse
as•per•sion
as•phalt (NOT ashphalt)
as•phal•tic
as•pho•del
as•phyxia
as•phyxi•ate
as•phyxia•tion
as•phyxia•tor
as•pic
as•pi•dis•tra
as•pir•ant
as•pi•rate
as•pi•ra•tion
as•pi•ra•tor
as•pire
as•pir•er
as•pi•rin (NOT asprin)
as•pir•ing
*asprin incorrect spelling of aspirin
asquint
ass
as•sail
assail•able
as•sail•ant
assail•ment
as•sas•sin
as•sas•si•nate
as•sas•si•na•tion
as•sault
as•sault•er
as•say test; cf essay
as•say•able
as•say•er
as•sem•blage
as•sem•ble

as•sem•bler
as•sem•bly (pl •blies)
as•sent consent; cf ascent
as•sen•ta•tion
as•sen•tient
as•sen•tor (or •sent•er)
as•sert
as•sert•er (or •ser•tor)
as•sert•ible
as•ser•tion
as•ser•tive
as•ser•tive•ness
as•sess
as•sess•able
as•sess•ment
as•ses•sor
as•set
as•sev•er•ate
as•sev•era•tion
as•si•du•ity (pl •ities)
as•sidu•ous
as•sidu•ous•ness
as•sign
as•sign•able
as•sig•na•tion
as•signee legal term
as•sign•er
as•sign•ment
as•sign•or legal term
as•simi•lable
as•simi•late
as•simi•la•tion

as•simi•la•tive (*or* •tory)
as•sist
as•sis•tance
as•sis•tant
as•sist•er
as•size
as•so•ci•able
as•so•ci•ate
as•so•cia•tion
as•so•cia•tive
as•so•nance
as•so•nant
as•sort
as•sorta•tive (*or* •sort•ive)
as•sort•ed
as•sort•ment
as•suage
as•suage•ment
as•suag•er
as•sum•able
as•sume
as•sumed
as•sum•ing
as•sump•tion
as•sump•tive
as•sur•able
as•sur•ance
as•sure
as•sured
as•sur•ed•ly
as•sur•er
*assymetric
  incorrect spelling
  of **asymmetric**
as•ter
as•ter•isk
astern

as•ter•oid
as•teroi•dal
as•the•nia (*or* •ny)
as•then•ic
asth•ma
asth•mat•ic
asthmati•cal•ly
as•tig•mat•ic
astig•ma•tism (*or* astig•mia)
astir
aston•ish
aston•ish•ing
aston•ish•ing•ly
aston•ish•ment
astound
astound•ed
astound•ing
astound•ing•ly
astrad•dle
as•tra•khan
as•tral
astray
astride
as•trin•gen•cy (*or* •gence)
as•trin•gent
as•tro•bi•ol•ogy
as•tro•dome
as•tro•dy•nam•ics
as•tro•labe
as•trolo•ger (*or* •gist)
as•tro•logi•cal
as•tro•logi•cal•ly
as•trol•ogy
as•tro•naut
as•tro•nau•tic (*or* •ti•cal)

as•tro•nau•tics
as•trono•mer
as•tro•nomi•cal (*or* •nom•ic)
as•tro•nomi•cal•ly
as•trono•my
as•tro•physi•cal
as•tro•physi•cist
as•tro•phys•ics
as•tute
as•tute•ly
as•tute•ness
asun•der
aswarm
asy•lum
asym•met•ric (*or* •ri•cal; *NOT* assymetric)
asym•met•ri•cal•ly
asym•me•try
asymp•to•mat•ic
asymp•to•mati•cal•ly
asyn•chro•nism
asyn•chro•nous
at
ata•vism
ata•vist
ata•vis•tic (*or* •vic)
ataxia (*or* ataxy)
atax•ic (*or* atac•tic)
ate
athe•ism
athe•ist
athe•is•tic (*or* •ti•cal)
athe•is•ti•cal•ly

ath•ero•ma (*pl*
  •mas *or* •mata)
ath•er•oma•tous
ath•ero•scle•ro•sis
  (*pl* •ses)
ath•ero•scle•rot•ic
ath•lete
ath•let•ic
ath•leti•cal•ly
ath•leti•cism
ath•let•ics
at•las
at•mos•phere
at•mos•pher•ic (*or*
  •pheri•cal)
at•mos•pheri•cal•ly
at•mos•pher•ics
at•oll
atom
atom•ic
atomi•cal•ly
ato•mic•ity
at•om•ism
at•om•ist
at•om•is•tic (*or*
  •ti•cal)
at•omi•za•tion
at•om•ize
at•om•iz•er
aton•able (*or*
  atone•)
aton•al
ato•nal•ity
ato•nal•ly
atone
atone•able *variant*
  spelling of
  atonable
atone•ment

aton•er
atop
atrium (*pl* atria)
atro•cious
atro•cious•ness
atroc•ity (*pl* •ities)
atroph•ic
at•ro•phy (*n, pl*
  •phies; *vb* •phies,
  •phy•ing, •phied)
at•ro•pine
atta•boy
at•tach
at•tach•able
at•ta•ché
at•tach•ment
  (*NOT*
  attachment)
at•tack
at•tack•er
at•tain
at•tain•abil•ity (*or*
  •able•ness)
at•tain•able
at•tain•ment
at•taint
at•tar (*or* ot•)
*attatchment
  incorrect spelling
  of attachment
at•tempt
at•tempt•able
at•tempt•er
at•tend
at•tend•ance
at•tend•ant
at•tend•er
at•ten•tion
at•ten•tive

at•ten•tive•ness
at•tenu•ant
at•tenu•ate
at•tenua•tion
at•test
at•test•able
at•test•ant
at•tes•ta•tion
at•test•er one who
  attests
at•test•or (*or*
  •test•ta•tor) legal
  term
at•tic
at•tire
at•ti•tude
at•ti•tu•di•nal
at•ti•tu•di•nize
at•ti•tu•di•niz•er
at•tor•ney
at•tor•ney
  gen•er•al (*pl*
  at•tor•neys
  general)
at•tract
at•tract•able
at•tract•ant
at•trac•tion
at•trac•tive
at•trac•tive•ly
at•trac•tive•ness
at•trac•tor (*or*
  •tract•er)
at•trib•ut•able
at•trib•ute
at•trib•ut•er (*or*
  •tribu•tor)
at•tribu•tion
at•tribu•tive

at•tri•tion
at•tri•tion•al
at•tune
atypi•cal
atypi•cal•ly
auber•gine (*Brit*) eggplant
auburn
auc•tion
auc•tion•eer
auda•cious
auda•cious•ness
audac•ity (*pl* •ities)
audibil•ity (*or* audible•ness)
audible
audi•ence
audio
audio•gen•ic
audi•om•e•ter
audi•om•e•try
audio•tape
audio•visual
audit
audi•tion
audi•tor
audi•to•rium (*pl* •riums *or* •ria)
audi•tory
auger boring tool; *cf* augur
aught anything; all; *cf* ought
aug•ment
aug•men•ta•tion
aug•menta•tive
aug•men•tor (*or* •ment•er)

augur predict; *cf* auger
augur•al
augu•ry (*pl* •ries)
¹August month
au'gust imposing
auk
aunt
auntie (*or* aunty; *pl* aunties)
aura (*pl* auras *or* aurae)
aural of the ear; *cf* oral
aural•ly
aure•ole (*or* aureo•la)
auri•cle chamber of heart; part of ear; *cf* oracle
auricu•lar
aurif•er•ous
auro•ra (*pl* •ras *or* •rae)
auro•ra aus•tra•lis
auro•ra bo•real•is
auro•ral
aus•cul•tate
aus•cul•ta•tion
aus•pi•cious
aus•pi•cious•ness
aus•tere
aus•tere•ness
aus•ter•ity (*pl* •ities)
aus•tral
Aus•tral•ian
Aus•trian
authen•tic

authen•ti•cal•ly
authen•ti•cate
authen•ti•ca•tion
au•then•ti•ca•tor
au•then•tic•ity
author
autho•rial
authori•tar•ian
authori•tari•an•ism
authori•ta•tive
authori•ta•tive•ness
author•ity (*pl* •ities)
authori•za•tion
author•ize
author•iz•er
author•ship
autism
autis•tic
auto•bi•og•ra•pher
auto•bio•graphi•cal
auto•bi•og•ra•phy (*pl* •phies)
auto•cade
autoc•ra•cy (*pl* •cies)
auto•crat
auto•crat•ic
auto•crati•cal•ly
auto•erot•ic
auto•eroti•cism (*or* •ero•tism)
autog•enous
auto•graft
auto•graph
auto•graph•ic
auto•graphi•cal•ly
autog•ra•phy
auto•hyp•no•sis

auto•hyp•not•ic
auto•hyp•noti•
  cal•ly
auto•im•mune
auto•im•mun•ity
auto•mat
automa•ta *pl of*
  automaton
auto•mate
auto•mat•ic
auto•mati•cal•ly
auto•ma•tion
automa•tism
automa•tist
automa•tize
automa•ton (*pl*
  •tons *or* automata)
automa•tous
auto•mo•bile
auto•mo•tive
auto•nom•ic
auto•nomi•cal•ly
autono•mist
autono•mous
autono•my (*pl*
  •mies)
auto•pi•lot
autop•sy (*pl* •sies)
auto•sug•ges•tion
auto•sug•ges•tive
auto•tim•er
autumn
autum•nal
aux•ilia•ry (*pl*
  •ries)
avail
avail•abil•ity
avail•able
ava•lanche

avant-garde
ava•rice
ava•ri•cious
avenge
aveng•er
av•enue
aver (aver•ring,
  averred)
av•er•age
aver•ment
averse
aver•sion
avert
avert•ible (*or* •able)
avian
aviary (*pl* aviaries)
  place for keeping
  birds; *cf* apiary
avi•ate
avia•tion
avia•tor
avi•cul•ture
avid
avid•ity
avid•ly
avid•ness
avi•on•ic
avi•on•ics
aviru•lent
avo•ca•do (*pl* •dos)
avo•cet
avoid
avoid•able
avoid•ance
avoid•er
avow
avow•able
avow•al
avowed

avowed•ly
avow•er
avul•sion
avun•cu•lar
await
awake (awak•ing,
  awoke *or* awaked,
  awok•en *or*
  awaked)
awak•en
award
award•able
aware
aware•ness
awash
away
awe wonder; *cf*
  oar; or; ore
awe-inspiring
awe•some
awe-stricken (*or*
  awe•, awe-struck,
  •struck)
aw•ful
aw•ful•ly
aw•ful•ness
awhile
awk•ward
awk•ward•ness
awl
awn•ing
awoke
awok•en
awry
ax (*Brit* axe)
axel ice-skating
  jump; *cf* axil; axle
ax•ial
axil angle between

leaf and stem; *cf*
  axel; axle
axi•om
axio•mat•ic (*or*
  •mati•cal)
axio•mati•cal•ly
axis (*pl* **axes**)
axle mechanical
  part; *cf* **axel; axil**
axo•lotl
aya•tol•lah
aye (*or* **ay**)
azalea
azi•muth
azi•muth•al
azo•ic
Az•tec
az•ure

B

baa (**baa•ing,**
  baaed)
bab•ble
bab•bler
babe
ba•biche
ba•boon
*****babtize** *incorrect*
  spelling of **baptize**
baby (*n, pl* **babies;**
  vb **babies,**
  ba•by•ing,
  ba•bied)
baby-boomer
ba•by•hood
ba•by•ish

baby-sit (**-sitting,**
  -sat)
baby-sitter
bac•ca•lau•re•ate
bac•ca•rat
bac•cha•nal
Bac•cha•na•lia (*pl*
  •lia *or* **•lias**)
bac•cha•na•lian
bach•elor (*NOT*
  batchelor)
ba•cil•lary (*or* **•lar**)
ba•cil•lus (*pl* **•cilli**)
back
back•ache
back-and-forth
back•bend
back•bite (**•bit•ing,**
  bit, bit•ten *or* **bit**)
back•board
back•bone
back•breaker
back•breaking
back•chat
back•date
back•door
back•drop
back•er
back•fire
back•gam•mon
back•ground
back•hand
back•hand•ed
back•handed•ly
back•handed•ness
back•hand•er
back•ing
back•lash
back•less

back•list
back•log
back•pack
back-pedal
  (**-pedaling,**
  -pedaled; *Brit*
  -pedalling,
  -pedalled)
back•scratch•er
back•side
back•sight
back-slapping (*adj*)
back•slide
  (**•slid•ing, •slid,**
  •slid *or* **•slid•den**)
back•slid•er
back•space
back•spin
back•stage
back stairs stairs at
  back of house
back•stairs
  indirect;
  underhand
back•stitch
back•stop
back•stroke
back•swept
back•swing
back talk (*n*) an
  impudent
  response
back-talk (*vb*) to
  answer back
back•track
back•up (*n*)
back•ward (*adj*)
back•ward (*Brit*
  •wards; *adv*)

back•ward•ness
back•wash
back•water
back•woods•man
(*pl* •men)
ba•con
bac•te•ria *pl of*
bacterium
bac•te•rial
bac•te•ri•cid•al
bac•te•ri•cide
bac•te•rio•logi•cal
bac•te•ri•olo•gist
bac•te•ri•ol•ogy
bac•te•rio•phage
bac•te•rio•sta•sis
bac•te•rio•stat•ic
bac•te•ri•um (*pl*
te•ria)
bad (worse, worst)
bad•dy (or •die; *pl*
•dies)
bade
badge
badg•er
badi•nage
bad•lands
bad•ly
bad•man (*pl* •men)
bad•min•ton
bad-mouth
bad•ness
baf•fle
baf•fle•ment
baf•fler
bag (bag•ging,
bagged)
baga•telle
ba•gel

bag•gage
bag•gi•ly
bag•gi•ness
bag•gy (•gi•er,
•gi•est)
bag•man (*pl* •men)
bag•pipe
ba•guette (or •guet)
bail (*n*) security for
prisoner; *cf* bale
bail (or bale; *vb*)
remove water
from boat
bail•able
bailee
bail•er (or bal•)
one that bails; *cf*
bailor; baler
bail•iff
bail•or provider of
security for
prisoner; *cf* bailer;
baler
bain-marie (*pl*
bains-marie)
bait enticement; to
torment; *cf* bate
baize
bake
bake•house
bak•er
bak•ery (*pl* •eries)
bala•cla•va
bal•ance
bal•ance•able
bal•anc•er
bal•co•nied
bal•co•ny (*pl* •nies)
bald

bal•der•dash
bald-headed
bald•ing
bald•ness
bale (*n*) block of
hay; *cf* bail
bale (*vb*) make
bales; jump from
aircraft; *variant
spelling of* bail
ba•leen
bale•ful
bale•ful•ly
bale•ful•ness
bal•er agricultural
machine; *variant
spelling of* bailer;
cf bailor
balk (or baulk)
balk•er (or baulk•)
ball
bal•lad
bal•lad•eer (or •ier)
bal•lad•ry
bal•last
bal•le•ri•na
bal•let
bal•let•ic
bal•leto•mane
bal•leto•ma•nia
bal•lis•tic
bal•lis•ti•cal•ly
bal•lis•tics
bal•loon
bal•loon•ist
bal•lot (•lot•ing,
•lot•ed)
ball•park
ball•point

ball•room
bal•ly•hoo (*n, pl* •hoos; *vb* •hoos, •hoo•ing, •hooed)
balm
balmi•ly
balmi•ness
balmy (balmi•er, balmi•est) soothing
balmy (*Brit* bar•my; balmi•er, balmi•est; *Brit* •mi•er, •mi•est) crazy
ba•lo•ney (*or* bo•)
bal•sa
bal•sam
bal•sam•ic
bal•us•trade
bam•bi•no (*pl* •nos *or* •ni)
bam•boo (*pl* •boos)
bam•boo•zle
bam•boo•zle•ment
bam•boo•zler
ban (ban•ning, banned)
ba•nal
ba•nal•ity
ba•na•na
band
band•age
ban•dan•na (*or* ban•dana)
band•box
ban•deau (*pl* •deaux)
ban•di•coot

ban•dit (*pl* •dits *or* •dit•ti)
ban•dit•ry
band•master
bands•man (*pl* •men)
band•stand
band•wagon
band•width
ban•dy (*adj* •di•er, •di•est; *vb* •dies, •dy•ing, •died)
bane
bang noise; *cf* bhang
bang•er
ban•gle
ban•ian *variant spelling of* banyan
ban•ish
ban•ish•ment
ban•is•ter (*or* ban•nis•)
ban•jo (*pl* •jos *or* •joes)
ban•jo•ist
bank
bank•able
bank•book
bank•er
bank•ing
bank•roll
bank•rupt
bank•rupt•cy (*pl* •cies)
banned
ban•ner
ban•ning
ban•nis•ter *variant*

spelling of banister
banns (*or* bans)
ban•quet feast
ban•quette seat
ban•shee (*or* •shie)
ban•tam
bantam•weight
ban•ter
ban•ter•er
Ban•tu (*pl* •tu *or* •tus)
ban•yan (*or* •ian)
bao•bab
bap•tism
bap•tis•mal
Bap•tist
bap•tist•ry (*or* •tis•tery; *pl* •ries *or* •teries)
bap•tize (*NOT* babtize)
bar (bar•ring, barred)
barb
bar•bar•ian
bar•bar•ian•ism
bar•bar•ic
bar•bari•cal•ly
bar•ba•rism
bar•bar•ity (*pl* •ities)
bar•ba•rize
bar•ba•rous
bar•ba•rous•ness
bar•be•cue (*or* •que; •cu•ing, •cued *or* •qu•ing, •qued)

bar•bel fish; bristle
bar•bell weight
bar•ber
barber•shop
bar•bi•can
bar•bi•tu•rate
bar•ca•role (*or* •rolle)
bard
bard•ic
bar•dola•try
bare uncovered; naked; expose; *cf* **bear**
bare•back (*or* •backed)
bare•faced
bare•foot (*or* •footed)
bare-handed
bare-headed (*or* •head)
bare•ly
bare•ness
bar•gain
barge
barge•man (*Brit* **bar•gee**; *pl* •men; *Brit* •gees)
barge•pole
bari•tone (*or* **bary•**)
bar•ium
bark dog's cry; outer layer of tree
bark (*Brit* **barque**) boat
bark•er
bar•ley
barley•corn

bar•maid
bar•man (*pl* •men)
bar mitz•vah
bar•my *Brit spelling of* **balmy** (crazy)
barn
bar•na•cle
barn•storm
barn•yard
baro•graph
ba•rom•e•ter
baro•met•ric (*or* •met•ri•cal)
bar•on
bar•on•ess
bar•on•et
bar•on•et•cy (*pl* •cies)
ba•ro•nial
baro•ny (*pl* •nies)
ba•roque
baro•scope
barque *Brit spelling of* **bark** (boat)
bar•rack (*vb*)
bar•racks (*n*)
bar•ra•cou•ta (*pl* •ta *or* •tas)
bar•ra•cu•da (*pl* •da *or* •das)
bar•rage
bar•ran•ca (*or* •co; *pl* •cas *or* •cos)
barred
bar•rel (•rel•ing, •reled; *Brit* •rel•ling, •relled)
barrel-chested

bar•ren
bar•ren•ness
bar•rens
bar•rette
bar•ri•cade
bar•ri•cad•er
bar•ri•er
bar•ring
bar•ris•ter (*Brit*) lawyer
bar•room
bar•row
bar•tend•er
bar•ter
bar•ter•er
ba•ry•tes
bary•tone *variant spelling of* **baritone**
ba•sal
ba•salt
basalt•ware
base
base•ball
base•board
base•born
base•less
base•line
base•man (*pl* •men)
base•ment
base•ness
ba•ses *pl of* **base** *or* **basis**
bash
bash•ful
bash•ful•ly
bash•ful•ness
ba•sic
ba•si•cal•ly

bas•il
ba•sil•i•ca (*pl* •cas
  or •cae)
ba•sin
ba•sis (*pl* •ses)
bask
bas•ket
basket•ball
bas•ket•ry
basket•work
bas-relief
bass voice; singer
bass (*pl* bass *or*
  basses) fish
bas•set
bas•soon
bas•soon•ist
bass•wood
bast fiber; *cf* baste
bas•tard
bas•tard•i•za•tion
bas•tard•ize
baste moisten
  meat; sew; *cf* bast
bast•ing
bas•tion
bat (bat•ting,
  bat•ted)
batch
*batchelor
  *incorrect spelling
  of* bachelor
bate restrain; *cf*
  bait
bat•ed
bath (*n*)
bathe (*vb*)
bath•er
ba•thet•ic

bath•house
bath•ing
ba•thos
bath•robe
bath•room
bath•tub
ba•thym•e•try
bathy•scaph (*or*
  •scaphe, •scape)
bathy•sphere
ba•tik
ba•tiste
ba•ton
bat•tal•ion
bat•ted
bat•ten
bat•ter
bat•ter•er
bat•tery (*pl* •teries)
bat•ting
bat•tle
battle-ax (*Brit*
  -axe)
bat•tle•dore
battle•field
bat•tle•ment
bat•tler
battle-scarred
battle•ship
bat•ty (•ti•er,
  •ti•est)
bat•wing (*adj*)
bau•ble
baulk *variant
  spelling of* balk
baux•ite
bawdi•ly
bawdi•ness
bawdy (*n, pl*

bawdies; *adj*
bawdi•er,
bawdi•est)
bawl
bawl•er
bay
bay•berry (*pl*
  •berries)
bayo•net (•net•ing,
  •net•ed *or*
  •net•ting, •net•ted)
bayou
bay•wood
ba•zaar (*or* •zar)
ba•zoo
ba•zoo•ka
be (be•ing, been)
beach shore; *cf*
  beech
beach•comber
beach•head
bea•con
bead
beadi•ly
beadi•ness
bead•ing
beady (beadi•er,
  beadi•est)
bea•gle
beak
beaked
beak•er
beaky (beaki•er,
  beaki•est)
beam
bean plant; seed; *cf*
  been
bean•bag
bean•ery (*pl* •eries)

beanie
bean•pole
bean•stalk
bear (bear•ing,
  bore, borne)
  support; convey;
  endure; cf bare
bear (bear•ing,
  bore, born) give
  birth to
bear (pl bears or
  bear) animal
bear•able
bear•ably
beard
beard•ed
beard•less
bear•er
bear•ish
bear•skin
beast
beast•li•ness
beast•ly (•lier,
  •liest)
beat (beat•ing,
  beat, beat•en or
  beat) strike; cf
  beet
beat•able
beat•er
bea•tif•ic
bea•tif•i•cal•ly
be•ati•fi•ca•tion
be•ati•fy (•fies,
  •fy•ing, •fied)
be•ati•tude
beat•nik
beau (pl beaus or
  beaux)

beau•jo•lais (or
  Beau•)
beau•te•ous
beau•ti•cian
beau•ti•fi•ca•tion
beau•ti•ful
beau•ti•ful•ly
beau•ti•fy (•fies,
  •fy•ing, •fied)
beau•ty (pl •ties)
bea•ver
be•bop
be•calmed
be•came
be•cause
bé•cha•mel
beck
beck•on
beck•on•er
be•come (•com•ing,
  •came)
be•com•ing•ly
bed (bed•ding,
  bed•ded)
be•daub
be•daz•zle
be•daz•zle•ment
bed•bug
bed•ded
bed•ding
be•deck
be•dev•il (•il•ing,
  •iled; Brit •il•ling,
  •illed)
be•dev•il•ment
be•dew
bed•fellow
bed•lam
Bedou•in (or

Bedu•in; pl •ins or
  •in)
bed•pan
bed•post
be•drag•gled
bed•rail
bed•rid•den (or
  bed•rid)
bed•rock
bed•roll
bed•room
bed•side
bed•sore
bed•spread
bed•stead
bed•time
Bedu•in variant
  spelling of
  Bedouin
bee
beech (pl beeches
  or beech) tree; cf
  beach
beech•nut
bee-eater
beef (pl beeves,
  beefs, or beef)
beef•bur•ger
beef•cake
beefi•ness
beef•steak
beefy (beefi•er,
  beefi•est)
bee•hive
bee•keeper
bee•line
been past participle
  of be; cf bean
beep

beep•er

beer

beery (beeri•er,
  beeri•est)

bees•wax

beet plant; cf beat

bee•tle insect; cf
  betel

beet•root (Brit) red
  beet

be•fall (•fal•ling,
  •fell, •fall•en)

be•fit (•fit•ting,
  •fit•ted)

be•fit•ting•ly

be•fog (•fog•ging,
  •fogged)

be•fore

before•hand

be•friend

be•fud•dle

beg (beg•ging,
  begged)

be•gan

be•get (•get•ting,
  •got, •got•ten or
  •got)

be•get•ter

beg•gar

beg•gar•li•ness

beg•gar•ly

beg•gary (pl
  •garies)

begged

beg•ging

be•gin (•gin•ning,
  •gan, •gun) start;
  cf beguine

be•gin•ner

be•gone

be•gonia

be•got

be•got•ten

be•grudge

be•grudg•ing•ly

be•guile

be•guile•ment

be•guil•er

be•guil•ing•ly

be•guine dance; cf
  begin

be•gun

be•half

be•have

be•hav•ior (Brit
  •iour)

be•hav•ior•al (Brit
  •iour•)

be•hav•ior•ism
  (Brit •iour•)

be•hav•ior•ist (Brit
  •iour•)

be•hav•ior•is•tic
  (Brit •iour•)

be•head

be•held

be•hind

behind•hand

be•hold (•hold•ing,
  •held)

be•hold•en

be•hold•er

be•hoove (Brit
  •hove)

beige (NOT biege)

be•ing

be•jew•el (•el•ing,

•eled; Brit •el•ling,
  •elled)

bel unit of power;
  cf bell; belle

be•la•bor (Brit
  •bour)

be•lat•ed

be•lat•ed•ly

be•lay (•lay•ing,
  •layed)

belch

be•lea•guer

bel•fry (pl •fries)

Bel•gian

be•lie (•ly•ing,
  •lied)

be•lief

be•li•er

be•liev•able

be•lieve

be•liev•er

be•lit•tle

be•lit•tle•ment

be•lit•tler

bell instrument; cf
  bel; belle

bel•la•don•na

bell-bottomed (or
  -bottom)

bell-bottoms

bell•boy

belle beautiful
  woman; cf bel;
  bell

bell•hop

bel•li•cose

bel•li•cos•ity

bel•lig•er•ence

bel•lig•er•en•cy

bel•lig•er•ent
bel•low
bel•low•er
bel•lows
bell•pull
bell•push
bel•ly (*n, pl* •lies;
   vb •lies, •ly•ing,
   •lied)
belly•ache
belly•button
bel•ly•ful
be•long
be•long•ings
be•lov•ed
be•low
belt
belt•way
be•moan
be•muse
be•mused
bench
bench•mark
bend (bend•ing,
   bent)
bendy (bendi•er,
   bendi•est)
be•neath
Ben•edic•tine
ben•edic•tion
ben•edic•tory
ben•efac•tion
ben•efac•tor
ben•efac•tress
ben•efice
be•nefi•cence
be•nefi•cent
ben•efi•cial
ben•efi•cial•ly

bene•fi•ciary (*pl*
   •ciaries)
ben•efit (•efit•ing,
   •efit•ed *or*
   •efit•ting,
   •efit•ted)
be•nevo•lence
be•nevo•lent
be•night•ed
be•nign
be•nig•nan•cy
be•nig•nant
be•nig•nity (*pl*
   •nities)
bent
bent•wood
be•numb
ben•zene chemical
   compound
ben•zine (*or* •zin)
   gasoline
   constituent
ben•zo•ic
ben•zo•in
ben•zol (*or* •zole)
be•queath
be•quest
be•rate
be•reave (•reav•ing,
   •reaved *or* •reft)
be•reave•ment
be•reft
be•ret
berg iceberg; *cf*
   burg
ber•ga•mot
beri•beri
ber•ret•ta (*or* be•)

*variant spellings
of* biretta
ber•ry (*n, pl* •ries;
   vb •ries, •ry•ing,
   •ried) fruit; pick
   fruit; *cf* bury
ber•serk
berth
ber•yl
be•seech
   (•seech•ing,
   •seeched *or*
   •sought)
be•set (•set•ting,
   •set)
be•side
be•sides
be•siege
be•sieg•er
be•smear
be•smirch
be•som
be•sot•ted
be•span•gle
be•spat•ter
be•spec•ta•cled
be•sprin•kle
best
bes•tial
bes•ti•al•ity (*pl*
   •ities)
bes•ti•al•ize
be•stir (•stir•ring,
   •stirred)
be•stow
be•stow•al (*or*
   •ment)
be•stow•er
be•strew

(•strew•ing,
•strewed, •strewn
or •strewed)
be•stride
(•strid•ing, •strode
or •strid,
•strid•den, •strode,
or •strid)
bet (bet•ting, bet or
bet•ted)
beta
be•take (•tak•ing,
•took, •tak•en)
be•tel plant; cf
beetle
bête noire (pl bêtes
noires)
be•tide
be•to•ken
be•took
be•tray
be•tray•al
be•tray•er
be•troth•al
be•trothed
bet•ter improved
bet•ter (or •tor)
one who bets
bet•ter•ment
be•tween
bev•el (•el•ing,
•eled; Brit •el•ling,
•elled)
bev•er•age
bevy (pl bevies)
be•wail
be•wail•er
be•ware
be•wil•der

be•wil•der•ing
be•wil•der•ment
be•witch
be•witch•ing•ly
be•yond
bez•el (or •il;
•el•ing, •eled,
•el•ling, •elled or
•il•ing, •illed,
•il•ling, •illed)
be•zique
bhang narcotic; cf
bang
bi•an•nual twice a
year; cf biennial
bi•an•nual•ly
bias (•as•ing, •ased
or •as•sing,
•assed)
bi•ath•lon
bib (bib•bing,
bibbed)
bib•ber
Bi•ble
bib•li•cal
bib•li•og•ra•ph•er
(or bib•lio•graph)
bib•lio•graph•ic (or
•graphi•cal)
bib•li•og•ra•phy
(pl •phies)
bib•li•ola•try
bib•lio•ma•nia
bib•lio•ma•ni•ac
bib•lio•phile (or
•phil)
bib•li•ophism
bibu•lous
bi•cam•er•al

bi•car•bo•nate
bi•cen•tenary (pl
•tenaries)
bi•cen•ten•nial
bi•ceps (pl •ceps or
•cepses)
bick•er
bick•er•er
bi•col•lat•er•al
bi•col•or (or •ored;
Brit •our or
•oured)
bi•con•cave
bi•con•cav•ity
bi•con•vex
bi•cus•pid
bi•cy•cle
bi•cy•clist (or •cler)
bid (bid•ding, bid
or bade, bid•den
or bid)
bid•dable
bid•der
bide (bid•ing,
bid•ed or bode,
bid•ed)
bi•det
*biege incorrect
spelling of beige
bi•en•nial every
two years; cf
biannual
bi•en•nial•ly
bi•fid
bi•fo•cal (adj)
bi•fo•cals (pl n)
bi•fur•cate
bi•fur•ca•tion

big (big•ger,
  big•gest)
biga•mist
biga•mous
biga•my (pl •mies)
big•ger
big•gest
big•gish
big•head
big•headed
big•headed•ness
big•horn (pl •horns
  or •horn)
bight bay; bend in
  rope; cf bite; byte
big•mouth
big•ot
big•ot•ed
big•ot•ry (pl •ries)
bi•jou (pl •jous or
  •joux)
bike
bik•er
bi•ki•ni (pl •nis)
bi•lat•er•al
bi•lat•er•al•ly
bile
bilge
bili•ary
bi•lin•gual
bi•lin•gual•ism
bili•ous
bil•ious•ness
bill
bill•board
bil•let
billet-doux (pl
  billets-doux)

bill•fish (pl •fish or
  •fishes)
bill•fold
bill•hook
bil•liard
bil•liards
bill•ing
bil•lion (pl •lions
  or •lion)
bil•lion•aire
bil•lionth
bil•low
bil•lowy
bil•ly (pl •lies)
bim•bo (pl •bos or
  •boes)
bi•me•tal•lic
bi•met•al•lism
bi•month•ly (pl
  •lies)
bin (bin•ning,
  binned)
bi•na•ry (pl •ries)
bin•aural
bind (bind•ing,
  bound)
bind•er
bind•ery (pl •eries)
bind•weed
binge
bin•na•cle
binned
bin•ning
bin•ocu•lar (adj)
bin•ocu•lars (n)
bi•no•mial
bio•as•say
bio•as•tro•nau•tics
bio•chemi•cal

bio•chemi•cal•ly
bio•chem•ist
bio•chem•is•try
bio•degrad•able
bio•deg•ra•da•tion
bio•di•ver•sity
bio•en•gi•neer
bio•en•gi•neer•ing
bio•ethi•cal
bio•eth•ics
bio•feed•back
bio•gas
bio•gen•esis
bio•genet•ic (or
  bio•geneti•cal,
  biog•enous)
bio•gen•ic
bio•geo•graphi•cal
bio•geog•ra•phy
bi•og•ra•pher
bio•graphi•cal
bi•og•ra•phy (pl
  •phies)
bio•logi•cal (or
  •log•ic)
bio•logi•cal•ly
bio•lo•gist
bi•ol•ogy
bio•lu•mi•nes•cence
bio•lu•mi•nes•cent
bio•mass
bio•met•ric (or
  •met•ri•cal)
bio•met•ri•cal•ly
bi•om•etry (or
  bio•met•rics)
bi•on•ic (adj)
bi•on•ics (n)
bio•physi•cal

bio•physi•cist
bio•phys•ics
bi•op•sy (*pl* •sies)
bio•rhythm
bio•sphere
bio•syn•the•sis
bio•syn•thet•ic
bio•syn•theti•cal•ly
bio•tech•no•
logi•cal
bio•tech•nolo•gist
bio•tech•nol•ogy
bi•ot•ic
bi•par•ti•san
bi•par•ti•san•ship
bi•par•tite
bi•par•ti•tion
bi•ped
bi•ped•al
bi•plane
bi•pod
bi•po•lar
bi•quar•ter•ly
bi•ra•cial
birch
bird
bird•bath
bird-brained
bird•cage
bird•house
bird•like
bird•lime
bird•seed
bird's-eye (*adj*)
bird•song
bird-watcher
bird-watching
bi•refrin•gence
bi•refrin•gent

bi•reme
bi•ret•ta (*or*
ber•ret•ta, be•)
birr make whirring
sound; *cf* **bur**;
burr
birth
birth•day
birth•mark
birth•place
birth•right
birth•stone
bis•cuit
bi•sect
bi•sec•tion
bi•sec•tor
bi•sex•ual
bi•sexu•al•ism (*or*
•ity)
bish•op
bish•op•ric
bis•muth
bi•son (*pl* •son)
bisque
bis•tro (*pl* •tros)
bi•sul•fate (*Brit*
•phate)
bi•sul•fide (*Brit*
•phide)
bi•sul•fite (*Brit*
•phite)
bi•sym•met•ric (*or*
•ri•cal)
bi•sym•met•ri•
cal•ly
bi•sym•met•ry
bit
bitch
bitchi•ly

bitchy (bitchi•er,
bitchi•est)
bite (bit•ing, bit,
bit•ten) grip with
teeth; *cf* **bight**;
byte
bit•ing•ly
bit•ten
bit•ter
bit•tern
bit•ter•ness
bitter•nut
bitter•sweet
bit•ty (•ti•er,
•ti•est)
bi•tu•men
bi•tu•mi•ni•za•tion
bi•tu•mi•nize
bi•tu•mi•nous
bi•va•lence (*or*
•len•cy; *pl* •lences
or •cies)
bi•va•lent
bi•valve
bi•val•vu•lar
bivou•ac (•ack•ing,
•acked)
bi•week•ly (*pl* •lies)
bi•year•ly
bi•zarre
blab (blab•bing,
blabbed)
blab•ber
black
black•ball
black•berry (*pl*
•berries)
black•bird
black•board

black•en
black•fish (pl •fish or •fishes)
black•fly (pl •flies)
Black•foot (pl •feet or •foot)
black•guard
black•guard•ly
black•head
black•hearted
black•ing
black•ish
black•jack
black•leg (•leg•ging, •legged)
black•list
black•mail
black•mail•er
black-market (vb)
black•ness
black•out
black•smith
black•tail
black•thorn
black•top
blad•der
blade
blain
blam•able (or blame•)
blame
blame•less
blame•less•ness
blame•worthi•ness
blame•worthy
blanch make white; cf blench
blanc•mange

bland
blan•dish
blan•dish•ment
bland•ness
blank
blan•ket
blank•ly
blare
bla•sé (or •se)
blas•pheme
blas•phem•er
blas•phe•mous
blas•phe•my (pl •mies)
blast
blasted
blast•ing
blast•off
blat (blat•ting, blat•ted)
bla•tan•cy
bla•tant
blath•er (or bleth•)
blaze
blaz•er
bla•zon
bla•zon•ry (pl •ries)
bleach
bleach•able
bleach•er
bleak
bleak•ness
blear
bleari•ness
bleary (bleari•er, bleari•est)
bleat
bleat•er

bleed (bleed•ing, bled)
bleed•er
bleep
blem•ish
blench shy away; cf blanch
blend
blend•er
bless (bless•ing, blessed or blest)
bless•ed (adj)
bless•ed•ness
blest
bleth•er variant of blather
blew
blight
blight•er
blimp
blind
blind•er
blind•fold
blind•ing
blind•ly
blind•ness
blind•worm
blink
blink•er (vb, n)
blink•ers (pl n)
blip (blip•ping, blipped)
bliss
bliss•ful
bliss•ful•ly
bliss•ful•ness
blis•ter
blis•ter•ing•ly
blithe

blithe•ness
blitz
blitz•krieg
bliz•zard
bloat
bloat•ed
bloat•er
blob (blob•bing,
blobbed)
bloc group of
nations
block chunk;
obstruct
block•ade
block•ad•er
block•age
block•bust•er
block•bust•ing
block•er
block•head
blond (fem blonde)
blond•ness (fem
blonde•ness)
blood
blood•curdling
blood•ed
blood•hound
bloodi•ly
bloodi•ness
blood•less
blood•letting
blood•root
blood•shed
blood•shot
blood•stain
blood•stained
blood•stock
blood•stone
blood•sucker

blood•thirsti•ly
blood•thirsti•ness
blood•thirsty
(•thirsti•er,
•thirsti•est)
bloody (adj
bloodi•er,
bloodi•est; vb
blood•ies,
bloody•ing,
blood•ied)
bloom
bloom•er
bloom•ers
bloop•er
blos•som
blot (blot•ting,
blot•ted)
blotch
blotchi•ly
blotchi•ness
blotchy (blotchi•er,
blotchi•est)
blot•ter
blouse
blou•son
blow (blow•ing,
blew, blown)
blow-by-blow
blow-dry (-dries,
-drying, -dried)
blow•er
blow•fish (pl •fish
or •fishes)
blow•hole
blow•lamp
blown
blow•out
blow•pipe

blow•torch
blow•up
blowzy (or blowsy;
blowzi•er,
blowzi•ier or
blowsi•er,
blowsi•est)
blub•ber
blub•bery
bludg•eon
blue (blue•ing or
blu•ing, blued)
blue•bell
blue•berry (pl
•berries)
blue•bill
blue•bird
blue-collar (adj)
blue•gill
blue•grass
blue•ness
blue•nose
blue-pencil (vb;
-penciling,
-penciled; Brit
-pencilling,
-pencilled)
blue•print
blues
blue•stocking
blue•weed
bluff
bluff•er
bluff•ness
blu•ish (or blue•)
blun•der
blun•der•buss
blun•der•er
blun•der•ing•ly

blunt
blunt•ness
blur (blur•ring, blurred)
blurb
blur•red•ness
blur•ry (•ri•er, •ri•est)
blurt
blush
blush•er
blush•ing•ly
blus•ter
blus•ter•er
blus•ter•ing•ly (or •ous•ly)
blus•tery (or •ter•ous)
boa
boar male pig; cf boor; bore
board
board•er
board•ing
board•room
board•walk
boar•ish coarse; sensual; cf boorish
boar•ish•ness
boast
boast•er
boast•ful
boast•ful•ly
boast•ful•ness
boast•ing•ly
boat
boat•er
boat•hook
boat•house

boat•ing
boat•load
boat•man (pl •men)
boat•swain (or bo•sun)
bob (bob•bing, bobbed)
bob•bin
bob•ble
bob•cat
bobo•link
bob•sled (Brit •sleigh)
bob•stay
bob•tail
bob•white
bode
bodge
bodg•er
bod•ice
bodi•less
bodi•ly
bod•kin
body (n, pl bodies; vb bodies, body•ing, bod•ied)
body•check (vb)
body•guard
body•work
bog (bog•ging, bogged)
bo•gey (or bogy; pl •geys or bogies) evil spirit; golf term; cf bogie
bogey•man (pl •men)
bog•gi•ness
bog•gle

bog•gy (•gi•er, •gi•est)
bo•gie wheeled undercarriage; cf bogey
bo•gus
bogy variant spelling of bogey
Bo•he•mian of Bohemia
bo•he•mian unconventional person
boil
boil•er
boiler•maker
boiler•plate
boiler•suit
bois•ter•ous
bois•ter•ous•ness
bola (or bolas; pl bolas or bolases)
bold
bold•face (adj)
bold•ness
bole tree trunk; cf bowl
boll
bo•lero (pl •leros)
boll
bol•lard
boll•worm
bo•lo•ney variant spelling of baloney
Bol•she•vik (pl •viks or •vi•ki)
Bol•she•vism
Bol•she•vist
bol•son
bol•ster

bolt
bolt•er
bo•lus (*pl* •luses)
bomb
bom•bard
bom•bar•dier
bom•bard•ment
bom•bast
bom•bas•tic
bom•bas•ti•cal•ly
bom•ba•zine (*or*
•sine)
bomb•er
bomb•shell
bomb•sight bomb-
aiming device
bomb site bomb-
destroyed area
bona fide (*adj*)
bona fides (*n*)
bo•nan•za
bon•bon
bond
bond•age
bond•ed
bond•holder
bone
bone•fish (*pl* •fish
or •fishes)
bone•head
bone•less
bone•set•ter
bone•shaker
bon•ey *variant
spelling of* bony
bone•yard
bon•fire
bong

bon•go (*pl* •gos *or*
•goes)
bon•ho•mie (*or*
•hom•mie)
boni•ness
bo•ni•to (*pl* •tos *or*
•toes)
bon mot (*pl* bons
mots *or* bon mots)
bon•net
bon•ny (*or* •nie;
•ni•er, •ni•est)
bon•sai (*pl* •sai)
bo•nus
bony (*or* bon•ey;
boni•er, boni•est)
boo (boo•ing,
booed)
boob
boo•by (*pl* •bies)
booby-trap (*vb*;
-trap•ping,
-trapped)
booed
boo•gie
boogie-woogie
boo•hoo (*n*, *pl*
•hoos; *vb* •hoos,
•hoo•ing, •hooed)
boo•ing
book
book•binder
book•bindery (*pl*
•binderies)
book•binding
book•case
bookie
book•ing
book•ish

book•ish•ness
book•keeper
book•keeping
book•let
book•maker
book•making
book•mark (*or*
•marker)
book•plate
book•seller
book•shelf (*pl*
•shelves)
book•shop
book•stall
book•stand
book•worm
boom
boom•er
boom•er•ang
boon
boon•docks
boon•dog•gle
boor unpleasant
person; *cf* boar;
bore
bore
boor•ish ill-
mannered;
insensitive; *cf*
boarish
boor•ish•ness
boost
boost•er
boot
boot•black
boot•ed
boo•tee (*or* •tie)
booth
boot•lace

boot•leg (•leg•ging, •legged)
boot•leg•ger
boot•less
boot•lick
boot•lick•er
boot•strap
boo•ty (*pl* •ties)
booze
booz•er
boozi•ness
boozy (boozi•er, boozi•est)
bop (bop•ping, bopped)
bo•rac•ic
bo•rax (*pl* •raxes or •ra•ces)
bor•del•lo (*pl* •los)
bor•der
bor•der•er
border•land
border•line
bore dull person; drill hole; *cf* **boar**; **boor**
bore•dom
bor•er
bo•ric
bor•ing
born given birth to; *cf* **borne**
born-again
borne carried; *cf* **born**
bo•ron
bor•ough
bor•row
bor•row•er

borscht (*or* **borsch, bortsch**)
bor•zoi (*pl* •zois)
bosh
Bos•nian
bos•om
bos•omy
boss
bos•sa nova
bossi•ly
bossi•ness
bossy (bossi•er, bossi•est)
bo•sun *variant spelling of* **boatswain**
bo•tani•cal (*or* •tan•ic)
bota•nist
bota•nize
bota•ny (*pl* •nies)
botch
botched
botch•er
botchy (botchi•er, botchi•est)
bot•fly (*pl* •flies)
both
both•er
both•era•tion
both•er•some
bot•tle
bottle-feed (-feed•ing, -fed)
bottle•neck
bottle•nose
bot•tom
bot•tom•less
bottom•most

botu•lism
bou•doir
bouf•fant
bou•gain•vil•lea (*or* •laea)
bough
bought
bouil•lon
boul•der
boule•vard
bounce
bounc•er
bounci•ly
bounci•ness
bounc•ing
bouncy (bounci•er, bounci•est)
bound
bounda•ry (*pl* •ries)
bound•en
bound•er
bound•less
boun•te•ous
boun•ti•ful
boun•ty (*pl* •ties)
bou•quet
bou•quet gar•ni (*pl* **bou•quets gar•nis**)
bour•bon
bour•geois (*fem* •geoise)
bour•geoi•sie
bour•geon *variant spelling of* **burgeon**
bourn (*Brit*) stream
bourne (*or* **bourn**) destination; boundary

bout
bou•tique
bou•zouki (*or*
  •souki; *pl* •zoukis
  or •soukis)
bo•vid
bo•vine
bow
bowd•ler•ism
bowd•leri•za•tion
bowd•ler•ize
bow•el (•el•ing,
  •eled *or* •el•ling,
  •elled)
bow•er
bower•bird
bow•fin
bowie knife
bow•ing
bow•knot
bowl basin;
  wooden ball; *cf*
  bole
bow•legged
bowl•er
bowl•ful
bow•line
bowl•ing
bowls
bow•man (*pl* •men)
bow•shot
bow•sprit
bow•string
  (•string•ing,
  •stringed *or*
  •strung)
bow•wow
box

box•berry (*pl*
  •berries)
box•car
box•er
box•ing
box•room
box•wood
boy child; *cf* buoy
boy•cott
boy•friend
boy•hood
boy•ish
boy•ish•ness
boy•sen•berry (*pl*
  •berries)
bra
brace
brace•let
brac•er
bra•chial
bra•chi•ate
bra•chia•tion
brachio•saur•us
brac•ing
brac•ing•ly
brack•en
brack•et
brack•ish
brack•ish•ness
bract
brad (brad•ding,
  brad•ded)
brad•awl
brag (brag•ging,
  bragged)
brag•gart
brag•ger
brag•ging•ly

Brah•man (*or* •min;
  pl •mans *or* •mins)
braid
braid•ed
braid•ing
Braille
brain
brain•child (*pl*
  •children)
brain-dead
braini•ness
brain•less
brain•less•ness
brain•sick
brain•storm
brain•storm•er
brain•storm•ing
brain•wash
brain•wash•er
brain•washing
brainy (braini•er,
  braini•est)
braise (*or* braize)
  cook; *cf* braze
brake
bram•ble
bran
branch
branch•ing
brand
bran•dish
brand-new
bran•dy (*pl* •dies)
brash
brash•ly
brash•ness
brass
brass•bound
bras•serie

bras•si•ca
bras•si•ca•ceous
bras•siere
brassi•ly
brassi•ness
brassy (brassi•er, brassi•est)
brat
brat•wurst
bra•va•do (pl •does or •dos)
brave
brave•ness
brav•ery (pl •eries)
bra•vo (pl •voes or •vos)
bra•vu•ra
brawl
brawl•er
brawn
brawni•ly
brawni•ness
brawny (brawni•er, brawni•est)
bray
bray•er
braze solder metal; cf braise
bra•zen
bra•zen•ness
braz•er one who brazes
bra•zi•er brass worker; charcoal-burning pot
Bra•zil•ian
Bra•zil nut
breach break; gap; cf breech

bread
bread•board
bread•crumb
bread•fruit (pl •fruits or •fruit)
bread•line
bread•nut
bread•root
breadth
bread•winner
break (break•ing, broke, brok•en)
break•able
break•age
break•away
break•down
break•er
break•fast
break-in (n)
break•neck
break-out (n)
break•point
break•through
break•up
break•water
bream (pl bream or breams)
breast
breast•bone
breast-feed (-feed•ing, -fed)
breast•pin
breast•plate
breast•stroke
breath
Breatha•lyz•er (Trademark)
breathe
breath•er

breathi•ly
breathi•ness
breath•ing
breath•less
breath•less•ness
breath•taking
breathy (breathi•er, breathi•est)
bred
breech part of gun; buttocks cf breach
breech•cloth
breeches
breech•loader
breech-loading (adj)
breed (breed•ing, bred)
breed•er
breeze
breezi•ly
breezi•ness
breezy (breezi•er, breezi•est)
Bren gun
brent (pl brents or brent)
br'er
breth•ren
breve
brev•ity (pl •ities)
brew
brew•er
brew•ery (pl •eries)
brew•ing
bri•ar variant spelling of brier
brib•able (or bribe•able)

bribe
brib•er
brib•ery (pl •eries)
bric-a-brac
brick
brick•layer
brick•laying
brick•work
brick•yard
brid•al
bride
bride•groom
brides•maid
bridge
bridge•able
bridge•board
bridge•head
bridge•work
bridg•ing
bri•dle
brief
brief•case
brief•ing
brief•ly
bri•er (or •ar)
brig
bri•gade
briga•dier
brig•and
bright
bright•en
bright•en•er
bright•ness
brights
bril•liance (or
  •lian•cy; pl
  •liances or •cies)
bril•liant
bril•lian•tine

brim (brim•ming,
  brimmed)
brim•ful (or •full)
brim•stone
brin•dle
brin•dled
brine
bring (bring•ing,
  brought)
brini•ness
brink
brink•man•ship
briny (brini•er,
  brini•est)
bri•oche
bri•quette (or
  •quet)
brisk
bris•tle
bris•tly (•tli•er,
  •tli•est)
Bri•tan•nic
Briti•cism
Brit•ish
Brit•ish•er
Brit•on
brit•tle
brit•tle•ness
broach raise topic;
  tap container; cf
  brooch
broad
broad•cast
  (cast•ing, •cast or
  •cast•ed)
broad•cast•er
broad•cloth
broad•en

broad•leaf (pl
  •leaves)
broad-leaved (or
  -leafed)
broad•loom
broad•ly
broad-minded
broad-minded•ness
broad•sheet
broad•side
broad•sword
bro•cade
broc•co•li
bro•chure
brogue
broil
broil•er
broke
bro•ken
broken-down
broken•hearted
bro•ker
bro•ker•age
bro•mide
bro•mine
bron•chi pl of
  bronchus
bron•chial
bronchi•ec•ta•sis
bron•chio•lar
bron•chi•ole
bron•chit•ic
bron•chi•tis
broncho•pneu•
  mo•nia
broncho•scope
bron•chos•co•py
bron•chus (pl •chi)

bron•co (or •cho; pl
•cos or •chos)
bronco•buster
bron•to•sau•rus (or
•to•saur)
bronze
bronzy
brooch piece of
jewelry; cf broach
brood
brood•er
broodi•ness
broody (broodi•er,
broodi•est)
brook
broom
broom•corn
broom•stick
broth
broth•el
broth•er
brother•hood
brother-in-law (pl
brothers-)
broth•er•li•ness
broth•er•ly
brought
brou•ha•ha
brow
brow•beat
(•beat•ing, •beat,
•beat•en or beat)
brown
browned-off
brownie
brown•ish
brown•out
brown•stone
browse

brows•er
bru•cel•lo•sis
bruise
bruised
bruis•er
bruis•ing
brunch
bru•nette (or •net)
brunt
brush
brush•er
brush-off
brush•up
brush•wood
brush•work
brusque
brusque•ness
bru•tal
bru•tal•ity (pl
•ities)
bru•tali•za•tion
bru•tal•ize
bru•tal•ly
brute
brut•ish
brut•ish•ness
bub•ble
bub•bler
bub•bly (•bli•er,
•bli•est)
bu•bon•ic
buc•cal of the
mouth; cf buckle
buc•ca•neer
buck
bucka•roo (or
bucke•; pl •roos)
buck•board
buck•et

buck•et•ful (pl •fuls
or buck•ets•ful)
buck•eye
buck•le clasp; cf
buccal
buck•ram
(ram•ing, •ramed)
buck•saw
buck•shee
buck•shot
buck•skin
buck•thorn
buck•tooth (pl
•teeth)
buck•wheat
bu•col•ic
bu•coli•cal•ly
bud (bud•ding,
bud•ded)
Bud•dhism
Bud•dhist
bud•ding
bud•dleia
bud•dy (or •die; pl
•dies)
budge
budg•eri•gar
budg•et
budgie
buff
buf•fa•lo (pl •loes,
•los, or •lo)
buff•er
buf•fet restaurant;
sideboard
buf•fet (•fet•ing,
•fet•ed) to batter;
a blow
buffle•head

buf•foon
buf•foon•ery
bug (bug•ging, bugged)
bug•bear
bugged
bug•ger
bug•gery
bug•ging
bug•gy (*n, pl* •gies; *adj* •gi•er, •gi•est)
bu•gle
bu•gler
build (build•ing, built)
build•er
build•ing
build•up
built
built-in
built-up
*buisness incorrect spelling of business
bul•bous
Bul•gar•ian
bulge
bulgi•ness
bulgy
bu•limia
bulk
bulk•head
bulki•ly
bulki•ness
bulky (bulki•er, bulki•est)
bull
bull•bat
bull•dog

bull•doze
bull•doz•er
bul•let
bul•le•tin
bullet•proof
bull•fight
bull•fighter
bull•fighting
bull•frog
bull•head
bul•lion
bull•ish
bull•necked
bull•ock
bull•pen
bull•ring
bull's-eye
bull•shit
bull•whip
bul•ly (*n, pl* •lies; *vb* •lies, •ly•ing, •lied)
bul•rush (*or* bull•)
bul•wark
bum (bum•ming, bummed)
bum•ble
bumble•bee
bum•bler
bum•mer
bump
bump•er
bumpi•ly
bumpi•ness
bump•kin
bump•tious
bump•tious•ness
bumpy (bumpi•er, bumpi•est)

bun
bunch
bunchi•ness
bunchy (bunchi•er, bunchi•est)
bun•combe *variant spelling of* bunkum
bun•dle
bun•dler
bung
bun•ga•low
bun•gee
bung•hole
bun•gle
bun•gler
bun•gling
bun•ion
bunk
bun•ker
bun•kum (*or* •combe)
bun•ny (*pl* •nies)
Bun•sen burn•er
bunt•ing
bunt•line
buoy float; *cf* boy
buoy•age
buoy•an•cy
buoy•ant
bur (bur•ring, burred) seed vessel; *cf* birr; burr
bur•ble
bur•bler
bur•bot (*pl* •bots *or* •bot)
bur•den

bur•den•some
bur•dock
bu•reau (*pl* •reaus
  or •reaux)
bu•reau•cra•cy (*pl*
  •cies)
bu•reau•crat
bu•reau•crat•ic
bu•reau•crati•
  cal•ly
bu•reau•crat•ism
bu•reauc•ra•ti•za•
  tion
bu•reau•cra•tize
bu•ret (*Brit* •rette)
burg town; *cf* berg
bur•geon (*or* bour•)
burg•er
bur•glar
bur•glar•ize
bur•glary (*pl*
  •glaries)
bur•gle (*Brit*)
  burglarize
bur•gun•dy (*or*
  Bur•; *pl* •dies)
bu•rial
buri•er
bu•rin
bur•lesque (*or*
  •lesk; •lesqu•ing,
  •lesqued *or*
  •lesk•ing, •lesked)
bur•li•ness
bur•ly (•li•er,
  •li•est)
Bur•mese (*or* •man;
  pl •mese *or* •mans)

burn (burn•ing,
  burnt *or* burned)
burn•er
burn•ing
bur•nish
burn•ish•able
burn•ish•er
bur•noose (*or*
  •nous)
burn•sides
burnt
burp
burr rough edge;
  small drill; dialect
  characteristic; *cf*
  birr; bur
burred
bur•ring
bur•ro (*pl* •ros)
  donkey
bur•row hole
bur•row•er
bur•ry (•ri•er,
  •ri•est)
bur•sa (*pl* •sae *or*
  •sas) anatomy
  term
bur•sar financial
  official
bur•sa•ry (*pl* •ries)
bur•si•tis
burst (burst•ing,
  burst *or* burst•ed)
bury (buries,
  bury•ing, bur•ied)
  inter; *cf* berry
bus (*n, pl* buses *or*
  busses; *vb* buses,
  bus•ing, bused *or*

busses, bus•sing,
  bussed)
bus•by (*pl* •bies)
bush
bush•el (•el•ing,
  •eled; *Brit* •el•ling,
  •elled)
bush•el•er (*Brit*
  •el•ler)
bush•fire
bushi•ness
bush•ing
bush•man (*pl* •men)
bush•master
bush•ranger
bush•tit
bush•whack
bush•whack•er
bushy (bushi•er,
  bushi•est)
busi•ly
busi•ness (*NOT*
  buisness) trade,
  etc.; *cf* busyness
business•like
business•man (*pl*
  •men)
business•woman
  (*pl* •women)
bus•ing (*or*
  bus•sing)
bust
bust•er
bus•tle
bus•tler
busty (busti•er,
  busti•est)
busy (*adj* busi•er,

busi•est; *vb* busies, busy•ing, busied)

busy•body (*pl* •bodies)

busy•ness state of being busy; *cf* business

but however; *cf* butt

bu•tane

butch

butch•er

butcher-bird

butch•ery (*pl* •eries)

but•ler

butt push; target; thick end; etc.; *cf* but

but•ter food

butt•er one that butts

butter•ball

butter•cup

butter•fat

butter•fingered

butter•fingers

butter•fish (*pl* •fish or •fishes)

butter•fly (*pl* •flies)

but•teri•ness

butter•milk

butter•nut

butter•scotch

but•tery (*pl* •teries)

but•tock

but•ton

button•hole

button•hook

button•mold (*Brit* •mould)

button•wood

but•tress

bux•om

bux•om•ness

buy (buys, buy•ing, bought)

buy•er

buzz

buz•zard

buzz•er

by

by-bidder

by-blow

by-election (or bye-)

by•gone

by•law (or bye•)

by-line

by•pass (•pass•ing, •passed or •past)

by•path

by-product

by•road

by•stander

by•street

byte computer term; *cf* bight; bite

by•way

by•word

Byz•an•tine

C

cab

ca•bal (•bal•ling, •balled)

ca•bal•le•ro (*pl* •ros)

caba•ret

cab•bage

cab•ba•la (*or* ca•ba•la, kab•ba•la, ka•ba•la)

cab•ba•lism (*or* caba•, kab•ba•, kaba•)

cab•ba•list (*or* caba•, kab•ba•, kaba•)

cab•ba•lis•tic (*or* caba•, kab•ba•, kaba•)

cab•by (*or* •bie; *pl* •bies)

cab•driver

cab•in

cabi•net

cabinet-maker

cabinet•work

cable

cable•way

cab•man (*pl* •men)

cabo•chon

ca•boo•dle

ca•boose

cab•ri•ole

ca•cao (*pl* •caos)

cacha•lot

cache

ca•chet

cach•in•nate

cach•in•na•tion

ca•cique

cack•le

cack•ler
caco•mis•tle (*or*
•mix•le)
ca•coph•o•nous
ca•coph•o•ny (*pl*
•nies)
cac•tus (*pl* •tuses
or •ti)
cad
ca•dav•er
ca•dav•er•ous
ca•dav•er•ous•ness
cad•die (*or* •dy; *n,
pl* •dies; *vb* •dies,
•dy•ing, •died)
golf term; *cf*
caddy
cad•dis fly
cad•dish
cad•dy (*pl* •dies)
tea container; *cf*
caddie
ca•dence
ca•dent
ca•den•za
ca•det
cadge
cadg•er
ca•dre
cae•cal *Brit
spelling of* cecal
cae•cum *Brit
spelling of* cecum
Cae•sar•ean
sec•tion *Brit
spelling of*
cesarean section
cae•sium *Brit
spelling of* cesium

cae•su•ra (*pl* •ras
or •rae)
ca•fé (*or* •fe)
cafe•te•ria
caf•feine (*or* •fein)
caf•tan *variant
spelling of* kaftan
cage
ca•gey (*or* •gy;
•gi•er, •gi•est)
ca•gi•ly
ca•gi•ness
ca•hoots
cai•man *variant
spelling of* cayman
cairn
cairn•gorm
cais•son
ca•jole
ca•jol•ery (*pl*
•eries)
Ca•jun (*or* •jan)
cake
cala•bash
cala•mine
ca•lami•tous
ca•lam•i•ty (*pl*
•ities)
cal•car•eous
cal•cif•er•ous
cal•ci•fi•ca•tion
cal•ci•fy (•fies,
•fy•ing, •fied)
cal•ci•na•tion
cal•cite
cal•cit•ic
cal•cium
cal•cu•la•bil•ity (*pl*
•ities)

cal•cu•lable
cal•cu•late
cal•cu•la•tion
cal•cu•la•tive
cal•cu•la•tor
cal•cu•lus (*pl*
•luses) math term
cal•cu•lus (*pl* •li)
stone in body
cal•dron *variant
spelling of*
cauldron
cal•en•dar dates; *cf*
colander
cal•en•der
smoothing
machine; *cf*
colander
cal•ends (*or*
kal•ends)
calf (*pl* calves)
calf•skin
cali•ber (*Brit* •bre)
cali•bered (*Brit*
•bred)
cali•brate
cali•bra•tion
cali•bra•tor (*or*
•brat•er)
cali•ces *pl of* calix
cali•co (*pl* •coes *or*
•cos)
cali•per (*Brit*
cal•li•per)
ca•liph (*or* ca•lif,
ka•lif, ka•liph,
kha•lif)
ca•li•phate (*or*

ca•li•fate,
ka•li•fate)
ca•lix (*pl* cali•ces)
chalice; *cf* calyx
calk *variant
spelling of* caulk
calk•er *variant
spelling of* caulker
call
cal•la
call•able
call•boy
call•er
cal•lig•ra•pher (*or*
•phist)
cal•li•graph•ic
cal•li•graphi•cal•ly
cal•lig•ra•phy (*pl*
•phies)
call•ing
cal•lio•pe
cal•li•per *Brit
spelling of* caliper
cal•los•ity (*pl*
•ities)
cal•lous unfeeling;
cf callus
cal•lous•ness
cal•low
cal•low•ness
call-up (*n*)
cal•lus (*pl* •luses)
hard skin; *cf*
callous
calm
calma•tive
calm•ly
calm•ness
calo•mel

ca•lor•ic
calo•ric•ity (*pl*
•ities)
calo•rie (*or* •ry; *pl*
•ries)
calo•rif•ic
calo•rim•eter
calo•ri•met•ric (*or*
•met•ri•cal)
calo•ri•met•ri•
cal•ly
calo•rim•etry
ca•lum•ni•ate
ca•lum•nia•tion
ca•lum•ni•ous (*or*
•nia•tory)
cal•um•ny (*pl*
•nies)
cal•va•ry (*pl* •ries)
calve (*vb*)
calves *pl of* calf
Cal•vin•ism
Cal•vin•ist
ca•lyp•so (*pl* •sos)
ca•lyx (*pl* ca•lyxes
or caly•ces) sepals
of plant; *cf* calix
cam
ca•ma•ra•de•rie
cam•ass (*or* •as)
cam•ber
cam•bium (*pl*
•biums *or* •bia)
Cam•bo•dian
cam•boose
cam•bric
cam•cord•er
came
cam•el

cam•el•eer
ca•mel•lia
Cam•em•bert
cameo (*n, pl*
cameos; *vb*
cameos,
cameo•ing,
cam•eoed)
cam•era
cam•er•al
camera•man (*pl*
•men)
cami•sole
camo•mile (*or*
chamo•)
camou•flage
camp
cam•paign
cam•paign•er
cam•pa•ni•le
cam•pa•nolo•gist
cam•pa•nol•ogy
camp•er
camp•fire
camp•ground
cam•phor
cam•pho•rat•ed
camp•ing
cam•pus (*pl* •puses)
cam•shaft
can (can•ning,
canned)
Ca•na•dian
ca•nal (•nal•ing,
•naled; *Brit*
•nal•ling, •nalled)
cana•li•za•tion
cana•lize
ca•na•pé

ca•nary (*pl* •naries)
ca•nas•ta
can•can
can•cel (•cel•ing, •celed; *Brit* •cel•ling, •celled)
can•cel•er (*Brit* •cel•ler)
can•cel•la•tion
can•cer
can•cer•ous
can•de•la
can•de•la•brum (or •bra; *pl* •bra, •brums, or •bras)
can•did
can•di•da
can•di•da•cy (or •da•ture)
can•di•date
can•did•ly
can•did•ness
can•died
can•dle
candle•light
candle•nut
candle•pin
candle•power
can•dler
candle•stick
candle•wick
candle•wood
can•dor (*Brit* •dour)
can•dy (*n, pl* •dies; *vb* •dies, •dy•ing, •died)
candy-striped
cane

cane•brake
can•er
ca•nine
can•ing
can•is•ter
can•ker
can•ker•ous
can•na
can•na•bis
canned
can•nel•lo•ni (or •ne•lo•ni)
can•ner
can•nery (*pl* •neries)
can•ni•bal
can•ni•bal•ism
can•ni•bal•is•tic
can•ni•bali•za•tion
can•ni•bal•ize
can•ni•ly
can•ni•ness
can•ning
can•non (*pl* •nons or •non) artillery; *cf* canon
can•non•ade
cannon•ball
can•non•eer
can•non•ry (*pl* •ries) artillery; *cf* canonry
can•not
ca•noe (•noe•ing, •noed)
ca•noe•ist
can•on priest; decree; *cf* cannon
ca•noni•cal

can•oni•za•tion
can•on•ize
can•on•ry (*pl* •ries) office of canon; *cf* cannonry
ca•noo•dle
cano•py (*n, pl* •pies; *vb* •pies, •py•ing, •pied)
cant sloping surface; insincere talk
can't cannot
can•ta•loupe (or •loup)
can•tan•ker•ous
can•tan•ker•ous• ness
can•ta•ta
can•teen
can•ter horse's gait; *cf* cantor
can•ti•cle
can•ti•lever
can•to (*pl* •tos)
can•ton
can•ton•al
Can•ton•ese (*pl* •ese)
can•ton•ment
can•tor religious singer; *cf* canter
can•vas cloth
can•vass (or •vas) solicit
can•vass•er
can•yon
cap (cap•ping, capped)

ca•pa•bil•i•ty (*pl*
•ities)
ca•pable
ca•pably
ca•pa•cious
ca•pa•cious•ness
ca•paci•tance
ca•paci•tor
ca•pac•i•ty (*pl*
•ities)
ca•pari•son
cape
ca•per
cape•skin
cap•il•lar•i•ty (*pl*
•ities)
ca•pil•lary (*pl*
•laries)
capi•tal city;
money; *cf* **capitol**
capi•tal•ism
capi•tal•ist
capi•tal•is•tic
capi•tali•za•tion
capi•tal•ize
capi•tal•ly
capi•ta•tion
capi•ta•tive
capi•tol building;
cf **capital**
ca•pitu•late
ca•pitu•la•tion
ca•pitu•la•tor
ca•pon
capo•ral tobacco;
cf **corporal;**
corporeal
capped
cap•per

cap•ping
cap•puc•ci•no (*pl*
•nos)
ca•price
ca•pri•cious
ca•pri•cious•ly
ca•pri•cious•ness
cap•ri•ole
cap•si•cum
cap•size
cap•stan
cap•stone (*or*
cope•)
cap•su•lar
cap•su•late (*or*
•lat•ed)
cap•su•la•tion
cap•sule
cap•sul•ize
cap•tain
cap•tain•cy (*or*
•tain•ship; *pl* •cies
or •ships)
cap•tion
cap•tious
cap•ti•vate
cap•ti•va•tion
cap•ti•va•tor
cap•tive
cap•tiv•i•ty (*pl*
•ities)
cap•tor
cap•ture
Capu•chin friar
capu•chin monkey
capy•ba•ra
car
cara•cal feline; *cf*
karakul

ca•ra•ca•ra
ca•rafe
cara•mel
cara•mel•ize
cara•pace
car•at unit of
weight for
precious stones;
cf caret; carrot;
karat
cara•van (•van•ing
or •van•ning,
•vaned *or* •vanned)
cara•van•se•rai (*or*
•sa•ry; *pl* •rai,
•rais, *or* •ries)
cara•way
car•bide
car•bine
car•bo•hy•drate
car•bo•lat•ed
car•bol•ic
car•bon
car•bo•na•ceous
car•bon•ate
car•bona•tion
car•bon•ic
car•bon•if•er•ous
car•boni•za•tion
car•bon•ize
car•bon•ous
car•box•yl•ic
car•boy
car•bun•cle
car•bun•cu•lar
car•bu•ra•tion
car•bu•ret
(•ret•ing, •ret•ed;

Brit •ret•ting,
•ret•ted)
car•bu•re•tor (*or*
•ter, •ra•tor; *Brit*
•ret•tor *or*
•ret•ter)
car•bu•ri•za•tion
car•bu•rize
car•cass (*Brit also*
•case)
car•cino•gen
car•ci•no•gen•ic
car•ci•no•ma (*pl*
•mas *or* •ma•ta)
card
car•da•mom (*or*
•mum, •mon)
card•board
card-carrying
car•di•ac
car•di•gan
car•di•nal
car•di•nal•ate (*or*
•ship)
car•di•nal•ly
card-index (*vb*)
card•ing
car•dio•gram
  record
car•dio•graph
  instrument
car•di•og•ra•pher
car•dio•graph•ic
  (*or* •graphi•cal)
car•di•og•ra•phy
car•dio•logi•cal
car•di•olo•gist
car•di•ol•ogy

car•dio•pul•mon•
  ary
car•dio•vas•cu•lar
card•sharp (*or*
  •sharper)
care
ca•reer
ca•reer•ist
care•free
care•ful
care•ful•ly
care•ful•ness
care•less
care•less•ness
car•er
ca•ress
ca•ress•er
ca•ress•ing•ly
car•et omission
  symbol; *cf* carat;
  carrot; karat
care•taker
care•worn
car•fare
car•go (*pl* •gos *or*
  •goes)
Car•ib (*pl* •ibs *or*
  •ib)
Car•ib•bean
cari•bou (*pl* •bous
  or •bou)
cari•ca•ture
cari•ca•tur•ist
caries (*pl* caries)
ca•ril•lon
  (•lon•ning,
  •lonned)
cari•ous
car•man (*pl* •men)

car•mina•tive
car•mine
car•nage
car•nal
car•nal•ity
car•nal•ly
car•na•tion
car•nel•ian *variant*
  spelling of
  cornelian
car•ni•val
car•ni•vore
car•nivo•rous
car•ob
car•ol (•ol•ing,
  •oled; *Brit*
  •ol•ling, •olled)
car•ol•er (*Brit also*
  •ol•ler)
caro•tene (*or* •tin)
ca•rot•id
ca•rous•al drinking
  party; *cf* carousel
ca•rouse
ca•rou•sel (*or*
  car•rou•) merry-
  go-round; *cf*
  carousal
ca•rous•er
carp
car•pal of the wrist
car•pel flower part
car•pen•ter
car•pen•try
car•pet
carpet•bag
carpet•bag•ger
car•port
car•pus (*pl* •pi)

car•riage
car•ri•er
car•ri•on
car•rot vegetable;
  cf carat; caret;
  karat
car•roty
car•rou•sel variant
  spelling of
  carousel
car•ry (•ries,
  •ry•ing, •ried)
carry•all
carry-over (n)
car•sick
car•sick•ness
cart
cart•age
carte blanche (pl
  cartes blanches)
car•tel
cart•ful
car•ti•lage
car•ti•lagi•nous
cart•load
car•tog•ra•pher
car•to•graph•ic
car•to•graphi•cal
car•tog•ra•phy
car•ton
car•toon
car•toon•ist
car•tridge
cart•wheel
carve
carv•er
carv•ing
cary•at•id (pl •ids
  or •ati•des)

cas•cade
cas•ca•ra
case
case-bound
case-harden
ca•sein
case•ment
case•work
case•work•er
cash
cash•able
cash-and-carry
cash•book
cash•ew
cash•ier
cash•mere
cas•ing
ca•si•no (pl •nos)
cask
cas•ket
cas•sa•va
cas•se•role
cas•sette
cas•sia
cas•sis
cas•sock priest's
  garment; cf
  hassock
cas•sou•let
cas•so•wary (pl
  •waries)
cast (cast•ing, cast)
  throw; cf caste
cas•ta•net
cast•away
caste Hindu class;
  cf cast
cas•tel•lat•ed
cas•tel•la•tion

cast•er one who
  casts; cf castor
cas•ter (or •tor)
  wheel on
  furniture
cas•ti•gate
cas•ti•ga•tion
cas•ti•ga•tor
cast•ing
cas•tle
cas•tled
cast-off (adj)
cast•off (n)
cas•tor plant oil; cf
  caster
cas•trate
cas•tra•tion
ca•sual
ca•su•al•ly
ca•su•al•ty (pl
  •ties)
ca•su•ist
ca•su•is•tic (or
  •ti•cal)
ca•su•ist•ry (pl
  •ries)
cat
cata•bol•ic
ca•tabo•lism
ca•tabo•lite
cata•clysm
cata•clys•mic (or
  •mal)
cata•comb
ca•tad•ro•mous
  migrating down
  river; cf
  anadromous
cata•lep•sy

cata•lep•tic
cata•log (or •logue;
•log•ing, •loged or
•logu•ing, logued)
cata•log•er (or
•log•ist, •logu•)
ca•tal•pa
ca•taly•sis (pl •ses)
cata•lyst
cata•lyt•ic
cata•lyze (Brit
•lyse)
cata•lyz•er (Brit
•lys•)
cata•ma•ran
cata•mount (or
•moun•tain)
cata•pult
cata•ract
ca•tarrh
ca•tarrh•al (or
•ous)
ca•tas•tro•phe
cata•stroph•ic
cata•strophi•cal•ly
cata•to•nia
cata•ton•ic
Ca•taw•ba (pl •bas
or •ba)
cat•bird
cat•boat
cat•call
catch (catch•ing,
caught)
catch-22
catch•able
catch•er
catchi•ness
catch•ing

catch•ment
catch•up variant of
ketchup
catch•word
catchy (catchi•er,
catchi•est)
cat•echism
cat•echis•mal
cat•echist (or
cate•chiz•er)
cat•echi•za•tion
cat•echize
cat•egori•cal (or
•egor•ic)
cat•egori•cal•ly
cat•ego•ri•za•tion
cat•ego•rize
cat•ego•ry (pl
•ries)
ca•ter
cater-cornered (or
catty-, kitty-)
ca•ter•er
ca•ter•ing
cat•er•pil•lar
cat•er•waul
cat•fish (pl •fish or
•fishes)
cat•gut
ca•thar•sis (pl •ses)
ca•thar•tic
ca•the•dral
cath•eter
cath•eteri•za•tion
cath•eter•ize
cath•ode
cath•od•ic
Catholic religion
catho•lic universal

Ca•tholi•cism
catho•lic•ity
cat•ion
cat•ion•ic
cat•kin
cat•like
cat•nap (vb
•nap•ping,
•napped)
cat•nip
cat-o'-nine-tails (pl
cat-o'-nine-tails)
cat's-eye
cat's-paw
cat•sup variant of
ketchup
cat•tery (pl •teries)
cat•ti•ly
cat•ti•ness
cat•tish
cat•tle
cattle•man (pl
•men)
cat•ty (•ti•er,
•ti•est)
catty-cornered
variant of cater-
cornered
cat•walk
Cau•ca•sian
Cau•ca•soid
cau•cus (pl •cuses)
cau•dal
cau•date (or
•dat•ed)
caught
caul•dron (or
cal•dron)
cau•li•flow•er

caulk (*or* calk)
caulk•er (*or* calk•er)
caus•al
cau•sal•i•ty (*pl* •ities)
cau•sal•ly
cau•sa•tion
causa•tive
cause cé•lè•bre (*pl* causes cé•lè•bres)
cause•way
caus•tic
caus•ti•cal•ly
caus•tic•i•ty (*or* •ness)
cau•teri•za•tion
cau•ter•ize
cau•tery (*pl* •teries)
cau•tion
cau•tion•ary
cau•tious
cau•tious•ly
cau•tious•ness
cav•al•cade
cava•lier
cava•lier•ism
cav•al•ry (*pl* •ries)
cav•al•ry•man (*pl* •men)
cave
ca•veat
cave-in (*n*)
cave•man (*pl* •men)
cav•er
cav•ern
cav•ern•ous
cavi•ar (*or* •are)

cav•il (•il•ing, •iled; *Brit* •il•ling, •illed)
cav•il•er (*Brit* •il•ler)
cavi•ta•tion
cav•ity (*pl* •ities)
ca•vort
ca•vy (*pl* •vies)
caw
cay low island; *cf* key; quay
cay•enne
cay•man (*or* cai•man; *pl* •mans)
cay•use (*pl* •use *or* •uses)
CD-video (*pl* -videos)
cease
cease•fire
cease•less
cease•less•ly
ce•cal (*Brit* cae•)
ce•cum (*Brit* cae•; *pl* •ca)
ce•dar tree; *cf* ceder
cede
ced•er one who cedes; *cf* cedar
ce•dil•la
ceil•ing
cel•an•dine
cel•ebrant
cel•ebrate
cel•ebra•tion
cel•ebra•tor
cel•ebra•tory

ce•leb•ri•ty (*pl* •rities)
ce•ler•ity
cel•ery
ce•les•tial
ce•les•tial•ly
ce•li•ac (*Brit* coe•)
celi•ba•cy (*pl* •cies)
celi•bate
cell
cel•lar storage room; *cf* seller
cel•lar•age
cel•list
cel•lo (*pl* •los *or* •li)
cel•lo•phane
cell•phone
cel•lu•lar
cel•lu•lite
cel•lu•loid
cel•lu•lose
Cel•sius
Celt (*or* Kelt)
Celt•ic (*or* Kelt•ic)
ce•ment
ce•men•ta•tion
ce•ment•er
cem•etery (*pl* •eteries)
ce•no•bite (*or* coe•)
ceno•taph
cen•ser incense container
cen•sor suppressor; to ban; *cf* sensor
cen•sor•able
cen•so•rial
cen•so•ri•ous
cen•so•ri•ous•ness

cen•sor•ship
cen•sual of a
census; *cf* sensual
cen•sur•able
cen•sure
cen•sus (*pl* •suses)
cent
cen•taur
cen•te•nar•ian
cen•ten•ary (*pl*
•aries)
cen•ten•nial
cen•ter (*Brit* •re)
center•board (*Brit*
centre•)
center•fold (*Brit*
centre•)
center•piece (*Brit*
centre•)
cen•ti•grade
cen•ti•gram (*or*
•gramme)
cen•ti•li•ter (*Brit*
•tre)
cen•time
cen•ti•me•ter (*Brit*
•tre)
cen•ti•pede
cen•tral
cen•tral•ism
cen•tral•i•ty (*pl*
•ities)
cen•trali•za•tion
cen•tral•ize
cen•tral•ly
cen•tric (*or* •tri•cal)
cen•tric•i•ty
cen•tri•fu•gal
cen•tri•fu•gal•ly

cen•trifu•ga•tion
cen•tri•fuge
cen•trip•etal
cen•trip•etal•ly
cen•trist
cen•tu•pli•cate
cen•tu•rion
cen•tu•ry (*pl* •ries)
ce•phal•ic
cepha•lo•pod
ce•ram•ic
ce•ram•ics
ce•ra•mist (*or*
ce•rami•cist)
ce•real crop; *cf*
serial
cer•ebel•lar
cer•ebel•lum (*pl*
•lums *or* •la)
ce•re•bral
ce•re•bral•ly
ce•re•bro•spi•nal
ce•re•bro•vas•
cu•lar
ce•re•brum (*pl*
•brums *or* •bra)
cer•emo•nial
cer•emo•ni•al•ism
cer•emo•ni•al•ist
cer•emo•nial•ly
cer•emo•ni•ous
cer•emo•ny (*pl*
•nies)
ce•rise
ce•rium
ce•rous
cer•tain
cer•tain•ly

cer•tain•ty (*pl*
•ties)
cer•ti•fi•able
cer•ti•fi•ably
cer•tifi•cate
cer•ti•fi•ca•tion
cer•ti•fy (•fies,
•fy•ing, •fied)
cer•ti•tude
ce•ru•lean
cer•vi•cal
cer•vix (*pl* •vixes
or •vi•ces)
ce•sar•ean sec•tion
(*Brit* Cae•sar•ean
sec•tion)
ce•sium (*Brit* cae•)
ces•sa•tion
ces•sion act of
ceding; *cf* session
cess•pool (*or* •pit)
ce•ta•cean
cha•blis (*or* Cha•)
chafe
chaf•er
chaff
chaff•er (*n*)
chaf•fer (*vb*)
chaf•finch
chaf•ing
Cha•gas' dis•ease
cha•grin
chain
chain-react
chain-smoke
chain-stitch
chain-store
chair
chair•borne

chair•man (pl
•men)
chair•man•ship
chair•person
chair•woman (pl
•women)
chaise longue (or
chaise lounge; pl
chaise longues,
chaises longues, or
chaise lounges)
chal•cedo•ny (pl
•nies)
cha•let
chal•ice goblet; cf
challis
chalk
chalk•board
chalki•ness
chalk•pit
chalky (chalki•er,
chalki•est)
chal•lenge
chal•lenge•able
chal•leng•er
chal•lis fabric; cf
chalice
cham•ber
cham•ber•lain
chamber•maid
cham•bray
cha•me•leon
cha•meleon•ic
cham•fer
cham•ois (pl •ois
or •oix)
chamo•mile variant
spelling of
camomile

cham•pagne wine
cham•paign open
country
cham•pion
cham•pi•on•ship
chance
chan•cel
chan•cel•lery (or
•lory; pl •leries or
•lories)
chan•cel•lor
chan•cery (pl
•ceries)
chanci•ly
chan•cre
chan•croid
chancy (chanci•er,
chanci•est)
chan•de•lier
chan•dler
chan•dlery (pl
•dleries)
change
change•abil•ity (or
•able•ness)
change•able
change•ably
change•ful
change•less
change•less•ness
change•ling
change•over
chang•er
chan•nel (•nel•ing,
•neled; Brit
•nel•ling, •nelled)
chan•nel•er (Brit
•nel•ler)
chan•nel•ize

chan•son
chant
chant•er
chan•teuse
chan•tey (or
chan•ty, shan•ty,
shan•tey; pl •teys
or •ties) song; cf
shanty
cha•os
cha•ot•ic
cha•oti•cal•ly
chap (chap•ping,
chapped)
chapa•re•jos (or
•ra•)
chap•ar•ral
chap•book
chap•el
chap•er•on (or
•one)
chap•er•on•age
chap•lain
chap•lain•cy (pl
•cies)
chapped
chaps short for
chaparejos
chap•stick
chap•ter
chapter•house
char (char•ring,
charred)
char•ac•ter
char•ac•ter•ful
char•ac•ter•is•tic
char•ac•ter•is•ti•
cal•ly

char•ac•teri•za•
tion
char•ac•ter•ize
char•ac•ter•less
cha•rade
char•coal
chard
charge
charge•abil•ity
charge•able
char•gé d'af•faires
(pl char•gés
d'af•faires)
charg•er
chari•ly
chari•ness
chari•ot
chari•ot•eer
cha•ris•ma (or
char•ism)
char•is•mat•ic
char•is•mati•cal•ly
chari•ta•ble
chari•table•ness
chari•tably
char•lty (pl •ities)
char•la•tan
char•la•tan•ism (or
•ry)
charle•ston
char•lotte
charm
charm•er
charm•ing
charm•ing•ly
char•nel
chart
chart•able
char•ter

char•tered
char•treuse
chary (chari•er,
chari•est)
chase
chas•er
chasm
Chas•sid (or
Cha•sid) variant
spellings of Hasid
chas•sis (pl •sis)
chaste
chaste•ly
chas•ten
chas•tis•able
chas•tise
chas•tise•ment
chas•ti•ty
chasu•ble
chat (chat•ting,
chat•ted)
cha•teau (or châ•;
pl •teaux or
•teaus)
chat•tel
chat•ter
chatter•box
chat•ter•er
chat•ti•ly
chat•ty (•ti•er,
•ti•est)
chauf•feur (fem
•feuse)
chau•vin•ism
chau•vin•ist
chau•vin•is•tic
chau•vin•is•ti•
cal•ly

cheap inexpensive;
cf cheep
cheap•en
cheap•ly
cheap•ness
cheap•skate
cheat
cheat•er
Che•chen (pl
•chens or •chen)
check pause;
pattern; etc.
check (Brit cheque)
bill of exchange
check•able
check•book (Brit
cheque•)
check•er one who
checks
check•er (Brit
che•quer) pattern
of squares, etc.
check•ered (Brit
che•quered)
checker•board
check•ers
check-in (n)
check•mate
check•out (n)
check•point
check•up (n)
Ched•dar (or
ched•)
cheek
cheek•bone
cheeki•ly
cheeki•ness
cheeky (cheeki•er,
cheeki•est)

cheep chirp; *cf*
  cheap
cheep•er
cheer
cheer•ful
cheer•ful•ly
cheer•ful•ness
cheeri•ly
cheeri•ness
cheer•leader
cheer•less
cheer•less•ness
cheery (cheeri•er,
  cheeri•est)
cheese
cheese•board
cheese•burger
cheese•cake
cheese•cloth
cheesi•ness
cheesy (cheesi•er,
  cheesi•est)
chee•tah (*or*
  che•tah)
chef
chef-d'oeuvre (*pl*
  chefs-d'oeuvre)
chemi•cal
chemi•cal•ly
che•mise
chem•ist
chem•is•try (*pl*
  •tries)
che•mo•re•cep•tor
  (*or* chemo•cep•tor)
che•mo•stat
chemo•syn•the•sis
  (*pl* •ses)
chemo•syn•the•tic

chemo•thera•pist
chemo•thera•py
chem•ur•gic (*or*
  •gi•cal)
chem•ur•gy
che•nille
cheque *Brit spelling
  of* check (bill of
  exchange)
cheque•book *Brit
  spelling of*
  checkbook
che•quer *Brit
  spelling of* checker
  (pattern of
  squares, etc.)
chequer•board *Brit
  spelling of*
  checkerboard
che•quered *Brit
  spelling of*
  checkered
cher•ish
cher•ish•able
cher•ish•er
Chero•kee (*pl*
  •kees *or* •kee)
che•root
cher•ry (*pl* •ries)
cher•ub (*pl* •ubs *or*
  cheru•bim)
che•ru•bic
Chesh•ire cheese
chess (*pl* chess *or*
  chesses)
chess•board
chess•man (*pl*
  •men)
chest

chest•ed
ches•ter•field
chesti•ly
chesti•ness
chest•nut
chesty (chesti•er,
  chesti•est)
che•tah *variant
  spelling of* cheetah
cheva•lier
che•viot
chev•ron
chew
chew•able
chew•er
chewy (chewi•er,
  chewi•est)
Chey•enne (*pl*
  •enne *or* •ennes)
chi
chi•an•ti
chia•ro•scu•ro (*pl*
  •ros)
chic
chi•cane
chi•ca•nery (*pl*
  •neries)
chick
chicka•dee
chicka•ree
Chicka•saw (*pl*
  •saws *or* •saw)
chick•en
chicken•hearted (*or*
  -livered)
chick•en pox
chick-pea
chick•weed
chi•cle

chico•ry (*or*
 chic•co•ry,
 chicko•ry; *pl* •ries)
chide (chid•ing;
 chid•ed *or* chid;
 chid•ed, chid, *or*
 chid•den)
chid•er
chief
chief•ly
chief•tain
chif•fon
chif•fo•nier (*or*
 •fon•nier)
chig•ger
chi•gnon
Chi•hua•hua
chil•blain
child (*pl* chil•dren)
child•bear•ing
child•bed
child•birth
child•care
child•hood
child•ish
child•ish•ly
child•ish•ness
child•less
child•less•ness
child•like
chil•dren *pl of* child
chill
chil•li (*or* chi•le,
 chi•li; *pl* •lies)
 pepper; *cf* chilly
chil•li con car•ne
chil•li•ness
chil•ly (•li•er,

 •li•est) cold; *cf*
 chilli
chime
chi•me•ra (*or*
 •mae•)
chim•ney
chimney•piece
chimney•pot
chimp
chim•pan•zee
chin (chin•ning,
 chinned)
chi•na
china•berry (*pl*
 •berries)
china•ware
chinch
chin•chil•la
chine
Chi•nese (*pl* •nese)
chink
chin•less
chinned
chin•ning
chino (*pl* chinos)
chi•noi•se•rie
Chi•nook (*pl*
 •nook *or* •nooks)
 American Indian
chi•nook wind
chin•qua•pin (*or*
 •ka•pin)
chintz
chintzy (chintzi•er,
 chintzi•est)
chip (chip•ping,
 chipped)
chip•board
chip•munk

Chip•pen•dale
chip•per
chip•ping
chip•py (*n, pl* •pies;
 adj •pi•er, •pi•est)
chi•ro•man•cy
chi•ropo•dist
chi•ropo•dy
chi•ro•prac•tic
chi•ro•prac•tor
chirp
chirp•er
chirpi•ly
chirpi•ness
chirpy (chirpi•er,
 chirpi•est)
chirr
chir•rup
chir•rup•er
chis•el (•el•ing,
 •eled; *Brit* •el•ling,
 •elled)
chis•el•er (*Brit*
 •el•ler)
chi-square
chit•chat
 (•chat•ting,
 •chat•ted)
chi•tin biochemical
 compound; *cf*
 chiton
chi•tin•ous
chi•ton mollusk; *cf*
 chitin
chit•ter
chit•ter•lings (*or*
 chit•lins,
 chit•lings)
chiv•al•ric

chiv•al•rous

chiv•al•ry (pl •ries)

chive (or chives)

chivy (or chiv•vy; n,
pl chivies or
chiv•vies; vb
chivies, chivy•ing,
chiv•ied or
chiv•vies,
chiv•vy•ing,
chiv•vied)

chlo•ral

chlo•rate

chlo•ric

chlo•ride

chlo•rin•ate

chlo•rina•tion

chlo•rina•tor

chlo•rine (or •rin)

chlo•rite

chloro•fluoro•
car•bon

chlo•ro•form

chlo•ro•phyll (or
•phyl)

chock

chock-a-block

chock-full (or
chock•ful)

choco•late

choco•laty

Choc•taw (pl
•taws or •taw)

choice

choice•ly

choice•ness

choir choral group;
cf quire

choir•boy

choir•master

choke

choke•berry (pl
•berries)

choke•cherry (pl
•cherries)

chok•er

chol•er anger; cf
collar

chol•era

chol•er•ic

cho•les•ter•ol (or
•ter•in)

chol•la

chomp

choose (choos•ing,
chose, cho•sen)

choos•er

choosi•ness

choosy (or
choos•ey;
choosi•er,
choosi•est)

chop (chop•ping,
chopped)

chop•logic

chop•per

chop•pi•ly

chop•pi•ness

chop•py (•pi•er,
•pi•est)

chop•stick

chop suey

cho•ral (adj)

cho•rale (n)

cho•ral•ly

chord math and
music term; cf
cord

chord•al

chor•date animal;
cf cordate

chore

cho•rea

cho•reo•graph

cho•re•og•ra•pher
(or cho•reg•
ra•pher)

cho•reo•graph•ic
(or cho•
regraph•ic)

cho•reo•graphi•
cal•ly (or
cho•regraphi•)

cho•re•og•ra•phy
(or cho•reg•
ra•phy; pl •phies)

cho•ric

chor•is•ter

chor•tle

cho•rus (n, pl
•ruses; vb •rus•ing
or •rus•sing,
•rused or russed)

chose

cho•sen

choux pastry; cf
shoe

chow

chow•chow (or
chow)

chow•der

chow mein

chrism

chris•ten

Chris•ten•dom

chris•ten•ing

Chris•tian

Chris•ti•an•ity
Chris•tian•iza•tion
Chris•tian•ize
Chris•tian•ly
Christ•like
Christ•mas
Christ•mas•sy
chro•mate
chro•mat•ic
chro•mati•cism
chro•mato•gram
chro•mato•graph•ic
chro•ma•tog•
 ra•phy
chrome
chro•mic
chro•mite
chro•mium
chro•mo•som•al
chro•mo•some
chro•mous
chron•ic
chroni•cal•ly
chro•nic•ity
chroni•cle
chroni•cler
chrono•graph
chrono•graph•ic
chrono•logi•cal
chrono•logi•cal•ly
chro•nolo•gist
chro•nol•ogy (pl
 •ogies)
chro•nom•eter
chrono•met•ric (or
 •ri•cal)
chrono•met•ri•
 cal•ly
chro•nom•etry

chrysa•lis (pl •lises,
 •lids, or chry•
 sali•des)
chry•san•the•mum
chub (pl chub or
 chubs)
chub•bi•ness
chub•by (•bi•er,
 •bi•est)
chuck
chuck•le
chuckle•head
chuck•ler
chuck•wal•la (or
 •awal•la)
chuff
chug (chug•ging,
 chugged)
chum (chum•ming,
 chummed)
chum•mi•ly
chum•mi•ness
chum•my (•mi•er,
 •mi•est)
chump
chunk
chunki•ness
chunky (chunki•er,
 chunki•est)
Church body of
 Christians
church building
church•goer
church•going
church•man (pl
 •men)
church•warden
church•woman (pl
 •women)

church•yard
churl
churl•ish
churl•ish•ly
churl•ish•ness
churn
chute slide; cf
 shoot
chut•ney
chutz•pah (or
 hutz•)
chyle intestinal
 fluid
chyme digested
 food
ci•ca•da (or
 ci•ca•la; pl •das,
 •dae or •las, •le)
cica•tri•cial
cica•trix (pl
 •tri•ces)
cic•ero•ne (pl •nes
 or •ni)
ci•der
ci•gar
ciga•rette (or •ret)
ciga•ril•lo (pl •los)
cilia pl of cilium
cili•ary
cili•ate (or •at•ed)
cil•ium (pl cilia)
cinch
cin•cho•na
cin•der
cine (or ciné)
cin•éaste (or •east)
cin•ema
cin•emat•ic
cin•emati•cal•ly

cin•emato•graph
cin•ema•tog•ra•pher
cin•emato•graph•ic
cin•ema•tog•ra•phy
cin•na•bar
cin•na•mon
cinque•foil
ci•pher (or cy•pher)
cir•ca
cir•ca•dian
cir•cle
cir•cler
cir•clet
cir•cuit
cir•cui•tous
cir•cui•tous•ly
cir•cuit•ry (pl •ries)
cir•cu•ity (pl •ities)
cir•cu•lar
cir•cu•lar•ity (or •ness)
cir•cu•lari•za•tion
cir•cu•lar•ize
cir•cu•lar•iz•er
cir•cu•late
cir•cu•la•tion
cir•cu•la•tive
cir•cu•la•tor
cir•cu•la•tory
cir•cum•am•bi•ent
cir•cum•am•bu•late
cir•cum•am•bu•la•tion
cir•cum•am•bu•la•tor
cir•cum•cise
cir•cum•ci•sion
cir•cum•fer•ence

cir•cum•fer•en•tial
cir•cum•flex
cir•cum•fluous (or •fluent)
cir•cum•lo•cu•tion
cir•cum•locu•tory
cir•cum•lu•nar
cir•cum•navi•gate
cir•cum•navi•ga•tion
cir•cum•navi•ga•tor
cir•cum•po•lar
cir•cum•scribe
cir•cum•scrip•tion
cir•cum•spect
cir•cum•spec•tion
cir•cum•spect•ly
cir•cum•stance
cir•cum•stan•tial
cir•cum•stan•ti•al•ity (pl •ities)
cir•cum•stan•tial•ly
cir•cum•stan•ti•ate
cir•cum•stan•tia•tion
cir•cum•vent
cir•cum•vent•er (or ven•tor)
cir•cum•ven•tion
cir•cum•vo•lu•tion
cir•cum•vo•lu•tory
cir•cus (pl •cuses)
cirque
cir•rhosed
cir•rho•sis
cir•rhot•ic
cir•ro•cu•mu•lus (pl •li)

cir•rose (or •rous, •rhose)
cir•ro•stra•tus (pl •ti)
cir•rus (or •rhus; pl •ri or •rhi)
cis•al•pine
cist box; cf cyst
Cis•ter•cian
cis•tern
cit•able (or cite•able)
cita•del
ci•ta•tion
cite quote; cf sight; site
citi•fy (or city•fy; •fies, •fy•ing, •fied)
citi•zen
citi•zen•ry (pl •ries)
citi•zen•ship
cit•rate
cit•ric
cit•ri•cul•ture
cit•rine
cit•ron
cit•ro•nel•la
cit•rus (pl •ruses)
city (pl cities)
civ•et
civ•ic
civi•cal•ly
civ•ics
civ•il
ci•vil•ian
ci•vil•ity (pl •ities)
civi•liz•able
civi•li•za•tion

civi•lize
civi•liz•er
civ•il•ly
civ•vy (*or* civie; *pl*
•vies *or* civies)
clack noise; *cf*
claque
clad (clad•ding,
clad)
claim
claim•able
claim•ant
claim•er
clair•voy•ance (*or*
•an•cy)
clair•voy•ant
clam (clam•ming,
clammed)
cla•mant
clam•bake
clam•ber
clam•mi•ly
clam•mi•ness
clam•my (•mi•er,
•mi•est)
clam•or (*Brit* •our)
clam•or•ous
clamp
clamp•down
clan
clan•des•tine
clang
clang•er that
which clangs;
mistake
clang•or (*or* •our)
loud noise
clang•or•ous (*or*
•our•ous)

clank
clan•nish
clans•man (*pl*
•men)
clans•woman (*pl*
•women)
clap (clap•ping,
clapped *or* clapt)
clap•board
clap•per
clap•trap
claque hired
applauders; *cf*
clack
clar•et
clari•fi•ca•tion
clari•fier
clari•fy (•fies,
•fy•ing, •fied)
clari•nct
clari•net•ist (*or*
•net•tist)
clari•on
clar•ity
clash
clash•er
clasp
clasp•er
class
class-conscious
class-conscious•
ness
clas•sic
clas•si•cal
clas•si•cal•ism
clas•si•cal•ity
clas•si•cal•ly
clas•si•cism

clas•si•cist (*or*
clas•si•cal•ist)
clas•sics
clas•si•fi•able
clas•si•fi•ca•tion
clas•si•fi•ca•tory
clas•si•fi•er
clas•si•fy (•fies,
•fy•ing, •fied)
classi•ness
class•less
class•less•ness
class•mate
class•room
classy (classi•er,
classi•est)
clat•ter
clat•tery
claus•al
clausc
claus•tro•pho•bia
claus•tro•pho•bic
claus•tro•pho•bi•
cal•ly
clavi•chord
clavi•chord•ist
clavi•cle
cla•vicu•lar
claw
clay
clay•bank
clay•ey
clay•like
clean
clean•able
clean-cut
clean•er
clean-limbed
clean•li•ness

clean•ly (•li•er, •li•est)
clean•ness
cleans•able
cleanse
cleans•er
clean-shaven
clean•up
clear
clear•ance
clear-cut
clear-eyed
clear•headed
clear•headed•ness
clear•ing
clear•ness
clear-sighted
cleat
cleav•able
cleav•age
cleave (cleav•ing; cleaved, cleft, or clove; cleft, cleaved, or clo•ven)
cleav•er
clef
cleft
clema•tis
clem•en•cy (pl •cies)
clem•ent
clem•en•tine
clench
cler•gy (pl •gies)
clergy•man (pl •men)
cler•ic
cler•i•cal

cleri•cal•ism
cleri•cal•ly
clerk
clerk•dom
clerk•ship
clev•er
clev•er•ly
clev•er•ness
clew yarn; cf clue
cli•ché
cli•chéd
click
click•er
cli•ent
cli•en•tele
cliff
cliff-hanger
cliff-hanging
cli•mac•ter•ic (n)
cli•mac•tic (or •ti•cal; adj)
cli•mate
cli•mat•ic (or •mati•cal or •mat•al)
cli•ma•ti•cal•ly
cli•ma•tolo•gist
cli•ma•tol•ogy
cli•max
climb ascend; cf clime
climb-down (n)
climb•er
clime climate; cf climb
clinch
clinch•er
cling (cling•ing, clung)

cling•er
clingi•ness (or cling•ing•ness)
cling•stone
clingy (clingi•er, clingi•est)
clin•ic
clini•cal
cli•ni•cian
clink
clink•er
clinker-built
clip (clip•ping, clipped)
clip•board
clip-clop
clip•per
clip•pers
clip•ping
clique
cli•quey (or •quy)
cli•quish
clito•ral
clito•ris
cloak
cloak-and-dagger (adj)
cloak•room
clob•ber
cloche
clock
clock•maker
clock•wise
clock•work
clod
clod•dish
clod•hop•per
clod•hop•ping

clog (clog•ging, clogged)
clog•gi•ness
clog•gy (•gi•er, •gi•est)
cloi•son•né
clois•ter
clois•tered
clomp
clo•nal
clone (or clon)
clonk
clop (clop•ping, clopped)
close
closed-circuit (adj)
close-down (n)
close•fisted
close-grained
close-knit
close•ly
close•ness
clos•er
clos•et
close-up (n)
clos•ing
clo•sure
clot (clot•ting, clot•ted)
cloth
cloth•bound
clothe (cloth•ing, clothed or clad)
clothes
clothes•horse
clothes•line
clothes•press
clothi•er
cloth•ing

clot•ted
clot•ting
clo•ture
cloud
cloud•burst
cloud-cuckoo-land
cloud•i•ly
cloudi•ness
cloud•less
cloud•scape
cloudy (cloudi•er, cloudi•est)
clout
clove
clo•ven
cloven-hoofed (or -footed)
clo•ver
clover•leaf (pl •leaves)
clown
clown•ery
clown•ish
cloy
cloy•ing•ly
cloy•ing•ness
club (club•bing, clubbed)
club•bable (or •able)
club•by (•bi•er, •bi•est)
club•footed
club•house
club•land
club•man (pl •men)
cluck
clue (clu•ing, clued) evidence; cf clew

clue•less
clump
clumpy (clumpi•er, clumpi•est)
clum•si•ly
clum•si•ness
clum•sy (•si•er, •si•est)
clung
clunk
clus•ter
clutch
clut•ter
coach
coach•er
coach•ing
coach•man (pl •men)
coach•work
co•ac•tion
co•ac•tive
co•ac•tiv•ity (pl •ities)
co•ad•ju•tant
co•agu•lable
co•agu•lant (or co•agu•la•tor)
co•agu•late
co•agu•la•tion
co•agu•la•tive
coal fuel; cf kohl
coa•lesce
coa•les•cence
coa•les•cent
coal•field
coa•li•tion
coa•li•tion•ist
coarse rough; cf course

coarse•ly
coars•en
coarse•ness
coast
coast•al
coast•er
coast•guard
coast•line
coat garment; cf
  cote
coat•ed
coa•ti (or
  coa•ti•mun•di,
  •mon•di; pl •tis or
  •dis)
coat•ing
coat•tail
co•author
coax
coax•er
co•ax•ial
cob (or cobb;
  cob•bing, cobbed)
co•balt
co•bal•tic
co•bal•tous
cob•ble
cob•bler
cobble•stone
cob•nut
co•bra
cob•web
cob•webbed
cob•web•by
co•ca
Coca-Cola
  (Trademark)
co•caine (or •cain)
co•cain•ism

coc•cal
coc•ci pl of coccus
coc•coid
coc•cus (pl •ci)
coc•cyg•eal
coc•cyx (pl •cyxes
  or •cy•ges)
cochi•neal
co•chlea (pl
  •chleae)
co•chlear
cock
cock•ade
cocka•tiel (or •teel)
cocka•too (pl
  •toos)
cock•crow
cock•er•el
cock•er span•iel
cock•eyed
cock•fight
cocki•ly
cocki•ness
cock•le
cockle•shell
cock•ney
cock•pit
cock•roach
cocks•comb (or
  cox•comb)
cock•sure
cock•tail
cocky (cocki•er,
  cocki•est)
co•co (pl •cos)
  palm tree
co•coa beverage
co•co•nut (or •coa•)
co•coon

cod (n, pl cod or
  cods)
co•da final part; cf
  coder
cod•dle
cod•dler
code
co•deine
cod•er person or
  device that codes;
  cf coda
co•dex (pl
  co•di•ces)
cod•fish (pl •fish
  or •fishes)
codg•er
codi•cil
codi•cil•lary
codi•fi•ca•tion
codi•fi•er
codi•fy (•fies,
  •fy•ing, •fied)
cod•ling
co-ed
co•ed•it
co•edi•tion
co•edi•tor
co•edu•ca•tion
co•edu•ca•tion•al
co•ef•fi•cient
coe•la•canth
coe•len•ter•ate
coe•li•ac Brit
  spelling of celiac
coe•no•bite variant
  spelling of
  cenobite
co•en•zyme
co•equal

co•equali•ty
co•equal•ly
co•erce
co•er•cible
co•er•cion
co•er•cion•ary
co•er•cion•ist
co•er•cive
co•er•cive•ness
co•eval
co•eval•ity
co•eval•ly
co•ex•ist
co•ex•ist•ence
co•ex•ist•ent
co•ex•tend
co•ex•ten•sion
co•ex•ten•sive
cof•fee
coffee•pot
cof•fer
cof•fin
cog (cog•ging,
  cogged)
co•gen•cy
co•gent
cogi•tate
cogi•ta•tion
cogi•ta•tive
cogi•ta•tor
Cog•nac (*or* cog•)
cog•nate
cog•na•tion
  relatedness
cog•ni•tion
  perception
cog•ni•tive
cog•ni•zable
cog•ni•zance

cog•ni•zant
cog•nize
co•gno•scen•te (*pl*
  •ti)
cog•wheel
co•hab•it
co•hab•itant (*or*
  •iter)
co•habi•ta•tion
co•habi•tee
co•heir
co•here
co•her•ence (*or*
  •en•cy)
co•her•ent
co•her•er
co•he•sion
co•he•sive
co•hort
coif•feur (*fem*
  •feuse) hairdresser
coif•fure hair style
coign (*or* coigne)
  variant spellings
  of quoin
coil
coil•er
coin currency; *cf*
  quoin
coin•age
co•in•cide
co•in•ci•dence
co•in•ci•dent
co•in•ci•den•tal
co•in•ci•den•tal•ly
coin•er
co•in•sur•ance
co•in•sure
coi•tal

coi•tion
coi•tus
coi•tus
  in•ter•rup•tus
coke
col
co•la (*or* ko•)
col•an•der sieve; *cf*
  calendar; calender
co•lati•tude
cold
cold-blooded
cold-blooded•ly
cold-blooded•ness
cold-hearted
cold-hearted•ly
cold-hearted•ness
cold•ish
cold•ly
cold•ness
cold-shoulder (*vb*)
cole•slaw
col•ic
col•icky
coli•seum (*or*
  col•os•seum)
co•li•tis (*or*
  colo•ni•tis)
col•labo•rate
col•labo•ra•tion
col•labo•ra•tive
col•labo•ra•tor
col•lage
col•lag•ist
col•lapse
col•laps•ible (*or*
  •able)
col•lar part of
  garment; *cf* choler

col•lar•bone
col•late
col•lat•er•al
col•lat•er•al•ly
col•la•tion
col•la•tive
col•la•tor
col•league
col•lect
col•lect•able (or •ible)
col•lec•tion
col•lec•tive
col•lec•tive•ly
col•lec•tiv•ism
col•lec•tiv•ist
col•lec•tiv•ity (pl •ities)
col•lec•tivi•za•tion
col•lec•tiv•ize
col•lec•tor
col•leen
col•lege
col•le•gial
col•legian
col•legi•ate
col•lide
col•lie
col•li•er
col•liery (pl •lieries)
col•lin•ear
col•lin•ear•ity
col•li•sion
col•lo•cate
col•lo•ca•tion
col•lo•dion (or •dium)
col•loid

col•loi•dal
col•lo•quial
col•lo•qui•al•ism
col•lo•qui•al•ly
col•lo•quium (pl •quiums or •quia)
col•lo•quy (pl •quies)
*collossus incorrect spelling of colossus
col•lude
col•lu•sion
col•lu•sive
co•logne
Co•lom•bian
co•lon (pl •lons) punctuation mark
co•lon (pl •lons or •la) large intestine
colo•nel officer; cf kernel
colo•nel•cy (or •ship; •cies or •ships)
co•lo•nial
co•lo•ni•al•ism
co•lo•ni•al•ist
co•lo•ni•al•ly
co•lon•ic
colo•nist
colo•ni•tis variant of colitis
colo•niz•able
colo•ni•za•tion
colo•nize
colo•niz•er
col•on•nade
col•on•nad•ed

colo•ny (pl •nies)
colo•phon
col•or (Brit •our)
col•or•able (Brit •our•)
col•or•ant
col•ora•tion
colo•ra•tu•ra (or col•ora•ture)
color-blind (Brit colour-)
col•ored (Brit •oured)
color•fast (Brit colour•)
col•or•ful (Brit •our•)
col•or•ful•ly (Brit •our•)
col•or•if•ic
col•or•im•eter
col•or•im•etry
col•or•ing (Brit •our•)
col•or•ist (Brit •our•)
col•or•ize (Brit •our•)
col•or•less (Brit •our•)
co•los•sal
co•los•sal•ly
co•los•sus (pl •si or •suses; NOT collossus)
co•los•to•my (pl •mies)
co•los•trum

col•our *Brit spelling of* color
colt
colt•er (*Brit* coul•)
colt•ish
col•um•bine
col•umn
co•lum•nar
col•umned (*or* •um•nat•ed)
col•um•nist
co•ma (*pl* •mas) unconsciousness
co•ma (*pl* •mae) cloud around comet
com•al
Co•man•che (*pl* •ches *or* •che)
co•ma•tose
comb
com•bat (•bat•ing, •bat•ed *or* •bat•ting, •bat•ted)
com•bat•able
com•bat•ant
com•bat•er
com•bat•ive
comb•er
com•bin•able
com•bi•na•tion
com•bi•na•tive (*or* •to•rial, •tory)
com•bine
com•bin•er
comb•ing
com•bust

com•bus•ti•bil•ity (*or* •tible•ness)
com•bus•tible
com•bus•tion
come (com•ing, came)
come•back
co•me•dian
co•me•dic (*or* •di•cal)
co•me•di•enne
come•down
com•edy (*pl* •edies)
come•ly (•li•er, •li•est)
come-on (*n*)
com•er
co•mes•tible
com•et
come•up•pance
com•fit candy
com•fort ease
com•fort•able
com•fort•ably
com•fort•er
com•fort•ing
com•fort•less
com•fy (•fi•er, •fi•est)
com•ic
comi•cal
comi•cal•ly
com•ing
com•ma
com•mand
com•man•dant
com•man•deer
com•mand•er
com•mand•er•ship

com•mand•ing
com•mand•ment
com•man•do (*pl* •dos *or* •does)
com•memo•rate
com•memo•ra•tion
com•memo•ra•tive (*or* •tory)
com•memo•ra•tor
com•mence
com•mence•ment
com•mend
com•mend•able
com•mend•ably
com•men•da•tion
com•menda•tory
com•men•sal
com•men•sal•ism (*or* •sal•ity)
com•men•su•rable
com•men•su•rate
com•men•su•ra•tion
com•ment
com•men•tary (*pl* •taries)
com•men•tate
com•men•ta•tor
com•ment•er
com•merce
com•mer•cial
com•mer•cial•ism
com•mer•cial•ist
com•mer•cial•is•tic
com•mer•ciali•za•tion
com•mer•cial•ize
com•mer•cial•ly
com•min•gle

com•mi•nute
com•mi•nu•tion
com•mis•er•ate
com•mis•era•tion
com•mis•era•tor
com•mis•sar
com•mis•sarial
com•mis•sariat
com•mis•sary (*pl*
•saries)
com•mis•sion
com•mis•sion•aire
com•mis•sion•al (*or*
•ary)
com•mis•sion•er
com•mit (•mit•ting,
•mit•ted)
com•mit•ment
(*NOT*
committment)
com•mit•tal
com•mit•tee
committee•man (*pl*
•men)
com•mit•ter
*committment
incorrect spelling
of committment
of* commitment
com•mode
com•mo•dious
com•mod•ity (*pl*
•ities)
com•mo•dore
com•mon
com•mon•er
com•mon•ly
com•mon•ness
common•place
common•wealth

com•mo•tion
com•mu•nal
com•mu•nal•ism
com•mu•nal•ist
com•mu•nal•ity
commu•nali•za•tion
com•mu•nal•ize
com•mu•nal•ly
com•mune
com•mu•ni•ca•bil•
ity (*or* •cable•ness)
com•mu•ni•cable
com•mu•ni•cant
com•mu•ni•cate
com•mu•ni•ca•tion
com•mu•ni•ca•tive
com•mu•ni•ca•tor
com•mu•ni•ca•tory
com•mun•ion
com•mun•ion•ist
com•mu•ni•qué
com•mun•ism
Com•mu•nist
political party
com•mu•nist
supporter of
communism
com•mu•nis•tic
com•mu•nity (*pl*
•nities)
com•mu•ni•za•tion
com•mu•nize
com•mut•able
com•mu•tate
com•mu•ta•tion
com•mu•ta•tor
com•mute
com•mut•er
com•pact

com•pact•ness
com•pan•ion
com•pan•ion•able
com•pan•ion•ably
com•pan•ion•ship
com•pan•ion•way
com•pa•ny (*pl*
•nies)
com•pa•ra•bil•ity
com•pa•rable
com•pa•rably
com•para•tive
com•para•tive•ly
com•pare
com•par•er
com•pari•son
com•part•ment
com•part•men•tal
com•part•men•tali•
za•tion
com•part•men•tal•
ize
com•pass
com•pass•able
com•pas•sion
com•pas•sion•ate
com•pat•ibil•ity
(*pl* •ities)
com•pat•ible
com•pat•ibly
com•pat•ri•ot
com•pat•ri•ot•ic
com•pel (•pel•ling,
•pelled)
com•pel•ler
com•pen•dious
com•pen•dium (*pl*
•diums *or* •dia)
com•pen•sate

com•pen•sa•tion
com•pen•sa•tor
com•pen•sa•to•ry
(*or* •tive)
com•pete
com•pe•tence
com•pe•tent
com•pe•tent•ly
com•pe•ti•tion
com•pet•i•tive
com•pet•i•tive•ness
com•pet•i•tor
com•pi•la•tion
com•pile
com•pil•er
com•pla•cen•cy (*or*
com•pla•cence; *pl*
•cencies *or*
•cences)
com•pla•cent self-
satisfied; *cf*
complaisant
com•plain
com•plain•ant
com•plain•er
com•plaint
com•plai•sance
com•plai•sant
willing to comply;
cf complacent
com•ple•ment
complete; that
which completes;
cf compliment
com•ple•men•tary
(*or* •tal)
completing; *cf*
complimentary
com•plete

com•plete•ly
com•plete•ness
com•ple•tion
com•plex
com•plex•ion
com•plex•i•ty (*pl*
•ities)
com•pli•ance (*or*
•an•cy)
com•pli•ant (*or*
•able)
com•pli•cate
com•pli•cat•ed
com•pli•ca•tion
com•plic•i•ty (*pl*
•ities)
com•pli•er
com•pli•ment
praise; *cf*
complement
com•pli•men•tary
flattering; free of
charge; *cf*
complementary
com•pline (*or* •plin)
com•ply (•plies,
•ply•ing, •plied)
com•po•nent
com•port
com•port•ment
com•pose
com•pos•er
com•pos•ite
com•po•si•tion
com•po•si•tion•al
com•pos•i•tor
com•pos men•tis
com•post
com•po•sure

com•pote
com•pound
com•pound•er
com•pre•hend
com•pre•hen•sibil•
ity (*or* •sible•ness)
com•pre•hen•sible
(*or* •hend•ible)
com•pre•hen•sibly
com•pre•hen•sion
com•pre•hen•sive
com•pre•hen•
sive•ly
com•press
com•press•ibil•ity
(*or* •ible•ness)
com•press•ible
com•pres•sion
com•pres•sive
com•pres•sor
com•pris•al
com•prise
com•pro•mise
com•pro•mis•er
comp•trol•ler
com•pul•sion
com•pul•sive
com•pul•sive•ly
com•pul•sory
com•pul•so•ri•ly
com•punc•tion
com•put•abil•ity
com•put•able
com•pu•ta•tion
com•pute
com•put•er
com•put•eri•za•tion
com•put•er•ize
com•rade

com•rade•ly
com•rade•ship
com•stock•ery
con (con•ning, conned)
con•cat•enate
con•cat•ena•tion
con•cave
con•cav•ity (*pl* •ities)
con•ceal
con•ceal•ment
con•cede
con•ced•er
con•ceit
con•ceit•ed
con•ceiv•able
con•ceiv•ably
con•ceive
con•cel•ebrate
con•cel•ebra•tion
*concensus
incorrect spelling
of consensus
con•cen•trate
con•cen•tra•tion
con•cen•tra•tor
con•cen•tric (or •tri•cal)
con•cen•tri•cal•ly
con•cen•tric•ity
con•cept
con•cep•tion
con•cep•tion•al
con•cep•tive
con•cep•tual
con•cep•tual•ly
con•cep•tual•ism
con•cep•tual•ist

con•cep•tuali•za•tion
con•cep•tual•ize
con•cern
con•cerned
con•cern•ed•ly
con•cern•ing
con•cert
con•cert•ed
concert•goer
con•cer•ti•na (•na•ing, •naed)
con•cer•to (*pl* •tos or •ti)
con•ces•sion
con•ces•sion•aire (or •er, •ary; *pl* •aires, •ers, or •aries)
con•ces•sion•ary
con•ces•sive
conch (*pl* conchs or conches)
con•cho•lo•gist
con•chol•ogy
con•cierge
con•cili•ate
con•cili•ation
con•cili•ator
con•cilia•tory (or •tive)
con•cise
con•cise•ness (or •ci•sion)
con•clave
con•clude
con•clu•sion
con•clu•sive
con•clu•sive•ly

con•coct
con•coct•er (or •coc•tor)
con•coc•tion
con•comi•tance
con•comi•tant
con•cord
con•cor•dance
con•cor•dant
con•cor•dat
con•course
con•crete
con•cre•tion
con•cu•bi•nage
con•cu•bine
con•cu•pis•cence
con•cu•pis•cent
con•cur (•cur•ring, •curred)
con•cur•rence (or •ren•cy; *pl* •rences or •cies)
con•cur•rent
con•cur•rent•ly
con•cuss
con•cus•sion
con•cus•sive
con•demn
con•demn•able
con•dem•na•tion
con•dem•na•tory
con•demn•er (or •or)
con•den•sabil•ity (or •sibil•ity)
con•dens•able (or •ible)
con•den•sate
con•den•sa•tion

con•dense
con•dens•er
con•de•scend
con•de•scend•ing
con•de•scen•sion
con•di•ment
con•di•tion
con•di•tion•al
con•di•tion•al•ity
con•di•tion•al•ly
con•di•tioned
con•di•tion•er
con•di•tion•ing
con•do•la•tory
con•dole
con•do•lence (*or* •dole•ment)
con•dol•er
con•dom
con•do•min•ium (*pl* •iums)
con•done
con•don•er
con•dor (*pl* •dors *or* •dores)
con•duce
con•du•cive
con•duct
con•duct•ance
con•duct•ible
con•duc•tion
con•duc•tive
con•duc•tiv•ity (*pl* •ities)
con•duc•tor (*fem* •tress)
con•duit
cone

co•ney *variant spelling of* cony
con•fabu•late
con•fabu•la•tion
con•fabu•la•tor
con•fec•tion
con•fec•tion•ary (*pl* •aries) place where confections are made
con•fec•tion•er
con•fec•tion•ery (*pl* •eries) candy
con•fed•era•cy (*pl* •cies)
con•fed•er•ate
con•fed•era•tion
con•fed•era•tion•ism
con•fed•era•tion•ist
con•fer (•fer•ring, •ferred)
con•feree (*or* •fer•ree)
con•fer•ence
con•fer•ment (*or* •fer•ral)
con•fer•rable
con•fer•rer
con•fess
con•fess•ant
con•fess•ed•ly
con•fes•sion
con•fes•sion•al
con•fes•sion•ary
con•fes•sor
con•fet•ti
con•fi•dant (*fem* •dante) person in

whom one confides; *cf* confident
con•fide
con•fi•dence
con•fi•dent self-assured; *cf* confidant
con•fi•den•tial
con•fi•den•ti•al•ity (*or* •tial•ness)
con•fi•den•tial•ly
con•fi•dent•ly
con•fid•er
con•fid•ing
con•fid•ing•ly
con•figu•ra•tion
con•figu•ra•tion•al (*or* •ra•tive)
con•fin•able (*or* •fine•able)
con•fine
con•fine•ment
con•firm
con•fir•ma•tion
con•firma•tory (*or* •tive)
con•fis•cable
con•fis•cate
con•fis•ca•tor
con•fis•ca•tory
con•fla•gra•tion
con•flict
con•flic•tion
con•flic•tive (*or* •tory)
con•flu•ence (*or* con•flux)
con•flu•ent

con•form
con•form•abil•ity
  (*or* •able•ness)
con•form•able
con•for•ma•tion
con•form•er
con•form•ist
con•form•ity (*or*
  •ance; *pl* •ities *or*
  •ances)
con•found
con•found•ed
con•fra•ter•nal
con•fra•ter•nity (*pl*
  •nities)
con•frere
con•front
con•fron•ta•tion (*or*
  con•front•ment)
con•fron•ta•tion•al
con•front•er
Con•fu•cian
Con•fu•cian•ism
con•fus•able
con•fuse
con•fus•ed•ly
con•fus•ing
con•fus•ing•ly
con•fu•sion
con•fu•ta•tion
con•fu•ta•tive
con•fute
con•fut•er
con•ga (•ga•ing,
  •gaed) dance; *cf*
  conger
con•geal
con•ge•ner•ic
con•genial

con•ge•nial•ity (*or*
  con•ge•nial•ness)
con•genial•ly
con•geni•tal
con•geni•tal•ly
con•ger eel; *cf*
  conga
con•gest
con•ges•tion
con•ges•tive
con•glom•er•ate
con•glom•era•tion
con•gratu•late
con•gratu•la•tion
con•gratu•la•tor
con•gratu•la•tory
con•gre•gate
con•gre•ga•tion
Con•gre•ga•tion•al
  evangelical
  Church
con•gre•ga•tion•al
  of a congregation
Con•gre•ga•tion•al
  •ism
Con•gre•ga•tion•al
  •ist
con•gre•ga•tor (*or*
  •gre•gant)
Con•gress US
  legislature
con•gress meeting
Con•gres•sion•al
con•gres•sion•al
Congress•man (*pl*
  •men)
Congress•woman
  (*pl* •women)
con•gru•ence (*or*

  •en•cy; *pl* •ences
  or •cies)
con•gru•ent
con•gru•ity (*pl*
  •ities)
con•gru•ous
con•ic (*or* coni•cal)
coni•fer
co•nif•er•ous
con•jec•tur•al
con•jec•ture
con•join
con•join•er
con•joint
con•ju•gable
con•ju•gal
con•ju•gal•ly
con•ju•gal•ity
con•ju•gate
con•ju•ga•tion
con•junct
con•junc•tion
con•junc•tion•al
con•junc•ti•va (*pl*
  •vas *or* •vae)
con•junc•ti•val
con•junc•tive
con•junc•ti•vi•tis
con•junc•ture
con•jura•tion
con•jure
con•jur•er (*or* •or)
conk
con•nate
con•nect
con•nect•ible (*or*
  •able)
con•nec•tion (*or*
  •nex•ion)

con•nec•tive
con•nect•or (or •er)
conned
con•nex•ion variant spelling of connection
con•ning
con•nip•tion
con•niv•ance (or •ence)
con•nive
con•niv•ent
con•niv•er
con•no•ta•tion
con•no•ta•tive (or con•no•tive)
con•note
con•nu•bial
con•nu•bi•al•ity
con•nu•bi•al•ly
con•quer
con•quer•or
con•quest
con•quls•ta•dor (pl •dors or •do•res)
con•san•guin•eous (or •guine)
con•san•guin•ity
con•science
conscience-stricken
con•sci•en•tious
con•sci•en•tious•ly
con•sci•en•tious•ness
con•scious
con•scious•ly
con•scious•ness
con•script

con•scrip•tion
con•se•crate
con•se•cra•tion
con•se•cra•tor
con•se•cra•tory (or •tive)
con•secu•tive
con•secu•tive•ly
con•sen•sual
con•sen•sus (NOT concensus)
con•sent
con•sent•er
con•se•quence
con•se•quent
con•se•quen•tial
con•se•quen•tial•ly
con•se•quen•ti•al•ity (or •tial•ness)
con•se•quent•ly
con•serv•able
con•serv•an•cy (pl •cies)
con•ser•va•tion
con•ser•va•tion•al
con•ser•va•tion•ist
con•serva•tism
con•serva•tive
con•serva•tory (pl •tories)
con•serve
con•serv•er
con•sid•er
con•sid•er•able
con•sid•er•ably
con•sid•er•ate
con•sid•era•tion
con•sid•er•er
con•sign

con•sign•able
con•signa•tion
con•signee
con•sign•ment
con•sign•or (or •er)
con•sist
con•sist•en•cy (or •ence; pl •cies or •ences)
con•sist•ent
con•sist•ent•ly
con•sol•able
con•so•la•tion
con•sola•tory
con•sole
con•sol•er
con•soli•date
con•soli•da•tion
con•soli•da•tor
con•som•mé (or •me)
con•so•nance (or •nan•cy; pl •nances or •cies)
con•so•nant
con•sort
con•sort•er
con•sor•tium (pl •tiums or •tia)
con•spicu•ous
con•spicu•ous•ly
con•spicu•ous•ness
con•spira•cy (pl •cies)
con•spira•tor
con•spira•to•rial (or con•spira•tory)
con•spira•to•rial•ly
con•spire

con•sta•ble
con•stabu•lary (*pl* •laries)
con•stan•cy
con•stant
con•stant•ly
con•stel•la•tion
con•ster•nate
con•ster•na•tion
con•sti•pate
con•sti•pat•ed
con•sti•pa•tion
con•stitu•en•cy (*pl* •cies)
con•stitu•ent
con•sti•tute
con•sti•tut•er (*or* •tu•tor)
con•sti•tu•tion
con•sti•tu•tion•al
con•sti•tu•tion•al•ism
con•sti•tu•tion•al•ist
con•sti•tu•tion•al•ity
con•sti•tu•tion•al•ly
con•sti•tu•tive
con•strain
con•strain•er
con•straint
con•strict
con•stric•tion
con•stric•tive
con•stric•tor
con•struct
con•struct•ible
con•struc•tion

con•struc•tion•al
con•struc•tive
con•struc•tor (*or* •ter)
con•strue (•stru•ing, •strued)
con•stru•er
con•sub•stan•tia•tion
con•sul
con•su•lar
con•su•late
con•sult
con•sul•tan•cy (*pl* •cies)
con•sul•tant
con•sul•ta•tion
con•sul•ta•tive (*or* ta•tory, con•sul•tive)
con•sult•er (*or* •sul•tor)
con•sum•able
con•sume
con•sum•er
con•sum•er•ism
con•sum•mate
con•sum•ma•tion
con•sum•ma•tive (*or* •tory)
con•sum•ma•tor
con•sump•tion
con•sump•tive
con•tact
con•tact•able
con•tac•tor
con•ta•gion
con•ta•gious
con•ta•gious•ness

con•tain
con•tain•er
con•tain•eri•za•tion
con•tain•er•ize
con•tain•ment
con•tami•nant
con•tami•nate
con•tami•na•tion
con•tami•na•tor
con•tem•plate
con•tem•pla•tion
con•tem•pla•tive
con•tem•pla•tor
con•tem•po•ra•neity
con•tem•po•ra•neous
con•tem•po•rari•ly
con•tem•po•rary (*pl* •raries)
con•tempt
con•tempt•ibil•ity (*or* •ible•ness)
con•tempt•ible
con•temp•tu•ous
con•temp•tu•ous•ly
con•tend
con•tend•er
con•tent
con•tent•ed
con•tent•ed•ly
con•tent•ed•ness
con•ten•tion
con•ten•tious
con•ten•tious•ness
con•tent•ment
con•ter•mi•nous (*or* co•)
con•test

con•test•able
con•test•ant
con•test•er
con•text
con•tex•tual
con•tex•tu•al•ize
con•ti•gu•ity
con•tigu•ous
con•ti•nence (or con•ti•nen•cy)
con•ti•nent
con•ti•nen•tal
con•tin•gence
con•tin•gen•cy (pl •cies)
con•tin•gent
con•tinu•able
con•tin•u•al•ity (or •al•ness)
con•tin•ual•ly
con•tinu•ance
con•tinu•ant
con•tinu•ation
con•tinue
con•tinu•er
con•tinu•ing
con•ti•nu•ity (pl •ities)
con•tinu•ous
con•tinu•um (pl •tinua or •tinu•ums)
con•tort
con•tor•tion
con•tor•tion•ist
con•tour
contra•band
contra•cep•tion

contra•cep•tive
con•tract
con•tract•ibil•ity (or •ible•ness)
con•tract•ible
con•trac•tile
con•trac•til•ity
con•trac•tion
con•trac•tor
con•trac•tual
con•trac•tual•ly
contra•dict
contra•dict•able
contra•dict•er (or •dic•tor)
contra•dic•tion
contra•dic•tory (pl •tories)
contra•dis•tinc•tion
contra•dis•tinc•tive
contra•in•di•cant
contra•in•di•cate
contra•in•di•ca•tion
con•tral•to (pl •tos or •ti)
con•trap•tion
con•tra•pun•tal
con•tra•pun•tal•ly
con•tra•pun•tist (or •tal•ist)
con•tra•ri•ety (pl •eties)
con•tra•ri•ly
con•tra•ri•ness
contrari•wise
con•tra•ry (pl •ries)
con•trast
con•trast•able

con•tra•vene
con•tra•ven•er
con•tra•ven•tion
con•tre•temps (pl •temps)
con•trib•ute
con•tri•bu•tion
con•tribu•tive
con•tribu•tor
con•tribu•tory (pl •tories)
con•trite
con•tri•tion
con•triv•ance
con•trive
con•trol (•trol•ling, •trolled)
con•trol•lable
con•trol•lably
con•trol•ler
con•tro•ver•sial
contro•ver•sial•ist
con•tro•ver•sial•ly
con•tro•ver•sy (pl •sies)
con•tro•vert
contro•vert•er
contro•vert•ible
con•tu•ma•cious
con•tu•ma•cy (pl •cies)
con•tu•me•li•ous
con•tu•me•ly (pl •lies)
con•tuse
con•tu•sion
co•nun•drum
con•ur•ba•tion
con•va•lesce

con•va•les•cence
con•va•les•cent
con•vec•tion
con•vec•tion•al
con•vec•tive
con•vec•tor
con•ven•able
con•vene
con•ven•er
con•ve•nience
con•ve•nient
con•ve•nient•ly
con•vent
con•ven•tion
con•ven•tion•al
con•ven•tion•al•ity
(pl •ities)
con•ven•tion•ali•
za•tion
con•ven•tion•al•ize
con•ven•tion•al•ly
con•verge
con•ver•gence (or
•gen•cy; pl •gences
or •cies)
con•ver•gent
con•vers•able
con•ver•sance (or
•san•cy)
con•ver•sant
con•ver•sa•tion
con•ver•sa•tion•al
con•ver•sa•tion•al•
ist (or •tion•ist)
con•ver•sa•tion•
al•ly
con•verse
con•verse•ly
con•vers•er

con•ver•sion
con•ver•sion•al (or
•ary)
con•vert
con•vert•er (or
•ver•tor)
con•vert•ibil•ity (or
•ible•ness)
con•vert•ible
con•vex
con•vex•ity (pl
•ities)
con•vey
con•vey•able
con•vey•ance
con•vey•anc•er
con•vey•anc•ing
con•vey•or (or •er)
con•vict
con•vict•able (or
•ible)
con•vic•tion
con•vince
con•vinc•er
con•vinc•ible
con•vinc•ing
con•vinc•ing•ly
con•viv•ial
con•viv•i•al•ity
con•viv•ial•ly
con•vo•ca•tion
con•vo•ca•tion•al
con•vo•ca•tor
con•voke
con•vok•er
con•vo•lute
con•vo•lut•ed
con•vo•lu•tion
con•voy

con•vul•sant
con•vulse
con•vul•sion
con•vul•sive
cony (or co•ney; pl
conies or •neys)
coo (coo•ing,
cooed)
cook
cook•book
cook•er
cook•ery (pl •eries)
cook•house
cookie (or cooky;
pl cookies)
cook•ing
cook•out
cool
cool•ant
cool•er
coolie (or cooly; pl
coolies)
cool•ly (adv)
cool•ness
coon
coon•skin
coon•tie
coop
co-op
coop•er
co•op•er•ate (or
co-op•)
co•op•era•tion (or
co-op•)
co•op•era•tive (or
co-op•)
co•op•era•tor (or
co-op•)
co-opt

co-option
co•or•di•nate (*or* co-or•)
co•or•di•na•tion (*or* co-or•)
co•or•di•na•tor (*or* co-or•)
coot
cootie
cop (cop•ping, copped)
co•pal
co•part•ner
cope
co•peck *variant spelling of* **kopeck**
cope•stone *variant spelling of* **capstone**
copi•er
co•pilot
cop•ing
co•pi•ous
co•pi•ous•ly
cop-out (*n*)
cop•per
copper•head
copper•plate
copper•smith
cop•pery
cop•pice
co•pra
copse (*or* cop•pice)
copu•la (*pl* •las *or* •lae) linking verb; *cf* **cupola**
copu•late
copu•la•tion
copy (*n, pl* copies;

vb copies, copy•ing, copied)
copy•book
copy•edit
copy•editor
copy•hold
copy•holder
copy•ist
copy•read
copy•reader
copy•right
copy•writer
copy•writing
coq au vin
co•quet•ry (*pl* •ries)
co•quette
co•quet•tish
cora•cle
cor•al animal; jewelry; *cf* **corral**
cor•al•line
cor an•glais (*pl* cors an•glais)
cor•bel (•bel•ing, •beled; *Brit* •bel•ling, •belled)
cord string; *cf* **chord**
cord•age
cor•date heart-shaped; *cf* **chordate**
cord•ed
cor•dial
cor•dial•ity (*pl* •ities)
cor•dial•ly
cord•ite

cord•less
cor•don
cor•don bleu (*pl* cor•dons bleus)
cor•du•roy
cord•wood
core
co•re•li•gion•ist
co•re•spon•dent adulterer; *cf* **correspondent**
cor•gi (*pl* •gis)
co•ri•an•der
cork
cork•age
cork•board
corked
cork•er
cork•screw
cork•wood
corky (corki•er, corki•est)
corm
cor•mo•rant
corn
corn•cob
corn•crib
cor•nea (*pl* •neas *or* •neae)
cor•neal
corned
cor•nel•ian (*or* car•)
cor•ner
corner•back
corner•stone
cor•net
cor•net•ist (*or* •net•tist)

corn•field

corn•flour (*Brit*)
  cornstarch

corn•flower plant

corn•husk

cor•nice

corn•starch

cor•nu•co•pia

corny (corni•er,
  corni•est)

co•rol•la

cor•ol•lary (*pl*
  •laries)

co•ro•na (*pl* •nas
  or •nae)

coro•nal

coro•nary (*pl*
  •naries)

coro•na•tion

coro•ner

coro•net

cor•po•ra *pl of*
  corpus

cor•po•ral NCO;
  of the body; *cf*
  corporeal; caporal

cor•po•ral•ity

cor•po•rate

cor•po•ra•tion

cor•po•ra•tive

cor•po•real
  physical; *cf*
  corporal; caporal

cor•po•re•al•ity (*or*
  •ness)

cor•po•re•al•ly

corps (*pl* corps)
  group of people

corpse dead body

cor•pu•lence (*or*
  •len•cy)

cor•pu•lent

cor•pus (*pl* •po•ra)

cor•pus•cle

cor•pus•cu•lar

cor•ral (•ral•ling,
  •ralled) animal
  enclosure; *cf* **coral**

cor•rect

cor•rect•able (*or*
  •ible)

cor•rec•tion

cor•rec•tive

cor•rect•ness

cor•rec•tor

cor•re•late

cor•re•la•tion

cor•rela•tive

cor•rela•tive•ness
  (*or* •tiv•ity)

cor•re•spond

cor•re•spon•dence

cor•re•spon•dent
  one who
  corresponds; *cf*
  corespondent

cor•ri•dor

cor•ri•gen•dum (*pl*
  •da)

cor•ri•gi•bil•ity

cor•ri•gible

cor•robo•rant

cor•robo•rate

cor•robo•ra•tion

cor•robo•ra•tive

cor•robo•ra•tor

cor•ro•dant (*or*
  •dent)

cor•rode

cor•rod•er

cor•rod•ibil•ity

cor•rod•ible

cor•ro•sion

cor•ro•sive

cor•ru•gate

cor•ru•gat•ed

cor•ru•ga•tion

cor•rupt

cor•rupt•er (*or*
  •rup•tor)

cor•rupt•ibil•ity (*or*
  •ible•ness)

cor•rup•tible

cor•rup•tion

cor•rup•tive

cor•rupt•ly

cor•sage

cor•sair

cor•set

cor•set•ry

cor•tege (*or* •tège)

cor•tex (*pl* •texes
  or •ti•ces)

cor•ti•cal

cor•ti•sone

co•run•dum

cor•us•cate

cor•us•ca•tion

cor•vette

cor•vine

co•ry•za

cos

co•se•cant (*or*
  co•sec)

co•sig•na•tory (*pl*
  •tories)

co•si•ly *Brit spelling of* **cozily**

co•sine

co•si•ness *Brit spelling of* **coziness**

cos•met•ic

cos•meti•cal•ly

cos•me•ti•cian

cos•mic (*or* •mi•cal)

cos•mogo•ny (*pl* •nies)

cos•mog•ra•phy

cos•mo•logi•cal (*or* •log•ic)

cos•molo•gist

cos•mol•ogy

cos•mo•naut

cos•mo•poli•tan

cos•mo•poli•tan•ism

cos•mos (*pl* •mos *or* •moses)

co•spon•sor

cos•set

cost (cost•ing, cost)

co•star (*or* co-star; •star•ring, •starred)

Cos•ta Ri•can

cost-effective

cost•ing

cost•li•ness

cost•ly (•li•er, •li•est)

cost-plus

cost-push

cos•tume

cos•tumier (*or* •tum•er)

co•sy *Brit spelling of* **cozy**

cot

co•tan•gent

cote shelter for doves; *cf* **coat**

co•ten•an•cy (*pl* •cies)

co•ten•ant

co•te•rie

co•ter•mi•nous *variant of* **conterminous**

cot•ta surplice; *cf* **cotter**

cot•tage

cot•tag•er

cot•ter (*or* •tar) securing pin; *cf* **cotta**

cot•ton

cotton•seed (*pl* •seeds *or* •seed)

cotton•tail

cotton•wood

cot•tony

coty•le•don

coty•le•don•ous

couch

cou•chette

cou•gar

cough

could

couldn't

cou•lomb

coul•ter *Brit spelling of* **colter**

coun•cil assembly

coun•ci•lor (*Brit* •cil•lor) council member

coun•sel (•sel•ing, •seled; *Brit* •sel•ling, •selled) advice; advise

coun•sel•or (*Brit* •sel•lor) adviser

count

count•able

count•down

coun•te•nance

count•er

counter•act

counter•ac•tion

counter•ac•tive

counter•at•tack

counter•bal•ance

counter•blast

counter•change

counter•charge

counter•check

counter•claim

counter•claim•ant

counter•clock•wise

counter•cul•ture

counter•es•pio•nage

counter•feit

counter•feit•er

counter•in•sur•gen•cy (*pl* •cies)

counter•in•tel•li•gence

counter•ir•ri•tant

counter•ir•ri•ta•tion

counter•mand

counter•meas•ure

counter•move

counter•of•fen•sive

counter•pane

counter•part

counter•plot
(•plot•ting,
•plot•ted)

counter•point

counter•poise

counter•pro•duc•
tive

counter•pro•pos•al

counter-
revo•lu•tion

counter-
revo•lu•tion•ary
(pl •aries)

counter•shaft

counter•sign

counter•sink
(•sink•ing, •sank,
•sunk)

counter•spy (pl
•spies)

counter•ten•or

counter•type

counter•vail

counter•weigh

counter•weight

counter•work

coun•tess

count•less

coun•tri•fy (or
•try•fy; •fies,
•fy•ing, •fied)

coun•try (pl •tries)

country•man (pl
•men)

country•side

country•woman (pl
•women)

coun•ty (pl •ties)

coup

coup de grâce (pl
coups de grâce)

coup d'état (pl
coups d'état or
coup d'états)

cou•pé (or coupe)

cou•ple

cou•pler

cou•plet

cou•pling

cou•pon

cour•age

cou•ra•geous

cou•ra•geous•ly

cour•gette (Brit)
zucchini

cou•ri•er

course direction,
etc.; cf coarse

course•work

court

cour•te•ous

cour•te•ous•ly

cour•te•san

cour•te•sy (pl •sies)

court•house

cour•ti•er

court•ly (•li•er,
•li•est)

court-martial (n, pl
court-martials or
courts-martial; vb

-martial•ing,
-martialed; Brit
-martial•ling,
-martialled)

court•room

court•ship

court•yard

cous•in relation; cf
cozen

cou•ture

cou•tu•rier (fem
•rière)

co•va•lence (Brit
•va•len•cy)

co•va•lent

cove

cov•en

cov•enant

cov•enan•tal

cov•enan•tee

cov•enant•er (or
•enan•tor)

cov•er

cov•er•age

cov•er•all

cov•er•ing

cov•er•let

cov•ert

cover-up (n)

cov•et

cov•etous

cov•etous•ly

cov•etous•ness

cow

cow•ard

cow•ard•ice

cow•ard•li•ness

cow•ard•ly

cow•bell

cow•bird
cow•boy
cow•catcher
cow•er
cow•girl
cow•hand
cow•herd
cow•hide
cowl
cow•lick
cowl•ing
cow•man (*pl* •men)
co-worker
cow•poke (*or* •puncher)
cow•pox
cow•ry (*or* •rie; *pl* •ries)
cow•slip
cox
cox•comb
cox•swain
coy
coy•ly
coy•ness
coy•ote (*pl* •otes *or* •ote)
coy•pu (*or* •pou; *pl* •pus, •pu *or* •pous, •pou)
co•zen to trick; *cf* cousin
co•zi•ly (*Brit* •si•)
co•zi•ness (*Brit* •si•)
co•zy (*Brit* •sy; *n,* *pl* •zies, *Brit* •sies; *adj* •zi•er, •zi•est, *Brit* •si•er, •si•est)

crab (crab•bing, crabbed)
crab•bed (*adj*)
crab•by (•bi•er, •bi•est)
crab•wise
crack
cracka•jack *variant spelling of* crackerjack
crack•brain
crack•brained
crack•down
cracked
crack•er
crack•er-bar•rel
cracker•jack (*or* cracka•)
crack•ing
crack•le
crack•ling
crack•pot
cra•dle
cradle•snatcher
cradle•song
craft
crafti•ly
crafti•ness
crafts•man (*pl* •men)
crafts•man•ship
crafty (crafti•er, crafti•est)
crag
crag•ged
crag•gy (•gi•er, •gi•est)
cram (cram•ming, crammed)

cramp
cramped
cram•pon
cran•ber•ry (*pl* •ries)
crane
cranes•bill
cra•nial
cra•nio•met•ric (*or* •ri•cal)
cra•ni•om•etry
cra•ni•oto•my (*pl* •mies)
cra•nium (*pl* •niums *or* •nia)
crank
crank•case
cranki•ly
cranki•ness
crank•pin
crank•shaft
cranky (cranki•er, cranki•est)
cran•nied
cran•ny (*pl* •nies)
crap (crap•ping, crapped)
crape *variant spelling of* crepe
crap•pie (*pl* •pies) fish
crap•py (•pi•er, •pi•est) worthless
craps
crap•shooter
crapu•lence
crapu•lous
crash
crash•ing

crash-land
crash land•ing
crass
crass•ness (or
    cras•si•tude)
crate
cra•ter
cra•ter•ous
cra•vat
crave
cra•ven
crav•ing
crawl
crawl•er
cray•fish (or craw•;
    pl •fish or •fishes)
cray•on
cray•on•ist
craze
crazed
cra•zi•ly
cra•zi•ness
cra•zy (adj •zi•er,
    •zi•est; n, pl •zies)
creak noise; cf
    creek
creaki•ness
creaky (creaki•er,
    creaki•est)
cream
cream•er
cream•ery (pl
    •eries)
creami•ness
creamy (creami•er,
    creami•est)
crease
crease•less
cre•ate

cre•ation
cre•ation•ism
cre•ation•ist
cre•ative
cre•ative•ly
cre•ativ•ity (or
    •ative•ness)
cre•ator
crea•ture
crèche
cre•dence
cre•den•tial
cred•ibil•ity (or
    •ible•ness)
cred•ible
cred•ibly
cred•it
cred•it•able
cred•it•able•ness
    (or •abil•ity)
cred•it•ably
credi•tor
cre•do (pl •dos)
cre•du•lity
credu•lous
Cree (pl Cree or
    Crees)
creed
creek inlet; cf
    creak
creel
creep (creep•ing,
    crept)
creep•er
creepi•ly
creepi•ness
creepy (creepi•er,
    creepi•est)
cre•mate

cre•ma•tion
cre•ma•tor
cre•ma•to•rium (pl
    •riums or •ria)
cre•ma•tory (adj)
crème cara•mel
crème de menthe
    (pl crèmes de
    menthe)
cre•nate (or
    •nat•ed)
cre•na•tion (or
    crena•ture)
cren•el•ate (Brit
    •el•late)
cren•el•a•tion (Brit
    •el•la•tion)
Cre•ole people
cre•ole language
creo•sol
    constituent of
    creosote; cf cresol
creo•sote
crepe (or crape,
    crêpe) fabric
crêpe pancake
crepe de chine (or
    crêpe de chine; pl
    crepes de chine or
    crêpes de chine)
crêpe su•zette (pl
    crêpes su•zettes)
crept
cre•pus•cu•lar
cre•scen•do (pl
    •dos, •does, or •di)
cres•cent
cres•cen•tic
cres•sol

disinfectant; *cf*
 creosol
cress
cres•set
crest
crest•ed
crest•fallen
crest•ing
cret•in
cret•in•ism
cret•in•ous
cre•tonne
cre•vasse glacier
 crack
crev•ice cleft
crew
crew•el yarn; *cf*
 cruel
crewel•work
crew neck (*or*
 crew•neck)
crib (**crib•bing**,
 cribbed)
crib•bage
crick
crick•et
cried
cri•er
crime
crimi•nal
crimi•nal•ity (*pl*
 •ities)
crimi•nal•ly
crimi•no•logi•cal
 (*or* **•log•ic**)
crimi•nolo•gist
crimi•nol•ogy
crimp
crim•son

cringe
crin•kle
crin•kly (**•kli•er**,
 •kli•est)
crino•line
crip•ple
crip•pling
cri•sis (*pl* **•ses**)
crisp
crisp•er
crisp•ness
crispy (**crispi•er**,
 crispi•est)
criss•cross
cri•te•ri•on (*pl* **•ria**
 or **•ri•ons**)
crit•ic
criti•cal
criti•cal•ly
criti•cism
criti•cize
criti•ciz•er
cri•tique
crit•ter
croak
croak•er
croaki•ly
croaki•ness
croaky (**croaki•er**,
 croaki•est)
Croa•tian
cro•chet (**•chet•ing**,
 •cheted)
 handicraft; *cf*
 crotchet
crock
crock•ery
croco•dile
croco•dil•ian

cro•cus (*pl* **•cuses**
 or **•ci**)
crois•sant
crone
cro•ny (*pl* **•nies**)
crook
crook•ed
crook•ed•ly
crook•ed•ness
croon
croon•er
crop (**crop•ping**,
 cropped)
crop-eared
crop•per
cro•quet (**•quet•ing**,
 •queted) game
cro•quette savory
 cake
cro•sier (*or* **•zier**)
cross
cross•bar
cross•beam
cross•bill
cross•bones
cross•bow
cross•breed
 (**•breed•ing**, **•bred**)
cross-check
cross-coun•try
cross-cur•rent
cross•cut
 (**•cut•ting**, **•cut**)
cross-ex•ami•
 na•tion
cross-ex•am•ine
cross-ex•am•in•er
cross-eye
cross-eyed

cross-fer•ti•li•za•tion

cross-fer•til•ize

cross•fire

cross-grained

cross•hatch

cross-index

cross•ing

cross-legged

cross-link

cross•over

cross•piece

cross-pol•li•nate

cross-pol•li•na•tion

cross-pur•poses

cross-ques•tion

cross-ques•tion•ing

cross-refer

cross-ref•er•ence

cross•road (or •roads)

cross-sec•tion•al

cross-stitch

cross•talk

cross•walk

cross•wind

cross•wise (or •ways)

cross•word

crotch

crotch•et musical note; cf crochet

crotch•ety

crouch

croup

crou•pi•er

crou•ton

crow (crow•ing, crowed or crew)

crow•bar

crowd

crowd•ed

crowd•ed•ness

crow•er

crow•foot (pl •foots or •feet)

crown

crow's-foot (pl -feet)

cro•zier variant spelling of crosier

cru•ces pl of crux

cru•cial

cru•cial•ly

cru•ci•ble

cru•ci•fier

cru•ci•fix

cru•ci•fix•ion

cru•ci•form

cru•ci•fy (•fies, •fy•ing, •fied)

crud (crud•ding, crud•ded)

crud•dy (•di•er, •di•est)

crude

crude•ly

crud•ity (or crude•ness; pl •ities or •nesses)

cru•el (•el•er, •el•est; Brit •el•ler, •el•lest) unkind; cf crewel

cru•el•ly

cru•el•ness

cru•el•ty (pl •ties)

cru•et

cruise sea trip; cf cruse

cruis•er

crul•ler

crumb

crum•ble

crum•bly (•bli•er, •bli•est)

crumby (crumbi•er, crumbi•est) full of crumbs

crum•my (•mi•er, •mi•est) inferior

crum•pet

crum•ple

crum•ply

crunch

crunchi•ly

crunchi•ness

crunchy (crunchi•er, crunchi•est)

cru•sade

cru•sad•er

cruse small pot; cf cruise

crush

crush•er

crust

crus•ta•cean

crust•ed

crusti•ly

crusti•ness

crusty (crusti•er, crusti•est)

crutch

crux (pl cruxes or cru•ces)

cry (n, pl cries; vb

cries, cry•ing,
cried)
cry•baby (*pl*
•babies)
cryo•bi•ol•o•gist
cryo•bi•ol•ogy
cryo•gen•ic
cryo•gen•ics
cry•on•ics
cryo•sur•gery
cryo•sur•gi•cal
cryo•thera•py
crypt
crypt•al of crypts
cryp•tic (or •ti•cal)
obscure
cryp•ti•cal•ly
cryp•to•gram
record
cryp•to•graph
instrument
cryp•tog•ra•pher
(or •phist)
cryp•to•graph•ic
cryp•tog•ra•phy (or
•tol•ogy)
cryp•tolo•gist
crys•tal
crys•tal•line
crys•tal•lin•ity
crys•tal•lize (or
•tal•ize)
crys•tal•log•ra•
pher
crys•tal•lo•graph•ic
crys•tal•log•ra•phy
crys•tal•loid
cub (cub•bing,
cubbed)

Cu•ban
cubby•hole
cube
cu•bic
cu•bi•cal of
volume
cu•bi•cle small
room
cub•ism
cub•ist
cu•bit
cu•boid
cuck•old
cuck•old•ry
cuckoo (*pl*
cuckoos)
cu•cum•ber
cud
cud•dle
cud•dle•some
cud•dly (•dli•er,
•dli•est)
cud•gel (•gel•ing,
•geled; *Brit*
•gel•ling, •gelled)
cud•gel•er (*Brit*
•gel•ler)
cue (cu•ing or
cue•ing, cued)
signal; shaft; *cf*
queue
cuff
cu•ing (or cue•ing)
cui•rass
cui•sine
cul-de-sac (*pl* culs-
de-sac or cul-de-
sacs)
culi•nary

cull
cull•er
cul•mi•nant
cul•mi•nate
cul•mi•na•tion
cu•lottes
cul•pa•bil•ity (*pl*
•ities)
cul•pable
cul•pably
cul•prit
cult
cult•ism
cult•ist
cul•ti•vable (or
cul•ti•vat•able)
cul•ti•vate
cul•ti•vat•ed
cul•ti•va•tion
cul•ti•va•tor
cul•tur•al
cul•tur•al•ly
cul•ture
cul•tured
cul•tur•ist
cul•vert
cum•ber
cum•ber•some (or
cum•brous)
cum•brance
cum•in
cum•mer•bund
cum•quat *variant
spelling of*
kumquat
cu•mu•late
cu•mu•la•tion
cu•mu•la•tive

cu•mu•lo•nim•bus
(pl •bi or •buses)
cu•mu•lo•stra•tus
(pl •ti)
cu•mu•lous (adj)
cu•mu•lus (n, pl •li)
cu•neal
cu•nei•form
cun•ni•lin•gus
cun•ning
cunt
cup (cup•ping,
cupped)
cup•bearer
cup•board
cup•cake
cu•pel (•pel•ing,
•peled; Brit
•pel•ling, •pelled)
cup•ful (pl •fuls or
cups•ful)
cu•pid•ity
cu•po•la dome; cf
copula
cupped
cup•ping
cu•pre•ous
cu•pric
cu•pro•nick•el
cu•prous
cur
cur•abil•ity
cur•able
cu•ra•çao (or •çoa)
cu•ra•cy (pl •cies)
cu•ra•re (or •ri)
cu•rate
cu•ra•tive
cu•ra•tor

cu•ra•to•rial
curb restrain;
restraint
curb (Brit kerb)
sidewalk edge
curb•ing (Brit
kerb•)
curb•stone (Brit
kerb•)
curd
curdi•ness
cur•dle
cur•dler
curdy (curdi•er,
curdi•est)
cur•able
cure
cure-all
cu•rette (or •ret;
•ret•ting, •ret•ted)
cu•ret•tage (or
•rette•ment,
•ret•ment)
cur•few
cu•ria (pl •riae)
cu•rio (pl •rios)
cu•ri•os•ity (pl
•ities)
cu•ri•ous
cu•ri•ous•ly
cu•ri•ous•ness
cu•rium
curl
curl•er
cur•lew
cur•li•cue (or •ly•)
curli•ness
curl•ing

curly (curli•er,
curli•est)
cur•mud•geon
cur•mud•geon•ly
cur•rant fruit; cf
current
cur•ren•cy (pl
•cies)
cur•rent flow; up-
to-date; cf currant
cur•ricu•lar
cur•ricu•lum (pl
•la or •lums)
cur•ricu•lum vi•tae
(pl •la vi•tae)
cur•ry (•ries,
•ry•ing, •ried)
groom horse;
flavor with curry
cur•ry (or •rie; pl
•ries) spicy food
curry•comb
curse
curs•ed (or curst;
adj)
cur•sive
cur•sor
cur•so•rial
cur•so•ri•ly
cur•so•ri•ness
cur•sory
curt
cur•tail
cur•tail•ment
cur•tain
curtain-raiser
curt•ly
curt•ness
curt•sy (or •sey; n,

pl •sies *or* •seys;
vb •sies, •sy•ing,
•sied *or* •seys,
•sey•ing, •seyed)
cur•va•ceous
cur•va•ture
curve
curved
cur•vi•lin•ear (*or*
•eal)
cur•vi•lin•ear•ity
curvi•ness
curvy (curvi•er,
curvi•est)
cush•ion
cush•iony
cushy (cushi•er,
cushi•est)
cusp
cus•pate (*or*
•pat•ed, cusped)
cus•pid
cuss
cuss•ed (*adj*)
cuss•ed•ness
cus•tard
cus•to•dial
cus•to•dian
cus•to•di•an•ship
cus•to•dy (*pl* •dies)
cus•tom
cus•tom•ari•ly
cus•tom•ary
custom-built
cus•tom•er
cus•tom•ize
custom-made
cut (cut•ting, cut)
cu•ta•ne•ous

cut•away
cut•back
cute
cute•ly
cute•ness
cu•ti•cle
cutie (*or* cutey)
cut•lass
cut•ler
cut•lery
cut•let
cut•off
cut•out
cut-rate (*Brit*
-price)
cut•ter
cut•throat
cut•ting
cut•tle
cuttle•bone
cuttle•fish (*pl* •fish
or •fishes)
cut•worm
cyan
cya•nate
cy•an•ic
cya•nide
cy•ano•gen
cya•no•sis
cya•not•ic
cy•ber•net•ic
cy•ber•net•ics
cy•cad
cyc•la•mate
cyc•la•men
cy•cle
cy•clic (*or* •cli•cal)
cy•cli•cal•ly
cy•clist

cy•cloid
cy•clone
cy•clon•ic (*or*
•cloni•cal,
•clo•nal)
cy•clo•pedia (*or*
•pae•dia)
cy•clo•pedic (*or*
•pae•dic)
cy•clo•tron
cyg•net young
swan; *cf* signet
cyl•in•der
cy•lin•dri•cal (*or*
•dric)
cy•lin•dri•cal•ly
cym•bal musical
instrument; *cf*
symbol
cym•bal•er (*or* •eer,
•bal•ist)
cyn•ic
cyni•cal
cyni•cal•ly
cyni•cism
cy•no•sure
cy•pher *variant*
spelling of cipher
cy•press
Cyp•rian
Cyp•ri•ot (*or* •ote)
Cy•ril•lic
cyst lump; sac; *cf*
cist
cyst•ic
cys•ti•tis
cy•to•logi•cal
cy•tolo•gist
cy•tol•ogy

cy•to•plasm
cy•to•plas•mic
czar (*or* tsar)
czar•ist (*or* tsar•ist)
Czech

D

dab (dab•bing,
  dabbed)
dab•ber
dab•ble
dab•bler
dace
dachs•hund
dac•tyl
dac•tyl•ic
dac•tylo•gram
dac•tyl•og•ra•phy
dad
dad•dy (*pl* •dies)
daddy-longlegs
daf•fo•dil
daft
dag•ger
da•guerreo•type
dahl•ia
dai•ly (*pl* •lies)
dain•ti•ly
dain•ti•ness
dain•ty (*n, pl* •ties;
  adj •ti•er, •ti•est)
dairy (*pl* dairies)
dairy•ing
dairy•man (*pl*
  •men)
dais
dai•sy (*pl* •sies)

daisy•wheel
dale
dal•li•ance
dal•ly (•lies,
  •ly•ing, •lied)
Dal•ma•tian
dam (dam•ming,
  dammed) river
  barrier; female
  parent; *cf* damn
dam•age
dam•age•able
dam•ag•er
dam•ages
dam•ask
dame
dammed
  obstructed; *cf*
  damned
dam•ming
  obstructing; *cf*
  damning
damn condemn; *cf*
  dam
dam•nable
dam•nably
dam•na•tion
dam•na•tory
damned
  condemned; *cf*
  dammed
damned•est
damn•ing
  damaging; *cf*
  damming
damp
damp•en
damp•en•er
damp•er

damp•ly
damp•ness
damp•proof
dam•sel
damsel•fly (*pl*
  •flies)
dam•son
dance
danc•er
danc•ing
dan•de•lion
dan•di•fi•ca•tion
dan•di•fy (•fies,
  •fy•ing, •fied)
dan•dle
dan•druff
dan•druffy
dan•dy (*n, pl* •dies;
  adj •dier, •di•est)
dan•dy•ish
dan•dy•ism
Dane
dan•ger
dan•ger•ous
dan•ger•ous•ly
dan•gle
dan•gler
Dan•ish
dank
dank•ness
dap•per
dap•ple
dapple-gray (*Brit*
  -grey)
dare
dare•devil
dar•er
dar•ing
dark

dark•en
dark•en•er
dark•ly
dark•ness
dark•room
dar•ling
darn
darned
darn•er
darn•ing
dart
dart•er
darts
dash
dash•board
dash•er
dash•ing
das•tard•ly
da•ta *pl of* datum
dat•able (*or* date•)
data•base
date
dat•ed
dat•ed•ness
date•less
date•line
dat•er
dat•ing
da•tive
da•tum (*pl* •ta *or*
•tums)
daub
daub•er
daugh•ter
daughter-in-law
(*pl* daughters-)
daugh•ter•li•ness
daugh•ter•ly
daunt

daunt•ing
daunt•less
dau•phin
dau•phine
dav•en•port
dav•it
daw
daw•dle
daw•dler
dawn
day
day•book
day•break
day•dream
day•dream•er
day•dream•ing
day•dreamy
day•flower
day•light
(•light•ing,
•light•ed *or* •lit)
day•long
day•time
day-to-day
day-trIpper
daze
daz•zle
dea•con
dea•con•ess
dea•con•ry (*pl*
•ries)
dea•con•ship
de•ac•tiv•ate
de•ac•ti•va•tion
de•ac•ti•va•tor
dead
dead•beat
dead•en
dead-end (*adj*)

dead•en•er
dead•head
dead•line
dead•li•ness
dead•lock
dead•ly (•li•er,
•li•est)
dead•ness
dead•pan
dead•wood
deaf
deaf•en
deaf-mute
deaf-mute•ness (*or*
-mut•ism)
deaf•ness
deal (deal•ing,
dealt)
deal•er
deal•ing
dealt
dean
dean•ery (*pl* •eries)
dean•ship
dear
dear•ly
dear•ness
dearth
death
death•bed
death•blow
death•less
death•li•ness
death•ly
death•trap
death•watch
de•ba•cle
de•bag (•bag•ging,
•bagged)

de•bar (•bar•ring, •barred)
de•bark
de•bar•ka•tion
de•bar•ment
de•base
de•base•ment
de•bat•able (or •bate•able)
de•bat•ably
de•bate
de•bat•er
de•bauch
debau•chee
de•bauch•er
de•bauch•ery (or •ment)
de•ben•ture
de•bili•tate
de•bili•ta•tion
de•bili•ta•tive
de•bil•ity (pl •ities)
deb•it
debo•nair (or •naire, deb•on•naire)
de•brief
de•bris (or dé•)
debt
debt•or
de•bug (•bug•ging, •bugged)
de•bunk
de•bunk•er
de•bus (•bus•ing, •bused or •bus•sing, •bussed)
de•but
debu•tante

dec•ade
deca•dence (or •den•cy)
deca•dent
de•caf•fein•ate
deca•gon
deca•he•dral
deca•he•dron (pl •drons or •dra)
de•cal•ci•fi•ca•tion
de•cal•ci•fi•er
de•cal•ci•fy (•fies, •fy•ing, •fied)
de•camp
de•cant
de•can•ta•tion
de•cant•er
de•capi•tate
de•capi•ta•tion
de•capi•ta•tor
de•car•bon•ate
de•car•bona•tion
de•cath•lete
de•cath•lon
de•cay
de•cease
de•ceased
de•ceit
de•ceit•ful
de•ceit•ful•ly
de•ceiv•able
de•ceive
de•ceiv•er
de•cel•er•ate
de•cel•era•tion
de•cel•era•tor
De•cem•ber
de•cen•cy (pl •cies)
de•cent

respectable; cf descent
de•cen•tral•ist
de•cen•trali•za•tion
de•cen•tral•ize
de•cep•tion
de•cep•tive
deci•bel
de•cid•able
de•cide
de•cid•ed
de•cid•ed•ly
de•cid•er
de•cidu•ous
deci•mal
deci•mali•za•tion
deci•mal•ize
deci•mate
deci•ma•tion
deci•ma•tor
deci•me•ter (Brit •tre)
de•ci•pher
de•ci•pher•able
de•ci•pher•er
de•ci•sion
de•ci•sive
de•ci•sive•ly
de•ci•sive•ness
deck
deck•house
deck•le (or •el)
deckle-edged
de•claim
de•claim•er
dec•la•ma•tion
de•clama•tory
de•clar•able
dec•la•ra•tion

de•clara•tive
de•clare
de•clar•er
de•clas•si•fi•able
de•clas•si•fi•ca•tion
de•clas•si•fy (•fies,
•fy•ing, •fied)
de•clen•sion
de•clin•able
dec•li•na•tion
de•cli•na•tory
de•cline
de•clivi•tous
de•cliv•ity (pl
•ities)
de•clutch
de•coct
de•coc•tion
de•code
de•cod•er
de•coke
dé•col•le•tage
dé•col•le•té (or
de•col•le•te)
de•colo•nize
de•col•or (Brit
•our)
de•col•or•ant
de•col•ori•za•tion
(or de•col•ora•
tion)
de•col•or•ize
de•com•mis•sion
de•com•pos•able
de•com•pose
de•com•pos•er
de•com•po•si•tion
de•com•press
de•com•pres•sion

de•com•pres•sive
de•com•pres•sor
de•con•gest•ant
de•con•se•crate
de•con•struct
de•con•tami•nant
de•con•tami•nate
de•con•tami•na•
tion
de•con•tami•na•tor
de•cor (or dé•)
deco•rate
deco•ra•tion
deco•ra•tive
deco•ra•tor
deco•rous
de•co•rum
de•coy
de•coy•er
de•crease
de•creas•ing•ly
de•cree (•cree•ing,
•creed)
de•cree•able
de•cre•er
de•crep•it
de•crepi•tude
de•cri•er
de•crimi•nali•za•
tion
de•crimi•nal•ize
de•cry (•cries,
•cry•ing, •cried)
de•crypt
de•cryp•tion
de•cus•sate
de•cus•sa•tion
dedi•cate
dedi•cat•ed

dedi•ca•tee
dedi•ca•tion
dedi•ca•tor
dedi•ca•tory (or
•tive)
de•duce
de•duc•ible
de•duct
de•duct•ible
de•duc•tion
de•duc•tive
deed
deem
deep
deep•en
deep-freeze (n)
deep-freeze (vb;
-freez•ing, -froze
or -freezed,
-frozen or -freezed)
deep-fry (-fries,
-frying, -fried)
deep-laid
deep•ness
deep-rooted (or
-seated)
deep-sea (adj)
deep-seated
deep-set
deer (pl deer or
deers)
deer•hound
deer•skin
deer•stalker
de-es•ca•late
de-es•ca•la•tion
de•face
de•face•ment
de•fac•er

de fac•to
defa•ma•tion
de•fama•to•ri•ly
de•fama•tory
de•fame
de•fam•er
de•fault
de•fault•er
de•feat
de•feat•er
de•feat•ism
de•feat•ist
def•ecate
def•eca•tion
de•fect
de•fec•tion
de•fec•tive
de•fec•tor
de•fend
de•fend•able
de•fend•ant
de•fend•er
de•fen•es•tra•tion
de•fense (*Brit* •fence)
de•fense•less (*Brit* •fence•)
de•fense•less•ness (*Brit* •fence•)
de•fen•sibil•ity (*or* •sible•ness)
de•fen•sible
de•fen•sibly
de•fen•sive
de•fen•sive•ly
de•fer (•fer•ring, •ferred)
def•er•ence
def•er•en•tial

def•er•en•tial•ly
de•fer•ment (*or* •fer•ral)
de•fer•rable (*or* •fer•able)
de•ferred
de•fer•rer
de•fi•ance
de•fi•ant
de•fi•ant•ly
de•fi•cien•cy (*pl* •cies)
de•fi•cient
defi•cit
de•fied
de•fi•er
de•fies
de•file
de•file•ment
de•fil•er
de•fin•able
de•fine
de•fin•er
defi•nite
defi•nite•ly
defi•nite•ness
defi•ni•tion
de•fini•tive
de•fini•tive•ly
de•flate
de•fla•tion
de•fla•tion•ary
de•fla•tion•ist
de•fla•tor
de•flect
de•flec•tion (*or* •flex•ion)
de•flec•tive
de•flec•tor

de•flo•ra•tion
de•flow•er
de•flow•er•er
de•fo•li•ant
de•fo•li•ate
de•fo•lia•tion
de•fo•lia•tor
de•for•est
de•for•es•ta•tion
de•form
de•for•ma•tion
de•formed
de•form•er
de•for•mi•ty (*pl* •ties)
de•fraud
de•fraud•er
de•fraud•ment
de•fray
de•fray•able
de•fray•al
de•fray•er
de•frock
de•frost
de•frost•er
deft
deft•ly
deft•ness
de•funct
de•funct•ness
de•fuse (*or* •fuze)
defy (•fies, •fy•ing, •fied)
de•gen•era•cy (*pl* •cies)
de•gen•er•ate
de•gen•er•ate•ness
de•gen•era•tion
de•gen•era•tive

de•glu•ti•nate
de•glu•ti•na•tion
  extraction of
  gluten
de•glu•ti•tion
  swallowing
de•gra•da•ble
deg•ra•da•tion
de•grade
de•grad•ed
de•grad•er
de•grad•ing
de•grease
de•gree
de•hisce
de•his•cence
de•his•cent
de•horn
de•hu•man•i•za•tion
de•hu•man•ize
de•hu•midi•fi•ca•
  tion
de•hu•midi•fi•er
de•hu•midi•fy
  (•fies, •fy•ing,
  •fied)
de•hy•drate
de•hy•dra•tion
de•hy•dra•tor
de•hyp•no•tize
de•ice
de•ic•er
dei•fi•ca•tion
dei•fy (•fies,
  •fy•ing, •fied)
deign
de•in•dus•tri•ali•
  za•tion
de•in•dus•tri•al•ize

de•ism
de•ist
de•ist•ic (or
  •is•ti•cal)
de•ity (pl •ities)
déjà vu
de•ject
de•ject•ed
de•ject•ed•ly
de•jec•tion
de ju•re
*delapidate
  incorrect spelling
  of dilapidate
de•lay
de•lay•er
de•lec•table
de•lec•table•ness
  (or •tabil•ity)
de•lec•tably
de•lec•ta•tion
del•egate
del•ega•tion
de•lete
del•ete•ri•ous
de•le•tion
deli (pl delis) *short*
  for delicatessen
de•lib•er•ate
de•lib•er•ate•ly
de•lib•era•tion
de•lib•era•tive
de•lib•era•tor
deli•ca•cy (pl •cies)
deli•cate
deli•ca•tes•sen
de•li•cious
de•li•cious•ness
de•light

de•light•ed
de•light•ful
de•light•ful•ly
de•light•ful•ness
de•lim•it (or
  •limi•tate)
de•limi•ta•tion
de•lin•eate
de•lin•ea•tion
de•lin•ea•tor
de•lin•quen•cy (pl
  •cies)
de•lin•quent
deli•quesce
deli•ques•cence
deli•ques•cent
de•liri•ous
de•liri•ous•ly
de•lir•ium (pl
  •lir•iums or •liria)
de•lir•ium tre•mens
de•liv•er
de•liv•er•able
de•liv•er•ance
de•liv•er•er
de•liv•ery (pl
  •eries)
dell
de•lo•cali•za•tion
de•lo•cal•ize
de•louse
del•phin•ium (pl
  •phin•iums or
  •phinia)
del•ta
del•ta•ic (or del•tic)
del•toid
de•lude
de•lud•er

del•uge
de•lu•sion
de•lu•sion•al
de•lu•sive
de•lu•so•ry
de•luxe
delve
delv•er
de•mag•neti•za•tion
de•mag•net•ize
de•mag•net•iz•er
dema•gog•ic (or •gogi•cal)
dema•gogue (or •gog)
dema•gogu•ery (or •ism)
dema•gogy (pl •gogies)
de•mand
de•mand•er
de•mand•ing
de•mar•cate
de•mar•ca•tion (or •ka•tion)
de•mar•ca•tor
de•ma•te•ri•ali•za•tion
de•ma•te•ri•al•ize
de•mean
de•mean•ing
de•mean•or (Brit •our)
de•ment
de•ment•ed
de•men•tia
dem•erara
de•mer•it

de•me•ri•to•ri•ous
demi•god (fem •god•dess)
demi•john
de•mili•ta•ri•za•tion
de•mili•ta•rize
demi•monde
de•min•er•al•iza•tion
de•min•er•al•ize
de•mise
de•mist•er
demo (pl demos)
de•mo•bi•li•za•tion
de•mo•bi•lize
de•moc•ra•cy (pl •cies)
Demo•crat
  political party
  member
demo•crat
  advocate of
  democracy
Demo•crat•ic
demo•crat•ic
demo•crati•cal•ly
de•moc•ra•ti•za•tion
de•moc•ra•tize
de•modu•late
de•modu•la•tion
de•modu•la•tor
de•mog•ra•pher (or •phist)
de•mo•graph•ic (or •graphi•cal)
de•mog•ra•phy
de•mol•ish

de•mol•ish•er
demo•li•tion
demo•li•tion•ist
de•mon
de•mo•ni•ac (or •nia•cal)
de•mo•nia•cal•ly
de•mon•ic
de•moni•cal•ly
de•mon•olo•gist
de•mon•ol•ogy
de•mon•strabil•ity (or •strable•ness)
de•mon•strable
de•mon•strably
dem•on•strate
dem•on•stra•tion
de•mon•stra•tive
de•mon•stra•tor
de•mor•al•iza•tion
de•mor•al•ize
de•mor•al•iz•er
de•mote
de•mo•tion
de•mount
de•mul•cent
de•mul•si•fi•ca•tion
de•mul•si•fi•er
de•mul•si•fy (•fies, •fy•ing, •fied)
de•mur (•mur•ring, •murred) object; objection
de•mure modest
de•mure•ly
de•mure•ness
de•mur•ral
de•mys•ti•fi•ca•tion

de•mys•ti•fy (•fies,
•fy•ing, •fied)
de•my•tholo•gize
den
de•na•tion•al•iza•
tion
de•na•tion•al•ize
de•natu•ral•iza•
tion
de•natu•ral•ize
de•na•tura•tion
de•na•ture (or
•tur•ize)
den•drite
den•drolo•gist
den•drol•ogy
den•gue
de•ni•able
de•ni•al
de•ni•er one who
denies
de•nier unit of
weight
deni•grate
deni•gra•tion
deni•gra•tor
den•im
de•ni•tri•fi•ca•tion
de•ni•tri•fy (•fies,
•fy•ing, •fied)
den•izen
de•nomi•nate
de•nomi•na•tion
de•nomi•na•tion•al
de•nomi•na•tion•al•
ism
de•nomi•na•tor
de•not•able
de•no•ta•tion

de•no•ta•tive
de•note
de•noue•ment
de•nounce
de•nounce•ment
de•nounc•er
dense
dense•ness
den•si•ty (pl •ties)
dent
den•tal
den•tate
den•ti•frice
den•tine (or •tin)
den•tist
den•tis•try
den•ti•tion
den•ture
de•nu•da•tion
de•nude
de•nud•er
de•nun•ci•ate
de•nun•cia•tion
de•nun•cia•tor
de•nun•cia•tory
de•ny (•nies,
•ny•ing, •nied)
de•odor•ant
de•odori•za•tion
de•odor•ize
de•odor•iz•er
de•oxi•di•za•tion
de•oxi•dize
de•oxi•diz•er
de•oxy•gen•ate
de•oxy•gena•tion
de•oxy•ri•bo•nu•
cle•ic acid
de•part

de•part•ment
de•part•men•tal
de•part•men•tali•
za•tion
de•part•ment•al•ize
de•part•men•tal•ly
de•par•ture
de•pend
de•pend•abil•ity (or
•able•ness)
de•pend•able
de•pend•ably
de•pend•ant variant
spelling of
dependent
de•pend•ence (or
•ance)
de•pend•en•cy (or
•an•cy; pl •cies)
de•pend•ent (or
•ant)
de•per•son•al•iza•
tion
de•per•son•al•ize
de•pict
de•pict•er (or
•pic•tor)
de•pic•tion
depi•late
depi•la•tion
depi•la•tor
de•pila•tory (pl
•tories)
de•plane
de•plet•able
de•plete
de•ple•tion
de•ple•tive
de•plor•able

de•plor•able•ness
(or •abil•ity)
de•plor•ably
de•plore
de•plor•er
de•ploy
de•ploy•ment
de•po•lari•za•tion
de•po•lar•ize
de•po•liti•cize
de•popu•late
de•popu•la•tion
de•port
de•port•able
de•por•ta•tion
de•por•tee
de•port•ment
de•pos•al
de•pose
de•pos•er
de•pos•it
de•posi•tary (pl
•taries) person; cf
depository
depo•si•tion
de•posi•tor
de•posi•tory (pl
•tories)
warehouse; cf
depositary
de•pot
dep•ra•va•tion
corruption; cf
deprivation
de•prave
de•praved
de•prav•er
de•prav•ity (pl
•ities)

dep•re•cate protest
against; cf
depreciate
dep•re•ca•tion
dep•re•ca•tor
dep•re•ca•tory
de•pre•cia•ble
de•pre•ci•ate lose
value; cf
deprecate
de•pre•cia•tion
de•pre•cia•tor
de•pre•cia•tory (or
•tive)
dep•re•date
dep•re•da•tion
de•press
de•pres•sant
de•pressed
de•press•ible
de•press•ing
de•press•ing•ly
de•pres•sion
de•pres•sive
de•pres•sor
de•pres•suri•za•
tion
de•pres•sur•ize
dep•ri•va•tion (or
de•priv•al) loss; cf
depravation
de•prive
de•prived
de•priv•er
depth
depu•ta•tion
de•pute
depu•tize
depu•ty (pl •ties)

de•rail
de•rail•ment
de•range
de•range•ment
der•by (pl •bies)
de•reg•is•ter
de•reg•is•tra•tion
de•regu•late
de•regu•la•tion
der•elict
der•elic•tion
de•re•strict
de•re•strict•ed
de•re•stric•tion
de•ride
de•rid•er
de ri•gueur
de•ris•ible
de•ri•sion
de•ri•sive (or •sory)
de•riv•able
deri•va•tion
deri•va•tion•al
de•riva•tive
de•rive
der•ma
der•mal
der•ma•ti•tis
der•ma•to•logi•cal
der•ma•tolo•gist
der•ma•tol•ogy
der•mis
dero•gate
dero•ga•tion
de•roga•tive
de•roga•tori•ly
de•roga•tory
der•rick
der•ring-do

der•rin•ger (*or* der•in•ger)
der•vish
de•sali•nate (*or* •nize)
de•sali•na•tion (*or* •ni•za•tion)
de•scale
des•cant (*or* dis•)
de•scend
de•scend•ant (*or* •ent)
de•scend•er
de•scend•ible (*or* •able)
de•scent going down; *cf* decent; dissent
de•scrib•able
de•scribe
de•scrib•er
de•scrip•tion
de•scrip•tive
de•scry (•scries, •scry•ing, •scried)
des•ecrate
des•ecra•tion
des•ecra•tor (*or* •ecrat•er)
de•seg•re•gate
de•seg•re•ga•tion
de•sen•si•ti•za•tion
de•sen•si•tize
de•sen•si•tiz•er
#des•ert plantless region
de•#sert abandon; merit; *cf* dessert
de•sert•ed

de•sert•er
de•sert•ifi•ca•tion
de•ser•tion
de•serve
de•serv•ed•ly
de•serv•ed•ness
de•serv•ing
des•ha•bille variant spelling of dishabille
des•ic•cate (*NOT* dessicate)
des•ic•ca•ted
des•ic•ca•tion
de•sign
des•ig•nate
des•ig•na•tion
des•ig•na•tive (*or* •tory)
des•ig•na•tor
dc•sign•ed•ly
de•sign•er
de•sign•ing
de•sir•abil•ity (*or* •sirable•ness)
de•sir•able
de•sir•ably
de•sire
de•sir•ous
de•sist
de•sist•ance (*or* •ence)
desk
desk•bound
desk•top
deso•late
deso•late•ly
deso•la•tion
de•spair

des•patch *variant spelling of* dispatch
des•pera•do (*pl* •does *or* •dos)
des•per•ate
des•per•ate•ly
des•pera•tion
de•spi•cabil•ity (*or* •cable•ness)
de•spic•able
de•spic•ably
de•spise
de•spis•er
de•spite
de•spoil
de•spoil•er
de•spoil•ment
de•spo•lia•tion
de•spond
de•spon•den•cy (*or* •ence)
de•spon•dent
des•pot
des•pot•ic
des•poti•cal•ly
des•pot•ism
des•sert sweet; *cf* desert
dessert•spoon
dessicate incorrect spelling of desiccate
des•ti•na•tion
des•tine
des•tined
des•ti•ny (*pl* •nies)
des•ti•tute
des•ti•tu•tion

de•stroy
de•stroy•able
de•stroy•er
de•struct
de•struc•tibil•ity
de•struc•tible
de•struc•tion
de•struc•tion•ist
de•struc•tive
de•struc•tive•ly
de•struc•tive•ness
  (or •tiv•ity)
des•ul•to•ri•ly
des•ul•to•ri•ness
des•ul•tory
de•tach
de•tach•able
de•tached
de•tach•ment
de•tail
de•tailed
de•tain
de•tainee
de•tain•ment
de•tect
de•tect•able (or
  •ible)
de•tec•tion
de•tec•tive
de•tec•tor
dé•tente
de•ten•tion
de•ter (•ter•ring,
  •terred)
de•ter•gent
de•te•rio•rate
de•te•rio•ra•tion
de•ter•ment
de•ter•min•able

de•ter•mi•nant
de•ter•mi•nate
de•ter•mi•na•tion
de•ter•mi•na•tive
de•ter•mine
de•ter•mined
de•ter•mined•ly
de•ter•min•er
de•ter•min•ism
de•ter•min•ist
de•ter•min•is•tic
de•ter•rence
de•ter•rent
de•test
de•test•able
de•tes•ta•tion
de•test•er
de•throne
de•throne•ment
deto•nate
deto•na•tion
deto•na•tor
de•tour
de•toxi•cant
de•toxi•cate
de•toxi•ca•tion
de•toxi•fi•ca•tion
de•toxi•fy (•fies,
  •fy•ing, •fied)
de•tract
de•trac•tion
de•trac•tive
de•trac•tor
de•train
det•ri•ment
det•ri•men•tal
det•ri•men•tal•ly
de•tri•tus
de•tu•mes•cence

deuce
deu•ced
deus ex machi•na
deu•te•ri•um
Deutsch•mark
de•valua•tion
de•value (or
  •valu•ate;
  •valu•ing, •val•ued
  or •at•ing, •ated)
dev•as•tate
dev•as•tat•ing
dev•as•ta•tion
dev•as•ta•tor
de•vel•op
de•vel•op•er
de•vel•op•ment
de•vel•op•men•tal
de•vel•op•men•
  tal•ly
de•vi•ance
de•vi•ant
de•vi•ate
de•via•tion
de•via•tor
de•via•tory
de•vice
  contrivance; plan;
  cf devise
dev•il (•il•ing, •iled;
  Brit •il•ling, •illed)
devil•fish (pl •fish
  or •fishes)
dev•il•ish
dev•il•ish•ly
dev•il•ish•ness
dev•il•ment
dev•il•try (Brit •ry;

pl •**tries**; *Brit*
•**ries)**
de•**vi•ous**
de•**vi•ous•ly**
de•**vi•ous•ness**
de•**vise** to plan;
leave by will; a
gift by will; *cf*
device
de•**vis•er** (*or*
•**vi•sor**) one who
devises; *cf* **divisor**
de•**vi•tal•ize**
de•**void**
de•**vo•lu•tion**
de•**volve**
de•**volve•ment**
de•**vote**
de•**vot•ed**
de•**vot•ed•ly**
devo•**tee**
de•**vo•tion**
de•**vo•tion•al**
de•**vour**
de•**vour•er**
de•**vour•ing•ly**
de•**vout**
de•**vout•ly**
de•**vout•ness**
dew
dew•**ber•ry** (*pl*
•**ries)**
dew•**claw**
dew•**drop**
dew•**lap**
dewy (dewi•**er**,
dewi•**est)**
dewy-eyed
dex•**ter•ity**

dex•**ter•ous** (*or*
dex•**trous)**
dex•**ter•ous•ness**
(*or* dex•**trous•**
ness)
dex•**tral**
dex•**trin**
dex•**trose**
dex•**trous** *variant*
spelling of
dexterous
dia•**be•tes**
dia•**be•tes**
mel•**li•tus**
dia•**bet•ic**
dia•**bol•ic**
dia•**boli•cal**
dia•**boli•cal•ly**
di•**abo•lism**
di•**abo•list**
di•**abo•lize**
dia•**chron•ic**
dia•**crit•ic**
dia•**criti•cal**
dia•**dem**
di•**aer•esis** *variant*
spelling of **dieresis**
di•**ag•nos•able** (*or*
•**nose•)**
di•**ag•nose**
di•**ag•no•sis** (*pl*
•**ses)**
di•**ag•nos•tic**
di•**ag•nos•ti•cal•ly**
di•**ag•nos•ti•cian**
di•**ag•nos•tics**
di•**ago•nal**
di•**ago•nal•ly**
dia•**gram**

(•**gram•ing,**
•**gramed**; *Brit*
•**gram•ming,**
•**grammed)**
dia•**gram•mat•ic**
dia•**gram•mati•**
cal•ly
dial (dial•**ing,**
dialed; *Brit*
dial•**ling,** dialled)
dia•**lect**
dia•**lec•tal**
dia•**lec•tic** (*adj, n*)
dia•**lec•ti•cal**
dia•**lec•ti•cal•ly**
dia•**lec•tics**
dial•**er** (*Brit* •**ler)**
dia•**logue** (*or* •**log)**
di•**aly•sis** (*pl* •**ses)**
dia•**lyt•ic**
dia•**lyze** (*Brit* •**lyse)**
dia•**lyz•er** (*Brit*
•**lys•)**
dia•**man•té**
di•**am•eter**
dia•**met•ric** (*or*
•**ri•cal)**
dia•**met•ri•cal•ly**
dia•**mond**
diamond•**back**
dia•**per**
di•**apha•nous**
di•**apha•nous•ness**
(*or* •**nei•ty)**
dia•**pho•resis**
dia•**pho•ret•ic**
dia•**phragm**
dia•**phrag•mat•ic**
dia•**rist**

di•ar•rhea (*Brit* •rhoea)
dia•ry (*pl* •ries)
Di•as•po•ra
di•as•to•le
dia•stol•ic
dia•tom
dia•to•ma•ceous
dia•tom•ic
dia•tribe
dib (dib•bing, dibbed)
dib•ble
dice
dic•er
di•choto•mous (*or* •cho•tom•ic)
di•choto•my (*pl* •mies)
dick•er
dicky (*or* dick•ey; *pl* dickies *or* dick•eys)
di•coty•le•don
di•coty•le•don•ous
dic•ta *pl of* dictum
dic•tate
dic•ta•tion
dic•ta•tor
dic•ta•to•rial
dic•ta•to•rial•ly
dic•ta•tor•ship
dic•tion
dic•tion•ary (*pl* •aries)
dic•tum (*pl* •tums *or* •ta)
did
di•dac•tic

di•dac•ti•cal•ly
di•dac•ti•cism
di•dac•tics
did•dle
didn't
die (*vb*; dy•ing, died) expire; *cf* dye
die (*n*) tool; *cf* dye
die-cast (-cast•ing, -cast)
die-hard
diel•drin
di•elec•tric
di•er•esis (*or* •aer•; *pl* •eses) phonetics symbol; *cf* diuresis
die•sel
diet
di•etary (*pl* •etaries)
di•et•er
di•etet•ic (*or* •ical)
di•etet•ics
di•eti•tian (*or* •cian)
dif•fer
dif•fer•ence
dif•fer•ent
dif•fer•en•tial
dif•fer•en•ti•ate
dif•fer•en•tia•tion
dif•fer•en•tia•tor
dif•fi•cult
dif•fi•cul•ty (*pl* •ties)
dif•fi•dence
dif•fi•dent

dif•fi•dent•ly
dif•fract
dif•frac•tion
dif•frac•tive
dif•fuse
dif•fuse•ly
dif•fuse•ness
dif•fus•er (*or* •fu•sor)
dif•fus•ibil•ity (*or* •ible•ness)
dif•fus•ible
dif•fu•sion
dif•fu•sive
dig (dig•ging, dug)
di•gest
di•gest•ant
di•gest•er
di•gest•ibil•ity (*or* •ible•ness)
di•gest•ible
di•ges•tion
di•ges•tive
dig•ger
dig•ging
dig•it
digi•tal
digi•tal•is
digi•tali•za•tion
digi•tal•ize
digi•tal•ly
digi•tate (*or* •tat•ed)
dig•iti•za•tion
dig•it•ize
dig•ni•fy (•fies, •fy•ing, •fied)
dig•ni•tary (*pl* •taries)

dig•ni•ty (*pl* •ities)
di•gress
di•gress•er
di•gres•sion
di•gres•sive
dike (*or* dyke)
di•lapi•date (*NOT* delapidate)
di•lapi•da•ted
di•lapi•da•tion
di•lat•able
di•la•ta•tion
di•late
di•la•tion
di•la•tive
di•la•tor
dila•to•ri•ness
di•la•tory
dil•do (*or* •doe; *pl* •dos *or* •does)
di•lem•ma
dil•et•tante (*pl* •tan•tes *or* •tan•ti)
dil•et•tant•ism (*or* tan•teism)
dili•gence
dili•gent
dili•gent•ly
dill
dil•ly (*pl* •lies)
dilly-dally (-dallies, -dally•ing, -dallied)
di•lute
di•lut•er (*or* •lu•tor)
di•lu•tion
dim (*adj* dim•mer, dim•mest; *vb*

dim•ming, dimmed)
dime
di•men•sion
di•men•sion•al
di•men•sion•less
di•min•ish
di•min•ish•ment
di•minu•en•do (*pl* •dos)
dimi•nu•tion
di•minu•tive
dim•ly
dimmed
dim•mer
dim•mest
dim•ming
dim•ness
dim•ple
dim•wit
dim-witted
dim-wit•ted•ness
din (din•ning, dinned)
dl•nar
dine eat; *cf* dyne
din•er
ding•bat
ding-dong
din•ghy (*pl* •ghies)
din•gi•ly
din•gi•ness
din•go (*pl* •goes)
din•gy (•gi•er, •gi•est)
dinky (dinki•er, dinki•est)
din•ner
di•no•saur

di•no•sau•rian
dint
di•oc•esan
dio•cese
di•ode
di•op•ter (*Brit* •tre)
dio•rama
di•ox•ide
di•ox•in
dip (dip•ping, dipped)
diph•the•ria (*NOT* diptheria)
diph•the•rial (*or* •the•rit•ic, •ther•ic)
diph•thong (*NOT* dipthong)
diph•thon•gal
di•ple•gia
di•ple•gic
di•plo•ma
di•plo•ma•cy (*pl* •cies)
dip•lo•mat
dip•lo•mat•ic (*or* •mati•cal)
dip•lo•mati•cal•ly
di•plo•ma•tist
di•po•lar
di•pole
dipped
dip•per
dip•ping
dip•so•ma•nia
dip•so•ma•ni•ac
dip•so•ma•nia•cal
dip•stick
*diptheria

*incorrect spelling
of* diphtheria

*dipthong *incorrect
spelling of*
diphthong

dip•tych
dire
di•rect
di•rec•tion
di•rec•tion•al
di•rec•tion•al•ly
di•rec•tive
di•rect•ly
di•rect•ness
di•rec•tor
di•rec•tor•ate
di•rec•to•ri•al
di•rec•tor•ship
di•rec•to•ry (*pl*
•tories)
dirge
dir•igible
dirndl
dirt
dirti•ly
dirti•ness
dirty (*adj* dirti•er,
dirti•est; *vb*
dirties, dirty•ing,
dirt•ied)
dis•abil•ity (*pl*
•ities)
dis•able
dis•abled
dis•able•ment
dis•abuse
dis•ac•cus•tom
dis•ad•van•tage
dis•ad•van•taged

dis•ad•van•ta•
geous
dis•af•fect
dis•af•fec•tion
dis•agree
(•agree•ing,
•agreed)
dis•agree•able
dis•agree•able•ness
dis•agree•ably
dis•agree•ment
dis•al•low
dis•al•low•able
dis•al•low•ance
dis•ap•pear
dis•ap•pear•ance
dis•ap•point
dis•ap•point•ed
dis•ap•point•ing
dis•ap•point•ment
dis•ap•pro•ba•tion
dis•ap•prov•al
dis•ap•prove
dis•ap•prov•er
dis•arm
dis•ar•ma•ment
dis•arm•er
dis•arm•ing
dis•ar•range
dis•ar•range•ment
dis•ar•ray
dis•as•sem•ble
dis•as•sem•bly
dis•as•so•ci•ate
dis•as•so•cia•tion
dis•as•ter
dis•as•trous
dis•avow
dis•avow•al

dis•avow•ed•ly
dis•avow•er
dis•band
dis•band•ment
dis•bar (•bar•ring,
•barred)
dis•bar•ment
dis•be•lief
dis•be•lieve
dis•be•liev•er
dis•be•liev•ing•ly
dis•burse
dis•burse•ment (*or*
•burs•al)
dis•burs•er
disc *Brit spelling of*
disk (circular
plate; record)
dis•cant *variant of*
descant
dis•card
dis•cern
dis•cern•er
dis•cern•ible (*or*
•able)
dis•cern•ing
dis•cern•ment
dis•charge
dis•charge•able
dis•charg•er
dis•ci•ple
dis•ci•ple•ship
dis•ci•plin•able
dis•ci•pli•nar•ian
dis•ci•pli•nary
dis•ci•pline
dis•ci•plin•er
dis•claim
dis•claim•er

dis•cla•ma•tion
dis•close
dis•clos•er
dis•clo•sure
dis•co (*pl* •cos)
dis•coid
dis•col•or (*Brit* •our)
dis•col•ora•tion
dis•col•or•ment (*Brit* •our•)
dis•com•fit disconcert; *cf* **discomfort**
dis•com•fi•ture
dis•com•fort make uncomfortable; *cf* **discomfit**
dis•com•mode
dis•com•pose
dis•com•pos•ed•ly
dis•com•po•sure
dis•con•cert
dis•con•cert•ed
dis•con•cert•ing•ly
dis•con•form•ity (*pl* •ities)
dis•con•nect
dis•con•nect•ed
dis•con•nec•tion (or •nex•ion)
dis•con•so•late
dis•con•so•la•tion (or •late•ness)
dis•con•tent
dis•con•tent•ed
dis•con•tent•ed•ness
dis•con•tent•ment

dis•con•tinu•ance
dis•con•tinua•tion
dis•con•tinue (•tinu•ing, •tinued)
dis•con•ti•nu•ity (*pl* •ities)
dis•con•tinu•ous
dis•cord
dis•cor•dance (or •dan•cy; *pl* •dances or •cies)
dis•cord•ant
dis•co•theque
dis•count
dis•count•able
dis•coun•te•nance
dis•count•er
dis•cour•age
dis•cour•age•ment
dis•cour•ag•er
dis•cour•ag•ing•ly
dis•course
dis•cours•er
dis•cour•te•ous
dis•cour•tesy (*pl* •tesies)
dis•cov•er
dis•cov•er•able
dis•cov•er•er
dis•cov•ery (*pl* •eries)
dis•cred•it
dis•cred•it•able
dis•cred•it•ably
dis•creet tactful; *cf* **discrete**
dis•creet•ly
dis•creet•ness

dis•crep•an•cy (*pl* •cies)
dis•crep•ant
dis•crete distinct; separate; *cf* **discreet**
dis•crete•ness
dis•cre•tion
dis•cre•tion•ari•ly (or •tion•al•ly)
dis•cre•tion•ary (or •al)
dis•cri•mi•nant
dis•crimi•nate
dis•crimi•nat•ing
dis•crimi•na•tion
dis•crimi•na•tor
dis•crimi•na•to•ri•ly (or dis•crimi•na•tive•ly)
dis•crimi•na•tory (or •tive)
dis•cur•sive
dis•cus (*pl* •cuses or •ci) disk
dis•cuss debate
dis•cus•sant (or •cuss•er)
dis•cuss•ible (or •able)
dis•cus•sion
dis•dain
dis•dain•ful
dis•dain•ful•ly
dis•ease
dis•eased
dis•em•bark
dis•em•bar•ka•tion

dis•em•bod•ied
dis•em•bodi•ment
dis•em•body
(•bodies,
•body•ing,
•bod•ied)
dis•em•bow•el
(•el•ing, •eled; *Brit*
•el•ling, •elled)
dis•em•bow•el•
ment
dis•en•chant
dis•en•chant•ment
dis•en•cum•ber
dis•en•cum•ber•
ment
dis•en•dow
dis•en•dow•er
dis•en•dow•ment
dis•en•fran•chise
dis•en•fran•chise•
ment
dis•en•gage
dis•en•gage•ment
dis•en•tan•gle
dis•en•tan•gle•ment
dis•en•ti•tle
dis•en•twine
dis•es•tab•lish
dis•es•tab•lish•
ment
dis•es•teem
dis•fa•vor (*Brit*
•vour)
dis•fig•ure
dis•fig•ure•ment
(or •ura•tion)
dis•fran•chise
dis•fran•chise•ment

dis•gorge
dis•gorge•ment
dis•grace
dis•grace•ful
dis•grace•ful•ly
dis•grac•er
dis•grun•tle
dis•grun•tled
dis•grun•tle•ment
dis•guis•able
dis•guise
dis•guis•er
dis•gust
dis•gust•ed•ly
dis•gust•ing
dish
dis•ha•bille (*or*
des•)
dis•har•mo•ni•ous
dis•har•mo•ny (*pl*
•nies)
dish•cloth
dis•heart•en
dis•heart•en•ment
dished
di•shev•el (•el•ing,
•eled; *Brit* •el•ling,
•elled)
di•shev•el•ment
dis•hon•est
dis•hon•est•ly
dis•hon•es•ty (*pl*
•ties)
dis•hon•or (*Brit*
•our)
dis•hon•or•able
(*Brit* •our•)
dis•hon•or•ably
(*Brit* •our•)

dis•hon•or•er (*Brit*
•our•)
dish•washer
dish•water
dis•il•lu•sion
dis•il•lu•sion•ment
dis•in•cen•tive
dis•in•cli•na•tion
dis•in•cline
dis•in•fect
dis•in•fect•ant
dis•in•fec•tion
dis•in•fec•tor
dis•in•fest
dis•in•fes•ta•tion
dis•in•genu•ous
dis•in•genu•ous•
ness
dis•in•her•it
dis•in•heri•tance
dis•in•te•grable
dis•in•te•grate
dis•in•te•gra•tion
dis•in•te•gra•tor
dis•in•ter
(•ter•ring, •terred)
dis•in•ter•est
dis•in•ter•est•ed
impartial; *cf*
uninterested
dis•in•ter•ment
dis•joint
dis•joint•ed
disk (*Brit* disc
except in
computer science)
disk•ette
dis•lik•able (*or*
•like•)

dis•like
dis•lo•cate
dis•lo•ca•tion
dis•lodge
dis•lodg•ment (*or* •lodge•)
dis•loy•al
dis•loy•al•ty (*pl* •ties)
dis•mal
dis•mal•ly
dis•mal•ness
dis•man•tle
dis•may
dis•mem•ber
dis•mem•ber•ment
dis•miss
dis•mis•sal
dis•miss•ible
dis•mis•sive
dis•mount
dis•obe•di•ence
dis•obe•di•ent
dis•obey
dis•obey•er
dis•oblige
dis•oblig•ing
dis•or•der
dis•or•dered
dis•or•der•li•ness
dis•or•der•ly
dis•or•gani•za•tion
dis•or•gan•ize
dis•or•gan•iz•er
dis•ori•ent (*or* dis•ori•en•tate)
dis•ori•en•ta•tion
dis•own
dis•own•ment

dis•par•age
dis•par•age•ment
dis•par•ag•er
dis•par•ate
dis•par•ity (*pl* •ities)
dis•pas•sion•ate
dis•patch (*or* des•)
dis•patch•er (*or* des•)
dis•pel (•pel•ling, •pelled)
dis•pel•ler
dis•pens•abil•ity (*or* •able•ness)
dis•pens•able
dis•pen•sary (*pl* •saries)
dis•pen•sa•tion
dis•pen•sa•tion•al
dis•pense
dis•pens•er
dis•per•sal
dis•per•sant
dis•perse
dis•pers•er
dis•per•sion
dis•per•sive
dis•pir•it
dis•pir•it•ed
dis•pir•it•ing
dis•place
dis•place•able
dis•place•ment
dis•plac•er
dis•play
dis•play•er
dis•please
dis•pleas•ure

dis•port
dis•pos•abil•ity (*or* •able•ness)
dis•pos•able
dis•pos•al
dis•pose
dis•posed
dis•pos•er
dis•po•si•tion
dis•pos•sess
dis•pos•ses•sion
dis•pos•ses•sor
dis•praise
dis•proof
dis•pro•por•tion
dis•pro•por•tion•al
dis•pro•por•tion•al•ly
dis•pro•por•tion•ate
dis•pro•por•tion•ate•ly
dis•prov•able
dis•prov•al
dis•prove
dis•put•abil•ity (*or* •able•ness)
dis•put•able
dis•put•ably
dis•pu•tant
dis•pu•ta•tion
dis•pu•ta•tious (*or* •tive)
dis•pute
dis•put•er
dis•quali•fi•able
dis•quali•fi•ca•tion
dis•quali•fi•er

dis•quali•fy (•fies,
•fy•ing, •fied)
dis•qui•et
dis•qui•et•ed•ly (or
dis•qui•et•ly)
dis•qui•et•ed•ness
(or dis•qui•et•
ness)
dis•qui•et•ing
dis•qui•etude
dis•qui•si•tion
dis•re•gard
dis•re•pair
dis•repu•tabil•ity
(or •table•ness)
dis•repu•table
dis•repu•tably
dis•re•pute
dis•re•spect
dis•re•spect•ful
dis•re•spect•ful•ly
dis•robe
dis•rupt
dis•rupt•er (or
•rup•tor)
dis•rup•tion
dis•rup•tive
dis•rup•tive•ly
dis•sat•is•fac•tion
dis•sat•is•fac•tory
dis•sat•is•fy (•fies,
•fy•ing, •fied)
dis•sect
dis•sec•tible
dis•sec•tion
dis•sec•tor
dis•sem•blance
dis•sem•ble
dis•sem•bler

dis•semi•nate
dis•semi•na•tion
dis•semi•na•tive
dis•semi•na•tor
dis•sen•sion
dis•sent disagree;
cf descent
dis•sent•er
dis•sen•tience
dis•sen•tient
dissenting
dis•sen•tious
argumentative
dis•ser•tate
dis•ser•ta•tion
dis•ser•vice
dis•sev•er
dis•sev•er•ance (or
•er•ment,
•era•tion)
dis•si•dence
dis•si•dent
dis•simi•lar
dis•simi•lar•ity (pl
•ities)
dis•simu•late
dis•simu•la•tion
dis•simu•la•tive
dis•simu•la•tor
dis•si•pate
dis•si•pat•ed
dis•si•pat•er (or
•pa•tor)
dis•si•pa•tion
dis•so•ci•abil•ity
(or •able•ness)
dis•so•ci•able
dis•so•ci•ate
dis•so•cia•tion

dis•so•cia•tive
dis•sol•ubil•ity (or
•uble•ness)
dis•sol•uble
dis•so•lute
dis•so•lute•ness
dis•so•lu•tion
dis•solv•abil•ity (or
•able•ness)
dis•solv•able
dis•solve
dis•sol•vent
dis•solv•er
dis•so•nance (or
•nan•cy)
dis•so•nant
dis•suade
dis•suad•er
dis•sua•sion
dis•sua•sive
dis•sua•sive•ness
dis•taff
dis•tal
dis•tance
dis•tant
dis•tant•ly
dis•taste
dis•taste•ful
dis•taste•ful•ly
dis•tem•per
dis•tend
dis•ten•sible
dis•ten•sion (or
•tion)
dis•till (Brit dis•til;
•til•ling, •tilled)
dis•till•able
dis•til•late

dis•til•la•tion (*or* dis•till•ment)
dis•til•ler
dis•til•lery (*pl* •leries)
dis•tinct
dis•tinct•ly
dis•tinc•tion
dis•tinc•tive
dis•tinc•tive•ly
dis•tinc•tive•ness
dis•tinct•ness
dis•tin•guish
dis•tin•guish•able
dis•tin•guish•ably
dis•tin•guished
dis•tort
dis•tort•ed
dis•tort•er
dis•tor•tion
dis•tract
dis•tract•ed
dis•tract•er
dis•tract•ibil•ity
dis•tract•ible
dis•trac•ting
dis•trac•tion
dis•trac•tive
dis•train
dis•train•able
dis•traught
dis•tress
dis•tressed
dis•tress•ful
dis•tress•ful•ly
dis•tress•ing
dis•trib•ut•able
dis•trib•ute
dis•tri•bu•tion

dis•tribu•tive
dis•tribu•tor
dis•trict
dis•trust
dis•trust•ful
dis•trust•ful•ly
dis•turb
dis•turb•ance
dis•turbed
dis•turb•er
dis•un•ion
dis•unite
dis•uni•ty (*pl* •ties)
dis•use
dis•used
ditch
dith•er
dith•er•er
dith•ery
dit•to (*n, pl* •tos; *vb* •tos, •to•ing, •toed)
dit•ty (*pl* •ties)
di•ure•sis increased urination; *cf* dieresis
di•uret•ic
di•ur•nal
di•ur•nal•ly
di•va (*pl* •vas *or* dive)
di•va•lent
di•van
dive (div•ing, dived *or* dove)
dive-bomb
div•er
di•verge
di•ver•gence (*or*

•gen•cy; *pl* •gences *or* •cies)
di•ver•gent
di•verse
di•ver•si•fi•ca•tion
di•ver•si•fi•er
di•ver•si•fy (•fies, •fy•ing, •fied)
di•ver•sion
di•ver•sion•ary (*or* •al)
di•ver•sity
di•vert
di•vert•er
di•vert•ible
di•vert•ing
di•ver•tisse•ment
di•vest
di•vesti•ture (*or* •ves•ture, •vest•ment)
di•vid•able
di•vide
divi•dend
di•vid•er
di•vin•able
divi•na•tion
divi•na•tory
di•vine
di•vin•er
div•ing
di•vin•ing
di•vin•ity (*pl* •ities)
di•vis•ibil•ity
di•vis•ible
di•vi•sion
di•vi•sion•al (*or* •ary)
di•vi•sive

di•vi•sive•ly
di•vi•sor math term; cf deviser
di•vorce
di•vor•cé (fem •cée)
div•ot
di•vulge
di•vul•gence (or •vulge•ment)
di•vulg•er
div•vy (n, pl •vies; vb •vies, •vy•ing, •vied)
Dix•ie
Dixie•land
diz•zi•ly
diz•zi•ness
diz•zy (adj •zi•er, •zi•est; vb •zies, •zy•ing, •zied)
djinni (or djinny, djinn, djin) variants of jinni
do (vb does, do•ing, did, done; n, pl dos or do's)
do (pl dos) musical note; cf doe, dough
do•able
dob•bin
Do•ber•man pin•scher
doc doctor; cf dock
do•cent
doc•ile
doc•ile•ly
do•cil•ity
dock wharf;

remove tail, part of law court; plant; cf doc
dock•age
dock•er
dock•et
dock•land
dock•yard
doc•tor
doc•tor•al
doc•tor•ate
doc•tri•naire
doc•tri•nair•ism
doc•tri•nal
doc•tri•nal•ity
doc•tri•nar•ian
doc•trine
docu•drama
docu•ment
docu•men•tary (pl •taries)
docu•men•ta•tion
dod•der
dod•der•er
dod•der•ing
dod•dery
do•deca•gon
do•de•cago•nal
do•deca•he•dral
do•deca•he•dron (pl •drons or •dra)
dodge
dodg•er
do•do (pl •dos or •does)
doe (pl does or doe) deer; cf do (musical note); dough

do•er
does present tense of do; pl of doe
doe•skin
doff
dog (dog•ging, dogged)
dog•cart
dog-ear
dog-eared
dog•fight
dog•fish (pl •fish or •fishes)
dog•ged (adj)
dog•ged•ly
dog•ged•ness
dog•ger•el (or dog•grel)
dog•gy (adj; •gi•er, •gi•est)
dog•gy (or •gie; n, pl •gies)
dog•house
do•gie
dog•ma (pl •mas or •ma•ta)
dog•mat•ic (or •mati•cal)
dog•mati•cal•ly
dog•ma•tism
dog•ma•tist
do-good•er
dog•sled
dog-tired
dog•trot
dog•wood
doi•ly (pl •lies)
do•ing
do-it-yourself (adj)

dol•ce vi•ta
dol•drums
dole
dole•ful
dole•ful•ly
dole•ful•ness
doll
dol•lar
dol•lar•fish (pl
•fish or •fishes)
doll•ish
dol•lop
dol•ly (n, pl •lies;
vb •ly•ing, •lied)
dol•man (pl •mans)
robe
dol•men tomb
do•lo•mite
dol•or (Brit •our)
dol•or•ous
dol•phin
dolt
dolt•ish
do•main
dome
dome•like
Domes•day variant
spelling of
Doomsday
do•mes•tic
do•mes•ti•ca•ble
do•mes•ti•cal•ly
do•mes•ti•cate
do•mes•ti•ca•tion
do•mes•ti•ca•tor
do•mes•ti•city (pl
•cities)
domi•cile
domi•cili•ary

domi•nance
domi•nant
domi•nate
domi•na•tion
domi•na•tor
domi•neer
Do•mini•can
do•min•ion
domi•no (pl •nos
or •noes)
don (don•ning,
donned)
do•nate
do•na•tion
do•na•tor
done completed; cf
dun
don•key
donned
don•ning
do•nor
don't
do•nut variant
spelling of
doughnut
doo•dad (Brit •dah)
doo•dle
doodle•bug
doo•dler
doom
doom-laden
Dooms•day (or
Domes•)
door
door•bell
do-or-die (adj)
door•frame
door•jamb
door•keeper

door•man (pl •men)
door•mat
door•nail
door•post
door•step
door•stop
door-to-door
door•way
door•yard
dope
do•pey (or •py;
•pi•er, •pi•est)
dopi•ness
Dop•pel•gäng•er
Dop•pler ef•fect
dor•man•cy
dor•mant
dor•mer
dor•mi•tory (pl
•tories)
dor•mouse (pl
•mice)
dor•sal
dor•sal•ly
do•ry (pl •ries)
dos•age
dose
dos•er
dos•si•er
dot (dot•ting,
dot•ted)
dot•age
do•tard
dote
dot•ing•ly
dot-matrix (adj)
dot•ted
dot•ter
dot•ti•ly

dot•ti•ness

dot•ting

dot•ty (•ti•er,
•ti•est)

dou•ble

double-bar•reled
(*Brit* -bar•relled)

double-bass (*adj*)

double-breast•ed

double-check (*vb*)

double-cross (*vb*)

double-dealer

double-deal•ing

double-decker

double-edged

dou•ble en•ten•dre

double-faced

double•header

double-hung

double-joint•ed

double-park (*vb*)

double-quick

double-space (*vb*)

dou•blet

double•think

double-time (*vb*)

dou•bly

doubt

doubt•able

doubt•er

doubt•ful

doubt•ful•ly

doubt•ful•ness

doubt•less

douche

dough bread;
money; *cf do*
(musical note);
doe

dough•boy

dough•nut (*or*
do•nut)

dough•ty (•ti•er,
•ti•est)

doughy (doughi•er,
doughi•est)

dour sullen; *cf*
dower

dour•ly

dour•ness

douse (*or* dowse)
drench; *cf dowse*

dous•er (*or* dows•)

dove bird; *past
tense of dive*

dove•cote (*or* •cot)

dove•tail

dov•ish

dowa•ger

dow•di•ly

dow•di•ness

dow•dy (*n, pl* •dies);
adj •di•er, •di•est)

dow•el (•el•ing,
•eled *or* •el•ling,
•elled)

dow•er widow's
inheritance; *cf*
dour

*dowery incorrect
spelling of* dowry

Dow-Jones
av•er•age

down

down-and-out

down•beat

down•cast

down•er

down•fall

down•fallen

down•grade

down•hearted

down•hearted•ly

down•hearted•ness

down•hill

downi•ness

down-load

down•market

down•pipe

down•pour

down•right

down•side

down•spout

Down's syn•drome

down•stage

down•stairs

down•state

down•stream

down•swing

down•time

down-to-earth

down•town

down•trod•den

down•turn

down•ward (*adj*)

down•ward (*Brit*
•wards; *adv*)

down•wind

downy (downi•er,
downi•est)

dow•ry (*pl* •ries;
NOT dowery)

dowse to divine
water; *variant
spelling of* douse

dows•er

dows•ing

dox•ol•o•gy (*pl*
•ogies)
doy•en (*fem* •enne)
doze
doz•en (*pl* •en *or*
•ens)
doz•enth
doz•er
dozy (dozi•er,
dozi•est)
drab (drab•ber,
drab•best)
drab•ly
drab•ness
drach•ma (*pl* •mas,
•mae, *or* •mai)
Dra•co•nian
draft sketch;
military selection;
money order
draft (*Brit* draught)
air current, drink,
load pulling
draftee
draft•er
drafti•ness (*Brit*
draughti•)
drafts•man (*pl*
•men)
drafts•man•ship
drafty (*Brit*
draughty;
drafti•er,
drafti•est; *Brit*
draughti•er,
draughti•est)
drag (drag•ging,
dragged)
drag•net

drag•on
dragon•fly (*pl*
•flies)
drag•on•ish
dra•goon
drain
drain•able
drain•age
drain•er
drain•pipe
drake
dram
dra•ma
dra•mat•ic
dra•mati•cal•ly
dra•mat•ics
**dra•ma•tis
per•so•nae**
drama•tist
drama•ti•za•tion
drama•tize
drama•tiz•er
drama•tur•gy
drank
drape
drap•er
dra•pery (*pl*
•peries)
drapes
dras•tic
dras•ti•cal•ly
drat
drat•ted
draught *Brit
spelling of* **draft**
(air current;
drink; load
pulling)
draughti•ness *Brit*

spelling of
drafti•ness
draughts (*Brit*)
checkers
draughty Brit
spelling of **drafty**
draw (draw•ing,
drew, drawn)
draw•able
draw•back
draw•bridge
drawee
draw•er
drawer•ful
draw•ing
draw•knife (*pl*
•knives) (*Brit*)
spokeshave
drawl
drawl•er
drawly
drawn
draw•string
dray cart; *cf* drey
dread
dread•ful
dread•ful•ly
dread•ful•ness
dread•locks
dread•nought
dream (dream•ing,
dreamt *or*
dreamed)
dream•er
dreami•ly
dreami•ness
dream•less
dream•like

dreamy (dreami•er,
  dreami•est)
dreari•ly
dreari•ness
dreary (dreari•er,
  dreari•est)
dredge
dredg•er
dreg
dreg•gy (•gi•er,
  •gi•est)
dregs
drench
drench•er
Dres•den chi•na
dress
dres•sage
dressed
dress•er
dressi•ness
dress•ing
dress•maker
dress•mak•ing
dressy (dressi•er,
  dressi•est)
drew
drey squirrel's
  nest; *cf* dray
drib•ble
drib•bler
dried
dri•er (*or* dry•)
  more dry; person
  or thing that
  dries; *cf* dryer
dri•est (*or* dry•)
drift
drift•er
drift•wood

drifty
drill
drill•able
drill•er
drill•ing
drill•master
dri•ly
drink (drink•ing,
  drank, drunk)
drink•able
drink•er
drip (drip•ping,
  dripped *or* dript)
drip-dry (*adj; vb*
  -dries, -drying,
  -dried)
drip-feed
drip•ping
drip•py (•pi•er,
  •pi•est)
drip•stone
driv•able (*or* drive•)
drive (driv•ing,
  drove, driv•en)
drive-in
driv•el (•el•ing,
  •eled; *Brit* •ell•ing,
  •elled)
driv•el•er (*Brit*
  •el•ler)
driv•en
driv•er
driv•er•less
drive•way
driv•ing
driz•zle
driz•zly
droll
droll•ery (*pl* •eries)

droll•ness
drol•ly
drom•edary (*pl*
  •edaries)
drone
drool
droop
droopi•ly
droopi•ness
droopy (droopi•er,
  droopi•est)
drop (drop•ping,
  dropped)
drop•let
drop•out
drop•per
drop•pings
drop•sy
dross
drought
drove
drov•er
drown
drowse
drowsi•ly
drowsi•ness
drowsy (drowsi•er,
  drowsi•est)
drub (drub•bing,
  drubbed)
drudge
drudg•ery (*pl*
  •eries)
drug (drug•ging,
  drugged)
drug•gist
drug•store
dru•id (*or* Dru•;
  fem •id•ess)

drum (drum•ming, drummed)
drum•beat
drum•fish (*pl* •fish or •fishes)
drum•mer
drum•stick
drunk
drunk•ard
drunk•en
drunk•en•ly
drunk•en•ness
dry (*adj* dri•er, dri•est *or* dry•er, dry•est; *vb* dries, dry•ing, dried)
dry•able
dry•ad (*pl* •ads or •ades)
dry-clean
dry-cleaner
dry-dock (*vb*)
dry•er machine for drying; *cf* drier
dry•ness
dual two; *cf* duel
dual•ism
dual•ist
dual•is•tic
dual•is•ti•cal•ly
du•al•ity (*pl* •ities)
dual-purpose
dub (dub•bing, dubbed)
dub•bin (*or* •bing)
du•bi•ety (*pl* •eties)
du•bi•ous
du•bi•ous•ly
du•bi•ous•ness

du•bi•table
du•cal
duch•ess
duchy (*pl* duchies)
duck
duck•board
duck•er
duck•ling
duck•weed
duct
duc•tile
duc•til•ity (*or* •tile•ness)
dud
dude
dudg•eon
due
duel (duel•ing, dueled; *Brit* duel•ling, duelled) fight; *cf* dual
duel•er (*or* •ist; *Brit* •ler *or* •list)
du•et (•et•ting, •et•ted)
du•et•tist
duf•fel (*or* •fle)
duf•fer
dug
du•gong
dug•out
duke
duke•dom
dul•cet
dul•ci•mer
dull
dull•ard
dull•ness (*or* dul•ness)

dul•ly in a dull way
du•ly appropriately
dumb
dumb•bell
dumb•found (*or* dum•)
dumb•ness
dumb•waiter
dum•dum
dum•my (*n, pl* •mies; *vb* •mies, •my•ing, •mied)
dump
dump•er
dumpi•ness
dump•ling
dumpy (dumpi•er, dumpi•est)
dun (dun•ning, dunned) demand payment; brown color; *cf* done
dunce
dunder•head
dune
dung
dun•ga•rees
dun•geon
dung•hill
dungy
dunk
dunk•er
dunned
dun•ning
duo (*pl* duos *or* dui)
duo•deci•mal of 12
duo•deci•mo (*pl* •mos) book size

duo•de•nal
duo•de•num (*pl*
•na *or* •nums)
duo•logue
dup•abil•ity
dup•able
dupe
dup•ery (*pl* •eries)
du•ple
du•plex
du•pli•cable (*or*
•pli•cat•able)
du•pli•cate
du•pli•ca•tion
du•pli•ca•tor
du•plic•ity (*pl*
•ities)
du•rabil•ity (*or*
•rable•ness)
du•rable
du•ra ma•ter
dur•ance
du•ra•tion
du•ress
dur•ing
dusk
duski•ness
dusky (duski•er,
duski•est)
dust
dust•bin
dust•er
dusti•ly
dusti•ness
dust•pan
dust•up
dusty (dusti•er,
dusti•est)
Dutch

Dutch•man (*pl*
•men)
du•ti•ful
du•ti•ful•ly
du•ti•ful•ness
du•ty (*pl* •ties)
duty-bound
duty-free
du•vet
dwarf (*pl* dwarfs
or dwarves)
dwarf•ish
dwarf•ish•ness
dwarf•ism
dwell (dwell•ing,
dwelt *or* dwelled)
dwell•er
dwell•ing
dwin•dle
dy•able (*or*
dye•able)
dye (dye•ing, dyed)
color; *cf* die
dye•ing coloring; *cf*
dying
dy•er
dye•stuff
dye•wood
dy•ing expiring; *cf*
dyeing
dyke *variant*
spelling of dike
dy•nam•ic
dy•nami•cal•ly
dy•nam•ics
dy•na•mism
dy•na•mist
dy•na•mite
dy•na•mo (*pl* •mos)

dy•na•mo•elec•tric
(*or* •tri•cal)
dy•na•mom•eter
dyn•ast
dy•nas•tic (*or*
•ti•cal)
dyn•as•ty (*pl* •ties)
dyne unit; *cf* dine
dys•en•tery
dys•func•tion
dys•func•tion•al
dys•lexia
dys•lex•ic
dys•pep•sia
dys•pep•tic
dys•pha•sia
dys•troph•ic
dys•tro•phy (*or*
•phia)

E

each
eager
eager•ly
eager•ness
eagle
eagle-eyed
eaglet
ear
ear•ache
ear•drum
eared
ear•flap
ear•ful
earl
earl•dom
ear•li•ness

ear•ly (•li•er,
•li•est)
ear•mark
ear•muff
earn
earn•er
ear•nest
ear•nest•ly
ear•nest•ness
earn•ings
ear•phone
ear•piece
ear-pierc•ing (*adj*)
ear•plug
ear•ring
ear•shot
ear•split•ting
earth
earth•born
earth•bound
earth•en
earthen•ware
earthi•ly
earthi•ness
earth•li•ness
earth•ling
earth•ly (•li•er,
•li•est) worldly; *cf*
earthy
earth•quake
earth•shak•ing
(*adj*)
earth•ward (*adj*)
earth•ward (*Brit*
•wards; *adv*)
earth•work
earth•worm
earthy (earthi•er,

earthi•est) of soil;
cf earthly
ear•wax
ear•wig
ease
easel
ease•ment
eas•er
easi•ly
easi•ness
east
east•bound
East•er
east•er•ly (*pl* •lies)
east•ern
east•ern•er
east•ern•most
east-northeast
east-southeast
east•ward (*adj*)
east•ward (*Brit*
•wards; *adv*)
east•ward•ly
easy (easi•er,
easi•est)
easy-going
eat (eat•ing, ate,
eat•en)
eat•able
eat•en
eat•er
eau de Co•logne (*pl*
eaux de Co•logne)
eau de Nile
eaves
eaves•drop
(•drop•ping,
•dropped)
eaves•dropper

ebb
eb•on•ize
eb•ony (*pl* •onies)
ebul•lience (*or*
•lien•cy)
ebul•lient
ec•cen•tric
ec•cen•tri•cal•ly
ec•cen•tri•city
(*pl* •cities)
ec•cle•si•as•tic
ec•cle•si•as•ti•cal
ec•cle•si•as•ti•
cal•ly
ec•cle•si•as•ti•cism
eche•lon
echid•na (*pl* •nas
or •nae)
echi•no•derm
echo (*n, pl* echoes;
vb echoes,
echo•ing, ech•oed)
echo•ic
echo•location
éclair
éclat
ec•lec•tic
ec•lec•ti•cism
eclipse
eclip•tic
eco•logi•cal (*or*
•log•ic)
eco•logi•cal•ly
ecolo•gist
ecol•ogy (*pl* •ogies)
econo•met•rics
eco•nom•ic
eco•nomi•cal
eco•nomi•cal•ly

eco•nom•ics
econo•mist
econo•mi•za•tion
econo•mize
econo•miz•er
econo•my (*pl* •mies)
eco•sphere
eco•sys•tem
eco•type
ec•sta•sy (*pl* •sies; *NOT* extasy)
ec•stat•ic
ec•stati•cal•ly
ec•to•derm
ec•to•der•mal (*or* •mic)
ec•to•morph
ec•to•mor•phic
ec•top•ic
ec•to•plasm
ecto•plas•mic
Ecua•do•rian (*or* •rean, •ran)
ecu•meni•cal (*or* •men•ic)
ecu•meni•cal•ly
ecu•meni•cism
ec•ze•ma
ec•zema•tous
Edam cheese
ed•dy (*n, pl* •dies; *vb* •dies, •dy•ing, •died)
edel•weiss
ede•ma (*pl* •mata) (*Brit* oede•)
edema•tous (*Brit* oedema•)

edge
cdg•er
edge•wise (*or* •ways)
edgi•ly
edgi•ness
edg•ing
edgy (edgi•er, edgi•est)
ed•ibil•ity (*or* •ible•ness)
ed•ible
edict
edi•fi•ca•tion
edifi•ca•tory
edi•fice
edi•fi•er
edi•fy (•fies, •fy•ing, •fied)
edi•fy•ing•ly
ed•it
edi•tion
edi•tor
edi•to•rial
edi•to•ri•ali•za•tion
edi•to•ri•al•ize
edi•to•ri•al•iz•er
edi•to•ri•al•ly
edi•tor•ship
edu•ca•bil•ity (*pl* •ities)
edu•cable
edu•cate
edu•cat•ed
edu•ca•tion
edu•ca•tion•al
edu•ca•tion•al•ist (*or* •tion•ist)
edu•ca•tion•al•ly

edu•ca•tive
edu•ca•tor
educe
educ•ible
eel
eel•grass
eel•like
e'er ever; *cf* air; ere; heir
eerie (*or* eery; eeri•er, eeri•est) weird; *cf* eyrie
eeri•ly
eeri•ness
ef•face
ef•face•able
ef•face•ment
ef•fac•er
ef•fect (*n*) result; (*vb*) cause; *cf* affect
ef•fect•er
ef•fect•ible
ef•fec•tive
ef•fec•tive•ly
ef•fec•tive•ness
ef•fec•tual
ef•fec•tu•al•ity (*or* •al•ness)
ef•fec•tu•al•ly
ef•femi•na•cy (*or* •nate•ness)
ef•femi•nate
ef•fer•ence
ef•fer•ent conducting outward; *cf* afferent
ef•fer•vesce

ef•fer•ves•cence
ef•fer•ves•cent
ef•fete
ef•fi•ca•cious
ef•fi•ca•cy (*or*
•cious•ness)
ef•fi•cien•cy (*pl*
•cies)
ef•fi•cient
ef•fi•cient•ly
ef•fi•gy (*pl* •gies)
ef•flo•resce
ef•flo•res•cence
ef•flo•res•cent
ef•flu•ence
ef•flu•ent
ef•flu•vial
ef•flu•vium (*pl* •via
or •viums)
ef•fort
ef•fort•ful
ef•fort•less
ef•fort•less•ly
ef•fort•less•ness
ef•fron•tery (*pl*
•teries)
ef•ful•gence
ef•ful•gent
ef•fu•sion
ef•fu•sive
ef•fu•sive•ly
ef•fu•sive•ness
eft
egali•tar•ian
egali•tari•an•ism
egg
egg•beater
egg•head
egg•nog

egg•plant
egg•shell
eggy
egis *variant
spelling of* aegis
eg•lan•tine
ego (*pl* egos)
ego•cen•tric
ego•cen•tric•ity
ego•cen•trism
ego•ism self-
interest; *cf*
egotism
ego•ist
ego•is•tic (*or*
•ti•cal)
ego•ma•nia
ego•ma•ni•ac
ego•ma•nia•cal
ego•tism self-
centeredness; *cf*
egoism
ego•tist
ego•tis•tic (*or*
•ti•cal)
ego•tis•ti•cal•ly
ego-trip (*vb*;
-trip•ping,
-tripped)
egre•gious
egress
egres•sion
egret
Egyp•tian
Egyp•tolo•gist
Egyp•tol•ogy
eh
eider
eider•down

eight
eight•een
eight•eenth
eight•fold
eighth
eighti•eth
eighty (*pl* eighties)
ei•ther
ejacu•late
ejacu•la•tion
ejacu•la•tory
eject
ejec•tion
ejec•tor
eke
elabo•rate
elabo•rate•ly
elabo•rate•ness
elabo•ra•tion
elabo•ra•tor
élan
eland
elapse
elas•tic
elas•ti•cal•ly
elas•tici•ty (*pl*
•ties)
elas•ti•cize
elate
elat•ed
ela•tion
el•bow
elbow•room
el•der
elder•berry (*pl*
•berries)
el•der•li•ness
el•der•ly
eld•est

elect
elect•able
elec•tion
elec•tion•eer
elec•tion•eer•er
elec•tion•eer•ing
elec•tive
elec•tor
elec•tor•al
elec•tor•ate
elec•tor•ship
elec•tric
elec•tri•cal
elec•tri•cal•ly
elec•tri•cian
elec•tric•ity
elec•tri•fi•ca•tion
elec•tri•fi•er
elec•tri•fy (•fies, •fy•ing, •fied)
elec•tro•car•dio• gram record
elec•tro•car•dio• graph instrument
elec•tro•car•dio• graph•ic (or •graphi•cal)
elec•tro•car•di•og• ra•phy
elec•tro•chemi•cal
elec•tro•chem• is•try
elec•tro•con•vul• sive
elec•tro•cute
elec•tro•cu•tion
elec•trode
elec•tro•en•cepha• lo•gram record

elec•tro•en•cepha• lo•graph instrument
elec•troly•sis
elec•tro•lyte
elec•tro•lyt•ic
elec•tro•ly•za•tion (Brit •sa•tion)
elec•tro•lyze (Brit •lyse)
elec•tro•mag•net
elec•tro•mag•net•ic
elec•tro•mag•neti• cal•ly
elec•tro•mag•ne• tism
elec•trom•eter
elec•tro•mo•tive
elec•tron
elec•tron•ic
elec•troni•cal•ly
elec•tron•ics
electro•plate
electro•posi•tive
electro•scope
electro•shock
electro•stat•ic
electro•stat•ics
electro•sur•gery
electro•sur•gi•cal
electro•thera•py (pl •pies)
electro•va•lence (or •len•cy; pl •lences or •cies)
electro•va•lent
el•egance (or •egan•cy; pl •egances or •cies)

el•egant
el•egant•ly
el•egi•ac
el•egia•cal•ly
el•egist
el•egize
el•egy (pl •egies)
el•ement
el•emen•tal
el•emen•ta•ri•ness
el•emen•tary
el•ephant (pl •ephants or •ephant)
el•ephan•tia•sis
el•ephan•tine
el•evate
el•evat•ed
el•eva•tion
el•eva•tor
elev•en
elev•enth
elf (pl elves)
elfin
elf•ish (or elv•)
elic•it evoke; cf illicit
elic•it•able
elici•ta•tion
elici•tor
elide
eli•gi•bil•ity
eli•gible
eli•gibly
elimi•nable
elimi•nate
elimi•na•tion
elimi•na•tor
eli•sion

elite (*or* **élite**)
elit•ism
elit•ist
elix•ir
elk
elk•hound
el•lipse flattened
  circle
el•lip•sis (*pl* **•ses**)
  missing words
el•lip•soid
el•lip•soi•dal
el•lip•tic
el•lip•ti•cal
el•lip•ti•cal•ly
elm
elo•cu•tion
elo•cu•tion•ary
elo•cu•tion•ist
elon•gate
elon•ga•tion
elope
elope•ment
elop•er
elo•quence
elo•quent
elo•quent•ly
else•where
elu•ci•date
elu•ci•da•tion
elu•ci•da•tive
elu•ci•da•tor
elude escape from;
  cf **allude**; **illude**
elud•er
elu•sion
elu•sive evasive; *cf*
  allusive; **illusive**
elu•sive•ness

elu•vial
elu•vium (*pl* **•via**)
  rock particles; *cf*
  alluvium
el•ver
elves *pl of* **elf**
elv•ish *variant*
  spelling of **elfish**
Ely•sian
ema•ci•ate
ema•ci•at•ed
ema•cia•tion
E-mail (*or* **e-**)
ema•nate
ema•na•tion
ema•na•tor
ema•na•tory
eman•ci•pate
eman•ci•pa•tion
eman•ci•pa•tive
eman•ci•pa•tor
emas•cu•late
emas•cu•la•tion
emas•cu•la•tive (*or*
  •tory)
emas•cu•la•tor
em•balm
em•balm•er
em•balm•ment
em•bank
em•bank•ment
***embarass**
  incorrect spelling
  of **embarrass**
em•bar•go (*n, pl*
  •goes; *vb* **•goes**,
  •go•ing, **•goed**)
em•bark
em•bar•ka•tion

em•bar•rass (*NOT*
  embarass)
em•bar•rass•ing
em•bar•rass•ment
em•bas•sy (*pl* **•sies**)
em•bat•tle
em•bed (**•bed•ding**,
  •bed•ded)
em•bel•lish
em•bel•lish•er
em•bel•lish•ment
em•ber
em•bez•zle
em•bez•zle•ment
em•bez•zler
em•bit•ter
em•bit•ter•ment
em•bla•zon
em•blem
em•blem•at•ic (*or*
  •ati•cal)
em•blema•tize (*or*
  •blem•ize)
em•bodi•ment
em•body (**•bod•ies**,
  •body•ing,
  •bod•ied)
em•bold•en
em•bol•ic
em•bo•lism
em•bo•lus (*pl* **•li**)
em•boss
em•boss•ment
em•brace
em•brace•able
em•brac•er
em•bra•sure
em•bro•ca•tion
em•broi•der

em•broi•der•er
em•broi•dery (*pl* •deries)
em•broil
em•broil•ment
em•bryo (*pl* •bryos)
em•bryo•logi•cal (*or* •log•ic)
em•bry•olo•gist
em•bry•ol•ogy
em•bry•on•ic (*or* •bryo•nal)
emend improve text; *cf* amend
emend•able
emen•da•tion
emen•da•tor
em•er•ald
emerge
emer•gence
emer•gen•cy (*pl* •cies)
emer•gent
emeri•tus (*pl* •ti)
emer•sion emerging; *cf* immersion
em•ery (*pl* •eries)
emet•ic
emi•grant
emi•grate leave country; *cf* immigrate
emi•gra•tion
émi•gré (*or* emi•)
emi•nence (*or* •nen•cy; *pl* •nences *or* •cies)

émi•nence grise (*pl* emi•nences grises)
emi•nent distinguished; *cf* immanent; imminent
emir (*or* amir)
emir•ate (*or* amir•)
em•is•sary (*pl* •saries)
emis•sion
emis•sive
emit (emit•ting, emit•ted)
emit•ter
emol•lience
emol•lient soothing
emolu•ment salary
emote
emo•tion
emo•tion•al
emo•tion•al•ism
emo•tion•ali•za•tion
emo•tion•al•ize
emo•tion•al•ly
emo•tive
emo•tive•ness (*or* •tiv•ity)
em•pan•el *variant spelling of* impanel
em•path•ic (*or* •pa•thet•ic)
em•pathi•cal•ly (*or* •pa•theti•cal•ly)
em•pa•thize
em•pa•thy
em•per•or
em•per•or•ship

em•pha•sis (*pl* •ses)
em•pha•size
em•phat•ic
em•phati•cal•ly
em•phy•sema
em•phy•sema•tous
em•pire
empire-build•ing (*adj*)
em•pir•ic
em•piri•cal
em•piri•cal•ly
em•piri•cism
em•piri•cist
em•place
em•place•ment
em•ploy
em•ploy•abil•ity
em•ploy•able
em•ployee (*or* •ploye)
em•ploy•er
em•ploy•ment
em•po•rium (*pl* •riums *or* •ria)
em•pow•er
em•pow•er•ment
em•press
emp•ti•ly
emp•ti•ness
emp•ty (*adj* •ti•er, •ti•est; *vb* •ties, •ty•ing, •tied)
empty-handed
empty-headed
em•py•rean
emu
emu•late
emu•la•tion

emu•la•tive
emu•la•tor
emul•si•fi•able
emul•si•fi•ca•tion
emul•si•fi•er
emul•si•fy (•fies,
  •fy•ing, •fied)
emul•sion
emul•sive
en•able
en•able•ment
en•abler
en•act
en•ac•tion
en•ac•tive
en•act•ment
en•ac•tor
en•ac•tory
enam•el (•el•ing,
  •eled; *Brit* •el•ling,
  •elled)
enam•el•er (*Brit*
  •el•ler)
enam•el•ist (*Brit*
  •el•list)
enamel•work
en•am•or (*Brit*
  •our)
en•am•ored (*Brit*
  •oured)
en•cage
en•camp
en•camp•ment
en•cap•su•late
en•cap•su•la•tion
en•case (*or* in•)
en•case•ment (*or*
  in•)
en•cash

en•cash•ment
en•cepha•li•tis
en•cepha•lo•gram
en•cepha•lo•graph
en•cepha•log•
  ra•phy
en•cepha•lo•my•
  eli•tis
en•chant
en•chant•er
en•chant•ing
en•chant•ing•ly
en•chant•ment
en•chant•ress
en•chi•la•da
en•ci•pher
en•cir•cle
en•cir•cle•ment
en•clave
en•close (*or* in•)
en•clo•sure (*or* in•)
en•code
en•code•ment
en•cod•er
en•co•mi•um
  (*pl* •miums *or*
  •mia)
en•com•pass
en•com•pass•ment
en•core
en•coun•ter
en•coun•ter•er
en•cour•age
en•cour•age•ment
en•cour•ag•er
en•cour•ag•ing•ly
en•croach
en•croach•er
en•croach•ment

en•crust (*or* in•)
en•crus•ta•tion (*or*
  in•)
en•crypt
en•cryp•tion
en•cum•ber
en•cum•brance
en•cyc•li•cal
en•cy•clo•pe•dia
  (*or* •pae•dia)
en•cy•clo•pe•dic (*or*
  •pae•dic)
en•cy•clo•pedi•
  cal•ly (*or* •pae•di•)
en•cy•clo•pe•dism
  (*or* •pae•dism)
en•cy•clo•pe•dist
  (*or* •pae•dist)
end
en•dan•ger
en•dear
en•dear•ing
en•dear•ing•ly
en•dear•ment
en•deav•or (*Brit*
  •our)
en•dem•ic
en•demi•cal•ly
end•game
end•ing
en•dive
end•less
end•less•ly
end•less•ness
end•most
endo•car•di•tis
endo•crine
endo•cri•nolo•gist
endo•cri•nol•ogy

en•do•derm
en•do•der•mal
en•do•don•tics
en•do•don•tist
en•dog•enous
en•do•me•trial
en•do•me•trio•sis
en•do•me•tri•um (*pl*
•tria)
en•do•morph
en•do•mor•phic
en•dor•phin
en•dors•able (*or*
in•)
en•dorse (*or* in•)
en•dor•see (*or* in•)
en•dorse•ment (*or*
in•)
en•dors•er (*or*
•dor•sor, in•)
endo•scope
en•dos•co•py
endo•skel•eton
endo•ther•mic (*or*
•mal)
en•dow
en•dow•er
en•dow•ment
end•plate
en•due (*or* in•;
•dues, •du•ing,
•dued)
en•dur•abil•ity (*or*
•dur•able•ness)
en•dur•able
en•dur•ance
en•dure
en•dur•ing
en•dur•ing•ly

end•wise (*or* •ways)
en•ema (*pl* •emas
or •emata)
en•emy (*pl* •emies)
en•er•get•ic
en•er•geti•cal•ly
en•er•get•ics
en•er•gize
en•er•giz•er
en•er•gy (*pl* •gies)
en•er•vate weaken;
cf innervate;
innovate
en•er•va•tion
en•er•va•tive
en fa•mille
en•fant ter•ri•ble
(*pl* en•fants
ter•ri•bles)
en•fee•ble
en•fee•ble•ment
en•fold
en•fold•er
en•fold•ment
en•force (*NOT*
inforce)
en•force•abil•ity
en•force•able
en•force•ment
en•forc•er
en•fran•chise
en•fran•chise•ment
en•fran•chis•er
en•gage
en•gaged
en•gage•ment
en•gag•er
en•gag•ing
en•gag•ing•ly

en•gen•der
en•gine
en•gi•neer
en•gi•neer•ing
Eng•lish
English•man (*pl*
•men)
English•woman (*pl*
•women)
en•gorge
en•gorge•ment
en•graft
en•grave
en•grav•er
en•grav•ing
en•gross
en•gross•ing•ly
en•gross•ment
en•gulf
en•gulf•ment
en•hance
en•hance•ment
en•hanc•er
enig•ma
enig•mat•ic (*or*
•mati•cal)
enig•mati•cal•ly
en•join
en•join•er
en•join•ment
en•joy
en•joy•able
en•joy•ably
en•joy•er
en•joy•ment
en•kin•dle
en•large
en•large•able
en•large•ment

en•larg•er
en•light•en
en•light•en•ment
en•list
en•list•er
en•list•ment
en•liv•en
en•liv•en•er
en•liv•en•ment
en masse
en•mesh
en•mity (*pl* •mities)
en•no•ble
en•no•ble•ment
en•no•bler
en•nui
enor•mity (*pl* •mities)
enor•mous
enor•mous•ly
enough
en pas•sant
en•plane
en•quire *variant*
  Brit spelling of
  inquire
en•quiry *variant*
  Brit spelling of
  inquiry
en•rage
en•rage•ment
en rap•port
en•rap•ture
en•rich
en•rich•er
en•rich•ment
en•robe
en•roll (*Brit* •rol;
  •rol•ling, •rolled)

en•rol•lee
en•rol•ler
en•roll•ment (*Brit*
  •rol•)
en route
en•sconce
en•sem•ble
en•shrine (*or* in•)
en•shrine•ment
en•shroud
en•sign
en•slave
en•slave•ment
en•slav•er
en•snare (*or* in•)
en•snare•ment
en•snar•er
en•sue (•su•ing,
  •sued)
en suite
en•sure make sure;
  cf insure
en•sur•er
en•tail
en•tail•ment
en•tan•gle
en•tan•gle•ment
entente cor•diale
en•ter
en•ter•able
en•ter•ic (*or* •al)
en•ter•i•tis
en•ter•prise
en•ter•pris•ing
en•ter•tain
en•ter•tain•er
en•ter•tain•ing
en•ter•tain•ing•ly
en•ter•tain•ment

en•thrall (*Brit*
  •thral; •thral•ling,
  •thralled)
en•thral•ling•ly
en•thrall•ment
  (*Brit* •thral•)
en•throne
en•throne•ment
en•thuse
en•thu•si•asm
en•thu•si•ast
en•thu•si•as•tic
en•thu•si•as•ti•
  cal•ly
en•tice
en•tice•ment
en•tic•er
en•tic•ing•ly
en•tire
en•tire•ly
en•tire•ness
en•tire•ty (*pl*
  •tireties)
en•ti•tle
en•ti•tle•ment
en•tity (*pl* •tities)
en•tomb
en•tomb•ment
ento•mo•logi•cal
  (*or* •log•ic)
ento•molo•gist
ento•mo•lo•gize (*or*
  •gise)
ento•mol•ogy study
  of insects; *cf*
  etymology
en•tou•rage
en•tr'acte
en•trails

en•train
en•tram•mel
(•mel•ing, •meled)
Brit •mel•ling,
•melled)
en•trance
en•trance•ment
en•tranc•ing•ly
en•trant
en•trap (•trap•ping,
•trapped)
en•trap•ment
en•trap•per
en•treat
en•treat•ing•ly
en•treaty (*pl*
•treaties)
en•tre•côte
en•trée
en•trench
en•trench•ment
en•tre nous
en•tre•pôt
en•tre•pre•neur
en•tre•pre•neur•ial
en•tre•pre•neur•ial•
ism (*or* •neur•ism)
en•tro•py (*pl* •pies)
en•trust
en•trust•ment
en•try (*pl* •tries)
en•twine
en•twine•ment
enu•mer•able
countable; *cf*
innumerable
enu•mer•ate
enu•mera•tion
enu•mera•tive

enu•mera•tor
enun•ci•ate
articulate; *cf*
annunciate
enun•cia•tion
enun•cia•tive (*or*
•tory)
enun•cia•tor
en•ure *variant
spelling of* inure
enu•resis
en'•vel•op (*vb*)
'en•velope (*n*)
en•vel•op•ment
en•vi•able
en•vi•able•ness
en•vi•ably
en•vi•er
en•vi•ous
en•vi•ous•ly
en•vi•ron•ment
en•vi•ron•men•tal
en•vi•ron•men•
tal•ism
en•vi•ron•men•
tal•ist
en•vi•ron•men•
tal•ly
en•vi•rons
en•vis•age
en•vis•age•ment
en•vi•sion
en•voy
en•vy (*n, pl* •vies;
vb •vies, •vy•ing,
•vied)
en•wrap (*or* in•;
•wrap•ping,
•wrapped)

en•zy•mat•ic (*or*
•zy•mic)
en•zyme
eohip•pus
Eolith•ic
eon (*Brit* aeon)
ep•au•let (*Brit*
•lette)
épée
ephem•era (*pl* •eras
or •erae) mayfly;
cf ephemeron
ephem•er•al
ephem•er•al•ity (*or*
•al•ness)
ephem•er•is (*pl*
•erides)
ephem•er•on (*pl*
•era *or* •er•ons)
transitory thing;
cf ephemera
epic
epi•cene
epi•cen•ter (*Brit*
•tre)
epi•cen•tral
epi•cure
epi•cu•rean
epi•cur•ism (*or*
•cu•re•an•ism)
epi•cy•cle
epi•cy•clic
epi•dem•ic
epi•de•mio•logi•cal
epi•de•mi•olo•gist
epi•de•mi•ol•ogy
epi•der•mal (*or*
•mic, •mous)
epi•der•mis

epi•dur•al
epi•glot•tis (*pl*
  •tises *or* •ti•des)
epi•gram saying; *cf*
  epigraph
epi•gram•mat•ic
epi•gram•mati•
  cal•ly
epi•gram•ma•tism
epi•gram•ma•tist
epi•graph
  inscription; *cf*
  epigram
epi•graph•ic (*or*
  •graphi•cal)
epig•ra•phist
epig•ra•phy
epi•lep•sy
epi•lep•tic
epi•lep•ti•form
epi•logue (*or* •log)
epi•neph•rine
Epipha•ny
  Christian festival
epipha•ny (*pl* •nies)
  manifestation
epi•phyte
epi•phyt•ic
epis•co•pa•cy (*pl*
  •cies)
epis•co•pal
epis•co•pa•lian
epis•co•pa•lian•ism
epis•co•pate
epi•sode
epi•sod•ic (*or*
  •sodi•cal)
epi•sodi•cal•ly
epis•te•mo•logi•cal

epis•te•molo•gist
epis•te•mol•ogy
epis•tle
epis•tler (*or* •to•ler,
  •to•list)
epis•to•lary (*or*
  epi•stol•ic,
  epis•to•la•tory)
epi•taph
epi•the•lial
epi•the•lium (*pl*
  •liums *or* •lia)
epi•thet
epi•thet•ic (*or* •ical)
epito•me
epi•tom•ic (*or* •ical)
epito•mi•za•tion
epito•mize
ep•och
ep•och•al
epoch-mak•ing
  (*adj*)
epo•nym
epony•mous (*or*
  epo•nym•ic)
epony•my
cpoxy
ep•si•lon
eq•uabil•ity (*or*
  •uable•ness)
eq•uable
eq•uably
equal (equal•ing,
  equaled; *Brit*
  equal•ling,
  equalled)
equali•ty (*pl* •ties)
equali•za•tion
equal•ize

equal•iz•er
equal•ly
equa•nim•ity
equani•mous
equat•abil•ity
equat•able
equate
equa•tion
equa•tor
equa•to•rial
eq•uer•ry (*pl* •ries)
eques•trian
eques•tri•an•ism
equi•dis•tance
equi•dis•tant
equi•lat•er•al
equi•li•brate
equi•li•bra•tion
equi•li•bra•tor
equili•brist
equi•lib•rium (*pl*
  •riums *or* •ria)
equine
equi•noc•tial
equi•nox
equip (equip•ping,
  equipped)
equi•page
equip•ment
equi•poise
equi•table
equi•tably
equi•ty (*pl* •ties)
equiva•lence (*or*
  •len•cy)
equiva•lent
equivo•cal
equivo•cal•ity (*or*
  •ca•cy)

equivo•cal•ly
equivo•cate
equivo•ca•tion
equivo•ca•tor
equivo•ca•tory
era
eradi•cable
eradi•cate
eradi•ca•tion
eradi•ca•tor
eras•able
erase
eras•er
era•sion
eras•ure
ere before; *cf* air;
  e'er; heir
erect
erect•able
erec•tile
erec•til•ity
erec•tion
erect•ness
erec•tor
erg
er•go
er•go•nom•ic
er•go•nom•ics
er•gono•mist
er•got
er•got•ism
eri•ca
er•mine (*pl* •mines
  or •mine)
erode
erod•ible
erog•enous
ero•sion
ero•sive

ero•sive•ness
erot•ic (*or*
  eroti•cal)
eroti•ca
eroti•cal•ly
eroti•cism
ero•to•ma•nia
ero•to•ma•ni•ac
err
er•ran•cy (*pl* •cies)
er•rand
er•rant
er•rant•ry (*pl*
  •tries)
er•ra•ta *pl of*
  erratum
er•rat•ic
er•rati•cal•ly
er•ra•tum (*pl* •ta)
er•ro•neous
er•ro•neous•ly
er•ro•neous•ness
er•ror
error-free
er•satz
erst•while
eruct
eruc•ta•tion
eru•dite
eru•di•tion
erupt break out; *cf*
  irrupt
erupt•ible
erup•tion
erup•tive
ery•sip•elas
eryth•ro•cyte
es•ca•drille aircraft

squadron; *cf*
  espadrille
es•ca•late
es•ca•la•tion
es•ca•la•tor
es•cal•lo•nia
es•cal•lope scallop
es•ca•lope veal
  slice
es•cap•able
es•ca•pade
es•cape
es•capee
es•cape•ment
es•cap•er
es•cap•ism
es•cap•ist
es•ca•polo•gist
es•ca•pol•ogy
es•carp•ment
es•cort
Es•ki•mo (*pl* •mos
  or •mo)
esopha•geal (*Brit*
  oesopha•)
esopha•gus (*Brit*
  oesopha•)
eso•ter•ic
eso•teri•cal•ly
eso•teri•cism
es•pa•drille canvas
  shoe; *cf* escadrille
es•pal•ier
es•pe•cial
es•pe•cial•ly
Es•pe•ran•to
es•pio•nage
es•pla•nade
es•pous•al

es•pouse
es•pous•er
es•pres•so (*pl* •sos;
 NOT expresso)
es•prit
es•prit de corps
espy (espies,
 espy•ing, espied)
es•quire
es•say
 composition;
 attempt; *cf* assay
es•say•ist
es•sence
es•sen•tial
es•sen•tial•ity (*or*
 •ness)
es•sen•tial•ly
es•tab•lish
es•tab•lish•ment
es•tab•lish•men•
 tar•ian
es•tab•lish•men•
 tar•ian•ism
es•tan•cia
es•tate
es•teem
es•ter
es•thete *variant*
 spelling of
 aesthete
es•thetic *variant*
 spelling of
 aesthetic
es•ti•mable
es•ti•mate
es•ti•ma•tion
es•ti•ma•tive
es•ti•ma•tor

es•ti•vate (*or* aes•)
es•ti•va•tion (*or*
 aes•)
Es•to•nian
es•trange
es•tranged
es•trange•ment
es•tro•gen (*Brit*
 oes•)
es•tro•gen•ic (*Brit*
 oes•)
es•trous (*Brit* oes•;
 adj)
es•trus (*Brit* oes•;
 n)
es•tua•rine
es•tu•ary (*pl* •aries)
eta
et cet•era
etch
etch•er
etch•ing
eter•nal
eter•nal•ity (*or*
 •ness)
eter•nali•za•tion
 (*or* eter•ni•)
eter•nal•ize (*or*
 eter•nize)
eter•nal•ly
eter•nity (*pl* •nities)
ethane
etha•nol
eth•ene *variant of*
 ethylene
ether anesthetic
ether (*or* aether)
 hypothetical
 medium

ethe•real
ethe•real•ity (*or*
 •ness)
ethe•reali•za•tion
ethe•real•ize
ethe•real•ly
ether•ic
etheri•fi•ca•tion
etheri•fy (•fies,
 •fy•ing, •fied)
eth•ic
ethi•cal
ethi•cal•ly
ethi•cal•ness (*or*
 •cali•ty)
ethi•cist
ethi•cize
eth•ics
Ethio•pian
eth•nic (*or* •ni•cal)
eth•ni•cal•ly
eth•nic•ity
eth•no•cen•tric
eth•no•cen•trism
eth•no•graph•ic (*or*
 •graphi•cal)
eth•nog•ra•phy
eth•no•log•ic (*or*
 •logi•cal)
eth•nolo•gist
eth•nol•ogy study
 of races; *cf*
 ethology
etho•log•ic (*or*
 •logi•cal)
etholo•gist
ethol•ogy study of
 animal behavior;
 cf ethnology

ethos
ethyl
eth•yl•ene (*or* eth•ene)
etio•late
etio•la•tion
etio•log•ic (*or* •logi•cal; *Brit* aetio•)
eti•olo•gist (*Brit* aeti•)
eti•ol•ogy (*Brit* aeti•)
eti•quette
ety•mo•logi•cal (*or* •log•ic)
ety•molo•gist
ety•mol•ogy (*pl* •ogies) study of words; *cf* entomology
euca•lyp•tus (*or* euca•lypt; *pl* •tuses, •ti, *or* •lypts)
Eucha•rist
euchre
Euclid•ean (*or* •ian)
eugen•ic (*or* eugeni•cal)
eugeni•cal•ly
eugeni•cist (*or* eugen•ist)
eugen•ics
eulo•gist (*or* •giz•er)
eulo•gis•tic (*or* •ti•cal)
eulo•gize

eulogy (*pl* eulogies)
eunuch
euphe•mism
euphe•mist
euphe•mis•tic (*or* •ti•cal)
euphe•mis•ti•cal•ly
euphe•mize
euphon•ic (*or* euphoni•cal)
euphoni•cal•ly
eupho•nious
eupho•nious•ly
eupho•nium
eupho•nize
eupho•ny (*pl* •nies)
euphor•bia
eupho•ria
euphor•ic
euphori•cal•ly
Eura•sian
eurhyth•mic (*or* euryth•)
eurhyth•mics (*or* euryth•)
Euro•cur•ren•cy (*pl* •cies)
Euro•dol•lar
Euro•mar•ket (*or* •mart)
Euro•pean
Eusta•chian tube
eutha•na•sia
euthen•ics
euthen•ist
evacu•ate
evacu•ation
evacu•ative
evacu•ator

evac•uee
evad•able (*or* •ible)
evade
evad•er
evad•ing•ly
evagi•nate
evagi•na•tion
evalu•ate
evalu•ation
evalu•ative
evalu•ator
eva•nesce
eva•nes•cence
eva•nes•cent
evan•geli•cal
evan•geli•cal•ism
evan•geli•cal•ly
evan•ge•lism
evan•ge•list
evan•ge•lis•tic
evan•ge•lis•ti•cal•ly
evan•ge•li•za•tion
evan•ge•lize
evan•ge•liz•er
evapo•rable
evapo•rate
evapo•ra•tion
evapo•ra•tive
evapo•ra•tor
eva•sion
eva•sive
eva•sive•ly
eva•sive•ness
eve
even
even•hand•ed
even•hand•ed•ness
eve•ning
even•ly

even•ness
even•song
event
even-tem•pered
event•ful
event•ful•ly
event•ful•ness
even•tide
even•tual
even•tu•al•ity (*pl* •ities)
even•tu•al•ly
even•tu•ate
even•tua•tion
ev•er
ever•green
ever•last•ing
ever•more
ever•sion
evert
every
every•body
every•day
every•one
every•thing
every•where
evict
evic•tion
evic•tor
evi•dence
evi•dent
evi•den•tial
evi•den•tial•ly
evi•dent•ly
evil
evil•doer
evil•do•ing
evil-eyed
evil•ly

evil-mind•ed
evil-mind•ed•ness
evil•ness
evince
evin•cible
evin•cive
evis•cer•ate
evis•cera•tion
evo•cable
evo•ca•tion
evoca•tive
evoca•tive•ness
evoke
evok•er
evo•lu•tion
evo•lu•tion•ary (*or* •al)
evo•lu•tion•ism
evo•lu•tion•ist
evolve
evolve•ment
evolv•er
ewe female sheep; *cf* yew; you
ew•er
ex•ac•er•bate
ex•ac•er•ba•tion
ex•act
ex•act•ing
ex•ac•tion
ex•acti•tude
ex•act•ly
ex•act•ness
ex•ac•tor (*or* •act•er)
ex•ag•ger•ate
ex•ag•ger•at•ed
ex•ag•ger•at•ed•ly
ex•ag•gera•tion

ex•ag•gera•tive (*or* •tory)
ex•ag•gera•tor
ex•alt
ex•al•ta•tion
ex•alt•ed
ex•alt•ed•ly
ex•alt•ed•ness
ex•alt•er
exam
ex•am•in•able
ex•ami•na•tion
ex•am•ine
ex•ami•nee
ex•am•in•er
ex•am•ple
ex•as•per•ate
ex•as•per•at•ing•ly
ex•as•pera•tion
ex•ca•vate
ex•ca•va•tion
ex•ca•va•tor
ex•ceed
ex•ceed•able
ex•ceed•ing•ly
ex•cel (•cel•ling, •celled)
ex•cel•lence
Ex•cel•len•cy (*or* •lence; *pl* •cies *or* •lences)
ex•cel•lent
ex•cel•si•or
ex•cept
ex•cept•ing
ex•cep•tion
ex•cep•tion•able objectionable

ex•cep•tion•al very good

ex•cep•tion•al•ity

excep•tion•al•ly

ex•cerpt book extract; *cf* exert; exsert

ex•cess

ex•ces•sive

ex•ces•sive•ly

ex•ces•sive•ness

ex•change

ex•change•abil•ity

ex•change•able

ex•chang•er

ex•che•quer

ex•cis•able

‡ex•cise tax

ex•‡ise to cut

ex•ci•sion

ex•cit•abil•ity (*or* •able•ness)

ex•cit•able

ex•cit•ably

ex•cit•ant (*or* •ci•ta•tive, •ci•ta•tory)

ex•ci•ta•tion

ex•cite

ex•cit•ed•ly

ex•cit•ed•ness

ex•cite•ment

ex•cit•ing

ex•cit•ing•ly

ex•claim

ex•cla•ma•tion

ex•clama•tory

ex•clave

ex•clud•able (*or* •ible)

ex•clude

ex•clud•er

ex•clu•sion

ex•clu•sion•ary

ex•clu•sion•ist

ex•clu•sive

ex•clu•sive•ly

ex•clu•sive•ness (*or* •sivi•ty)

ex•com•mu•ni•cable

ex•com•mu•ni•cate

ex•com•mu•ni•ca•tion

ex•com•mu•ni•ca•tive (*or* •tory)

ex•com•mu•ni•ca•tor

ex•co•ri•ate

ex•co•ria•tion

ex•cre•ment

ex•cre•men•tal (*or* •ti•tious)

ex•cres•cence

ex•cres•cent

ex•cre•ta

ex•cre•tal

ex•crete

ex•cret•er

ex•cre•tion

ex•cre•tory

ex•cru•ci•at•ing

ex•cru•ci•at•ing•ly

ex•cul•pate

ex•cul•pa•tion

ex•cul•pa•tory

ex•cur•sion

ex•cur•sion•ist

ex•cur•sive

ex•cur•sive•ness

ex•cus•able

ex•cus•ably

ex•cuse

ex•ecrable

ex•ecrable•ness

ex•ecrate

ex•ecra•tion

ex•ecra•tive (*or* •tory)

ex•ecut•able

ex•ecu•tant

ex•ecute

‡ex•ecut•er one who executes something; *cf* executor

ex•ecu•tion

ex•ecu•tion•er

ex•ecu•tive

ex•‡ecu•tor trustee of will; *cf* executer

ex•ecu•to•rial

ex•ecu•trix (*pl* •tri•ces *or* •trixes)

ex•egesis (*pl* •egeses)

ex•em•plar

ex•em•pla•ri•ly

ex•em•pla•ri•ness

ex•em•pla•ry

ex•em•pli•fi•ca•tion

ex•em•pli•fi•er

ex•em•pli•fy (•fies, •fy•ing, •fied)

ex•empt

ex•empt•ible
ex•emp•tion
ex•er•cis•able
ex•er•cise train;
  use; *cf* exorcise
ex•er•cis•er
ex•ert make effort;
  cf excerpt; exsert
ex•er•tion
ex•er•tive
ex•fo•li•ate
ex•fo•lia•tion
ex gra•tia
ex•hal•ant
ex•ha•la•tion
ex•hale
ex•haust
ex•haust•ibil•ity
ex•haust•ible
ex•haus•tion
ex•haus•tive
ex•haus•tive•ly
ex•haus•tive•ness
ex•hib•it
ex•hi•bi•tion
ex•hi•bi•tion•ism
ex•hi•bi•tion•ist
ex•hibi•tive
ex•hibi•tor (*or*
  •hib•it•er)
ex•hibi•tory
ex•hila•rate
ex•hil•arat•ing•ly
ex•hila•ra•tion
ex•hila•ra•tive (*or*
  •tory)
ex•hila•ra•tor
ex•hort
ex•hor•ta•tion

ex•hor•ta•tive (*or*
  •tory)
ex•hort•er
ex•hu•ma•tion
ex•hume
exi•gen•cy (*or*
  exi•gence; *pl* •cies
  or •gences)
exi•gent urgent; *cf*
  exiguous
exi•gu•ity (*or*
  ex•igu•ous•ness)
ex•igu•ous meager;
  cf exigent
ex•ile
ex•ist
ex•is•tence
ex•is•tent
ex•is•ten•tial
ex•is•ten•tial•ism
ex•is•ten•tial•ist
ex•is•ten•tial•ly
exit
ex li•bris
exo•dus
ex of•fi•cio
ex•og•enous
ex•on•er•ate
ex•on•era•tion
ex•on•era•tor
ex•or•bi•tance
ex•or•bi•tant
ex•or•cise (*or* •cize)
  expel evil spirit; *cf*
  exercise
ex•or•cis•er (*or*
  •ciz•er)
ex•or•cism
ex•or•cist

exo•skel•eton
exo•ther•mic (*or*
  •mal)
ex•ot•ic
ex•oti•ca
ex•oti•cal•ly
ex•oti•cism
ex•pand
ex•pand•able
ex•pand•er
ex•panse
ex•pan•sibil•ity
ex•pan•sible
ex•pan•sion
ex•pan•sion•ary
ex•pan•sion•ism
ex•pan•sion•ist
ex•pan•sion•is•tic
ex•pan•sive
ex•pan•sive•ly
ex•pan•sive•ness
ex•pa•ti•ate
  enlarge upon; *cf*
  expiate
ex•pa•tia•tion
ex•pa•tia•tor
ex•pat•ri•ate
ex•pat•ria•tion
ex•pect
ex•pect•able
ex•pec•tan•cy (*or*
  •tance; *pl* •cies *or*
  •tances)
ex•pec•tant
ex•pec•tant•ly
ex•pec•ta•tion
ex•pec•to•rant
ex•pec•to•rate
ex•pec•to•ra•tion

ex•pe•di•en•cy (*or*
•di•ence; *pl* •cies
or •ences)
ex•pe•di•ent
ex•pe•dite
ex•pe•dit•er (*or*
•di•tor)
ex•pe•di•tion
ex•pe•di•tion•ary
ex•pe•di•tious
ex•pe•di•tious•ness
ex•pel (•pel•ling,
•pelled)
ex•pel•lable
ex•pel•lant (*or*
•lent)
ex•pel•lee
ex•pel•ler
ex•pend
ex•pend•abil•ity
ex•pend•able
ex•pend•er
ex•pendi•ture
ex•pense
ex•pen•sive
ex•pen•sive•ly
ex•pen•sive•ness
ex•pe•ri•ence
ex•pe•ri•en•tial
ex•peri•ment
ex•peri•men•tal
ex•peri•men•tal•
ism
ex•peri•men•tal•ist
ex•peri•men•tal•ly
ex•peri•men•ta•
tion
ex•peri•ment•er
ex•pert

ex•per•tise
ex•pert•ness
ex•pi•able
ex•pi•ate atone; *cf*
expatiate
ex•pia•tion
ex•pia•tor
ex•pia•tory
ex•pi•ra•tion
ex•pira•tory
ex•pire
ex•pi•ry (*pl* •ries)
ex•plain
ex•plain•able
ex•plain•er
ex•pla•na•tion
ex•plana•tory (*or*
•tive)
ex•ple•tive
ex•pli•cable
ex•pli•cate
ex•pli•ca•tion
ex•pli•ca•tive (*or*
•tory)
ex•pli•ca•tor
ex•plic•it
ex•plic•it•ly
ex•plic•it•ness
ex•plode
ex•ploit
ex•ploit•able (*or*
•ploita•tive)
ex•ploi•ta•tion
ex•plo•ra•tion
ex•plora•tory (*or*
•tive)
ex•plore
ex•plor•er
ex•plo•sion

ex•plo•sive
ex•plo•sive•ly
ex•plo•sive•ness
ex•po•nent
ex•po•nen•tial
ex•po•nen•tial•ly
ex•port
ex•port•able
ex•por•ta•tion
ex•port•er
ex•pos•able
ex•pos•al
ex•pose
ex•po•sé
ex•posed
ex•pos•er
ex•po•si•tion
ex•po•si•tion•al
ex•posi•tor
ex•posi•tory (*or*
•tive)
ex•pos•tu•late
ex•pos•tu•la•tion
ex•pos•tu•la•tor
ex•pos•tu•la•tory
(*or* •tive)
ex•po•sure
ex•pound
ex•pound•er
ex•press
ex•press•er
ex•press•ible
ex•pres•sion
ex•pres•sion•ism
ex•pres•sion•ist
ex•pres•sion•is•tic
ex•pres•sion•less
ex•pres•sive
ex•pres•sive•ly

ex•pres•sive•ness
ex•pres•siv•ity
ex•press•ly
*expresso *incorrect spelling of* espresso
ex•press•way
ex•pro•pri•able
ex•pro•pri•ate
ex•pro•pria•tion
ex•pro•pria•tor
ex•pul•sion
ex•pul•sive
ex•punc•tion
ex•punge
ex•pur•gate
ex•pur•ga•tion
ex•pur•ga•tor
ex•pur•ga•to•ry (*or* •to•rial)
ex•quis•ite
ex•quis•ite•ly
ex•quis•ite•ness
ex•san•gui•nate
ex•san•gui•nation
ex•sert *protrude; cf* excerpt; exert
ex•ser•tion
*extasy *incorrect spelling of* ecstasy
ex•tant *surviving; cf* extent
ex•tem•po•ra•neous (*or* •po•rary)
ex•tem•po•rari•ly
ex•tem•po•re
ex•tem•po•ri•za•tion

ex•tem•po•rize
ex•tem•po•riz•er
ex•tend
ex•tend•er
ex•tend•ibil•ity (*or* •abil•ity)
ex•tend•ible (*or* •able)
ex•ten•sibil•ity (*or* •sible•ness)
ex•ten•sible (*or* •sile)
ex•ten•sion
ex•ten•sive
ex•ten•sive•ly
ex•ten•sive•ness
ex•tent *range; scope cf* extant
ex•tenu•ate
ex•tenu•ation
ex•tenu•ator
ex•tenu•atory
ex•te•ri•or
ex•ter•mi•nable
ex•ter•mi•nate
ex•ter•mi•na•tion
ex•ter•mi•na•tor
ex•tern (*or* •terne)
ex•ter•nal
ex•ter•nal•ism
ex•ter•nal•ist
ex•ter•nal•ity (*pl* •ities)
ex•ter•nali•za•tion
ex•ter•nal•ize
ex•ter•nal•ly
ex•tinct
ex•tinc•tion
ex•tinc•tive

ex•tin•guish
ex•tin•guish•able
ex•tin•guish•ant
ex•tin•guish•er
ex•tin•guish•ment
ex•tir•pate
ex•tir•pa•tion
ex•tir•pa•tor
ex•toll (*Brit* •tol; •tol•ling, •tolled)
ex•tol•ler
ex•tol•ment
ex•tort
ex•tort•er
ex•tor•tion
cx•tor•tion•ary
ex•tor•tion•ate
ex•tor•tion•ist (*or* •er)
ex•tra
ex•tract
ex•tract•abil•ity (*or* •ibil•ity)
ex•tract•able (*or* •ible)
ex•trac•tion
ex•trac•tive
ex•trac•tor
extra•cur•ricu•lar
extra•dit•able
extra•dite
extra•di•tion
extra•ju•di•cial
extra•mari•tal
extra•mu•ral
ex•tra•neous
ex•tra•neous•ness
extraor•di•nari•ly

extraor•di•nari•
ness
extraor•di•nary
(*NOT*
extrordinary)
ex•trapo•late
ex•trapo•la•tion
ex•trapo•la•tive (*or*
•tory)
ex•trapo•la•tor
extra•sen•sory
extra•ter•res•trial
extra•ter•ri•to•rial
extra•ter•ri•to•ri•
al•ity
ex•trava•gance
ex•trava•gant
ex•trava•gant•ly
ex•trava•gan•za
extra•ve•hicu•lar
ex•tra•vert *variant
spelling of*
extrovert
ex•treme
ex•treme•ly
ex•treme•ness
ex•trem•ism
ex•trem•ist
ex•trem•ity (*pl*
•ities)
ex•tri•cable
ex•tri•cate
ex•tri•ca•tion
ex•trin•sic
ex•trin•si•cal•ly
*extrordinary
*incorrect spelling
of* extraordinary

ex•tro•ver•sion (*or*
•tra•)
ex•tro•ver•sive (*or*
•tra•)
ex•tro•vert (*or*
•tra•)
ex•tro•vert•ed (*or*
•tra•)
ex•trude
ex•tru•sion
ex•tru•sive
exu•ber•ance (*or*
•ancy)
exu•ber•ant
exu•date
exu•da•tion
exu•da•tive
ex•ude
ex•ult
ex•ult•ant
ex•ul•ta•tion
ex•ult•ing•ly
ex•ur•bia
eye (eye•ing *or*
ey•ing, eyed)
eye•ball
eye•brow
eye-catcher
eye-catching
eye•cup
eyed
eye•dropper
eye•ful
eye•glass
eye•glasses
eye•hole
eye•ing (*or* ey•ing)
eye•lash
eye•less

eye•let small hole;
cf islet
eye•lev•el (*adj*)
eye•lid
eye•liner
eye-opener
eye•piece
eye•shade
eye•shot
eye•sight
eye•sore
eye•strain
eye•tooth (*pl*
•teeth)
eye•wash
eye•witness
ey•rie (*or* ey•ry,
aerie; *pl* ey•ries *or*
aeries) eagle's
nest; *cf* airy; eerie

F

fa
fab
fa•ble
fa•bled
fab•ric
fab•ri•cate
fab•ri•ca•tion
fab•ri•ca•tor
fabu•list
fabu•lous
fabu•lous•ly
fa•cade (*or* •cade)
face
face•less
face-lift

face-off
fac•er
face-saving
fac•et (*vb* •et•ing,
 •et•ed *or* •et•ting,
 •et•ted)
fa•ce•tious
fa•ce•tious•ly
fa•ce•tious•ness
fa•cia *variant
 spelling of* fascia
fa•cial
fa•cial•ly
fac•ile
fac•ile•ly
fac•ile•ness
fa•cili•tate
fa•cili•ta•tion
fa•cili•ta•tive
fa•cili•ta•tor
fa•cil•ity (*pl* •ities)
fac•ing
fac•simi•le (•le•ing,
 •led)
fact
fac•tion
fac•tion•al
fac•tion•al•ism
fac•tion•al•ist
fac•tious factional;
 cf factitious
fac•tious•ness
fac•ti•tious
 contrived; *cf*
 factious; fictitious
fac•ti•tious•ness
fac•tor
fac•tor•able
fac•torial

fac•to•ri•al•ly
fac•tori•za•tion
fac•tor•ize
fac•to•ry (*pl* •ries)
fac•to•tum
fac•tual
fac•tu•al•ly
fac•tu•al•ness (or
 •ity)
fac•ul•ty (*pl* •ties)
fad
fad•dish
fad•dism
fad•dist
fad•dy (•di•er,
 •di•est)
fade
fade-in (*n*)
fade-out (*n*)
fad•er
fad•ing
fae•cal *Brit spelling
 of* fecal
fae•ces *Brit
 spelling of* feces
fae•rie (*or* •ry; *pl*
 •ries) fairyland; *cf*
 fairy
fag (fag•ging,
 fagged)
fag•ot (*or* fag•got)
fag•ot•ing (*or*
 •got•)
Fahr•en•heit
fa•ience (*or*
 faï•ence)
fail be
 unsuccessful
fail•ing

faille fabric
fail-safe
fail•ure
faint indistinct;
 collapse; *cf* feint
faint•hearted
faint•ly
faint•ness
fair just; not dark;
 event; *cf* fare
fair•ground
fair•ing
fair•ish
fair•ly
fair-minded
fair-minded•ness
fair•ness
fair-spoken
fair•way
fair-weather (*adj*)
fairy (*pl* fairies)
 supernatural
 being; *cf* faerie
fairy•land
fait ac•com•pli (*pl*
 faits ac•com•plis)
faith
faith•ful
faith•ful•ly
faith•ful•ness
faith•less
faith•less•ness
fake
fak•er one who
 fakes
fak•ery
fa•kir (*or* •qir,
 •quir, •keer) holy
 man

fal•con
fal•con•er
fal•con•ry
fal•deral (*or*
  fal•derol,
  fol•derol,
fall (fall•ing, fell,
  fall•en)
fal•la•cious
fal•la•cious•ness
fal•la•cy (*pl* •cies)
fall•back
fall•en
fall•er
fall•fish (*pl* •fish,
  •fishes)
fal•libil•ity (*or*
  •lible•ness)
fal•lible
fal•libly
fal•lo•pian tube
fall•out
fal•low
fal•low•ness
false
false•hood
false•ly
false•ness
fal•set•to (*pl* •tos)
fal•si•fi•able
fal•si•fi•ca•tion
fal•si•fi•er
fal•si•fy (•fies,
  •fy•ing, •fied)
fal•sity (*pl* •sities)
fal•ter
fal•ter•er
fal•ter•ing•ly
fame

fa•mil•ial
fa•mil•iar
fa•mil•iar•ity (*pl*
  •ities)
fa•mil•iari•za•tion
fa•mil•iar•ize
fa•mil•iar•ly
fami•ly (*pl* •lies)
fam•ine
fam•ish
fa•mous
fa•mous•ly
fan (fan•ning,
  fanned)
fa•nat•ic
fa•nati•cal
fa•nati•cal•ly
fa•nati•cism
fa•nati•cize
fan•cied
fan•ci•er
fan•ci•ful
fan•ci•ful•ly
fan•ci•ful•ness
fan•ci•ly
fan•ci•ness
fan•cy (*adj* •ci•er,
  •ci•est; *n, pl* •cies;
  vb •cies, •cy•ing,
  •cied)
fancy-free
fancy•work
fan•dan•go (*pl*
  •gos)
fan•fare
fang
fanged
fan-jet
fan•light

fanned
fan•ner
fan•ning
fan•ny (*pl* •nies)
fan•tail
fan-tailed
fan•ta•sia (*or* •sie)
fan•ta•size
fan•tas•tic (*or*
  •ti•cal)
fan•tas•ti•cal•ly
fan•ta•sy (*or* phan•;
  n, pl •sies; *vb* •sies,
  •sy•ing, •sied)
fan•zine
fa•qir (*or* •quir)
  variant spellings
  of fakir
far (far•ther,
  far•thest *or*
  fur•ther, fur•thest)
far•ad
far•away
farce
far•ceur (*fem*
  •ceuse)
far•ci•cal
far•ci•cal•ity (*or*
  •ness)
far•ci•cal•ly
fare payment;
  food; to manage;
  cf fair
fare•well
far-fetched
far-flung
fari•na•ceous
farm
farm•able

farm•er
farm•house
farm•ing
farm•land
farm•stead
farm•yard
far•ness
far-off
far-out
far•ra•go (*pl* •goes)
far-reaching
far•row
far•seeing
far•sighted
far•sighted•ly
far•sighted•ness
fart
far•ther (*or* fur•)
  more distant; *cf*
  further
farther•most
far•thest (*or* fur•)
far•thing
fas•cia (*or* fa•cia;
  pl •ciae *or* •cias)
fas•ci•nate
fas•ci•nat•ing•ly
fas•ci•na•tion
fas•cism
fas•cist
fa•scis•tic
fash•ion
fash•ion•able
fash•ion•ably
fash•ion•able•ness
fast
fast•back
fas•ten
fas•ten•er

fas•ten•ing
fast•er
fast-food (*adj*)
fast-forward (*vb*)
fas•tidi•ous
fas•tidi•ous•ly
fas•tidi•ous•ness
fast•ness
fat (fat•ter,
  fat•test)
fa•tal
fa•tal•ism
fa•tal•ist
fa•tal•is•tic
fa•tal•is•ti•cal•ly
fa•tal•ity (*pl* •ities)
fa•tal•ly
fat•back
fate destiny; *cf* fete
fat•ed
fate•ful
fate•ful•ly
fate•ful•ness
fat•head
fat•headed
fa•ther
father•hood
father-in-law (*pl*
  fathers-)
father•land
fa•ther•less
fa•ther•li•ness
fa•ther•ly
fath•om (*pl* •oms
  or •om)
fath•om•able
fath•om•less
fati•gabil•ity
fa•tig•able

fa•tigue (•tigu•ing,
  •tigued)
fat•ness
fat-soluble
fat•ted
fat•ten
fat•ten•able
fat•ten•er
fat•ti•ly
fat•ti•ness
fat•tish
fat•ty (*adj* •ti•er,
  •ti•est; *n, pl* •ties)
fa•tu•ity (*pl* •ities)
fatu•ous
fatu•ous•ly
fatu•ous•ness
fau•cet
fault
fault•finder
fault•finding
faulti•ly
faulti•ness
fault•less
fault•less•ly
faulty (faulti•er,
  faulti•est)
faun Roman deity;
  cf fawn
fau•na (*pl* •nas *or*
  •nae)
fau•nal
faux pas (*pl* faux
  pas)
fa•vor (*Brit* •vour)
fa•vor•able (*Brit*
  •vour•)
fa•vor•ably (*Brit*
  •vour•)

fa•vor•able•ness
(*Brit* •vour•)
fa•vor•er (*Brit*
•vour•)
fa•vor•ite (*Brit*
•vour•)
fa•vor•it•ism (*Brit*
•vour•)
fawn animal;
color; cringe; *cf*
faun
fawn•er
fawn•ing•ly
fax
fay fairy; *cf* fey
faze
fe•al•ty (*pl* •ties)
fear
fear•ful
fear•ful•ly
fear•ful•ness
fear•less
fear•less•ly
fear•less•ness
fear•some
fear•some•ly
fear•some•ness
fea•sibil•ity (*or*
•sible•ness)
fea•sible
fea•sibly
feast
feast•er
feat exploit; *cf* feet
feath•er
feather•bed
(•bed•ding,
•bed•ded)
feather•brain

feather•brained
feath•er•ing
feather•stitch
feather•weight
feath•ery
fea•ture
feature-length (*adj*)
fea•ture•less
fea•ture•less•ness
fe•brile
Feb•ru•ary (*pl*
•aries *or* •arys)
fe•cal (*Brit* fae•)
fe•ces (*Brit* fae•)
feck•less
feck•less•ness
fe•cund
fe•cun•date
fe•cun•da•tion
fe•cun•dity
fed
fed•er•al
fed•er•al•ly
fed•er•al•ism
fed•er•al•ist
fed•er•al•is•tic
fed•er•ali•za•tion
fed•er•al•ize
fed•er•ate
fed•era•tion
fed•era•tive
fee (fee•ing, feed)
fee•ble
feeble•minded
feeble•minded•ly
feeble•minded•ness
fee•ble•ness
fee•bly
feed (feed•ing, fed)

feed•back
feed•er
feel (feel•ing, felt)
feel•er
feel-good (*adj*)
feel•ing
feel•ing•ly
feet *pl of* foot; *cf*
feat
feign
feign•er
feint mock action;
printing term; *cf*
faint
feis•ty (•ti•er,
•ti•est)
feld•spar (*or*
fel•spar)
fe•lici•tate
fe•lici•ta•tion
fe•lici•ta•tor
fe•lici•tous
fe•lic•ity (*pl* •ities)
fe•line
fe•lin•ity (*or*
•line•ness)
fell
fell•able
fel•la•tio
fell•er
fel•low
fel•low•ship
fel•on
fe•lo•ni•ous
fe•lo•ni•ous•ness
felo•ny (*pl* •nies)
fel•spar *variant
spelling of*
feldspar

felt
felt•ing
fe•male
fe•male•ness
femi•nine
femi•nin•ity
femi•nism
femi•nist
femi•ni•za•tion
femi•nize
femme fa•tale (*pl* femmes fa•tales)
femo•ral
fe•mur (*pl* •murs or femo•ra)
fen
fence
fenc•er
fenc•ing
fend
fend•er
fend•ered
fe•nes•trat•ed (or •trate)
fen•es•tra•tion
fen•nel
fe•ral (or •rine)
fer-de-lance (*pl* fer-de-lance)
fer•ment undergo fermentation; *cf* foment
fer•ment•able
fer•men•ta•tion
fer•menta•tive
fer•ment•er
fern
fern•ery (*pl* •eries)
ferny

fe•ro•cious
fe•ro•cious•ly
fe•roc•ity (or •ro•cious•ness)
fer•ret
fer•ric
Fer•ris wheel
fer•rite
fer•ro•mag•net•ic
fer•ro•mag•net•ism
fer•rous
fer•rule metal cap; *cf* ferule
fer•ry (*n, pl* •ries; *vb* •ries, •ry•ing, •ried)
fer•tile
fer•til•ity (or •tile•ness)
fer•ti•li•za•tion
fer•ti•lize
fer•ti•liz•er
fer•ule flat cane; *cf* ferrule
fer•ven•cy
fer•vent (or •vid)
fer•vent•ly (or •vid•ly)
fer•vor (*Brit* •vour)
fes•tal
fes•ter
fes•ti•val
fes•tive
fes•tive•ly
fes•tive•ness
fes•tiv•ity (*pl* •ities)
fes•toon
feta

fe•tal (*Brit also* foe•)
fetch
fetch•er
fetch•ing
fete (or fête) entertainment; *cf* fate
fet•id (*Brit also* foet•)
fet•ish (or •ich)
fet•ish•ism (or •ich•)
fet•ish•ist (or •ich•)
fet•lock (or fetter•)
fe•tor (*Brit also* foe•)
fet•ter
fet•tle
fe•tus (*Brit also* foe•; *pl* •tuses)
feud
feu•dal
feu•dal•ism
feu•dal•ist
feu•dal•is•tic
feud•ist
fe•ver
fe•vered
fe•ver•ish (or •ous)
fe•ver•ish•ly
fe•ver•ish•ness
fever•wort
few
fey whimsical; *cf* fay
fez (*pl* fezzes or fezes)
fi•an•cé (*fem* •cée)

fi•as•co (*pl* •cos or
•coes)
fib (fib•bing,
fibbed)
fib•ber
fi•ber (*Brit* •bre)
fiber•board (*Brit*
fibre•)
fi•bered (*Brit*
•bred)
fiber•fill (*Brit*
fibre•)
fiber•glass (or
•glas; *Brit* fibre•)
fiber-optic (*Brit*
fibre-; *adj*)
fiber optics (*Brit*
fibre optics; *n*)
fiber•scope (*Brit*
fibre•)
fi•broid
fi•bro•sis
fi•bro•si•tis
fi•brous
fi•brous•ness
fibu•la (*pl* •lae or
•las)
fiche (*pl* fiche or
fiches)
fick•le
fick•le•ness
fick•ly
fic•tion
fic•tion•al
fic•tion•ali•za•tion
(or •tion•iza•tion)
fic•tion•al•ize (or
•tion•ize)
fic•ti•tious not

genuine; *cf*
factitious
fic•ti•tious•ness
fid•dle
fid•dler
fiddle•sticks
fid•dling
fid•dly (•dli•er,
•dli•est)
fi•del•i•ty (*pl* •ities)
fidg•et
fidg•ety
fi•du•ciary (*pl*
•ciaries)
fie
fief
fief•dom
field
field•er
field•work
fiend
fiend•ish
fiend•ish•ly
fiend•ish•ness
fierce
fierce•ly
fierce•ness
fi•eri•ly
fi•eri•ness
fi•ery
fi•es•ta
fife
fif•teen
fif•teenth
fifth
fif•ti•eth
fif•ty (*pl* •ties)
fifty-fifty
fig

fight (fight•ing,
fought)
fight•er
fig•ment
fig•ura•tive
fig•ura•tive•ly
fig•ure
fig•ured
figure•head
figu•rine
fig•wort
fila•gree *variant
spelling of* **filigree**
fila•ment
fila•men•tous
fil•bert
filch
filch•er
file
file•fish (*pl* •fish or
•fishes)
fil•er
fi•let mi•gnon (*pl*
fi•lets mi•gnons)
fil•ial
fil•ial•ly
fil•ial•ness
fili•bus•ter
fili•bus•ter•er
fili•bus•ter•ism
fili•gree (or fila•,
filla•; •gree•ing,
•greed)
fil•ings
fill
filla•gree *variant
spelling of* **filigree**
filled
fill•er

fil•let
fill-in (*n*)
fill•ing
fil•lip (*or* fil•ip)
fil•ly (*pl* •lies)
film
film•goer
film•ic
filmi•ness
film•set (•set•ting,
•set)
film•setter
filmy (filmi•er,
filmi•est)
filo (*or* fil•lo)
fil•ter separating
device; *cf* philtre
fil•ter•able (*or*
fil•trable)
filter-tipped
filth
filthi•ly
filthi•ness
filthy (filthi•er,
filthi•est)
fil•trable *variant of*
filterable
fil•trate
fil•tra•tion
fin (fin•ning,
finned)
appendage;
provide with fins,
etc.; *cf* Finn
fin•able (*or* fine•)
fi•nal
fi•na•le
fi•nal•ist
fi•nal•ity (*pl* •ities)

fi•na•li•za•tion
fi•nal•ize
fi•nal•ly
fi•nals
fi•nance
fi•nan•cial
fi•nan•cial•ly
fi•nan•cier
finch
find (find•ing,
found)
find•er
find•ing
fine
fine•able *variant*
spelling of finable
fine-cut
fine-draw
(-draw•ing, -drew,
-drawn)
fine-grained
fine•ly
fine•ness
fin•ery (*pl* •eries)
fine•spun
fi•nesse
fine-tooth (*or*
-toothed) comb
fine-tune
fin•ger
finger•board
fin•gered
fin•ger•ing
fin•ger•ling
finger•nail
finger•print
finger•stall
finger•tip
fi•nial

fin•icki•ness
fin•icky (*or*
•ick•ing)
fin•ish complete;
end; *cf* Finnish
fin•ish•er
fi•nite
fi•nite•ly
Finn native of
Finland; *cf* fin
finned
Finn•ish of
Finland; *cf* finish
fin•ny (•ni•er,
•ni•est)
fiord *variant*
spelling of fjord
fir tree; *cf* fur
fire
fire•able
fire•arm
fire•ball
fire•bird
fire•boat
fire•bomb
fire•box
fire•brand
fire•break
fire•brick
fire•bug
fire•cracker
fire•damp
fire•dog
fire-eater
fire-eating
fire•fighter
fire•fly (*pl* •flies)
fire•guard
fire•light

fire•man (pl •men)
fire•place
fire•proof
fir•er
fire•side
fire•storm
fire•trap
fire•warden
fire•weed
fire•wood
fire•work
fir•ing
fir•kin
firm
fir•ma•ment
firm•ly
firm•ness
firm•ware
first
first-born
first-class (adj)
first-degree (adj)
first•hand
first•ly
first-nighter
first-rate
firth (or frith)
fis•cal
fish (pl fish or fishes)
fish•bowl
fish•er
fisher•man (pl •men)
fish•ery (pl •eries)
fish•eye
fish•hook
fishi•ly
fishi•ness

fish•ing
fish•net
fish•plate
fish•tail
fish•wife (pl •wives)
fishy (fishi•er, fishi•est)
fis•sile
fis•sion
fis•sion•able
fis•sure
fist
fisti•cuffs
fis•tu•la (pl •las or •lae)
fit (vb fit•ting, fit•ted or fit; adj fit•ter, fit•test)
fit•ful
fit•ful•ly
fit•ful•ness
fit•ly
fit•ness
fit•ted
fit•ter
fit•ting
fit•ting•ly
five
five•fold
five•penny
five•pins
fiv•er
five-star (adj)
fix
fix•able
fix•ate
fixa•tion
fixa•tive
fixed

fix•ed•ly
fix•ed•ness
fix•er
fix•ings
fix•ity (pl •ities)
fix•ture
fizz
fizz•er
fizzi•ness
fiz•zle
fizzy (fizzi•er, fizzi•est)
fjord (or fiord)
flab
flab•ber•gast
flab•bi•ly
flab•bi•ness
flab•by (•bi•er, •bi•est)
flac•cid
flac•cid•ity (or •ness)
flack variant spelling of flak
flag (flag•ging, flagged)
flag•el•lant (or •la•tor)
flag•el•late
flag•el•la•tion
flag•el•lum (pl •la or •lums)
flagged
flag•ger
flag•ging
flag•on
flag•pole
fla•gran•cy (or •grance)

fla•grant
fla•gran•te
de•lic•to
fla•grant•ly
flag•ship
flag•staff (*pl*
•staffs *or* •staves)
flag•stone
flag-waver
flag-waving
flail
flair talent; *cf* flare
flak (*or* flack)
flake
flaki•ness
flaky (flaki•er,
flaki•est)
flam•bé (*or* •bée;
•bé•ing, •béed)
flam•boy•ance (*or*
•an•cy)
flam•boy•ant
flame
fla•men•co (*pl*
•cos)
flame•proof
flam•er
flame•throw•er
flam•ing
fla•min•go (*pl* •gos
or •goes)
flam•mabil•ity
flam•mable
flamy (flami•er,
flami•est)
flan
flange
flank
flank•er

flan•nel (•nel•ing,
•neled; *Brit*
•nel•ling, •nelled)
flan•nel•ette (*or*
•et)
flan•nel•ly
flap (flap•ping,
flapped)
flap•jack
flap•per
flare flame; widen;
cf flair
flare-up (*n*)
flash
flash•back
flash•bulb
flash•er
flashi•ly
flashi•ness
flash•ing
flash•light
flashy (flashi•er,
flashi•est)
flask
flat (flat•ter,
flat•test)
flat•boat
flat•fish (*pl* •fish
or •fishes)
flat•foot (*pl* •feet)
fallen arches
flat•foot (*pl* •foots)
police officer
flat-footed
flat-footed•ly
flat-footed•ness
flat•iron
flat•ness
flat•ten

flat•ter
flat•ter•er
flat•ter•ing
flat•ter•ing•ly
flat•tery (*pl* •teries)
flat•tish
flat•top
flatu•lence (*or*
•len•cy)
flatu•lent
flat•ware
flat•wise (*Brit*
•ways)
flat•worm
flaunt
flaunt•er
flaunt•ing•ly
flaunty (flaunti•er,
flaunti•est)
flau•tist *variant of*
flutist
fla•vor (*Brit* •vour)
fla•vor•er (*Brit*
•vour•)
fla•vor•ful (*Brit*
•vour•)
fla•vor•ing (*Brit*
•vour•)
fla•vor•less (*Brit*
•vour•)
fla•vor•some (*Brit*
•vour•)
flaw
flaw•less
flaw•less•ly
flax
flax•en (*or* flaxy)
flax•seed
flay

flay•er
flea
flea•bag
flea•bite
flea-bitten
fleck
flec•tion (*Brit*
 flex•ion) bending;
 a bend; *cf* **flexion**
fled
fledge
fledg•ling (*or*
 fledge•)
flee (flee•ing, fled)
flies
fleece
fleeci•ness
fleecy (fleeci•er,
 fleeci•est)
fle•er
fleet
fleet•ing
fleet•ing•ly
fleet•ness
Flem•ing
Flem•ish
flesh
fleshi•ness
flesh•ly (•li•er,
 •li•est)
fleshy (fleshi•er,
 fleshi•est)
fleur-de-lis (*or* -lys;
 pl fleurs-de-lis,
 -lys *or* fleur-de-lis,
 -lys)
flew *past tense of*
 fly; *cf* **flu**; **flue**
flex

flex•ibil•ity (*or*
 •ible•ness)
flex•ible
flex•ibly
flex•ion bending a
 limb; *cf* flection
flex•time (*or* flexi•)
flex•or
lib•ber•ti•gib•bet
flick
flick•er
flick•er•ing•ly
flick•ery
fli•er (*or* fly•)
flies
flight
flighti•ly
flighti•ness
flight•less
flighty (flighti•er,
 flighti•est)
flim•flam
 (•flam•ming,
 •flammed)
flim•si•ly
flim•si•ness
flim•sy (•si•er,
 •si•est)
flinch
flinch•ing•ly
fling (fling•ing,
 flung)
fling•er
flint
flinti•ness
flinty (flinti•er,
 flinti•est)
flip (flip•ping,
 flipped)

flip-flop
 (-flop•ping,
 -flopped)
flip•pan•cy
flip•pant
flip•pant•ly
flip•per
flirt
flir•ta•tion
flir•ta•tious
flir•ta•tious•ness
flirt•er
flit (flit•ting,
 flit•ted)
flit•ter
float
float•abil•ity
float•able
float•age *variant
 spelling of* flotage
floata•tion *variant
 spelling of*
 flotation
float•er
float•ing
floc•cu•la•tion
floc•cu•lence (*or*
 •len•cy)
floc•cu•lent
flock
floe ice; *cf* flow
flog (flog•ging,
 flogged)
flog•ger
flog•ging
flood
flood•er
flood•gate
flood•light

(•light•ing,
•light•ed or •lit)
floor
floor•age
floor•board
floor•ing
floo•zy (or •zie,
•sy, •sie; pl •zies
or •sies)
flop (flop•ping,
flopped)
flop•pi•ly
flop•pi•ness
flop•py (•pi•er,
•pi•est)
flo•ra (pl •ras or
•rae)
flo•ral
flo•ral•ly
Flor•en•tine
flo•res•cence
flowering; cf
fluorescence
flo•ret
flo•ri•cul•ture
flor•id
flo•rid•ity (or
•ness)
flor•id•ly
flo•rist
floss
flossy (flossi•er,
flossi•est)
flo•tage (or
float•age)
flo•ta•tion (or
floata•tion)
flo•til•la
flot•sam

flounce
floun•der to
struggle; cf
founder
flour foodstuff; cf
flower
flour•ish
flour•ish•er
floury (flouri•er,
flouri•est)
flout
flout•er
flow liquid
movement; cf floe
flow•er part of
plant; cf flour
flower•bed
flow•ered
flow•er•er
flow•er•et
flow•eri•ness
flow•er•ing
flow•er•less
flower•like
flower•pot
flow•ery
flow•ing
flown
flu illness; cf flew;
flue
fluc•tu•ate
fluc•tua•tion
flue pipe; cf flew;
flu
flu•en•cy
flu•ent
flu•ent•ly
fluff
fluffi•ly

fluffi•ness
fluffy (fluffi•er,
fluffi•est)
flu•id
flu•id•ics
flu•id•ity (or •ness)
flu•idi•za•tion
flu•id•ize
flu•id•ly (or
flu•id•al•ly)
fluke
fluki•ness
fluky (or fluk•ey;
fluki•er, fluki•est)
flum•mery (pl
•meries)
flum•mox
flung
flunk
flunky (or flunk•ey;
pl flunkies or •eys)
fluo•resce
fluo•res•cence
radiation
emission; cf
florescence
fluo•res•cent
fluori•date
fluori•da•tion
fluo•ride
fluori•nate
fluori•na•tion
fluo•rine (or •rin)
fluo•rite
fluoro•car•bon
fluoro•scope
fluoro•scop•ic
fluo•ros•co•py
flur•ry (n, pl •ries;

vb •ries, •ry•ing,
•ried)
flush
flush•er
flus•ter
flute
flut•ed
flut•ing
flut•ist (or flaut•)
flut•ter
flut•ter•ing•ly
flut•tery
flu•vial (or
•via•tile)
flux
fly (n, pl flies; vb
flies, fly•ing, flew,
flown)
fly•able
fly•away
fly•blow
(•blow•ing, •blew,
•blown)
fly•by
fly-by-night
fly•catcher
fly•er variant
spelling of flier
fly-fish
fly-fishing
fly•ing
fly•leaf (pl •leaves)
fly•over (Brit •past)
fly•paper
fly•trap
fly•weight
fly•wheel
foal
foam

foami•ness
foamy (foami•er,
foami•est)
fob (fob•bing;
fobbed)
fo•cal
fo•cal•ly
fo•cus (n, pl •cuses
or •ci; vb •cuses,
•cus•ing, •cused or
•cusses, •cus•sing,
•cussed)
fo•cus•able
fo•cus•er
fod•der
foe
foe•tal variant Brit
spelling of fetal
foet•id variant Brit
spelling of fetid
foe•tor variant Brit
spelling of fetor
foe•tus variant Brit
spelling of fetus
fog (fog•ging,
fogged)
fog•bound
fo•gey (or •gie)
variant spellings
of fogy
fogged
fog•gi•ly
fog•gi•ness
fog•ging
fog•gy (•gi•er,
•gi•est)
fog•horn
fogy (or fo•gie,

fo•gey; pl fogies or
•geys)
fo•gy•ish (or •gey•)
foi•ble
foil
foist
fold
fold•able
fold•away
fold•ed
fold•er
fol•derol variant
spelling of falderal
fold•ing
fo•li•age
fo•li•ate (or •at•ed)
fo•lia•tion
fo•lic acid
fo•lio (n, pl •lios; vb
•lios, •lio•ing,
•lioed)
folk (pl folk or
folks)
folk•lore
folk•lor•ist
folk•si•ness
folk•sy (•si•er,
•si•est)
fol•li•cle
fol•licu•lar
fol•low
fol•low•er
fol•low•ing
follow-through (n)
follow-up (n)
fol•ly (pl •lies)
fo•ment instigate;
cf ferment
fo•men•ta•tion

fo•ment•er
fond
fon•dant
fon•dle
fon•dler
fond•ness
fon•due (*or* •du)
font baptismal
  bowl
font (*Brit* fount)
  printing term
food
foodie
food•stuff
fool
fool•ery (*pl* •eries)
fool•har•di•ness
fool•hardy
  (•hardi•er,
  hardi•est)
fool•ish
fool•ish•ly
fool•ish•ness
fool•proof
fools•cap paper
fool's cap dunce
  cap
foot (*pl* feet)
foot•age
foot-and-mouth
  disease
foot•ball
foot•ball•er
foot•board
foot•bridge
foot•fall
foot•gear
foot•hill
foot•hold

foot•ing
foot•lights
foot•ling
foot•loose
foot•man (*pl* •men)
foot•mark
foot•note
foot•path
foot•plate
foot•print
foot•rest
foot•sie (*or* •sy)
foot•sore
foot•step
foot•stool
foot•wear
foot•work
fop
fop•pery (*pl*
  •peries)
fop•pish
fop•pish•ness
for indicates a
  recipient,
  purpose, etc., *cf*
  fore; four
for•age
for•ag•er
for•as•much as
for•ay
for•bade (*or* •bad)
for•bear (•bear•ing,
  •bore, •borne) to
  refrain; *variant
  spelling of*
  forebear
for•bear•ance
for•bear•ing•ly
for•bid (•bid•ding,

  •bade *or* •bad,
  •bid•den *or* •bid)
for•bid•dance
for•bid•den
for•bid•der
for•bid•ding•ly
for•bore
for•borne
force
force•able able to
  be forced; *cf*
  forcible
forced
force-feed
  (-feeding, -fed)
force•ful
force•ful•ly
force•ful•ness
force•meat
for•ceps (*pl* •ceps
  or •ci•pes)
forc•er
for•cible involving
  force; forceful; *cf*
  forceable
for•cibly
forc•ing•ly
ford
ford•able
fore toward the
  front; *cf* for; four
fore-and-aft (*adj*)
fore•arm
fore•bear (*or* for•)
  ancestor; *cf*
  forbear
fore•bode
fore•bod•ing
fore•cast

(•cast•ing, •cast or
•cast•ed)
fore•cast•er
fore•cas•tle
fore•close
fore•clo•sure
fore•court
fore•father
fore•fend *variant spelling of* forfend
fore•finger
fore•foot (*pl* •feet)
fore•front
fore•gather *variant spelling of* forgather
fore•go (•goes, •go•ing, •went, •gone) precede; *variant spelling of* forgo
fore•ground
fore•hand
fore•head
for•eign
for•eign•er
for•eign•ness
fore•judge (*or* for•)
fore•judg•ment (*Brit also* •judge•)
fore•know (•know•ing, •knew, •known)
fore•knowl•edge
fore•leg
fore•limb
fore•lock
fore•man (*pl* •men)
fore•mast

fore•most
fore•name
fore•named
fore•noon
fo•ren•sic
fo•ren•si•cal•ly
fo•ren•sics
fore•or•dain
fore•paw
fore•play
fore•quar•ter
fore•run (•run•ning, •ran, •run)
fore•run•ner
fore•sail
fore•see (•see•ing, •saw, •seen)
fore•see•able
fore•seen
fore•seer
fore•shad•ow
fore•shock
fore•shore
fore•short•en
fore•side
fore•sight
fore•sighted
fore•sighted•ness
fore•skin
for•est
for•est•al (*or* fo•res•tial)
fore•stall
fore•stall•er
fore•stall•ment
for•esta•tion
for•est•ed
for•est•er
for•est•ry

fore•swear *variant spelling of* forswear
fore•taste
fore•tell (•tell•ing, •told)
fore•tell•er
fore•thought
fore•to•ken
fore•told
for•ev•er
forever•more
fore•warn
fore•warn•er
fore•went
fore•word preface; *cf* forward
for•feit
for•feit•able
for•feit•er
for•fei•ture
for•fend (*or* fore•)
for•gath•er (*or* fore•)
for•gave
forge
forge•able
forg•er
forg•ery (*pl* •geries)
for•get (•get•ting, •got, •got•ten *or* •got)
for•get•ful
for•get•ful•ly
for•get•ful•ness
forget-me-not
for•get•table
for•get•ter

forg•ing
for•giv•able
for•giv•ably
for•give (•giv•ing,
•gave, •giv•en)
for•give•ness
for•giv•er
for•giv•ing•ly
for•go (or fore•;
•goes, •go•ing,
•went, •gone) give
up; cf forego
for•go•er (or fore•)
for•got
for•got•ten
for•judge variant
spelling of
forejudge
fork
forked
fork•ful (pl •fuls or
forks•ful)
fork•lift
for•lorn
for•lorn•ly
form
form•able
for•mal
for•mal•de•hyde
for•ma•lin
for•mal•ism
for•mal•ist
for•mal•is•tic
for•mal•ity (pl
•ities)
for•mali•za•tion
for•mal•ize
for•mal•iz•er
for•mal•ly in a

formal way; cf
formerly
for•mal•ness
for•mat (•mat•ting,
•mat•ted)
for•ma•tion
forma•tive
forma•tive•ly
form•er one that
forms
for•mer past
for•mer•ly in the
past; cf formally
for•mic acid
For•mi•ca
(Trademark)
for•mi•dabil•ity (or
•dable•ness)
for•mi•dable
for•mi•dably
form•less
form•less•ness
for•mu•la (pl •las
or •lae)
for•mu•laic
for•mu•late
for•mu•la•tion
for•mu•la•tor
for•ni•cate
for•ni•ca•tion
for•ni•ca•tor
for•sake (•sak•ing,
•sook, •sak•en)
for•sak•en
for•sak•er
for•sook
for•sooth
for•swear (or fore•;

•swear•ing,
•swore, •sworn)
for•swear•er
for•sworn
for•sythia
fort fortified
building; cf fought
forte strength
for•te musical term
forth forward; cf
fourth
forth•com•ing
forth•right
forth•right•ness
forth•with
for•ti•eth
for•ti•fi•able
for•ti•fi•ca•tion
for•ti•fi•er
for•ti•fy (•fies,
•fy•ing, •fied)
for•tis•si•mo (pl
•mos or •mi)
for•ti•tude
fort•night
fort•night•ly (pl
•lies)
FORTRAN (or
Fortran)
for•tress
for•tui•tous
for•tui•tous•ly
for•tui•tous•ness
for•tu•ity (pl •ities)
for•tu•nate
for•tu•nate•ly
for•tune
fortune-teller
fortune-telling

for•ty (*pl* •ties)
forty-niner
fo•rum (*pl* •rums or •ra)
for•ward (*adj*) to the front; *cf* **foreword**
for•ward (*Brit* •wards; *adv*)
for•ward•ness
for•went
fos•sil
fos•sili•za•tion
fos•sil•ize
fos•ter
fos•ter•er
fought *past tense of* **fight**; *cf* **fort**
foul bad; *cf* **fowl**
fou•lard
foul•ly
foul•mouthed
foul•ness
foul-up (*n*)
found
foun•da•tion
foun•da•tion•al
found•er one who founds; to sink; *cf* **flounder**
found•ing
found•ling
found•ry (*pl* •ries)
fount source; *Brit spelling of* **font**
foun•tain
fountain•head

four number; *cf* **for**; **fore**
four•fold
four•post•er
four•score
four•some
four•square
four•teen
four•teenth
fourth 4th; *cf* **forth**
fourth•ly
four-wheel drive
fowl (*pl* **fowl** or **fowls**) chicken; *cf* **foul**
fox (*pl* **foxes** or **fox**)
fox•glove
fox•hound
foxi•ly
foxi•ness
fox•tail
fox-trot (-trot•ting, -trot•ted)
foxy (foxi•er, foxi•est)
foy•er
fra•cas (*pl* •cases; *Brit* •cas)
frac•tion
frac•tion•al (*or* •ary)
frac•tion•al•ly
frac•tion•ate
frac•tiona•tion
frac•tiona•tor
frac•tioni•za•tion
frac•tion•ize
frac•tious

frac•ture
frag (frag•ging, fragged)
frag•ile
frag•ile•ly
fra•gil•ity (*or* •gile•ness)
frag•ment
frag•men•tal
frag•men•tal•ly
frag•men•tari•ly
frag•men•tari•ness
frag•men•tary
frag•men•ta•tion
fra•grance (*or* •gran•cy; *pl* •grances *or* •cies)
fra•grant
frail
frail•ly
frail•ness
frail•ty (*pl* •ties)
fram•able (*or* frame•)
frame
frame•less
fram•er
frame-up
frame•work
fram•ing
franc currency; *cf* **frank**
frank
fran•chise
Fran•cis•can
fran•gi•pani (*or* •pan•ni; *pl* •panis, •pani *or* •nis, •ni)
Frank Germanic people

frank straight-
forward; to mark
mail; *cf* **franc**
frank•able
frank•fur•ter
frank•in•cense
Frank•ish
frank•ly
frank•ness
fran•tic
fran•ti•cal•ly (*or*
fran•tic•ly)
fra•ter•nal
fra•ter•nal•ly
fra•ter•ni•ty (*pl*
•nities)
frat•er•ni•za•tion
frat•er•nize
frat•er•niz•er
frat•ri•cide
Frau (*pl* Frau•en
or Fraus)
fraud
fraudu•lence (*or*
•len•cy)
fraudu•lent
fraudu•lent•ly
fraught
Fräu•lein (*pl* •lein
or •leins)
fray
fraz•zle
freak
freaki•ly
freaki•ness
freak•ish
freak•ish•ness
freaky (freaki•er,
freaki•est)

freck•le
freck•led (*or* •ly)
free (*adj* fre•er,
fre•est; *vb*
free•ing, freed)
free•base
free•bie (*or* •bee)
free•boot•er
free•born
free•dom
free-for-all (*n, adj*)
free-form (*adj*)
free•hand drawn
without instru-
ments
free•handed
generous
free•hold
free•hold•er
free•lance
free•lanc•er
free•load
free•load•er
free•ly
free•man (*pl* •men)
Free•ma•son
Free•ma•son•ry
free•sia
free-spoken
free•standing
free•stone
free•style
free•thinker
free•thinking
free•way
free•wheel
free•wheeling
freez•able
freeze (freez•ing,

froze, fro•zen)
chill; *cf* **frieze**
freeze-dry (-dries,
-drying, -dried)
freez•er
freeze-up (*n*)
freez•ing
freight
freight•age
freight•er
French
French•man (*pl*
•men)
French•woman (*pl*
•women)
fre•net•ic
fre•neti•cal•ly
fren•zied•ly
fren•zy (*n, pl* •zies;
vb •zies, •zy•ing,
•zied)
fre•quen•cy (*pl*
•cies) physics and
statistics term
fre•quen•cy (*or*
fre•quence; *pl*
•cies *or* •quences)
frequent
occurrence
fre•quent
fre•quent•able
fre•quent•er
fre•quent•ly
fres•co (*n, pl* •coes
or •cos; *vb* •coes,
•co•ing, •coed)
fresh
fresh•en
fresh•en•er

fresh•man (*pl*
  •men)
fresh•ness
fresh•water (*adj*)
fret (fret•ting,
  fret•ted)
fret•ful
fret•ful•ly
fret•ful•ness
fret•ted
fret•work
Freud•ian
fri•abil•ity (*or*
  •able•ness)
fri•able
fri•ar monk; *cf*
  fryer
fri•ary (*pl* •aries)
fric•as•see
  (•see•ing, •seed)
fric•tion
fric•tion•al
Fri•day
fridge
fried
friend
friend•less
friend•less•ness
friend•li•ness
friend•ly (•li•er,
  •li•est)
friend•ship
fri•er *variant*
  spelling of fryer
fries
frieze ornament; *cf*
  freeze
frig•ate
fright

fright•en
fright•en•able
fright•en•er
fright•en•ing
fright•en•ing•ly
fright•ful
fright•ful•ly
frig•id
fri•gid•ity (*or*
  frig•id•ness)
frill
frilled
frilli•ness
frilly (frilli•er,
  frilli•est)
fringe
frip•pery (*pl*
  •peries)
Fris•bee
  (*Trademark*)
frisk
frisk•er
friski•ly
friski•ness
frisky (friski•er,
  friski•est)
fris•son
frith *variant of*
  firth
fri•til•lary (*pl*
  •laries)
frit•ter
friv•ol (•ol•ing,
  •oled; *Brit*
  •ol•ling, •olled)
friv•ol•er (*Brit*
  •ol•ler)
fri•vol•ity (*pl* •ities)
frivo•lous

frivo•lous•ly
frivo•lous•ness
frizz
friz•zi•ness
friz•zle
friz•zy (*or* •zly;
  •zi•er, •zi•est *or*
  •zli•er, •zli•est)
fro
frock
frog (frog•ging,
  frogged)
frog•man (*pl* •men)
frog-march
frol•ic (•ick•ing,
  •icked)
frol•ick•er
frol•ic•some (*or*
  frol•icky)
from
frond
front
front•age
front•al
fron•tal•ly
fron•tier
fron•tiers•man (*pl*
  •men)
fron•tiers•woman
  (*pl* •women)
fron•tis•piece
front-page (*adj, vb*)
front-runner
front•ward (*Brit*
  •wards)
frost
frost•bite (•bit•ing,
  •bit, •bit•ten)
frost•ed

frosti•ly
frosti•ness
frost•ing
frosty (frosti•er, frosti•est)
froth
frothi•ly
frothi•ness
frothy (frothi•er, frothi•est)
frown
frown•er
frown•ing•ly
frowzi•ness
frowzy (or frowsy; frowzi•er, frowzi•est or frowsi•er, frows•iest)
froze
fro•zen
fro•zen•ness
fruc•ti•fy (•fies, •fy•ing, •fied)
fruc•tose
fru•gal
fru•gal•ly
fru•gal•ity (or •ness)
fruit
frui•tar•ian
fruit•cake
fruit•er
fruit•ful
fruit•ful•ly
fruit•ful•ness
fruiti•ness
frui•tion
fruit•less

fruit•less•ly
fruity (fruiti•er, fruiti•est)
frump
frump•ish (or frumpy)
frump•ish•ness (or frumpi•ness)
frus•trate
frus•trat•er
frus•trat•ing•ly
frus•tra•tion
fry (n, pl fries; vb fries, fry•ing, fried)
fry•er (or fri•) one that fries; cf friar
fry•ing
fuch•sia (NOT fushia)
fuck
fuck•er
fuck•up
fud•dle
fuddy-duddy (pl -duddies)
fudge
Fueh•rer variant spelling of Führer
fuel (fuel•ing, fueled; Brit fuel•ling, fuelled)
fuel•er (Brit fuel•ler)
fu•gi•tive
fu•gi•tive•ly
fugue
Füh•rer (or Fueh•)

ful•crum (pl •crums or •cra)
ful•fill (Brit •fil; •fil•ling, •filled)
ful•fill•er
ful•fill•ment (Brit •fil•)
full
full•back
full-blooded
full-blown
full-bodied
full•er
full-faced
full-fledged (Brit fully fledged)
full-frontal (adj)
full-length (adj)
full•ness (or ful•ness)
full-scale
full-size (or -sized)
full-time (adj)
full-timer
ful•ly
ful•mar
ful•mi•nate
ful•mi•na•tion
ful•mi•na•tor
ful•ness variant spelling of fullness
ful•some
ful•some•ly
ful•some•ness
fum•ble
fum•bler
fum•bling•ly
fume
fum•er

fu•mi•gant
fu•mi•gate
fu•mi•ga•tion
fu•mi•ga•tor
fum•ing
fumy (fumi•er, fumi•est)
fun (fun•ning, funned)
func•tion
func•tion•al (or •ary)
func•tion•al•ism
func•tion•al•ist
func•tion•al•ly
func•tion•ary (or •aire, •naire; pl •aries, •aires, or •naires)
fund
fun•da•ment
fun•da•men•tal
fun•da•men•tal•ism
fun•da•men•tal•ist
fun•da•men•tal•ity (or •ness)
fun•da•men•tal•ly
fund•ed
fund-raiser
fund-raising
funds
fu•ner•al
fu•ner•ary
fu•ne•real
fun•fair
fun•gal
fun•gi pl of fungus
fun•gi•cid•al
fun•gi•cide

fun•goid
fun•gous (adj)
fun•gus (n; pl •gi or •guses)
fu•nicu•lar
funk
funk•er
funky (funki•er, funki•est)
fun•nel (•nel•ing, •neled; Brit •nel•ling, •nelled)
fun•ni•ly
fun•ni•ness
fun•ny (•ni•er, •ni•est)
fur (fur•ring, furred) animal hair; trim with fur; cf fir
fur•be•low
fur•bish
fur•bish•er
fu•ri•ous
fu•ri•ous•ly
furl
fur•long
fur•lough
fur•nace
fur•nish
fur•nish•er
fur•nish•ings
fur•ni•ture
fu•ror (Brit fu•ro•re)
furred
fur•ri•er
fur•ri•ery (pl •eries)

fur•ri•ness
fur•ring
fur•row
fur•ry (•ri•er, •ri•est)
fur•ther additional; variant of farther
fur•ther•ance
fur•ther•er
further•more (adv)
further•most (adj)
fur•thest
fur•tive
fur•tive•ly
fur•tive•ness
fury (pl furies)
furze
fuse melt, blend, etc.; circuit breaker; cf fuze
fu•se•lage
*fushia incorrect spelling of fuchsia
fu•sibil•ity (or fusible•ness)
fu•sible
fu•sil•lade
fu•sion
fuss
fuss•er
fussi•ly
fussi•ness
fussy (fussi•er, fussi•est)
fus•tian
fus•ti•ness
fus•ty (•ti•er, •ti•est)
fu•tile

fu•tile•ly
fu•til•ity (*pl* •ities)
fu•ton
fu•ture
fu•tur•ism
fu•tur•ist
fu•tur•is•tic
fu•tur•is•ti•cal•ly
fu•tur•ity (*pl* •ities)
fu•tur•olo•gist
fu•tur•ol•ogy
fuze (*Brit* **fuse**) detonator; *cf* **fuse**
fuzz
fuzzi•ly
fuzzi•ness
fuzzy (**fuzzi•er,** **fuzzi•est**)
fyke

G

gab (**gab•bing,** **gabbed**)
gab•ar•dine (*or* •er•)
gab•ber
gab•ble
gab•bler
gab•er•dine *variant spelling of* **gabardine**
gab•fest
ga•ble
ga•bled
gad (**gad•ding,** **gad•ded**)
gad•about

gad•der
gad•fly (*pl* •flies)
gadg•et
gadg•et•ry
gad•wall (*pl* •walls *or* •wall)
Gael•ic
gaff angling pole; nautical boom
gaffe blunder
gaf•fer
gag (**gag•ging,** **gagged**)
gaga
gage pledge; greengage; *variant spelling of* **gauge**
gage•able *variant spelling of* **gaugeable**
gag•er *variant spelling of* **gauger**
gagged
gag•ger
gag•ging
gag•gle
gag•man (*pl* •men)
gag•ster
gai•ety (*or* **gay•**; *pl* •eties)
gail•lard *variant spelling of* **galliard**
gai•ly (*or* **gay•**)
gain
gain•able
gain•er
gain•ful
gain•ful•ly
gain•ful•ness

gain•li•ness
gain•ly
gain•say (•say•ing, •said)
gain•say•er
gait walk; *cf* **gate**
gai•ter
gala
ga•lac•tic
gala•vant *variant spelling of* **gallivant**
Gal•axy solar system
gal•axy (*pl* •axies) any star system; distinguished gathering
gale
gall
gal•lant
gal•lant•ly
gal•lant•ry (*pl* •ries)
gall•blad•der
gal•leon
gal•ler•ied
gal•lery (*pl* •leries)
gal•ley
gall•fly (*pl* •flies)
gal•liard (*or* **gail•**)
gal•li•mau•fry (*pl* •fries)
gall•ing
gal•li•nule
gal•li•vant (*or* **gala•vant**)
gal•li•wasp

gall•nut (or gall-apple)

gal•lon

gal•loot variant spelling of galoot

gal•lop horse's gait; cf galop

gal•lop•er

gal•lows (pl •lowses or •lows)

gall•stone

ga•loot (or gal•loot)

ga•lop dance; cf gallop

ga•lore

ga•loshes (or go•)

ga•lumph (or gal•lumph)

gal•van•ic (or •vani•cal)

gal•vani•cal•ly

gal•va•ni•za•tion

gal•va•nize

gal•va•niz•er

gal•va•nom•eter

gam•bit

gam•ble bet; cf gambol

gam•bler

gam•bling

gam•boge

gam•bol (•bol•ing, •boled; Brit •bol•ling, •bolled) frolic; cf gamble

game

game•cock

game•keeper

game•keeping

gam•elan

game•ly

game•ness

games•man•ship

game•ster

ga•met•ic

gam•ete

gam•ey variant spelling of gamy

gam•in street urchin

gam•ine boyish girl

gami•ness

gam•ing

gam•ma

gam•mon

gam•ut

gamy (or gam•ey; gami•er, gami•est)

gan•der

ga•nef

gang group; cf gangue

gang•buster

gang•land

gan•gling (or •gly)

gan•gli•on (pl •glia or •gli•ons)

gan•gli•on•ic

gang•plank

gan•grene

gan•gre•nous

gang•ster

gangue (or gang) worthless ore; cf gang

gang•way

gan•net (pl •nets or •net)

gant•let variant spelling of gauntlet

gan•try (or •tree; pl •tries or •trees)

gaol variant Brit spelling of jail

gap (gap•ping, gapped)

gape

gap•er

gap•ing

gap•py (•pi•er, •pi•est)

gar (pl gar or gars) variant of garfish

ga•rage

garb

gar•bage

gar•ble

gar•bler

gar•den

gar•den•er

gar•denia

gar•den•ing

gar•fish (pl •fish or •fishes)

gar•gan•tuan

gar•gle

gar•goyle

gar•goyled

gar•ish

gar•ish•ness

gar•land

gar•lic

gar•licky

gar•ment

gar•ner

gar•net

gar•nish

gar•nish•er

gar•ni•ture

ga•rotte *variant spelling of* garrotte

gar•pike

gar•ret

gar•ri•son

gar•rotte (*or* gar•rote, ga•rotte)

gar•rot•ter (*or* gar•rot•er, ga•rot•ter)

gar•ru•lous

gar•ru•lous•ness (*or* gar•ru•lity)

gar•ter

gas (*n, pl* gases *or* gasses; *vb* gases *or* gas•ses, gas•sing, gassed)

gas•bag

gas-cooled

gas•eous

gas•eous•ness

gash

gasi•fi•ca•tion

gasi•fi•er

gasi•fy (•fies, •fy•ing, •fied)

gas•ket

gas•light

gas•lit

gas•man (*pl* •men)

gaso•line (*or* •lene)

gas•om•eter

gasp

gasp•er

gassed

gas•ser

gas•si•ness

gas•sing

gas•sy (•si•er, •si•est)

gasteropod incorrect spelling of gastropod

gas•tight

gas•tric

gas•tri•tis

gas•tro•en•teri•tis

gas•tro•in•tes•ti•nal

gas•tro•nome (*or* •trono•mer, •trono•mist)

gas•tro•nom•ic (*or* •nomi•cal)

gas•tro•nomi•cal•ly

gas•trono•mist

gas•trono•my

gas•tro•pod (*NOT* gasteropod)

gas•tropo•dous

gas•works

gate *barrier; opening; cf* gait

gâ•teau (*or* ga•; *pl* •teaux *or* •teaus)

gate-crash

gate•crasher

gated

gate•house

gate•keeper

gate-leg (*or* -legged) table

gate•post

gate•way

gath•er

gath•er•er

gath•er•ing

gauche

gauche•ly

gauche•ness

gau•cherie

gau•cho (*pl* •chos)

gaudi•ly

gaudi•ness

gaudy (gaudi•er, gaudi•est)

gauf•fer *variant spelling of* goffer

gauge (*or* gage; *NOT* guage) scale; to measure; *cf* gage

gauge•able (*or* gage•)

gaug•er (*or* gag•)

gaunt

gaunt•let (*or* gant•)

gaunt•ness

gauss (*pl* gauss *or* gausses)

gauze

gauzi•ness

gauzy (gauzi•er, gauzi•est)

gave

gav•el (•el•ing, •eled *or* •el•ling, •elled)

ga•votte

gawk

gawki•ly (*or* gawk•ish•)

gawki•ness (*or* gawk•ish•)

gawky (*or* gawk•ish; gawki•er, gawki•est)

gay

gay•ety *variant spelling of* gaiety

gay•ly *variant spelling of* gaily

gay•ness

gaze

ga•ze•bo (*or* •za•, •zee•; *pl* •bos *or* •boes)

ga•zelle (*pl* •zelles *or* •zelle)

gaz•er

ga•zette

gaz•et•teer

gaz•pa•cho (*pl* •chos)

gear

gear•box

gear•ing

gear•shift

gear•wheel

gecko (*pl* geckos *or* geckoes)

gee (gee•ing, geed)

geek

geese

gee•zer old man; *cf* geyser

Geiger count•er

gei•sha (*pl* •sha *or* •shas)

gel (gel•ling, gelled) jellylike substance; form gel; *variant spelling of* jell

gela•tin (*or* •tine)

ge•lati•ni•za•tion

ge•lati•nize

ge•lati•nous

geld (geld•ing, geld•ed *or* gelt)

gelled

gel•ling

gel•se•mium (*pl* •miums *or* •mia)

gem (gem•ming, gemmed)

gem•olo•gist (*or* gem•molo•)

gem•ol•ogy (*or* gem•mol•)

gem•stone

ge•müt•lich

gen•darme

gen•dar•me•rie (*or* •ry; *pl* •ries)

gen•der

gender-bender

gene

ge•nea•logi•cal (*or* •log•ic)

ge•nealo•gist

ge•neal•ogy (*pl* •ogies)

gen•era *pl of* genus

gen•er•al

gen•er•al•is•si•mo (*pl* •mos)

gen•er•al•ist

gen•er•al•ity (*pl* •ities)

gen•er•ali•za•tion

gen•er•al•ize

gen•er•al•iz•er

gen•er•al•ly

gen•er•al•ness

gen•er•al•ship

gen•er•ate

gen•era•tion

gen•era•tive

gen•era•tor

ge•ner•ic (*or* neri•cal)

ge•neri•cal•ly

gen•er•os•ity (*pl* •ities)

gen•er•ous

gen•er•ous•ly

gen•esis (*pl* •eses)

ge•net•ic (*or* neti•cal)

ge•neti•cal•ly

ge•neti•cist

ge•net•ics

gen•ial cheerful

ge•nial of the chin

ge•ni•al•ity (*or* gen•ial•ness)

ge•nial•ly

ge•nie (*pl* •nies *or* •nii)

geni•tal

geni•tals (*or* •ta•lia)

geni•tive

genito•uri•nary

ge•nius (*pl* •niuses
  or •nii)

geno•cid•al

geno•cide

ge•nome (or •nom)

gen•re

gent

gen•teel

gen•teel•ly

gen•tian

Gen•tile

gen•til•ity (*pl*
  •ities)

gen•tle

gentle•folk (or
  •folks)

gentle•man (*pl*
  •men)

gentle•man•li•ness

gentle•man•ly

gen•tle•ness

gentle•woman (*pl*
  •women)

gen•tly

gen•tri•fi•ca•tion

gen•tri•fy (•fies,
  •fy•ing, •fied)

gen•try

genu•flect

genu•flec•tion (*Brit*
  also •flex•ion)

genu•flec•tor

genu•ine

genu•ine•ly

genu•ine•ness

ge•nus (*pl* gen•era
  or ge•nuses)

geo•cen•tric

geo•cen•tri•cal•ly

geo•des•ic (or
  •desi•cal)

geod•esy (or
  geo•det•ics)

geo•det•ic (or
  •deti•cal)

ge•og•ra•pher

geo•graphi•cal (or
  •graph•ic)

geo•graphi•cal•ly

ge•og•ra•phy (*pl*
  •phies)

geo•logi•cal (or
  •log•ic)

geo•logi•cal•ly

ge•olo•gist (or
  •ger)

ge•olo•gize

ge•ol•ogy (*pl*
  •ogies)

geo•mag•net•ic

geo•mag•ne•tism

geo•man•cer

geo•man•cy

geo•man•tic (or
  •manti•cal)

ge•om•eter (or
  •om•etri•cian)

geo•met•ric (or
  •ri•cal)

geo•met•ri•cal•ly

ge•om•etrize

ge•om•etry

geo•physi•cal

geo•physi•cist

geo•phys•ics

geor•gette

geo•sta•tion•ary

geo•ther•mal (or
  •mic)

ge•ra•nium

ger•bil (or •bille)

ger•fal•con *variant
  spelling of*
  gyrfalcon

geri•at•ric

geria•tri•cian (or
  geri•at•rist)

geri•at•rics

ger•kin *variant
  spelling of* gherkin

germ

Ger•man

ger•mane

ger•mane•ly

ger•mane•ness

Ger•man•ic

ger•mi•cid•al

ger•mi•cide

ger•mi•nal

ger•mi•nal•ly

ger•mi•nate

ger•mi•na•tion

ger•mi•na•tive

ger•mi•na•tor

ge•ron•to•logi•cal

ger•on•tolo•gist

ger•on•tol•ogy

ger•ry•man•der

ger•und

ges•so (*pl* •soes)

ge•stalt (*pl* •stalts
  or •stal•ten)

Ge•sta•po

ges•tate

ges•ta•tion

ges•ta•tion•al

ges•tic•u•late
ges•tic•u•la•tion
ges•tic•u•la•tive
ges•tic•u•la•tor
ges•tur•al
ges•ture
ges•tur•er
get (get•ting, got *or* got•ten)
get•able
get-at•able
get•away (*n*)
get-out (*n*)
get•ter
get-together
get-up (*n*)
get-up-and-go (*or* -get; *n*)
gew•gaw
gey•ser hot spring; *cf* geezer
Gha•na•ian (*or* Gha•nian)
ghast•li•ness
ghast•ly (•li•er, •li•est)
ghee (*or* ghi)
gher•kin (*or* ger•) pickled cucumber; *cf* jerkin
ghet•to (*pl* •tos *or* •toes)
ghost
ghost•like
ghost•li•ness
ghost•ly (•li•er, •li•est)
ghost•write

(•writ•ing, •wrote, •writ•ten)
ghost•writer
ghoul
ghoul•ish
GI (*pl* GIs *or* GI's)
gi•ant
gi•ant•ess
gi•ant•ism *variant of* gigantism
gib (gib•bing, gibbed)
gib•ber
gib•ber•ish
gib•bet (•bet•ing, •bet•ed *or* •bet•ting, •bet•ted)
gib•bing
gib•bon
gib•bous (*or* •bose)
gibe (*or* jibe) taunt; *cf* gybe
gib•er (*or* jib•)
gib•lets
gid•di•ly
gid•di•ness
gid•dy (*adj* •di•er, •di•est; *vb* •dies, •dy•ing, •died)
gift
gift•ed
gift•ed•ness
gift wrap (wrap•ping, wrapped)
gig (gig•ging, gigged)
gi•gan•tic
gi•gan•ti•cal•ly

gi•gan•tism (*or* gi•ant•ism)
gig•gle
gig•gler
gig•gly
gigo•lo (*pl* •los)
gild (gild•ing, gild•ed *or* gilt) cover with gold; *cf* guild
gild•er one who gilds; *variant spelling of* guilder
gild•ing
gill
gilled
gil•ly•flower (*or* •li•)
gilt covered in gold; gilding substance; security; pig; *cf* guilt
gilt-edged
gim•crack
gim•let
gim•mick
gim•mick•ry
gim•micky
gin (gin•ning, ginned)
gin•ger
gin•ger•bread
gin•ger•ly
gin•gery
ging•ham
gin•gi•vi•tis
gink•go (*or* ging•ko; *pl* •goes)

or •gos, •koes *or*
•kos)
gin•seng
gip•sy *variant*
spelling of gypsy
gi•raffe (*pl* •raffes
or •raffe)
gird (gird•ing,
gird•ed *or* girt)
gird•er
gir•dle
gir•dler
girl
girl•friend
girl•hood
girlie (*or* girly; *pl*
girlies)
girl•ish
girl•ish•ness
girt
girth
gis•mo (*or* giz•; *pl*
•mos)
gist
giv•able (*or*
give•able)
give (giv•ing, gave,
giv•en)
give-and-take (*n*)
give•away (*n*)
giv•en
giv•er
giz•mo *variant*
spelling of gismo
giz•zard
gla•cé (•cé•ing,
•céed)
gla•cial
gla•cial•ly

gla•ci•ate
gla•cia•tion
gla•cier ice sheet;
cf glazier
gla•ci•olo•gist (*or*
gla•cial•ist)
gla•ci•ol•ogy
glad (glad•der,
glad•dest)
glad•den
glad•den•er
glade
gladia•tor
gladia•to•rial
gladio•lus (*pl* •li *or*
•luses)
glad•ly
glad•ness
glad•some
glam•or *variant*
spelling of
glamour
glam•ori•za•tion
glam•or•ize (*or*
•our•)
glam•or•iz•er
glam•or•ous (*or*
•our•)
glam•or•ous•ness
(*or* •our•)
glam•our (*or* •or)
glance
glanc•ing
gland
glan•ders
glan•du•lar (*or*
•lous)
glare
glar•ing

glar•ing•ly
glary
glas•nost
glass
glass•blower
glass•blowing
glasses
glass•ful
glass•house
glassi•ly
glassi•ness
glass•maker
glass•making
glass•ware
glass•work
glass•worker
glass•works
glass•wort
glassy (glassi•er,
glassi•est)
glau•co•ma
glau•coma•tous
glau•cous
glaze
glaz•er one that
glazes
gla•zier
glassworker; *cf*
glacier
gla•ziery
glaz•ing
gleam
gleam•ing
glean
glean•able
glean•er
glean•ings
glee
glee•ful

glee•ful•ly
glee•ful•ness
glen
glib (glib•ber, glib•best)
glib•ly
glib•ness
glide
glid•er
glid•ing
glim•mer
glim•mer•ing
glimpse
glint
glis•ten
glis•ten•ing
glis•ter
glitch
glit•ter
glit•te•ra•ti (pl n)
glit•tery
glitzy (glitzi•er, glitzi•est)
gloam•ing
gloat
gloat•er
gloat•ing•ly
glob
glob•al
glob•ali•za•tion
glob•al•ly
glo•bate (or •bat•ed)
globe
globe•flower
globe•trotter
globe•trotting
glo•boid
globu•lar (or •lous)

glob•ule
globu•lin
glock•en•spiel
gloom
gloom•ful
gloomi•ly
gloomi•ness
gloomy (gloomi•er, gloomi•est)
glo•ri•fi•ca•tion
glo•ri•fi•er
glo•ri•fy (•fies, •fy•ing, •fied)
glo•ri•ous
glo•ri•ous•ly
glo•ri•ous•ness
glo•ry (n, pl •ries; vb •ries, •ry•ing, •ried)
gloss
glos•sa•rist
glos•sa•ry (pl •ries)
glos•sa•tor
gloss•er
glossi•ly
glossi•ness
glossy (adj glossi•er, glossi•est; n, pl glossies)
glot•tal
glot•tis (pl •tises or •ti•des)
glove
glov•er
glow
glow•er
glow•er•ing•ly
glow•worm

glox•inia
glu•cose
glue (glu•ing or glue•ing, glued)
glu•er
glu•ey (glui•er, glui•est)
glum (glum•mer, glum•mest)
glum•ly
glum•ness
glut (glut•ting, glut•ted)
glu•ta•mate
glu•ten
glu•ten•ous of gluten
glu•ti•nous (or •nose) sticky
glu•ti•nous•ness (or •nos•ity)
glut•ton
glut•ton•ous
glut•tony (pl •tonies)
glyc•er•in (or •ine)
glyc•er•ol
gly•col
G-man (pl -men)
gnarl
gnarled (or gnarly)
gnash
gnat
gnat•catcher
gnaw (gnaw•ing, gnawed, gnawed or gnawn)
gnaw•able
gnaw•er

gneiss rock; *cf* nice

gnoc•chi (*pl n*)

gnome

gno•mic (*or •mi•cal*)

gno•mi•cal•ly

gnom•ish

gno•sis (*pl •ses*)

gnos•tic (*or •ti•cal; adj*)

Gnos•tic (*n*)

Gnos•ti•cism

gnu (*pl* gnus *or* gnu) antelope; *cf* knew; new

go (*vb* goes, go•ing, went, gone; *n, pl* goes)

goad

go-ahead (*n, adj*)

goal

goalie

goal•keeper

goal•keeping

goal•less

goal•mouth

goat

goatee

goat•herd

goat•ish

goat•skin

goat's-rue

goat•sucker

gob

gob•bet

gob•ble

gob•ble•de•gook (*or •dy•*)

gob•bler

go-between

gob•let

gob•lin

goby (*pl* goby *or* gobies)

go-cart

god (god•ding, god•ded)

god•child (*pl •children*)

god•damn (*or •dam*)

god•damned (*or •damn, •dam*)

god•daughter

god•dess

go•detia

god•father

God-fearing

god•forsaken

god•head

god•hood

god•less

god•less•ness

god•like

god•li•ness

god•ly (•li•er, •li•est)

god•mother

god•parent

god•send

god•son

god•wit

goer

go•fer errand runner; *cf* gopher

gof•fer (*or* gauf•) to crimp; *cf* gopher

go-getter

gog•gle

goggle-eyed

gog•gles

go•ing

goi•ter (*Brit •tre*)

goi•trous (*or •ter•ous*)

gold

gold•beater

gold•beating

gold•en

golden•eye (*pl •eyes or •eye*)

golden•rod

golden•seal

gold•eye (*pl •eyes or •eye*)

gold•finch

gold•fish (*pl •fish or •fishes*)

goldi•locks (*or goldy•*)

gold-plate (*vb*)

gold•smith

gold•thread

go•lem

golf

golf•er

go•li•ath

gol•li•wog (*or •wogg*)

go•loshes *variant spelling of* galoshes

gom•bo *variant spelling of* gumbo

gon•ad

gon•ad•al (*or*

go•na•dial,
go•nad•ic)
gon•do•la
gon•do•lier
gone
gon•er
gong
gon•or•rhea (*Brit* •rhoea)
gon•or•rheal (*Brit* •rhoeal)
goo
goo•ber
good (bet•ter, best)
good-bye
good-for-nothing (*adj, n*)
good-hearted
good-humored (*Brit* -humoured)
good-humored•ly (*Brit* -humoured•)
good•ish
good•li•ness
good-looking
good•ly (•li•er, •li•est)
good-natured
good-natured•ly
good•ness
good-night
goods
good-sized
good-tempered
good•will
goody (*pl* goodies)
goody-goody (*pl* -goodies)

goo•ey (gooi•er, gooi•est)
goof
goofi•ly
goofi•ness
goofy (goofi•er, goofi•est)
goon
goop
goose (*pl* geese)
goose•berry (*pl* •berries)
goose•foot (*pl* •foots)
goose•grass
goose-step (-stepping, -stepped)
goosy (*or* goos•ey; goosi•er, goosi•est)
go•pher animal; *cf* gofer; goffer
gore
gorge
gor•geous
gor•geous•ly
gor•geous•ness
gorg•er
Gor•gon•zo•la cheese
go•ril•la ape; *cf* guerrilla
gori•ly
gori•ness
gor•mand *variant spelling of* gourmand
gor•man•dize eat

greedily; *cf* gourmandise
gor•man•diz•er
gorse
gory (gori•er, gori•est)
gosh
gos•hawk
gos•ling
Gos•pel New Testament book
gos•pel truth; doctrine
gos•pel•er (*Brit* •pel•ler)
gos•sa•mer
gos•sip (•sip•ing, •siped *or* •sip•ping, •sipped)
gos•sip•er
gossip•monger
gos•sipy
got
got•ten
gouache
gouge
goug•er
gou•lash
gourd
gour•mand (*or* gor•) greedy person; *cf*
gourmet
gour•man•dise love of food; *cf*
gormandize
gour•mand•ism
gour•met epicure; *cf* gourmand

gout
gouti•ness
gouty
gov•ern
gov•ern•abil•ity (or •able•ness)
gov•ern•able
gov•ern•ance
gov•er•ness
gov•ern•ment
gov•ern•men•tal
gov•er•nor
gov•er•nor•ship
gown
goy (pl goys or goy•im)
grab (grab•bing, grabbed)
grab•ber
grace
grace•ful
grace•ful•ly
grace•ful•ness
grace•less
gra•cious
gra•cious•ly
gra•cious•ness
grack•le
gra•date
gra•da•tion
gra•da•tion•al
grade
grad•er
gra•di•ent
grad•ual
gradu•al•ism
gradu•al•ist
gradu•al•is•tic
gradu•al•ly

gradu•al•ness
gradu•ate
gradua•tion
gradua•tor
graf•fi•tist
graf•fi•to (pl •ti)
graft
graft•er
graft•ing
grain
grain•er
graini•ness
grain•ing
grainy (graini•er, graini•est)
gram (Brit also gramme)
gram•mar
gram•mar•ian
gram•mati•cal
gram•mati•cal•ly
gramme variant Brit spelling of gram
gramo•phone (Brit) phonograph
gram•pus (pl •puses)
grana•dil•la
gra•na•ry (pl •ries)
grand
grand•aunt variant of great-aunt
grand•child (pl •children)
grand•dad
grand•daughter
gran•dee
gran•deur

grand•father
gran•dilo•quence
gran•dilo•quent
grand•di•ose
gran•di•ose•ly
gran•di•os•ity
grand•ma (or •mama, •mam•ma)
grand•mother
grand•mother•ly
grand•nephew variant of great-nephew
grand•niece variant of great-niece
grand•pa
grand•parent
grand•son
grand•stand
grand•uncle variant of great-uncle
grange
gran•ite
gra•nit•ic (or gran•it•oid)
gran•ny (or •nie; pl •nies)
gra•no•la
grant
grant•able
grantee
grant•er one who grants
grant•or legal term
granu•lar
granu•lar•ity
granu•late
granu•la•tion

gran•ule

granu•lo•ma (*pl* •mas *or* •ma•ta)

granu•loma•tous

grape

grape•fruit (*pl* •fruit *or* •fruits)

grape•shot

grape•vine

grap•ey (*or* grapy)

graph

graph•ic (*or* graphi•cal)

graphi•cal•ly

graph•ic•ness

graph•ics

graph•ite

gra•phit•ic

gra•pholo•gist

gra•phol•ogy

grap•nel

grap•ple

grap•pler

grapy *variant spelling of* grapey

grasp

grasp•able

grasp•er

grasp•ing

grass

grass•hopper

grassi•ness

grass•land

grass•quit

grassy (grassi•er, grassi•est)

grate framework; to rub; *cf* great

grate•ful

grate•ful•ly

grate•ful•ness

grat•er grating implement; *cf* greater

grati•fi•ca•tion

grati•fi•er

grati•fy (•fies, •fy•ing, •fied)

grati•fy•ing•ly

gra•tin

grat•ing

grat•ing•ly

gra•tis

grati•tude

gra•tui•tous

gra•tui•tous•ly

gra•tu•ity (*pl* •ities)

grave

grave ac•cent

grav•el (•el•ing, •eled; *Brit* •el•ling, •elled)

grav•el•ly

grav•en

grave•ly

grave•ness

graves

grave•stone

grave•yard

grav•id

gravi•tate

gravi•ta•tion

gravi•ta•tion•al

gravi•ta•tion•al•ly

grav•ity (*pl* •ities)

gra•vy (*pl* •vies)

gray (*Brit* grey)

gray•back (*Brit* grey•)

gray•beard (*Brit* grey•)

gray•hound *variant spelling of* greyhound

gray•ish (*Brit* grey•)

gray•lag (*Brit* grey•)

gray•ling (*pl* •ling *or* •lings)

gray•ness (*Brit* grey•)

graze

graz•er

graz•ing

grease

grease•paint

greas•er

grease•wood

greasi•ly

greasi•ness

greasy (greasi•er, greasi•est)

great large; *cf* grate

great-aunt (*or* grand•)

great•coat

great•er larger; *cf* grater

great•est

great-grand•child (*pl* •children)

great-grand• daughter

great-grand•father

great-grand•mother
great-grand•parent
great-grand•son
great•ly
great-nephew (*or* grand•)
great•ness
great-niece (*or* grand•)
great-uncle (*or* grand•)
grebe (*pl* grebe *or* grebes)
Gre•cian
greed
greedi•ly
greedi•ness
greedy (greedi•er, greedi•est)
Greek
green
green•back
green•bottle
green•brier
green•ery (*pl* •eries)
green-eyed
green•fly (*pl* •flies)
green•gage
green•heart
green•horn
green•house
green•ing
green•ish
green•ling
green•mail
green•ness
green•room

green•stick frac•ture
green•stuff
greet
greet•er
greet•ing
gre•gari•ous
gre•gari•ous•ness
grem•lin
gre•nade
grena•dier
grew
grey *Brit spelling of* gray
grey•back *Brit spelling of* grayback
grey•beard *Brit spelling of* graybeard
grey•hound (*or* gray•)
grey•lag *Brit spelling of* graylag
grid (grid•ding, grid•ded)
grid•dle
grid•iron
grief
griev•ance
grieve
griev•er
griev•ing
griev•ous
griev•ous•ly
grif•fin (*or* grif•fon, gryph•on) winged monster

grif•fon dog; vulture
grill broil; cross-examine; gridiron
grille (*or* grill) metal screen
grilled
grill•er
grill•room
grim (grim•mer, grim•mest)
gri•mace
gri•mac•er
gri•mac•ing•ly
grime
grim•ly
grim•ness
grimy (grim•ier, grim•iest)
grin (grin•ning, grinned)
grind (grind•ing, ground)
grin•delia
grind•er
grind•stone
grin•go (*pl* •gos)
grin•ner
grip (grip•ping, gripped)
gripe
grip•er complainer; *cf* gripper
grip•ing•ly
grip•per one that grips; *cf* griper
grip•ping
grip•ping•ly

gris•li•ness

gris•ly (•li•er,
•li•est) gruesome;
cf gristly; grizzly

grist

gris•tle

gris•tli•ness

gris•tly having
gristle; *cf* grisly;
grizzly

grist•mill

grit (grit•ting,
grit•ted)

grits

grit•ti•ly

grit•ti•ness

grit•ty (•ti•er,
•ti•est)

griz•zle

griz•zled

griz•zler

griz•zly (*adj* •zli•er,
•zli•est; *n, pl*
•zlies) gray-
haired; bear; *cf*
grisly; gristly

groan complain;
noise; *cf* grown

groan•er

groat old coin

groats crushed
grain

gro•cer

gro•cery (*pl*
•ceries)

grog

grog•gi•ly

grog•gi•ness

grog•gy (•gi•er,
•gi•est)

groin abdominal
region; vault

groin (*Brit* groyne)
jetty

grom•met (*or*
grum•)

groom

groom•er

groom•ing

grooms•man (*pl*
•men)

groove

groovy (groovi•er,
groovi•est)

grope

grop•er

gros•beak

gros•grain

gross

gross•ly

gross•ness

gro•tesque

gro•tesque•ly

gro•tesque•ness

grot•to (*pl* •toes *or*
•tos)

grouch

grouchi•ly

grouchi•ness

grouchy
(grouch•ier,
grouch•iest)

ground

ground•hog

ground•ing

ground•less

ground•ling

ground•nut

ground•sel

ground•sheet

grounds•keeper

ground•speed

ground•work

group

group•er (*pl* •er *or*
•ers)

groupie

group•ing

grouse (*pl* grouse
or grouses) bird

grouse complaint;
complain

grous•er

grout

grove

grov•el (•el•ing,
•eled; *Brit* •el•ling,
•elled)

grov•el•er (*Brit*
•el•ler)

grov•el•ing•ly (*Brit*
•el•ling•ly)

grow (grow•ing,
grew, grown)

grow•able

grow•er

growl

growl•er

grown developed;
cf groan

grown-up

growth

groyne *Brit spelling*
of groin (jetty)

grub (grub•bing,
grubbed)

grub•ber
grub•bi•ly
grub•bi•ness
grub•by
  (grub•bi•er,
  grub•bi•est)
grub•stake
grudge
grudg•er
grudg•ing
grudg•ing•ly
gru•el
gru•el•ing (*Brit*
  •el•ling)
grue•some
gruff
gruff•ly
gruff•ness
gru•gru
grum•ble
grum•bler
grum•bling•ly
grum•bly
grum•met *variant*
  spelling of
  grommet
grump
grumpi•ly (*or*
  grump•ish•ly)
grumpi•ness (*or*
  grump•ish•ness)
grumpy (*or*
  grump•ish;
  grumpi•er,
  grumpi•est)
grun•ion
grunt
grunt•er
Gru•yère cheese

gryph•on *variant*
  spelling of griffin
gua•ca•mo•le (*or*
  •cha•)
gua•co (*pl* •cos)
guage incorrect
  spelling of gauge
guaia•cum (*or*
  guaio•)
guan
gua•na•co (*pl* •cos
  or •co)
gua•no (*pl* •nos)
guar•an•tee
  (•tee•ing, •teed)
  promise; *cf*
  guaranty
guar•an•tor
guar•an•ty (*pl*
  •ties) legal term;
  cf guarantee
guard
guard•able
guard•ed
guard•ed•ly
guard•ed•ness
guard•er
guard•house
guard•ian
guard•ian•ship
guard•rail
guard•room
guards•man (*pl*
  •men)
gua•va
gua•yu•le
gu•ber•na•to•rial
gudg•eon
guern•sey

guer•ril•la (*or*
  gue•ril•la) fighter;
  cf gorilla
guer•ril•la•ism (*or*
  gue•)
guess
guess•able
guess•er
guess•ti•mate
guess•work
guest
guest•house
guff
guf•faw
guid•able
guid•ance
guide
guide•book
guide•line
guide•post
guid•er
guid•ing
guild (*or* gild)
  organization; *cf*
  gild
guil•der (*or* gild•er,
  gul•den; *pl* •ders,
  •der *or* •dens,
  •den) currency; *cf*
  gilder
guile
guile•ful
guile•ful•ly
guile•ful•ness
guile•less
guil•lemot
guil•lo•tine
guilt guiltiness;
  remorse; *cf* gilt

guilti•ly
guilti•ness
guilt•less
guilty (guilti•er,
  guilti•est)
guinea
guinea pig
guise
gui•tar
guitar•fish (pl •fish
  or •fishes)
gui•tar•ist
gulch
gul•den variant of
  guilder
gulf
gulf•weed
gull
gul•let
gul•li•bil•ity (or
  •la•)
gul•lible (or •lable)
gul•libly (or •lably)
gull-wing (adj)
gul•ly (n, pl •lies;
  vb •lies, •ly•ing,
  •lied)
gulp
gulp•er
gum (gum•ming,
  gummed)
gum•bo (or gom•;
  pl •bos)
gum•boil
gum•drop
gum•mi•ly
gum•mi•ness
gum•my (•mi•er,
  •mi•est)

gum•shoe
gun (gun•ning,
  gunned)
gun•boat
gun•cotton
gun•fight
gun•fighter
gun•fire
gun•flint
gun•man (pl •men)
gun•metal
gunned
gun•nel fish;
  variant spelling of
  gunwale
gun•ner
gun•nery
gun•ning
gun•ny (pl •nies)
gun•play
gun•point
gun•powder
gun•runner
gun•running
gun•shot
gun-shy
gun•slinger
gun•smith
gun•smithing
gun•wale (or •nel)
  nautical term; cf
  gunnel
gup•py (pl •pies)
gur•gle
gur•nard (pl •nard
  or •nards)
guru (pl gurus)
gush
gush•er

gush•ing•ly
gushy (gushi•er,
  gushi•est)
gus•sct
gust
gusti•ly
gusti•ness
gus•to (pl •toes)
gusty (gusti•er,
  gusti•est)
gut (gut•ting,
  gut•ted)
gut•bucket
gut•less
gutsy (gutsi•er,
  gutsi•est)
gutta-percha
gut•ted
gut•ter
gut•ter•ing
gutter•snipe
gut•ting
gut•tur•al
gut•tur•al•ly
gut•tur•al•ness (or
  •ity, •ism)
guy
guz•zle
guz•zler
gybe (or jibe)
  nautical term; cf
  gibe
gym
gym•na•sium (pl
  •siums or •sia)
gym•nast
gym•nas•tic
gym•nas•ti•cal•ly
gym•nas•tics

gy•ne•co•logi•cal (or •log•ic; *Brit* •nae•)
gy•ne•colo•gist (*Brit* •nae•)
gy•ne•col•ogy (*Brit* •nae•)
gyp•sophi•la
gyp•sum
gyp•sy (or gip•; *pl* •sies)
gy•rate
gy•ra•tion
gy•ra•tor
gy•ra•tory
gyr•fal•con (or ger•)
gyro (*pl* gyros)
gy•ro•com•pass
gy•ro•scope
gy•ro•scop•ic
gy•ro•sta•bi•liz•er
gy•ro•stat

H

ha (or hah)
ha•beas cor•pus
hab•er•dash•er
hab•er•dash•ery (*pl* •eries)
ha•bili•tate
ha•bili•ta•tion
hab•it
hab•it•abil•ity (or •able•ness)
hab•it•able
hab•it•ably

hab•it•ant
habi•tat
habi•ta•tion
hab•it•ed
habit-forming
ha•bitu•al
ha•bitu•al•ly
ha•bitu•al•ness
ha•bitu•ate
ha•bitua•tion
ha•bitué (or •bitue)
haci•en•da
hack
hacka•more
hack•berry (*pl* •berries)
hack•er
hack•ing
hack•le
hack•les
hack•ney
hack•neyed
hack•saw
hack•work
had
had•dock
hadj *variant spelling of* hajj
hadj•i *variant spelling of* hajji
hadn't
haema• (or haemo•) *Brit equivalents of the prefixes* hema• *or* hemo•
haft
hag

hag•fish (*pl* •fish or •fishes)
Hag•ga•dah (or •da; *pl* •dahs, •das, or •doth)
hag•gard
hag•gard•ness
hag•gis
hag•gish
hag•gle
hag•gler
hagi•og•ra•pher (or •phist)
hagio•graph•ic (or •graphi•cal)
hagi•og•ra•phy (*pl* •phies)
hagio•log•ic (or •logi•cal)
hagi•olo•gist
hagi•ol•ogy (*pl* •ogies)
hag•ridden
hah *variant spelling of* ha
ha-ha (or haw-haw)
Hai•da (*pl* •da or •das)
hai•ku (or hok•ku; *pl* •ku)
hail frozen rain; greet; *cf* hale
hail•er
hail•stone
hail•storm
hair threadlike growth; *cf* hare
hair•ball
hair•brained

hair•brush
hair•cloth
hair•cut
hair•do (*pl* •dos)
hair•dresser
hair•dressing
hairi•ness
hair•less
hair•like
hair•line
hair•net
hair•piece
hair•pin
hair-raising
hairs•breadth (or
  hair's-, hair•)
hair•splitter
hair•splitting
hair•spring
hair•style
hair•stylist
hair•weaving
hair•worm
hairy (hairi•er,
  hairi•est)
hajj (or hadj; *pl*
  hajjes or hadjes)
haj•ji (or hadji,
  haji)
hake (*pl* hake or
  hakes)
ha•kim (or •keem)
ha•la•vah *variant*
  of halvah
hal•berd (or •bert)
hal•cy•on
hale healthy; to
  haul; *cf* hail
half (*pl* halves)

half-and-half
half•back
half-breed
half-baked
half-caste
half-day
half•hearted
half•hearted•ly
half•hearted•ness
half-hour
half-hourly
half-life
half-light
half-mast
half-moon
half-naked
half-open
half-price
half-shut
half-timbered (or
  -timber)
half-time (*adj*)
half•tone
half-truth
half•way
half-wit
half-witted
half-witted•ly
half-witted•ness
half-yearly
hali•but (*pl* •but or
  •buts)
hal•ide
hali•to•sis
hall
hal•le•lu•jah
  variant of alleluia
hal•liard *variant*
  spelling of halyard

hall•mark
hal•lo *variant*
  spelling of halloo
  or hello
hal•loo (or •lo; *n, pl*
  •loos or •los; *vb*
  •loos, •loo•ing,
  •looed; *or* •los,
  •lo•ing, •loed)
  shout; *cf* hello
hal•low
hal•lowed
hal•lowed•ness
Hal•low•e'en (or
  Hal•low•een)
hal•lu•ci•nate
hal•lu•ci•na•tion
hal•lu•ci•na•tor
hal•lu•ci•na•tory
hal•lu•cino•gen
hal•lu•ci•no•gen•ic
hall•way
halm *variant*
  spelling of haulm
halo (*n, pl* halos or
  haloes; *vb* haloes
  or halos, halo•ing,
  haloed)
halo•gen
halt
hal•ter
halt•ing
halt•ing•ly
hal•vah (or hal•va,
  ha•la•vah)
halve
hal•yard (or
  hal•liard)

ham (ham•ming, hammed)
ham•burg•er
ham•let
ham•mer
ham•mer•er
hammer•head
hammer•toe
ham•mock
ham•my (ham•mi•er, ham•mi•est)
ham•per
ham•per•er
ham•ster
ham•string (•string•ing, •strung)
hand
hand•bag
hand•ball
hand•ball•er
hand•barrow
hand•bell
hand•bill
hand•book
hand•breadth (or hands•)
hand•cart
hand•clasp
hand•craft
hand•cuff
hand-feed (-feed•ing, -fed)
hand•ful
hand•grip
hand•gun
hand•hold
handi•cap

(•cap•ping, •capped)
handi•cap•per
handi•craft
handi•crafts•man (pl •men)
handi•ly
handi•ness
handi•work
hand•ker•chief (NOT hanker-chief)
han•dle
han•dle•able
handle•bar
han•dled
han•dler
hand•less
han•dling
hand•made
hand•maid (or •maiden)
hand-me-down
hand•out
hand•pick
hand•picked
hand•rail
hand•saw
hand•set
hand•shake
hands-off (adj)
hand•some good-looking; cf hansom
hand•some•ly
hand•some•ness
hands-on (adj)
hand•spike
hand•spring

hand•stand
hand-to-hand
hand-to-mouth
hand•writing
hand•written
handy (handi•er, handi•est)
handy•man (pl •men)
hang (hang•ing, hung or hanged)
han•gar aircraft shed; cf hanger
hang•dog
hanged killed; cf hung
hang•er support; one that hangs; cf hangar
hanger-on (pl hangers-on or hanger-ons)
hang•man (pl •men)
hang•nail
hang•out
hang•over
hang-up (n)
hank
han•ker
*hankerchief incorrect spelling of handkerchief
han•ker•er
hanky (or han•key, han•kie; pl han•kies)
hanky-panky (or hankey-pankey)

han•som carriage;
  cf handsome
Ha•nuk•kah
hap•haz•ard
hap•haz•ard•ness
hap•less
hap•less•ness
hap•pen
hap•pen•ing
hap•pen•stance
hap•pi•ly
hap•pi•ness
hap•py (•pi•er,
  •pi•est)
happy-go-lucky
hara-kiri (*or* hari-
  kari)
ha•rangue
ha•rangu•er
ha•rass (*NOT*
  harrass)
ha•rass•er
ha•rass•ment
har•bin•ger
har•bor (*Brit*
  •bour)
har•bor•age (*Brit*
  •bour•)
har•bor•er (*Brit*
  •bour•)
har•bor•less (*Brit*
  •bour•)
hard
hard•back
hard-bitten
hard•board
hard-boiled
hard-core (*adj*)
hard•en

hard•ened
hard•en•er
hard•en•ing
hard•hack
hard•headed
hard•headed•ly
hard•headed•ness
hard•heads
hard•hearted
hard•hearted•ly
hard•hearted•ness
hard-hitting
har•di•hood
har•di•ly
har•di•ness
hard-lin•er
hard•ly
hard•ness
hard-nosed
hard•pan
hard-pressed
hard-shell
hard•ship
hard•tack
hard•top
hard•ware
hard-wearing
hard•wood
hard-working
har•dy (•di•er,
  •di•est)
hare animal; *cf*
  hair
hare•bell
hare•brained
hare•lip
hare•lipped
har•em
hari•cot

*hari•dan *incorrect*
  spelling of
  harridan
hari-kari *variant*
  spelling of hara-
  kiri
hark
hark•en *variant*
  spelling of
  hearken
har•lequin
har•lequin•ade
har•lot
har•lot•ry
harm
harm•er
harm•ful
harm•ful•ly
harm•ful•ness
harm•less
harm•less•ly
harm•less•ness
har•mon•ic
har•moni•ca
har•moni•cal•ly
har•mon•ics
har•mo•ni•ous
har•mo•ni•ous•ly
har•mo•nist
har•mo•nis•tic
har•mo•nium
har•mo•ni•za•tion
har•mo•nize
har•mo•niz•er
har•mo•ny (*pl*
  •nies)
har•ness
har•ness•er
harp

harp•er (*or* •ist)
har•poon
har•poon•er (*or* •eer)
harp•si•chord
harp•si•chord•ist
har•py (*pl* •pies)
*harrass *incorrect spelling of* harass
har•ri•dan (*NOT* haridan)
har•ri•er
har•row
har•row•er
har•row•ing
har•ry (•ries, •ry•ing, •ried)
harsh
harsh•ly
harsh•ness
hart (*pl* hart *or* harts) male deer; *cf* heart
harum-scarum
har•vest
har•vest•er
har•vest•ing
harvest•man (*pl* •men)
has
has-been (*n*)
hash
hash•ish
Ha•sid (*or* Has•sid, Chas•sid, Cha•sid; *pl* •si•dim)
Ha•sid•ic (*or* Has•sid•ic,

Chas•sid•ic, Cha•sid•ic)
Has•id•ism (*or* Has•sid•ism, Chas•sid•ism, Cha•sid•ism)
hasn't
hasp
has•sle
has•sock *kneeling cushion; cf* cassock
haste
has•ten
hasti•ly
hasti•ness
has•ty (•ti•er, •ti•est)
hat (hat•ting, hat•ted)
hat•able *variant spelling of* hateable
hat•band
hat•box
hatch
hatch•back
hatch•er
hatch•ery (*pl* •eries)
hatch•et
hatch•ing
hatch•way
hate
hate•able (*or* hat•)
hate•ful
hate•ful•ly
hate•ful•ness
hater

hat•less
hat•pin
ha•tred
hat•ter
haugh•ti•ly
haugh•ti•ness
haugh•ty (•ti•er, •ti•est)
haul
haul•age
haul•er (*Brit* •ier)
haulm (*or* halm)
haunch
haunched
haunt
haunt•ed
haunt•er
haunt•ing
haute cou•ture
haute cui•sine
hau•teur
have (has, hav•ing, had)
ha•ven
have-not (*n*)
haven't
hav•er•sack
hav•ing
hav•oc (•ock•ing, •ocked)
haw
Ha•wai•ian
hawk
hawk•er
hawk-eyed
hawk•ing
hawk•ish
hawks•bill
hawk•weed

haw•ser
haw•thorn
hay dried grass; *cf*
  hey
hay•fork
hay•maker
hay•making
hay•mow
hay•rack
hay•rick
hay•seed
hay•stack
hay•wire
haz•ard
hazard-free
haz•ard•ous
haz•ard•ous•ness
haze
ha•zel
hazel•nut
ha•zi•ly
ha•zi•ness
hazy (ha•zi•er,
  ha•zi•est)
H-bomb
he
head
head•ache
head•achy
head•band
head•board
head-butt (*vb*)
head•cheese
head•count
head•dress
head•ed
head•er
head•first
head•gear

head-hunt
head•hunter
head•hunting
headi•ly
headi•ness
head•ing
head•land
head•less
head•light (*or*
  •lamp)
head•line
head•lin•er
head•lock
head•long
head•man (*pl*
  •men)
head•master (*fem*
  •mistress)
head•master•ship
  (*fem* •mistress•)
head-on
head•phones
head•piece
head•quarters
head•rest
head•room
head•sail
head•scarf (*pl*
  •scarves *or*
  •scarfs)
head•set
head•ship
head•stall
head•stand
head•stone
head•stream
head•strong
head•waiter

head•ward (*Brit*
  •wards)
head•waters
head•way
head•word
head•work
heady (headi•er,
  headi•est)
heal cure; *cf* heel
heal•able
heal•er
heal•ing•ly
health
health•ful
healthi•ly
healthi•ness
healthy (healthi•er,
  healthi•est)
heap
heap•ing
hear (hear•ing,
  heard) listen to; *cf*
  here
hear•able
heard listened to;
  cf herd
hear•er
hearing-impaired
hark•en (*or* hark•)
hear•say
hearse
heart bodily organ;
  cf hart
heart•ache
heart•beat
heart•break
heart•breaker
heart•breaking
heart•breaking•ly

heart•broken
heart•burn
heart•en
heart•en•ing
heart•felt
hearth
hearth•stone
hearti•ly
hearti•ness
heart•land
heart•less
heart•less•ly
heart•less•ness
heart•rending
hearts•ease
heart•sick
heart•sickness
heart•strings
heart•throb
heart-to-heart
heart•warming
heart•wood
hearty (heart•ier, hearti•est)
heat
heat•ed
heat•ed•ly
heat•er
heath
heath•berry (pl •berries)
hea•then (pl •thens or •then)
heath•er
heath•ery
heat•ing
heat•stroke
heave (heav•ing, heaved or hove)

heav•en
heav•en•li•ness
heav•en•ly
heaven-sent
heaven•ward (*adj*)
heaven•ward (*Brit* •wards; *adv*)
heavi•ly
heavi•ness
heavy (*adj* heavi•er, heavi•est; *n, pl* heavies)
heavy-duty
heavy-footed
heavy-handed
heavy-handed•ly
heavy-handed•ness
heavy-hearted
heavy•set
heavy•weight
heb•doma•dal (*or* •dary)
heb•etude
He•bra•ic (*or* •brai•cal)
He•brew
heck
heck•le
heck•ler
hect•are
hec•tic
hec•ti•cal•ly
hec•to•gram
hec•tor
he'd
hedge
hedge•hog
hedge•hop

(•hop•ping, •hopped)
hedge•hopper
hedg•er
hedge•row
hedgy
he•do•nism
he•do•nist
heebie-jeebies
heed
heed•ful
heed•ful•ly
heed•ful•ness
heed•less
heed•less•ly
heed•less•ness
heel part of foot; *cf* heal
heel•ball
heeled
heel•less
heft
hefti•ly
hefti•ness
hefty (hefti•er, hefti•est)
heg•emon•ic (*or* •emoni•cal)
he•gemo•ny
heif•er
height
height•en
hei•nous
hei•nous•ness
heir inheritor; *cf* air; e'er; ere
heir•dom
heir•ess
heir•loom

heir•ship
heist
heist•er
held
he•li•an•thus (pl •thuses)
heli•cal
heli•ces pl of helix
heli•chry•sum
heli•cop•ter
helio•cen•tric
helio•cen•tri•cal•ly
helio•cen•tric•ity (or helio•cen•tri•cism)
helio•graph
helio•trope
heli•port
he•lium
he•lix (pl heli•ces or he•lixes)
hell
he'll
hell•ben•der
hell-bent
hell•cat
hell-diver
hel•le•bore
hell•fire
hell•gram•mite
hell•hole
hell•hound
hel•lion
hell•ish
hell•ish•ly
hel•lo (or hal•lo, hul•lo; pl •los) greeting; cf halloo
helm

hel•met
hel•met•ed
hel•minth
hel•min•thic
helms•man (pl •men)
help
help•able
help•er
help•ful
help•ful•ly
help•ful•ness
help•ing
help•less
help•less•ly
help•less•ness
help•mate
helter-skelter
hem (hem•ming, hemmed)
he•mal (Brit hae•)
he-man (pl -men)
hema•tite (Brit haema•)
hema•tit•ic (Brit haema•)
hema•to•log•ic (or •logi•cal; Brit haema•)
hema•tolo•gist (Brit haema•)
hema•tol•ogy (Brit haema•)
hema•to•ma (Brit haema•; pl •mas or •mata)
hemi•plegia
hemi•ple•gic
he•mip•ter•ous

hemi•sphere
hemi•spher•ic (or •spheri•cal)
hem•line
hem•lock
hem•mer
hemo•di•aly•sis (Brit haemo•)
hemo•glo•bin (Brit haemo•)
he•moly•sis (Brit hae•; pl •ses)
hemo•lyt•ic (Brit haemo•)
hemo•phile (Brit haemo•)
hemo•philia (Brit haemo•)
hemo•phili•ac (Brit haemo•)
hemo•phil•ic (Brit haemo•)
hem•or•rhage (Brit haem•)
hem•or•rhag•ic (Brit haem•)
hem•or•rhoids (Brit haem•)
hem•or•rhoi•dal (Brit haem•)
hem•or•rhoid•ec•to•my (Brit haem•; pl •mies)
hemo•sta•sis (Brit haemo•)
hemo•stat•ic (Brit haemo•)
hemp
hemp•en

hem•stitch
hen
hence
hence•forth
hence•forward (or •forwards)
hench•man (pl •men)
hen•coop
hen•house
hen•na
hen•peck
hen•pecked
hen•ry (pl •ry, •ries, or •rys)
he•pat•ic
he•pat•i•ca
hepa•ti•tis
hep•ta•gon
hep•tago•nal
her
her•ald
he•ral•dic
her•ald•ry (pl •ries)
herb
her•ba•ceous
herb•age
herb•al
herb•al•ist
her•bar•ium (pl •iums or •baria)
her•bi•ci•dal
herbi•cide
her•bi•vore
her•bivo•rous
herby (herbi•er, herbi•est)
her•cu•lean

herd group; cf heard
herd•er
herds•man (pl •men)
here at this place; cf hear
here•abouts (or •about)
here•after
here•by
he•redi•tabil•ity
he•redi•table
he•redi•tary
he•red•ity (pl •ities)
here•in
here•in•after
here•in•to
here•of
here•on
her•esy (pl •esies)
her•etic
he•reti•cal
he•reti•cal•ly
here•to
here•to•fore
here•under
here•unto
here•upon
here•with
her•it•abil•ity
her•it•able
heri•tage
her•maph•ro•dite
her•maph•ro•dit•ic
her•maph•ro•dit•ism
her•meneu•tic

her•meneu•tics
her•met•ic air-tight; cf hermitic
her•meti•cal•ly
her•mit
her•mit•age
her•mit•ic hermitlike; cf hermetic
her•miti•cal•ly
her•mit•like
her•nia (pl •nias or •niae)
her•ni•at•ed
hero (pl heroes)
he•ro•ic
he•roi•cal•ly
he•ro•ics
hero•in drug
hero•ine heroic female
hero•ism
her•on
her•on•ry (pl •ries)
hero-worship (vb; -worship•ing, -worshiped; Brit -worship•ping, -worshipped)
her•pes
her•pes sim•plex
her•pes zos•ter
her•pet•ic
her•pe•tolo•gist
her•pe•tol•ogy
Herr (pl Her•ren)
her•ring (pl •ring or •rings)
herring•bone

hers
her•self
hertz (pl hertz)
hes more than one
  male
he's he is; he has
hesi•tan•cy
hesi•tant
hesi•tant•ly
hesi•tate
hesi•tat•er
hesi•tat•ing•ly
hesi•ta•tion
hes•sian
hetero•dox
hetero•doxy (pl
  •doxies)
hetero•dyne
hetero•geneity
hetero•ge•neous of
  different parts
heter•oge•nous of
  different origin
hetero•sex•ism
hetero•sex•ual
hetero•sexu•al•ity
hetero•sex•ual•ly
heu•ris•tic
heu•ris•ti•cal•ly
hew (hew•ing,
  hewed, hewed or
  hewn) cut; cf hue
hew•er
hex
hexa•gon
hex•ago•nal
hex•ago•nal•ly
hexa•gram
hex•am•eter

hey exclamation;
  cf hay
hey•day
hi hello; cf hie;
  high
hia•tus (pl •tuses
  or •tus)
hi•ber•nate
hi•ber•na•tion
hi•ber•na•tor
hi•bis•cus
hic•cup (or •cough;
  •cup•ing, •cuped,
  •cup•ping,
  •cupped, or
  •cough•ing,
  •coughed)
hick
hick•ey (or hicky;
  pl •eys or hickies)
hicko•ry (pl •ries)
hid
hid•able
hid•den
hide (hid•ing, hid,
  hid•den or hid)
hide-and-seek (or
  -and-go-seek)
hide•away
hide•bound
hid•eous
hid•eous•ly
hid•eous•ness (or
  hid•eos•ity)
hide•out
hid•er
hid•ing
hie (hie•ing or

hy•ing, hied)
hurry; cf hi; high
hi•er•arch
hi•er•ar•chal
hi•er•ar•chi•cal (or
  hi•er•ar•chic)
hi•er•ar•chi•cal•ly
hi•er•ar•chism
hi•er•ar•chy (pl
  •chies)
hi•ero•glyph
hi•ero•glyph•ic
hi•ero•glyph•ics
hi•ero•glyph•ist
hi•fa•lu•tin variant
  spelling of
  highfalutin
hi-fi
higgledy-piggledy
high tall; cf hi; hie
high•ball
high•bind•er
high•born
high•boy
high•bred
high•brow
high-class
high•fa•lu•tin (or
  hi•)
high-fidelity (adj)
high-flier (or
  •flyer)
high-flying
high-flown
high-grade (adj)
high-handed
high-handed•ly
high-handed•ness
high-hat (vb;

-hat•ting,
-hat•ted)
high•land
high•land•er
inhabitant of
highland
Highland•er
inhabitant of
Scottish
Highlands
high-level (*adj*)
high•life
high•light
high•ly
high-minded
high-minded•ness
high•ness high
condition
High•ness title for
royalty
high-octane
high-pitched
high-powered (*or*
-power)
high-pressure (*adj*;
vb)
high-rise
high-risk
high•road (*Brit*)
highway
high-school (*adj*)
high-spirited
high-spirited•ness
high-strung (*Brit*
highly strung)
high•tail
high-tech (*or* hi-)
high-tension (*adj*)
high-toned

high•way
highway•man (*pl*
•men)
hi•jack
hi•jack•er
hike
hik•er
hi•lari•ous
hi•lari•ous•ly
hi•lar•ity
hill
hill•bil•ly (*pl* •lies)
hill•fort
hill•ock
hill•ocked (*or*
•ocky)
hill•side
hilly (hilli•er,
hilli•est)
hilt
him that male
person; *cf* **hymn**
him•self
hind (*adj* hind•er,
hind•most *or*
hinder•most; *n*, *pl*
hinds *or* hind)
hin•der obstruct
hind•er at the rear
hin•der•er
Hin•di language; *cf*
Hindu
hind•most (*or*
hinder•most)
hind•quarter
hin•drance
hind•sight
Hin•du (*or* •doo; *pl*

•dus *or* •doos)
people; *cf* **Hindi**
Hin•du•ism
hinge
hin•ny (*n*, *pl* •nies;
vb •nies, •ny•ing,
•nied)
hint
hint•er
hinter•land
hip (hip•ping,
hipped)
hip•bone
hip•pie (*or* •py; *pl*
•pies)
hip•po (*pl* •pos)
hippo•drome
hippo•pota•mus (*pl*
•muses *or* •mi)
hip•py *variant
spelling of* **hippie**
hir•able (*or* hire•)
hire
hire•ling
hir•er
hir•sute
hir•sute•ness
his
His•pan•ic
hiss
hiss•er
his•ta•mine
his•to•gram
his•to•logi•cal (*or*
•log•ic)
his•tolo•gist
his•tol•ogy
his•to•rian

his•tor•ic famous; important

his•tori•cal concerned with history

his•tori•cal•ly

his•tori•cism

his•tori•cist

his•to•ric•ity

his•to•ri•og•ra•pher

his•to•rio•graph•ic

his•to•ri•og•ra•phy

his•to•ry (pl •ries)

his•tri•on•ic (or •oni•cal)

his•tri•oni•cal•ly

his•tri•on•ics

hit (hit•ting, hit)

hit-and-run (adj)

hitch

hitch•er

hitch•hike

hitch•hik•er

hi-tech variant spelling of **high-tech**

hith•er

hither•to

hit-or-miss (adj)

hit•ter

hive bee colony

hives skin condition

ho exclamation; cf **hoe**

ho•act•zin variant spelling of **hoatzin**

hoar

hoard store; cf **horde**

hoard•er

hoard•ing

hoar•frost

hoari•ly

hoari•ness

hoarse grating; cf **horse**

hoarse•ly

hoars•en

hoarse•ness

hoary (hoari•er, hoari•est)

ho•at•zin (or •act•; pl •zins or •zi•nes)

hoax

hoax•er

hob (hob•bing, hobbed)

hob•ble

hob•bler

hob•by (pl •bies)

hobby•horse

hob•by•ist

hob•goblin

hob•nail

hob•nailed

hob•nob (•nob•bing, •nobbed)

hobo (pl hoboes or hobos)

hock

hock•ey

hocus-pocus (-pocus•ing, -pocused or

-pocus•sing, -pocussed)

hod (hod•ding, hod•ded)

hodge•podge (Brit **hotch•potch**) mixture; cf **hotchpotch**

hoe (hoe•ing, hoed) gardening tool; to weed; cf **ho**

hoe•down

hoer

hog (hog•ging, hogged)

ho•gan

hog•back

hog•fish (pl •fish or •fishes)

hogged

hog•ger

hog•ging

hog•gish

hog•gish•ly

hog•gish•ness

hog•nose

hog•nut

hogs•head

hog-tie (-tying, -tied)

hog•wash

hog•weed

hoick

hoi pol•loi

hoist

hoist•er

hoity-toity

hok•ku variant spelling of **haiku**

ho•kum
hold (hold•ing, held)
hold•able
hold•er
hold•fast
hold•ing
hold•over
hold•up
hole cavity; *cf* whole
holey having holes; *cf* holy; wholly
holi•day
holier-than-thou
ho•li•ly
Ho•li•ness pope's title
ho•li•ness holy state
ho•lism
ho•lis•tic
ho•lis•ti•cal•ly
hol•lan•daise sauce
hol•ler
hol•low
hollow-eyed
hol•low•ly
hol•low•ness
hol•ly (*pl* •lies)
hol•ly•hock
holo•caust
holo•caus•tal (or •caus•tic)
holo•gram three-dimensional image
holo•graph

handwritten document
holo•graph•ic
ho•log•ra•phy
hol•ster
hol•stered
holy (*adj* ho•li•er, ho•li•est; *n, pl* holies) saintly; sacred; *cf* holey; wholly
hom•age
hom•bre
hom•burg
home
home•body
home•boy
home•bred
home•brew
home•coming
home•grown
home•land
home•less
home•less•ness
home•li•ness
home•ly (•li•er, •li•est) ugly; (*Brit*) unpretentious; *cf* homy
home•made
home•making
homeo•path•ic
homeo•pathi•cal•ly
homeopa•thist
homeopa•thy
home•owner
hom•er
home•sick
home•sick•ness

home•spun
home•stead
home•stead•er
home•stretch
home•ward (*adj*)
home•ward (*Brit* •wards; *adv*)
home•work
homey *variant spelling of* homy
homey•ness *variant spelling of* hominess
homi•ci•dal
homi•ci•dal•ly
homi•cide
homi•let•ic (*or* •leti•cal)
homi•list
homi•ly (*pl* •lies)
homi•ness (*or* homey•ness)
hom•ing
homi•nid
homi•noid
homi•ny
hom•mos *variant of* hummus
homoeo• *variant Brit spelling of words beginning* homeo•
homo•erotic
homo•eroti•cism (*or* •ero•tism)
homo•genei•ty
homo•ge•neous uniform; *cf* homogenous

homo•ge•neous•ly
ho•mog•eni•za•tion
ho•mog•enize
ho•mog•eniz•er
ho•mog•enous
similar through
common
ancestry; *cf*
homogeneous
ho•mog•eny
homo•graph
homo•graph•ic
homo•log *variant*
spelling of
homologue
ho•molo•gize
ho•molo•giz•er
ho•molo•gous
homo•logue (*or*
•log)
ho•mol•ogy (*pl*
•ogies)
homo•nym
homo•nym•ic
homo•phobe
homo•pho•bia
homo•pho•bic
homo•phone
homo•phon•ic
Homo sa•pi•ens
homo•sex•ual
homo•sexu•al•ity
homo•sex•ual•ly
ho•mun•cu•lus (*pl*
•li)
homy (*or* homey;
homi•er, homi•est)
cosy; *cf* homely
hon•cho (*n, pl*

•chos; *vb* •chos,
•cho•ing, •choed)
Hon•du•ran
hone
hon•est
hon•est•ly
hon•es•ty (*pl* •ties)
hon•ey
honey•bee
honey•bunch (*or*
•bun)
honey•comb
honey•dew
honey•eater
hon•eyed (*or* •ied)
honey•moon
honey•moon•er
honey•sucker
honey•suckle
hon•ied *variant*
spelling of
honeyed
honk
honk•er
hon•ky (*or* •key,
•kie; *pl* •kies)
honky-tonk
hon•or (*Brit* •our)
hon•or•able (*Brit*
•our•)
hon•or•able•ness
(*Brit* •our•)
hon•or•ably (*Brit*
•our•)
hono•rar•ium (*pl*
•rar•iums *or*
•raria)
hon•or•ary

hon•or•er (*Brit*
•our•)
hon•or•if•ic
hon•or•ifi•cal•ly
hon•our *Brit*
spelling of honor
hooch
hood
hood•ed
hood•like
hood•lum
hood•lum•ism
hoo•doo (*pl* •doos)
hoo•doo•ism
hood•wink
hood•wink•er
hoo•ey
hoof (*pl* hooves *or*
hoofs)
hoofed
hoof•er
hoo-ha
hook
hook•ah
hooked
hook•er
hook•nose
hook•nosed
hook•worm
hooky (*or* hookey)
hoo•li•gan
hoo•li•gan•ism
hoop circle; *cf*
whoop
hooped
hoop•la
hoo•rah (*or* •ray)
variants of hurrah
hoose•gow

hoot
hoot•en•an•ny (*or* hoot•nan•ny; *pl* •nies)
hoot•er
hooves
hop (hop•ping, hopped)
hope
hope•ful
hope•ful•ly
hope•ful•ness
hope•less
hope•less•ly
hope•less•ness
hop•er
Hopi (*pl* Hopi *or* Hopis)
hop•per
hop•ping
hop•scotch
horde mob; *cf* hoard
ho•ri•zon
hori•zon•tal
hori•zon•tal•ity (*or* •ness)
hori•zon•tal•ly
hor•mo•nal
hor•mone
horn
horn•beam
horn•bill
horn•blende
horn•book
horned
hor•net
horni•ly
horni•ness

horn•less
horn•pipe
horn-rimmed
horn•tail
horn•wort
horny (horni•er, horni•est)
horo•log•ic (*or* •logi•cal)
ho•rolo•gist (*or* •ger)
ho•rol•ogy
horo•scope
horo•scop•ic
ho•ros•co•py (*pl* •pies)
hor•ren•dous
hor•ren•dous•ly
hor•ri•ble
hor•ri•bly
hor•rid
hor•rid•ness
hor•rif•ic
hor•rlfi•cal•ly
hor•ri•fy (•fies, •fy•ing, •fied)
hor•ri•fy•ing•ly
hor•ripi•la•tion
hor•ror
horror-stricken (*or* -struck)
hors de com•bat
hors d'oeu•vre (*pl* hors d'oeu•vres *or* hors d'oeu•vre)
horse (*pl* horses *or* horse) animal; *cf* hoarse
horse•back

horse•flesh
horse•fly (*pl* •flies)
horse•hair
horse•hide
horse•leech
horse•less
horse•man (*pl* •men)
horse•man•ship
horse•play
horse•power (*pl* •power)
horse•radish
horse•shoe (•shoe•ing, •shoed)
horse•tail
horse•weed
horse•whip (•whip•ping, •whipped)
horse•whip•per
horse•woman (*pl* •women)
horsi•ness
horsy (*or* hors•ey; horsi•er, horsi•est)
hor•ti•cul•tur•al
hor•ti•cul•tur•al•ly
hor•ti•cul•ture
hor•ti•cul•tur•ist
ho•san•na (*or* •nah)
hose
ho•sier
ho•siery
hos•pice
hos•pi•table
hos•pi•tably
hos•pi•tal

hos•pi•tal•er (*Brit* •tal•ler)
hos•pi•tal•i•ty (*pl* •ities)
hos•pi•tali•za•tion
hos•pi•tal•ize
host
hos•ta
hos•tage
hos•tel lodging; *cf* hostile
hos•tel•er (*Brit* •tel•ler)
hos•tel•ing (*Brit* •tel•ling)
hos•tel•ry (*pl* •ries)
host•ess
hos•tile antagonistic; *cf* hostel
hos•tile•ly
hos•til•i•ty (*pl* •ities)
hot (*adj* hot•ter, hot•test; *vb* hot•ting, hot•ted)
hot•bed
hot-blooded
hot-blooded•ness
hotch•potch soup; *cf* hodgepodge
hot•dog (*vb*; •dog•ging, •dogged)
ho•tel
ho•tel•ier
hot•foot
hot•head
hot-headed

hot-headed•ly
hot-headed•ness
hot•house
hot•ly
hot•ness
hot•shot
hot-tempered
hot•tish
hot-wire (*adj*; *vb*)
hound
hound•er
hour time; *cf* our
hour•glass
hour•ri (*pl* •ris)
hour•ly
louse
house•boat
house•bound
house•boy
house•break•er
house•breaking
house•broken
house•coat
house•father
house•fly (*pl* •flies)
house•guest
house•hold
house•holder
house•husband
house•keeper
house•keeping
house•maid
house•man (*pl* •men)
house•master
house•mistress
house•mother
house•plant
house-proud

house•room
house•top
house•warming
house•wife (*pl* •wives)
house•wife•li•ness
house•wife•ly
house•wif•ery
house•work
house•worker
hous•ing
hous•to•nia
hove
hov•el (•el•ing, •eled; *Brit* •el•ling, •elled)
hov•er
hover•craft
hov•er•er
how
how•be•it
how•dah
how•dy
how•ever
how•it•zer
howl
howl•er
howl•ing
how•so•ever
hoy•den
hoy•den•ish
hub
hubble-bubble
hub•bub
hub•by (*pl* •bies)
hub•cap
hu•bris (*or* hy•)
hu•bris•tic
huck•le

huckle•berry (*pl*
 •berries)
huck•ster
hud•dle
hud•dler
hue color; outcry;
 cf hew
hued
huff
huffi•ly
huffi•ness
huffy (huffi•er,
 huffi•est)
hug (hug•ging,
 hugged)
huge
huge•ly
huge•ness
hug•gable
hug•ger
hugger-mugger
huh
hulk
hulk•ing
hull
hul•la•ba•loo (*or*
 •bal•loo; *pl* •loos)
hul•lo variant
 spelling of hello
hum (hum•ming,
 hummed)
hu•man
hu•mane
hu•mane•ly
hu•mane•ness
hu•man•ism
hu•man•ist
hu•man•ist•ic
hu•mani•tar•ian

hu•mani•tari•
 an•ism
hu•mani•tari•an•ist
hu•man•ity (*pl*
 •ities)
hu•mani•za•tion
hu•man•ize
hu•man•iz•er
human•kind
hu•man•ly
hu•man•ness
hu•man•oid
hum•ble
hum•ble•ness
hum•bler
hum•bling
hum•bly
hum•bug
 (•bug•ging,
 •bugged)
hum•bug•ger
hum•ding•er
hum•drum
hu•mer•al
hu•mer•us (*pl*
 •meri) arm bone;
 cf humorous
hu•mid
hu•midi•fi•ca•tion
hu•midi•fi•er
hu•midi•fy (•fies,
 •fy•ing, •fied)
hu•midi•stat
hu•mid•ity
hu•mid•ness
hu•mili•ate
hu•mili•at•ing•ly
hu•milia•tion
hu•milia•tor

hu•milia•tory
hu•mil•ity (*pl*
 •ities)
hummed
hum•mer
hum•ming
humming•bird
hum•mock
hum•mocky
hum•mus (*or*
 hom•mos) food; *cf*
 humus
hu•mor (*Brit*
 •mour)
hu•mor•ist
hu•mor•less (*Brit*
 •mour•)
hu•mor•less•ness
 (*Brit* •mour•)
hu•mor•ous funny;
 cf humerus
hu•mor•ous•ly
hu•mor•ous•ness
hu•mour *Brit*
 spelling of humor
hump
hump•back
hump•backed
humph
humpy (humpi•er,
 humpi•est)
hu•mus soil; *cf*
 hummus
hunch
hunch•back
hunch•backed
hun•dred (*pl* •dreds
 or •dred)
hun•dredth

hundred•weight (*pl* •weight *or* •weights)

hung suspended; *cf* hanged

Hun•gar•ian

hun•ger

hun•gri•ly

hun•gri•ness

hun•gry (•gri•er, •gri•est)

hunk

hunk•er

hunky-dory

hunt

hunt•ed

hunt•er

hunt•ing

hunts•man (*pl* •men)

hur•dle

hur•dler

hurdy-gurdy (*pl* -gurdies)

hurl

hurl•er

hurl•ing

hurly-burly (*pl* -burlies)

Hu•ron (*pl* •rons *or* •ron)

hur•rah (*or* •ray, hoo•ray, hoo•rah)

hur•ri•cane

hur•ried

hur•ried•ly

hur•ry (*vb* •ries, •ry•ing, •ried; *n, pl* •ries)

hurt (hurt•ing, hurt)

hur•ter

hurt•ful

hurt•ful•ly

hurt•ful•ness

hur•tle

hus•band

hus•band•less

hus•band•ry

hush

hush-hush

husk

huski•ly

huski•ness

husky (*adj* huski•er, huski•est; *n, pl* huskies)

hus•sar

hus•sy (*pl* •sies)

hus•tle

hus•tler

hut (hut•ting, hut•ted)

hutch

hutz•pah *variant spelling of* chutzpah

hya•cinth

hy•aena *variant spelling of* hyena

hy•brid

hy•brid•ism

hy•brid•ity

hy•brid•iz•able

hy•bridi•za•tion

hy•brid•ize

hy•brid•iz•er

hy•bris *variant spelling of* hubris

hy•dra (*pl* •dras *or* •drae)

hy•dran•gea

hy•drant

hy•dras•tis

hy•drate

hy•drat•ed

hy•dra•tion

hy•dra•tor

hy•drau•lic

hy•drau•li•cal•ly

hy•drau•lics

hy•dride

hy•dro (*pl* •dros)

hydro•car•bon

hydro•cephal•ic

hydro•cepha•lus (*or* •cephaly)

hydro•chlo•ric acid

hydro•chlo•ride

hydro•cor•ti•sone

hydro•dy•nam•ic

hydro•dy•nam•ics

hydro•elec•tric

hydro•elec•tric•ity

hydro•foil

hydro•gen

hydro•gen•ate

hydro•gena•tion

hydro•gena•tor

hydro•geni•za•tion

hydro•gen•ize

hy•drog•enous

hy•drog•ra•pher

hydro•graph•ic (*or* •graphi•cal)

hy•drog•ra•phy

hydro•log•ic (*or*
  •logi•cal)
hy•drolo•gist
hy•drol•ogy
hy•droly•sis
hydro•lyz•able
  (*Brit* •lys•)
hydro•ly•za•tion
  (*Brit* •sa•tion)
hydro•lyze (*Brit*
  •lyse)
hydro•lyz•er (*Brit*
  •lys•er)
hydro•mechani•cal
hydro•mechan•ics
hy•drom•eter
hydro•met•ric (*or*
  •met•ri•cal)
hy•drom•etry
hydro•path•ic (*or*
  •pathi•cal)
hy•dropa•thist (*or*
  hydro•path)
hy•dropa•thy
hydro•phil•ic
hydro•pho•bia
hydro•pho•bic
hydro•plane
hydro•pon•ic
hydro•pon•ics
hydro•pow•er
hydro•scope
hydro•sphere
hydro•stat
hydro•stat•ic
hydro•stat•ics
hydro•thera•peu•tic
hydro•thera•pist
hydro•thera•py

hy•drous
hy•drox•ide
hy•drox•yl
hy•ena (*or* •aena)
hy•giene
hy•gien•ic
hy•gieni•cal•ly
hy•gien•ics
hy•gien•ist
hygrom•eter
hygro•met•ric
hygrom•etry
hygro•scope
hygro•scop•ic
hyla
hy•men
hy•men•al
hy•menop•ter•an
  (*or* •on; *pl* •tera,
  •ter•ans, *or*
  •ter•ons)
hy•menop•ter•ous
hymn song; *cf* him
hym•nal
hym•nist (*or*
  hym•no•dist)
hym•nolo•gist
hym•nol•ogy
hyo•scine
hype
hy•per
hyper•ac•tive
hyper•ac•tiv•ity
hyper•bo•la (*pl*
  •las *or* •lae)
  geometric curve
hyper•bo•le
  exaggeration

hyper•bol•ic (*or*
  •boli•cal)
hyper•bo•lize
hyper•bo•rean
hyper•criti•cal
  overcritical; *cf*
  hypocritical
hyper•criti•cal•ly
hyper•criti•cism
hyper•gly•cemia
  (*Brit* •cae•mia)
hyper•gly•cemic
  (*Brit* •cae•mic)
hyper•icum
hyper•in•fla•tion
hyper•opia (*Brit*
  hyper•metro•pia)
hyper•op•ic
hyper•sen•si•tive
hyper•sen•si•tiv•ity
hyper•son•ic
hyper•ten•sion
hyper•ten•sive
hyper•text
hyper•ther•mla (*or*
  •ther•my)
hyper•thy•roid
hyper•thy•roid•ism
hyper•ton•ic
hyper•ven•ti•late
hyper•ven•ti•la•tion
hy•phen
hy•phen•ate
hy•phena•tion
hyp•no•sis (*pl* •ses)
hyp•no•thera•py
hyp•not•ic
hyp•noti•cal•ly
hyp•no•tism

hyp•no•tist
hyp•no•tize
hypo (*pl* hypos)
hypo•al•ler•gen•ic
hypo•chon•dria
hypo•chon•dri•ac
hypo•chon•dria•
    cal•ly
hy•poc•ri•sy (*pl*
    •sies)
hypo•crite
hypo•crit•i•cal
    insincere; *cf*
    hypercritical
hypo•criti•cal•ly
hypo•der•mic
hypo•gly•cemia
    (*Brit* •cae•mia)
hypo•gly•cemic
    (*Brit* •cae•mic)
hypo•ten•sion
hypo•ten•sive
hy•pot•enuse (*or*
    •poth•)
hypo•thala•mus (*pl*
    •mi)
hypo•ther•mia
hy•poth•esis (*pl*
    •eses)
hy•poth•esize
hypo•theti•cal
hypo•theti•cal•ly
hypo•thy•roid
hypo•thy•roid•ism
hypo•ton•ic
hy•poxia
hy•pox•ic
hys•sop

hys•ter•ec•to•my
    (*pl* •mies)
hys•te•re•sis
hys•te•ria
hys•ter•ic
hys•teri•cal
hys•teri•cal•ly
hys•ter•ics

I

I (*pl* I's *or* Is)
iamb (*or* iam•bus;
    pl iambs, iam•bi,
    or iam•buses)
iam•bic
ibex (*pl* ibexes,
    ibi•ces, *or* ibex)
    goat
ibis (*pl* ibises *or*
    ibis) bird
ice
ice•berg
ice•bound
ice•box
ice•breaker
ice•cap
ice cream
Ice•land•ic
ice-skate (*vb*)
ich•neu•mon
ich•thy•olo•gist
ich•thy•ol•ogy
ich•thyo•saur (*or*
    •sau•rus; *pl* •saurs,
    •sau•ruses, *or*
    •sau•ri)
ici•cle

ici•cled
ici•ly
ici•ness
ic•ing
icon (*or* ikon)
icon•ic
icono•clasm
icono•clast
icono•clas•tic
icono•clas•ti•cal•ly
ico•nog•ra•pher
ico•nog•ra•phy (*pl*
    •phies)
ico•sa•he•dral
ico•sa•he•dron (*pl*
    •drons *or* •dra)
icy (ici•er, ici•est)
I'd
id
idea
ideal
ideal•ism
ideal•ist
ideal•is•tic
ideal•is•ti•cal•ly
ideali•za•tion
ideal•ize
ideal•iz•er
ideal•ly
idée fixe (*pl* idées
    fixes)
iden•ti•cal
iden•ti•cal•ly
iden•ti•cal•ness
iden•ti•fi•able
iden•ti•fi•ca•tion
iden•ti•fi•er
iden•ti•fy (•fies,
    •fy•ing, •fied)

iden•tity (*pl* •tities)
ideo•gram (*or* •graph)
ideo•logi•cal (*or* •log•ic)
ideo•logi•cal•ly
ideolo•gist (*or* ideo•logue)
ideol•ogy (*pl* •ogies)
ides
idio•cy (*pl* •cies)
idi•om
idio•mat•ic (*or* •mati•cal)
idio•mati•cal•ly
idio•syn•cra•sy (*pl* •sies)
idio•syn•crat•ic
idio•syn•crati•cal•ly
idi•ot
idi•ot•ic
idi•oti•cal•ly
idle lazy; *cf* idol; idyll
idle•ness
idler
idly
idol image; *cf* idle; idyll
idola•ter (*fem* •tress)
idola•trize
idola•trous
idola•try (*pl* •tries)
idoli•za•tion
idol•ize
idol•iz•er

idyll (*or* idyl) poem; *cf* idle; idol
idyl•lic
idyl•li•cal•ly
if
ig•loo (*or* iglu; *pl* •loos *or* iglus)
ig•ne•ous
ig•nit•able (*or* •ible)
ig•nite
ig•nit•er (*or* •ni•tor)
ig•ni•tion
ig•no•bil•ity (*or* •ble•ness)
ig•no•ble
ig•no•bly
ig•no•mini•ous
ig•no•mini•ous•ly
ig•no•miny (*pl* •minies)
ig•nor•able
ig•no•ra•mus (*pl* •muses *or* •mi)
ig•no•rance
ig•no•rant
ig•nore
ig•nor•er
igua•na
iguano•don
ikon *variant spelling of* icon
ilang-ilang *variant spelling of* ylang-ylang
ile•ac (*or* •al) of ileum; *cf* iliac
ile•um (*pl* ilea)

small intestine; *cf* ilium
ilex
ili•ac of ilium; *cf* ileac
ili•um (*pl* ilia) pelvic bone; *cf* ileum
ilk
I'll
ill
ill-advised
ill-assorted
ill-bred
ill-breeding
ill-considered
ill-defined
ill-disposed
il•legal
il•legal•ity (*pl* •ities)
il•legali•za•tion
il•legal•ize
il•legal•ly
il•leg•ibil•ity (*or* •ible•ness)
il•leg•ible
il•leg•ibly
il•legiti•ma•cy (*or* •mate•ness)
il•legiti•mate
il•legiti•mate•ly
ill-fated
ill-favored (*Brit* -favoured)
ill-founded
ill-gotten
ill-humored (*Brit* -humoured)

il•lib•er•al
il•lib•er•al•ity (or
•ness, •ism)
il•lic•it illegal; cf
elicit
il•lim•it•abil•ity (or
•able•ness)
il•lim•it•able
il•lit•era•cy (pl
•cies)
il•lit•er•ate
ill-judged
ill-mannered
ill-natured
ill•ness
il•logi•cal
il•logi•cal•ity (or
•ness)
il•logi•cal•ly
ill-omened
ill-starred
ill-tempered
ill-timed
ill-treat
ill-treatment
il•lude deceive; cf
allude; elude
il•lu•mi•nate
il•lu•mi•na•tion
il•lu•mi•na•tive
il•lu•mi•na•tor
il•lu•mine
ill-use (vb)
ill-use (or -usage;
n)
il•lu•sion delusion;
cf allusion
il•lu•sion•ary (or
•al)

il•lu•sion•ism
il•lu•sion•ist
il•lu•sion•is•tic
il•lu•sive illusory;
cf allusive; elusive
il•lu•so•ri•ly
il•lu•so•ri•ness
il•lu•sory
il•lus•trat•able
il•lus•trate
il•lus•tra•tion
il•lus•tra•tive
il•lus•tra•tor
il•lus•tri•ous
I'm
*imaculate
incorrect spelling
of immaculate
im•age
im•age•ry (pl •ries)
im•agi•nable
im•agi•nably
im•agi•nari•ly
im•agi•nary
im•agi•na•tion
im•agi•na•tive
im•agi•na•tive•ly
im•agi•na•tive•ness
im•ag•ine
im•ag•in•er
ima•go (pl •goes or
•gi•nes)
imam (or imaum)
im•bal•ance
im•becile
im•becil•ity (pl
•ities)
im•bibe
im•bib•er

im•bi•bi•tion
im•bro•glio (pl
•glios)
im•bue (•bu•ing,
•bued)
*imigrate incorrect
spelling of
immigrate
imi•tabil•ity (or
•table•ness)
imi•table
imi•tate
imi•ta•tion
imi•ta•tive
imi•ta•tor
im•macu•la•cy (or
•late•ness)
im•macu•late
(NOT imaculate)
im•ma•nence (or
•nen•cy)
im•ma•nent
existing within; cf
eminent; imminent
im•ma•te•rial
im•ma•te•ri•al•ism
im•ma•te•ri•al•ist
im•ma•te•ri•al•ity
(or •ness)
im•ma•te•ri•al•ize
im•ma•ture
im•ma•tu•rity (or
•ture•ness)
im•mea•sur•abil•ity
(or •able•ness)
im•mea•sur•able
immense; cf
unmeasurable
im•mea•sur•ably

im•me•dia•cy (*or* •di•ate•ness)
im•me•di•ate
im•me•di•ate•ly
im•me•mo•rial
im•me•mo•ri•al•ly
im•mense
im•mense•ly
im•men•si•ty (*pl* •ties)
im•merse
im•mers•ible
im•mer•sion immersing; *cf* emersion
im•mi•grant
im•mi•grate (*NOT* imigrate) enter country; *cf* emigrate
im•mi•gra•tion
im•mi•gra•tory
im•mi•gra•tor
im•mi•nence
im•mi•nent impending; *cf* eminent; immanent
im•mi•nent•ly
im•mis•ci•bil•ity
im•mis•ci•ble
im•mis•ci•bly
im•mo•bile
im•mo•bil•ity
im•mo•bi•li•za•tion
im•mo•bi•lize
im•mo•bi•liz•er
im•mod•er•ate
im•mod•er•ate•ly

im•mod•era•tion (*or* •er•ate•ness)
im•mod•est
im•mod•es•ty
im•mo•late
im•mo•la•tion
im•mo•la•tor
im•mor•al morally bad; *cf* amoral
im•mor•al•ity (*pl* •ities)
im•mor•al•ly
im•mor•tal
im•mor•tal•ity
im•mor•tali•za•tion
im•mor•tal•ize
im•mor•tal•ly
im•mov•abil•ity (*or* •mov•able•ness)
im•mov•able (*or* •move•)
im•mov•ably
im•mune
im•mu•nity (*pl* •nities)
im•mu•ni•za•tion
im•mu•nize
im•mu•niz•er
im•mu•no•de•fi•cien•cy (*pl* •cies)
im•mu•no•log•ic (*or* •logi•cal)
im•mu•nolo•gist
im•mu•nol•ogy
im•mu•no•sup•pressed
im•mu•no•sup•pres•sion

im•mu•no•sup•pres•sive
im•mu•no•thera•py
im•mure
im•mu•tabil•ity (*or* •table•ness)
im•mu•table
im•mu•tably
imp
im•pact
im•pact•ed
im•pac•tion
im•pair
im•pair•ment
im•pa•la (*pl* •las *or* •la)
im•pale
im•pale•ment
im•pal•er
im•pal•pa•bil•ity
im•pal•pable
im•pal•pably
im•pan•el (*or* em•; •el•ing, •eled; *Brit* •el•ling, •elled)
im•part
im•part•er
im•par•tial
im•par•ti•al•ity (*or* •ness)
im•par•tial•ly
im•pass•abil•ity (*or* •able•ness)
im•pass•able impossible to cross; *cf* impassible
im•pass•ably
im•passe

im•pas•sible
  unfeeling; *cf*
  impassable
im•pas•sible•ness
im•pas•sibly
im•pas•sioned
im•pas•sive
im•pas•sive•ly
im•pas•sive•ness
  (*or* •siv•ity)
im•pa•tience lack
  of patience
im•pa•tiens (*pl*
  •tiens) plant
im•pa•tient
im•pa•tient•ly
im•peach
im•peach•abil•ity
im•peach•able
im•peach•er
im•peach•ment
im•pec•cabil•ity
im•pec•cable
im•pec•cably
im•pecu•nious
im•pecu•nious•ness
  (*or* •nios•ity)
im•ped•ance
  electrical
  resistance; *cf*
  impediment
im•pede
im•ped•er
im•pedi•ment
  hindrance; *cf*
  impedance
im•pedi•men•ta
im•pel (•pel•ling,
  •pelled)

im•pel•lent
im•pel•ler (*or* •lor)
im•pend
im•pend•ence (*or*
  •en•cy; *pl* •ences
  or •cies)
im•pend•ing
im•pen•etrabil•ity
im•pen•etrable
im•pen•etrably
im•peni•tence (*or*
  •ten•cy,
  •tent•ness)
im•peni•tent
im•pera•tive
im•per•cep•tibil•ity
  (*or* •tible•ness)
im•per•cep•tible
im•per•cep•tibly
im•per•cep•tion
im•per•cep•tive
im•per•cep•tiv•ity
  (*or* •tive•ness)
im•per•fect
im•per•fec•tion
im•per•fect•ly
im•per•fo•rate
im•pe•rial
im•pe•ri•al•ism
im•pe•ri•al•ist
im•pe•ri•al•is•tic
im•pe•ri•al•is•ti•
  cal•ly
im•pe•ri•al•ly
im•per•il (•il•ing,
  •iled; *Brit* •il•ling,
  •illed)
im•pe•ri•ous
im•pe•ri•ous•ly

im•pe•ri•ous•ness
im•per•ish•abil•ity
  (*or* •able•ness)
im•per•ish•able
im•per•ma•nence
  (*or* •nen•cy)
im•per•ma•nent
im•per•me•abil•ity
  (*or* •able•ness)
im•per•me•able
im•per•mis•sible
im•per•son•al
im•per•son•al•ity
im•per•son•al•ly
im•per•son•ate
im•per•sona•tion
im•per•sona•tor
im•per•ti•nence (*or*
  •nen•cy)
im•per•ti•nent
im•per•ti•nent•ly
im•per•turb•abil•
  ity (*or* •able•ness)
im•per•turb•able
im•per•turb•ably
im•per•vi•ous
im•peti•go
im•petu•os•ity (*or*
  •ous•ness)
im•petu•ous
im•petu•ous•ly
im•pe•tus (*pl*
  •tuses)
im•pi•ety (*pl* •eties)
im•pinge
im•pinge•ment
im•ping•er
im•pi•ous
imp•ish

im•plac•abil•ity (*or* •able•ness)
im•plac•able
im•plac•ably
im•plant
im•plan•ta•tion
im•plau•sibil•ity (*or* •sible•ness)
im•plau•sible
im•plau•sibly
im•ple•ment (*NOT* impliment)
im•ple•men•ta•tion
im•ple•ment•er (*or* •men•tor)
im•pli•cate
im•pli•ca•tion
im•plic•it
im•plic•it•ness (*or* •plic•ity)
im•plied
*impliment
incorrect spelling of implement
im•plode
im•plore
im•plor•ing•ly
im•plo•sion
im•ply (•plies, •ply•ing, •plied)
im•po•lite
im•po•lite•ly
im•po•lite•ness
im•poli•tic
im•poli•tic•ly
im•pon•der•abil•ity (*or* •able•ness)
im•pon•der•able
im•pon•der•ably

im•port
im•port•able
im•por•tance
im•por•tant
im•por•tant•ly
im•por•ta•tion
im•port•er
im•por•tu•nate
im•por•tune
im•por•tun•er
im•por•tu•nity (*pl* •nities)
im•pose
im•pos•er
im•pos•ing
im•pos•ing•ly
im•po•si•tion
im•pos•sibil•ity (*pl* •ities)
im•pos•sible
lm•pos•sibly
im•pos•tor (*or* •ter)
im•pos•ture
im•po•tence (*or* •ten•cy, •tent•ness)
im•po•tent
im•pound
im•pound•able
im•pound•age (*or* •ment)
im•pound•er
im•pov•er•ish
im•pov•er•ish•ment
im•prac•ti•cabil•ity (*or* •cable•ness)
im•prac•ti•cable
not feasible
im•prac•ti•cably

im•prac•ti•cal not practical
im•prac•ti•cal•ity (*or* •ness)
im•prac•ti•cal•ly
im•pre•cate
im•pre•ca•tion
im•pre•ca•tory
im•pre•cise
im•pre•cise•ly
im•pre•ci•sion (*or* •cise•ness)
im•preg•nabil•ity (*or* •nable•ness)
im•preg•nable (*or* im•preg•na•table)
im•preg•nate
im•preg•na•tion
im•preg•na•tor
im•pre•sa•rio (*pl* •rios)
im•press
im•press•er
im•press•ible
im•pres•sion
im•pres•sion•abil•ity (*or* •able•ness)
im•pres•sion•able
im•pres•sion•al
im•pres•sion•ism
im•pres•sion•ist
im•pres•sion•is•tic
im•pres•sive
im•pres•sive•ly
im•pres•sive•ness
im•pri•ma•tur
im•print
im•print•ing
im•pris•on

im•pris•on•ment
im•prob•a•bil•i•ty (*or*
•able•ness)
im•prob•a•ble
im•prob•a•bly
im•pro•bi•ty (*pl*
•bi•ties)
im•promp•tu
im•prop•er
im•prop•er•ly
im•pro•pri•e•ty (*pl*
•e•ties)
im•prov•a•ble
im•prove
im•prove•ment
im•prov•er
im•provi•dence
im•provi•dent
im•provi•sa•tion
im•provi•sa•tion•al
im•pro•vise
im•pro•vis•er (*or*
•vi•sor)
im•pru•dence
im•pru•dent
unwise; *cf*
impudent
im•pru•dent•ly
im•pu•dence (*or*
•den•cy)
im•pu•dent
impertinent; *cf*
imprudent
im•pu•dent•ly
im•pugn
im•pugn•a•ble
im•pugn•ment
im•pugn•er
im•pulse

im•pul•sion
im•pul•sive
im•pul•sive•ly
im•pul•sive•ness
im•pu•ni•ty (*pl*
•ni•ties)
im•pure
im•pu•ri•ty (*pl*
•ri•ties)
im•pu•ta•tion
im•pute
in within; *cf* inn
in•abil•i•ty (*pl*
•ities)
in ab•sen•tia
in•ac•ces•si•bil•i•ty
(*or* •sible•ness)
in•ac•ces•si•ble
in•ac•ces•si•bly
in•ac•cu•ra•cy (*pl*
•cies)
in•ac•cu•rate
in•ac•cu•rate•ly
in•ac•tion
in•ac•ti•vate
in•ac•ti•va•tion
in•ac•tive
in•ac•tiv•i•ty (*or*
•tive•ness)
in•ad•e•qua•cy (*pl*
•cies)
in•ad•e•quate
in•ad•e•quate•ly
in•ad•mis•si•bil•i•ty
in•ad•mis•si•ble
in•ad•mis•si•bly
in•ad•ver•tence (*or*
•ten•cy; *pl* •tences
or •cies)

in•ad•ver•tent
in•ad•ver•tent•ly
in•ad•vis•abil•i•ty
(*or* •able•ness)
in•ad•vis•able
in•ad•vis•ably
in•alien•abil•i•ty (*or*
•able•ness)
in•alien•able
in•alien•ably
in•amo•ra•ta (*masc*
•to; *pl* •tas *or* •tos)
in•ane
in•ane•ly
in•ani•mate
in•ani•mate•ness
(*or* •ma•tion)
ina•ni•tion
inan•i•ty (*pl* •ities)
in•ap•pli•cabil•i•ty
(*or* •cable•ness)
in•ap•pli•ca•ble
in•ap•po•site
in•ap•pre•cia•ble
in•ap•pre•cia•tive
in•ap•pro•pri•ate
in•ap•pro•pri•ate•ly
in•ap•pro•pri•ate•
ness
in•apt inappropri-
ate; *cf* inept
in•ap•ti•tude (*or*
•apt•ness)
in•ar•ticu•late
in•ar•ticu•late•ly
in•ar•tis•tic
in•ar•tis•ti•cal•ly
in•at•ten•tion (*or*
•tive•ness)

in•at•ten•tive
in•at•ten•tive•ly
in•audibil•ity (*or*
•audible•ness)
in•audible
in•audibly
in•augu•ral
in•augu•rate
in•augu•ra•tion
in•augu•ra•tor
in•aus•pi•cious
in-between (*adj, n*)
in•bound
in•born
in•bred
in•breed (•breed•
ing, •bred)
in•built
Inca (*pl* Inca *or*
Incas)
in•cal•cu•labil•ity
(*or* •lable•ness)
in•cal•cu•lable
In•cal•cu•lably
in cam•era (*adv,
adj*)
in•can•desce
in•can•des•cence
(*or* •cen•cy)
in•can•des•cent
in•can•ta•tion
in•ca•pabil•ity (*pl*
•ities)
in•ca•pable
in•ca•pably
in•ca•paci•tate
in•ca•paci•ta•tion
in•ca•pac•ity (*pl*
•ities)

in•car•cer•ate
in•car•cera•tion
in•car•cera•tor
in•car•nate
in•car•na•tion
in•case *variant
spelling of* encase
in•case•ment
variant spelling of
encasement
in•cau•tious
in•cau•tious•ness
(*or* •cau•tion)
in•cen•dia•rism
in•cen•di•ary (*pl*
•aries)
in•cense
in•cen•tive
in•cep•tion
in•cep•tive
in•ces•sant
in•ces•sant•ly
in•cest
in•ces•tu•ous
in•ces•tu•ous•ly
inch
in•cho•ate
in•choa•tion
in•ci•dence
in•ci•dent
in•ci•den•tal
in•ci•den•tal•ly
in•cin•er•ate
in•cin•era•tion
in•cin•era•tor
in•cipi•ence (*or*
•en•cy)
in•cipi•ent
in•cise

in•ci•sion
in•ci•sive
in•ci•sor
in•cite provoke; *cf*
insight
in•cite•ment
in•ci•vil•ity (*pl*
•ities)
in•clem•en•cy (*or*
•ent•ness)
in•clem•ent
in•cli•na•tion
in•cline
in•clin•er
in•close *variant
spelling of* enclose
in•clo•sure *variant
spelling of*
enclosure
in•clud•able (*or*
•ible)
in•clude
in•clu•sion
in•clu•sive
in•cog•nl•to (*fem*
•ta; *pl* •tos *or* •tas)
in•co•her•ence (*or*
•en•cy, •ent•ness)
in•co•her•ent
in•co•her•ent•ly
in•come
in•com•er
in•com•ing
in•com•mode
in•com•mo•di•ous
in•com•mu•ni•cable
in•com•mu•ni•
ca•do

in•com•mu•ni•ca•
tive
in•com•pa•rabil•ity
(or •rable•ness)
in•com•pa•rable
in•com•pa•rably
in•com•pat•ibil•ity
(or •ible•ness)
in•com•pat•ible
in•com•pat•ibly
in•com•pe•tence (or
•ten•cy)
in•com•pe•tent
in•com•pe•tent•ly
in•com•plete
in•com•plete•ly
in•com•plete•ness
(or •ple•tion)
in•com•pre•hen•
sibil•ity (or
•sible•ness)
in•com•pre•hen•
sible
in•com•pre•hen•
sibly
in•com•pre•hen•
sion
in•com•pre•hen•
sive
in•con•ceiv•abil•ity
(or •able•ness)
in•con•ceiv•able
in•con•ceiv•ably
in•con•clu•sive
in•con•gru•ity (pl
•ities)
in•con•gru•ous (or
•ent)
in•con•gru•ous•ly

in•con•gru•ous•ness
(or •gru•ence)
in•con•se•quence
in•con•se•quen•tial
(or •quent)
in•con•se•quen•
tial•ly
in•con•sid•er•able
in•con•sid•er•ate
in•con•sid•er•ate•
ness
in•con•sist•en•cy
(pl •cies)
in•con•sist•ent
in•con•sol•abil•ity
(or •able•ness)
in•con•sol•able
in•con•sol•ably
in•con•spicu•ous
in•con•spicu•ous•ly
in•con•spicu•ous•
ness
in•con•stan•cy (pl
•cies)
in•con•stant
in•con•test•abil•ity
(or •able•ness)
in•con•test•able
in•con•test•ably
in•con•ti•nence (or
•nen•cy)
in•con•ti•nent
in•con•tro•vert•ibil•
ity (or •ible•ness)
in•con•tro•vert•ible
in•con•tro•vert•ibly
in•con•ven•ience
in•con•ven•ient
in•cor•po•rable

in•cor•po•rate
in•cor•po•rat•ed
in•cor•po•ra•tion
in•cor•po•real
in•cor•po•real•ly
in•cor•po•reity (or
•real•ity)
in•cor•rect
in•cor•rect•ly
in•cor•rect•ness
in•cor•ri•gibil•ity
(or •gible•ness)
in•cor•ri•gible
in•cor•ri•gibly
in•cor•rupt•ibil•ity
(or •ible•ness)
in•cor•rupt•ible
in•cor•rupt•ibly
in•creas•able
in•crease
in•creas•er
in•creas•ing•ly
in•cred•ibil•ity (or
•ible•ness)
in•cred•ible
unbelievable; cf
incredulous
in•cred•ibly
in•cre•du•lity
in•credu•lous
skeptical; cf
incredible
in•cre•ment
in•cre•men•tal
in•crimi•nate
in•crimi•na•tion
in•crimi•na•tor
in•crimi•na•tory

in•crust *variant spelling of* encrust
in•crus•ta•tion *variant spelling of* encrustation
in•cu•bate
in•cu•ba•tion
in•cu•ba•tor
in•cu•bus (*pl* •bi *or* •buses)
in•cul•cate
in•cul•ca•tion
in•cul•ca•tor
in•cul•pable
in•cul•pate
in•cul•pa•tion
in•cum•ben•cy (*pl* •cies)
in•cum•bent
in•cu•nabu•lum (*pl* •la)
in•cur (•cur•ring, •curred)
in•cur•able not curable; *cf* incurrable
in•cu•ri•ous
in•cu•ri•ous•ly
in•cur•rable liable to incur; *cf* incurable
in•cur•sion
in•cur•sive
in•debt•ed
in•debt•ed•ness
in•de•cen•cy (*pl* •cies)
in•de•cent
in•de•cent•ly

in•de•ci•pher•able
in•de•ci•sion
in•de•ci•sive
in•de•ci•sive•ly
in•de•ci•sive•ness
in•deco•rous
in•de•co•rum
in•deed
in•de•fati•gabil•ity (*or* •gable•ness)
in•de•fati•gable
in•de•fati•gably
in•de•fen•sible
in•de•fin•able
in•de•fin•ably
in•defi•nite
in•defi•nite•ly
in•del•ibil•ity (*or* •ible•ness)
in•del•ible
in•del•ibly
in•deli•ca•cy (*pl* •cies)
in•deli•cate
in•dem•nl•fi•ca•tion
in•dem•ni•fy (•fies, •fy•ing, •fied)
in•dem•nity (*pl* •nities)
in•dent
in•den•ta•tion
in•den•ture
in•de•pend•ence
in•de•pend•en•cy (*pl* •cies)
in•de•pend•ent
in•de•pend•ent•ly
in-depth

in•de•scrib•abil•ity (*or* •able•ness)
in•de•scrib•able
in•de•scrib•ably
in•de•struc•tibil•ity (*or* •tible•ness)
in•de•struc•tible
in•de•struc•tibly
in•de•ter•min•able
in•de•ter•mi•na•cy (*or* •na•tion, •nate•ness)
in•de•ter•mi•nate
in•dex (*pl* •dexes *or* •di•ces)
in•dex•ation
in•dex•er
In•dian
in•di•cate
in•di•ca•tion
in•dica•tive
in•di•ca•tor
in•dica•tory
in•di•ces *pl of* index
in•dict accuse; *cf* indite
in•dict•able
in•dict•er (*or* •or)
in•dict•ment
in•dif•fer•ence
in•dif•fer•ent
in•dif•fer•ent•ly
in•di•gence
in•dig•enous
in•dig•enous•ness (*or* in•di•gen•ity)
in•di•gent
in•di•gest•ibil•ity (*or* •ible•ness)

in•di•gest•ible
in•di•ges•tion
in•dig•nant
in•dig•nant•ly
in•dig•na•tion
in•dig•nity (*pl*
•nities)
in•di•go (*pl* •gos *or*
•goes)
in•di•rect
in•di•rect•ly
in•di•rect•ness
in•dis•cern•ible
in•dis•cern•ibly
in•dis•ci•pline
in•dis•creet tactless
in•dis•crete
undivided
in•dis•cre•tion
in•dis•crimi•nate
in•dis•crimi•nate•ly
in•dis•crimi•na•tion
in•dis•pens•abil•ity
(*or* •able•ness)
in•dis•pens•able
in•dis•pens•ably
in•dis•pose
in•dis•posed
in•dis•po•si•tion
in•dis•put•abil•ity
(*or* •able•ness)
in•dis•put•able
in•dis•put•ably
in•dis•sol•ubil•ity
(*or* •uble•ness)
in•dis•sol•uble
in•dis•sol•ubly
in•dis•tinct
in•dis•tinct•ly

in•dis•tinguish•
abil•ity (*or*
•able•ness)
in•dis•tinguish•
able
in•dis•tinguish•
ably
in•dite write; *cf*
indict
in•dium
in•di•vid•ual
in•di•vidu•al•ism
in•di•vidu•al•ist
in•di•vidu•al•is•tic
in•di•vidu•al•is•ti•
cal•ly
in•di•vidu•al•ity
(*pl* •ities)
in•di•vidu•ali•za•
tion
in•di•vidu•al•ize
in•di•vid•ual•ly
in•di•vis•ibil•ity (*or*
•ible•ness)
in•di•vis•ible
in•di•vis•ibly
in•doc•tri•nate
in•doc•tri•na•tion
in•doc•tri•na•tor
Indo-European
in•do•lence
in•do•lent
in•do•lent•ly
in•domi•tabil•ity
(*or* •table•ness)
in•domi•table
in•domi•tably
In•do•nesian
in•door (*adj*)

in•doors (*adv*)
in•dorse *variant*
spelling of endorse
in•drawn
in•du•bi•tabil•ity
(*or* •table•ness)
in•du•bi•table
in•du•bi•tably
in•duce
in•duce•ment
in•duc•er
in•duc•ible
in•duct
in•duc•tee
*inducter *incorrect*
spelling of
inductor
in•duc•tion
in•duc•tive
in•duc•tor (*NOT*
inducter)
in•due *variant*
spelling of endue
in•dulge
in•dul•gence (*or*
•gen•cy; *pl* •gences
or •cies)
in•dul•gent
in•dul•gent•ly
in•dulg•er
in•dus•trial
in•dus•tri•al•ism
in•dus•tri•al•ist
in•dus•tri•ali•za•
tion
in•dus•tri•al•ize
in•dus•tri•al•ly
in•dus•tri•ous
in•dus•tri•ous•ly

in•dus•try (*pl*
•tries)
in•dus•try•wide
in•ebri•ate
in•ebri•at•ed
in•ebria•tion
in•ebri•ety
in•ed•ibil•ity
in•ed•ible
in•edu•cable
in•ef•fabil•ity (*or*
•fable•ness)
in•ef•fable
in•ef•fably
in•ef•fec•tive
in•ef•fec•tual
in•ef•fec•tu•al•ity
(*or* •ness)
in•ef•fec•tual•ly
in•ef•fi•ca•cious
in•ef•fi•ca•cy (*or*
•ca•cious•ness)
in•ef•fi•cien•cy (*pl*
•cies)
in•ef•fi•cient
in•ef•fi•cient•ly
in•elas•tic
in•elas•tic•ity
in•el•egance (*or*
•egan•cy)
in•el•egant
in•eli•gibil•ity (*or*
•gible•ness)
in•eli•gible
in•eluc•tabil•ity
in•eluc•table
in•eluc•tably
in•ept

incompetent; *cf*
inapt
in•epti•tude
in•ept•ly
in•ept•ness
in•equal•ity (*pl*
•ities)
in•equi•table
in•equi•ty (*pl* •ties)
injustice; *cf*
iniquity
in•eradi•cable
in•eradi•cably
in•ert
in•er•tia
in•er•tial
in•ert•ly
in•es•cap•able
in•es•cap•ably
in•es•sen•tial
in•es•ti•mabil•ity
(*or* •mable•ness)
in•es•ti•mable
in•es•ti•mably
in•evi•tabil•ity (*or*
•table•ness)
in•evi•table
in•evi•tably
in•ex•act
in•ex•acti•tude
in•ex•cus•able
in•ex•cus•ably
in•ex•haust•ibil•ity
(*or* •ible•ness)
in•ex•haust•ible
in•ex•haust•ibly
in•ex•is•tence (*or*
•ten•cy)
in•ex•is•tent

in•exo•rabil•ity (*or*
•rable•ness)
in•exo•rable
in•exo•rably
in•ex•pen•sive
in•ex•pe•ri•ence
in•ex•pe•ri•enced
in•ex•pert
in•ex•pli•cabil•ity
(*or* •cable•ness)
in•ex•pli•cable
in•ex•pli•cably
in•ex•press•ibil•ity
(*or* •ible•ness)
in•ex•press•ible
in•ex•press•ibly
in•ex•pres•sive
in•ex•tin•guish•
able
in ex•tre•mis
in•ex•tri•cable
in•ex•tri•cably
in•fal•libil•ity (*or*
•lible•ness)
in•fal•lible
in•fal•libly
in•fa•mous
in•fa•mous•ly
in•fa•my (*pl* •mies)
in•fan•cy (*pl* •cies)
in•fant
in•fan•ta Spanish
princess
in•fan•te Spanish
prince
in•fan•ti•cide
in•fan•tile
in•fan•ti•lism

in•fan•try (*pl* •tries)
in•fantry•man (*pl* •men)
in•farct
in•farc•tion
in•fatu•ate
in•fatu•at•ed
in•fatua•tion
in•fect
in•fec•tion
in•fec•tious
in•fec•tious•ness
in•fec•tive
in•fec•tive•ness (or •tiv•ity)
in•fec•tor (or •fect•er)
in•fe•lici•tous
in•fe•lic•ity (*pl* •ities)
in•fer (•fer•ring, •ferred)
in•fer•able (or •ible, •rible)
in•fer•ence
in•fer•en•tial
in•fe•ri•or
in•fe•ri•or•ity
in•fer•nal
in•fer•nal•ly
in•fer•no (*pl* •nos)
in•ferred
in•fer•ring
in•fer•tile
in•fer•til•ity
in•fest
in•fes•ta•tion
in•fi•del

in•fi•del•ity (*pl* •ities)
in•field
in•fighting
in•fill
in•fil•trate
in•fil•tra•tion
in•fil•tra•tor
in•fi•nite
in•fi•nite•ly
in•fini•tesi•mal
in•fini•tesi•mal•ly
in•fini•tive
in•fin•ity (*pl* •ities)
in•firm
in•fir•ma•ry (*pl* •ries)
in•fir•mity (*pl* •mities)
in•firm•ly
in fla•gran•te de•lic•to
in•flame
in•flam•er
in•flam•mabil•ity (or •mable•ness)
in•flam•mable
in•flam•ma•tion
in•flam•ma•to•ri•ly
in•flam•ma•tory
in•flat•able
in•flate
in•flat•ed
in•flat•er (or •fla•tor)
in•fla•tion
in•fla•tion•ary
in•flect

in•flec•tion (or •flex•ion)
in•flec•tive
in•flex•ibil•ity (or •ible•ness)
in•flex•ible
in•flex•ibly
in•flex•ion *variant spelling of* inflection
in•flict
in•flict•er (or •flic•tor)
in•flic•tion
in-flight (*adj*)
in•flo•res•cence
in•flow
in•flu•ence
in•flu•en•tial
in•flu•en•tial•ly
in•flu•en•za
in•flux
*inforce *incorrect spelling of* enforce
in•form
in•for•mal
in•for•mal•ity (*pl* •ities)
in•for•mal•ly
in•form•ant
in•for•ma•tion
in•forma•tive (or •tory)
in•forma•tive•ly
in•formed
in•form•er
in•frac•tion
in•fra dig
infra•red

infra•son•ic
infra•struc•ture
in•fre•quen•cy (or •quence)
in•fre•quent
in•fre•quent•ly
in•fringe
in•fringe•ment
in•fring•er
in•furi•ate
in•furi•at•ing•ly
in•fuse
in•fus•er
in•fus•ibil•ity (or •ible•ness)
in•fus•ible
in•fu•sion
in•ge•nious skillful; cf ingenuous
in•gé•nue (or •ge•)
in•ge•nu•ity (pl •ities)
in•ge•nu•ous naive; cf ingenious
in•gest
in•ges•tion
in•glo•ri•ous
in•going
in•got
in•grain
in•grained
in•grate
in•gra•ti•ate
in•gra•ti•at•ing (or in•gra•tia•tory)
in•gra•tia•tion
in•grati•tude
in•gre•di•ent
in•gress

in•gres•sion
in-group
in•growing
in•grown
in•gui•nal
in•hab•it
in•hab•it•abil•ity
in•hab•it•able
in•habi•tan•cy (or •tance)
in•habi•tant
in•hal•ant
in•ha•la•tion
in•hale
in•hal•er
in•har•mo•ni•ous
in•her•ence (or •en•cy)
in•her•ent
in•her•ent•ly
in•her•it
in•her•it•abil•ity (or •able•ness)
in•her•it•able
in•hcri•tance
in•heri•tor
in•hib•it
in•hib•it•er (or •hibi•tor)
in•hi•bi•tion
in•hibi•tive (or •tory)
in•hibi•tor
in•hos•pi•table
in•hos•pi•tably
in•hos•pi•tal•ity
in-house
in•hu•man
in•hu•mane

in•hu•man•ity (pl •ities)
in•imi•cal
in•imi•cal•ly
in•imi•tabil•ity (or •table•ness)
in•imi•table
in•imi•tably
in•iqui•tous
in•iquity (pl •iquities) sin; cf inequity
ini•tial (•tial•ing, •tialed; Brit •tial•ling, •tialled)
ini•tial•ly
ini•ti•ate
ini•tia•tion
ini•tia•tive
ini•tia•tor
ini•tia•tory
in•ject
in•ject•able
in•jec•tion
in•jec•tor
in•ju•di•cious
in•junc•tion
in•jure
in•jur•er
in•ju•ri•ous
in•ju•ry (pl •ries)
in•jus•tice
ink
ink•berry (pl •berries)
inki•ness
ink•ling
ink•stand
ink•well

inky (inki•er, inki•est)
in•laid
in•land
in-law
in•lay (•lay•ing, •laid)
in•lay•er
in•let (•let•ting, •let)
in loco pa•ren•tis
in•mate
in me•mo•ri•am
in-migrant
in-migrate
in-migration
in•most
inn hotel; cf in
in•nards
in•nate
in•nate•ly
in•ner
inner-city (adj)
inner•most
in•ner•vate supply with nerves; cf enervate; innovate
in•ner•va•tion
in•ning
inn•keeper
in•no•cence
in•no•cent
in•no•cent•ly
*innoculate
   incorrect spelling
   of inoculate
in•nocu•ous
in•nocu•ous•ly
in•nocu•ous•ness

in•no•vate
   introduce new
   ideas; cf enervate;
   innervate
in•no•va•tion
in•no•va•tive (or •tory)
in•no•va•tor
in•nu•en•do (pl •dos or •does)
In•nu•it (or Inu•it; pl •it or •its)
in•nu•mer•abil•ity (or •able•ness)
in•nu•mer•able (or •ous)
   uncountable; cf enumerable
in•nu•mer•ably
in•nu•mer•ate
in•ocu•late (NOT innoculate)
in•ocu•la•tion
in•ocu•la•tor
in•of•fen•sive
in•op•er•able
in•op•era•tive
in•op•por•tune
in•op•por•tune•ness (or •tun•ity)
in•or•di•na•cy (or •nan•cy, •nate•ness)
in•or•di•nate
in•or•di•nate•ly
in•or•gan•ic
in•or•gani•cal•ly
in•pa•tient

in•put (•put•ting, •put)
in•quest
in•qui•etude
in•quire (Brit also en•)
in•quir•er (Brit also en•)
in•quiry (Brit also en•; pl •quiries)
in•qui•si•tion
in•qui•si•tion•al
in•quisi•tive
in•quisi•tive•ly
in•quisi•tive•ness
in•quisi•tor
in•quisi•to•rial
in•quisi•to•rial•ly
in•road
in•rush
in•sa•lu•bri•ous
in•sane
in•sane•ly
in•sani•tari•ness (or •ta•tion)
in•sani•tary
in•san•ity (pl •ities)
in•sa•tiabil•ity (or •tiable•ness, •tiate•ness)
in•sa•tiable (or •tiate)
in•sa•tiably (or •ti•ate•ly)
in•scape
in•scribe
in•scrib•er
in•scrip•tion
in•scrip•tion•al

in•scru•tabil•ity (*or* •table•ness)
in•scru•table
in•sect
in•sec•ti•cide
in•sec•ti•vore
in•sec•tivo•rous
in•se•cure
in•se•cu•rity (*pl* •rities)
in•semi•nate
in•semi•na•tion
in•semi•na•tor
in•sen•sate
in•sen•sibil•ity (*or* •sible•ness)
in•sen•sible
in•sen•sibly
in•sen•si•tive
in•sen•si•tiv•ity
in•sen•tience (*or* •tien•cy)
in•sen•tient
in•sepa•rabil•ity (*or* •rable•ness)
in•sepa•rable
in•scpa•rably
in•sert
in•ser•tion
in•set (•set•ting, •set *or* •set•ted)
in•shore
in•side
in•sid•er
in•sidi•ous
in•sidi•ous•ly
in•sight under-standing; *cf* incite
in•sight•ful

in•sig•nia (*or* •ne; *pl* •nias *or* •nia)
in•sig•nifi•cance (*or* •can•cy)
in•sig•nifi•cant
in•sin•cere
in•sin•cere•ly
in•sin•cer•ity (*pl* •ities)
in•sinu•ate
in•sinua•tion
in•sinua•tor
in•sip•id
in•si•pid•ity (*or* •ness)
in•sist
in•sis•tence (*or* •ten•cy)
in•sis•tent
in•sis•tent•ly
in•sist•er
in situ
in•snare *variant spelling of* ensnare
in•so•bri•ety
in•so•far
in•so•late expose to sun; *cf* insulate
in•so•la•tion
in•sole
in•so•lence
in•so•lent
in•sol•ubil•ity (*or* •uble•ness)
in•sol•uble
in•sol•ubly
in•solv•abil•ity
in•solv•able
in•sol•ven•cy

in•sol•vent
in•som•nia
in•som•ni•ac
in•so•much
in•sou•ci•ance
in•sou•ci•ant
in•spect
in•spec•tion
in•spec•tor
in•spec•tor•ate
in•spec•tor•ship
in•spi•ra•tion
in•spi•ra•tion•al
in•spira•tory
in•spire
in•spir•ing
in•spir•it
in•stabil•ity (*pl* •ities)
in•stall (*or* •stal; •stall•ing, •stalled *or* •stal•ling, •stalled)
in•stal•la•tion
ln•stall•er
in•stall•ment (*Brit* •stal•)
in•stance
in•stant
in•stan•ta•neous
in•stan•ta•neous•ness (*or* •ta•neity)
in•stant•ly
in•state
in•state•ment
in•stead
in•step
in•sti•gate
in•sti•ga•tion

in•sti•ga•tor
in•still (*Brit* •stil;
•still•ing, •stilled;
Brit stil•ling,
•stilled)
in•stil•la•tion
in•still•er
in•still•ment (*Brit*
•stil•)
in•stinct
in•stinc•tive (*or*
•tual)
in•stinc•tive•ly
in•sti•tute
in•sti•tu•tion
in•sti•tu•tion•al
in•sti•tu•tion•
al•ism
in•sti•tu•tion•ali•
za•tion
in•sti•tu•tion•al•ize
in•sti•tu•tor
in-store (*adj*)
in•struct
in•struct•ible
in•struc•tion
in•struc•tion•al
in•struc•tive
in•struc•tor
in•stru•ment
in•stru•men•tal
in•stru•men•tal•ist
in•stru•men•tal•ity
(*pl* •ities)
in•stru•men•tal•ly
in•stru•men•ta•tion
in•sub•or•di•nate
in•sub•or•di•na•
tion

in•sub•stan•tial
in•sub•stan•ti•al•ity
in•sub•stan•tial•ly
in•suf•fer•able
in•suf•fer•ably
in•suf•fi•cien•cy (*or*
•cience; *pl* •cies *or*
•ciences)
in•suf•fi•cient
in•suf•fi•cient•ly
in•su•lar
in•su•lar•ity (*or*
•ism)
in•su•late isolate;
cf insolate
in•su•la•tion
in•su•la•tor
in•su•lin
in•sult
in•sult•er
in•sult•ing
in•sult•ing•ly
in•su•per•abil•ity
(*or* •able•ness)
in•su•per•able
in•su•per•ably
in•sup•port•able
in•sup•port•ably
in•sur•abil•ity
in•sur•able
in•sur•ance
in•sure protect
against loss; *cf*
ensure
in•sured
in•sur•er
in•sur•gence
in•sur•gen•cy (*pl*
•cies)

in•sur•gent
in•sur•mount•able
in•sur•mount•ably
in•sur•rec•tion
in•sur•rec•tion•ist
in•sus•cep•tibil•ity
in•sus•cep•tible
in•tact
in•ta•glio (*pl* •glios
or •gli)
in•take
in•tan•gibil•ity (*or*
•gible•ness)
in•tan•gible
in•tan•gibly
in•te•ger
in•te•gral
in•te•gral•ly
in•te•grate
in•te•grat•ed
in•te•gra•tion
in•te•gra•tor
in•teg•rity
in•tegu•ment
in•tel•lect
in•tel•lec•tual
in•tel•lec•tu•al•ism
in•tel•lec•tu•al•ity
(*or* •ness)
in•tel•lec•tu•al•ize
in•tel•lec•tu•al•ly
in•tel•li•gence
in•tel•li•gent
in•tel•li•gent•ly
in•tel•li•gent•sia
in•tel•li•gibil•ity
(*or* •gible•ness)
in•tel•li•gible
in•tel•li•gibly

in•tem•per•ance
in•tem•per•ate
in•tend
in•tend•ed
in•tense
in•ten•si•fi•ca•tion
in•ten•si•fi•er
in•ten•si•fy (•fies, •fy•ing, •fied)
in•ten•si•ty (*pl* •sities)
in•ten•sive
in•ten•sive•ly
in•tent
in•ten•tion
in•ten•tion•al
in•ten•tion•al•ly
in•tent•ly
in•ter (•ter•ring, •terred)
inter•act
inter•ac•tion
inter•ac•tive
inter•agen•cy
in•ter alia
inter•breed (•breed•ing, •bred)
inter•ca•lary
inter•cede
inter•ced•er
inter•cel•lu•lar
inter•cept
inter•cep•tion
inter•cep•tive
inter•cep•tor (*or* •cept•er)
inter•ces•sion
inter•ces•sion•al (*or* inter•ces•sory)

inter•ces•sor
inter•change
inter•change•abil•ity (*or* •able•ness)
inter•change•able
inter•change•ably
inter•city
inter•col•le•giate
inter•com
inter•com•mu•ni•cate
inter•com•mu•ni•ca•tion
inter•con•nect
inter•con•nec•tion
inter•con•ti•nen•tal
inter•course
inter•cul•tur•al
inter•de•nomi•na•tion•al
inter•de•part•men•tal
inter•de•pen•dence (*or* •den•cy)
inter•de•pen•dent
inter•dict
inter•dic•tion
inter•dic•tive (*or* •tory)
inter•dis•ci•pli•nary
in•ter•est
in•ter•est•ed
in•ter•est•ed•ly
in•ter•est•ing
inter•face
inter•fa•cial
inter•fac•ing
inter•faith (*adj*)

inter•fere
inter•fer•ence
inter•fer•er
inter•fer•ing
inter•fer•on
inter•fuse
inter•fu•sion
inter•ga•lac•tic
inter•gla•cial
inter•gov•ern•men•tal
in•te•rim
in•te•ri•or
inter•ject
inter•jec•tion
inter•lace
inter•lace•ment
inter•lard
inter•lay (•lay•ing, •laid)
inter•leave
inter•line
inter•lin•er
inter•lin•ing
inter•link
inter•lock
inter•lock•er
inter•lo•cu•tion
inter•locu•tor
inter•locu•tory
inter•lop•er
inter•lude
inter•mar•riage
inter•mar•ry (•ries, •ry•ing, •ried)
inter•me•dia•cy
inter•me•di•ary (*pl* •aries)
inter•me•di•ate

in•ter•me•di•a•tor

in•ter•ment burial;
 cf internment

inter•mez•zo (*pl*
 •zos *or* •zi)

in•ter•mi•na•ble

in•ter•mi•na•ble•
 ness (*or* •nabil•ity)

in•ter•mi•na•bly

inter•min•gle

inter•mis•sion

inter•mit
 (•mit•ting,
 •mit•ted)

inter•mit•tence (*or*
 •ten•cy)

inter•mit•tent

inter•mix

inter•mix•ture

inter•mo•lec•u•lar

in•tern (*or* •terne)

in•ter•nal

in•ter•nal•ity (*or*
 •ness)

in•ter•nali•za•tion

in•ter•nal•ize

in•ter•nal•ly

inter•na•tion•al

inter•na•tion•
 al•ism

inter•na•tion•al•ist

inter•na•tion•al•ity

inter•na•tion•ali•
 za•tion

inter•na•tion•al•ize

inter•na•tion•al•ly

inter•ne•cine

in•terne *variant
 spelling of* intern

in•ternee

in•tern•ment
 confinement; *cf*
 interment

in•tern•ship (*or*
 •terne•)

inter•pen•etrate

inter•pen•etra•tion

inter•per•son•al

inter•plan•etary

inter•play

in•ter•po•late

in•ter•po•la•tion

in•ter•po•la•tor

inter•pose

inter•po•si•tion

in•ter•pret

in•ter•pret•abil•ity
 (*or* •able•ness)

in•ter•pret•able

in•ter•pre•ta•tion

in•ter•pre•ta•tive

in•ter•pret•er

in•ter•pre•tive

inter•ra•cial

inter•ra•cial•ly

inter•reg•nal

inter•reg•num (*pl*
 •nums *or* •na)

inter•re•late

inter•re•la•tion

inter•re•la•tion•
 ship

in•ter•ro•gate

in•ter•ro•ga•tion

in•ter•ro•ga•tion•al

in•ter•ro•ga•tive

in•ter•ro•ga•tor

in•ter•roga•tory
 (*pl* •tories)

in•ter•rupt

in•ter•rupt•er (*or*
 •rup•tor)

in•ter•rupt•ible

in•ter•rup•tion

in•ter•rup•tive

inter•sect

inter•sec•tion

inter•sec•tion•al

inter•space

inter•spa•tial (*or*
 •cial)

inter•sperse

inter•sper•sion (*or*
 •sal)

inter•state between
 states; *cf*
 intrastate

inter•stel•lar

in•ter•stice

in•ter•sti•tial (*or*
 •cial)

inter•twine

in•ter•val

inter•vene

inter•ven•er (*or*
 •ve•nor)

inter•ven•tion

inter•ven•tion•al

inter•ven•tion•ism

inter•ven•tion•ist

inter•view

inter•viewee

inter•view•er

inter•war

inter•weave
 (•weav•ing, •wove

or •weaved,
•wo•ven *or*
•weaved)
in•tes•ta•cy
in•tes•tate
in•tes•ti•nal
in•tes•tine
in•ti•fa•da
in•ti•ma•cy (*pl*
•cies)
in•ti•mate
in•ti•mate•ly
in•ti•ma•tion
in•timi•date
in•timi•da•tion
in•timi•da•tor
into
in•tol•er•abil•ity
(*or* •able•ness)
in•tol•er•able
in•tol•er•ably
in•tol•er•ance
in•tol•er•ant
in•to•nate
in•to•na•tion
in•tone
in•ton•er
in toto
in•toxi•cant
in•toxi•cate
in•toxi•ca•tion
in•trac•tabil•ity (*or*
•table•ness)
in•trac•table
in•trac•tably
intra•mu•ral
intra•mus•cu•lar
in•tran•si•gence (*or*
•gen•cy)

in•tran•si•gent
in•tran•si•tive
intra•state *within a*
state; cf interstate
intra•uter•ine
intra•ve•nous
intravert incorrect
spelling of
introvert
in-tray
in•trep•id
in•tre•pid•ity (*or*
•trep•id•ness)
in•trep•id•ly
in•tri•ca•cy (*pl*
•cies)
in•tri•cate
in•trigue
(•trigu•ing,
•trigued)
in•trigu•er
in•trigu•ing•ly
in•trin•sic
in•trin•si•cal•ly
in•tro (*pl* •tros)
intro•duce
intro•duc•er
intro•duc•tion
intro•duc•tory
intro•spec•tion
intro•spec•tive
intro•ver•sion
intro•vert (*NOT*
intravert)
in•trude
in•trud•er
in•tru•sion
in•tru•sive
in•tu•it

in•tu•it•able
in•tui•tion
in•tui•tion•al
in•tui•tive
in•tui•tive•ly
in•tui•tive•ness
Inu•it *variant*
spelling of **Innuit**
in•un•date
in•un•da•tion
in•un•da•tor
in•ure (*or* en•)
in•ured•ness (*or*
en•)
in•vade
in•vad•er
'in•va•lid *disabled*
person
in•'val•id *not valid*
in•vali•date
in•vali•da•tion
in•vali•da•tor
in•va•lid•ism *being*
an invalid
in•va•lid•ity (*or*
•val•id•ness) *being*
not valid
in•valu•able
in•valu•ably
in•vari•abil•ity (*or*
•able•ness)
in•vari•able
in•vari•ably
in•va•sion
in•va•sive
in•vec•tive
in•veigh
in•vei•gle
in•vei•gle•ment

in•vei•gler
in•vent
in•ven•tion
in•ven•tive
in•ven•tive•ly
in•ven•tive•ness
in•ven•tor
in•ven•tory (*n, pl*
•tories; *vb* •tories,
•tory•ing, •toried)
in•verse
in•ver•sion
in•vert
in•ver•te•brate
in•vert•er (*or*
•ver•tor)
in•vert•ibil•ity
in•vert•ible
in•vest
in•vest•able (*or*
•ible)
in•ves•ti•gate
in•ves•ti•ga•tion
in•ves•ti•gative (*or*
•ga•tory)
in•ves•ti•ga•tor
in•ves•ti•ture
in•vest•ment
in•ves•tor
in•vet•er•ate
in•vi•abil•ity (*or*
•able•ness)
in•vi•able
in•vidi•ous
in•vigi•late
in•vigi•la•tion
in•vigi•la•tor
in•vig•or•ate
in•vig•or•at•ing

in•vig•ora•tion
in•vig•ora•tor
in•vin•cibil•ity (*or*
•cible•ness)
in•vin•cible
in•vin•cibly
in•vio•labil•ity (*or*
•lable•ness)
in•vio•lable
in•vio•lably
in•vio•la•cy (*or*
•late•ness)
in•vio•late
in•vis•ibil•ity (*or*
•ible•ness)
in•vis•ible
in•vis•ibly
in•vi•ta•tion
in•vite
in•vit•er
in•vit•ing
in vi•tro
in•vo•cable
in•vo•ca•tion
in•voca•tory
in•voice
in•voke
in•vok•er
in•vol•un•tari•ly
in•vol•un•tari•ness
in•vol•un•tary
in•vo•lute (*or*
lut•ed)
in•vo•lu•tion
in•volve
in•volved
in•volve•ment
in•vul•ner•abil•ity
(*or* •able•ness)

in•vul•ner•able
in•vul•ner•ably
in•ward (*adj*)
in•ward (*Brit*
•wards; *adv*)
in•ward•ly
in•wrap *variant*
spelling of enwrap
in•wrought
iodide
iodine
iodi•za•tion
iodize
ion electrically
charged atom; *cf*
iron
ion•ic
ioni•za•tion
ion•ize
iono•sphere
iono•spher•ic
iota
IOU (*pl* IOUs)
ip•ecac (*or*
•ecacu•an•ha)
ipso fac•to
Ira•nian
Iraqi (*pl* Iraqis)
iras•cibil•ity (*or*
•cible•ness)
iras•cible
iras•cibly
irate
irate•ly
ire
iri•des•cence
iri•des•cent (*NOT*
irridescent)
irid•ium

iris (*pl* irises *or* iris) flower

iris (*pl* irises *or* iri•des) part of eye

Irish

irk

irk•some

iron metal; *cf* ion

iron•clad

iron•er

iron•ic (*or* ironi•cal)

ironi•cal•ly

iron•ing

iro•nist

iron•smith

iron•stone

iron•ware

iron•wood

iron•work

iro•ny (*pl* •nies) sarcasm

irony containing iron

Iro•quoi•an

Iro•quois (*pl* •quois)

ir•ra•di•ate

ir•ra•dia•tion

ir•ra•dia•tive

ir•ra•dia•tor

ir•ra•tion•al

ir•ra•tion•al•ity (*or* •ism)

ir•ra•tion•al•ly

ir•rec•on•cil•abil•ity (*or* •able•ness)

ir•rec•on•cil•able

ir•rec•on•cil•ably

ir•re•cov•er•able

ir•re•cov•er•ably

ir•re•deem•abil•ity (*or* •able•ness)

ir•re•deem•able

ir•re•deem•ably

ir•re•den•tism

ir•re•den•tist

ir•re•duc•ibil•ity (*or* •ible•ness)

ir•re•duc•ible

ir•re•duc•ibly

ir•refu•tabil•ity (*or* •table•ness)

ir•refu•table

ir•refu•tably

ir•regu•lar

ir•regu•lar•ity (*pl* •ities)

ir•regu•lar•ly

ir•rel•evance (*or* •evan•cy; *pl* •evances *or* •cies)

ir•rel•evant

ir•re•li•gious

ir•re•medi•able

ir•re•medi•ably

ir•re•mov•able

ir•re•mov•ably

ir•repa•rabil•ity (*or* •rable•ness)

ir•repa•rable

ir•repa•rably

ir•re•place•able

ir•re•press•ibil•ity (*or* •ible•ness)

ir•re•press•ible

ir•re•press•ibly

ir•re•proach•abil•ity (*or* •able•ness)

ir•re•proach•able

ir•re•proach•ably

ir•re•sist•ibil•ity (*or* •ible•ness)

ir•re•sist•ible

ir•re•sist•ibly

ir•reso•lute

ir•reso•lute•ness (*or* •lu•tion)

ir•re•solv•abil•ity (*or* •able•ness)

ir•re•solv•able

ir•re•spec•tive

ir•re•spon•sibil•ity (*or* •sible•ness)

ir•re•spon•sible

ir•re•spon•sibly

ir•re•triev•abil•ity (*or* •able•ness)

ir•re•triev•able

ir•re•triev•ably

ir•rev•er•ence

ir•rev•er•ent (*or* •eren•tial)

ir•re•vers•ibil•ity (*or* •ible•ness)

ir•re•vers•ible

ir•re•vers•ibly

ir•revo•cabil•ity (*or* •cable•ness)

ir•revo•cable

ir•revo•cably

*irridescent *incorrect spelling of* iridescent

ir•ri•gable

ir•ri•gate

ir•ri•ga•tion
ir•ri•ga•tor
ir•ri•tabil•ity (pl •ities)
ir•ri•table
ir•ri•tably
ir•ri•tant
ir•ri•tate
ir•ri•tat•ing•ly
ir•ri•ta•tion
ir•ri•ta•tor
ir•rupt enter or increase suddenly; cf erupt
ir•rup•tion
ir•rup•tive
is
isin•glass
Is•lam
Is•lam•ic
is•land
is•land•er
isle island; cf aisle
is•let small island; cf eyelet
isn't
iso•bar
iso•bar•ic
isoch•ro•ous
iso•elec•tric
iso•late
iso•la•tion
iso•la•tion•ism
iso•la•tion•ist
iso•la•tor
iso•mer
iso•mer•ic
isom•er•ism
iso•met•ric

iso•morph
iso•mor•phic (or •phous)
iso•mor•phism
isos•celes
iso•therm
iso•ther•mal
iso•tope
iso•top•ic
is•sue (•su•ing, •sued)
is•su•er
isth•mian
isth•mus (pl •muses or •mi)
it
Ital•ian
ital•ic
itali•ci•za•tion
itali•cize
itch
itchi•ness
itch•ing
itchy (itchi•er, itchi•est)
item
itemi•za•tion
item•ize
it•er•ate
it•era•tion (or •er•ance)
it•era•tive
itin•er•an•cy (or •era•cy; pl •cies)
itin•er•ant
itin•er•ary (pl •aries)
it'll
its of it

it's it is
it•self
I've
ivied
ivo•ry (pl •ries)
ivy (pl ivies)

J

jab (jab•bing, jabbed)
jab•ber
jab•ber•er
jab•bing
jabi•ru
jabo•ran•di
jaca•mar
ja•ça•na (or •ca•)
jaca•ran•da
ja•cinth
jack
jack•al
jacka•napes
jack•ass
jack•boot
jack•daw
jack•et
jack•et•ed
jack•fish (pl •fish or •fishes)
jack•hammer
jack-in-the-box (pl jack-in-the-boxes or jacks-in-the-box)
jack•knife (pl •knives)
jack-of-all-trades

(*pl* jacks-of-all-
 trades)
jack-o'-lantern
jack•pot
jack•rabbit
jack•screw
jack•shaft
jack•smelt (*pl*
 •smelt)
Jaco•bean
Jaco•bite
Ja•cuz•zi
 (*Trademark*)
jade
jad•ed
jag (jag•ging,
 jagged)
jag•ged (*adj*)
jag•ged•ly
jag•ged•ness
jag•ging
jag•gy (•gi•er,
 •gi•est)
jag•uar
ja•gua•ron•di (*or*
 •run•; *pl* •dis)
jail (*Brit also* gaol)
jail•bird (*Brit also*
 gaol•)
jail•break (*Brit
 also* gaol•)
jail•er (*Brit also*
 •or, gaol•er)
jail•house
ja•la•peño (*or*
 •peno; *pl* •peños *or*
 •penos)
ja•lopy (*or* •lop•py;

pl •lopies *or*
 •loppies)
jalou•sie shutter; *cf*
 jealousy
jam (jam•ming,
 jammed) wedge;
 crowd; preserve;
 cf jamb
Ja•mai•can
jamb (*or* jambe)
 part of frame; *cf*
 jam
jam•ba•laya
jam•bo•ree
jammed
jam•mer
jam•ming
jam-packed
jan•gle
jani•tor
Janu•ary (*pl* •aries
 or •arys)
ja•pan (•pan•ning,
 •panned)
Japa•nese
jape
jap•er
ja•poni•ca
jar (jar•ring,
 jarred)
jar•di•nière (*or*
 •niere)
jar•gon
jar•goni•za•tion
jar•gon•ize
jarred
jar•ring
jar•ring•ly
jas•mine

jas•per
jaun•dice
jaunt
jaun•ti•ly
jaun•ty (•ti•er,
 •ti•est)
jave•lin
jaw
jaw•bone
jaw•breaker
jay
jay•walk
jay•walk•er
jazz
jazzi•ly
jazzi•ness
jazzy (jazzi•er,
 jazzi•est)
jeal•ous
jeal•ous•ly
jeal•ousy (*pl*
 •ousies) suspicion;
 cf jalousie
jeans
Jeep (*Trademark*)
jeer
jeer•er
jeer•ing•ly
je•had *variant
 spelling of* jihad
je•june naive
je•ju•num small
 intestine
jell (*or* gel; jel•ling,
 jelled *or* gel•ling,
 gelled) congeal; *cf*
 gel
jel•lied
jel•li•fi•ca•tion

jel•li•fy (•fies, •fy•ing, •fied)

Jell-O (*Trademark*)

jel•ly (*n, pl* •lies; *vb* •lies, •ly•ing, •lied)

jelly•fish (*pl* •fish *or* •fishes)

jem•my *Brit spelling of* jimmy

jen•ny (*pl* •nies)

jeop•ar•dize

jeop•ar•dy (*pl* •ardies)

jer•boa

jerk

jerk•er

jerki•ly

jer•kin jacket; *cf* gherkin

jerk•water

jerky (jerki•er, jerki•est)

jerry-build (-build•ing, -built)

jer•sey

jest

jest•er

Jesu•it

Jesu•it•ic (*or* •iti•cal)

jet (jet•ting, jet•ted)

jet-lagged

jet•lin•er

jet•port

jet-propelled

jet•sam (*or* •som)

jet•set•ter

jet-ski (-skiing, -skied)

jet•ti•son

jet•ty (*pl* •ties)

Jew

jew•el (•el•ing, •eled; *Brit* •el•ling, •elled)

jew•el•er (*Brit* •el•ler)

jew•el•ry (*Brit* •el•lery)

Jew•ess

jew•fish (*pl* •fish *or* •fishes)

Jew•ish

Jew•ish•ness

Jew•ry (*pl* •ries)

Jew's harp (*or* Jews' harp)

jib (jib•bing, jibbed)

jib•ber

jibe *variant spelling of* gibe *or* gybe

jif•fy (*or* jiff; *pl* jiffies *or* jiffs)

jig (jig•ging, jigged)

jig•ger

jig•gered

jig•ging

jig•gle

jig•gly

jig•saw

ji•had (*or* je•)

jilt

jilt•er

jim•my (*Brit* jem•; *n, pl* •mies; *vb* •mies, •my•ing, •mied)

jim•son•weed

jin•gle

jin•gly (•gli•er, •gli•est)

jin•go (*pl* •goes)

jin•go•ism

jin•go•ist

jin•go•is•tic

jinks high spirits; *cf* jinx

jinni (*or* jinn, djinni, djinn; *pl* jinn, jinns *or* djinn, djinns)

jinx bad luck; *cf* jinks

ji•pi•ja•pa

jit•ter

jitter•bug (•bug•ging, •bugged)

jit•tery

jiu•jit•su *variant spelling of* jujitsu

jive

job (job•bing, jobbed)

job•ber

job•holder

job-hunt

job•less

job•less•ness

jock

jock•ey

jock•strap

jo•cose

jo•cose•ly

jo•cose•ness (or
jo•cos•ity)

jocu•lar

jocu•lar•ity

jocu•lar•ly

joc•und

jo•cun•dity (pl
•dities)

jodh•purs

jog (jog•ging,
jogged)

jog•ger

jog•gle

jog•trot (•trot•ting,
•trot•ted)

John Dory (pl
John Dories)

John•ny (or
john•nie; pl •nies)

Johnny-come-
lately (pl Johnny-
come-latelies or
Johnnies-come-
lately)

joie de vi•vre

join

join•er

join•ery

joint

joint•ed

joint•er

joint•ly

join•ture

joint•worm

joist

jo•joba

joke

jok•er

jok•ey (or joky;
joki•er, joki•est)

jok•ing•ly

jol•li•fi•ca•tion

jol•li•fy (•fies,
•fy•ing, •fied)

jol•lity (pl •lities)

jol•ly (adj •li•er,
•li•est; vb •lies,
•ly•ing, •lied; n, pl
•lies)

jolt

jolty

jon•quil

josh

joss stick

jos•tle

jos•tler

jot (jot•ting,
jot•ted)

jot•ter

joule

jour•nal

jour•nal•ese

jour•nal•ism

jour•nal•ist

jour•nal•is•tic

jour•nal•is•ti•cal•ly

jour•ney

jour•ney•er

journey•man (pl
•men)

joust

joust•er

jo•vial

jo•vi•al•ity (or
•ness)

jo•vial•ly

jowl

joy

joy•ful

joy•ful•ly

joy•ful•ness

joy•less

joy•less•ness

joy•ous

joy•ous•ly

joy•ous•ness

joy•ride (•rid•ing,
•rode, •rid•den)

joy•rider

joy•stick

ju•bi•lance (or
•lan•cy)

ju•bi•lant

ju•bi•lant•ly

ju•bi•la•tion

ju•bi•lee

Ju•da•ic (or
•dai•cal)

Ju•da•ism

Ju•dai•za•tion

Ju•da•ize

jud•der

judge

judge•able

judg•er

judge•ship

judg•ing•ly

judg•ment (Brit
also judge•)

judg•men•tal (Brit
also judge•)

ju•di•ca•ture

ju•di•cial of the
law; cf judicious

ju•di•cial•ly

ju•di•ciary (*pl*
•ciaries)
ju•di•cious wise; *cf*
judicial
ju•di•cious•ly
ju•di•cious•ness
judo
judo•ist
jug (jug•ging,
jugged)
jug•ful (*pl* •fuls)
jugged
jug•ger•naut
jug•ging
jug•gle
jug•gler
jug•glery
jugu•lar
juice
juici•ly
juici•ness
juicy (juici•er,
juici•est)
ju•jit•su (*or*
ju•jut•su, jiu•)
juju
ju•jube
juke•box
ju•lep
ju•li•enne
July (*pl* Julys)
jum•ble
jum•bo (*pl* •bos)
jump
jump•able
jump•er
jumpi•ly
jumpi•ness
jump-off (*n*)

jump-start
jumpy (jumpi•er,
jumpi•est)
jun•co (*pl* •cos *or*
•coes)
junc•tion
junc•tion•al
junc•ture
June
Jung•ian
jun•gle
jun•gly (•gli•er,
•gli•est)
jun•ior
ju•ni•per
junk
jun•ket
jun•ket•er (*or*
•ke•teer)
junkie (*or* junky; *pl*
junkies)
junk•yard
Ju•no•esque
jun•ta
ju•ridi•cal (*or*
•rid•ic)
ju•ris•dic•tion
ju•ris•dic•tion•al
ju•ris•pru•dence
ju•ris•pru•dent
ju•ris•pru•den•tial
ju•rist
ju•ris•tic (*or*
•ti•cal)
ju•ror
jury (*pl* juries)
jury•man (*pl* •men)
jury•woman (*pl*
•women)

just
jus•tice
jus•tice•ship
jus•ti•fi•abil•ity (*or*
•able•ness)
jus•ti•fi•able
jus•ti•fi•ably
jus•ti•fi•ca•tion
jus•ti•fi•ca•tory (*or*
•tive)
jus•ti•fi•er
jus•ti•fy (•fies,
•fy•ing, •fied)
just•ly
just•ness
jut (jut•ting,
jut•ted)
jute
ju•venile
ju•venilia
jux•ta•pose
jux•ta•po•si•tion
jux•ta•po•si•tion•al

K

kab•ba•la (*or*
ka•ba•la) *variant
spellings of*
cabbala
kaf•tan (*or* caf•)
kai•ser
kale (*or* kail)
ka•lei•do•scope
ka•lei•do•scop•ic
ka•lei•do•scopi•
cal•ly

kal•ends *variant spelling of* **calends**
ka•lif (*or* **•liph**) *variant spellings of* **caliph**
kal•mia
ka•mi•ka•ze
kan•ga•roo (*pl* **•roos**)
kao•lin (*or* **•line**)
ka•pok
ka•put (*or* **•putt**)
kara•kul (*or* **cara•**) sheep; *cf* **caracal**
karao•ke
kar•at (*Brit* **car•**) unit of weight for gold; *cf* **carat**; **caret**; **carrot**
ka•ra•te
kar•ma
kar•mic
ka•ty•did
kay•ak
ka•zoo (*pl* **•zoos**)
ke•bab (*or* **•bob**)
kcd•geree
keel
keel•haul
keel•son (*or* **kel•**)
keen
keen•ly
keen•ness
keep (**keep•ing**, **kept**)
keep•er
keep•sake
keg
keis•ter (*or* **kees•**)

kelp
kel•son *variant spelling of* **keelson**
Kelt *variant spelling of* **Celt**
kel•ter *variant Brit spelling of* **kilter**
Kelt•ic *variant spelling of* **Celtic**
kel•vin
ken (**ken•ning**, **kenned** *or* **kent**)
ken•do
ken•nel (**•nel•ing**, **•neled**; *Brit* **•nel•ling**, **•nelled**)
keno
kept
kera•tin
ke•rat•ini•za•tion
ke•rat•in•ize
kerb *Brit spelling of* **curb** (sidewalk edge)
kerb•stone *Brit spelling of* **curbstone**
ker•chief (*pl* **•chiefs** *or* **•chieves**)
ker•nel grain; *cf* **colonel**
kero•sene (*or* **•sine**)
kes•trel
ketch
ketch•up (*or* **catch•up**, **cat•sup**)
ke•tone
ket•tle
kettle•drum

kettle•drummer
kettle•ful (*pl* **•fuls**)
key instrument; musical notes; *cf* **cay**; **quay**
key•board
key•hole
key•note
key•pad
key•punch
key•stone
key•stroke
kha•ki (*pl* **•kis**)
kha•lif *variant spelling of* **caliph**
khan
khan•ate
kib•butz (*pl* **•but•zim**)
kib•butz•nik
kib•itz (*or* **kib•bitz**)
ki•bosh
kick
kick•able
kick•back
kick•er
kick•off
kick•shaw
kick•stand
kid (**kid•ding**, **kid•ded**)
kid•der
kid•dy (*or* **•die**; *pl* **•dies**)
kid•nap (**•nap•ing**, **•naped**; *Brit* **•nap•ping**, **•napped**)

kid•nap•er (*Brit* •nap•per)
kid•ney
kid•skin
ki•lim
kill
kill•deer (*pl* •deers *or* •deer)
kill•er
kil•li•fish (*pl* •fish *or* •fishes)
kill•ing
kill•joy
kiln
kilo (*pl* kilos)
kilo•byte
kilo•calo•rie
kilo•gram (*or* •gramme)
kilo•hertz
kilo•joule
kilo•meter (*Brit* •metre)
kilo•met•ric (*or* •ri•cal)
kilo•ton
kilo•volt
kilo•watt
kilowatt-hour
kilt
kilt•ed
kil•ter (*Brit also* kel•)
ki•mo•no (*pl* •nos)
ki•mo•noed
kin
kind
kin•der•gar•ten
kind•hearted

kind•hearted•ly
kind•hearted•ness
kin•dle
kin•dler
kind•li•ness
kin•dling
kind•ly (•li•er, •li•est)
kind•ness
kin•dred
kin•dred•ness (*or* kin•dred•ship)
kin•emat•ic (*or* •emati•cal)
kin•emat•ics
kin•escope
ki•net•ic
ki•neti•cal•ly
ki•net•ics
kin•folk (*or* •folks, kins•)
king
king•bird
king•bolt
king•cup
king•dom
king•fish (*pl* •fish *or* •fishes)
king•fisher
king•let
king•li•ness
king•ly (•li•er, •li•est)
king•maker
king•pin
king•ship
king-size (*or* -sized)
king•wood
kink

kin•ka•jou
kinki•ly
kinki•ness
kinky (kinki•er, kinki•est)
kins•folk *variant of* kinfolk
kin•ship
kins•man (*pl* •men)
kins•woman (*pl* •women)
ki•osk
kip•per
kirsch (*or* kirsch• was•ser)
kis•met
kiss
kiss•able
kiss•er
kit (kit•ting, kit•ted)
kitch•en
kitch•en•ette (*or* •et)
kitchen•ware
kite
kith
kitsch
kitschy
kit•ted
kit•ten
kit•ten•ish
kit•ten•ish•ness
kit•ting
kit•ti•wake
kit•ty (*pl* •ties)
kiwi (*pl* kiwis)
Klax•on (*Trademark*)

klep•to•ma•nia
klep•to•ma•ni•ac
*Klu Klux Klan
incorrect spelling
of Ku Klux Klan
klutz
knack
knack•wurst (*or*
knock•)
knap•sack
knap•weed
knave rogue; *cf*
nave
knav•ery (*pl* •eries)
knav•ish
knav•ish•ness
knead mix; *cf*
kneed; need
knead•er
knee (knee•ing,
kneed)
knee•cap
(•cap•ping,
•capped)
kneed *past tense of*
knee; *cf* knead;
need
knee-deep
knee-high (*adj, n*)
knee•hole
knee-jerk (*adj*)
kneel (kneel•ing,
knelt *or* kneeled)
kneel•er
knee-length (*adj*)
knee•pad
knell
knelt

knew *past tense of*
know; *cf* gnu; new
Knick•er•bock•er
New Yorker
knick•er•bock•ers
breeches
knick•ers
knick•knack (*or*
nick•nack)
knife (*pl* knives)
knife-edge
knight soldier; *cf*
night
knight-errant (*pl*
knights-)
knight•hood
knight•li•ness
knight•ly
knish
knit (knit•ting, knit
or knit•ted) inter-
twine yarn; bind;
cf nit
knit•ter
knit•ting
knit•wear
knives *pl of* knife
knob (knob•bing,
knobbed)
projection; *cf* nob
knob•bly (•bli•er,
•bli•est)
knob•by (•bi•er,
•bi•est)
knock
knock•about
knock•down
knock•er
knock-knee

knock-kneed
knock-off (*n*)
knock•out
knock•up
knock•wurst
variant spelling of
knackwurst
knoll
knot (knot•ting,
knot•ted) tie; *cf*
not
knot•grass
knot•hole
knot•ted
knot•ter
knot•ti•ly
knot•ti•ness
knot•ting
knot•ty (•ti•er,
•ti•est)
knot•weed
know (know•ing,
knew, known)
know•able
know•er
know-how
know•ing
know•ing•ly
know•ing•ness
know-it-all (*Brit*
know-all)
knowl•edge
knowl•edge•able
(*or* •edg•able)
knowl•edge•ably
known
know-nothing
knuck•le
knuckle•bone

knuckle-duster
knuckle•head
knuck•ly
knurl
knurled
KO (*vb* KO's,
  KO'ing, KO'd; *n*,
  pl KO's)
koa
koa•la
kohl cosmetic; *cf*
  coal
kohl•ra•bi (*pl* •bies)
ko•la *variant
  spelling of* cola
koo•doo *variant
  spelling of* kudu
kook
kooka•bur•ra
kooky (*or* kookie;
  kooki•er,
  kooki•est)
ko•peck (*or* •pek,
  co•peck)
Ko•ran
Ko•ran•ic
Ko•rean
ko•sher
kow•tow
kow•tow•er
kraal
krait
Krem•lin
krill (*pl* krill)
Krish•na
Kriss Krin•gle
Kru•ger•rand
kryp•ton
ku•dos

kudu (*or* koo•doo;
  pl kudu, kudus *or*
  •doo, •doos)
Ku Klux Klan
  (*NOT* Klu Klux
  Klan)
Ku Klux•er (*or* Ku
  Klux Klan•ner)
küm•mel
kum•quat (*or* cum•)
kung fu
Kurd
Kurd•ish
Ku•wai•ti

L

laa•ger (*or* la•)
  African camp; *cf*
  lager
lab
la•bel (•bel•ing,
  •beled; *Brit*
  •bel•ling, •belled)
la•bel•er (*Brit*
  •bel•ler)
la•bia *pl of* labium
la•bial
la•bium (*pl* •bia)
la•bora•tory (*pl*
  •tories)
la•bor (*Brit* •bour)
la•bored (*Brit*
  •boured)
la•bor•er (*Brit*
  •bour•)
labor-intensive
  (*Brit* labour-)

la•bo•ri•ous
la•bo•ri•ous•ly
la•bo•ri•ous•ness
la•bor•ite (*Brit*
  •bour•)
labor•saving (*Brit*
  labour-saving)
la•bour *Brit
  spelling of* labor
Lab•ra•dor
re•triev•er
la•bur•num
laby•rinth
laby•rin•thine (*or*
  •thian, •thic)
lac resin; *cf* lack
lace
lac•er•ate
lac•era•tion
lac•era•tive
lace•wing
lac•ey *variant
  spelling of* lacy
lach•ry•mose
lach•ry•mose•ly
lach•ry•mos•ity
laci•ness
lac•ing
lack want; *cf* lac
lacka•dai•si•cal
lacka•dai•si•cal•ly
lacka•dai•si•cal•
  ness
lack•ey
lack•luster (*Brit*
  •lustre)
la•con•ic
la•coni•cal•ly
lac•quer

lac•quer•er
lac•ri•mal
lac•ri•ma•tion
la•crosse
lac•tate
lac•ta•tion
lac•teal
lac•tic
lac•tose
la•cu•na (*pl* •nae
or •nas)
lacy (or lac•ey;
laci•er, laci•est)
lad
lad•der
lad•die
lade (lad•ing,
lad•ed, lad•en or
lad•ed) load
cargo; *cf* laid
lad•er
la-di-da (or la-de-,
lah-di-dah)
la•dies *pl of* lady
lad•ing
La•di•no (*pl* •nos)
language; person
la•di•no (*pl* •nos)
clover
la•dle
ladle•ful (*pl* •fuls)
la•dler
lady (*pl* la•dies)
lady•bug (*Brit*
•bird)
lady-in-waiting (*pl*
ladies-)
lady-killer
lady•like

lady•love
la•dy•ship
lady's slipper (or
lady-slipper)
lady's-smock
lag (lag•ging,
lagged)
la•ger beer; *cf*
laager
lag•gard
lag•gard•ly
lag•gard•ness
lagged
lag•ging
la•gniappe
la•goon
lah-di-dah *variant*
spelling of la-di-da
laic (or lai•cal)
lai•cism
lai•ci•za•tion
lai•cize
laid (*NOT* layed)
past tense and
past participle of
lay; *cf* lade
laid-back
lain *past participle*
of lie; *cf* lane
lair
laird
lais•sez faire (*Brit*
also lais•ser faire)
la•ity
lake
lake•front
lak•er
lake•side
lal•apa•loo•za (or

lal•la•pa•) *variant*
spellings of
lollapalooza
lal•ly•gag (or lol•;
•gag•ging,
•gagged)
lam (lam•ming,
lammed) beat;
escape; *cf* lamb
lama Tibetan
priest; *cf* llama
la•ma•sery (*pl*
•series)
lamb young sheep;
cf lam
lam•baste (or
•bast)
lamb•da
lam•ben•cy
lam•bent
lamb•kin
lamb•skin
lamé fabric
lame disabled;
disable
lame•ly
lame•ness
la•ment
lam•en•table
lam•en•tably
la•men•ta•tion
la•ment•ed
la•ment•er
lami•na (*pl* •nae or
•nas)
lami•nar (or •nose)
lami•nate
lami•na•ted
lami•na•tion

Lam•mas
lamp
lamp•black
lamp•light
lam•poon
lam•poon•er (or •ist)
lam•poon•ery
lamp•post
lam•prey
lamp•shade
lance
lance•let
lan•ceo•late
lanc•er soldier
lan•cers dance
lan•cet
lance•wood
land
lan•dau
land•ed
land•fall
land•fill
land•form
land-grant (adj)
land•holder
land•ing
land•lady (pl •ladies)
land•locked
land•lord
land•lub•ber
land•mark
land•mass
land•owner
land•owning
land•scape
land•scap•ist
land•slide

land•slip
lands•man (pl •men)
land•ward
lane road; cf lain
lan•guage
lan•guid
lan•guid•ly
lan•guish
lan•guish•er
lan•guor
lan•guor•ous
lan•iard variant spelling of lanyard
lank
lanki•ly
lanki•ness
lank•ly
lank•ness
lanky (lanki•er, lanki•est)
lano•lin (or •line)
lan•tern
lantern-jawed
lan•tha•nide
lan•tha•num
lan•yard (or •iard)
Lao (pl Lao or Laos)
La•odi•cean
Lao•tian
lap (lap•ping, lapped) circuit; part of body; to wrap; drink; cf Lapp
lap•board
la•pel
la•pelled

lapi•dar•ian
lapi•dary (pl •daries)
la•pis la•zu•li
Lap•land•er
Lapp native of Lapland; cf lap
lapped
lap•per
lap•pet
lap•ping
lapse
lapsed
lap•top
lap•wing
lar•ce•ner (or •nist)
lar•ce•nous
lar•ceny (pl •cenies)
larch
lard
lar•der
lar•don (or •doon)
lardy
large
large•ly
large-minded
large•ness
large-scale
lar•gess (or •gesse)
larg•ish
lar•go (pl •gos)
lari•at
lark
lark•er
lark•spur
larky (larki•er, larki•est)
lar•ri•gan

lar•va (*pl* •vae or •vas) preadult animal; *cf* lava; laver

lar•val

la•ryn•geal (or •gal)

la•ryn•ges *pl of* larynx

lar•yn•gi•tis

lar•ynx (*pl* la•ryn•ges or lar•ynxes)

la•sa•gne (or •gna)

las•civ•i•ous

las•civ•i•ous•ly

las•civ•i•ous•ness

la•ser

lash

lash•er

lash•ing

lass

Las•sa fe•ver

las•sie

las•si•tude

las•so (*n, pl* •sos or •soes; *vb* •sos or •soes, •so•ing, •soed)

las•so•er

last

last-ditch (*adj*)

last•er

last•ing

last•ing•ly

last•ly

latch

latch•key

late

late•comer

*lateish incorrect spelling of latish

late•ly

la•ten•cy (*pl* •cies)

late•ness

la•tent

lat•er

lat•er•al

lat•er•al•ly

lat•est

la•tex (*pl* •texes or lati•ces)

lath (*pl* laths or lath) wood strip

lathe machine

lath•er

lati•meria

Lat•in

Lat•in•ate

Lat•ini•za•tion

Lat•in•ize

La•ti•no (*pl* •nos)

lat•ish (*NOT* lateish)

lati•tude

lati•tu•di•nal

lati•tu•di•nar•ian

lati•tu•di•nari•an•ism

lat•ke

la•trine

lat•ter

latter-day

lat•ter•ly

latter•most

lat•tice

lat•ticed

lattice•work

Lat•vian

laud

laud•abil•ity (or •able•ness)

laud•able

laud•ably

lau•da•num

lauda•tory (or •tive)

laugh

laugh•able

laugh•ably

laugh•er

laugh•ing

laugh•ing•ly

laughing•stock

laugh•ter

launch

launch•er

laun•der

laun•der•er

laun•dress

Laun•dro•mat (*Trademark*)

laun•dry (*pl* •dries)

laundry•man (*pl* •men)

laundry•woman (*pl* •women)

lau•re•ate

lau•re•ate•ship

lau•rel (•rel•ing, •reled; *Brit* •rel•ling, •relled)

lau•rus•ti•nus

lava molten rock; *cf* larva; laver

lava•tory (*pl* •tories)

lav•en•der

la•ver seaweed;

vessel; *cf* **larva;**
lava
lav•ish
lav•ish•ly
lav•ish•ness
law rule, etc.; *cf*
lore
law-abiding
law•breaker
law•breaking
law•ful
law•ful•ly
law•ful•ness
law•giver
law•giving
law•less
law•less•ly
law•less•ness
law•maker
law•man (*pl* •men)
lawn
law•suit
law•yer
lax
laxa•tive
lax•ity (*or*
lax•ness)
lax•ly
lay (lay•ing, laid)
place on surface;
nonclerical;
ballad; *cf* **lei**
lay•away
*layed *incorrect*
spelling of* **laid**
lay•er
lay•er•ing
lay•ette
lay•ing

lay•man (*pl* •men)
lay•off
lay•out
lay•over
lay•shaft
lay-up (*n*)
lay•woman (*pl*
•women)
laze
la•zi•ly
la•zi•ness
lazy (la•zi•er,
la•zi•est)
lazy•bones
lea (*or* ley)
meadow; *cf* **lee**
leach percolate; *cf*
leech
leach•er
lead (lead•ing, led)
guide; *cf* **lied**
(song)
lead (lead•ing,
lead•ed) metal; *cf*
led
lead•en
lead•en•ly
lead•en•ness
lead•er one that
leads; *cf* **lieder**
(songs)
lead•er•ship
lead-in (*n*)
lead•ing
lead•off
lead•wort
leaf (*pl* leaves)
leaf•age
leaf•hopper

leafi•ness
leaf•let
leaf-stalk
leafy (leafi•er,
leafi•est)
league (leagu•ing,
leagued)
leak hole; escape;
cf **leek**
leak•age
leak•er
leaki•ness
leaky (leaki•er,
leaki•est)
lean (lean•ing,
leaned; *Brit*
lean•ing, leant *or*
leaned) incline;
thin; *cf* **lien**
lean•ness
leant *a Brit past
tense of* **lean;** *cf*
lent
lean-to (*pl* -tos)
leap (leap•ing,
leaped *or* leapt)
leap•er
leap•frog
(•frog•ging,
•frogged)
leapt
learn (learn•ing,
learned *or* learnt)
learn•able
learned (*adj*)
learn•ed•ly
learn•ed•ness
learn•er
learn•ing

learnt

leary *variant spelling of* leery

leas•able

lease

lease•back

lease•hold

lease•holder

leas•er

leash

least

least•wise (*Brit* •ways)

leath•er

leather•back

leath•eri•ness

leather•jacket

leather•neck

leather•wood

leather•work

leath•ery

leave (leav•ing, left)

leaved

leav•en

leav•en•ing

leav•er

leaves *pl of* leaf *or* leave; *present tense of* leave

leave-taking

leav•ing

Leba•nese

lech•er

lech•er•ous

lech•ery (*pl* •eries)

lec•tern

lec•ture

lec•tur•er

lec•ture•ship

led *past tense of* lead (guide); *cf*

lead (metal)

le•der•ho•sen

ledge

ledged

ledg•er

lee sheltered side; *cf* lea

leech bloodsucker; *cf* leach

leek vegetable; *cf* leak

leer

leery (*or* leary; leeri•er, leeri•est *or* leari•er, leari•est)

lees

lee•ward

lee•way

left

left-hand (*adj*)

left-handed

left-handed•ly

left-handed•ness

left-hand•er

left•ism

left•ist

left•over (*adj*)

left•overs (*pl n*)

left•ward (*adj*)

left•ward (*Brit* •wards; *adv*)

left-wing (*adj*)

left-wing•er

lefty (*pl* lefties)

leg (leg•ging, legged)

lega•cy (*pl* •cies)

le•gal

le•gal•ese

le•gal•ism

le•gal•ist

le•gal•is•tic

le•gal•is•ti•cal•ly

le•gal•ity (*pl* •ities)

le•gali•za•tion

le•gal•ize

le•gal•ly

leg•ate envoy

lega•tee recipient of legacy

le•ga•tion

le•ga•to (*pl* •tos)

leg•end

leg•end•ary (*adj*)

leg•end•ry (*n*)

leg•er•de•main

legged *past tense of* leg

#eg•ged having legs

leg•gi•ness

leg•ginged (*or* •gined)

leg•gings (*or* •gins)

leg•gy (•gi•er, •gi•est)

leg•ibil•ity (*or* •ible•ness)

leg•ible

leg•ibly

le•gion

le•gion•ary (*pl* •aries)

le•gion•naire

leg•is•late

leg•is•la•tion
leg•is•la•tive
leg•is•la•tor
leg•is•la•ture
le•giti•ma•cy (*or* •mate•ness)
le•giti•mate
le•giti•mate•ly
le•giti•ma•tize *variant of* legitimize
le•giti•mi•za•tion
le•giti•mize (*or* •ma•tize)
leg•less
leg•man (*pl* •men)
leg-pull
leg•room
leg•ume
le•gu•mi•nous
leg•work
lei Hawaiian garland; *cf* lay
lei•sure
lei•sured
lei•sure•li•ness
lei•sure•ly
leit•mo•tiv (*or* •tif)
lem•ming
lem•on
lem•on•ade
lem•ony
le•mur
lend (lend•ing, lent)
lend•er
length
length•en
length•en•er
lengthi•ly

lengthi•ness
length•wise (*or* •ways)
lengthy (lengthi•er, lengthi•est)
le•ni•en•cy (*or* •ni•ence; *pl* •cies *or* •ences)
le•ni•ent
le•ni•ent•ly
lens
lens•man (*pl* •men)
Lent time of penance
lent *past tense of* lend; *cf* leant
Lent•en
len•til
len•to (*pl* •tos)
leo•nine
leop•ard
leop•ard•ess
leo•tard
lep•er
lepi•dop•ter•an (*pl* •ter•ans *or* •tera)
lepi•dop•ter•ist
lepi•dop•ter•ous
lep•re•chaun
lep•ro•sy
lep•rous
les•bian
les•bi•an•ism
lese ma•jes•ty (*or* lèse ma•jes•té; *pl* •ties *or* •tés)
le•sion
less (less•er, least)
les•see

less•en decrease; *cf* lesson
less•er less great; *cf* lessor
les•son instruction; *cf* lessen
les•sor one who grants lease; *cf* lesser
lest
let (let•ting, let)
let•down
le•thal
le•thal•ly
le•thar•gic
le•thar•gi•cal•ly
leth•ar•gy (*pl* •gies)
let•ter
let•tered
letter•head
let•ter•ing
letter-perfect
letter•press
let•ter•set
let•ting
let•tuce
let•up
leu•ke•mia (*Brit* •kae•mia)
leuko•cyte (*Brit* leuco•)
le•vee embankment; *cf* levy
lev•el (•el•ing, •eled; *Brit* •el•ling, •elled)
level-headed
level-headed•ly
level-headed•ness

lev•el•er (*Brit* •el•ler)
lev•el•ly
lev•er
lev•er•age
lev•er•et
levi•able
le•via•than
levi•er
Le•vi's (*Trademark*)
levi•tate
levi•ta•tion
levi•ta•tor
lev•ity (*pl* •ities)
levy (*vb* levies, levy•ing, levied; *n*, *pl* levies) tax; *cf* levee
lewd
lewd•ly
lewd•ness
lexi•cal
lexi•cog•ra•pher
lexi•co•graph•ic (*or* •graphi•cal)
lexi•cog•ra•phy
lexi•co•logi•cal
lexi•colo•gist
lexi•col•ogy
lexi•con (*pl* •ca *or* •cons)
ley *variant spelling of* lea; *cf* lee
li•abil•ity (*pl* •ities)
li•able
li•aise
liai•son
lia•na (*or* li•ane)

liar one who lies; *cf* lyre
li•ba•tion
li•ba•tion•al (*or* •ary)
li•bel (•bel•ing, •beled; *Brit* •bel•ling, •belled)
li•bel•er (*or* •bel•ist; *Brit* •bel•ler *or* •bel•ist)
li•bel•ous (*Brit* •bel•lous)
lib•er•al
lib•er•al•ism
lib•er•al•ist
lib•er•al•is•tic
lib•er•al•ity (*pl* •ities)
lib•er•ali•za•tion
lib•er•al•ize
lib•er•al•iz•er
lib•er•al•ly
lib•er•al•ness
lib•er•ate
lib•er•a•tion
lib•era•tor
lib•er•tar•ian freethinker; *cf* libertine
lib•er•tar•ian•ism
lib•er•tine dissolute person; *cf* libertarian
lib•er•tin•ism (*or* •age)
lib•er•ty (*pl* •ties)
li•bidi•nal
li•bidi•nous

li•bi•do (*pl* •dos)
li•brar•ian
li•brar•ian•ship
li•brary (*pl* •braries)
li•bret•tist
li•bret•to (*pl* •tos *or* •ti)
Liby•an
lice *pl of* louse
li•cence *Brit spelling of* license (*n*)
li•cens•able
li•cense (*vb*)
li•cense (*Brit* •cence; *n*)
li•cen•see (*or* •cee)
li•cens•er (*or* •cenc•, •cen•sor)
li•cen•sure
li•cen•ti•ate licence holder
li•cen•tious promiscuous
li•cen•tious•ness
li•chee *variant spellings of* litchi
li•chen plant; *cf* liken
li•chen•ous
lich-gate (*or* lych-)
lic•it
lick
lick•er
lickety-split
lick•ing
lick•spittle

lico•rice (*Brit* li•quo•)
lid
lid•ded
lid•less
lie (ly•ing, lied) tell untruth; *cf* lye
lie (ly•ing, lay, lain) recline; *cf* lye
lied told untruth
lied (*pl* lied•er) song; *cf* lead (guide)
lien property right; *cf* lean
lieu
lieu•ten•an•cy
lieu•ten•ant
life (*pl* lives)
life•blood
life•boat
life•guard
life•less
life•less•ly
life•less•ness
life•like
life•line
life•long for life; *cf* livelong
lif•er
life•saver
life•saving
life-size (*or* -sized)
life•style
life•time
life•work
lift
lift•able
lift•er

lift•off
liga•ment
liga•men•tous (*or* •tal, •ta•ry)
liga•ture
light (light•ing, light•ed *or* lit)
light•en
light•en•er
light•en•ing making lighter; *cf* lightning
light•er
light-fingered
light-footed
light-headed
light-headed•ly
light-headed•ness
light-hearted
light-hearted•ly
light-hearted•ness
light•house
light•ing
light•ish
light•ly
light•ness
light•ning light flash; *cf* lightening
light-sensitive (*adj*)
light•ship
light•weight
light-year
lig•ne•ous
lig•ni•fi•ca•tion
lig•ni•fy (•fies, •fy•ing, •fied)
lig•nite
lig•num vi•tae
lik•able (*or* like•)

lik•able•ness (*or* like•)
like
like•li•hood (*or* •ness)
like•ly (•li•er, •li•est)
like-minded
like-minded•ly
like-minded•ness
lik•en compare; *cf* lichen
like•ness
like•wise
lik•ing
li•lac
lilt
lilt•ing
lily (*pl* lilies)
lily-livered
lima bean
limb arm or leg; *cf* limn
lim•ber
limb•less
lim•bo (*pl* •bos)
lime
lime•ade
lime•kiln
lime•light
lim•er•ick
lime•stone
lime•water
lim•ey Briton; *cf* limy
lim•it
lim•it•able
limi•ta•tion
lim•it•ed

lim•it•er

lim•it•less

limn to draw; *cf* **limb**

lim•ner

limou•sine

limp

limp•er

lim•pet

lim•pid

lim•pid•ity (*or* •ness)

limp•ing•ly

limp•kin

limp•ness

limy (limi•er, limi•est) of lime; *cf* limey

lin•age (*or* line•) number of lines; *cf* lineage

linch•pin pin for wheel; *cf* lynch

linc•tus (*pl* •tuses)

lin•den

line (lin•ing, lined)

lin•eage descent from ancestor; *cf* linage

lin•eal

lin•eal•ly directly; *cf* linearly

linea•ment facial feature; *cf* liniment

lin•ear

lin•ear•ity

lin•ear•ly in a line; *cf* lineally

lin•eate (*or* •eat•ed)

lin•eation

line•backer

line•man (*pl* •men) footballer; one who repairs power lines; *cf* linesman

lin•en

lin•er

lines•man (*pl* •men) sporting official; one who repairs power lines; *cf* lineman

line•up

ling heather

ling (*pl* ling *or* lings) fish

ling•cod (*pl* •cod *or* •cods)

lin•ger

lin•ger•er

lin•gerie

lin•ger•ing•ly

lin•go (*pl* •goes)

lin•gua fran•ca (*pl* lin•gua fran•cas *or* lin•guae fran•cae)

lin•gual

lin•gual•ly

lin•guist

lin•guis•tic

lin•guis•ti•cal•ly

lin•guis•tics

lini•ment topical medicine; *cf* lineament

lin•ing

link

link•able

link•age

link•man (*pl* •men)

links golf course; *cf* lynx

link•up

link•work

lin•net

li•no•cut

li•no•leum

lin•seed

lint

lin•tel

lin•teled (*Brit* •telled)

lion

li•on•ess

lion•fish (*pl* •fish *or* •fishes)

lion-hearted

li•oni•za•tion

li•on•ize

li•on•iz•er

lip (lip•ping, lipped)

li•pid

lipo•suc•tion

Lip•pi•zan•er (*or* •za•na, Lip•iz• zan•er, Lip•piz• zan•er)

lip•py (•pi•er, •pi•est)

lip-read (-read•ing, -read)

lip-reader

lip•stick

lip-sync (*or* •sync, •synch)
liq•ue•fac•tion
liq•ue•fi•able
liq•ue•fi•er
liq•ue•fy (•fies, •fy•ing, •fied)
li•queur *sweet alcoholic spirit; cf* liquor
liq•uid
liq•ui•date
liq•ui•da•tion
liq•ui•da•tor
li•quid•ity (*pl* •ities)
liq•uid•ize
liq•uid•iz•er
liq•ui•fy *variant spelling of* liquefy
liq•uor *any alcoholic drink; cf* liqueur
li•quo•rice *Brit spelling of* licorice
lira (*pl* lire *or* liras)
lirio•den•dron (*pl* •drons *or* •dra)
lisle
lisp
lisp•er
lis•som (*or* •some)
lis•som•ness (*or* •some•)
list
list•ed
lis•ten
lis•ten•er
lis•teria

list•ing
list•less
list•less•ly
list•less•ness
lit
lita•ny (*pl* •nies)
li•tchi (*or* •chee, ly•chee; *pl* •tchis, •chees, *or* •chees)
li•ter (*Brit* •tre)
lit•era•cy
lit•er•al *of words or letters; cf* littoral
lit•er•al•ism
lit•er•al•ist
lit•er•al•is•tic
lit•er•al•ly
lit•er•al•ness (*or* •ity)
lit•er•ari•ness
lit•er•ary
lit•er•ate
lit•era•ti (*pl n*)
lit•era•ture
lithe
lithe•ly
lithe•ness
lith•ium
li•tho (*pl* •thos)
litho•graph
li•thog•ra•pher
litho•graph•ic (*or* •graphi•cal)
litho•graphi•cal•ly
li•thog•ra•phy
Lithua•nian
liti•gant

liti•gate
liti•ga•tion
liti•ga•tor
li•ti•gious
lit•mus
li•tre *Brit spelling of* liter
lit•ter
litter•bug
lit•tle
lit•to•ral *of the shore; cf* literal
li•tur•gi•cal (*or* •gic)
li•tur•gi•cal•ly
lit•ur•gy (*pl* •gies)
liv•able (*or* live•)
live
live•able *variant spelling of* livable
lived-in
live-in (*adj*)
live•li•hood
live•li•ness
live•long *very long; entire; cf* lifelong
live•ly (•li•er, •li•est)
liv•en
liv•en•er
liv•er
liv•er•ish
liv•er•ish•ness
liver•wort *plant*
liver•wurst *sausage*
liv•ery (*pl* •eries)
lives *pl of* life; *present tense of* live

live•stock
liv•id
liv•id•ly
liv•id•ness (or
  li•vid•ity)
liv•ing
liz•ard
lla•ma animal; cf
  lama
lla•no (pl •nos)
lo exclamation; cf
  low
load burden, etc.;
  cf lode
load•ed
load•er
load•ing
load•star variant
  spelling of
  lodestar
load•stone variant
  spelling of lode-
  stone
loaf (pl loaves)
loaf•er
loam
loami•ness
loamy (loami•er,
  loami•est)
loan something
  lent; lend cf lone
loan•able
loan•er
loan•word
loath (or loth)
  reluctant
loathe to hate
loath•ing
loath•ly

loath•some
loath•some•ness
loaves pl of loaf
lob (lob•bing,
  lobbed)
lo•bar
lo•bate (or •bat•ed)
lobbed
lob•bing
lob•by (n, pl •bies;
  vb •bies, •by•ing,
  •bied)
lob•by•er
lob•by•ist
lobe
lo•belia
lob•lol•ly (pl •lies)
lo•boto•my (pl
  •mies)
lob•ster (pl •sters
  or •ster)
lo•cal (adj)
lo•cale (n)
lo•cal•ity (pl •ities)
lo•cali•za•tion
lo•cal•ize
lo•cal•ly
lo•cat•able
lo•cate
lo•cat•er (or
  •ca•tor)
lo•ca•tion
loci pl of locus
lock
lock•able
lock•er
lock•et
lock•jaw
lock•out (n)

lock•smith
lock•up (n)
lo•cos (pl locos or
  locoes)
lo•co•mo•tion
lo•co•mo•tive
lo•co•weed
lo•cus (pl •ci)
lo•cust
lo•cu•tion
lode ore deposit; cf
  load
lode•star (or load•)
lode•stone (or
  load•)
lodge
lodge•able
lodg•er
lodg•ing
lodg•ings
lodg•ment (or
  lodge•)
loft
lofti•ly
lofti•ness
lofty (lofti•er,
  lofti•est)
log (log•ging,
  logged)
lo•gan•ber•ry (pl
  •berries)
loga•rithm
loga•rith•mic (or
  •mi•cal)
loga•rith•mi•cal•ly
log•book
logged
log•ger
log•ger•head

log•gia (*pl* •gias *or*
  •gie)
log•ging
log•ic
logi•cal
logi•cal•ity (*or*
  •ness)
logi•cal•ly
lo•gi•cian
lo•gis•tic
lo•gis•ti•cal
lo•gis•ti•cal•ly
log•is•ti•cian
lo•gis•tics
log•jam
logo (*pl* logos)
log•roll•ing
log•wood
logy (logi•er,
  logi•est)
loin
loin•cloth
loi•ter
loi•ter•er
loll
lol•la•pa•loo•za
  (*or* lal•apa•,
  lal•la•pa•)
loll•er
lol•li•pop
lol•lop
lol•ly•gag *variant
  spelling of*
  lallygag
lone solitary; *cf*
  loan
lone•li•ness
lone•ly (•li•er,
  •li•est)

lone•ness
lon•er
lone•some
lone•some•ly
lone•some•ness
long
long•boat
long•bow
long•cloth
long-distance (*adj*)
long-drawn-out (*or*
  long-drawn)
lon•gev•ity
long-haired
long•hand
long•horn
long•ing
long•ing•ly
long•ish
lon•gi•tude
lon•gi•tu•di•nal
lon•gi•tu•di•nal•ly
long johns
long-lived
long-range (*adj*)
long•ship
long•shore
long•shore•man (*pl*
  •men)
long-sighted
long-sighted•ness
long•spur
long-standing
long-suffering
long-term
long•time (*adj*)
long-winded
long-winded•ly
long-winded•ness

long•wise (*Brit*
  •ways)
loo•fah (*or* •fa,
  luf•fa)
look
look-alike
look•er
looker-on (*pl*
  lookers-)
look-in (*n*)
look•out
look-over (*n*)
look-see
loom
loon
looni•ness
loony (*or* loo•ney;
  adj looni•er,
  looni•est; *n, pl*
  loonies *or* •neys)
loop
loop•er
loop•hole
loopi•ness
loopy (loopi•er,
  loopi•est)
loose
loose-jointed
loose-leaf (*adj*)
loose•ly
loos•en
loose•ness
loose•strife
loose-tongued
loot spoils; *cf* lute
loot•er
lop (lop•ping,
  lopped)
lope

lop-eared
lop•er
lopped
lop•per
lop•ping
lop•sided
lop•sided•ly
lop•sided•ness
lo•qua•cious
lo•quac•ity (or
lo•qua•cious•ness)
lo•quat
Lord God
lord nobleman
lord•li•ness
lord•ling
lord•ly (•li•er,
•li•est)
lord•ship
lore knowledge; cf
law
lor•gnette
lori•keet
lor•ry (pl •ries)
(Brit) truck
lory (pl lories)
parrot
los•able (or lose•)
lose (los•ing, lost)
los•er
los•ing
loss
lost
lot (lot•ting, lot•ted)
loth variant
spelling of loath
lo•tion
lo•tos variant
spelling of lotus

lot•ted
lot•tery (pl •teries)
lot•ting
lot•to
lo•tus (or •tos)
lotus-eater (or
lotos-)
loud
loud•ish
loud•ly
loud•mouth
loud•ness
loud•speaker
lounge
loung•er
lounge•wear
lour variant
spelling of lower
(look menacing)
louse (pl lice)
lousi•ly
lousi•ness
lousy (lousi•er,
lousi•est)
lout
lout•ish
lout•ish•ness
lou•ver (Brit •vre)
lou•vered (Brit
•vred)
lov•abil•ity (or
love•)
lov•able (or love•)
lov•ably (or love•)
lov•age
love
love•bird
love•less
love•li•ness

love•lock
love•lorn
love•ly (adj •li•er,
•li•est; n, pl •lies)
love•making
lov•er
love•sick
love•sick•ness
lovey-dovey
lov•ing
lov•ing•ly
lov•ing•ness
low not high; to
moo; cf lo
low•born
low•boy
low•bred
low•brow
low•down (n)
low-down (adj)
low•er less high;
make less high
low•er (or lour)
look menacing
low•er•able
lower•case (adj, vb)
lower-class (adj)
low•er•ing•ly (or
lour•)
lower•most
low•est
low-grade (adj)
low-key (or -keyed)
low•land
low•land•er
low-level (adj)
low•li•ness
low•ly (•li•er,
•li•est)

low-lying
low-minded
low•ness
low-pitched
low-pressure (*adj*)
low-rise (*adj*)
low-spirited
low-tension (*adj*)
lox (*pl* **lox** *or* **loxes**)
loy•al
loy•al•ism
loy•al•ist
loy•al•ly
loy•al•ty (*pl* •ties)
loz•enge
luau
lub•ber
lub•ri•cant
lu•bri•cate
lu•bri•ca•tion
lu•bri•ca•tor
lu•bric•i•ty (*pl* •ities)
lu•bri•cous (*or* •cious)
lu•cid
lu•cid•ity (*or* •ness)
lu•cid•ly
luck
lucki•ly
lucki•ness
luck•less
luck•less•ness
lucky (lucki•er, lucki•est)
luc•ra•tive
lu•cra•tive•ly
lu•cra•tive•ness

lu•cre
lu•di•crous
luf•fa *variant spelling of* **loofah**
lug (lug•ging, lugged)
luge
lug•gage
lugged
lug•ging
lu•gu•bri•ous
lug•worm
luke•warm
lull
lulla•by (*n*, *pl* •bies; *vb* •bies, •by•ing, •bied)
lulu
lum•ba•go
lum•bar *of the back*
lum•ber *timber; move awkwardly*
lum•ber•er
lum•ber•ing
lumber•jack
lumber•jacket
lumber•yard
lu•mi•nance
lu•mi•nary (*pl* •naries)
lu•mi•nesce
lu•mi•nes•cence
lu•mi•nes•cent
lu•mi•nos•ity (*pl* •ities)
lu•mi•nous
lu•mi•nous•ly
lump

lump•ec•to•my (*pl* •mies)
lump•er
lump•fish (*pl* •fish *or* •fishes)
lumpi•ly
lumpi•ness
lump•ish
lumpy (lumpi•er, lumpi•est)
luna *moth*; *cf* lunar
lu•na•cy (*pl* •cies)
lu•nar *of the moon*; *cf* luna
lu•nate (*or* •nat•ed)
lu•na•tic
lunch
lunch•eon
lunch•eon•ette
lunch•er
lunch•room
lunch•time
lu•nette
lung
lunge
lung•er
lung•fish (*pl* •fish *or* •fishes)
lung•ful (*pl* •fuls *or* lungs•)
lung•worm
lung•wort
lu•pine (*Brit* •pin) *plant*
lu•pine *wolflike*
lu•pus *skin disease*
lurch
lurch•er
lure

lur•er
lu•rid
lu•rid•ly
lu•rid•ness
lurk
lurk•er
lus•cious
lus•cious•ness
lush
lush•ly
lush•ness
lust
lus•ter (*Brit* •tre)
lus•ter•less (*Brit* •tre•)
luster•ware (*Brit* lustre•)
lust•ful
lust•ful•ly
lust•ful•ness
lusti•ly
lusti•ness
lus•tre *Brit spelling of* luster
lus•trous
lusty (lusti•er, lusti•est)
lute musical instrument; *cf* loot
lu•te•nist (*or* •ta•, lut•ist)
Lu•ther•an
Lu•ther•an•ism
lux (*pl* lux *or* luxes)
luxu•ri•ance
luxu•ri•ant
luxu•ri•ant•ly

luxu•ri•ate
luxu•ri•ous
luxu•ri•ous•ly
luxu•ry (*pl* •ries)
ly•can•thrope
ly•can•thro•py
ly•ceum
ly•chee *variant spelling of* litchi
lych-gate *variant spelling of* lich-gate
lye alkaline solution; *cf* lie
ly•ing
lying-in (*pl* lyings-in *or* lying-ins)
Lyme dis•ease
lymph
lym•phat•ic
lym•pho•ma (*pl* •ma•ta *or* •mas)
lynch kill; *cf* linchpin
lynch•er
lynch•ing
lynx (*pl* lynxes *or* lynx) cat; *cf* links
lyre musical instrument; *cf* liar
lyre•bird
lyr•ic
lyri•cal
lyri•cal•ly
lyri•cism
lyri•cist
lyr•ist

M

ma
Ma'am
mac (*or* mack) mackintosh; *cf* Mach
ma•ca•bre
mac•ad•am road surface
maca•da•mia nut
mac•ad•ami•za•tion
mac•ad•am•ize
ma•caque
maca•ro•ni (*pl* •nis *or* •nies)
maca•roon
ma•caw
mace
mac•er•ate
mac•era•tion
Mach number indicating speed of sound; *cf* mac
ma•chete
Machia•vel•lian (*or* •vel•ian)
ma•chin•able (*or* •chine•)
machi•nate
machi•na•tion
machi•na•tor
ma•chine
machine-gun (*vb*; -gun•ning, -gunned)
machine-readable

ma•chin•ery (pl •eries)
ma•chin•ist
ma•chis•mo
macho (pl machos)
mack variant spelling of mac
mack•er•el (pl •el or •els)
mack•in•tosh (or mac•in•)
mac•ra•mé (or •me)
macro•bi•ot•ic
macro•cosm
macro•cos•mic
macro•cos•mi•cal•ly
macro•eco•nom•ic
macro•eco•nom•ics
macro•mo•lecu•lar
macro•mol•ecule
mac•ron
macro•scop•ic (or •scopi•cal)
macro•scopi•cal•ly
mad (mad•der, mad•dest)
mad•am (pl mes•dames or mad•ams) term of address; brothel keeper
mad•ame (pl mes•dames) (French) lady; Mrs
mad•cap
mad•den
mad•den•ing

mad•der
mad•dest
made
Ma•dei•ra
mad•emoi•selle (pl mad•emoi•selles or mes•de•moi•selles)
made-to-order
made-up (adj)
mad•house
mad•ly
mad•man (pl •men)
mad•ness
Ma•don•na (or ma•)
mad•ras
mad•ri•gal
mad•ri•gal•ist
ma•dro•ña (or •ño, •ne; pl •ñas, •ños, or •nes)
mad•woman (pl •women)
mael•strom
mae•nad (or me•nad)
maes•tro (pl •tros or •tri)
Ma•fia (or Maf•fia)
ma•fio•so (pl •sos or •si)
mag
maga•zine
ma•gen•ta
mag•got
mag•goti•ness
mag•goty

magi pl of magus
mag•ic (•ick•ing, •icked)
magi•cal
magi•cal•ly
ma•gi•cian
mag•is•te•rial
mag•is•te•rial•ly
mag•is•tra•cy (or •ture; pl •cies or •tures)
mag•is•trate
mag•ma (pl •mas or •mata)
mag•na cum lau•de
mag•na•nim•ity (pl •ities)
mag•nani•mous
mag•nani•mous•ly
mag•nate powerful person; cf magnet
mag•ne•sia
mag•ne•sium
mag•net iron-attracting metal; cf magnate
mag•net•ic
mag•neti•cal•ly
mag•net•ics
mag•net•ism
mag•net•iz•able
mag•neti•za•tion
mag•net•ize
mag•net•iz•er
mag•ne•to (pl •tos)
mag•ni•fi•able
Mag•nifi•cat
mag•ni•fi•ca•tion
mag•nifi•cence

mag•nifi•cent
splendid; *cf*
munificent
mag•nifi•cent•ly
mag•ni•fi•er
mag•ni•fy (•fies,
•fy•ing, •fied)
mag•nilo•quence
mag•nilo•quent
mag•ni•tude
mag•ni•tu•di•nous
mag•no•lia
mag•num (*pl*
•nums)
mag•num opus
mag•pie
magus (*pl* magi)
ma•ha•ra•jah (or
•ja)
ma•ha•ra•ni (or
•nee) maharajah's
wife
ma•ha•ri•shi
Hindu teacher
ma•hat•ma
Ma•hi•can (or
Mo•; *pl* •cans or
•can)
mah•jong (or mah-
jongg)
ma•hoga•ny (*pl*
•nies)
ma•ho•nia
maid
maid•en
maiden•hair
maiden•head
maid•en•hood
maid•en•li•ness

maid•en•ly
maid•servant
mai•hem *variant
spelling of* **may-
hem**
mail transported
letters; armor; *cf*
male
mail•able
mail•bag
mail•box
mail•er
mail•man (*pl* •men)
mail-order (*adj*)
mail•room
mail•sack
mail•shot
maim
maim•er
main chief; *cf* **mane**
main•frame
main•land
main•line (*adj, vb*)
main•lin•er
main•ly
main•mast
main•sail
main•spring
main•stay
main•stream
main•tain
main•tain•able
main•tain•er
main•te•nance
ma•ioli•ca *variant
spelling of*
majolica
mai•son•ette (or
•son•nette)

maî•tre d'hô•tel (or
maî•tre d'; *pl*
maî•tres d'hô•tel
or mai•tre d's)
maize cereal; *cf*
maze
ma•jes•tic (or
•ti•cal)
ma•jes•ti•cal•ly
Maj•es•ty (*pl* •ties)
title for royalty
maj•es•ty dignity
ma•joli•ca (or
•ioli•)
ma•jor
ma•jor•do•mo (*pl*
•mos)
ma•jor•ette
ma•jori•tar•ian
ma•jor•ity (*pl*
•ities)
major-league (*adj*)
make (mak•ing,
made)
make-believe (or
-belief; *n*)
make•fast
mak•er
make•over
make•shift
make•up
make•weight
mak•ing
mal•ab•sorp•tion
mala•chite
mal•ad•just•ed
mal•ad•just•ment
mal•ad•min•is•ter

mal•ad•min•is•tra•tion
mal•ad•min•is•tra•tor
mala•droit
mala•droit•ness
mala•dy (*pl* •dies)
ma•laise
mala•mute (*or* mal•emute)
mala•prop•ian
mala•prop•ism (*or* mala•prop)
mal•ap•ro•pos
ma•laria
ma•lar•ial (*or* •lar•ian, •lari•ous)
ma•lar•key (*or* •ky)
Ma•lay
Ma•lay•an
Ma•lay•sian
mal•con•tent
male of men; *cf* mail
mal•edic•tion
mal•edic•tive (*or* •tory)
mal•efac•tion
mal•efac•tor
ma•lef•ic
ma•lefi•cence
ma•lefi•cent
mal•emute *variant spelling of* malamute
male•ness
ma•levo•lence
ma•levo•lent
ma•levo•lent•ly

mal•for•ma•tion
mal•formed
mal•func•tion
mal•ice
ma•li•cious
ma•li•cious•ly
ma•li•cious•ness
ma•lign
ma•lig•nan•cy (*or* •nance; *pl* •cies or •nances)
ma•lig•nant
ma•lign•er
ma•lig•ni•ty (*pl* •nities)
ma•lin•ger
ma•lin•ger•er
mall promenade; shopping complex; *cf* maul
mal•lard (*pl* •lard *or* •lards)
mal•le•abil•ity (*or* •able•ness)
mal•le•able
mal•le•ably
mal•let
mal•low
malm•sey
mal•nour•ished
mal•nu•tri•tion
mal•odor•ous
mal•prac•tice
mal•prac•ti•tion•er
malt
malt•ed
Mal•tese (*pl* •tese)
Mal•thu•sian
Mal•thu•sian•ism

malti•ness
malt•ing
malt•ose
mal•treat
mal•treat•er
mal•treat•ment
malty (malti•er, malti•est)
mama (*or* mam•ma, mom•ma)
mam•ba snake
mam•bo (*pl* •bos) dance
ma•mey (*or* mam•mee) fruit; *cf* mammy
mam•ma *variant spelling of* mama
mam•mal
mam•ma•lian
mam•ma•ry
mam•mee *variant spelling of* mamey
mam•mo•gram
mam•mog•ra•phy
mam•mon
mam•moth
mam•my (*or* •mie; *pl* •mies) mother; *cf* mamey
man (*n, pl* men; *vb* man•ning, manned)
mana power; *cf* manna
mana•cle
man•age

man•age•abil•ity
(*or* •able•ness)
man•age•able
man•age•ably
man•age•ment
man•ag•er
man•ag•er•ess
mana•gerial
mana•geri•al•ly
man•ag•ing
mana•kin bird; *cf*
manikin;
mannequin
ma•ña•na
man-at-arms (*pl*
men-)
mana•tee
man•chi•neel
man•da•la
Man•da•rin
language
man•da•rin official;
fruit; duck
man•da•tary
variant spelling of
mandatory (*n*)
man•date
man•da•to•ri•ly
man•da•tory
obligatory
man•da•tory (*or*
•tary; *pl* •tories *or*
•taries*) mandate
holder
man•di•ble
man•dibu•lar
man•do•la
man•do•lin (*or*
•line)

man•do•lin•ist
man•drake (*or*
man•drago•ra)
man•drel (*or* •dril)
spindle
man•drill monkey
mane long hair; *cf*
main
man-eater
maned
ma•nège (*or* •nege)
riding school; *cf*
ménage
ma•neu•ver (*Brit*
•noeu•vre)
ma•neu•ver•abil•ity
(*Brit*
•noeu•vrabil•)
ma•neu•ver•able
(*Brit* •noeu•vrable)
ma•neu•ver•er (*Brit*
•noeu•vrer)
man•ful
man•ful•ly
man•ful•ness
man•ga•nate
man•ga•nese
mange
man•ger
man•gi•ness
man•gle
man•gler
man•go (*pl* •goes
or •gos)
man•grove
man•gy (*or* •gey;
•gi•er, •gi•est)
man•handle
man•hole

man•hood
man-hour
man•hunt
man hunt•er
ma•nia
ma•ni•ac
ma•nia•cal
ma•nia•cal•ly
man•ic
manic-depressive
mani•cure
mani•cur•ist
mani•fest
mani•fest•able
mani•fes•ta•tion
mani•fest•ly
mani•fes•to (*pl*
•toes *or* •tos)
mani•fold
mani•kin (*or*
mana•kin,
man•ni•kin)
dwarf; *cf*
manakin;
mannequin
mani•oc (*or*
manio•ca)
ma•nipu•labil•ity
ma•nipu•lat•able
(*or* •nipu•lable)
ma•nipu•late
ma•nipu•la•tion
ma•nipu•la•tive
ma•nipu•la•tor
ma•nipu•la•tory
mani•tou (*or* •tu,
•to; *pl* •tous, •tou,
•tus, •tu, *or* •tos,
•to)

man•kind
man•like
man•li•ness
man•ly (•li•er,
•li•est)
man-made
man•na celestial
food; cf mana
manned
man•ne•quin
model; cf
manakin; manikin
man•ner behavior;
cf manor
man•nered
man•ner•ism
man•ner•ist
man•ner•is•tic (or
•ti•cal)
man•ner•is•ti•cal•ly
man•ner•less
man•ner•less•ness
man•ner•li•ness
man•ner•ly
man•nish
man•nish•ly
man•nish•ness
ma•noeu•vrable
Brit spelling of
maneuverable
ma•noeu•vre Brit
spelling of
maneuver
man-of-war (pl
men-)
ma•nom•e•ter
mano•met•ric (or
•ri•cal)
ma•nom•e•try

man•or estate; cf
manner
ma•no•rial
man•power
man•qué
man•sard
man•servant (pl
men•servants)
man•sion
man-sized (or -size)
man•slaughter
man•ta
man•tel (or •tle)
frame around
fireplace; cf
mantle
mantel•piece
mantel•shelf (pl
•shelves)
man•til•la
man•tis (pl •tises
or •tes)
man•tle cloak;
region below
earth's crust;
cf mantel
man•tra
man•trap
manu•al
manu•al•ly
manu•fac•tory (pl
•tories)
manu•fac•tur•able
manu•fac•ture
manu•fac•tur•er
manu•fac•tur•ing
manu•mis•sion
manu•mit

(•mit•ting,
•mit•ted)
ma•nure
manu•script
Manx
many (more, most)
many-sided
many-sided•ness
Mao•ism
Mao•ist
Mao•ri (pl •ris or
•ri)
map (map•ping,
mapped)
ma•ple
map•pable
mar (mar•ring,
marred)
mara•bou (or
•bout)
ma•raca
mara•schi•no (pl
•nos)
mara•thon
ma•raud
ma•raud•er
mar•ble
mar•bled
mar•bling
mar•bly
mar•ca•site
March month
march walk, etc.
march•er
mar•chion•ess
Mar•di Gras
mare (pl mares)
female horse

mare (*pl* ma•ria)
lunar plain
mar•ga•ri•ta
cocktail; *cf*
marguerite
mar•ga•rite
mineral; *cf*
marguerite
mar•gin
mar•gin•al
mar•gi•na•lia
mar•gin•al•ly
mar•gin•ali•za•tion
mar•gin•al•ize
mar•gue•rite
flower; *cf*
margarite
mari•gold
mari•jua•na (*or*
•hua•)
ma•rim•ba
ma•ri•na
mari•nade (*n*)
mari•nate (*or*
•nade; *vb*)
mari•na•tion
ma•rine
mari•ner
mari•on•ette
mari•po•sa
mari•tal
mari•time
mar•jo•ram
mark spot, sign,
etc.; *cf* marque
mark•down
marked
mark•ed•ly
mark•ed•ness

mark•er
mar•ket
mar•ket•abil•ity
(*or* •able•ness)
mar•ket•able
mar•ket•er
mar•ket•ing
market•place
mark•ing
marks•man (*pl*
•men)
marks•man•ship
mark•up
marl
mar•lin (*pl* •lin *or*
•lins) fish
mar•line (*or* •lin)
rope
mar•line•spike (*or*
•lin•, •ling•)
marly
mar•ma•lade
mar•mo•real (*or*
•rean)
mar•mo•set
mar•mot
maro•cain
ma•roon
ma•rooned
marque brand of
car; *cf* mark
mar•quee tent;
canopy; *cf*
marquis
mar•quess British
nobleman; *cf*
marquis
mar•que•try (*or*

•que•te•rie; *pl*
•tries *or* •ries)
mar•quis (*pl*
•quises *or* •quis)
continental
European
nobleman; *cf*
marquee;
marquess
mar•quise gem-
stone; wife of
marquis
mar•ram
Mar•ra•no (*pl*
•nos)
marred
mar•rer
mar•riage
mar•riage•abil•ity
(*or* •able•ness)
mar•riage•able
mar•ried
mar•ring
mar•ron gla•cé (*pl*
mar•rons gla•cés)
mar•row
marrow•bone
marrow•fat
mar•ry (•ries,
•ry•ing, •ried)
marsh
mar•shal (•shal•
ing, •shaled; *Brit*
•shal•ling,
•shalled) to
organize; officer;
cf martial
mar•shal•er (*Brit*
•shal•ler)

mar•shal•cy (*or* •shal•ship*)
marshi•ness
marsh•land
marsh•mal•low candy
marsh mal•low plant
marshy (marshi•er, marshi•est)
mar•su•pial
mart
mar•ten (*pl* •tens *or* •ten) mammal; *cf* martin
mar•tial warlike; *cf* marshal
mar•tial•ism
mar•tial•ist
mar•tial•ly
Mar•tian
mar•tin bird; *cf* marten
mar•ti•net
Mar•ti•ni (*Trade-mark*) vermouth
mar•ti•ni (*pl* •nis) cocktail
mar•tyr
mar•tyr•dom
mar•tyred
mar•tyr•ize
mar•tyri•za•tion
mar•vel (•vel•ing, •veled; *Brit* •vel•ling, •velled)
mar•vel•ous (*Brit* •vel•lous)
Marx•ism

Marx•ist
mar•zi•pan
mas•cara
mas•cot
mas•cu•line
mas•cu•lin•ity (*or* •line•ness)
mas•cu•li•ni•za•tion
mas•cu•lin•ize
ma•ser
mash
mash•er
mask disguise; to cover; *variant spelling of* masque
masked
mask•er *variant spelling of* masquer
mas•ki•nonge *variant spelling of* muskellunge
maso•chism
maso•chist
maso•chis•tic
Ma•son freemason
ma•son stone worker
Mason-Dixon Line
Ma•son•ic
ma•son•ry (*pl* •ries)
masque (*or* mask) entertainment; *cf* mask
mas•quer (*or* mask•er)
mas•quer•ade
mas•quer•ad•er

Mass church service
mass large amount, etc.
mas•sa•cre
mas•sa•crer
mas•sage
mas•sag•er (*or* •ist)
mas•sa•sau•ga
massed
mas•seur (*fem* •seuse)
mas•sif landform
mas•sive huge
mas•sive•ly
mas•sive•ness (*or* •siv•ity)
mass-produce
mass-produc•er
massy (massi•er, massi•est)
mast
mas•tec•to•my (*pl* •mies)
mas•ter
mas•ter-at-arms (*pl* masters-)
mas•ter•ful
mas•ter•ful•ly
mas•ter•ful•ness
mas•ter•li•ness
mas•ter•ly
master•mind
master•piece
mas•ter•ship
master•stroke
master•work
mas•tery (*pl* •teries)

mast•head
mas•tic
mas•ti•cate
mas•ti•ca•tion
mas•ti•ca•tor
mas•ti•ca•tory
mas•tiff
mas•to•don
mas•toid
mas•tur•bate
mas•tur•ba•tion
mas•tur•ba•tor
mat (mat•ting, mat•ted) floor covering; tangle
mat (or matt, matte; mat•ting, mat•ted) lacking gloss; provide with mat surface; cf matte
mata•dor
match
match•board
match•box
match•less
match•less•ness
match•maker
match•making
match•stick
match•wood
mate partner, etc.
maté (or mate) tea
ma•te•rial
ma•te•ri•al•ism
ma•te•ri•al•ist
ma•te•ri•al•is•tic
ma•te•ri•al•ity (pl •ities)

ma•te•ri•ali•za•tion
ma•te•ri•al•ize
ma•te•ri•al•ly
ma•ter•nal
ma•ter•nal•ism
ma•ter•nal•is•tic
ma•ter•nal•ly
ma•ter•nity
math (Brit maths)
math•emati•cal (or •emat•ic)
math•emati•cal•ly
math•ema•ti•cian
math•emat•ics
mati•née (or •nee)
mat•ins
ma•tri•arch
ma•tri•ar•chal (or •chic)
ma•tri•ar•chy (pl •chies)
ma•tri•ces pl of matrix
mat•ri•cid•al
mat•ri•cide
ma•tricu•late
ma•tricu•la•tion
ma•tricu•la•tor
mat•ri•lin•eal
mat•ri•mo•nial
mat•ri•mo•nial•ly
mat•ri•mo•ny (pl •nies)
ma•trix (pl •tri•ces or •trixes)
ma•tron
ma•tron•li•ness
ma•tron•ly
matt (or matte)

variant spellings of mat (lacking gloss)
matte smelting material; cf mat
mat•ted
mat•ter
matter-of-course (adj)
matter-of-fact (adj)
mat•ting
mat•tock
mat•tress
matu•ra•tion
ma•ture
ma•ture•ly
ma•ture•ness
ma•tur•ity
maud•lin
maul to batter; a hammer; cf mall
maul•er
maun•der
maun•der•er
maun•dy
mau•so•leum (pl •leums or •lea)
mauve
mav•er•ick
maw
mawk•ish
mawk•ish•ly
mawk•ish•ness
max•il•la (pl •lae or •las)
max•il•lary (pl •laries)
max•im

maxi•ma *pl of*
  maximum
maxi•mal
maxi•mal•ly
maxi•mi•za•tion
maxi•mize
maxi•miz•er
maxi•mum (*pl*
  •mums *or* •ma)
May
may (might)
Maya (*pl* Maya *or*
  Mayas)
Ma•yan
may•be (*adv*)
may•flower
may•fly (*pl* •flies)
may•hem (*or* mai•)
mayn't
may•on•naise
may•or
may•or•al
may•or•al•ty (*pl*
  •ties)
may•or•ess
may•or•ship
may•pole
may•weed
maze labyrinth;
  confusing net-
  work; *cf* maize
ma•zu•ma
ma•zur•ka (*or*
  •zour•)
Mc•Car•thy•ism
me pronoun; *cf* mi
mea cul•pa
mead
mead•ow

meadow•lark
meadow•sweet
mea•ger (*Brit* •gre)
meal
meal•worm
mealy (meali•er,
  meali•est)
mealy•mouthed
mean (mean•ing,
  meant) intend;
  miserly; mid-
  point; *cf* mien
me•ander
me•ander•er
me•ander•ing•ly
meanie *variant*
  spelling of meany
mean•ing
mean•ing•ful
mean•ing•ful•ly
mean•ing•ful•ness
mean•ing•less
mean•ing•less•ness
mean•ly
mean•ness
means (*pl* means)
meant
mean•time
mean•while
meany (*or* meanie;
  pl meanies)
mea•sles
mea•sly (•sli•er,
  •sli•est)
meas•ur•abil•ity
  (*or* •able•ness)
meas•ur•able
meas•ur•ably
meas•ure

meas•ured
meas•ure•less
meas•ure•ment
meas•ur•er
meat food; *cf* meet;
  mete
meat•ball
meati•ly
meati•ness
meaty (meati•er,
  meati•est)
me•chan•ic
me•chani•cal
me•chani•cal•ly
me•chan•ics
mecha•nism
mecha•nis•tic
mecha•ni•za•tion
mecha•nize
mecha•niz•er
med•al (*vb* •al•ing,
  •aled; *Brit*
  •al•ling, •alled)
  award; *cf* meddle
med•al•ist (*Brit*
  •al•list)
me•dal•lion
med•dle interfere;
  cf medal
med•dler inter-
  ferer; *cf* medlar
med•dle•some
med•dle•some•ness
med•dling•ly
me•dia *pl of* me-
  dium, *esp. in com-*
  munications sense
me•di•aeval *variant*

spelling of medi-
eval
me•dial
me•dial•ly
me•dian
me•di•ate
me•di•a•tion
me•dia•tive (*or*
•tory, •to•rial)
me•dia•tor
med•ic doctor
med•ic (*Brit* •dick)
plant
medi•cable
medi•cal
medi•cal•ly
me•dica•ment
medi•cate
medi•ca•tion
medi•ca•tive
me•dici•nal
me•dici•nal•ly
medi•cine
med•ick *Brit*
spelling of medic
(plant)
medi•co (*pl* •cos)
me•di•eval (*or*
•aeval)
me•di•eval•ism (*or*
•aeval•)
me•di•eval•ist (*or*
•aeval•)
me•di•eval•ly (*or*
•aeval•)
me•dio•cre
me•di•oc•rity (*pl*
•rities)
medi•tate

medi•ta•tion
medi•ta•tive
medi•ta•tive•ly
medi•ta•tor
me•dium (*pl* •dia
or •diums)
med•lar fruit; *cf*
meddler
med•ley
me•dul•la (*pl* •las
or •lae)
me•dul•lary (*or*
•lar)
me•du•sa (*pl* •sas
or •sae)
meek
meek•ly
meek•ness
*meer *incorrect*
spelling of mere
meer•kat
meer•schaum
meet (meet•ing,
met) come to-
gether; suitable;
cf meat; mete
meet•er
meet•ing
mega
mega•bit
mega•buck
mega•byte
mega•cy•cle
mega•death
mega•hertz
mega•lith
mega•lith•ic
mega•lo•ma•nia
mega•lo•ma•ni•ac

mega•lo•saur
mega•phone
mega•star
mega•ton
mega•volt
mega•watt
meio•sis (*pl* •ses)
mei•ot•ic
Meis•sen ware
mela•mine
mel•an•cho•lia
mel•an•cho•li•ac
mel•an•chol•ic
mel•an•choli•cal•ly
mel•an•choly (*pl*
•cholies)
mé•lange
mela•nin
mela•no•ma (*pl*
•mas *or* •mata)
meld
me•lee (*or* mê•lée)
mel•lif•er•ous (*or*
•lif•ic) producing
honey
mel•lif•lu•ous (*or*
•lu•ent) sweet-
sounding
mel•lif•lu•ous•ly
mel•lif•lu•ous•ness
(*or* •lu•ence)
mel•low
mel•low•ness
me•lo•deon
me•lod•ic
me•lodi•cal•ly
me•lo•di•ous
me•lo•di•ous•ly
me•lo•di•ous•ness

melo•dra•ma
melo•dra•mat•ic
melo•dra•mati•
cal•ly
melo•drama•tist
melo•drama•tize
melo•dy (*pl* •dies)
mel•on
melt (melt•ing,
melt•ed, melt•ed
or mol•ten)
melt•able
melt•age
melt•down
melt•er
melt•ing•ly
melt•water
mem•ber
mem•ber•ship
mem•brane
mem•bra•nous
me•men•to (*pl* •tos
or •toes)
me•men•to mori (*pl*
me•men•to mori)
memo (*pl* memos)
mem•oir
memo•ra•bilia (*pl*
n)
memo•rabil•ity (*or*
•rable•ness)
memo•rable
memo•rably
memo•ran•dum (*pl*
•dums *or* •da)
me•mo•rial
me•mo•ri•al•ist
me•mo•ri•ali•za•
tion

me•mo•ri•al•ize
memo•riz•able
memo•ri•za•tion
memo•rize
memo•riz•er
memo•ry (*pl* •ries)
men
men•ace
men•ac•er
men•ac•ing•ly
me•nad *variant*
spelling of maenad
mé•nage
household; *cf*
manège
mé•nage à trois (*pl*
mé•nages à trois)
me•nag•erie
men•ar•che
mend
mend•able
men•da•cious
men•da•cious•ly
men•dac•ity (*pl*
•ities) untruth-
fulness; *cf* mendi-
cancy
mend•er
men•di•can•cy (*or*
men•dic•ity)
begging; *cf*
mendacity
men•di•cant
mend•ing
men•folk (*or*
•folks)
men•ha•den (*pl*
•den *or* •dens)
me•nial

me•nial•ly
me•nin•geal
men•in•gi•tis
me•ninx (*pl*
me•nin•ges)
me•nis•cus (*pl* •ci
or •cuses)
meno•pau•sal
meno•pause
me•no•rah
men•ses
men•strual
men•stru•ate
men•strua•tion
women's monthly
bleeding
men•su•ra•tion
measuring
mens•wear (*or*
men's wear)
men•tal
men•tal•ity (*pl*
•ities)
men•tal•ly
men•thol
men•tho•la•ted
men•tion
men•tion•able
men•tor
menu
meow (*or* miaou,
miaow)
Meph•is•to•phe•
lean (*or* •lian)
mer•can•tile
mer•can•til•ism
mer•can•til•ist
mer•ce•nari•ly
mer•ce•nari•ness

mer•ce•nary (*pl*
•naries)
mer•cer
mer•ceri•za•tion
mer•cer•ize
mer•chan•dise
mer•chan•dis•er
mer•chant
mer•chant•able
mer•ci•ful
mer•ci•ful•ly
mer•ci•ful•ness
mer•ci•less
mer•ci•less•ly
mer•cu•rial
mer•cu•rial•ly
mer•cu•ric
mer•cu•rous
mer•cu•ry (*or* •ries)
mer•cy (*pl* •cies)
mere (*NOT* meer)
mere•ly
mer•etri•cious
insincere; *cf*
meritorious
mer•gan•ser (*pl*
•sers *or* •ser)
merge
mer•gence
mer•ger
me•rid•ian
me•ridio•nal
me•ringue
mer•it
meri•toc•ra•cy (*pl*
•cies)
meri•to•ri•ous
praiseworthy; *cf*
meretricious

mer•lin
mer•maid
mer•man (*pl* •men)
mer•ri•ly
mer•ri•ment
mer•ri•ness
mer•ry (•ri•er,
•ri•est)
merry-go-round
merry•maker
merry•making
me•sa
mes•cal cactus;
alcohol
mes•ca•line drug
mes•dames *pl of*
madame
mes•de•moi•selles
pl of mademoiselle
mes•em•bry•an•
the•mum
mesh
meshy
mes•mer•lc
mes•meri•cal•ly
mes•mer•ism
mes•mer•ist
mes•meri•za•tion
mes•mer•ize
mes•mer•iz•er
Meso•lith•ic
meso•morph
meso•mor•phic
me•son
meso•sphere
mes•quite
mess
mes•sage

Mes•sei•gneurs *pl*
of Monseigneur
mes•sen•ger
Mes•si•ah
mes•si•an•ic (*or*
Mes•)
mes•sieurs *pl of*
monsieur
messi•ly
messi•ness
Messrs. *pl of* Mr.
messy (messi•er,
messi•est)
mes•ti•zo (*fem* •za;
pl •zos, •zoes, *or*
•zas)
met
meta•bol•ic
meta•boli•cal•ly
me•tabo•lism
me•tabo•lite
me•tabo•lize
meta•car•pal
meta•car•pus (*pl*
•pi) hand bones;
cf metatarsus
met•al (•al•ing,
•aled; *Brit* •al•
ling, •alled) sub-
stance; cover with
metal; *cf* mettle
met•al•ist (*Brit*
•al•list)
met•ali•za•tion
(*Brit* met•al•li•)
met•al•ize (*Brit*
•al•lize)
me•tal•lic (*or*
•tal•ic)

me•tal•li•cal•ly
met•al•lif•er•ous
met•al•lur•gic (or •gi•cal)
met•al•lur•gi•cal•ly
met•al•lur•gist
met•al•lur•gy
metal•work
metal•worker
metal•working
meta•mor•phic (or •phous)
meta•mor•phism
  rock-forming process; cf
  metamorphosis
meta•mor•phose
meta•mor•pho•sis (pl •ses)
  transformation; cf
  metamorphism
meta•phor
meta•phor•ic (or •phori•cal)
meta•phori•cal•ly
Meta•physi•cal
  denoting poetic group
meta•physi•cal of metaphysics
meta•physi•cal•ly
meta•phys•ics
me•tas•ta•sis (pl •ses)
me•tas•ta•size
meta•tar•sal
meta•tar•sus (pl •si) foot bones; cf
  metacarpus

mete allot; cf meat; meet
me•teor
me•teor•ic
me•teori•cal•ly
me•teor•ite
me•teor•it•ic
me•teor•oid
me•teoro•logi•cal (or •log•ic)
me•teoro•logi•cal•ly
me•teor•olo•gist
me•teor•ol•ogy
  study of weather; cf **metrology**
me•ter instrument
me•ter (Brit •tre) unit; verse rhythm
metha•done (or •don)
meth•ane
metha•nol
meth•od
me•thodi•cal (or •thod•ic)
me•thodi•cal•ly
me•thodi•cal•ness
Meth•od•ism
Meth•od•ist
meth•odi•za•tion
meth•od•ize
meth•od•iz•er
meth•odo•logi•cal
meth•odo•logi•cal•ly
meth•od•olo•gist

meth•od•ol•ogy (pl •ogies)
me•thyl
meth•yl•ate
meth•yla•tion
me•ticu•lous
me•ticu•lous•ly
me•ticu•lous•ness (or •los•ity)
mé•tier (or me•)
mé•tis (pl •tis)
me•tre Brit spelling of **meter** (unit; verse rhythm)
met•ric
met•ri•cal
met•ri•cal•ly
met•ri•ca•tion
met•ri•cize (Brit •cate)
met•ro•logi•cal
me•trolo•gist
me•trol•ogy (pl •ogies) study of measurement; cf **meteorology**
met•ro•nome
me•tropo•lis (pl •lises)
met•ro•poli•tan
met•ro•poli•tan•ism
met•tle courage; cf **metal**
met•tle•some
mew cat's cry; cf **mu**
mewl cry; cf **mule**
mewl•er

Mexi•can
me•zu•zah (*or* •za;
pl •zahs, •zas,
•zoth, *or* •zot)
mez•za•nine
mez•zo (*pl* •zos)
mezzo-soprano (*pl*
-sopranos)
mez•zo•tint
mi musical note; *cf*
me
miaou (*or* miaow)
variant spellings
of meow
mi•as•ma (*pl*
•ma•ta *or* •mas)
mi•as•mal (*or*
•mat•ic, •mic)
mica
mi•ca•ceous
mice
Mich•ael•mas
Mick•ey Finn
mick•ey mouse
(*adj*)
Mic•mac (*pl* •mac
or •macs)
mi•crobe
mi•cro•bial (*or*
•bic)
mi•cro•bi•cide
micro•bio•logi•cal
(*or* •log•ic)
micro•bi•olo•gist
micro•bi•ol•ogy
micro•chip
micro•cir•cuit
micro•cir•cuit•ry
micro•cli•mate

micro•cli•mat•ic
micro•com•put•er
micro•copy (*pl*
•copies)
micro•cosm (*or*
•cos•mos)
micro•cos•mic (*or*
•cos•mi•cal)
micro•dot
micro•eco•nom•ic
micro•eco•nom•ics
micro•elec•tron•ic
micro•elec•tron•ics
micro•fiche (*pl*
•fich *or* •fiches)
micro•film
micro•graph
mi• #rom•eter
measuring
instrument
#micro•meter (*Brit*
•metre) unit of
length
mi•cron (*pl* •crons
or •cra)
micro•or•gan•ism
micro•phone
micro•phon•ic
micro•pho•to•
graph
micro•pro•ces•sor
micro•scope
micro•scop•ic (*or*
•scopi•cal)
micro•scopi•cal•ly
mi•cros•co•pist
mi•cros•co•py
micro•sec•ond
micro•struc•ture

micro•sur•gery
micro•sur•gi•cal
micro•wave
mic•tu•rate
mic•tu•ri•tion
mid•air
mid•course
mid•day
mid•dle
middle-aged
middle•brow
middle-class (*adj*)
middle-distance
(*adj*)
middle•man (*pl*
•men)
middle-of-the-road
(*adj*)
middle•weight
mid•dling
mid•field
midge
midg•et
midi
mid•land
mid•line
mid•lev•el
mid•life
mid•morn•ing
mid•most
mid•night
mid•point
mid•range
mid•riff
mid•sec•tion
mid•ship
mid•ship•man (*pl*
•men)
mid•ships

midst
mid•sum•mer
mid•term
mid•town
mid•way
mid•week
mid•wife (*pl* •wives)
mid•wife•ry
mid•win•ter
mid•year
mien bearing; *cf* mean
might *past tense of* may; strength; *cf* mite
mighti•ly
mighti•ness
mighty (mighti•er, mighti•est)
mi•gnon•ette
mi•graine
mi•grain•ous
mi•grant
mi•grate
mi•gra•tion
mi•gra•tor
mi•gra•tory
mike
mil•age *variant spelling of* mileage
milch
mild
mil•dew
mil•dewy
mild•ly
mild•ness
mile

mile•age (*or* mil•age)
mile•post
mil•er
mile•stone
mil•foil
mi•lieu (*pl* •lieus *or* •lieux)
mili•tan•cy (*or* •tant•ness)
mili•tant
mili•tant•ly
mili•tari•ly
mili•ta•rism
mili•ta•rist
mili•ta•ris•tic
mili•ta•ris•ti•cal•ly
mili•ta•ri•za•tion
mili•ta•rize
mili•tary (*pl* •tary *or* •taries)
mili•tate
mili•ta•tion
mi•li•tia
mi•li•tia•man (*pl* •men)
milk
milk•er
milk•fish (*pl* •fish *or* •fishes)
milki•ly
milki•ness
milk•maid
milk•man (*pl* •men)
milk•sop
milk•weed
milk•wort
milky (milki•er, milki•est)

Milky Way
mill
mill•able
mill•board
milled
mille-feuille
mil•le•nary (*pl* •naries) a thousand; *cf* millinery
mil•len•nial
mil•len•ni•al•ist
mil•len•nium (*pl* •nia *or* •niums)
mil•le•pede *variant spelling of* millipede
mill•er
mil•let
mil•li•bar
mil•li•gram (*or* •gramme)
mil•li•li•ter (*Brit* •tre)
mil•li•meter (*Brit* •metre)
mil•li•ner
mil•li•nery hat making; *cf* millenary
mill•ing
mil•lion (*pl* •lions *or* •lion)
mil•lion•aire (*or* •lion•naire)
mil•lion•air•ess
mil•lionth
mil•li•pede (*or* •le•pede, •le•ped)
mil•li•sec•ond

mill•pond
mill•race
mill•stone
mill•stream
mill•wright
milque•toast
milt
mil•ter
mime
mimeo•graph
mim•er
mi•me•sis
mi•met•ic
mi•meti•cal•ly
mim•ic (•ick•ing, •icked)
mim•ick•er
mim•ic•ry (pl •ries)
mi•mo•sa
mina variant spelling of myna
min•able (or mine•able)
mina•ret
mina•to•ri•ly (or •ri•al•ly)
mina•tory (or •to•rial)
mince
mince•meat
minc•er
minc•ing
minc•ing•ly
mind
mind-altering
mind-bending
mind-blowing
mind-boggling
mind•ed

mind•er
mind•ful
mind•ful•ly
mind•ful•ness
mind•less
mind•less•ly
mind•less•ness
mind-numbing
mind-set
mine
mine•able variant spelling of minable
mine•field
mine•lay•er
min•er one who mines; cf minor
min•er•al
min•er•ali•za•tion
min•er•al•ize
min•er•al•ogi•cal (or •og•ic)
min•er•alo•gist
min•er•al•ogy (NOT miner-ology)
min•estro•ne
mine•sweeper
mine•sweeping
Ming
min•gle
mini (pl minis)
minia•ture (NOT miniture)
minia•tur•ist
minia•turi•za•tion
minia•tur•ize
mini•bar
mini•bus
mini•com•put•er

min•im
mini•ma pl of minimum
mini•mal
mini•mal•ist
mini•mal•ly
mini•mi•za•tion
mini•mize
mini•miz•er
mini•mum (pl •mums or •ma)
min•ing
min•ion
*miniscule incorrect spelling of minuscule
mini•series
mini•skirt
min•is•ter
min•is•te•rial
min•is•te•rial•ly
min•is•trant
min•is•tra•tion
mln•is•tra•tlve
min•is•try (pl •tries)
*miniture incorrect spelling of miniature
mini•vet
mink (pl mink or minks) weaselike animal
min•ke whale
min•now (pl •nows or •now)
mi•nor lesser; cf miner

mi•nor•ity (*pl*
•ities)
minor-league (*adj*)
min•ster
min•strel
min•strel•sy (*pl*
•sies)
mint
minty (minti•er,
minti•est)
minu•et
mi•nus
mi•nus•cule (*NOT*
miniscule)
#min•ute 60
seconds
mi•#hute very small
#min•ute•ly every
minute
mi•#hute•ly in great
detail
mi•nute•ness
min•utes
mi•nu•tiae (*pl n*)
minx
mira•cle
mi•racu•lous
mi•racu•lous•ly
mi•rage
mire
mirky *variant
spelling of* murky
mir•ror
mirth
mirth•ful
mirth•ful•ly
mirth•less
mirth•less•ly
miry

mis•ad•ven•ture
mis•ad•vise
mis•align
mis•align•ment
mis•al•li•ance
mis•an•thrope (*or*
•thro•pist)
mis•an•throp•ic (*or*
•thropi•cal)
mis•an•thropi•
cal•ly
mis•an•thro•pist
variant of misan-
thrope
mis•an•thro•py
mis•ap•pli•ca•tion
mis•ap•ply (•plies,
•ply•ing, •plied)
mis•ap•pre•hend
mis•ap•pre•hen•
sion
mis•ap•pro•pri•ate
mis•ap•pro•pria•
tion
mis•be•got•ten
mis•be•have
mis•be•hav•er
mis•be•hav•ior
(*Brit* •iour)
mis•cal•cu•late
mis•cal•cu•la•tion
mis•car•riage
mis•car•ry (•ries,
•ry•ing, •ried)
mis•cast (•cast•ing,
•cast)
mis•ce•gena•tion
mis•ce•genet•ic
mis•cel•la•nea

mis•cel•la•neous
mis•cel•la•nist
mis•cel•la•ny (*pl*
•nies)
mis•chance
mis•chief
mis•chie•vous
mis•chiev•ous•ly
mis•chiev•ous•ness
mis•cible capable
of mixing; *cf*
missable
mis•con•ceive
mis•con•cep•tion
mis•con•duct
mis•con•struc•tion
mis•con•strue
(•stru•ing, •strued)
mis•copy (•copies,
•copy•ing,
•cop•ied)
mis•count
mis•cre•ance (*or*
•an•cy)
mis•cre•ant
mis•deal (•deal•ing,
•dealt)
mis•deed
mis•de•mean•or
(*Brit* •our)
mis•di•ag•nose
mis•di•ag•no•sis
(*pl* •ses)
mis•dial (•dial•ing,
•dialed; *Brit*
•dial•ling, •dialled)
mis•di•rect
mis•di•rec•tion
mise-en-scène

mi•ser
mis•er•able
mis•er•able•ness
mis•er•ably
mis•eri•cord (or •corde)
mi•ser•li•ness
mi•ser•ly
mis•ery (pl •eries)
mis•fire
mis•fit (•fit•ting, •fit•ted)
mis•for•tune
mis•give (•giv•ing, •gave, •giv•en)
mis•giv•ings
mis•gov•ern
mis•gov•ern•ment
mis•gov•er•nor
mis•guid•ance
mis•guide
mis•guid•ed
mis•guid•ed•ly
mis•han•dle
mis•hap
mis•hear (•hear•ing, •heard)
mis•hit (•hit•ting, •hit)
mish•mash
mis•in•form
mis•in•form•ant (or •form•er)
mis•in•for•ma•tion
mis•in•ter•pret
mis•in•ter•pre•ta•tion
mis•in•ter•pret•er
mis•judge

mis•judg•er
mis•judg•ment (Brit also •judge•)
mis•lay (•lay•ing, •laid)
mis•lead (•lead•ing, •led)
mis•lead•er
mis•man•age
mis•man•age•ment
mis•man•ag•er
mis•match
mis•no•mer
mi•sogy•nist
mi•sogy•nous
mi•sogy•ny
mis•per•cep•tion
mis•place
mis•place•ment
mis•print
mis•pro•nounce
mis•pro•nun•cia•tion
mis•quo•ta•tion
mis•quote
mis•read (•read•ing, •read)
mis•rep•re•sent
mis•rep•re•sen•ta•tion
mis•rep•re•sent•er
mis•rule
Miss title of address
miss fail, etc.
miss•able able to be missed; cf miscible

mis•sal prayer book; cf missile
mis•shape (•shap•ing, •shaped or •shap•en)
mis•sile weapon; cf missal
miss•ing
mis•sion
mis•sion•ary (pl •aries)
mis•sion•er
mis•sis (or •sus)
mis•sive
mis•speak (•speak•ing, •spoke, •spoken)
mis•spell (•spell•ing, •spelled or •spelt)
mis•spend (•spend•ing, •spent)
mis•state
mis•state•ment
mis•step
mis•sus variant spelling of missis
missy (pl missies)
mist
mis•tak•able (or •take•)
mis•take (•tak•ing, •took or •tak•en)
mis•tak•en•ly
mis•teach (•teach•ing, •taught)

mis•ter

misti•ly

mis•time

misti•ness

mis•tle•toe

mis•took

mis•tral wind; cf
mistrial

mis•treat

mis•treat•ment

mis•tress

mis•tri•al void
trial; cf mistral

mis•trust

mis•trust•ful

mis•trust•ful•ly

mis•trust•ful•ness

misty (misti•er,
misti•est)

mis•under•stand
(•stand•ing,
•stood)

mis•us•age

mis•use

mis•us•er

mite arachnid;
small
contribution, etc.;
cf might

mi•ter (Brit •tre)

miter•wort (Brit
mitre•)

miti•gable

miti•gate

miti•gat•ing

miti•ga•tion

miti•ga•tive (or
•tory)

miti•ga•tor

mi•to•sis (pl •ses)

mi•tot•ic

mi•tre Brit spelling
of miter

mitt

mit•ten

mix

mix•able

mixed

mixed-up

mix•er

mix•ing

Mix•tec (pl •tec or
•tecs)

mix•ture

mix-up (n)

miz•zen (or miz•en)

miz•zen•mast (or
miz•en•)

mne•mon•ic (NOT
nemonic)

mne•moni•cal•ly

mne•mon•ics

moa

moan lament;
grumble; cf mown

moan•er

moan•ing•ly

moat ditch; cf mote

mob (mob•bing,
mobbed)

mob•ber

mo•bile

mo•bil•ity

mo•bi•liz•able

mo•bi•li•za•tion

mo•bi•lize

mob•ster

moc•ca•sin

mo•cha coffee; cf
mocker

mock

mock•able

mock•er one who
mocks; cf mocha

mock•ery (pl
•eries)

mock-heroic

mock-heroically

mocking•bird

mock•ing•ly

mock-up (n)

mod•al of mode; cf
model

mo•dal•ity (pl
•ities)

mo•dal•ly

mode

mod•el (•el•ing,
•eled; Brit •el•ling,
•elled) represen-
tation, etc.; make
or act as model;
cf modal

mod•el•er (Brit
•el•ler)

mo•dem

mod•er•ate

mod•er•ate•ly

mod•er•ate•ness

mod•era•tion

mod•era•tor

mod•ern

mod•ern•ism

mod•ern•ist

mod•ern•is•tic

mod•ern•is•ti•cal•ly

mo•der•ni•ty (*pl* •nities)
mod•erni•za•tion
mod•ern•ize
mod•ern•iz•er
mod•ern•ness
mod•est
mod•est•ly
mod•es•ty (*pl* •ties)
modi•cum
modi•fi•able
modi•fi•ca•tion
modi•fi•ca•tory (or •tive)
modi•fi•er
modi•fy (•fies, •fy•ing, •fied)
mod•ish
mod•ish•ness
modu•lar
modu•late
modu•la•tion
modu•la•tive (or •tory)
modu•la•tor
mod•ule
modu•lus (*pl* •li)
mo•dus op•eran•di (*pl* modi op•eran•di)
mo•dus vi•ven•di (*pl* modi vi•ven•di)
Mo•gul (or •ghul) Muslim Indian ruler; *cf* **Mongol**
mo•gul important person
mo•hair
Mo•ham•med•an

(or **Mu•ham•mad•**)
Mo•ha•ve (or •ja•; *pl* •ve or •ves)
Mo•hawk (*pl* •hawks or •hawk)
Mo•hi•can *variant spelling of* **Mahican**
moi•ety (*pl* •eties)
moire fabric
moi•ré having watered pattern
moist
mois•ten
moist•en•er
moist•ness
mois•ture
mois•tur•ize
mois•tur•iz•er
Mo•ja•ve *variant spelling of* **Mohave**
mola (*pl* mola or molas) fish
mo•lar tooth; chemistry term
mo•lar•ity
mo•las•ses
mold (*Brit* mould)
mold•able (*Brit* mould•)
mold•er (*Brit* mould•)
moldi•ness (*Brit* mouldi•)
mold•ing (*Brit* mould•)
moldy (*Brit*

mouldy; moldier, moldi•est; *Brit* mouldi•er, mouldi•est)
mole
mo•lecu•lar
mol•ecule
mole•hill
mole•skin
mo•lest
mo•les•ta•tion
mo•lest•er
moll
mol•li•fi•able
mol•li•fi•ca•tion
mol•li•fi•er
mol•li•fy (•fies, •fy•ing, •fied)
mol•lusk (*Brit* •lusc)
mol•lus•kan (*Brit* •can)
mol•ly (or •lie; *pl* •lies)
molly•coddle
molt (*Brit* moult)
mol•ten
molt•er (*Brit* moult•)
mo•lyb•de•num
mom
mo•ment
mo•men•tari•ly
mo•men•tary
mo•men•tous
mo•men•tous•ly
mo•men•tum (*pl* •ta or •tums)

mom•ma *variant of* mama
mon•ad (*pl* •ads or mona•des)
mon•arch
mo•nar•chal (*or* •chi•al)
mo•nar•chic (*or* •chi•cal)
mon•ar•chism
mon•ar•chist
mon•ar•chis•tic
mon•ar•chy (*pl* •chies)
mo•nar•da
mon•as•te•rial
mon•as•tery (*pl* •teries)
mo•nas•tic (*or* •ti•cal)
mo•nas•ti•cal•ly
mo•nas•ti•cism
Mon•day
mon•etar•ism
mon•etar•ist
mon•etary
mon•eti•za•tion
mon•etize
mon•ey (*pl* •eys or monies)
mon•eyed (*or* •ied)
money•grubber
money•grubbing
money•lender
money•lending
money•maker
money•making
money-spinner
money•wort

Mon•gol native of Mongolia; *cf* Mogul
Mon•go•lian
mon•goose (*pl* •gooses)
mon•grel
mon•grel•ly
mon•ism
mon•ist
mo•nis•tic
moni•tor
moni•to•rial
moni•tor•ship
moni•tory (*or* •to•rial)
monk
mon•key
monk•fish (*pl* •fish or •fishes)
monk•hood being a monk
monk•ish
monks•hood plant
mono•chro•mat•ic (*or* mono•chro•ic)
mono•chro•mati•cal•ly
mono•chrome
mono•chro•mic (*or* •mi•cal)
mono•cle
mono•cled
mono•coty•le•don
mono•coty•le•don•ous
mo•nocu•lar
mono•cul•ture
mo•noga•mist

mo•noga•mous
mo•noga•my having one spouse; *cf* monogyny
mono•gram
mono•grammed
mono•graph
mo•nog•ra•pher
mo•nogy•nist
mo•nogy•nous
mo•nogy•ny having one female part-ner; *cf* monogamy
mono•lin•gual
mono•lith
mono•lith•ic
mono•lithi•cal•ly
mo•nolo•gist
mono•logue (*or* •log)
mono•ma•nia
mono•ma•ni•ac
mono•ma•nia•cal
mono•phon•ic
mono•plane
mo•nopo•lism
mo•nopo•list
mo•nopo•lis•tic
mo•nopo•lis•ti•cal•ly
mo•nopo•li•za•tion
mo•nopo•lize
mo•nopo•liz•er
mo•nopo•ly (*pl* •lies)
mono•rail
mono•ski (*vb* •skis,

•ski•ing, •skied; *n,*
pl •skis)
mono•so•dium
glu•ta•mate
mono•syl•lab•ic
mono•syl•la•ble
mono•the•ism
mono•the•ist
mono•the•is•tic
mono•tone
mono•ton•ic
mo•noto•nous
mo•noto•nous•ly
mo•noto•ny (*pl*
•nies)
mono•type
mon•ox•ide
Mon•sei•gneur (*pl*
Mes•sei•gneurs)
French title
mon•sieur (*pl*
mes•sieurs)
Mon•si•gnor (*pl*
•gnors *or* •gnori)
ecclesiastical title
mon•soon
mon•ster
mon•strance
mon•stros•ity (*pl*
•ities)
mon•strous
mon•strous•ly
mon•strous•ness
mon•tage
mont•bre•tia
month
month•ly (*pl* •lies)
monu•ment
monu•men•tal

monu•men•tal•ity
monu•men•tal•ly
moo
mooch
mooch•er
mood state of mind
moodi•ly
moodi•ness
mooed *past tense of*
moo
moody (moodi•er,
moodi•est)
moon
moon•beam
moon•eye
moon•faced
moon•fish (*pl*
•fishes *or* •fish)
moon•flower
mooni•ly
mooni•ness
moon•less
moon•light
moon•light•er
moon•light•ing
moon•lit
moon•rise
moon•scape
moon•set
moon•shine
moon•shiner
moon•shot
moon•stone
moon•struck (*or*
•strick•en)
moon•walk
moon•wort
moony (mooni•er,
mooni•est)

Moor African
Muslim
moor open ground;
attach boat; *cf*
more
moor•age
moor•hen
moor•ing
moor•ings
Moor•ish
moose (*pl* moose)
large deer; *cf*
mousse
moot
mop (mop•ping,
mopped)
mop•board
mope
moped *past tense of*
mope
mo•ped motorbike
mop•er
mopped
mop•pet
mop•ping
mopy (*or* mop•ey;
mopi•er, mopi•est)
mo•quette
mo•raine
mor•al ethical;
lesson
mo•rale confidence
mor•al•ism
mor•al•ist
mor•al•is•tic
mor•al•is•ti•cal•ly
mor•al•ity (*pl*
•ities)
mor•ali•za•tion

mor•al•ize
mor•al•iz•er
mor•al•iz•ing•ly
mor•al•ly
mo•rass
mora•to•rium (*pl*
•ria *or* •riums)
mo•ray
mor•bid
mor•bid•i•ty
mor•bid•ly
mor•bid•ness
mor•dan•cy
mor•dant
more *comparative*
of much; *cf* moor
mo•rel
mo•rel•lo (*pl* •los)
more•over
mo•res (*pl n*)
mor•ga•nat•ic
mor•ga•nati•cal•ly
morgue
mori•bund
mori•bun•dity
Mor•mon
Mor•mon•ism
morn morning; *cf*
mourn
morn•ing
morning-after (*adj*)
morning-glory (*pl*
-glories)
Mo•roc•can
mo•roc•co
mor•on
mo•ron•ic
mo•roni•cal•ly
mo•rose

mo•rose•ly
mo•rose•ness
mor•phine (*or*
•phia)
mor•pho•log•ic (*or*
•logi•cal)
mor•phol•o•gy
mor•row
Morse code
mor•sel
mor•tal
mor•tal•i•ty (*pl*
•ities)
mor•tal•ly
mor•tar
mortar•board
mort•gage
mort•gage•able
mort•ga•gee
mort•gag•or (*or*
•er)
mor•tice *variant*
spelling of mortise
mor•ti•cian
mor•ti•fi•ca•tion
mor•ti•fi•er
mor•ti•fy (•fies,
•fy•ing, •fied)
mor•ti•fy•ing•ly
mor•tise (*or* •tice)
mor•tu•ary (*pl*
•aries)
mo•sa•ic (•ick•ing,
•icked)
mos•cha•tel
mo•selle (*or* Mo•)
mo•sey
Mos•lem *variant*
spelling of Muslim

mosque
mos•qui•to (*pl*
•toes *or* •tos)
moss
moss•back
moss•bunk•er
mossi•ness
mossy (mossi•er,
mossi•est)
most
most•ly
mote tiny speck; *cf*
moat
mo•tel
mo•tet
moth
moth•ball
moth-eaten
moth•er
moth•er•hood
mother-in-law (*pl*
mothers-)
mother•land
moth•er•less
moth•er•li•ness
moth•er•ly
mother-of-pearl
mother•wort
moth•proof
mothy (mothi•er,
mothi•est)
mo•tif theme; *cf*
motive
mo•tile
mo•til•i•ty
mo•tion
mo•tion•less
mo•tion•less•ness
mo•ti•vate

mo•ti•va•tion

mo•ti•va•tion•al

mo•tive reason;
causing motion;
cf motif

mo•tive•less

mo•tiv•i•ty

mot juste (*pl* mots
justes)

mot•ley

mot•mot

mo•to•cross

mo•tor

motor•bike

motor•boat

motor•bus

motor•cade

motor•car

motor•cycle

motor•cyclist

mo•tor•ist

mo•tori•za•tion

mo•tor•ize

motor•man (*pl*
•men)

motor•way (*Brit*)
expressway

mott•le

mot•to (*pl* •toes or
•tos)

moue

mould *Brit spelling
of* mold

mould•er *Brit spell-
ing of* molder

mouldy *Brit spell-
ing of* moldy

moult *Brit spelling
of* molt

mound

mount

mount•able

moun•tain

moun•tain•eer

moun•tain•eer•ing

moun•tain•ous

mountain•top

moun•tebank

mount•ed

mount•er

mount•ing

mourn grieve; *cf*
morn

mourn•er

mourn•ful

mourn•ful•ly

mourn•ful•ness

mourn•ing

mouse (*pl* mice)
rodent; *cf* mousse

mous•er

mouse•trap

mous•ey *variant
spelling of* mousy

mousi•ness

mous•sa•ka

mousse food; *cf*
moose; mouse

mous•tache *Brit
spelling of*
mustache

mousy (or mous•ey;
mousi•er,
mousi•est)

mouth (*n, vb*)

*mouthe *incorrect
spelling of* mouth
(*vb*)

mouth•er

mouth•ful (*pl* •fuls)

mouth•part

mouth•piece

mouth-to-mouth

mouth•wash

mouth•water•ing

mov•abil•ity (*or*
•able•ness, move•)

mov•able (*or*
move•)

mov•ably

move (mov•ing,
moved)

move•ment

mov•er

movie

movie•mak•er

mov•ing

mov•ing•ly

mow (mow•ing,
mowed, mowed *or*
mown)

mow•er

mown *past tense of*
mow; *cf* moan

moxie

moz•za•rel•la

Mr. (*pl* Messrs.)

Mrs. (*pl* Mmes.)

Ms. (*pl* Mss. or
Mses.)

mu Greek letter; *cf*
mew

much (more, most)

much•ness

mu•ci•lage

mu•ci•lagi•nous

muck

muck•er
mucki•ly
mucki•ness
muck•rake
muck•rak•er
mucky (mucki•er,
 mucki•est)
mu•cos•ity
mu•cous (or •cose;
 adj)
mu•cus (n)
mud (mud•ding,
 mud•ded)
mud•cat
mud•died
mud•di•ly
mud•di•ness
mud•dle
mud•dled•ness
muddle•headed
muddle•headed•
 ness
mud•dler
mud•dling•ly
mud•dy (adj •di•er,
 •di•est; vb •dies,
 •dy•ing, •died)
mud•fish (pl •fish
 or •fishes)
mud•guard (Brit)
 fender
mud•pack
mud•skipper
mud•slinger
mud•slinging
mud•stone
mues•li
mu•ez•zin
muff

muf•fin
muf•fle
muf•fler
muf•ti (pl •tis)
mug (mug•ging,
 mugged)
mug•ger
mug•gi•ly
mug•gi•ness
mug•gy (•gi•er,
 •gi•est)
mug•wort
mug•wump
Mu•ham•mad•an
 variant spelling of
 Mohammedan
mu•ja•he•din (or
 •hi•, •he•deen,
 •hi•deen; pl n)
mu•lat•to (pl •tos
 or •toes)
mul•berry (pl
 •berries)
mulch soil enricher
mulct cheat
mule animal;
 slipper; cf mewl
mu•le•teer
mul•ish
mul•ish•ness
mull
mul•lah (or •la)
mul•lein (or •len)
mul•ler
mul•let (pl •let or
 •lets)
mul•li•ga•taw•ny
mul•lion
mul•lioned

multi•ac•cess
multi•cel•lu•lar
multi•chan•nel
multi•col•ored (Brit
 •oured)
multi•cul•tur•al
multi•cul•tur•al•
 ism
multi•di•rec•tion•al
multi•dis•ci•pli•
 nary
multi•fac•et•ed
multi•far•i•ous
multi•far•i•ous•ness
multi•form
multi•for•mity
multi•gen•era•
 tion•al
multi•lat•er•al
multi•lat•er•al•ly
multi•lin•gual
multi•me•dia
multi•mil•lion
multi•mil•lion•aire
multi•na•tion•al
multi•pack
multi•par•ty
multi•ple
multiple-choice
 (adj)
multi•plex
multi•pli•able
multi•pli•cand
multi•pli•ca•tion
multi•plic•i•ty (pl
 •ities)
multi•pli•er
multi•ply (•plies,
 •ply•ing, •plied)

multi•pro•ces•sor
multi•pro•gram•ing (*Brit* •gram•ming)
multi•pur•pose
multi•ra•cial
multi•role
multi•screen
multi•stage
multi•sto•ry (*Brit* •rey)
multi•tude
multi•tu•di•nous
multi•user (*adj*)
mum silent
mum (*or* mumm; mum•ming, mummed) act in mummer's play
mum•ble
mum•bler
mum•bling•ly
mum•bo jum•bo (*pl* mum•bo jum•bos)
mum•mer
mum•mery (*pl* •meries)
mum•mi•fi•ca•tion
mum•mi•fy (•fies, •fy•ing, •fied)
mum•my (*pl* •mies)
mumps
munch
munch•er
mun•dane
mun•dane•ly
mun•dan•ity (*pl* •ities)
mung bean (*or* mung)

mu•nici•pal
mu•nici•pal•ity (*pl* •ities)
mu•nici•pali•za•tion
mu•nici•pal•ize
mu•nici•pal•ly
mu•nifi•cence (*or* •cent•ness)
mu•nifi•cent generous; *cf* **magnificent**
mu•ni•tion
munt•jac (*or* •jak)
mu•ral
mu•ral•ist
mur•der
mur•der•er (*fem* •ess)
mur•der•ous
mur•der•ous•ness
murk (*or* mirk)
murki•ly (*or* mirki•)
murki•ness (*or* mirki•)
murky (*or* mirky; murki•er, murki•est *or* mirki•er, mirki•est)
mur•mur
mur•mur•er
mur•mur•ous
murre
mus•ca•dine
mus•cat
mus•ca•tel (*or* •del, •dell, •delle)

mus•cle tissue; strength; *cf* **mussel; muzzle**
muscle-bound
muscle•man (*pl* •men)
mus•cly
mus•co•va•do (*or* mus•ca•; *pl* •does)
Mus•co•vite
Mus•co•vy duck
mus•cu•lar
mus•cu•lar•ity
mus•cu•la•ture
muse
mus•er
mu•seum
mush
mushi•ly
mushi•ness
mush•room
mushy (mushi•er, mushi•est)
mu•sic
mu•si•cal of music
mu•si•cale concert
mu•si•cal•ly
mu•si•cal•ness (*or* •ity)
mu•si•cian
mu•si•cian•ly
mu•si•cian•ship
mu•si•co•logi•cal
mu•si•colo•gist
mu•si•col•ogy
musk
mus•kel•lunge (*or* mas•ki•nonge; *pl*

•lunge, •lunges *or*
•nonge, •nonges)
mus•ket
mus•ket•eer
mus•ket•ry
muski•ness
musk•melon
musk•rat (*pl* •rats
or •rat)
musky (muski•er,
muski•est)
Mus•lim (*or*
Mos•lem; *pl* •lims,
•lim *or* •lems,
•lem)
Mus•lim•ism (*or*
Mos•lem•)
mus•lin
mus•quash
muss
mus•sel mollusk; *cf*
muscle; muzzle
must
mus•tache (*Brit*
mous•)
mus•ta•chio (*or*
mous•; *pl* •chi•os)
mus•ta•chi•oed (*or*
mous•)
mus•tang
mus•tard
mus•ter
musti•ly
musti•ness
mustn't
mus•ty (•ti•er,
•ti•est)
mu•tabil•ity (*or*
•table•ness)

mu•table
mu•ta•gen
mu•ta•gen•ic
mu•tant
mu•tate
mu•ta•tion
mute
mute•ly
mute•ness
mu•ti•late
mu•ti•la•tion
mu•ti•la•tor
mu•ti•neer
mu•ti•nous
mu•ti•nous•ly
mu•ti•ny (*n, pl*
•nies; *vb* •nies,
•ny•ing, •nied)
mut•ism
mut•ter
mut•ter•er
mut•ton
mu•tu•al
mu•tu•al•ity (*or*
•ness)
mu•tu•al•ize
mu•tu•al•ly
Mu•zak (*Trade-
mark*)
muz•zi•ly
muz•zi•ness
muz•zle animal's
nose and mouth;
to restrain; *cf*
muscle; mussel
muz•zler
muz•zy (•zi•er,
•zi•est)
my

my•al•gia
my•al•gic
my•celium (*pl*
•celia)
my•colo•gist
my•col•ogy
my•eli•tis
myna (*or* my•nah,
mina)
myo•pia
my•op•ic
my•opi•cal•ly
myri•ad
myrrh
myr•tle
my•self
mys•te•ri•ous
mys•te•ri•ous•ly
mys•te•ri•ous•ness
mys•tery (*pl*
•teries)
mys•tic
mys•ti•cal
mys•ti•cal•ly
mys•ti•cism
mys•ti•fi•ca•tion
mys•ti•fi•er
mys•ti•fy (•fies,
•fy•ing, •fied)
mys•tique
myth
mythi•cal
mythi•cal•ly
mythi•cist (*or*
•ciz•er)
mythi•cize
mytho•logi•cal
my•tholo•gist
my•tholo•gize

my•tholo•giz•er
my•thol•ogy (*pl*
•ogies)
myxo•ma•to•sis
(*NOT* myxa-
matosis)

N

nab (nab•bing,
nabbed)
na•celle
na•cre
na•cho (*pl* •chos)
na•dir
nae•vus *Brit
spelling of* nevus
nag (nag•ging,
nagged)
nag•ger
Na•huatl (*pl* •huatl
or •huatls)
Na•hua•tlan
nai•ad (*pl* •ads *or*
•ades)
na•if (*or* •ïf)
*variant spellings
of* naive
nail
nail-biting
nail•brush
nail•er
na•ive (*or* •ïve, •if,
•ïf)
na•ive•ly
na•ive•ty (*or*
•ive•té, •ïve•té; *pl*
•ties *or* •tés)

na•ked
na•ked•ness
nam•able (*or*
name•)
namby-pamby (*pl*
-pambies)
name
name-dropper
name-dropping
name•less
name•ly
name•plate
name•sake
name•tag
nan•ny (*pl* •nies)
na•no•meter (*Brit*
•metre)
nap (nap•ping,
napped)
na•palm
nape
naph•tha
naph•tha•lene (*or*
•line)
nap•kin
napped
nap•py (•pi•er,
•pi•est)
nap•py (*or* •pie; *pl*
•pies)
nap•time
nar•cis•sism (*or*
nar•cism)
nar•cis•sist
nar•cis•sis•tic
nar•cis•sus (*pl* •si
or •suses)
nar•co•lep•sy
nar•co•lep•tic

nar•co•sis (*pl* •ses)
nar•cot•ic
nar•coti•cal•ly
nar•co•tism
nar•co•ti•za•tion
nar•co•tize
Nar•ra•gan•set (*or*
•sett; *pl* •set, •sets
or •sett, •setts)
nar•rat•able
nar•rate
nar•ra•tion
nar•ra•tive
nar•ra•tor (*or*
•rat•er)
nar•row
nar•row•cast
(•cast•ing, •cast *or*
•casted)
narrow-gauge (*or*
-gauged)
narrow-minded
narrow-minded•
ness
nar•row•ness
nar•whal (*or* •wal,
•whale)
na•sal
na•sal•ity
na•sali•za•tion
na•sal•ize
na•sal•ly
nas•cence (*or*
•cen•cy)
nas•cent
nas•ti•ly
nas•ti•ness
na•stur•tium

nas•ty (*adj* •ti•er,
•ti•est; *n*, *pl* •ties)
na•tal
na•tal•i•ty (*pl* •ities)
na•tion
na•tion•al
na•tion•al•ism
na•tion•al•ist
na•tion•al•is•tic
na•tion•al•i•ty (*pl*
•ities)
na•tion•ali•za•tion
na•tion•al•ize
na•tion•al•ly
na•tion•hood
nation•wide
na•tive
native-born
na•tiv•ism
na•tiv•ist
na•tiv•is•tic
Na•tiv•i•ty Christ's
birth
na•tiv•i•ty (*pl* •ities)
birth or origin
nat•ter•jack
nat•ti•ly
nat•ti•ness
nat•ty (•ti•er,
•ti•est)
natu•ral
natu•ral•ism
artistic move-
ment; *cf* naturism
natu•ral•ist
natu•ral•is•tic
natu•ral•is•ti•cal•ly
natu•rali•za•tion
natu•ral•ize

natu•ral•ly
natu•ral•ness
na•ture
na•tur•ism nudism;
cf naturalism
na•tur•ist
na•turo•path
na•turo•path•ic
na•tur•opa•thy
naught (*Brit*
nought)
naugh•ti•ly
naugh•ti•ness
naugh•ty (•ti•er,
•ti•est)
nau•sea
nau•se•ate
nau•se•at•ing
nau•sea•tion
nau•seous
nau•seous•ness
nau•ti•cal
nau•ti•cal•ly
nau•ti•loid
nau•ti•lus (*pl*
•luses *or* •li)
Nava•ho (*or* •jo; *pl*
•ho, •hos *or* •jo,
•jos)
na•val of ships; *cf*
navel
nave part of a
church; *cf* knave
na•vel umbilicus;
cf naval
na•vicu•lar
navi•gabil•ity (*or*
•gable•ness)
navi•gable

navi•gably
navi•gate
navi•ga•tion
navi•ga•tion•al
navi•ga•tor
navy (*pl* navies)
nay no; *cf* nee;
neigh
Nazi (*pl* Nazis)
Na•zism (*or*
•zi•ism)
Ne•an•der•thal (*or*
•tal)
neap
Nea•poli•tan
near
near•by
near•ly
near•ness
near•side
near•sighted
near•sighted•ness
neat
neat•en
neath
neat•ly
neat•ness
neb•bish
nebu•la (*pl* •lae *or*
•las)
nebu•lar
nebu•li•za•tion
nebu•lize
nebu•liz•er
nebu•los•ity (*pl*
•ities)
nebu•lous
nebu•lous•ness
nec•es•sari•ly

nec•es•sary (*pl* •saries)
ne•ces•si•tate
ne•ces•sita•tion
ne•ces•si•ta•tive
ne•ces•si•tous
ne•ces•sity (*pl* •sities)
neck
neck•band
neck•cloth
neck•er•chief (*pl* •chiefs *or* •chieves)
neck•lace
neck•line
neck•piece
neck•tie
neck•wear
nec•ro•man•cer
nec•ro•man•cy
nec•ro•man•tic
nec•ro•philia (*or* ne•crophi•lism)
nec•ro•phili•ac (*or* •phile)
nec•ro•phil•ic
ne•cropo•lis (*pl* •lises, •li, •les, *or* •leis)
ne•crose (*vb*)
ne•cro•sis (*pl* •ses)
ne•crot•ic
nec•tar
nec•tar•ous
nec•tar•ine
nec•ta•ry (*pl* •ries)
nee (*or* née) indi- cating maiden

name; *cf* nay; neigh
need require; requirement; *cf* knead; kneed
need•ful
need•ful•ly
need•ful•ness
needi•ness
nee•dle
needle•craft
needle•point
need•less
need•less•ness
needle•woman (*pl* •women)
needle•work
needn't
needy (needi•er, needi•est)
ne'er-do-well
ne•fari•ous
ne•fari•ous•ness
ne•gate
ne•ga•tion
nega•tive
nega•tive•ness
nega•tiv•ism
nega•tiv•ist
nega•tiv•ity
ne•ga•tor (*or* •gat•er)
ne•ga•tory
ne•glect
ne•glect•er (*or* •glec•tor)
ne•glect•ful
ne•glect•ful•ly
ne•glect•ful•ness

neg•li•gee (or •gée, •gé)
neg•li•gence
neg•li•gent
neg•li•gibil•ity (or •gible•ness)
neg•li•gible
neg•li•gibly
ne•go•tiabil•ity
ne•go•tiable
ne•go•ti•ant
ne•go•ti•ate
ne•go•tia•tion
ne•go•tia•tor
Ne•gress
Ne•gri•tude (or ne•)
Ne•gro (*pl* •groes)
Ne•groid
neigh sound of a horse; *cf* nay; nee
neigh•bor (*Brit* •bour)
neigh•bor•hood (*Brit* •bour•)
neigh•bor•ing (*Brit* •bour•)
neigh•bor•li•ness (*Brit* •bour•)
neigh•bor•ly (*Brit* •bour•)
nei•ther not either; *cf* nether
nel•son
nema•tode
ne•mesia
nem•esis (*pl* •eses)
*nemonic *incorrect*

spelling of **mne-
monic**
neo•clas•si•cal (*or*
•**sic**)
neo•clas•si•cism
neo•clas•si•cist
neo•co•lo•nial
neo•co•lo•nial•ism
neo•co•lo•nial•ist
neo•con•serva•tism
neo•con•serva•tive
**neo•im•pres•sion•
ism**
neo•lib•er•al
neo•lib•er•al•ism
neo•lith
Neo•lith•ic
ne•olo•gism (*or*
ne•ol•ogy; *pl*
•**gisms** *or* •**ogies**)
ne•olo•gist
ne•olo•gize
ne•ol•ogy *variant
of* **neologism**
neon
neo•na•tal
neo•nate
neo-Nazi (*pl*
-**Nazis**)
neo•phyte
neo•phyt•ic
neo•plasm
Nepa•lese (*pl* •**lese**)
Ne•pali (*pl* •**pali** *or*
•**palis**)
neph•ew
ne•phri•tis
ne•phrolo•gist
ne•phrol•ogy

ne plus ul•tra
ne•pot•ic (*or*
nepo•tis•tic)
nepo•tism
nepo•tist
nerd (*or* **nurd**)
nerve
nerve•less
nerve•less•ness
nerve-racking (*or*
-**wracking**)
nervi•ly
nervi•ness
ner•vous
ner•vous•ly
ner•vous•ness
nervy (**nervi•er,
nervi•est**)
ne•science
ne•scient
nest
nest•er
nes•tle
nes•tler
nest•ling young
bird
nes•tling *present
participle of* **nestle**
net (**net•ting,
net•ted**) mesh;
catch in net
net (*Brit also* **nett;
net•ting, net•ted**)
remaining; earn
as profit
net•ball
neth•er lower; *cf*
neither
nether•most

ne•tsu•ke (*pl* •**ke**
or •**kes**)
nett *variant Brit
spelling of* **net**
net•ted
net•ting
net•tle
net•tle•some
net•work
neu•ral
neu•ral•gia
neu•ral•gic
neu•ras•the•nia
neu•ras•then•ic
neu•ri•tis
neu•ro•logi•cal
neu•rolo•gist
neu•rol•ogy
neu•ron (*Brit also*
•**rone**)
neu•ropa•thy
**neu•ro•physio•logi•
cal**
**neu•ro•physi•olo•
gist**
**neu•ro•physi•ol•
ogy**
neu•ro•sci•ence
neu•ro•sis (*pl* •**ses**)
neu•ro•sur•geon
neu•ro•sur•gery
neu•ro•sur•gi•cal
neu•rot•ic
neu•roti•cal•ly
neu•roti•cism
neu•ro•vas•cu•lar
neu•ter
neu•tral
neu•tral•ism

neu•tral•ist
neu•tral•ity (*pl*
•ities)
neu•trali•za•tion
neu•tral•ize
neu•tral•iz•er
neu•tral•ly
neu•tri•no (*pl* •nos)
neu•tron
nev•er
never•more
never•the•less
ne•vus (*Brit* nae•;
pl •vi)
new recent; *cf* gnu;
knew
new•born
new•com•er
new•el
new•fan•gled
new•ish
new•ly
newly•wed
new•ness
news
news•boy
news•cast
news•cast•er
news•dealer (*Brit*
•agent)
news•desk
news•hawk
newsi•ness
news•letter
news•maker
news•man (*pl*
•men)
news•paper

news•paper•man
(*pl* •men)
new•speak
news•print
news•reel
news•stand
news•worthi•ness
news•worthy
newsy (newsi•er,
newsi•est)
newt
new•ton
New Yorker
next
next-door (*adj*)
nex•us (*pl* nex•uses
or nex•us)
nib (nib•bing,
nibbed)
nib•ble
nib•bler
nice pleasing; *cf*
gneiss
nice•ly
nice•ness
ni•cety (*pl* •ceties)
niche
nick
nick•el (•el•ing,
•eled; *Brit* •el•ling,
•elled)
nickel•odeon
nick•er
nick•nack *variant*
spelling of
knickknack
nick•name
ni•co•tia•na
nico•tine

nico•tin•ic
nico•tin•ism
nic•ti•tate (*or*
nic•tate)
nic•ti•ta•tion (*or*
nic•ta•tion)
niece
nif•ti•ly
nif•ti•ness
nif•ty (•ti•er,
•ti•est)
nig•gard
nig•gard•li•ness
nig•gard•ly
nig•ger
nig•gle
nig•gler
nig•gling
nig•gly
nigh
night darkness; *cf*
knight
night•cap
night•clothes
night•club
night•dress
night•fall
night•gown
night•hawk
night•in•gale
night•jar
night•life
night-light
night•long
night•ly
night•mare
night•mar•ish
night•shade
night•shirt

night•spot
night•time
night•wear
ni•hil•ism
ni•hil•ist
ni•hil•is•tic
nil
nim•ble
nim•ble•ness
nim•bly
nim•bo•stra•tus (pl •ti)
nim•bus (pl •bi or •buses)
Nim•by (pl •bies)
niminy-piminy
nin•com•poop
nine
nine•fold
nine•pins
nine•teen
nine•teenth
nine•ti•eth
nine•ty (pl •ties)
nin•ja (pl •ja or •jas)
nin•ny (pl •nies)
ninth
nip (nip•ping, nipped)
nip•per
nip•pi•ly
nip•ple
nip•py (•pi•er, •pi•est)
nir•va•na
nir•va•nic
nit insect egg; cf knit

ni•ter (Brit •tre)
nit•pick
nit•pick•er
ni•trate
ni•tra•tion
ni•tre Brit spelling of niter
ni•tric
ni•tride
ni•tri•fi•ca•tion
ni•tri•fy (•fies, •fy•ing, •fied)
ni•trite
ni•tro•gen
ni•trog•eni•za•tion
ni•trog•en•ize
ni•trog•enous
ni•tro•glyc•er•in (or •ine)
ni•trous
nit•ty (•ti•er, •ti•est)
nitty-gritty
nit•wit
ni•val
no (pl noes or nos)
no-account (adj, n)
nob head; cribbage term; cf knob
no•belium
No•bel prize
no•bil•ity (pl •ities)
no•ble
noble•man (pl •men)
no•ble•ness
no•blesse oblige
noble•woman (pl •women)

no•bly
no•body (pl •bodies)
noc•tam•bu•lism (or •la•tion)
noc•tam•bu•list
noc•turn part of Catholic matins; cf nocturne
noc•tur•nal
noc•tur•nal•ity
noc•tur•nal•ly
noc•turne musical piece; cf nocturn
nocu•ous
nod (nod•ding, nod•ded)
no•dal
no•dal•ity
nod•dy (pl •dies)
node
nodu•lar (or •lose, •lous)
nod•ule
Noel (or Noël)
no-fault (adj)
nog (nog•ging, nogged)
no-go
nog•gin
no-hit•ter
noise
noise•less
noise•less•ness
noi•sette
noisi•ly
noisi•ness
noi•some
noi•some•ness

noisy (noisi•er,
noisi•est)
no•mad
no•mad•ic
no•madi•cal•ly
no•mad•ism
no-man's-land
nom de plume (*pl*
noms de plume)
no•men•cla•ture
nomi•nal
nomi•nal•ism
nomi•nal•ist
nomi•nal•is•tic
nomi•nal•ly
nomi•nate
nomi•na•tion
nomi•na•tor
nomi•nee
no•na•gen•ar•ian
non•ag•gres•sion
non•ago•nal
non•al•co•hol•ic
non•aligned
non•ap•pear•ance
non•as•sess•able
non•at•ten•dance
nonce
non•cha•lance
non•cha•lant
non•cha•lant•ly
non•com•bat•ant
non•com•mis•
 sioned of•fi•cer
non•com•mit•tal
non•com•peti•tive
non•com•pli•ance
non com•pos
 men•tis

non•con•duc•tor
non•con•form•ism
Non•con•form•ist
 dissenting
 Protestant
non•con•form•ist
 one who does not
 conform
non•con•form•ity
non•con•sti•tu•
 tion•al
non•con•ta•gious
non•con•tribu•tory
non•co•op•era•tion
non•co•op•era•tive
non•co•op•era•tor
non•cor•rod•ing
non•de•nomi•na•
 tion•al
non•de•script
non•drink•er
non•driv•er
none not any; *cf*
 nun
non•en•tity (*pl*
 •tities)
non•es•sen•tial
none•such (*or* non•)
none•the•less
non•event
non•ex•is•tence
non•ex•is•tent
non•fa•tal
non•fer•rous
non•fic•tion
non•fic•tion•al
non•flam•mable
non•iden•ti•cal
non•in•fec•tious

non•in•flam•mable
non•in•ter•ven•tion
non•in•ter•ven•
 tion•al
non•in•ter•ven•
 tion•ist
non•in•va•sive
non•ir•ri•tant
non•judg•men•tal
 (*or* •judge•)
non•ma•lig•nant
non•medi•cal
non•mem•ber
non•nego•tiable
non•nu•cle•ar
no-nonsense (*adj*)
non•op•era•tion•al
non•pa•reil
non•par•tici•pat•
 ing
non•par•ti•san (*or*
 •zan)
non•par•ty
non•pay•ment
non•plus (*n*, *pl*
 •pluses; *vb* •pluses,
 •plus•ing, •plused;
 Brit •plusses,
 •plus•sing,
 •plussed)
non•poi•son•ous
non•po•liti•cal
non•pro•duc•tive
non•pro•duc•tive•
 ness
non•pro•duc•tiv•ity
non•prof•it (*Brit*
 non-profit-
 making)

non•pro•gres•sive
non•pro•lif•era•tion
non•rep•re•sen•ta•
  tion•al
non•resi•dence (*or*
  •den•cy)
non•resi•dent
non•resi•den•tial
non•re•sis•tant
non•re•turn•able
non•sec•tar•ian
non•sense
non•sen•si•cal
non•sen•si•cal•ly
non•sen•si•cal•ness
  (*or* •ity)
non se•qui•tur
non•slip
non•smok•er
non•smok•ing
non•spe•cif•ic
non•stan•dard
non•start•er
non•stick
non•stop
non•such *variant*
  spelling of
  nonesuch
non•swim•mer
non•tech•ni•cal
non•tox•ic
non•un•ion
non•ver•bal
non•vio•lence
non•vio•lent
non•vot•er
noo•dle
nook
noon

noon•day
no one
noon•ing
noon•time (*or* •tide)
noose
no-par (*or* no-par-
  value; *adj*)
nor
Nor•dic
norm
nor•mal
nor•mal•ity (*or* •cy)
nor•mali•za•tion
nor•mal•ize
nor•mal•ly
Nor•man
nor•ma•tive
Norse
Norse•man (*pl*
  •men)
north
north•bound
north•east
north•east•er
north•east•er•ly
  (*pl* •lies)
north•east•ern
north•er•ly (*pl*
  •lies)
north•ern
north•ern•er
north•ern•most
north-northeast
north-northwest
North Pole
north•ward (*adj*)
north•ward (*Brit*
  •wards; *adv*)
north•west

north•west•er
north•west•er•ly
  (*pl* •lies)
north•west•ern
Nor•we•gian
nose
nose•bag
nose•band
nose•bleed
nose-dive (*vb*
  -diving, -dived *or*
  -dove)
nose•gay
nos•ey *variant*
  spelling of nosy
nos•ey par•ker
nosh
no-show
nosi•ly
nosi•ness
nos•tal•gia
nos•tal•gic
nos•tal•gi•cal•ly
nos•tril
nos•trum
nosy (*or* nos•ey;
  nosi•er, nosi•est)
not in no way; *cf*
  knot
nota bene
no•tabil•ity (*pl*
  •ities)
no•table
no•table•ness
no•tably
no•tar•ial
no•ta•ry (*pl* •ries)
no•ta•ry pub•lic
  (*pl* no•ta•ries)

pub•lic *or* no•ta•ry
  pub•lics)
no•tate
no•ta•tion
no•ta•tion•al
notch
note
note•book
note•case
not•ed
note•paper
note•worthi•ly
note•worthi•ness
note•worthy
noth•ing
noth•ing•ness
no•tice
no•tice•able
no•tice•ably
no•ti•fi•able
no•ti•fi•ca•tion
no•ti•fi•er
no•ti•fy (•fies,
  •fy•ing, •fied)
not•ing
no•tion
no•tion•al
no•tion•al•ly
no•to•ri•ety (*or*
  no•to•ri•ous•ness)
no•to•ri•ous
not•withstanding
nou•gat
nought *Brit spelling*
  of naught
noun
nour•ish
nour•ish•er
nour•ish•ing

nour•ish•ment
nou•veau riche (*pl*
  nou•veaux riches)
nova (*pl* novas *or*
  no•vae)
nov•el
nov•el•ette (*or* •et)
nov•el•ist
nov•eli•za•tion
nov•el•ize
no•vel•la (*pl* •las
  or •le)
nov•el•ty (*pl* •ties)
No•vem•ber
nov•ice
no•vi•tiate (*or*
  •ciate)
now
nowa•days
no•way (*or* •ways)
no•where
no-win (*adj*)
no•wise
nox•ious
nox•ious•ness
noz•zle
nth
nu
nu•ance
nub
nub•bin
nub•ble
nub•by (*or* •bly;
  •bi•er, •bi•est *or*
  •bli•er, •bli•est)
nu•bile
nu•bil•i•ty
nu•clear
nu•cleate

nu•clei *pl of*
  nucleus
nu•cleic acid
nu•cleon
nu•cleus (*pl* •clei
  or •cleuses)
nude
nudge
nudg•er
nud•ism
nud•ist
nu•dity (*pl* •dities)
nug•get
nui•sance
nuke
null
nul•li•fi•ca•tion
nul•li•fi•er
nul•li•fy (•fies,
  •fy•ing, •fied)
nul•lity (*pl* •lities)
numb
num•ber numeral
numb•er more
  numb
num•ber•less
numb•ness
numb•skull *variant*
  spelling of
  numskull
nu•mer•able
nu•mer•acy
nu•mer•al
nu•mer•ary *of*
  numbers; *cf*
  nummary
nu•mer•ate
nu•mera•tion
nu•mera•tive

nu•mera•tor
nu•meri•cal (*or* •mer•ic)
nu•meri•cal•ly
nu•mero•logi•cal
nu•mer•ol•ogy
nu•mer•ous
nu•mer•ous•ness
nu•mi•nous
nu•mis•mat•ic
nu•mis•mat•ics (*or* •ma•tol•ogy)
nu•mis•ma•tist (*or* •ma•tolo•gist)
num•ma•ry of coins; *cf* numerary
num•mu•lar
num•skull (*or* numb•)
nun female in religious order; *cf* none
nun•cio (*pl* •cios)
nun•like
nun•nery (*pl* •neries)
nup•tial
nurd *variant spelling of* nerd
nurse
nurs•ling (*or* nurse•)
nurse•maid
nurs•er
nur•sery (*pl* •series)
nursery•man (*pl* •men)
nurs•ing
nur•ture

nur•tur•er
nut (nut•ting, nut•ted)
nut•brown
nut•cracker
nut•gall
nut•hatch
nut•meg
nu•tri•ent
nu•tri•ment
nu•tri•tion
nu•tri•tion•al
nu•tri•tion•ist
nu•tri•tious
nu•tri•tious•ness
nu•tri•tive
nut•shell
nut•ted
nut•ti•ly
nut•ti•ness
nut•ting
nut•ty (•ti•er, •ti•est)
nut•wood
nux vomi•ca (*pl* nux vomi•ca)
nuz•zle
ny•lon
nymph
nymph•al (*or* nym•phean)
nymph•like
nym•pho (*pl* •phos)
nym•pho•ma•nia
nym•pho•ma•ni•ac
nym•pho•ma•nia• cal
nys•tag•mus

O

O *variant spelling of* oh
oaf (*pl* oafs)
oaf•ish
oaf•ish•ly
oaf•ish•ness
oak (*pl* oaks *or* oak)
oak•en
oakum
oar rowing implement; *cf* awe; or; ore
oared
oar•lock
oars•man (*pl* •men)
oars•man•ship
oasis (*pl* oases)
oat
oat•cake
oat•en
oath (*pl* oaths)
oat•meal
ob•bli•ga•to *variant spelling of* obligato
ob•du•ra•cy (*or* •rate•ness)
ob•du•rate
ob•du•rate•ly
obeah *variant of* obi
obe•di•ence
obe•di•ent
obe•di•ent•ly
obei•sance
obei•sant

ob•elisk
ob•elus (*pl* •eli)
obese
obe•sity (*or* obese•ness)
obey
obey•er
ob•fus•cate
ob•fus•ca•tion
ob•fus•ca•tory
obi (*or* obeah; *pl* obis *or* obeahs)
obitu•ar•ist
obitu•ary (*pl* •aries)
ob•ject
ob•jec•ti•fi•ca•tion
ob•jec•ti•fy (•fies, •fy•ing, •fied)
ob•jec•tion
ob•jec•tion•abil•ity (*or* •able•ness)
ob•jec•tion•able
ob•jec•tion•ably
ob•jec•tive
ob•jec•tive•ly
ob•jec•tiv•ism
ob•jec•tiv•ity (*or* •tive•ness)
ob•jet d'art (*pl* ob•jets d'art)
ob•late
ob•la•tion
ob•li•gable
ob•li•gate
ob•li•ga•tion
obliga•tive
ob•li•ga•to (*or*

ob•bli•; *pl* •tos *or* •ti)
ob•li•ga•tor
obliga•to•ri•ly
ob•liga•tory
oblige
oblig•er
oblig•ing
oblig•ing•ly
oblique
oblique•ly
oblique•ness
obliqui•ty (*pl* •ties)
oblit•erate
oblit•era•tion
oblit•era•tor
oblivi•on
oblivi•ous
oblivi•ous•ly
oblivi•ous•ness
ob•long
ob•lo•quy (*pl* •quies)
ob•nox•ious
ob•nox•ious•ly
ob•nox•ious•ness
oboe
obo•ist
ob•scene
ob•scene•ly
ob•scen•ity (*pl* •ities)
ob•scu•ran•tism
ob•scu•ran•tist
ob•scure
ob•scu•rity (*pl* •rities)
ob•se•qui•ous
ob•se•qui•ous•ly

ob•se•qui•ous•ness
ob•se•quy (*pl* •quies)
ob•serv•able
ob•serv•ably
ob•ser•vance
ob•ser•vant
ob•ser•vant•ly
ob•ser•va•tion
ob•ser•va•tion•al
ob•ser•va•tory (*pl* •tories)
ob•serve
ob•serv•er
ob•sess
ob•ses•sion
ob•ses•sion•al
ob•ses•sion•al•ly
ob•ses•sive
ob•ses•sive•ly
ob•ses•sive•ness
ob•sid•ian
ob•so•les•cence
ob•so•les•cent
ob•so•lete
ob•so•lete•ness
ob•sta•cle
ob•stet•ric (*or* •ri•cal)
ob•stet•ri•cal•ly
ob•ste•tri•cian
ob•stet•rics
ob•sti•na•cy (*pl* •cies)
ob•sti•nate
ob•strep•er•ous
ob•strep•er•ous• ness
ob•struct

ob•struct•er (*or* •struc•tor)
ob•struc•tion
ob•struc•tion•ism
ob•struc•tion•ist
ob•struc•tive
ob•struc•tive•ness
ob•tain
ob•tain•abil•ity
ob•tain•able
ob•trude
ob•trud•er
ob•tru•sion
ob•tru•sive
ob•tru•sive•ly
ob•tru•sive•ness
ob•tuse
ob•tuse•ness
ob•verse
ob•ver•sion
ob•vi•ate
ob•via•tion
ob•vi•ous
ob•vi•ous•ly
ob•vi•ous•ness
oca (*or* oka)
oca•ri•na
oc•ca•sion
oc•ca•sion•al
oc•ca•sion•al•ly
Oc•ci•dent
oc•ci•den•tal (*or* Oc•)
oc•cipi•tal
oc•ci•put (*pl* •puts *or* •cipi•ta)
oc•clude
oc•clu•sion
oc•cult

oc•cult•ism
oc•cult•ist
oc•cu•pan•cy (*pl* •cies)
oc•cu•pant
oc•cu•pa•tion
oc•cu•pa•tion•al
oc•cu•pi•er
oc•cu•py (•pies, •py•ing, •pied)
oc•cur (•cur•ring, •curred)
oc•cur•rence
oc•cur•rent
ocean
ocean•ar•ium (*pl* •ar•iums *or* •aria)
ocean•going
oce•an•ic
ocean•og•ra•pher
ocean•og•ra•phy
oce•lot
ocher (*or* ochre)
ocher•ous (*or* ochery, ochre•ous, ochrous, ochry)
o'clock
oco•til•lo (*pl* •los)
oc•ta•gon (*or* •tan•gle; *NOT* octogon)
oc•tago•nal
oc•tago•nal•ly
oc•ta•he•dral
oc•ta•he•dron (*pl* •drons *or* •dra)
oc•tane
oc•tave
oc•ta•vo (*pl* •vos)

oc•tet
Oc•to•ber
oc•to•genar•ian (*or* oc•tog•enary; *pl* •ians *or* •enaries)
*octogon *incorrect spelling of* octagon
oc•to•pus (*pl* •puses *or* •pi)
ocu•lar
ocu•list
odd
odd•ball
odd•ity (*pl* •ities)
odd•ly
odd•ment
odd•ness
odds-on (*adj*)
ode
odi•ous
odi•ous•ness
odium
odom•eter
odor (*Brit* odour)
odor•if•er•ous
odor•less (*Brit* odour•)
odor•ous
odour *Brit spelling of* odor
od•ys•sey
oede•ma *Brit spelling of* edema
oedi•pal (*or* •pean)
Oedi•pus com•plex
o'er over; *cf* or; ore
oesopha•gus *Brit spelling of* esophagus

oes•tro•gen *Brit spelling of* estrogen

oes•trous *Brit spelling of* estrous

oes•trus *Brit spelling of* estrus

oeuvre

of

off

of•fal

off•beat

off-center (*Brit* -centre)

off•cut

of•fend

of•fend•er

of•fense (*Brit* •fence)

of•fen•sive

of•fen•sive•ly

of•fen•sive•ness

of•fer

of•fer•er (*or* •or)

of•fer•ing

of•fer•tory (*pl* •tories)

off•hand

off•handed

off•handed•ly

off•handed•ness

of•fice

of•fic•er

of•fi•cial
authorized; officer; *cf* officious

of•fi•cial•dom

of•fi•cial•ese

of•fi•cial•ly

of•fi•ci•ate

of•fi•cia•tion

of•fi•cia•tor

of•fi•cious
obtrusive; *cf* official

of•fi•cious•ness

off•ing

off•ish

off-key (*adj*)

off-line (*adj*)

off-load

off-peak

off•print

off-putting

off-season

off•set (•set•ting, •set)

off•shoot

off•shore

off•side

off•spring

off•stage

off-white

oft

of•ten

ogle

ogler

ogre (*fem* ogress)

ogre•ish

oh (*or* O; *pl* ohs, O's, *or* Os) exclamation; *cf* owe

ohm

ohm•age

ohm•meter

oil

oil•bird

oil•can

oil•cloth

oil-fired

oili•ly

oili•ness

oil•man (*pl* •men)

oil•skin

oil•stone

oily (oili•er, oili•est)

oint•ment

OK (*or* okay; *n, pl* OK's *or* okays; *vb* OK'ing, OK'ed *or* okay•ing, okayed)

oka *variant spelling of* oca

oka•pi (*pl* •pis *or* •pi)

okay *variant of* OK

okra

old

old•en

old•er

old-fashioned

old•ness

old-time

old-timer

old-world

ole•agi•nous

ole•an•der

ole•as•ter

ol•fac•tory (*pl* •tories)

oli•garch

oli•gar•chic (*or* •chi•cal)

oli•gar•chy (*pl* •chies)

ol•ive
olo•ro•so (pl •sos)
Olym•pi•ad
Olym•pian
Olym•pic
oma•sum (pl •sa)
om•buds•man (pl •men)
omega
ome•let (or •lette)
omen
omi•nous
omi•nous•ly
omis•sible
omis•sion
omit (omit•ting, omit•ted)
omit•ter
om•ni•bus (pl •buses)
om•nipo•tence
om•nipo•tent
om•ni•pres•ence
om•ni•pres•ent
om•nis•cience
om•nis•cient
om•ni•vore
om•niv•or•ous
on
onan•ism
once
once-over (n)
onco•gene
on•co•gen•ic (or on•cog•enous)
on•colo•gist
on•col•ogy
on•coming

one number; cf won
one-horse (adj)
Onei•da (pl •da or •das)
one-liner
one-man (adj)
one•ness
oner•ous
oner•ous•ness
one•self (or one's self)
one-sided
one-sided•ly
one-sided•ness
one-step
one-time
one-to-one
one-track
one-up (-up•ing, -upped)
one-upmanship
one-way
on•going
on•ion
onion•skin
on•iony
on-line
on•looker
on•looking
only
ono•mato•poeia
ono•mato•poe•ic (or •poei•cal, •po•et•ic)
ono•mato•poei•cal• ly (or •po•eti• cal•ly)
on•rush

on•set
on•shore
on•side
on•slaught
on•stage
onto
on•to•logi•cal
on•to•logi•cal•ly
on•tol•ogy
onus (pl onuses)
on•ward (adj)
on•ward (Brit •wards; adv)
onyx gemstone; cf oryx
ooh
oom•pah
oomph
ooze
oozi•ness
oozy (oozi•er, oozi•est)
opac•ity (pl •ities)
opah
opal
opal•es•cence
opal•es•cent
opal•ine
opaque (opaqu•ing, opaqued)
opaque•ly
opaque•ness
open
open-and-shut
open-ended
open•er
open-eyed
open•handed
open•handed•ness

open•hearted
open•hearted•ness
open•ing
open•ly
open-minded
open-minded•ness
open-mouthed
open•ness
open•work
op•era
op•er•abil•ity
op•er•able
op•er•ant
op•er•ate
op•er•at•ic
op•er•ati•cal•ly
op•er•at•ics
op•era•tion
op•era•tion•al
op•era•tion•al•ly
op•era•tive
op•era•tor
oper•cu•lum (pl •la
  or •lums)
op•er•et•ta
op•er•et•tist
ophid•ian
oph•thal•mia
oph•thal•mic (NOT
  opthalmic)
oph•thal•molo•gist
oph•thal•mol•ogy
  (NOT opthal-
  mology)
oph•thal•mo•scope
opi•ate
opine
opin•ion

opin•ion•at•ed (or
  opin•iona•tive)
opium
opos•sum (pl
  •sums or •sum)
op•po•nen•cy
op•po•nent
op•por•tune
op•por•tune•ness
op•por•tun•ism
op•por•tun•ist
op•por•tun•is•tic
op•por•tun•is•ti•
  cal•ly
op•por•tu•nity (pl
  •nities)
op•pos•abil•ity
op•pos•able
op•pos•ably
op•pose
op•pos•er
op•po•site on the
  other side of; cf
  apposite
op•po•site•ness
op•po•si•tion
op•po•si•tion•al
op•press
op•pres•sion
op•pres•sive
op•pres•sive•ly
op•pres•sive•ness
op•pres•sor
op•pro•bri•ous
op•pro•brium
op•pugn
opt
*opthalmic

incorrect spelling
  of ophthalmic
*opthalmology
incorrect spelling
  of ophthalmology
op•tic
op•ti•cal
op•ti•cal•ly
op•ti•cian
op•tics
op•ti•mal
op•ti•mal•ly
op•ti•mism
op•ti•mist
op•ti•mis•tic (or
  •ti•cal)
op•ti•mis•ti•cal•ly
op•ti•mi•za•tion
op•ti•mize
op•ti•mum (pl •ma
  or •mums)
op•tion
op•tion•al
op•tion•al•ly
op•tom•etrist
op•tom•etry
opu•lence (or
  •len•cy)
opu•lent
opus (pl opera or
  opuses)
or alternatively; cf
  awe; oar; o'er; ore
ora•cle shrine;
  prophecy; etc.; cf
  auricle
oracu•lar
oral of the mouth;
  cf aural

oral•ly
or•ange
or•ange•ade
or•ang•ery (*or* •erie; *pl* •eries)
orange•wood
orang•utan (*or* •outang)
orate
ora•tion
ora•tor
ora•tori•cal (*or* •tor•ic)
ora•to•rio (*pl* •rios)
ora•tory (*pl* •tories)
orb
or•bicu•lar (*or* •late, •lat•ed)
or•bit
or•bit•al
or•bit•er
orc
or•chard
or•ches•tra
or•ches•tral
or•ches•trate
or•ches•tra•tion
or•ches•tra•tor (*or* •trat•er)
or•chid
or•chi•da•ceous
or•chis
or•chi•tis
or•dain
or•dain•er
or•dain•ment
or•deal
or•der

or•der•li•ness
or•der•ly (*pl* •lies)
or•di•nal
or•di•nance decree; *cf* ordnance
or•di•nand
or•di•nari•ly
or•di•nari•ness
or•di•nary (*pl* •naries)
or•di•nate
or•di•na•tion
ord•nance weaponry; *cf* ordinance
or•dure
ore mineral; *cf* awe; oar; or; o'er
orega•no
or•gan
or•gan•dy (*Brit* •die; *pl* •dies)
or•gan•ic
or•gani•cal•ly
or•gan•ism
or•gan•ist
or•gani•za•tion
or•gani•za•tion•al
or•gan•ize
or•gan•iz•er
or•gan•za
or•gasm
or•gas•mic (*or* •tic)
or•gi•as•tic
orgy (*or* orgie; *pl* orgies)
ori•el window; *cf* oriole
Ori•ent (*n*)

ori•ent (*or* ori•en•tate; *vb*)
ori•en•tal (*or* Ori•)
Ori•en•tal•ism
Ori•en•tal•ist
ori•en•tali•za•tion (*or* Ori•)
ori•en•tal•ize (*or* Ori•)
ori•en•tate *variant of* orient (*vb*)
ori•en•ta•tion
ori•en•ta•tion•al
ori•en•teer•ing
ori•fice
ori•ga•mi paper folding
origa•num marjoram or oregano
ori•gin
origi•nal
origi•nal•ity (*pl* •ities)
origi•nal•ly
origi•nate
origi•na•tion
origi•na•tor
ori•ole bird; *cf* oriel
ori•son
or•mo•lu
or•na•ment
or•na•men•tal
or•na•men•tal•ly
or•na•men•ta•tion
or•nate
or•nate•ly
or•nate•ness

or•nitho•logi•cal
or•ni•tholo•gist
or•ni•thol•ogy
oro•gen•ic (or •gen•et•ic)
orog•eny (or oro•gen•esis; pl •enies or •eses)
oro•tund
or•phan
or•phan•age
or•rery (pl •reries)
or•ris (or •rice)
or•ris•root
ortho•don•tic
ortho•don•tics
or•tho•don•tist
Ortho•dox religion
ortho•dox (pl •dox or •doxes) conforming; one who conforms
ortho•doxy (pl •doxies)
or•thog•ra•pher (or •phist)
ortho•graph•ic (or •graphi•cal)
ortho•graphi•cal•ly
or•thog•ra•phy (pl •phies)
ortho•pe•dic (Brit •pae•)
ortho•pe•dics (Brit •pae•)
ortho•pe•dist (Brit •pae•)
or•thop•tic
or•thop•tics

or•thop•tist
or•to•lan
oryx (pl oryxes or oryx) antelope; cf onyx
Osage (pl Osages or Osage)
Os•car (Trademark)
os•cil•late fluctuate regularly; cf osculate
os•cil•la•tion
os•cil•la•tor
os•cil•la•tory
os•cil•lo•scope
os•cu•late kiss; math term; cf oscillate
os•cu•la•tion
os•cu•la•tory
osier
os•mium
os•mo•sis (pl •ses)
os•mot•ic
os•moti•cal•ly
os•mun•da (or •mund)
os•prey
os•seous
os•si•cle
os•si•fi•ca•tion
os•si•fy (•fies, •fy•ing, •fied)
os•so buc•co (or os•so bu•co)
os•su•ary (pl •aries)
os•teal

os•ten•sibil•ity
os•ten•sible
os•ten•sibly
os•ten•sive
os•ten•ta•tion
os•ten•ta•tious
os•teo•ar•thrit•ic
os•teo•ar•thri•tis
os•teolo•gist
os•teol•ogy
os•teo•ma•la•cia
os•teo•my•eli•tis
os•teo•path (or •te•opa•thist)
os•teo•path•ic
os•te•opa•thy
os•teo•poro•sis
os•tra•cism
os•tra•cize
os•tra•ciz•er
os•trich (pl •triches or •trich)
oth•er
oth•er•ness
other•wise
other•worldli•ness
other•worldly
oti•ose
oti•os•ity
oti•tis
oto•lar•yn•golo•gist
oto•lar•yn•gol•ogy
otolo•gist
otol•ogy
ot•ter (pl •ters or •ter)
Ot•to•man (or Oth•man; pl

•mans) Turk;
Turkish
ot•to•man (*pl*
•mans) sofa
ouch
ought should; *cf*
aught
Oui•ja (*Trade-*
mark)
ounce
our of us; *cf* hour
ours
our•selves
oust
out
out-and-out
out•back
out•bal•ance
out•bid (•bid•ding,
•bid, •bid•den *or*
•bid)
out•bluff
out•board
out•bound
out•break
out•breed
(•breed•ing, •bred)
out•building
out•burst
out•cast
out•class
out•come
out•crop
(•crop•ping,
•cropped)
out•cross
out•cry (*n, pl*
•cries; *vb* •cries,
•cry•ing, •cried)

out•date
out•dat•ed
out•dis•tance
out•do (•does,
•do•ing, •did,
•done)
out•door (*adj*)
out•doors (*adv*)
out•er
outer•most
out•face
out•fall
out•field
out•field•er
out•fit (•fit•ting,
•fit•ted)
out•flank
out•flow
out•fox
out•go (•goes,
•go•ing, •went,
•gone)
out•go•ing (*adj*)
out•go•ings
out•grow
(•grow•ing, •grew,
•grown)
out•growth
out•gun (•gun•ning,
•gunned)
out•house
out•ing
out•land•ish
out•land•ish•ly
out•land•ish•ness
out•last
out•law
out•law•ry (*pl*
•ries)

out•lay (•lay•ing,
•laid)
out•let
out•line
out•live
out•look
out•lying
out•man
(•man•ning,
•manned)
out•ma•neu•ver
(*Brit* •noeu•vre)
out•mod•ed
out•num•ber
out-of-doors
out-of-the-way
out•patient
out•post
out•pour
out•pouring
out•put (•put•ting,
•put•ted *or* •put)
out•rage
out•ra•geous
out•ra•geous•ly
out•ra•geous•ness
out•rank
outré
out•ride (•rid•ing,
•rode, •rid•den)
out•rid•er
out•rig•ger
out•right
out•ri•val (•val•ing,
•valed; *Brit*
•val•ling, •valled)
out•run (•run•ning,
•ran, •run)
out•run•ner

out•sell (•sell•ing, •sold)

out•set (or •setting)

out•shine (•shin•ing, •shone or •shined)

out•shoot (•shoot•ing, •shot)

out•side

out•sid•er

out•size (or •sized)

out•skirts

out•smart

out•spoken

out•spread (•spread•ing, •spread)

out•standing

out•standing•ly

out•stare

out•station

out•stay

out•stretched

out•strip (•strip•ping, •stripped)

out•talk

out•think (•think•ing, •thought)

out•vote

out•ward (adj)

out•ward (Brit •wards; adv)

out•ward•ly

out•wear (•wear•ing, •wore, •worn)

out•weigh

out•wit (•wit•ting, •wit•ted)

out•work (•work•ing, •worked or •wrought)

out•worker

ouzel (or ousel)

ouzo (pl ouzos) drink

ova pl of ovum

oval

oval•ness

ovar•ian

ova•ry (pl •ries)

ovate

ova•tion

oven

oven•bird

oven-ready

oven•ware

over

over•abun•dance

over•abun•dant

over•achieve

over•act

over•ac•tive

over•age

over•all

over•alls

over•am•bi•tious

over•anx•ious

over•arm

over•ate

over•awe

over•bal•ance

over•bear (•bear•ing, •bore, •borne)

over•bear•ing•ly

over•bid (•bid•ding, •bid, •bid•den or •bid)

over•blown

over•board

over•book

over•build (•build•ing, •built)

over•bur•den

over•came

over•ca•pac•ity

over•cast

over•cau•tious

over•charge

over•cloud

over•coat

over•come (•com•ing, •came, •come)

over•com•pen•sate

over•com•pen•sa•tion

over•con•fi•dent

over•cook

over•criti•cal

over•criti•cize

over•crop (•crop•ping, •cropped)

over•crowd

over•crowd•ing

over•cul•ti•vate

over•devel•op

over•devel•op•ment

over•do (•does, •do•ing, •did, •done) do to excess; cf overdue

over•dos•age
over•dose
over•draft
over•draw
(•draw•ing, •drew,
•drawn)
over•dress
over•drive
(•driv•ing, •drove,
•driv•en)
over•due past the
due time; *cf*
overdo
over•eat (•eat•ing,
•ate, •eat•en)
over•em•pha•size
over•em•phat•ic
over•en•thu•si•asm
over•en•thu•si•as•
tic
over•en•thu•si•as•
ti•cal•ly
over•es•ti•mate
over•es•ti•ma•tion
over•ex•cite
over•ex•pose
over•ex•po•sure
over•feed
(•feed•ing, •fed)
over•fill
over•fish
over•flow
(•flow•ing,
•flowed, •flown)
over•fly (•flies,
•fly•ing, •flew,
•flown)
over•fond
over•full

over•garment
over•gen•er•ous
over•ground
over•grow
(•grow•ing, •grew,
•grown)
over•growth
over•hang
(•hang•ing, •hung)
over•haul
over•head
over•heads
over•hear
(•hear•ing, •heard)
over•heat
over•hung
over•in•dulge
over•in•dul•gence
over•in•dul•gent
over•is•sue (•sues,
•su•ing, •sued)
over•joyed
over•kill
over•land
over•lap (•lap•ping,
•lapped)
over•lay (•lay•ing,
•laid)
over•leaf
over•lie (•ly•ing,
•lay, •lain)
over•load
over•long
over•look
over•ly
over•man
(•man•ning,
•manned)
over•mantel

over•mas•ter
over•matter
over•much
over•night
over•pass
(•pas•sing,
•passed, •past)
over•pay (•pay•ing,
•paid)
over•pay•ment
over•pitch
over•play
over•popu•late
over•popu•la•tion
over•pow•er
over•pow•er•ing
over•print
over•pro•duce
over•pro•duc•tion
over•pro•tect
over•pro•tec•tion
over•pro•tec•tive
over•quali•fied
over•ran
over•rate
over•reach
over•re•act
over•re•ac•tion
over•ride (•rid•ing,
•rode, •rid•den)
over•rid•er
over•ripe
over•rode
over•rule
over•run
(•run•ning, •ran,
•run)
over•seas

over•see (•see•ing, •saw, •seen)
over•seer
over•sell (•sell•ing, •sold)
over•sen•si•tive
over•sew (•sew•ing, •sewed, •sewed or •sewn)
over•sexed
over•shad•ow
over•shoe
over•shoot (•shoot•ing, •shot)
over•sight
over•sim•pli•fi•ca•tion
over•sim•pli•fy (•fies, •fy•ing, •fied)
over•size
over•sized
over•skirt
over•sleep (•sleep•ing, •slept)
over•spe•ciali•za•tion
over•spe•cial•ize
over•spend (•spend•ing, •spent)
over•spill (•spill•ing, •spilled or •spilt)
over•staff
over•state
over•state•ment
over•stay
over•steer

over•step (•step•ping, •stepped)
over•stretch
over•strung
over•sub•scribe
overt
over•take (•tak•ing, •took, •tak•en)
over•tax
over-the-counter (adj)
over•throw (•throw•ing, •threw, •thrown)
over•time
over•tire
over•tired
overt•ly
over•tone
over•took
over•ture
over•turn
over•use
over•view
over•ween•ing
over•weight
over•whelm
over•whelm•ing
over•wind (•wind•ing, •wound)
over•winter
over•work
over•write (•writ•ing, •wrote, •writ•ten)
over•wrought

ovi•duct
ovine
ovipa•rous
ovoid
ovu•late
ovu•la•tion
ovule
ovum (pl ova)
ow cry of pain
owe be obliged to pay, etc.; cf oh
ow•ing
owl
owl•et
owl•ish
own
own•er
own•er•ship
ox (pl oxen)
ox•al•ic acid
ox•blood
ox•bow
oxen pl of ox
ox•eye
ox•hide
oxi•dant
oxi•da•tion
ox•ide
oxi•di•za•tion
oxi•dize
oxi•diz•er
ox•lip
ox•pecker
ox•tail
oxy•acety•lene
oxy•gen
oxy•gen•ate (or •ize)
oxy•gena•tion

oxy•gen•ic (*or* ox•yg•enous)
oxy•mo•ron (*pl* •mo•ra)
oyez (*or* oyes; *pl* oyes•ses)
oys•ter
oyster•catcher
ozone
ozone-friendly
ozon•ic (*or* ozo•nous)
ozo•no•sphere

P

pa
pace
pace•maker
pac•er
pace•setter
pachou•li *variant spelling of* patchou•li
pachy•derm
pachy•der•ma•tous
Pa•cif•ic ocean, etc.
pa•cif•ic conciliatory
pa•cifi•cal•ly
paci•fi•ca•tion
paci•fi•er
paci•fism
paci•fist
paci•fy (•fies, •fy•ing, •fied)
pack

pack•age
pack•ag•er
pack•ag•ing
pack•er
pack•et
pack•horse
pack•ing
pack•sack
pack•saddle
pact
pad (pad•ding, pad•ded)
pad•ding
pad•dle
paddle•fish (*pl* •fish *or* •fishes)
pad•dler
pad•dock
pad•dy (*pl* •dies)
pad•lock
pa•dre
paean (*or* pean) song of praise; *cf* peon
paed•er•ast *variant spelling of* pederast
pae•di•at•rics *Brit spelling of* pediatrics
pae•do•phile *Brit spelling of* pedophile
pa•el•la
paeo•ny *variant spelling of* peony
pa•gan
pa•gan•ism
page

pag•eant
pag•eant•ry (*pl* •ries)
page•boy
pagi•nate
pagi•na•tion
pa•go•da
paid
pail bucket; *cf* pale
pail•ful (*pl* •fuls)
pail•lasse *variant spelling of* palliasse
pain hurt; *cf* pane
pained
pain•ful
pain•ful•ly
pain•ful•ness
pain•killer
pain•kill•ing
pain•less
pain•less•ly
pain•less•ness
pains•taking
pains•taking•ly
paint
paint•brush
paint•er
paint•er•ly
paint•ing
paint•work
painty
pair two similar things; *cf* pare
pais•ley
pa•ja•ma (*Brit* py•; *adj*)
pa•ja•mas (*Brit* py•; *n*)

Pa•ki•stani
pal (pal•ling, palled) friend; to befriend; cf **pall**
pal•ace
pala•din
palaeo• *Brit spelling of words beginning with* paleo•
pal•at•abil•ity (*or* •able•ness)
pal•at•able
pal•at•ably
pala•tal
pal•ate roof of mouth; cf **palette**; **pallet**
pa•la•tial
pa•la•tial•ly
pa•la•tial•ness
pa•lati•nate
pa•lav•er
pale lacking color; wooden post; cf **pail**
pale•face
pale•ly
pale•ness
paleo•an•thro•pol•ogy (*Brit* palaeo•)
pale•og•ra•pher (*Brit* palae•)
pale•og•ra•phy (*Brit* palae•)
Paleo•lith•ic (*Brit* Palaeo•)
pale•on•to•logi•cal (*Brit* palae•)

pale•on•tolo•gist (*Brit* palae•)
pale•on•tol•ogy (*Brit* palae•)
Pal•es•tin•ian
pal•ette (*or* pal•let) artist's board; cf **palate**; **pallet**
pal•ette knife (*pl* pal•ette knives)
pali•mo•ny
pal•imp•sest
pal•in•drome
pal•in•drom•ic
pal•ing
pali•sade
pal•ish
pall coffin cover; to be boring; cf **pal**; **pawl**
pal•la•dium (*pl* •dia *or* •diums)
pall•bearer
palled *past tense of* **pal** *or* **pall**
pal•let straw bed; potter's knife; machine part; *variant spelling of* palette; cf **palate**
pal•li•asse (*or* pail•lasse)
pal•li•ate
pal•lia•tion
pal•lia•tive
pal•lia•tor
pal•lid
pal•lor

pal•ly (•li•er, •li•est)
palm
pal•mate (*or* •mat•ed)
pal•met•to (*pl* •tos *or* •toes)
palm•ist
palm•is•try
palmy (palmi•er, palmi•est)
pal•my•ra
palo•mi•no (*pl* •nos)
pa•loo•ka
pal•pabil•ity (*or* •pable•ness)
pal•pable
pal•pably
pal•pate examine medically; cf **palpitate**
pal•pa•tion
pal•pi•tate beat rapidly; cf **palpate**
pal•pi•ta•tion
pal•sied
pal•sy (*n, pl* •sies; *vb* •sies, •sy•ing, •sied)
pal•tri•ness
pal•try (•tri•er, •tri•est)
pam•pas
pam•pean
pam•per
pam•per•er
pam•pero (*pl* •peros)

pam•phlet
pam•phlet•eer
pan (pan•ning, panned)
pana•cea
pana•cean
pa•nache
pana•ma
Pana•ma•nian
Pan-Ameri•can
Pan-Ameri•can•ism
pana•tela (*or* •tel•la, pane•)
pan•cake
pan•chro•mat•ic
pan•cre•as
pan•cre•at•ic
pan•da animal; *cf* pander
*pandamonium *incorrect spelling of* pandemonium
pan•dem•ic
pan•de•mo•nium (*or* •dae•; *NOT* pandamonium)
pan•der gratify weakness; pimp; *cf* panda
pan•der•er
pan•dow•dy (*pl* •dies)
pane sheet of glass; *cf* pain
pan•egyr•ic
pan•egyr•ist
pan•egy•rize
pan•el (•el•ing, •eled; *Brit* •el•ling, •elled)
pan•el•ist (*Brit* •el•list)
pane•tela *variant spelling of* panatela
pan•ful (*pl* •fuls)
pang
pan•go•lin
pan•han•dle
pan•ic (•ick•ing, •icked)
pan•icky
pani•cle
panic-stricken (*or* -struck)
pan•nier (*or* pan•ier)
pa•no•cha (*or* •che, pe•nu•che)
pano•plied
pano•ply (*pl* •plies)
pano•ra•ma
pano•ram•ic
pano•rami•cal•ly
pan•pipes
pan•sy (*pl* •sies)
pant
pan•ta•loon pantomime character
pan•ta•loons men's trousers
pan•tech•ni•con
pan•the•ism
pan•the•ist
pan•the•is•tic (*or* •ti•cal)
pan•the•is•ti•cal•ly
pan•the•on
pan•ther (*pl* •thers *or* •ther)
panties
pan•tile
pan•to•graph
pan•to•mime
pan•to•mim•ist
pan•try (*pl* •tries)
pants
pant•suit (*or* pants suit)
panty•hose (*or* panty hose)
pap
papa
pa•pa•cy (*pl* •cies)
pa•pal
pa•pal•ly
pa•pa•raz•zo (*pl* •zi)
pa•paw (*or* paw•)
pa•pa•ya (*or* pa•paia)
pa•per
paper•back
paper•board
paper•boy
pa•per•er
paper•girl
paper•hanger
paper•hanging
pa•peri•ness
paper•weight
paper•work
pa•pery
pa•pier-mâ•ché
pa•pil•la (*pl* •lae)

pap•il•lary (*or* •late, •lose)
pap•il•lo•ma (*pl* •ma•ta *or* •mas)
pa•pist
pa•pis•ti•cal (*or* •pis•tic)
pa•pist•ry
pa•poose (*or* pap•poose)
pap•py (•pi•er, •pi•est)
pap•ri•ka
pa•py•rus (*pl* •ri *or* •ruses)
par accepted standard; *cf* parr
para (*pl* paras *or* para)
par•able
pa•rabo•la
para•bol•ic
para•chute
para•chut•ist
pa•rade
pa•rad•er
para•digm
para•dig•mat•ic
para•dise
para•di•sia•cal (*or* •disi•ac)
para•dox
para•doxi•cal
para•doxi•cal•ly
para•drop
par•af•fin (*or* •fine)
para•gon
para•graph
Para•guay•an

para•keet (*or* par•ra•)
par•al•lax
par•al•lel (•lel•ing, •leled)
par•al•lel•epi•ped
par•al•lel•ism
par•al•lelo•gram
pa•raly•sis (*pl* •ses)
para•lyt•ic
para•lyti•cal•ly
para•ly•za•tion (*Brit* •sa•tion)
para•lyze (*Brit* •lyse)
para•lyz•er (*Brit* •lys•er)
para•med•ic
para•medi•cal
pa•ram•eter
para•met•ric (*or* •ri•cal)
para•mili•tary (*pl* •taries)
para•mount
par•amour
para•noia
para•noi•ac
para•noid (*or* •noi•dal)
para•nor•mal
para•pet
para•pet•ed
para•pher•na•lia
para•phrase
para•phras•tic
para•plegia
para•plegic
para•psy•chol•ogy

para•site
para•sit•ic
para•siti•cal•ly
para•sit•ism
para•si•tize
para•si•tolo•gist
para•si•tol•ogy
para•sol
para•troop•er
para•troops
para•ty•phoid
par avi•on
par•boil
par•cel (•cel•ing, •celed; *Brit* •cel•ling, •celled)
parch
parch•ment
par•don
par•don•able
par•don•ably
par•don•er
pare trim; *cf* pair
par•egor•ic
pa•rei•ra
par•ent
par•ent•age
pa•ren•tal
pa•ren•thesis (*pl* •theses)
pa•ren•thesize
par•en•thet•ic
par•en•theti•cal•ly
par•ent•hood
par•ent•ing
par•er
par ex•cel•lence
par•fait
par•fleche

pa•ri•ah
pa•ri•etal
par•ing
par•ish
pa•rish•ion•er
Pa•ri•sian
par•ity (*pl* •ities)
park
par•ka
park•ing
par•kin•son•ism
Par•kin•son's
 dis•ease
park•land
park•way
par•lance
par•lay double up
 in betting
par•ley discuss
par•ley•er
par•lia•ment
par•lia•men•tar•ian
par•lia•men•ta•ry
par•lor (*Brit* •lour)
par•lous
Par•me•san cheese
pa•ro•chial
pa•ro•chial•ism
pa•ro•chial•ly
pa•rod•ic (*or*
 •rodi•cal)
paro•dist
paro•dy (*n, pl* •dies;
 vb •dies, •dy•ing,
 •died)
pa•role
pa•rolee
pa•rot•id
par•ox•ysm

par•ox•ys•mal (*or*
 •mic)
par•quet
par•que•try (*pl*
 •tries)
parr (*pl* parr *or*
 parrs) salmon; *cf*
 par
par•ra•keet *variant
 spelling of*
 parakeet
par•ri•cid•al
par•ri•cide killing
 of parent; *cf*
 patricide
par•rot
par•ry (*vb* •ries,
 •ry•ing, •ried; *n, pl*
 •ries)
parse
par•sec
pars•er
par•si•mo•nious
par•si•mo•ny
pars•ley
pars•nip
par•son
par•son•age
part
par•take (•tak•ing,
 •took, •tak•en)
par•tak•er
part•ed
par•terre
par•theno•gen•esis
par•theno•genet•ic
par•theno•geneti•
 cal•ly
Par•thian

par•tial
par•tial•ity (*pl*
 •ities)
par•tial•ly
par•tial•ness
par•tici•pant
par•tici•pate
par•tici•pa•tion (*or*
 •tici•pance)
par•tici•pa•tor
par•ti•cipi•al
par•ti•ci•ple
par•ti•cle
parti-colored (*Brit*
 -coloured)
par•ticu•lar
par•ticu•lar•ism
par•ticu•lar•ist
par•ticu•lar•ity (*pl*
 •ities)
par•ticu•lari•za•
 tion
par•ticu•lar•ize
par•ticu•lar•ly
par•ticu•late
part•ing
par•ti•san (*or* •zan)
par•ti•san•ship (*or*
 •zan•ship)
par•ti•tion
par•ti•tion•er one
 that partitions
par•ti•tion•ist
 proponent of
 political partition
part•ly
part•ner
part•ner•ship
par•took

par•tridge (*pl* •tridge *or* •tridges)
part-time (*adj*)
part-timer
par•tu•ri•ent
par•tu•ri•tion
par•ty (*n, pl* •ties; *vb* •ties, •ty•ing, •tied)
par•ty poop•er
par•venu (*fem* •venue)
pas•cal unit
pas•chal of Easter
pas de deux (*pl* pas de deux)
Pash•to (*or* Push•tu)
pasque•flow•er
pass
pass•able able to be passed; *cf* passible
pass•ably
pas•sage
passage•way
pass•book
pas•sé
passed *past tense of* pass; *cf* past
pas•sen•ger
passe-par•tout
passer•by (*pl* passers•by)
pas•ser•ine
pas•sibil•ity
pas•sible sensitive; *cf* passable
pas•sim

pass•ing
Pas•sion Christ's sufferings
pas•sion strong emotion
pas•sion•ate
pas•sion•ate•ly
passion•flower
passion•fruit
pas•sion•less
Passion•tide
pas•sive
pas•sive•ness (*or* pas•siv•ity)
pas•siv•ism
pas•siv•ist
pass•key
Pass•over
pass•port
*passtime *incorrect spelling of* pastime
pass•word
past
pas•ta
paste
paste•board
pas•tel drawing crayon; *cf* pastille
pas•tel•ist (*or* •tel•list)
pas•tern
paste-up (*n*)
pas•teuri•za•tion
pas•teur•ize (*NOT* pasturize)
pas•teur•iz•er
pas•tiche
pas•tille (*or* •til) lozenge; *cf* pastel

pas•time (*NOT* passtime)
pasti•ness
pas•tis
pas•tor
pas•to•ral of shepherds or pastors
pas•to•rale (*pl* •rales *or* •ra•li) musical piece
pas•to•ral•ly
pas•tor•ate
pas•tra•mi
pas•try (*pl* •tries)
pas•tur•age
pas•ture
*pasturize *incorrect spelling of* pasteurize
pas•ty (*n, pl* •ties; *adj* •ti•er, •ti•est)
pat (pat•ting, pat•ted)
patch
patch•able
patch•er
patchi•ly
patchi•ness
patchou•li (*or* •ly, pachou•)
patch•work
patchy (patchi•er, patchi•est)
pate the head
pâté food
pâté de foie gras (*pl* pâtés de foie gras)

pa•tel•la (*pl* •lae)
pa•tel•lar
pat•en (*or* •in)
  plate for
  Eucharist; *cf*
  patten
pat•en•cy
pat•ent
pat•ent•able
pat•en•tee
pat•ent•ly
pat•en•tor
pa•ter•fa•mili•as
  (*pl* pa•tres•
  fa•mili•as)
pa•ter•nal
pa•ter•nal•ism
pa•ter•nal•ist
pa•ter•nal•is•tic
pa•ter•nal•is•ti•
  cal•ly
pa•ter•nal•ly
pa•ter•nity
pat•er•nos•ter
path
pa•thet•ic
pa•theti•cal•ly
path•finder
path•finding
patho•gen
patho•gen•ic
patho•logi•cal (*or*
  •log•ic)
patho•logi•cal•ly
pa•tholo•gist
pa•thol•ogy (*pl*
  •ogies)
pa•thos
path•way

pa•tience
pa•tient
pa•tient•ly
pat•in *variant*
  spelling of **paten**
pati•na (*pl* •nas *or*
  •nae)
pa•tio (*pl* •tios)
pa•tis•serie (*or* pâ•)
pa•tois (*pl* pa•tois)
pa•trial
pa•tri•arch
pa•tri•ar•chal
pa•tri•arch•ate
pa•tri•ar•chy (*pl*
  •chies)
pa•tri•cian
pat•ri•cid•al
pat•ri•cide killing
  one's father; *cf*
  parricide
pat•ri•lin•eal
pat•ri•mo•nial
pat•ri•mo•ny (*pl*
  •nies)
pa•tri•ot
pat•ri•ot•ic
pat•ri•ot•ism
pa•trol (•trol•ling,
  •trolled)
pa•trol•ler
patrol•man (*pl*
  •men)
pa•tron
pat•ron•age
pa•tron•al
pa•tron•ess
pa•tron•ize
pa•tron•iz•er

pa•tron•iz•ing
pa•tron•iz•ing•ly
pat•ro•nym•ic
pat•ted
pat•ten wooden
  clog; *cf* **paten**
pat•ter
pat•tern
pat•ting
pat•ty (*or* •tie; *pl*
  •ties)
pau•city
paunch
paunchi•ness
paunchy
  (paunchi•er,
  paunchi•est)
pau•per
pau•per•ism
pau•per•ize
pause
paus•er
pa•vane (*or* •van)
pave
pave•ment
pa•vil•ion
pav•ing
Pav•lo•va
Pav•lo•vian
paw
pawl part of
  ratchet; *cf* **pall**
pawn
pawn•age
pawn•broker
pawn•broking
Paw•nee (*pl* •nee
  or •nees)
pawn•shop

paw•paw *variant spelling of* papaw
pay (pay•ing, paid)
pay•able
pay•day
payee
pay•er
pay•load
pay•master
pay•ment
pay•off
pay•ola
pay•phone
pay•roll
pea (*pl* peas *or* pease)
peace
peace•able
peace•able•ness
peace•ful
peace•ful•ly
peace•ful•ness
peace•maker
peace•time
peach
peachi•ness
peachy (peachi•er, peachi•est)
pea•cock (*pl* •cocks *or* •cock)
pea•fowl (*pl* •fowls *or* •fowl)
pea•hen
peak summit; to sicken; *cf* peek; peke
peaked pointed
peak•ed of sickly appearance

peaky (peaki•er, peaki•est)
peal loud sound; *cf* peel
pean *variant spelling of* paean; *cf* peon
pea•nut
pear
pearl jewel; *cf* purl
pearl•er
pearl•ite *variant spelling of* perlite
pearl•ized
pearly (pearli•er, pearli•est)
peas•ant
peas•ant•ry
pea•shooter
peat
peaty
peb•ble
peb•bling
peb•bly
pe•can nut; *cf* pekan
pec•ca•dil•lo (*pl* •los *or* •loes)
pec•ca•ry (*pl* •ries *or* •ry)
pec•ca•vi (*pl* •vis)
peck
peck•er
peck•ing
pec•tic
pec•tin
pec•to•ral
pe•cu•liar

pe•cu•li•ar•ity (*pl* •ities)
pe•cu•liar•ly
pe•cu•ni•ari•ly
pe•cu•ni•ary
peda•gog•ic (*or* •gogi•cal)
peda•gogi•cal•ly
peda•gog•ics
peda•gogue (*or* •gog)
peda•go•gy
ped•al (•al•ing, •aled; *Brit* •al•ling, •alled) foot lever; operate pedals; of the foot; *cf* peddle
ped•al•er (*Brit* •al•ler) one who pedals; *cf* peddler
ped•alo (*pl* •alos *or* •aloes) pedal boat
ped•ant
pe•dan•tic
pe•dan•ti•cal•ly
ped•ant•ry (*pl* •ries)
ped•dle sell; *cf* pedal
ped•dler drugs seller
ped•dler (*Brit* •lar) hawker
ped•er•ast (*or* paed•)
ped•er•as•tic (*or* paed•)

ped•er•as•ty (*or* paed•)

ped•es•tal

pe•des•trian

pe•des•tria•ni•za•tion

pe•des•tri•an•ize

pe•di•at•ric (*Brit* pae•)

pe•dia•tri•cian (*Brit* pae•)

pe•di•at•rics (*Brit* pae•)

pedi•cure

pedi•gree

pedi•greed

pedi•ment

pedi•ment•al

ped•lar *Brit spelling of* peddler (hawker)

pe•dolo•gist

pe•dol•ogy study of soils

pe•dol•ogy (*Brit* pae•) study of children

pe•dom•eter

pe•do•phile (*Brit* pae•)

pe•do•philia (*Brit* pae•)

pee (pee•ing, peed)

peek peep; *cf* peak; peke

peel rind; to remove rind; *cf* peal

peel•er

peel•ing

peen

peep

peep•er

peep•hole

peer a noble; an equal; to look; *cf* pier

peer•age

peer•ess

peer•less

peeve

peev•ish

peev•ish•ly

peev•ish•ness

pee•wee *variant spelling of* pewee

pee•wit (*or* pe•wit)

peg (peg•ging, pegged)

peg•board

pe•jo•ra•tive (*NOT* perjorative)

pek•an an animal; *cf* pecan

peke Pekingese dog; *cf* peak; peek

Pe•king•ese (*or* •kin•; *pl* •ese)

pel•age

pel•ar•go•nium

peli•can

pel•la•gra

pel•let

pel•li•cle

pell-mell

pel•lu•cid

pel•lu•cid•ity (*or* •ness)

pel•met

pelt

pel•vic

pel•vis (*pl* •vises *or* •ves)

pem•mi•can (*or* pemi•can)

pen (pen•ning, penned) writing tool; write

pen (pen•ning, penned *or* pent) enclosure; enclose

pe•nal

pe•nali•za•tion

pe•nal•ize

pen•al•ty (*pl* •ties)

pen•ance

pence

pen•cel (*or* •sil) small flag; *cf* pencil

pen•chant

pen•cil (•cil•ing, •ciled; *Brit* •cil•ling, •cilled) writing tool, etc.; *cf* pencel

pen•cil•er (*Brit* •cil•ler)

pend

pen•dant (*or* •dent) necklace

pen•dent (*or* •dant) dangling

pend•ing

pen•du•lous

pen•du•lum

pen•etrabil•ity

pen•etrable
pen•etrant
pen•etrate
pen•etra•tion
pen•etra•tor
pen•guin
peni•cil•lin
pen•in•su•la
pen•in•su•lar
pe•nis (*pl* •nises or •nes)
peni•tence
peni•tent
peni•ten•tial
peni•ten•tia•ry (*pl* •ries)
pen•knife (*pl* •knives)
pen•man (*pl* •men)
pen•man•ship
pen•nant ship's flag; *cf* pennon
pcnned
pen•nies
pen•ni•less
pen•ni•less•ness
pen•ning
pen•non long flag; *cf* pennant
pen•ny (*pl* •nies or pence)
pen•ny•cress
penny-pinching
penny•roy•al
penny•wort
penny•worth
pe•nolo•gist
pe•nol•ogy
pen-pushing

pen•sil *variant spelling of* pencel
pen•sion
pen•sion•able
pen•sion•er
pen•sive
pen•sive•ly
pen•sive•ness
pen•ste•mon
pent
pen•ta•cle
Pen•ta•gon US defense headquarters
pen•ta•gon five-sided polygon
pen•tago•nal
pen•ta•gram
pen•tam•eter
Pen•ta•teuch
pen•tath•lete
pen•tath•lon
Pen•te•cost
Pen•te•cos•tal
pent•house
pent-up
pe•nu•che *variant of* panocha
pe•nul•ti•mate
pe•nul•ti•mate•ly
pe•num•bra (*pl* •brae or •bras)
pe•num•bral (or •brous)
pe•nu•ri•ous
penu•ry
peon (*pl* peons or peo•nes) Spanish-

American worker; *cf* paean
peo•ny (or paeo•; *pl* •nies)
peo•ple
pep (pep•ping, pepped)
pep•per
pepper•corn
pepper•grass
pepper•mint
pep•pery
pep•py (•pi•er, •pi•est)
pep•sin (or •sine)
pep•tic
pep•tide
Pe•quot (*pl* •quot or •quots)
per
per•am•bu•late
per•am•bu•la•tion
per•am•bu•la•tor
per•am•bu•la•tory
per an•num
per capi•ta
per•ceiv•able
per•ceive
per•cent
per•cent•age
per•cen•tile
per•cep•tibil•ity (or •tible•ness)
per•cep•tible
per•cep•tibly
per•cep•tion
per•cep•tion•al
per•cep•tive
per•cep•tive•ly

per•cep•tiv•i•ty (*or* •tive•ness)
per•cep•tual
perch (*pl* perch *or* perches) fish
perch (*pl* perches) resting place; to rest
per•chance
perch•er
per•cipi•ence
per•cipi•ent
per•co•late
per•co•la•tion
per•co•la•tive
per•co•la•tor
per•cuss
per•cus•sion
per•cus•sion•ist
per•cus•sive
per•di•tion
per•egri•nate
per•egri•na•tion
per•egri•na•tor
per•egrine
pe•rei•ra
pe•remp•to•ri•ly
pe•remp•to•ri•ness
pe•remp•tory
per•en•nial
per•en•nial•ly
per•estroi•ka
per•fect
per•fect•er
per•fect•ibil•ity
per•fect•ible
per•fec•tion
per•fec•tion•ism
per•fec•tion•ist

per•fect•ly
per•fidi•ous
per•fidi•ous•ness
per•fi•dy (*pl* •dies)
per•fo•rate
per•fo•ra•tion
per•force
per•form
per•form•able
per•for•mance
per•form•er
per•form•ing
per•fume
per•fum•er
per•fum•ery (*pl* •eries)
per•func•to•ri•ly
per•func•to•ri•ness
per•func•tory
per•fuse
per•fu•sion
per•go•la
per•haps
peri•anth
peri•car•dium (*pl* •dia)
peri•dot
peri•he•lion (*pl* •lia)
per•il
per•il•ous
per•il•ous•ly
per•il•ous•ness
pe•rim•eter
peri•met•ric (*or* •ri•cal)
pe•rim•etry
peri•neal
peri•neum (*pl* •nea)

pe•ri•od
pe•ri•od•ic
pe•ri•odi•cal
pe•ri•odi•cal•ly
pe•rio•dic•ity (*pl* •ities)
perio•don•tal
perio•don•tics
peri•pa•tet•ic
peri•pa•teti•cal•ly
pe•riph•er•al
pe•riph•er•al•ly
pe•riph•ery (*pl* •eries)
pe•riph•ra•sis (*pl* •ses)
peri•phras•tic
peri•phras•ti•cal•ly
peri•scope
peri•scop•ic
per•ish
per•ish•abil•ity (*or* •able•ness)
per•ish•able
per•ish•ing
peri•stal•sis (*pl* •ses)
peri•stal•tic
peri•to•neal
peri•to•neum (*pl* •nea *or* •neums)
peri•to•ni•tis
peri•wig
peri•win•kle
*perjorative
incorrect spelling of pejorative
per•jure
per•jur•er

per•jury (pl •juries)
perk
perki•ly
perki•ness
perky (perki•er, perki•est)
per•lite (or pearl•)
perm
per•ma•frost
per•ma•nence
per•ma•nen•cy (pl •cies)
per•ma•nent
per•ma•nent•ly
per•man•ga•nate
per•me•abil•ity (pl •ities)
per•me•able
per•me•ant
per•me•ate
per•mea•tion
per•mea•tor
per•mis•sibil•ity
per•mis•sible
per•mis•sion
per•mis•sive
per•mis•sive•ness
per•mit (•mit•ting, •mit•ted)
per•mit•ter
per•mu•tate
per•mu•ta•tion
per•ni•cious
per•ni•cious•ness
per•nick•eti•ness
per•nick•ety
pero•rate
pero•ra•tion
per•ox•ide

per•pen•dicu•lar
per•pen•dicu•lar•ity
per•pe•trate
per•pe•tra•tion
per•pe•tra•tor
per•pet•ual
per•pet•ual•ly
per•petu•ate
per•petua•tion
per•pe•tu•ity (pl •ities)
per•plex
per•plex•ity (pl •ities)
per•qui•site
Per•rier (Trademark)
per•ry (pl •ries)
per se
per•se•cute
per•se•cu•tion
per•se•cu•tive (or •tory)
per•se•cu•tor
per•sever•ance
per•se•ver•ant
per•severe
Per•sian
per•si•flage
per•sim•mon
per•sist
per•sis•tence (or •ten•cy)
per•sis•tent
per•sis•tent•ly
per•sist•er
per•son

per•so•na (pl •nae or •nas)
per•son•able
per•son•able•ness
per•son•age
per•so•na gra•ta
per•son•al
per•son•al•ity (pl •ities)
per•son•ali•za•tion
per•son•al•ize
per•son•al•ly
per•so•na non gra•ta
per•soni•fi•ca•tion
per•soni•fy (•fies, •fy•ing, •fied)
per•son•nel
per•spec•tive
per•spi•ca•cious
per•spi•cac•ity (or •ca•cious•ness)
per•spi•ra•tion
per•spire
per•suad•able (or per•sua•sible)
per•suade
per•suad•er
per•sua•si•bil•ity
per•sua•sion
per•sua•sive
per•sua•sive•ly
per•sua•sive•ness
*persue incorrect spelling of pursue
pert
per•tain
per•ti•na•cious

per•ti•nac•ity (*or* •na•cious•ness)
per•ti•nence
per•ti•nent
pert•ly
pert•ness
per•turb
per•turb•able
per•tur•ba•tion
per•tus•sis
pe•rus•al
pe•ruse
pe•rus•er
Pe•ru•vian
per•vade
per•vad•er
per•va•sion
per•va•sive
per•va•sive•ness
per•verse
per•verse•ly
per•verse•ness
per•ver•sion
per•ver•sity (*pl* •sities)
per•ver•sive
per•vert
per•vert•ed
per•vert•ed•ly
per•vert•ed•ness
per•vert•er
per•vert•ible
per•vi•ous
per•vi•ous•ness
Pe•sach
pe•seta
pesky (peski•er, peski•est)
peso (*pl* pesos)

pes•sa•ry (*pl* •ries)
pes•si•mism
pes•si•mist
pes•si•mis•tic
pes•si•mis•ti•cal•ly
pest
pes•ter
pes•ter•er
pes•ter•ing•ly
pes•ti•cid•al
pes•ti•cide
pes•ti•lence
pes•ti•lent
pes•ti•len•tial
pes•tle
pet (pet•ting, pet•ted)
pet•al
pet•aled (*Brit* •alled)
petal•like
pe•tard
pe•ter
pethi•dine
peti•ole
pe•tit bour•geois (*pl* pe•tits bour•geois)
pe•tite
pe•tite bour•geoisie
pe•tit four (*pl* pe•tits fours *or* pe•tit fours)
pe•ti•tion
pe•ti•tion•ary
pe•ti•tion•er
pet•it point
pe•tits pois

pe•trel bird; *cf* petrol
Pe•tri dish
pet•ri•fac•tion (*or* pet•ri•fi•ca•tion)
pe•tri•fi•er
pet•ri•fy (•fies, •fy•ing, •fied)
pet•ro•chemi•cal
pet•ro•dol•lar
pet•rol (*Brit*) gasoline; *cf* petrel
pe•tro•leum
pe•trolo•gist
pe•trol•ogy
pet•ti•coat
pet•ti•fog (•fog• ging, •fogged)
pet•ti•fog•ger
pet•ti•ly
pet•ting
pet•tish
pet•tish•ness
pet•ty (•ti•er, •ti•est)
petu•lance (*or* •lan•cy)
petu•lant
pe•tu•nia
pew
pe•wee (*or* pee•)
pe•wit *variant spelling of* peewit
pew•ter
pe•yo•te (*or* pe•yotl)
pfen•nig (*pl* •nig, •nigs, *or* •ni•ge)
phago•cyte

pha•lanx (*pl*
pha•lanxes *or*
pha•lan•ges)
phal•lic
phal•lus (*pl* •li *or*
•luses)
phan•tasm
phan•tas•ma•go•ria
(*or* •gory)
phan•tas•ma•gor•ic
(*or* •gori•cal)
phan•tas•mal (*or*
•mic)
phan•tom
Phar•aoh
Phar•aon•ic
Phari•sa•ic (*or*
•sai•cal)
Phari•see
phar•ma•ceu•ti•cal
(*or* •tic)
phar•ma•ceu•tics
phar•ma•cist
phar•ma•co•logi•
cal
phar•ma•colo•gist
phar•ma•col•ogy
phar•ma•co•poeia
(*or* •peia)
phar•ma•cy (*pl*
•cies)
phar•yn•geal (*or*
pha•ryn•gal)
phar•yn•gi•tis
phar•ynx (*pl*
pha•ryn•ges *or*
phar•ynxes)
phase
pha•sic

pheas•ant
phe•no•bar•bi•tal
(*Brit* •tone)
phe•nol
phe•nol•ic
phe•nom•ena *pl of*
phenomenon
phe•nom•enal
phe•nom•enal•ism
phe•nom•enal•ist
phe•nom•enal•ly
phe•nom•enol•ogy
phe•nom•enon (*pl*
•ena *or* •enons)
phe•nyl
phero•mone
phew
phial (*or* vial)
phila•del•phus
phi•lan•der
phi•lan•der•er
phil•an•throp•ic (*or*
•thropi•cal)
phil•an•thropi•
cal•ly
phi•lan•thro•pist
phi•lan•thro•py (*pl*
•pies)
phila•tel•ic
phi•lat•elist
phi•lat•ely
phil•har•mon•ic
phi•lip•pic
Phil•is•tine (*or*
phil•)
Phil•is•tin•ism (*or*
phil•)
philo•den•dron (*pl*
•drons *or* •dra)

philo•logi•cal
phi•lolo•gist (*or*
•ger)
phi•lol•ogy
phi•loso•pher
philo•soph•ic
philo•sophi•cal (*or*
•soph•ic)
philo•sophi•cal•ly
philo•sophi•cal•
ness
phi•loso•phi•za•
tion
phi•loso•phize
phi•loso•phiz•er
phi•loso•phy (*pl*
•phies)
phil•ter (*Brit* •tre)
love potion; *cf*
filter
phle•bit•ic
phle•bi•tis
phlegm
phleg•mat•ic (*or*
•mati•cal)
phleg•mati•cal•ly
phlo•em
phlox (*pl* phlox *or*
phloxes)
pho•bia
pho•bic
phoe•nix
phone
phone-in (*n*)
pho•neme
pho•nemic
pho•net•ic
pho•neti•cal•ly
pho•neti•cian

pho•net•ics
pho•ney *variant spelling of* phony
phon•ic
pho•ni•ness
pho•no•graph
pho•no•logi•cal
pho•nolo•gist
pho•nol•ogy
pho•ny (*or* •ney; *adj* •ni•er, •ni•est; *n, pl* •nies *or* •neys)
phos•phate
phos•phor (*or* •phore)
phos•pho•resce
phos•pho•res•cence
phos•pho•res•cent
phos•phor•ic
phos•pho•rous (*adj*)
phos•pho•rus (*n*)
pho•to (*pl* •tos)
photo•cell
photo•chemi•cal
photo•chem•ist
photo•chem•is•try
photo•copi•er
photo•copy (*n, pl* •copies; *vb* •copies, •copy•ing, •cop•ied)
photo•elec•tric (*or* •tri•cal)
photo•elec•tri•cal•ly
photo•elec•tric•ity
photo•gen•ic
photo•geni•cal•ly

photo•graph
pho•tog•ra•pher
photo•graph•ic
photo•graphi•cal•ly
pho•tog•ra•phy
photo•gra•vure
photo•jour•nal•ism
photo•jour•nal•ist
photo•litho•graph
photo•li•thog•ra•phy
pho•tom•eter
photo•met•ric
pho•tom•etry
pho•ton
photo-offset
photo•sen•si•tive
photo•sen•si•tiv•ity
Photo•stat (*Trademark*) machine
photo•stat (*n, vb*) photocopy
photo•syn•the•sis
photo•syn•the•size
photo•syn•thet•ic
photo•type•set•ting
phras•al
phrase
phra•seo•logi•cal
phra•seol•ogy (*pl* •ogies)
phras•ing
phreno•logi•cal
phre•nolo•gist
phre•nol•ogy
phy•lac•tery (*pl* •teries)
phy•lum (*pl* •la)
physi•at•rics

phys•ic (•ick•ing, •icked)
physi•cal
physi•cal•ly
physi•cal•ness
phy•si•cian
physi•cist
phys•ics
physi•og•nom•ic (*or* •nomi•cal)
physi•og•no•mist
physi•og•no•my (*pl* •mies; *NOT* physionomy)
physio•logi•cal
physio•logi•cal•ly
physi•olo•gist
physi•ol•ogy
*physionomy *incorrect spelling of* physiognomy
physio•thera•pist
physio•thera•py
phy•sique
phyto•plank•ton
pi (*pl* pis)
pia•nis•si•mo (*pl* •mi *or* •mos)
pia•nist
pia•nis•tic
pi•ano (*pl* •anos)
pi•ano•for•te
pi•as•sa•va (*or* •ba)
pi•az•za (*pl* •zas *or* •ze)
pica printer's measure; *cf* pika
pica•dor (*pl* •dors *or* •do•res)

pica•resque of type of fiction; *cf* **picturesque**

pica•yune

pic•ca•lil•li

pic•co•lo (*pl* •los)

pick

picka•back *variant of* **piggyback**

pick•able

pick•ax (*Brit* •axe)

pick•er

pick•er•el (*pl* •el *or* •els)

pickerel•weed

pick•et

pick•et•er

pick•et•ing

pick•ings

pick•le

pick•led

pick•lock

pick-me-up

pick•pocket

pick•up

picky (picki•er, picki•est)

pic•nic (•nick•ing, •nicked)

pic•nick•er

pic•to•graph (*or* •gram)

pic•to•graph•ic

pic•to•rial

pic•to•rial•ly

pic•ture

pic•tur•esque strikingly

pleasing; *cf* **picaresque**

pic•tur•esque•ness

pid•dle

pid•dling

pidg•in language; *cf* **pigeon**

pie

pie•bald

piece

pièce de ré•sis•tance (*pl* pièces de ré•sis•tance)

piece•meal

piece•work

pie•crust

pied

pied-à-terre (*pl* pieds-à-terre)

pie-eyed

pier landing place; pillar; *cf* **peer**

pierce

pierc•able

pierc•er

pierc•ing

pierc•ing•ly

Pier•rot

pie•tà

pi•etism

pi•ety (*pl* •eties)

pi•ezo•elec•tric

pi•ezo•elec•tric•ity

pif•fle

pif•fling

pig (pig•ging, pigged)

pi•geon bird; *cf* **pidgin**

pigeon•hole

pigeon-toed

pig•fish (*pl* •fish *or* •fishes)

pig•gery (*pl* •geries)

pig•gish

pig•gish•ness

pig•gy (*n, pl* •gies; *adj* •gi•er, •gi•est)

piggy•back (*or* picka•back)

pig-headed

pig-headed•ness

pig•let

pig•like

pig•meat

pig•ment

pig•men•tary

pig•men•ta•tion

pig•ment•ed

pig•my *variant spelling of* **pygmy**

pig•nut

pig•skin

pig•stick•er

pig•stick•ing

pig•sty (*pl* •sties)

pig•tail

pig•tailed

pig•weed

pika animal; *cf* **pica**

pike (*pl* pikes) spear

pike (*pl* pike *or* pikes) fish

pik•er

pike•staff

pi•las•ter

pi•lau (*or* •laf, •laff, •law)

pil•chard

pile

piles (*pl n*)

pile•up

pil•fer

pil•fer•age

pil•fer•er

pil•grim

pil•grim•age

pil•ing

pill

pil•lage

pil•lag•er

pil•lar

pill•box

pil•lion

pil•lo•ry (*n, pl* •ries; *vb* •ries, •ry•ing, •ried)

pil•low

pillow•case (*or* •slip)

pi•lot

pi•lot•age

pi•men•to (*pl* •tos *or* •to) spice

pi•mien•to (*pl* •tos) sweet pepper

pimp

pim•per•nel

pim•ple

pim•pled

pim•pli•ness

pim•ply (•pli•er, •pli•est)

pin (pin•ning, pinned)

piña co•lada

pina•fore

pin•ball

pince-nez (*pl* pince-nez)

pin•cer

pin•cers

pinch

pinch•beck

pin•cushion

pine

pin•eal gland

pine•ap•ple

piney *variant spelling of* piny

pin•fish (*pl* •fish *or* •fishes)

ping

ping•er

Ping-Pong (*Trademark*)

pin•head

pin•hole

pin•ion

pink

pinkie (*or* pinky; *pl* pinkies) little finger; *cf* pinky

pink•ish

pink•ness

pinko (*pl* pinkos *or* pinkoes)

pink•root

pinky pinkish;

variant spelling of pinkie

pin•nace

pin•na•cle

pin•nate (*or* •nat•ed)

pinned

pin•ner

pin•ning

pin•point

pin•prick

pin•stripe

pin•striped

pint

pin•tail (*pl* •tails *or* •tail)

pin•to (*pl* •tos *or* •toes)

pint-sized (*or* -size)

pin-up (*n*)

pin•wheel

piny (*or* piney; pini•er, pini•est)

Pin•yin

pion

pio•neer

pi•ous

pi•ous•ly

pi•ous•ness

pip (pip•ping, pipped)

pipe

pipe•fish (*pl* •fish *or* •fishes)

pipe•fitting

pipe•line

pip•er

pi•pette (*or* •pet)

pip•ing

pip•is•trelle (*or* •trel)

pip•it

pipped

pip•pin

pip•ping

pip•sis•se•wa

pip•squeak

pi•quan•cy (*or* •quant•ness)

pi•quant

pique (piqu•ing, piqued)

pi•quet

pi•ra•cy (*pl* •cies)

pi•ra•nha (*or* •ña)

pi•rate

pi•rat•ic (*or* •rati•cal)

pi•rati•cal•ly

pirou•ette

pis•ca•to•rial (*or* •tory)

pis•ci•na (*pl* •nae)

pis•cine

piss

pis•ta•chio (*pl* •chios)

piste

pis•til flower part

pis•tol (•tol•ing, •toled; *Brit* •tol•ling, •tolled) gun

pis•ton

pit (pit•ting, pit•ted)

pita fiber; flat bread; *cf* pitta

pit-a-pat (-patting, -patted)

pitch

pitch-black

pitch-blende

pitch-dark

pitch•er

pitch•fork

pitchy (pitchi•er, pitchi•est)

pit•eous

pit•eous•ly

pit•eous•ness

pit•fall

pith

pit•head

pithi•ly

pithi•ness

pithy (pithi•er, pithi•est)

piti•able

piti•able•ness

piti•ably

piti•ful

piti•ful•ly

piti•ful•ness

piti•less

piti•less•ly

piti•less•ness

pi•ton

pit•ta bird; *cf* pita

pit•tance

pitter-patter

pi•tui•tary (*pl* •taries)

pity (*n, pl* pities; *vb* pities, pity•ing, pit•ied)

pity•ing•ly

piv•ot

piv•ot•al

pix pictures; *cf* pyx

pix•el

pixie (*or* pixy; *pl* pixies) fairy; *cf* pyxie

pixi•lat•ed (*or* pix•il•lat•ed)

pi•zazz (*or* piz•zazz)

piz•za

piz•ze•ria

piz•zi•ca•to (*pl* •ti)

pla•cabil•ity

pla•cable easily placated; *cf* placeable

plac•ard

pla•cate

pla•ca•tion

placa•tory (*or* •tive)

place position; *cf* plaice

place•able easily placed; *cf* placable

pla•ce•bo (*pl* •bos *or* •boes)

place•ment

pla•cen•ta (*pl* •tas *or* •tae)

pla•cen•tal

plac•er

plac•id

pla•cid•ity (*or* •ness)

plac•id•ly

plac•ing

plack•et

*plad *incorrect spelling of* plaid

pla•gia•rism

pla•gia•rist

pla•gia•ris•tic

pla•gia•rize

pla•gia•riz•er

plague (plagu•ing, plagued)

plagu•er

plaice (*pl* plaice *or* plaices) fish; *cf* place

plaid (*NOT* plad)

plain simple; unattractive; treeless region; *cf* plane

plain•chant

plain•ly

plain•ness

plains•man (*pl* •men)

plain•song

plain•spoken

plaint

plain•tiff legal term

plain•tive melancholy

plain•tive•ly

plain•tive•ness

plait braid; *cf* plat

plan (plan•ning, planned)

pla•nar

plane aircraft; level; tool; tree; *cf* plain

pla•ner

plan•et

plan•etar•ium (*pl* •etar•iums *or* •etaria)

plan•etary (*pl* •etaries)

plan•gen•cy

plan•gent

plank

plank•ing

plank•ton

plank•ton•ic

planned

plan•ner

plan•ning

plant

plant•able

plan•tain

plan•tar of sole of foot; *cf* planter

plan•ta•tion

plant•er plantation owner; *cf* plantar

plaque

plash

plashy (plashi•er, plashi•est)

plas•ma

plas•ter

plaster•board

plas•tered

plas•ter•er

plas•ter•ing

plas•tic

plas•ti•cal•ly

Plas•ti•cine (*Trademark*)

plas•tic•ity

pla•ner

plas•ti•ci•za•tion

plas•ti•cize

plas•ti•ciz•er

plat small plot; *cf* plait

plat•an plane tree; *cf* platen

plat du jour (*pl* plats du jour)

plate

pla•teau (*pl* •teaus *or* •teaux)

plat•ed

plate•ful (*pl* •fuls)

plate•let

plat•en printing plate; typewriter roller; *cf* platan

plat•form

plat•ing

plati•num

platinum-blond (*fem* -blonde)

plati•tude

plati•tu•di•nize

plati•tu•di•niz•er

plati•tu•di•nous

Pla•ton•ic of Plato

pla•ton•ic nonerotic

pla•toni•cal•ly

Pla•to•nism

pla•toon

plat•ter

platy (*pl* platy, platys, *or* platies)

platy•pus (*pl* •puses)

plau•dit

plau•sibil•ity (*or* •sible•ness)
plau•sible
plau•sibly
play
play•able
play•act
play•act•ing
play•actor
play•back
play•bill
play•boy
play•er
play•fellow
play•ful
play•ful•ly
play•ful•ness
play•goer
play•ground
play•group
play•house
play•let
play•mate
play-off (*n*)
play•pen
play•room
play•suit
play•thing
play•time
play•wright
pla•za
plea
pleach
plead (plead•ing, plead•ed *or* pled)
plead•able
plead•er
pleas•able
pleas•ant

pleas•ant•ly
pleas•ant•ness
pleas•ant•ry (*pl* •ries)
please
pleased
pleas•er
pleas•ing
plea•sur•able
plea•sur•ably
plea•sure
pleat
pleat•er
pleb
ple•be•ian
ple•be•ian•ism
plebi•scite
plec•trum (*pl* •tra *or* •trums)
pledge
pledgee
pledg•er (*or* •or, pledge•or)
ple•na•ry
pleni•po•ten•ti•ary (*pl* •aries)
pleni•tude
plen•te•ous
plen•te•ous•ness
plen•ti•ful
plen•ti•ful•ly
plen•ti•ful•ness
plen•ty (*pl* •ties)
ple•num (*pl* •nums *or* •na)
pletho•ra
pleu•ra (*pl* •rae *or* •ras)
pleu•ral

pleu•ri•sy
pleu•rit•ic
plex•us (*pl* •uses *or* •us)
pli•abil•ity (*or* able•ness)
pli•able
pli•an•cy (*or* •ant•ness)
pli•ant
pli•er (*Brit also* ply•) one who plies
pli•ers tool
plight
plight•er
Plim•soll mark
plinth
plod (plod•ding, plod•ded)
plod•der
plod•ding•ly
plonk
plop (plop•ping, plopped)
plot (plot•ting, plot•ted)
plot•ter
plough *Brit spelling of* plow
plov•er (*pl* •er *or* •ers)
plow (*Brit* plough)
plow•boy (*Brit* plough•)
plow•er (*Brit* plough•)
plow•man (*Brit* plough•; *pl* •men)

plow•share (*Brit* plough•)
ploy
pluck
pluck•er
plucki•ly
plucki•ness
plucky (plucki•er, plucki•est)
plug (plug•ging, plugged)
plug-in (*adj*)
plum fruit; *cf* plumb
plum•age
plumb work as plumber; experience misery; *cf* plum
plumb•able
plum•ba•go (*pl* •gos)
plumb•er
plumb•ery (*pl* •eries)
plumb•ing
plume
plum•met
plum•my (•mi•er, •mi•est)
plump
plump•ness
plumy (plumi•er, plumi•est)
plun•der
plun•der•able
plun•der•er
plunge
plung•er

plunk
plu•per•fect
plu•ral
plu•ral•ism
plu•ral•ist
plu•ral•ity (*pl* •ities)
plu•rali•za•tion
plu•ral•ize
plu•ral•ly
plus (*pl* pluses or plusses)
plush
plushi•ness
plush•ness
plushy (plushi•er, plushi•est)
plu•toc•ra•cy (*pl* •cies)
plu•to•crat
plu•to•crat•ic (or •crati•cal)
plu•to•crati•cal•ly
plu•ton•ic
plu•to•nium
plu•vial
ply (*vb* plies, ply•ing, plied; *n, pl* plies)
ply•er *variant Brit spelling of* plier
Plym•outh Breth•ren
ply•wood
pneu•mat•ic
pneu•mati•cal•ly
pneu•mo•co•nio•sis
pneu•mo•nia
pneu•mon•ic
poach

poach•er
poach•ing
po•chard (*pl* •chards or •chard)
pock
pock•et
pocket•book
pock•et•ful (*pl* •fuls or pock•ets•ful)
pocket-knife (*pl* •knives)
pock•mark
pock•marked
pod (pod•ding, pod•ded)
podgi•ness
podgy (podgi•er, podgi•est)
po•di•at•ric
po•dia•trist
po•dia•try
po•dium (*pl* •diums or •dia)
poem
po•esy (*pl* •esies)
poet
po•et•as•ter
po•et•ess
po•et•ic (or •eti•cal)
po•eti•cal•ly
po•eti•cize (or po•et•ize)
po•et•ics
poet lau•reate (*pl* poets lau•reate or poet lau•reates)
po•et•ry
po-faced

po•go stick
po•grom
poi (*pl* poi *or* pois)
poi•gnan•cy
poi•gnant
poi•gnant•ly
poin•set•tia
point
point-blank
point•ed
point•ed•ly
point•ed•ness
point•er
poin•til•lism
poin•til•list
point•ing
point•less
point•less•ly
point•less•ness
point-of-sale (*pl* points-)
pointy (pointi•er, pointi•est)
poise
poised
poi•son
poi•son•er
poi•son•ous
poi•son•ous•ness
poke
poke•berry (*pl* •berries)
pok•er
poker-faced
poke•weed
poki•ly
poki•ness
poky (*or* pokey; poki•er, poki•est)

po•lar
po•lar•ity (*pl* •ities)
po•lari•za•tion
po•lar•ize
po•lar•iz•er
Po•lar•oid (*Trademark*)
Pole Polish native
pole long piece of wood, etc.; end of axis
pole•ax (*Brit* •axe)
pole•cat (*pl* •cats *or* •cat)
po•lem•ic
po•lemi•cal
po•lemi•cal•ly
po•lemi•cist (*or* •lem•ist)
po•lem•ics
po•len•ta
pole-vault (*vb*)
po•lice
police•man (*pl* •men)
police•woman (*pl* •women)
poli•cy (*pl* •cies)
policy•holder
po•lio
po•lio•my•eli•tis
Po•lish of Poland
pol•ish make smooth; smooth-ness; etc.
pol•ish•er
po•lite
po•lite•ly
po•lite•ness

poli•tic shrewd
po•liti•cal of politics
po•liti•cal•ly
poli•ti•cian
po•liti•ci•za•tion
po•liti•cize
po•litick•ing
po•liti•co (*pl* •cos *or* •coes)
poli•tics
pol•ka (•ka•ing, •kaed)
poll
pol•lack (*or* •lock; *pl* •lack *or* •lock)
pol•lard
polled
pol•len
pol•li•nate (*or* •lenate)
pol•li•na•tion
pol•li•na•tor
poll•ing
pol•lock *variant spelling of* pollack
poll•ster
pol•lu•tant
pol•lute
pol•lut•er
pol•lu•tion
polo
polo•naise
pol•ter•geist
pol•troon
poly (*pl* polys)
poly•an•drous
poly•an•dry

poly•an•thus (*pl*
•thuses *or* •thi)
poly•chro•mat•ic
(*or* •mic, •mous)
poly•chro•ma•tism
poly•chrome
poly•clin•ic
poly•es•ter
po•lyga•mist
po•lyga•mous
po•lyga•my
poly•glot
poly•glot•ism (*or*
•glot•tism)
poly•gon
po•lygo•nal
poly•graph
po•lygy•nist
po•lygy•nous
po•lygy•ny
poly•he•dral
poly•he•dron (*pl*
•drons *or* •dra)
poly•math
poly•math•ic
poly•mer
poly•mer•ic
po•lym•eri•za•tion
poly•mer•ize
poly•mor•phism
poly•mor•phous (*or*
•phic)
Poly•ne•sian
poly•no•mial
pol•yp
poly•phon•ic
po•lypho•ny (*pl*
•nies)
poly•pro•pyl•ene

poly•sty•rene
poly•syl•lab•ic
poly•syl•lable
poly•tech•nic
poly•the•ism
poly•the•ist
poly•the•is•tic
poly•thene
poly•un•satu•rat•ed
poly•ure•thane
poly•vi•nyl
    chlo•ride
pom•ace
po•made
po•man•der
pom•egran•ate
pom•elo (*pl* •elos)
Pom•era•nian
pom•mel part of
    saddle; *cf* **pummel**
pomp
pom•pa•no (*pl* •no
    or •nos)
pom-pom cannon
pom•pon (*or* •pom)
    globular tuft;
    flower
pom•pos•ity (*pl*
    •ities)
pomp•ous
pomp•ous•ly
pomp•ous•ness
pon•cho (*pl* •chos)
pond
pon•der
pon•der•able
pon•der•er
pon•der•ous
pon•der•ous•ly

pon•der•ous•ness
pond•weed
pone
pong
pon•tiff
pon•tifi•cal
pon•tifi•cal•ly
pon•tifi•cate
pon•toon
pony (*pl* ponies)
pony•tail
pooch
poo•dle
pooh
pooh-pooh
pool
poop
pooper-scooper
poor needy;
    unfortunate; *cf*
    pore; pour
poor•house
poor•ly
poor•ness
pop (pop•ping,
    popped)
pop•corn
pope
pop•ery
pop•eyed
pop•gun
pop•in•jay
pop•ish
pop•ish•ness
pop•lar
pop•lin
pop•over
popped
pop•per

pop•pet
pop•ping
pop•ple
pop•py (*pl* •pies)
pop•py•cock
poppy•head
popu•lace
popu•lar
popu•lar•ity
popu•lari•za•tion
popu•lar•ize
popu•lar•iz•er
popu•lar•ly
popu•late
popu•la•tion
popu•lism
popu•list
popu•lous
popu•lous•ness
pop-up (*adj*, *n*)
por•ce•lain
porch
por•cine
por•cu•pine
pore examine; small hole; *cf* poor; pour
por•gy (*pl* •gy or •gies)
pork
pork•er
porki•ness
pork•pie
porky (porki•er, porki•est)
porn (*or* por•no)
por•nog•ra•pher
por•no•graph•ic

por•no•graphi•cal•ly
por•nog•ra•phy
po•ros•ity (*pl* •ities)
po•rous
po•rous•ness
por•phy•rit•ic
por•phy•ry (*pl* •ries)
por•poise (*pl* •poises or •poise)
por•ridge
port
por•tabil•ity (*or* •table•ness)
port•able
por•tage
por•tal
port•cul•lis
por•tend
por•tent
por•ten•tous
por•ten•tous•ness
por•ter
por•ter•age
porter•house
port•fo•lio (*pl* •lios)
port•hole
por•ti•co (*pl* •coes or •cos)
por•tion
port•li•ness
port•ly (•li•er, •li•est)
port•man•teau (*pl* •teaus or •teaux)
por•trait
por•trait•ist

por•trai•ture
por•tray
por•tray•able
por•tray•al
por•tray•er
Por•tu•guese (*pl* •guese)
por•tu•laca
pose
pos•er one who poses; problem
po•seur affected person
pos•it postulate; *cf* posset
po•si•tion
po•si•tion•al
posi•tive
posi•tive•ly
posi•tive•ness
posi•tiv•ism
posi•tiv•ist
posi•tiv•is•tic
posi•tron
pos•se
pos•sess
pos•sessed
pos•ses•sion
pos•ses•sive
pos•ses•sive•ly
pos•ses•sive•ness
pos•ses•sor
pos•ses•so•ry
pos•set hot drink; *cf* posit
pos•sibil•ity (*pl* •ities)
pos•sible
pos•sibly

pos•sum
post
post•age
post•al
post•bag (*Brit*) mailbag
post•box (*Brit*) mailbox
post•card
post•code (*Brit*) zip code
post•coit•al
post•date
post•doc•tor•al
post•cr
poste res•tante
pos•teri•or
pos•ter•ity
pos•tern
post•gradu•ate
post•haste
post•hu•mous (*NOT* postu-mous)
post•hu•mous•ly
pos•til•ion (or •til•lion)
post•im•pres•sion•ism
post•im•pres•sion•ist
post•ing
post•man (*pl* •men)
post•mark
post•master
post•me•rid•ian (*adj*)
post me•rid•iem
post•mil•len•nial

post•mod•ern•ism
post•mod•ern•ist
post•mor•tem
post•na•tal
post•nup•tial
post•op•era•tive
post•paid
post•pon•able
post•pone
post•pone•ment
post•pon•er
post•posi•tive
post•pran•dial
post•script
post-traumatic stress dis•order
pos•tu•lan•cy (or •lant•ship; *pl* •cies or •ships)
pos•tu•lant
pos•tu•late
pos•tu•la•tion
pos•tu•la•tor
postumous incorrect spelling of **posthumous**
pos•tur•al
pos•ture
pos•tur•er
post•vi•ral
post•war
posy (*pl* posies)
pot (pot•ting, pot•ted)
po•table
po•tage
pot•ash
po•tas•sium
po•ta•to (*pl* •toes)

pot•bel•lied
pot•belly (*pl* •bellies)
pot•boiler
po•teen (or •theen)
po•ten•cy (or •tence; *pl* •ten•cies or •tences)
po•tent
po•ten•tate ruler; *cf* potentiate
po•ten•tial
po•ten•ti•al•ity (*pl* •ities)
po•ten•tial•ly
po•ten•ti•ate increase effectiveness; *cf* potentate
po•ten•til•la
pot•ful (*pl* •fuls)
po•theen *variant spelling of* poteen
poth•er
pot•herb
pot•hole
pot•hook
pot•hunter
po•tion
pot•latch
pot•luck
pot•pour•ri (*pl* •ris)
pot•sherd (or •shard)
pot•ted
pot•ter
pot•tery (*pl* •teries)
pot•ting
pot•ty (*pl* •ties)

pouch
pouched
pouf (*or* pouffe)
poult
poul•ter•er
poul•tice
poul•try
pounce
pound
pound•er
pour flow; *cf* poor;
  pore
pour•er
pout
pout•er
pout•ing•ly
pouty (pouti•er,
  pouti•est)
pov•er•ty
poverty-stricken
pow
pow•der
pow•dery
pow•er
power•boat
pow•er•ful
pow•er•ful•ly
pow•er•ful•ness
power•house
pow•er•less
pow•er•less•ness
pow•wow
pox
prac•ti•cabil•ity (*or*
  •cable•ness)
prac•ti•cable
prac•ti•cably
prac•ti•cal

prac•ti•cal•ity (*or*
  •cal•ness)
prac•ti•cal•ly
prac•tice (*n*)
prac•tice (*Brit*
  •tise; *vb*)
prac•ticed (*Brit*
  •tised)
prac•ti•tion•er
prag•mat•ic
prag•mati•cal•ly
prag•ma•tism
prag•ma•tist
prai•rie
praise
prais•er
praise•worthi•ness
praise•worthy
pra•line
pram
prance
pranc•er
prank
prank•ish
prank•ster
prate
prat•tle
prat•tler
prawn
pray utter prayer;
  cf prey
prayer petition
pray•er one who
  prays
prayer•ful
prayer•ful•ly
preach
preach•er
pre•ado•les•cence

pre•ado•les•cent
pre•am•ble
pre•am•bu•lary
pre•am•pli•fi•er
pre•ar•range
pre•ar•range•ment
pre•ar•rang•er
preb•end
pre•ben•dal
preb•en•dary (*pl*
  •daries)
pre•can•cel
  (•cel•ing, •celed;
  Brit •cel•ling,
  •celled)
pre•can•cel•la•tion
pre•cari•ous
pre•cari•ous•ly
pre•cari•ous•ness
pre•cast (•cast•ing,
  •cast)
preca•tory (*or*
  •tive)
pre•cau•tion
pre•cau•tion•ary
  (*or* •tion•al)
pre•cede come
  before; *cf* proceed
pre•cedence
pre•cedent
pre•ced•ing
pre•cen•tor cleric;
  cf preceptor
pre•cept
pre•cep•tor
  teacher; *cf*
  precentor
pre•cep•to•rial (*or*
  •to•ral)

pre•ces•sion
  rotation; motion
  of equinoxes; *cf*
  procession
pre•ces•sion•al
pre-Chris•tian
pre•cinct
pre•ci•os•ity (*pl*
  •ities)
pre•cious
pre•cious•ness
preci•pice
pre•cipi•tance (*or*
  •tan•cy)
pre•cipi•tant
pre•cipi•tate
pre•cipi•ta•tion
pre•cipi•ta•tor
pre•cipi•tous
pre•cipi•tous•ness
pré•cis (*pl* •cis)
pre•cise
pre•cise•ly
pre•cise•ness
pre•ci•sion
pre•clini•cal
pre•clude
pre•clu•sion
pre•clu•sive
pre•co•cious
pre•co•cious•ly
pre•co•cious•ness
  (*or* pre•coc•ity)
pre•cog•ni•tion
pre•cog•ni•tive
pre•con•ceive
pre•con•cep•tion
pre•con•demn
pre•con•di•tion

pre•con•tract
pre•cook
pre•cur•sor
pre•cur•sory (*or*
  •sive)
pre•date precede
pre•da•tion
  predatory action
preda•tor
preda•to•ri•ly
preda•to•ri•ness
preda•tory
pre•de•cease
pre•de•ces•sor
pre•des•ti•na•tion
pre•des•tine (*or*
  •ti•nate)
pre•de•ter•min•able
pre•de•ter•mi•nate
pre•de•ter•mi•na•
  tion
pre•de•ter•mine
predi•cable
pre•dica•ment
predi•cate
predi•ca•tion
pred•ica•tive
pre•dict
pre•dict•abil•ity
pre•dict•able
pre•dict•ably
pre•dic•tion
pre•dic•tive
pre•dic•tive•ly
pre•dic•tor
pre•di•lec•tion
pre•dis•pose
pre•dis•po•si•tion

pre•domi•nance (*or*
  •nan•cy)
pre•domi•nant
pre•domi•nant•ly
pre•domi•nate
pre•domi•na•tion
pre•domi•na•tor
pree•mie (*or*
  pre•mie)
pre•emi•nence
pre•emi•nent
pre•emi•nent•ly
pre•empt
pre•emp•tion
pre•emp•tive
pre•emp•tor
pre•emp•tory
preen
preen•er
pre•ex•ist
pre•ex•is•tence
pre•fab
pre•fab•ri•cate
pre•fab•ri•ca•tion
pref•ace
prefa•tory
pre•fect
pre•fec•to•rial
pre•fec•ture
pre•fer (•fer•ring,
  •ferred)
pref•er•able
pref•er•ably
pref•er•ence
pref•er•en•tial
pref•er•en•tial•ly
pre•fer•ment
pre•fer•rer
pre•fig•ure

pre•fix
pre•form
pre•for•ma•tion
preg•na•ble
preg•nan•cy (*pl* •cies)
preg•nant
pre•heat
pre•hen•sile
pre•hen•sion
pre•his•tor•ic (*or* •tori•cal)
pre•his•tori•cal•ly
pre•his•to•ry (*pl* •ries)
pre•judge
pre•judg•er
pre•judg•ment (*Brit also* •judge•ment)
preju•dice
preju•di•cial
prela•cy (*pl* •cies)
prel•ate
pre•limi•nari•ly
pre•limi•nary (*pl* •naries)
prel•ude
pre•mari•tal
prema•ture
prema•ture•ly
prema•tu•rity (*or* •ture•ness)
pre•med
pre•medi•cal
pre•medi•ca•tion
pre•medi•tate
pre•medi•ta•tion
pre•men•stru•al

pre•mie *variant spelling of* preemie
pre•mier first in importance
pre•miere first performance
prem•ier•ship
prem•ise state as premiss; *variant spelling of* premiss
prem•ises land and buildings
prem•iss (*or* •ise) logical statement
pre•mium
pre•mo•lar
pre•mo•ni•tion
pre•moni•tory
pre•na•tal
pre•nomi•nal
pre•oc•cu•pa•tion (*or* •pan•cy)
pre•oc•cu•py (•pies, •py•ing, •pied)
pre•or•dain
pre•or•di•na•tion
prep (prep•ping, prepped)
pre•pack
pre•pack•age
pre•paid
prepa•ra•tion
pre•para•to•ri•ly
pre•para•tory
pre•pare
pre•par•ed•ness
pre•pay (•pay•ing, •paid)
pre•pay•able

pre•pay•ment
pre•pon•der•ance (*or* •an•cy)
pre•pon•der•ant
pre•pon•der•ate
prepo•si•tion
prepo•si•tion•al
pre•pos•sess
pre•pos•ses•sion
pre•pos•ter•ous
pre•pos•ter•ous•ly
prepped
prep•ping
prep•py (*or* •pie; *pl* •pies)
pre•puce
Pre-Ra•phael•ite
pre•re•cord
pre•requi•site
pre•roga•tive
pres•age
pres•byo•pia
pres•by•op•ic
pres•by•ter
Pres•by•te•ri•an
Pres•by•teri•an•ism
pres•by•tery (*pl* •teries)
pre•school
pres•cience
pres•cient
pre•scribe give ruling; order use of drug; *cf* pro•scribe
pre•script
pre•scrip•tion
pre•scrip•tive

pres•ence
'pres•ent the time
 now; in existence
 now; gift
pre•'sent to give
pre•sent•able
pre•sent•able•ness
 (or •abil•ity)
pre•sent•ably
pres•en•ta•tion
pres•en•ta•tion•al
present-day (adj)
pre•sent•er
pre•sen•tient
pre•sen•ti•ment
pres•ent•ly
pre•sent•ment
pre•serv•abil•ity
pre•serv•able
pres•er•va•tion
pre•serva•tive
pre•serve
pre•serv•er
pre•set (•set•ting,
 •set)
pre•shrunk
pre•side
presi•den•cy (pl
 •cies)
presi•dent
president-elect
presi•den•tial
pre•sid•er
pre•sid•ium (pl
 •sid•iums or
 •sidia)
press
press-gang
press•ing

press•ing•ly
press•man (pl
 •men)
press•room
press-up (n; Brit)
 push-up
pres•sure
pres•suri•za•tion
pres•sur•ize
press•work
pres•ti•digi•ta•tion
pres•ti•digi•ta•tor
pres•tige
pres•tig•ious
pres•tig•ious•ness
pres•to (pl •tos)
pre•stressed
pre•sum•able
pre•sum•ably
pre•sume
pre•sum•er
pre•sump•tion
pre•sump•tive
pre•sump•tu•ous
pre•sump•tu•ous•ly
pre•sump•tu•ous•
 ness
pre•sup•pose
pre•sup•po•si•tion
pre•tax
pre•tend
pre•tend•er
pre•tense (Brit
 •tence)
pre•ten•sion
pre•ten•tious
pre•ten•tious•ly
pre•ten•tious•ness
pre•ter•natu•ral

pre•ter•natu•ral•
 ism
pre•ter•natu•ral•ly
pre•text
pret•ti•fy (•fies,
 •fy•ing, •fied)
pret•ti•ly
pret•ti•ness
pret•ty (adj •ti•er,
 •ti•est; vb •ties,
 •ty•ing, •tied)
pret•zel
pre•vail
pre•vail•ing•ly
preva•lence (or
 •lent•ness)
preva•lent
pre•vari•cate
pre•vari•ca•tion
pre•vari•ca•tor
pre•vent
pre•vent•able (or
 •ible)
pre•vent•ably
pre•ven•ta•tive
 variant of
 preventive
pre•vent•er
pre•vent•ible
 variant spelling of
 preventable
pre•ven•tion
pre•ven•tive (Brit
 also •ta•tive)
pre•ven•tive•ly
pre•view (or •vue)
pre•vi•ous
pre•vi•ous•ly
pre•vi•ous•ness

pre•vue *variant spelling of* **preview**
pre•war
prey victim; to hunt; victimize; *cf* **pray**
prey•er
price
price•less
price•less•ness
pricey (*or* pricy; prici•er, prici•est)
prick
prick•er
prick•le
prick•li•ness
prick•ly (•li•er, •li•est)
pricy *variant spelling of* **pricey**
pride
pride•ful
prie-dieu (*pl* -dieus *or* -dieux)
pri•er (*or* pry•) one who pries; *cf* **prior**
priest
priest•ess
priest•hood
priest•li•ness
priest•ly (•li•er, •li•est)
prig
prig•gery (*or* prig•gish•ness)
prig•gish
prim (*adj* prim•mer, prim•mest; *vb*

prim•ming, primmed)
pri•ma bal•leri•na
pri•ma•cy (*pl* •cies)
pri•ma don•na (*pl* pri•ma don•nas)
pri•mae•val *variant spelling of* **primeval**
pri•ma fa•cie
pri•mal
pri•mari•ly
pri•ma•ry (*pl* •ries)
pri•mate
prime
prime•ness
pri•mer introductory text
prim•er person or thing that primes
pri•me•val (*or* •mae•)
pri•me•val•ly
prim•ing
primi•tive
primi•tive•ly
primi•tive•ness
primi•tiv•ism
primi•tiv•ist
prim•ly
prim•ness
pri•mo•geni•tary
pri•mo•geni•tor
pri•mo•geni•ture
pri•mor•dial
primp
prim•rose
primu•la
pri•mum mo•bi•le

Pri•mus (*Trademark*)
prince
prince•dom
prince•li•ness
prince•ling
prince•ly (•li•er, •li•est)
prin•cess
prin•ci•pal foremost; head person; *cf* **principle**
prin•ci•pal•ity (*pl* •ities)
prin•ci•pal•ly
prin•ci•ple standard; *cf* **principal**
prin•ci•pled
prink
print
print•able
print•er
print•ing
print•maker
print•out
pri•or earlier; abbot's deputy; *cf* **prier**
pri•or•ess
pri•ori•tize
pri•or•ity (*pl* •ities)
pri•ory (*pl* •ories)
prise *variant spelling of* **prize** (pry)
prism
pris•mat•ic

pris•on
pris•on•er
pris•si•ly
pris•si•ness
pris•sy (•si•er,
•si•est)
pris•tine
pri•va•cy (pl •cies)
pri•vate
pri•va•teer
pri•vate•ly
pri•va•tion
priva•tive
pri•vati•za•tion
pri•vat•ize
priv•et
privi•lege
privi•leged
privy (n, pl privies;
adj privi•er,
privi•est)
prize award
prize (or prise) pry
prize•fight
prize•fighter
prize•winner
prize•winning
pro (pl pros)
pro•ac•tive
prob•abil•ity (pl
•ities)
prob•able
prob•ably
pro•bate
pro•ba•tion
pro•ba•tion•al (or
•tion•ary)
pro•ba•tion•er
probe

prob•er
pro•bity
prob•lem
prob•lem•at•ic (or
•ati•cal)
prob•lem•ati•cal•ly
pro•bos•cis (pl
•cises or •ci•des)
pro•ce•dur•al
pro•ce•dure
pro•ceed (NOT
procede) carry
on; cf precede
pro•ceed•ing
pro•ceed•ings
pro•ceeds (n)
pro•cess
pro•ces•sion
pro•ces•sion•al
pro•ces•sor
pro•claim
proc•la•ma•tion
pro•clama•tory
pro•cliv•ity (pl
•ities)
pro•con•sul
pro•cras•ti•nate
pro•cras•ti•na•tion
pro•cras•ti•na•tor
pro•cre•ate
pro•crea•tion
pro•crea•tive
pro•crea•tor
Pro•crus•tean (or
pro•)
proc•tor
proc•to•rial
pro•cur•able
procu•ra•tion

procu•ra•tor
pro•cure
pro•cure•ment (or
•cur•ance, •cur•al)
pro•cur•er (fem
•ess)
prod (prod•ding,
prod•ded)
prod•der
prodi•gal
prodi•gal•ity (pl
•ities)
prodi•gal•ly
pro•di•gious
pro•di•gious•ly
pro•di•gious•ness
prodi•gy (pl •gies)
pro•duce
pro•duc•er
pro•duc•ible
prod•uct
pro•duc•tion
pro•duc•tive
pro•duc•tive•ly
prod•uc•tiv•ity (or
•tive•ness)
pro•fane
pro•fane•ness
pro•fan•er
pro•fan•ity (pl
•ities)
pro•fess
pro•fess•ed•ly
pro•fes•sion
pro•fes•sion•al
pro•fes•sion•al•ism
pro•fes•sion•al•ly
pro•fes•sor
prof•es•so•rial

pro•fes•sor•ship
prof•fer
prof•fer•er
pro•fi•cien•cy (*pl* •cies)
pro•fi•cient
pro•fi•cient•ly
pro•file
prof•it
prof•it•abil•ity
prof•it•able
prof•it•ably
profi•teer
prof•it•er
pro•fit•er•ole
prof•it•less
profit-sharing (*adj*)
prof•li•ga•cy
prof•li•gate
pro for•ma
pro•found
pro•found•ly
pro•found•ness
pro•fun•dity (*pl* •dities)
pro•fusc
pro•fuse•ly
pro•fuse•ness
pro•fu•sion
pro•geni•tive
pro•geni•tor
prog•eny (*pl* •enies)
pro•ges•ter•one
pro•ges•to•gen (*or* pro•ges•tin)
prog•no•sis (*pl* •ses)
prog•nos•tic
prog•nos•ti•cate

prog•nos•ti•ca•tion
prog•nos•ti•ca•tor
pro•gram (•gram• ing, •gramed *or* •gram•ming, •grammed) computer term
pro•gram (*Brit* •gramme; •gram• ing, •gramed *or* •gram•ming, •grammed) schedule; broad-cast; etc.
pro•gram•mable (*or* •gram•able)
pro•gram•mat•ic
pro•gram•mer (*or* •gram•er)
pro•gress
pro•gres•sion
pro•gres•sive
pro•gres•sive•ly
pro•hib•it
pro•hib•it•er (*or* •hibi•tor)
pro•hi•bi•tion
pro•hi•bi•tion•ary
pro•hi•bi•tion•ism
pro•hi•bi•tion•ist
pro•hibi•tive (*or* •tory)
pro•hibi•tive•ly
proj•ect
pro•jec•tile
pro•jec•tion
pro•jec•tion•ist
pro•jec•tive
pro•jec•tor

pro•lapse
prole
pro•letar•ian (*or* •letary; *pl* •ians *or* •letaries)
pro•letar•ian•ism
pro•letari•at
pro-life
pro•lif•er•ate
pro•lif•era•tion
pro•lif•era•tive
pro•lif•ic
pro•lifi•cal•ly
pro•lix
pro•lix•ity (*or* •ness)
pro•logue (*or* •log; •logu•ing, •logued *or* •log•ing, •loged)
pro•long
pro•lon•ga•tion
prom
prom•enade
prom•enad•er
Pro•me•thean
promi•nence
promi•nent
promi•nent•ly
promis•cu•ity (*pl* •ities)
pro•mis•cu•ous
pro•mis•cu•ous•ly
prom•ise
prom•is•er (*or* in *legal contexts* promi•sor)
prom•is•ing
prom•is•sory

pro•mo (*pl* •mos)
prom•on•tory (*pl*
•tories)
pro•mot•able
pro•mote
pro•mot•er
pro•mo•tion
pro•mo•tion•al
pro•mo•tive
prompt
prompt•book
prompt•er
promp•ti•tude
prompt•ly
prompt•ness
prom•ul•gate
prom•ul•ga•tion
prom•ul•ga•tor
pro•nate
pro•na•tion
prone
prone•ness
prong
prong•horn (*pl*
•horn *or* •horns)
pro•nomi•nal
pro•noun
pro•nounce
pro•nounce•able
pro•nounced
pro•nounc•ed•ly
pro•nounce•ment
pro•nounc•er
pron•to
proof
proof•read
(•read•ing, •read)
proof•reader

prop (prop•ping,
propped)
propa•gable
propa•gan•da
propa•gan•dism
propa•gan•dist
propa•gan•dize
propa•gate
propa•ga•tion
propa•ga•tive
propa•ga•tor
pro•pane
pro•pel (•pel•ling,
•pelled)
pro•pel•lant (*or*
•lent; *n*)
pro•pel•lent (*or*
•lant; *adj*)
pro•pel•ler (*or* •lor)
pro•pene
pro•pen•sity (*pl*
•sities)
prop•er
prop•er•ly
prop•er•ness
prop•er•tied
prop•er•ty (*pl* •ties)
proph•ecy (*or* •esy;
pl •ecies *or* •esies)
proph•esi•er
proph•esy (*or* •ecy;
•esies, •esy•ing,
•esied *or* •ecies,
•ecy•ing, •ecied)
proph•et (*fem*
•et•ess)
pro•phet•ic
pro•pheti•cal•ly
pro•phy•lac•tic

pro•phy•lax•is (*pl*
•laxes)
pro•pin•quity
pro•pi•ti•able
pro•pi•ti•ate
pro•pi•tia•tion
pro•pi•tia•tor
pro•pi•tia•tory
pro•pi•tious
pro•pi•tious•ness
prop•jet
pro•po•nent
pro•por•tion
pro•por•tion•al
pro•por•tion•al•ity
pro•por•tion•al•ly
pro•por•tion•ate
pro•por•tion•ate•ly
pro•po•sable
pro•po•sal
pro•pose
pro•pos•er
propo•si•tion
propo•si•tion•al
pro•pound
pro•pri•etary (*pl*
•etaries)
pro•pri•etor (*fem*
•etress)
pro•pri•etor•ial
pro•pri•ety (*pl*
•eties)
pro•pul•sion
pro•pul•sive (*or*
•sory)
pro•pyl•ene
pro rata
pro•rate
pro•ra•tion

pro•ro•ga•tion
pro•rogue
pro•sa•ic
pro•sai•cal•ly
pro•sa•ic•ness
pros and cons
pro•sce•nium (*pl*
•scenia or
•sce•niums)
pro•sciut•to (*pl* •ti
or •tos)
pro•scribe
prohibit; *cf*
prescribe
pro•scrip•tion
pro•scrip•tive
prose
pros•ecut•able
pros•ecute
pros•ecu•tion
pros•ecu•tor
pros•elyte
pros•elyt•ism
pros•elyti•za•tion
pros•elyt•ize
pros•clyt•iz•er
prosi•ly
prosi•ness
pro•sod•ic
proso•dist
proso•dy (*pl* •dies)
pros•pect
pros•pec•tive
pros•pec•tor
pro•spec•tus (*pl*
•tuses)
pros•per
pros•per•ity (*pl*
•ities)

pros•per•ous
pros•per•ous•ly
pros•tate gland; *cf*
prostrate
pros•tat•ic
pros•the•sis (*pl*
•ses) artificial
body part; *cf*
prothesis
pros•thet•ic
pros•thet•ics
pros•ti•tute
pros•ti•tu•tion
pros•trate face
down; *cf* prostate
pros•tra•tion
prosy (prosi•er,
prosi•est)
pro•tago•nism
pro•tago•nist
pro•tea
pro•tean
pro•tect
pro•tec•tion
pro•tec•tion•ism
pro•tec•tion•ist
pro•tec•tive
pro•tec•tive•ly
pro•tec•tive•ness
pro•tec•tor
pro•tec•tor•al
pro•tec•tor•ate
pro•té•gé (*fem*
•gée)
pro•tein
pro•teina•ceous (or
•tein•ic)
pro tem (or pro
tem•po•re)

pro•test
Prot•es•tant
religion
pro•test•ant
protester
Prot•es•tant•ism
pro•tes•ta•tion
pro•test•er (or
•tes•tor)
pro•test•ing•ly
proth•esis
linguistics and
ecclesiastic term;
cf prosthesis
pro•thet•ic
pro•to•col
pro•ton
proto•plasm
proto•plas•mic (or
•mal)
proto•ty•pal (or
•typi•cal)
proto•type
proto•zoan (or
•zo•on; *n, pl*
•zoans or •zoa)
proto•zoan (or
•zoal, zoic; *adj*)
pro•tract
pro•tract•ed•ly
pro•trac•tile (or
•tract•ible)
pro•trac•tion
pro•trac•tor
pro•trude
pro•tru•dent
pro•tru•sible
pro•tru•sion
pro•tru•sive

pro•tu•ber•ance (*or*
•an•cy; *pl* •ances
or •cies)
pro•tu•ber•ant
proud
proud•ly
proud•ness
prov•abil•ity
prov•able
prove (prov•ing,
proved, proved *or*
prov•en)
prov•enance
Pro•ven•çal of
Provence
Pro•ven•çale
cookery term
prov•en•der
prov•erb
pro•ver•bial
pro•ver•bial•ly
pro•vide
provi•dence
provi•dent
provi•den•tial
provi•den•tial•ly
pro•vid•er
prov•ince
pro•vin•cial
pro•vin•cial•ism
pro•vin•ci•al•ity
pro•vi•sion
pro•vi•sion•al (*or*
•ary)
pro•vi•sion•al•ly
pro•vi•sion•er
pro•vi•sions
pro•vi•so (*pl* •sos
or •soes)

pro•vi•so•ri•ly
pro•vi•sory
provo•ca•tion
pro•voca•tive
pro•voca•tive•ly
pro•voca•tive•ness
pro•voke
pro•vok•ing•ly
pro•vost
prow
prow•ess
prowl
prowl•er
proxi•mal•ly
proxi•mate
proxi•mate•ly
prox•im•ity
proxy (*pl* proxies)
prude
pru•dence
pru•dent
pru•den•tial
pru•dent•ly
prud•ery (*pl* •eries)
prud•ish
prud•ish•ly
prud•ish•ness
prune
prun•er
pru•ri•ence
pru•ri•ent lewd; *cf*
purulent
Prus•sian
prus•sic acid
pry (*vb* pries,
pry•ing, pried; *n*,
pl pries)
pry•er *variant
spelling of* prier

psalm
psalm•book
psalm•ic
psalm•ist
psalmo•dy (*pl*
•dies)
Psalms Old
Testament book
Psal•ter (*or* psal•)
psalmbook
pse•pholo•gist
pse•phol•ogy
pseud (*n, adj*)
pseu•do (*adj*)
pseudo•nym
pseu•dony•mous
pseudo•po•dium
(*pl* •dia)
psi
psit•ta•co•sis
pso•ria•sis
pso•ri•at•ic
psych
psy•che
psyche•delia
psyche•del•ic
psyche•deli•cal•ly
psy•chi•at•ric
psy•chi•at•ri•cal•ly
psy•chia•trist
psy•chia•try
psy•chic
psy•chi•cal
psy•cho (*pl* •chos)
psycho•analy•sis
psycho•ana•lyst
psycho•ana•lyt•ic
(*or* •lyti•cal)

psycho•ana•lyti•cal•ly
psycho•ana•lyze (*Brit* •lyse)
psycho•bab•ble
psycho•dra•ma
psycho•dra•mat•ic
psycho•ki•nesis
psycho•ki•net•ic
psycho•logi•cal
psycho•logi•cal•ly
psy•cholo•gist
psy•cholo•gize
psy•chol•ogy (*pl* •ogies)
psycho•met•ric (*or* •ri•cal)
psycho•met•rics (*or* psy•chom•etry)
psycho•path
psycho•path•ic
psycho•pathi•cal•ly
psy•chopa•thy
psycho•sex•ual
psycho•sexu•al•ly
psy•cho•sis (*pl* •ses)
psycho•so•cial
psycho•so•mat•ic
psycho•thera•peu•tic
psycho•thera•pist
psycho•thera•py
psy•chot•ic
psy•choti•cal•ly
ptar•mi•gan (*pl* •gan *or* •gans)
pteri•do•phyte
ptero•dac•tyl

ptero•saur
Ptol•ema•ic
pto•maine (*or* •main)
pub
pu•ber•ty
pu•bes•cence
pu•bes•cent
pu•bic
pu•bis (*pl* •bes)
pub•lic
pub•li•can
pub•li•ca•tion
pub•li•cist
pub•lic•ity
pub•li•cize
pub•lic•ly
public-spirited
pub•lish
pub•lish•able
pub•lish•er
puc•coon
puce
puck
puck•er
puck•ish
puck•ish•ly
puck•ish•ness
pud•ding
pud•dle
pud•dler
pud•dly
pu•den•dal
pu•den•dum (*pl* •da)
pudgi•ness
pudgy (pudgi•er, pudgi•est)
Pueb•lo (*pl* •lo *or*

•los) American Indian
pueb•lo (*pl* •los) village
pu•er•ile
pu•er•ile•ly
pu•er•il•ity (*pl* •ities)
pu•er•per•al
Puer•to Ri•can
puff
puff•ball
puff•bird
puff•er
puffi•ly
puf•fin
puffi•ness
puffy (puffi•er, puffi•est)
pug (pug•ging, pugged)
pu•gi•lism
pu•gi•list
pu•gi•lis•tic
pug•na•cious
pug•na•cious•ly
pug•nac•ity (*or* •na•cious•ness)
pug-nosed
puke
pul•chri•tude
pul•chri•tudi•nous
Pu•lit•zer prize
pull
pul•let
pul•ley
pull•out
pull•over
pul•lu•late

pul•lu•la•tion
pul•mo•nary
pulp
pulpi•ness
pul•pit
pulp•wood
pulpy (pulpi•er,
  pulpi•est)
pul•sar
pul•sate
pul•sa•tion
pul•sa•tor
pul•sa•tory
pulse
pul•veri•za•tion
pul•ver•ize
pul•ver•iz•er
puma (pl pumas or
  puma)
pum•ice
pum•mel (•mel•ing,
  •meled; Brit
  •mel•ling, •melled)
  to pound; cf
  pommel
pump
pum•per•nick•el
pump•kin
pumpkin•seed
pun (pun•ning,
  punned)
punch
punch•ball
punch-drunk
punch•er
punch-out (n)
punchy (punchi•er,
  punchi•est)
punc•tili•ous

punc•tili•ous•ly
punc•tili•ous•ness
punc•tu•al
punc•tu•al•ity
punc•tu•al•ly
punc•tu•ate
punc•tua•tion
punc•tur•able
punc•ture
pun•dit
pung
pun•gen•cy
pun•gent
pu•ni•ness
pun•ish
pun•ish•able
pun•ish•er
pun•ish•ing•ly
pun•ish•ment
pu•ni•tive (or •tory)
pu•ni•tive•ness
punk
punned
pun•ner
pun•net
pun•ning
pun•ster
punt
punt•er
puny (pu•ni•er,
  pu•ni•est)
pup (pup•ping,
  pupped)
pupa (pl pupae or
  pupas)
pu•pal
pu•pate
pu•pa•tion
pu•pil

pu•pil•lary (or
  •pi•lary)
pup•pet
pup•pe•teer
pup•pet•ry
pup•ping
pup•py (pl •pies)
pup•py•hood
pup•py•ish
pur•blind
pur•chas•able
pur•chase
pur•chas•er
pur•dah
pure
pure•bred
pu•rée (or •ree;
  •rée•ing, •réed or
  •ree•ing, •reed)
pure•ly
pure•ness
pur•ga•tion
pur•ga•tive
pur•ga•to•rial
pur•ga•tory
purge
purg•er
pu•ri•fi•ca•tion
pu•rifi•ca•tory
pu•ri•fi•er
pu•ri•fy (•fies,
  •fy•ing, •fied)
Pu•rim
pur•ism
pur•ist
pu•rist•ic
Pu•ri•tan extreme
  Protestant

pu•ri•tan strictly moral person
pu•ri•tani•cal (*or* •tan•ic)
pu•ri•tani•cal•ness
pu•ri•tan•ism
pu•rity
purl knitting stitch; *cf* **pearl**
pur•lieu
pur•lin (*or* •line)
pur•loin
pur•ple
pur•plish
pur•port
pur•port•ed•ly
pur•pose
pur•pose•ful
pur•pose•ful•ly determinedly; *cf* **purposely**
pur•pose•ful•ness
pur•pose•less
pur•pose•less•ness
pur•pose•ly intentionally; *cf* **purposefully**
pur•pos•ive
purr
purse
purs•er
purs•lane
pur•su•ance
pur•su•ant
pur•sue (•su•ing, •sued; *NOT* persue)
pur•su•er
pur•suit

pu•ru•lence (*or* •len•cy)
pu•ru•lent of pus; *cf* **prurient**
pur•vey
pur•vey•ance
pur•vey•or
pus matter from wound; *cf* **puss**
push
push•er
pushi•ly
pushi•ness
push•ing
push•ing•ly
push•over
Push•tu *variant of* **Pashto**
push-up (*n*)
pushy (pushi•er, pushi•est)
pu•sil•la•nim•ity
pu•sil•lani•mous
puss cat; *cf* **pus**
pus•sy (•si•er, •si•est) full of pus
pussy (*or* pussy•cat; *pl* pussies *or* •cats)
pussy•foot
pus•tu•lar
pus•tu•late
pus•tu•la•tion
pus•tule
put (put•ting, put) to place, etc.; *cf* **putt**
pu•ta•tive
put-down (*n*)

put-off (*n*)
put-on (*n*)
put•out
pu•tre•fac•tion
pu•tre•fac•tive (*or* •fa•cient)
pu•tre•fy (•fies, •fy•ing, •fied; *NOT* putrify)
pu•tres•cence
pu•tres•cent
pu•trid
pu•trid•ity (*or* •trid•ness)
*****putrify** *incorrect spelling of* **putrefy**
putt golf stroke; *cf* **put**
put•tee (*or* •ty; *pl* •tees *or* •ties) leg cloth
putt•er golf club
put•ter placer
put•ter (*Brit* pot•) work slowly; dawdle
putt•ing golf stroke
put•ting placing
put•ty (*n, pl* •ties; *vb* •ties, •ty•ing, •tied)
put-up (*adj*)
puz•zle
puz•zle•ment
puz•zler
puz•zling•ly
Pyg•my (*or* Pig•; *pl* •mies) African race

pyg•my (or pig•; pl
•mies) dwarf
py•ja•mas Brit
spelling of
pajamas
py•lon
py•ra•can•tha
pyra•mid
pyr•ami•dal (or
pyra•midi•cal,
pyra•mid•ic)
pyre
py•re•thrum
py•ret•ic
Py•rex (Trade-
mark)
py•rexia
py•rite
py•ri•tes (pl •tes)
pyro•ma•nia
pyro•ma•ni•ac
pyro•tech•nic (or
•ni•cal)
pyro•tech•nics
Pyr•rhic
Py•thago•rean
py•thon
pyx container for
Eucharist; cf pix
pyxie shrub; cf
pixie

Q

quack
quack•ery (pl
•eries)
quad

quad•ra•genar•ian
quad•ran•gle
quad•ran•gu•lar
quad•rant
quad•ra•phon•ic (or
•ri•)
quad•ra•phon•ics
(or •ri•)
quad•rat•ic
quad•ren•nial
quad•ren•nial•ly
quad•ri•cen•ten•
nial
quad•ri•lat•er•al
quad•rille
quad•ri•plegia
quad•ri•plegic
quad•ru•ped
quad•ru•ped•al
quad•ru•ple
quad•ru•plet
quad•ru•pli•cate
quad•ru•pli•ca•tion
quad•ru•plic•ity
(pl •ities)
quaff
quaff•er
quag•mire
qua•hog (or •haug)
quail (pl quail or
quails)
quaint
quaint•ly
quaint•ness
quake
quake•proof
Quak•er
Quak•er•ism
quaki•ness

quaky (quaki•er,
quaki•est)
quali•fi•able
quali•fi•ca•tion
quali•fi•ca•tory
quali•fied
quali•fi•er
quali•fy (•fies,
•fy•ing, fied)
quali•ta•tive
qual•ity (pl •ities)
qualm
qualm•ish
quan•da•ry (pl
•ries)
quango (pl
quangos)
quan•ta pl of
quantum
quan•ti•fi•able
quan•ti•fi•ca•tion
quan•ti•fi•er
quan•ti•fy (•fies,
•fy•ing, •fied)
quan•ti•ta•tive (or
quan•ti•tive)
quan•tity (pl
•tities)
quan•ti•za•tion
quan•tize
quan•tum (pl •ta)
quar•an•tine
quark
quar•rel (•rel•ing,
•reled; Brit
•rel•ling, •relled)
quar•rel•er (Brit
•rel•ler)
quar•rel•some

quar•ry (*n, pl* •ries;
vb •ries, •ry•ing,
•ried)
quart
quar•ter
quarter•back
quarter•deck
quar•tered
quarter•final
quarter-hour
quar•ter•ing
quar•ter•ly (*pl*
•lies)
quarter•master
quar•ters
quar•tet (*or* •tette)
quar•tile
quar•to (*pl* •tos)
quartz
quartz•ite
qua•sar
quash
qua•si
quas•sia
qua•ter•cen•te•nary
(*pl* •naries)
qua•ter•nary (*pl*
•naries)
quat•rain
qua•ver
qua•ver•ing•ly
qua•very
quay landing
place; *cf* cay; key
quay•age
quay•side
quea•si•ly
quea•si•ness

quea•sy (•si•er,
•si•est)
Quech•ua (*pl* •ua
or •uas)
Quech•uan
queen
queen•li•ness
queen•ly (•li•er,
•li•est)
queer
queer•ly
queer•ness
quell
quell•er
quench
quench•able
quench•er
queru•lous
queru•lous•ly
queru•lous•ness
que•ry (*n, pl* •ries;
vb •ries, •ry•ing,
•ried)
quest
quest•er
ques•tion
ques•tion•able
ques•tion•able•ness
(*or* •abil•ity)
ques•tion•ably
ques•tion•er
ques•tion•ing
ques•tion•ing•ly
ques•tion•less
ques•tion•naire
quet•zal (*pl* •zals
or •zales)
queue (queu•ing *or*

queue•ing, queued)
line; pigtail; *cf* cue
quib•ble
quib•bler
quiche (*pl* quiche
or quiches)
quick
quick•en
quick-freeze
(-freez•ing, -froze,
-fro•zen)
quickie
quick•lime
quick•ly
quick•ness
quick•sand
quick•silver
quick•step
(•step•ping,
•stepped)
quick-tempered
quick-witted
quick-witted•ly
quick-witted•ness
quid
quid•dity (*pl*
•dities)
quid pro quo (*pl*
quid pro quos)
qui•es•cence (*or*
•cen•cy)
qui•es•cent
qui•et
qui•et•ly
qui•et•ness
qui•etude
quill
quill•wort
quilt

quilt•er
quilt•ing
quin
quince
quin•cen•te•nary
(pl •naries)
quin•cunx
qui•nine
quin•qua•genar•ian
quin•quen•nial
quin•quen•nial•ly
quin•sy
quin•tes•sence
quin•tes•sen•tial
quin•tes•sen•tial•ly
quin•tet (or •tette)
quin•tu•ple
quin•tu•plet
quin•tu•pli•cate
quin•tu•pli•ca•tion
quip (quip•ping,
  quipped)
quip•ster
quire set of paper;
  cf choir
quirk
quirki•ly
quirki•ness
quirky (quirki•er,
  quirki•est)
quis•ling
quit (quit•ting,
  quit•ted or quit)
quit•claim
quite
quits
quit•ter
quiv•er
quiv•er•ing•ly

quiv•ery
quix•ot•ic (or
  •oti•cal)
quix•oti•cal•ly
quixo•tism
quiz (n, pl quiz•zes;
  vb quiz•zes,
  quiz•zing, quizzed)
quiz•master
quiz•zer
quiz•zi•cal
quiz•zi•cal•ly
quod erat de•mon•
  stran•dum
quoin (or coign,
  coigne) angle of
  building; cf coin
quoit ring
quoits game
quo•rum
quo•ta
quot•abil•ity
quot•able
quo•ta•tion
quote
quo•tient

R

rab•bi (or •bin; pl
  •bis or •bins)
rab•bini•cal (or
  •bin•ic)
rab•bit
rab•ble
rabble-rouser
rabble-rousing
Rab•elai•sian

rab•id
ra•bid•ity (or
  rab•id•ness)
ra•bid•ly
ra•bies
rac•coon (or
  ra•coon)
race
race•course
race•goer
race•horse
rac•er
race•track
race•way
ra•cial
ra•cial•ism variant
  of racism
ra•cial•ly
raci•ly
raci•ness
rac•ing
rac•ism (or
  ra•cial•ism)
rac•ist (or
  ra•cial•ist)
rack frame;
  toothed bar; to
  strain; etc.; cf
  wrack
rack (or wrack)
  destruction, esp.
  in rack and ruin
rack•et disturb-
  ance; dishonest
  practice
rack•et (or
  rac•quet) bat
rack•eteer

rack•ets (*or*
  rac•quets) game
rack•ety
rac•on•teur
ra•coon *variant*
  spelling of raccoon
rac•quet *variant*
  spelling of racket
racy (raci•er,
  raci•est)
ra•dar
rad•dled
ra•dial
ra•dial•ly
radial-ply
ra•di•ance (*or*
  •an•cy; *pl* •ances
  or •cies)
ra•di•ant
ra•di•ant•ly
ra•di•ate
ra•dia•tion
ra•dia•tor
radi•cal basic; ex-
  treme; chemistry
  term; *cf* radicle
radi•cal•ism
radi•cal•ly
radi•cal•ness
ra•dic•chio (*pl*
  •chios)
radi•cle embryonic
  plant root; *cf*
  radical
ra•dii *pl of* radius
ra•dio (*n, pl* •dios;
  vb •dios, •dio•ing,
  •di•oed)
radio•ac•tive

radio•ac•tiv•ity
radio•car•bon
radio•com•mu•ni•
  ca•tion
radio•graph
ra•di•og•ra•pher
radio•graph•ic
ra•di•og•ra•phy
radio•iso•tope
radio•logi•cal
ra•di•olo•gist
ra•di•ol•ogy
radio•phon•ic
radio•phoni•cal•ly
ra•di•opho•ny
radio•scope
radio•scop•ic
radio•scopi•cal•ly
ra•dio•sco•py
radio•sen•si•tive
radio•sen•si•tiv•ity
radio•tele•gram
radio•tele•graph
radio•tele•graph•ic
radio•teleg•ra•phy
radio•tele•phone
radio•thera•peu•tic
radio•thera•pist
radio•thera•py
rad•ish
ra•dium
ra•dius (*pl* •dii *or*
  •di•uses)
ra•don
raf•fia (*or* raphia)
raff•ish
raff•ish•ly
raff•ish•ness
raf•fle

raf•fler
raft
raft•er
rag (rag•ging,
  ragged)
raga•muf•fin
rag•bag
rage
rag•ga
ragged teased
rag•ged tattered
rag•ged•ly
rag•ged•ness
rag•ing
rag•lan
ra•gout
rag•time
rag•weed
rag•wort
raid
raid•er
rail
rail•car
rail•er
rail•ing
rail•lery (*pl* •leries)
rail•road
rail•way
rain precipitation;
  cf reign; rein
rain•bow
rain•coat
rain•drop
rain•fall
raini•ness
rain•maker
rain•making
rain•proof
rain•storm

rain•water
rain•wear
rainy (raini•er,
  raini•est)
rais•able (or raise•)
raise elevate; cf
  raze
rais•er lifter; cf
  razer; razor
rai•sin
rai•siny
rai•son d'être (or
  rai•son d'etre; pl
  rai•sons d'être or
  rai•sons d'etre)
rake
rake-off (n)
rak•er
rak•ish
rak•ish•ly
rak•ish•ness
ral•ly (n, pl •lies; vb
  •lies, •ly•ing, •lied)
RAM random-
  access memory
ram (ram•ming,
  rammed) male
  sheep; to force; to
  strike
Rama•dan
ram•ble
ram•bler
ram•bling
ram•bu•tan
ram•ekin (or
  •equin)
ramie (or ramee)
rami•fi•ca•tion

rami•fy (•fies,
  •fy•ing, •fied)
rammed
ram•mer
ram•ming
ramp
ram•page
ram•pag•er
ram•pan•cy
ram•pant
ram•pant•ly
ram•part
ram•rod
ram•shack•le
ran
ranch
ranch•er
ran•che•ro (pl •ros)
ran•cho (pl •chos)
ran•cid
ran•cid•ness (or
  •ity)
ran•cor (Brit •cour)
ran•cor•ous
ran•cor•ous•ly
ran•cor•ous•ness
rand
randi•ly
randi•ness
ran•dom
ran•dom•ly
ran•dom•ness
randy (randi•er,
  randi•est)
rang
range
rang•er
rangi•ly
rangi•ness

rangy (rangi•er,
  rangi•est)
rank
rank•er
rank•ing
ran•kle
rank•ness
ran•sack
ran•sack•er
ran•som
ran•som•er
rant
rant•er
rant•ing•ly
rap (rap•ping,
  rapped) strike; cf
  wrap
ra•pa•cious
ra•pa•cious•ly
ra•pac•ity (or
  •pa•cious•ness)
rape
rape•seed
raphia variant
  spelling of raffia
rap•id
rapid-fire (adj)
ra•pid•ity (or
  rap•id•ness)
rap•id•ly
rap•ids
ra•pi•er
rap•ist
rapped past tense
  of rap; cf rapt;
  wrapped
rap•per one that
  raps; cf wrapper
rap•ping

rap•port
rap•proche•ment
rapt engrossed; cf
    rapped; wrapped
rap•ture
rap•tur•ous
rap•tur•ous•ly
rara avis (pl ra•rae
    aves or rara
    avis•es)
rare
rare•bit variant of
    (Welsh) rabbit
rar•efac•tion (or
    •efi•ca•tion)
rar•efy (or •ify;
    •efies, •efy•ing,
    •efied or •ifies,
    •ify•ing, •ified)
rare•ly
rare•ripe
rar•ing
rar•ity (pl •ities)
ras•cal
ras•cal•ly
rase variant
    spelling of raze
rash
rash•er
rash•ly
rash•ness
rasp
rasp•berry (pl
    •berries)
rasp•er
rasp•ing (or raspy)
Ras•ta•far•ian (or
    Ras•ta)

rat (rat•ting,
    rat•ted)
rat•abil•ity (or
    •able•ness, rate•)
rat•able (or rate•)
rat•ably (or rate•)
rata•fia (or •fee)
ra•tan variant
    spelling of rattan
rat-a-tat-tat (or
    rat-a-tat)
ra•ta•touille
ratch•et
rate
rate•able variant
    spelling of ratable
ra•tel
rate•payer
rat•fink
rat•fish (pl •fish or
    •fishes)
ra•ther
rati•fi•able
rati•fi•ca•tion
rati•fi•er
rati•fy (•fies,
    •fy•ing, •fied)
rat•ing
ra•tio (pl •tios)
ra•tion
ra•tion•al using
    reason
ra•tion•ale basis
ra•tion•al•ism
ra•tion•al•ist
ra•tion•al•is•tic
ra•tion•al•is•ti•
    cal•ly

ra•tion•al•ity (pl
    •ities)
ra•tion•ali•za•tion
ra•tion•al•ize
ra•tion•al•iz•er
ra•tion•al•ly
ra•tions
rat•tan (or ra•tan)
rat•ted
rat•ter
rat•ti•ly
rat•ti•ness
rat•ting
rat•tle
rat•tler
rattle•snake
rat•tling
rat•tly (•tli•er,
    •tli•est)
rat•trap
rat•ty (•ti•er,
    •ti•est)
rau•cous
rau•cous•ly
rau•cous•ness (or
    rau•city)
raun•chy (•chi•er,
    •chi•est)
rav•age
rav•ag•er
rave
rav•el (•el•ing,
    •eled; Brit •el•ling,
    •elled)
rav•el•er (Brit
    •el•ler)
ra•ven bird
rav•en to plunder
rav•en•ing

rav•en•ous
rav•en•ous•ly
rav•en•ous•ness
rav•er
ra•vine
rav•ing
ra•vio•li (*pl* •li *or*
•lis)
rav•ish
rav•ish•er
rav•ish•ing
raw
raw•boned
raw•hide
raw•ness
ray beam of light;
fish; *cf* re
ray•on
raze (*or* rase)
destroy; *cf* raise
raz•er (*or* ras•)
demolisher; *cf*
raiser
ra•zor shaver; *cf*
raiser
razor•back
razor•bill
razz•ma•tazz (*Brit
also* razza•,
razzle-dazzle)
re musical note;
concerning; *cf* ray
re•ab•sorb
reach
reach•able
reach•er
re•act act in
response
re-act act again

re•ac•tion
re•ac•tion•ary (*pl*
•aries)
re•ac•ti•vate
re•ac•ti•va•tion
re•ac•tive
re•ac•tiv•ity (*or*
•tive•ness)
re•ac•tor
read (read•ing,
read) peruse; *cf*
reed
read•abil•ity (*or*
•able•ness)
read•able
read•ably
re•ad•dress
read•er
read•er•ship
read•ily
readi•ness
re•adjust
re•adjust•ment
re•ad•mis•sion
re•ad•mit
(•mit•ting,
•mit•ted)
re•ad•mit•tance
read•out
ready (*adj* readi•er,
readi•est; *vb*
readies, ready•ing,
readied)
ready-made
re•affirm
re•affir•ma•tion
re•agent
real actual; true; *cf*
reel

re•align
re•align•ment
re•al•ism
re•al•ist
re•al•is•tic
re•al•is•ti•cal•ly
re•al•ity (*pl* •ities)
actuality; *cf* realty
re•al•iz•able
re•al•iza•tion
re•al•ize
re•allo•cate
re•allo•ca•tion
re•al•ly
realm
Re•al•po•li•tik
real-time (*adj*)
re•al•tor
re•al•ty (*pl* •ties)
property; *cf*
reality
ream
ream•er
re•ani•mate
re•ani•ma•tion
reap
reap•er
re•appear
re•appear•ance
re•apply (•applies,
•apply•ing,
•applied)
re•appoint
re•appoint•ment
re•apprais•al
re•appraise
rear
rear•er
rear•guard

re•arm
re•arma•ment
rear•most
re•arrange
re•arrange•ment
rear•ward (*adj*)
rear•ward (*Brit* •wards; *adv*)
rea•son
rea•son•able
rea•son•ably
rea•soned
rea•son•er
rea•son•ing
re•as•sem•ble
re•assur•ance
re•assure
re•assur•ing
re•awak•en
re•awak•en•ing
re•bate
¹reb•el (*n*)
re•²bel (*vb* •bel•ling, •belled)
re•bel•lion
re•bel•lious
re•bel•lious•ly
re•bel•lious•ness
re•birth
re•born
re•bound
re•buff
re•build (•build•ing, •built)
re•buke
re•buk•er
re•buk•ing•ly
re•but (•but•ting, •but•ted)

re•but•tal
re•cal•ci•trance (*or* •tran•cy)
re•cal•ci•trant
re•call
re•cant
re•can•ta•tion
re•cant•er
re•cap (•cap•ping, •capped)
re•ca•pitu•late
re•ca•pitu•la•tion
re•cap•ture
re•cede
re•ceipt
re•ceiv•able
re•ceive (*NOT* recieve)
re•ceiv•er
re•ceiv•er•ship
re•cent
re•cent•ly
re•cent•ness (*or* •cen•cy)
re•cep•ta•cle
re•cep•tion
re•cep•tion•ist
re•cep•tive
re•cep•tiv•ity (*or* •tive•ness)
re•cep•tor
re•cess
re•ces•sion
re•ces•sion•al
re•ces•sive
re•ces•sive•ness
re•charge
re•cher•ché
re•cidi•vism

re•cidi•vist
re•cidi•vis•tic (*or* •cidi•vous)
*recieve *incorrect spelling of* receive
reci•pe
re•cipi•ent
re•cip•ro•cal
re•cip•ro•cal•ity (*or* •ness)
re•cip•ro•cal•ly
re•cip•ro•cate
re•cip•ro•ca•tion
reci•proc•ity (*pl* •ities)
re•cit•al
reci•ta•tion
reci•ta•tive (*or* •ta•ti•vo)
re•cite
re•cit•er
reck•less
reck•less•ly
reck•less•ness
reck•on
reck•on•er
reck•on•ing
re•claim
re•claim•able
re•claim•ant (*or* •er)
rec•la•ma•tion
re•cline
re•clin•er
re•cluse
re•clu•sive
rec•og•ni•tion
rec•og•niz•abil•ity
rec•og•niz•able

rec•og•niz•ably
rec•og•nize
re•coil
rec•ol•lect
rec•ol•lec•tion
rec•ol•lec•tive
re•com•mence
re•com•mence•
  ment
rec•om•mend
rec•om•mend•able
rec•om•men•da•
  tion
rec•om•menda•tory
rec•om•mend•er
rec•om•pense
rec•on•cil•abil•ity
rec•on•cil•able
rec•on•cil•ably
rec•on•cile
rec•on•cilia•tion
rec•on•cilia•tory
re•con•dite
re•con•dite•ly
re•con•dite•ness
re•con•di•tion
re•con•di•tion•er
re•con•nais•sance
rec•on•noi•ter (*Brit*
  •tre)
re•con•sid•er
re•con•sid•era•tion
re•con•sti•tute
re•con•sti•tut•ed
re•con•sti•tu•tion
re•con•struct
re•con•struc•tible
re•con•struc•tion
re•con•struc•tive

re•con•struc•tor
re•con•vene
#ec•ord (*n*)
re•#ord (*vb*)
re•cord•able
re•cord•er
re•cord•ing
re•count relate
re-count count
  again
re•coup
re•coup•able
re•course
re•cov•er regain
re-cov•er cover
  again
re•cov•er•abil•ity
re•cov•er•able
re•cov•er•er
re•cov•ery (*pl*
  •eries)
re-create
rec•rea•tion
  enjoyment
re-creation new
  creation
rec•rea•tion•al
rec•re•men•tal
re•crimi•nate
re•crimi•na•tion
re•crimi•na•tive (*or*
  •tory)
re•crimi•na•tor
re•cruit
re•cruit•able
re•cruit•er
re•cruit•ment
rec•ta *pl of* rectum
rec•tal

rec•tan•gle
rec•tan•gu•lar
rec•ti•fi•able
rec•ti•fi•ca•tion
rec•ti•fi•er
rec•ti•fy (•fies,
  •fy•ing, •fied)
rec•ti•tude
rec•to (*pl* •tos)
rec•tor
rec•tory (*pl* •tories)
rec•tum (*pl* •tums
  or •ta)
re•cum•bence (*or*
  •ben•cy)
re•cum•bent
re•cu•per•ate
re•cu•pera•tion
re•cu•pera•tive
re•cu•pera•tor
re•cur (•cur•ring,
  •curred)
re•cur•rence
re•cur•rent
re•cur•rent•ly
re•cy•clable
re•cy•cle
re•cy•cling
red (red•der,
  red•dest)
red-blooded
red•breast
red•brick
red•bud
red•bug
red•cap
red•den
red•dish
re•deco•rate

re•deco•ra•tion
re•deem
re•deem•able (*or* re•demp•tible)
re•deem•er
re•deem•ing
re•demp•tion
re•demp•tion•al
re•demp•tion•er
re•deploy
re•deploy•ment
re•devel•op
re•devel•op•er
re•devel•op•ment
red•eye
red-faced
red•fin (*pl* •fin *or* •fins)
red•fish (*pl* •fish *or* •fishes)
red-handed
red•head
red-headed
red-hot
re•dial (•dial•ing, •dialed; *Brit* •dial•ling, •dialled)
re•di•rect
re•di•rec•tion
re•dis•cov•er
re•dis•cov•ery (*pl* •eries)
re•dis•trib•ute
re•dis•tri•bu•tion
red-letter (*adj*)
red•neck
red•ness
redo (re•does,

•do•ing, •did, •done)
redo•lence (*or* •len•cy)
redo•lent
re•dou•ble
re•doubt•able
re•doubt•ably
red•poll
re•draft
re•draw (•draw•ing, •drew, •drawn)
re•dress put right
re-dress dress again
red•root
red•skin
red•start
re•duce
re•duc•er
re•duc•ibil•ity
re•duc•ible
re•duc•tio ad ab•sur•dum
re•duc•tion
re•dun•dan•cy (*pl* •cies)
re•dun•dant
re•dun•dant•ly
red•wood
re•echo (•echoes, •echo•ing, •echoed)
reed grass; musical instrument; *cf* read
reedi•ness
re•edu•cate
re•edu•ca•tion

reedy (reedi•er, reedi•est)
reef
reef•er
reek smell; *cf* wreak
reel spool; whirl; dance; *cf* real
re•elect
re•elec•tion
reel•er
re•em•ploy
re•em•ploy•ment
re•en•act
re-enforce enforce again; *cf* reinforce
re-enforce•ment
re•en•ter
re•en•try (*pl* •tries)
re•es•tab•lish
re•ex•am•ina•tion
re•ex•am•ine
re•ex•port
re•ex•por•ta•tion
re•fec•tory (*pl* •tories)
re•fer (•fer•ring, •ferred)
ref•er•able (*or* re•fer•rable)
ref•eree (•eree•ing, •ereed)
ref•er•ence
ref•er•en•dum (*pl* •dums *or* •da)
ref•er•ent
ref•er•en•tial of a reference; *cf* reverential

re•fer•ral
re•fer•rer
re•fill
re•fill•able
re•fin•able
re•fine
re•fined
re•fine•ment
re•fin•er
re•fin•ery (pl •eries)
re•fit (•fit•ting, •fit•ted)
re•flate
re•fla•tion
re•flect
re•flec•tance
re•flec•tion (*Brit also* •flex•ion)
re•flec•tion•al
re•flec•tive
contemplative; able to reflect; *cf* reflexive
re•flec•tive•ly
re•flec•tive•ness (*or* •tiv•ity)
re•flec•tor
re•flex
re•flex•ive
grammar term; *cf* reflective
re•flex•olo•gist
re•flex•ol•ogy
re•for•esta•tion
re•form improve
re-form form again
re•form•able
Ref•or•ma•tion

religious movement
ref•or•ma•tion
radical improvement
re-formation
forming again
ref•or•ma•tion•al
re•forma•tive
re•forma•tory (pl •tories)
re•form•er
re•fract
re•frac•tion
re•frac•tive
re•frac•tive•ness (*or* •tiv•ity)
re•frac•tor
re•frac•to•ri•ly
re•frac•to•ri•ness
re•frac•tory (pl •tories)
re•frain
re•freeze (•freez•ing, •froze, •fro•zen)
re•fresh
re•fresh•er
re•fresh•ing
re•fresh•ing•ly
re•fresh•ment
re•frig•er•ate
re•frig•era•tion
re•frig•era•tor
re•fu•el (•el•ing, •eled; *Brit* •el•ling, •elled)
ref•uge
refu•gee

re•fund
re•fund•able
re•fund•er
re•fur•bish
re•fur•bish•ment
re•fus•able
re•fus•al
re•#use decline
#ef•use rubbish
refu•tabil•ity
refu•table
refu•ta•tion
re•fute
re•gain
re•gain•able
re•gal royal
re•gale amuse
re•ga•lia
re•gal•ity (pl •ities)
re•gal•ly
re•gard
re•gard•ful
re•gard•ing
re•gard•less
re•gards
re•gat•ta
re•gen•cy (pl •cies)
re•gen•er•ate
re•gen•era•tion
re•gen•era•tive
re•gen•era•tor
re•gent
reg•gae
regi•cide
re•gime (*or* ré•)
administration
regi•men course of treatment
regi•ment

reg•i•men•tal
regi•men•ta•tion
re•gion
re•gion•al
re•gion•al•ism
re•gion•al•ist
re•gion•al•ly
reg•is•ter
reg•is•tra•ble
reg•is•trar
reg•is•tra•tion
reg•is•try (*pl* •tries)
re•gress
re•gres•sion
re•gres•sive
re•gres•sive•ly
re•gres•sive•ness
re•gret (•gret•ting,
  •gret•ted)
re•gret•ful
re•gret•ful•ly
re•gret•ful•ness
re•gret•table
re•gret•tably
re•group
re•growth
regu•lable
regu•lar
regu•lar•ity (*pl*
  •ities)
regu•lari•za•tion
regu•lar•ize
regu•late
regu•la•tion
regu•la•tive (*or*
  •tory)
regu•la•tor
re•gur•gi•tate
re•gur•gi•ta•tion

re•ha•bili•tate
re•ha•bili•ta•tion
re•ha•bili•ta•tive
re•hash
re•hears•al
re•hearse
re•heat
re•house
reign rule; *cf* rain;
  rein
re•im•burs•able
re•im•burse
re•im•burse•ment
re•im•port
re•im•por•ta•tion
re•im•pose
re•im•po•si•tion
rein long strap;
  restrain; *cf* rain;
  reign
re•in•car•nate
re•in•car•na•tion
rein•deer (*pl* •deer
  or •deers)
re•in•force
  strengthen; *cf* re-
  enforce
re•in•force•ment
re•in•state
re•in•state•ment
re•in•sur•ance
re•in•sure
re•in•tro•duce
re•in•tro•duc•tion
re•in•vent
re•is•sue (•su•ing,
  •sued)
re•it•er•ate
re•it•era•tion

re•it•era•tive
re•ject
re•ject•er (*or*
  •jec•tor)
re•jec•tion
re•joice
re•joic•ing
re•join
re•join•der
re•ju•venate
re•ju•vena•tion
re•ju•vena•tor
re•kin•dle
re•la•bel (•bel•ing,
  •beled; *Brit*
  •bel•ling, •belled)
re•lapse
re•laps•er
re•lat•able
re•late
re•lat•ed
re•lat•ed•ness
re•lat•er one that
  relates; *cf* relator
re•la•tion
re•la•tion•ship
rela•tive
rela•tive•ly
rela•tiv•ity (*pl*
  •ities)
re•la•tor legal
  term; *cf* relater
re•lax
re•lax•ant
re•laxa•tion
re•laxed
re•lax•er
re•lax•ing
re•lay convey

re-lay (-lay•ing, -laid) lay again
re-lease set free
re-lease lease again
re•leas•er
rel•egate
rel•ega•tion
re•lent
re•lent•less
re•lent•less•ly
re•lent•less•ness
rel•evance (*or* •evan•cy)
rel•evant
re•li•abil•ity (*or* •able•ness)
re•li•able
re•li•ably
re•li•ance
re•li•ant
rel•ic
re•lief
re•liev•able
re•lieve
re•liev•er
re•li•gion
re•ligi•os•ity
re•li•gious
re•li•gious•ly
re•li•gious•ness
re•lin•quish
re•lin•quish•ment
reli•quary (*pl* •quaries)
rel•ish
re•live
re•load
re•lo•cate
re•lo•ca•tion

re•luc•tance (*or* •tan•cy)
re•luc•tant
re•luc•tant•ly
rely (re•lies, rely•ing, re•lied)
re•made
re•main
re•main•der
re•main•ing
re•mains
re•make (•mak•ing, •made)
re•mand
re•mark
re•mark•able
re•mark•ably
re•mar•riage
re•mar•ry (•ries, •ry•ing, •ried)
re•match
re•medi•able
re•medial
re•medial•ly
rem•edy (*n, pl* •edies; *vb* •edies, •edy•ing, •edied)
re•mem•ber
re•mem•brance
re•mind
re•mind•er
remi•nisce
remi•nis•cence
remi•nis•cent
remi•nis•cent•ly
re•miss
re•mis•sion (*or* •mit•tal)
re•mis•sive

re•miss•ness
re•mit (•mit•ting, •mit•ted)
re•mit•table
re•mit•tal
re•mit•tance
rem•nant
re•mod•el (•el•ing, •eled; *Brit* •el•ling, •elled)
re•mold (*Brit* •mould)
re•mon•strance
re•mon•strate
re•mon•stra•tion
re•mon•stra•tor
re•morse
re•morse•ful
re•morse•ful•ly
re•morse•less
re•morse•less•ly
re•morse•less•ness
re•mote
remote-controlled
re•mote•ly
re•mote•ness
re•mould *Brit spelling of* remold
re•mount
re•mov•able (*or* •move•)
re•mov•al
re•move
re•mov•er
re•mu•ner•ate
re•mu•nera•tion
re•mu•nera•tive
Re•nais•sance historical period

re•nais•sance (*or* •nas•cence) revival

re•nal

re•name

rend (rend•ing, rent)

ren•der

ren•der•ing

ren•dez•vous (*pl* •vous)

ren•di•tion

ren•egade

re•nege

re•new

re•new•abil•ity

re•new•able

re•new•al

ren•net

re•nounce

reno•vate

reno•va•tion

reno•va•tor

re•nown

re•nowned

rent

rent•able

rent•al

rent-free

re•num•ber

re•nun•cia•tion

re•open

re•or•der

re•or•gani•za•tion

re•or•gan•ize

rep

re•paint

re•pair

re•pair•able able to

be repaired; *cf* reparable

re•pair•er

re•pair•man (*pl* •men)

repa•rable able to be made good; *cf* repairable

repa•rably

repa•ra•tion

rep•ar•tee

re•past

re•pat•ri•ate

re•pat•ria•tion

re•pay (•pay•ing, •paid)

re•pay•able

re•pay•ment

re•peal

re•peat

re•peat•able

re•peat•ed

re•peat•ed•ly

re•pel (•pel•ling, •pelled)

re•pel•len•cy

re•pel•lent (*or* •lant)

re•pent

re•pen•tance

re•pen•tant

re•pent•er

re•per•cus•sion

re•per•cus•sive

rep•er•toire stock of plays, songs, etc.

rep•er•tory (*pl* •tories) theatrical company

rep•eti•tion

rep•eti•tious

re•peti•tive

re•peti•tive•ly

re•phrase

re•place

re•place•able

re•place•ment

re•play

re•plen•ish

re•plen•ish•ment

re•plete

re•ple•tion

rep•li•ca

rep•li•cate

rep•li•ca•tion

re•ply (*vb* •plies, •ply•ing, •plied; *n,* *pl* •plies)

re•port

re•port•able

re•port•age

re•port•ed•ly

re•port•er

re•pose

re•po•si•tion

re•posi•tory (*pl* •tories)

re•pos•sess

re•pos•ses•sion

re•pos•ses•sor

rep•re•hend

rep•re•hen•sible

rep•re•hen•sibly

rep•re•hen•sion

rep•re•sent correspond to

re-present present
again
rep•re•sen•ta•tion
rep•re•senta•tive
rep•re•senta•tive•ly
rep•re•senta•tive•
ness
re•press restrain
re-press press
again
re•press•ible
re•pres•sion
re•pres•sive
re•pres•sive•ly
re•pres•sive•ness
re•pres•sor
re•prieve
rep•ri•mand
re•print
re•pri•sal
re•prise
re•pro (pl •pros)
re•proach
re•proach•able
re•proach•ful
re•proach•ful•ly
re•proach•ful•ness
rep•ro•bate
rep•ro•ba•tion
re•pro•duce
re•pro•duc•er
re•pro•duc•ibil•ity
re•pro•duc•ible
re•pro•duc•tion
re•pro•duc•tive
re•pro•graph•ic
re•prog•ra•phy
re•proof rebuke

re-proof renew
texture
re•prove
re•prov•ing•ly
rep•tile
rep•til•ian
re•pub•lic
Re•pub•li•can of
the political party
re•pub•li•can of a
republic
re•pub•li•ca•tion
re•pub•lish
re•pub•lish•able
re•pu•di•ate
re•pu•dia•tion
re•pug•nance (or
•nan•cy; pl
•nances or
•nan•cies)
re•pug•nant
re•pug•nant•ly
re•pulse
re•puls•er
re•pul•sion
re•pul•sive
re•pul•sive•ly
re•pul•sive•ness
repu•tabil•ity (or
•table•ness)
repu•table
repu•tably
repu•ta•tion
re•pute
re•put•ed
re•put•ed•ly
re•quest
requi•em
re•quire

re•quire•ment
requi•site
requi•si•tion
requi•si•tion•er (or
•ist)
re•quit•able
re•quit•al
re•quite
re•read (•read•ing,
•read)
rere•dos
re•route
re•sal•able (or
•sale•)
re•sale
re•scind
res•cu•able
res•cue (•cu•ing,
•cued)
res•cu•er
re•search
re•search•er
re•sem•blance
re•sem•ble
re•sem•bler
re•sent
re•sent•ful
re•sent•ful•ly
re•sent•ful•ness
re•sent•ment
re•serv•able
res•er•va•tion
re•serve
re•served
re•serv•ed•ly
re•serv•ed•ness
re•serv•er
re•serv•ist
res•er•voir

re•set (•set•ting, •set)
re•set•ter
re•set•tle
re•set•tle•ment
re•shape
re•shuf•fle
re•side
resi•dence
resi•den•cy (pl •cies)
resi•dent
resi•den•tial
re•sid•ual
re•sidu•ary
resi•due
re•sidu•um (pl •sidua)
re•sign give up
re-sign sign again
res•ig•na•tion
re•signed
re•sign•ed•ly
re•sil•ience (or •ien•cy)
re•sil•ient
re•sil•ient•ly
res•in gumlike substance; cf rosin
res•in•ous
res•in•ous•ness
re•sist
re•sis•tance
re•sis•tant (or •sis•tive)
re•sist•er opposer; cf resistor
re•sist•ibil•ity
re•sist•ible

re•sist•ibly
re•sis•tor electrical component; cf resister
re•sit (•sit•ting, •sat)
reso•lute
reso•lute•ly
reso•lute•ness
reso•lu•tion
re•solv•abil•ity (or •able•ness)
re•solv•able
re•solve
reso•nance
reso•nant
reso•nant•ly
reso•nate
reso•na•tion
re•sort holiday town; to use
re-sort sort again
re•sound
re•sound•ing
re•sound•ing•ly
re•source
re•source•ful
re•source•ful•ly
re•source•ful•ness
re•source•less
re•spect
re•spect•abil•ity (pl •ities)
re•spect•able
re•spect•ably
re•spect•er
re•spect•ful
re•spect•ful•ly
re•spect•ful•ness

re•spect•ing
re•spec•tive
re•spec•tive•ly
res•pi•ra•tion
res•pi•ra•tor
re•spira•tory
re•spire
res•pite
re•splen•dence (or •den•cy)
re•splen•dent
re•splen•dent•ly
re•spond
re•sponse
re•spon•sibil•ity (pl •ities)
re•spon•sible
re•spon•sibly
re•spon•sive
re•spon•sive•ly
re•spon•sive•ness
re•spray
rest repose; remainder; etc.; cf wrest
res•tau•rant
res•tau•ra•teur
rest•ful
rest•ful•ly
rest•ful•ness
rest•ing
res•ti•tu•tion
res•tive
res•tive•ness
rest•less
rest•less•ly
rest•less•ness
re•stock

re•stor•able
res•to•ra•tion
re•stora•tive
re•store
re•stor•er
re•strain
re•strain•able
re•strain•ed•ly
re•strain•er
re•straint
re•strict
re•strict•ed•ly
re•strict•ed•ness
re•stric•tion
re•stric•tive
re•stric•tive•ly
re•stric•tive•ness
re•struc•ture
re•style
re•sult
re•sult•ant
re•sum•able
re•sume restart
ré•su•mé (or
  re•su•me,
  re•su•mé)
  summary
re•sump•tion
re•sump•tive
re•sur•face
re•sur•gence
re•sur•gent
res•ur•rect
Res•ur•rec•tion
  rising of Christ
res•ur•rec•tion
  revival
re•sus•ci•tate
re•sus•ci•ta•tion

re•sus•ci•ta•tor
re•tail
re•tail•er
re•tain
re•tain•able
re•tain•er
re•take (•tak•ing,
  •took, •tak•en)
re•tali•ate
re•talia•tion
re•talia•tive (or
  •tory)
re•talia•tor
re•tard
re•tard•ant
re•tar•da•tion (or
  •tard•ment)
re•tard•ed
retch vomit; cf
  wretch
re•tell (•tell•ing,
  •told)
re•ten•tion
re•ten•tive
re•ten•tive•ly
re•ten•tive•ness
re•think
  (•think•ing,
  •thought)
reti•cence (or
  •cen•cy)
reti•cent
reti•cent•ly
reti•na (pl •nas or
  •nae)
reti•nal
reti•nue
re•tire
re•tire•ment

re•tir•er
re•tir•ing
re•tir•ing•ly
re•tort
re•touch
re•touch•er
re•trace
re•trace•able
re•tract
re•tract•abil•ity (or
  •ibil•)
re•tract•able (or
  •ible)
re•trac•tile
re•trac•til•ity
re•trac•tion
re•trac•tive
re•trac•tor
re•train
re•tread (•tread•
  ing, •tread•ed) put
  new tread on tire
re-tread (-treading,
  -trod, -trod•den)
  retrace one's steps
re•treat
re•trench
re•trench•ment
re•tri•al
ret•ri•bu•tion
re•tribu•tive (or
  •tory)
re•triev•abil•ity
re•triev•able
re•triev•ably
re•triev•al
re•trieve
re•triev•er
retro•ac•tive

retro•grade
retro•gress
retro•gres•sion
retro•gres•sive
retro•gres•sive•ly
retro-rocket
retro•spect
retro•spec•tion
retro•spec•tive
retro•spec•tive•ly
re•trous•sé
retro•ver•sion
retro•vert•ed
re•try (•tries,
 •try•ing, •tried)
re•turn
re•turn•able
re•turnee
re•turn•er
re•type
re•uni•fi•ca•tion
re•uni•fy (•fies,
 •fy•ing, •fied)
re•union
re•unite
re•up•hol•ster
re•us•abil•ity (*or*
 •able•ness)
re•us•able
re•use
rev (rev•ving,
 revved)
re•valua•tion
re•value (•valu•ing,
 •valued)
re•vamp
re•veal
re•veal•able
re•veal•er

re•veal•ing
re•veal•ing•ly
rev•eil•le
rev•el (•el•ing,
 •eled; *Brit* •el•ling,
 •elled)
rev•ela•tion
rev•el•er (*Brit*
 •el•ler)
rev•el•ry (*pl* •ries)
rev•enant
re•venge
re•venge•ful
re•venge•ful•ly
re•veng•er
rev•enue
re•ver•ber•ant
re•ver•ber•ant•ly
re•ver•ber•ate
re•ver•bera•tion
re•ver•bera•tor
re•vere venerate; *cf*
 revers
rev•er•ence
rev•er•end de-
 serving reverence;
 clergyman
rev•er•ent feeling
 reverence
rev•er•en•tial
 showing rever-
 ence; *cf* referential
rev•er•en•tial•ly
rev•er•ent•ly
rev•er•ent•ness
rev•erie (*or* •ery; *pl*
 •eries)
re•vers (*pl* •vers)

lapel; *cf* revere;
 reverse
re•ver•sal
re•verse opposite;
 cf revers
re•vers•er
re•vers•ibil•ity
re•vers•ible
re•vers•ibly
re•ver•sion
re•vert
re•vert•ible
rev•ery *variant
 spelling of* reverie
re•view survey;
 critical opinion; *cf*
 revue
re•view•able
re•view•er
re•vile
re•vile•ment
re•vil•er
re•vis•abil•ity
re•vis•able
re•vise
re•vis•er (*or*
 •vi•sor)
re•vi•sion
re•vi•sion•al (*or*
 •ary)
re•vi•sion•ism
re•vi•sion•ist
re•vi•so•ry
re•vi•tali•za•tion
re•vi•tal•ize
re•viv•able
re•viv•al
re•viv•al•ism
re•viv•al•ist

re•viv•al•is•tic
re•vive
re•viv•er
revo•cable (*or* re•vok•able)
revo•ca•tion
re•voca•tive (*or* revo•ca•tory)
re•vok•able *variant spelling of* revocable
re•voke
re•vok•er
re•volt
re•volt•ing
re•volt•ing•ly
revo•lu•tion
revo•lu•tion•ari•ly
revo•lu•tion•ary (*pl* •aries)
revo•lu•tion•ist
revo•lu•tion•ize
revo•lu•tion•iz•er
re•volv•able
re•volve
re•volv•er
re•volv•ing
re•vue entertainment; *cf* review
re•vul•sion
re•ward
re•ward•ing
re•ward•ing•ly
re•wind (•wind•ing, •wound)
re•wire
re•word
re•work

re•write (•writ•ing, •wrote, •writ•ten)
re•zone
rhap•sod•ic
rhap•sodi•cal•ly
rhap•so•dist
rhap•so•dize
rhap•so•dy (*pl* •dies)
rhea
rheo•stat
rhe•sus
rheto•ric
rhe•tori•cal
rhe•tori•cal•ly
rhe•tori•cian
rheu•mat•ic
rheu•mati•cal•ly
rheu•mat•ics
rheu•ma•tism
rheu•ma•toid (*or* •toi•dal)
rhine•stone
rhi•no (*pl* •nos *or* •no)
rhi•noc•er•os (*pl* •er•os, •er•oses, *or* •eri)
rhi•no•plas•ty (*pl* •ties)
rhi•zome
rho Greek letter; *cf* roe; row
rho•do•den•dron
rhom•bic
rhom•boid
rhom•boi•dal
rhom•bus (*pl* •buses *or* •bi)

rhu•barb
rhum•ba *variant spelling of* rumba
rhyme identical-sounding word; verse; *cf* rime
rhyme•ster (*or* rhym•er)
rhythm
rhyth•mic (*or* •mi•cal)
rhyth•mi•cal•ly
rhyth•mic•ity
ri•ata
rib (rib•bing, ribbed)
rib•ald
rib•ald•ry (*pl* •ries)
rib•bon
ribbon•fish (*pl* •fish *or* •fishes)
rice
rice•bird
ric•er
rich
riches
rich•ly
rich•ness
Rich•ter scale
rick
rick•eti•ness
rick•ets
rick•ety
rick•rack (*or* ric•rac)
rick•shaw (*or* •sha)
rico•chet (•chet•ing, •chet•ed)

or •chet•ting,
•chet•ted)
ri•cot•ta
ric•tus (*pl* •tus *or*
•tuses)
rid (rid•ding, rid *or*
rid•ded)
rid•able (*or* ride•)
rid•dance
rid•den
rid•dle
rid•dler
ride (rid•ing, rode,
rid•den)
ride•able *variant*
spelling of ridable
rid•er
rid•er•less
ridge
ridge•pole (*or*
•tree)
ridgy
ridi•cule
ri•dicu•lous
ri•dicu•lous•ly
ri•dicu•lous•ness
rid•ing
ries•ling (*or* Ries•)
rife
rife•ness
rif•fle shuffle; *cf*
rifle
riff•raff
ri•fle gun; ransack;
cf riffle
rifle•bird
ri•fler
ri•fle•ry
rift

rig (rig•ging,
rigged)
riga•ma•role
variant spelling of
rigmarole
rig•ger one who
rigs; *cf* rigor
rig•ging
right just; true;
authority; rectify;
not left; *cf* rite;
write
right-angled (*or*
-angle)
righ•teous
righ•teous•ly
righ•teous•ness
right•ful
right•ful•ly
right•ful•ness
right-hand (*adj*)
right-handed
right-handedly
right-handed•ness
right-hander
right•ism
right•ist
right•ly
right-minded
right-minded•ly
right-minded•ness
right•ness
right-on
right•ward (*adj*)
right•ward (*Brit*
•wards; *adv*)
right-wing (*adj*)
right-winger
rig•id

ri•gidi•fy (•fies,
•fy•ing, •fied)
ri•gid•ity (*or* •ness)
rig•id•ly
rig•ma•role (*or*
riga•)
rig•or chilliness;
muscular rigidity
rig•or (*Brit* •our)
harshness; *cf*
rigger
rig•or mor•tis
rig•or•ous
rig•or•ous•ly
rig•or•ous•ness
rig•our *Brit*
spelling of rigor
(harshness)
rile
rill
rill•et
rim (rim•ming,
rimmed)
rime frost; *cf*
rhyme
rimy (rimi•er,
rimi•est)
rind
ring (ring•ing,
rang, rung)
produce sound; *cf*
wring
ring (ring•ing,
ringed) circular
band; to encircle;
cf wring
ring•er
ring-fence (*vb*)
ring•ing

ring•leader
ring•let
ring•master
ring•neck
ring-necked (or
-neck)
ring•side
ring•tail
ring-tailed
ring•worm
rink
rinse
rins•er
riot
ri•ot•er
ri•ot•ous
ri•ot•ous•ly
ri•ot•ous•ness
rip (rip•ping,
ripped)
rip•cord
ripe
ripe•ly
rip•en
rip•en•er
ripe•ness
rip-off (n)
ri•poste (or •post)
ripped
rip•per
rip•ping
rip•ple
rip•pler
rip•plet
rip•ply
rip-roaring
rip•saw
rip•tide

rise (ris•ing, rose,
ris•en)
ris•er
ris•ibil•ity (pl
•ities)
ris•ible
ris•ibly
ris•ing
risk
risk•er
risk•ily
riski•ness
risky (riski•er,
riski•est)
involving risk; cf
risqué
ri•sot•to (pl •tos)
ris•qué improper;
cf risky
ris•sole
rite religious
procedure; cf
right; write
ritu•al
ritu•al•ism
ritu•al•ist
ritu•al•is•tic
ritu•al•is•ti•cal•ly
ritu•al•ize
ritu•al•ly
ritzy (ritzi•er,
ritzi•est)
ri•val (•val•ing,
•valed; Brit
•val•ling, •valled)
ri•val•ry (pl •ries)
riv•er
river•bed
river•boat

river•head
river•side
riv•et
riv•et•er
rivu•let
roach cockroach
roach (pl roach or
roaches) fish
road
road•block
road•holding
road•house
roadie
road•runner
road•side
road•stead
road•ster
road•way
road•work
road•worthi•ness
road•worthy
roam
roam•er
roan
roar
roar•er
roar•ing
roast
roast•er
roast•ing
rob (rob•bing,
robbed)
roba•lo (pl •los or
•lo)
rob•ber
rob•bery (pl
•beries)
rob•bing
robe

rob•in
ro•binia
ro•ble
ro•bot
ro•bot•ic
ro•bot•ics
ro•bust
ro•bust•ly
ro•bust•ness
roc legendary bird
rock hard mass;
  sway
rocka•bil•ly
rock-and-roll (or
  rock 'n' roll)
rock-and-roller (or
  rock 'n' roller)
rock-bottom (adj)
rock•er
rock•ery (pl •eries)
rock•et
rock•et•ry
rock•fish (pl •fish
  or •fishes)
rocki•ly
rocki•ness
rock•ling (pl •lings
  or •ling)
rocky (rocki•er,
  rocki•est)
ro•co•co
rod
rode
ro•dent
ro•denti•cide
ro•deo (pl •deos)
roe fish ovary or
  testis; deer; cf rho;
  row

roe•buck (pl •buck
  or •bucks)
roent•gen (or rönt•)
rogue
ro•guery (pl
  •gueries)
ro•guish
ro•guish•ly
ro•guish•ness
rois•ter
roist•er•er
role (or rôle) part;
  function; cf roll
role-playing
roll cylinder; move
  by turning; bread;
  cf role
roll•back
roll•er
roller-skate (vb)
rol•lick
rol•lick•ing
roll•ing
roll•mops (pl
  •mops)
roll•out
roll•over
roly-poly (pl
  -polies)
ro•maine
Ro•man of Rome
ro•man type style
ro•mance
Ro•ma•nian (or
  Ru•)
ro•man•tic
ro•man•ti•cal•ly
ro•man•ti•cism
ro•man•ti•cist

ro•man•ti•ci•za•
  tion
ro•man•ti•cize
Roma•ny (or
  Rom•ma•ny; pl
  •nies)
Romeo (pl
  Romeos)
romp
ron•deau (pl
  •deaux) poem
ron•do (pl •dos)
  musical work
rönt•gen variant
  spelling of
  roentgen
roof (pl roofs)
roof•ing
rook
rook•ery (pl •eries)
rookie
room
room•er lodger; cf
  rumor
room•ette
room•ful (pl •fuls)
roomi•ly
roomi•ness
room•mate
roomy (roomi•er,
  roomi•est)
roor•back
roost
roost•er
root plant part;
  source; cf route
rope
rope•walk
ropi•ly

ropi•ness
ropy (*or* rop•ey;
  ropi•er, ropi•est)
ror•qual
Ror•schach test
ro•sary (*pl* •saries)
rose plant
rosé wine
ro•seate
rose•bay
rose•bud
rose•bush
rose-colored (*Brit*
  -coloured)
rose•fish (*pl* •fish
  or •fishes)
rose•hip (*or* rose
  hip)
rose•mary (*pl*
  •maries)
ro•sette
rose•wood
Rosh Ha•sha•nah
  (*or* Rosh
  Ha•sha•na, Rosh
  Ha•sho•na, Rosh
  Ha•sho•nah)
rosi•ly
ros•in type of
  resin; *cf* resin
rosi•ness
rosin•weed
ros•iny
ros•ter
ros•trum (*pl*
  •trums *or* •tra)
rosy (rosi•er,
  rosi•est)

rot (rot•ting,
  rot•ted)
rota
ro•ta•ry (*pl* •ries)
ro•tat•able
ro•tate
ro•ta•tion
ro•ta•tion•al
ro•ta•tor
ro•ta•tory
rote
rot•gut
ro•tis•serie
ro•tor
rot•ted
rot•ten
rot•ten•ly
rot•ten•ness
rot•ting
Rott•wei•ler
ro•tund
ro•tun•da
ro•tun•dity (*or*
  •tund•ness)
rouche *variant
  spelling of* ruche
roué
rouge
rough coarse;
  approximate; *cf*
  ruff
rough•age
rough-and-ready
rough-and-tumble
rough•cast
  (•cast•ing, •cast)
rough•en
rough•ly
rough•ness

rough•shod
rough-spoken
rou•lade
rou•lette
round
round•about
round•ed
round•er
round•ish
round•ly
round•ness
round-shouldered
round-the-clock
  (*adj*)
round•up
round•worm
rouse
rous•er
rous•ing
rous•ing•ly
roust
rout defeat
route road; course;
  cf root
rout•er
rou•tine
rou•tine•ly
roux (*pl* roux) fat-
  and-flour paste;
  cf rue
rove
rov•er
row line; propel
  boat; quarrel;
  noise; *cf* rho; roe
row•an
row•boat
row•di•ly

row•di•ness (*or* •dy•ism)
row•dy (•di•er, •di•est)
row•er
roy•al
roy•al•ist
roy•al•ly
roy•al•ty (*pl* •ties)
rub (rub•bing, rubbed)
rub•ber
rub•ber•ize
rubber•neck
rubber-stamp (*vb*)
rub•bery
rub•bing
rub•bish
rub•ble
rub•bly
rub•down
rube
ru•bel•la German measles
ru•beo•la measles
ru•bi•cund
ru•bric
ruby (*pl* rubies)
ruche (*or* rouche)
ruch•ing
ruck
ruck•sack
ruck•us (*pl* •uses)
ruc•tion
rud•beckia
rudd (*pl* rudd *or* rudds)
rud•der
rud•di•ly

rud•di•ness
rud•dy (•di•er, •di•est)
rude
rude•ly
rude•ness
ru•di•ment
ru•di•men•ta•ri•ly (*or* •men•tal•ly)
ru•di•men•ta•ry (*or* •men•tal)
rue (ru•ing, rued) regret; plant; *cf*
roux
rue•ful
rue•ful•ly
rue•ful•ness
ruff raised collar; bird; cards term; *cf* rough
ruf•fian
ruf•fi•an•ism
ruf•fi•an•ly
ruf•fle
rug
rug•by
rug•ged
rug•ged•ly
rug•ged•ness
ruin
ru•ina•tion
ru•in•er
ru•ing
ru•in•ous
ru•in•ous•ly
rul•able
rule
rul•er
rul•ing

rum
Ru•ma•nian
variant spelling of
Romanian
rum•ba (*or* rhum•)
rum•ble
rum•bler
rum•bly
rum•bus•tious
rum•bus•tious•ly
rum•bus•tious•ness
ru•mi•nant
ru•mi•nate
ru•mi•na•tion
ru•mi•na•tive
ru•mi•na•tive•ly
ru•mi•na•tor
rum•mage
rum•mag•er
rum•my (*n, pl* •mies; *adj* •mi•er, •mi•est)
ru•mor (*Brit* •mour) gossip; *cf*
roomer
rump
rum•ple
rum•pus (*pl* •puses)
run (run•ning, ran, run)
run•about
run•away
run•back
run•down (*n*)
run-down (*adj*)
rune
rung
ru•nic
run-in (*n*)

run•ner
runner-up (*pl* runners-up)
run•ning
run•ny (•ni•er, •ni•est)
run•off
run-of-the-mill
runt
run-through (*n*)
runt•ish
runty
run-up (*n*)
run•way
rup•ture
ru•ral
ru•ral•ism
ru•ral•ist (*or* •ite)
ru•ral•ity
ru•rali•za•tion
ru•ral•ize
ru•ral•ly
ruse
rush
rush•er
rushy (rushi•er, rushi•est)
rusk
rus•set
Rus•sian
rust
rus•tic
rus•ti•cal•ly
rus•ti•cate
rus•ti•ca•tion
rus•tic•ity
rusti•ly
rusti•ness
rus•tle

rus•tler
rust•proof
rusty (rusti•er, rusti•est)
rut (rut•ting, rut•ted)
ru•ta•ba•ga
ruth•less
ruth•less•ly
ruth•less•ness
rut•ted
rut•ting
rut•ty (•ti•er, •ti•est)
rye cereal; whiskey; *cf* wry
rye•grass

S

saba•dil•la
Sab•bath seventh day
sab•bath rest period
Sab•bati•cal (*or* •bat•ic) of the Sabbath
sab•bati•cal academic leave
sa•ber (*Brit* •bre)
sa•ble (*pl* •bles *or* •ble)
sab•ot
sabo•tage
sabo•teur
sa•bre *Brit spelling of* saber

sac biological pouch; *cf* sack
saca•ton
sac•cha•rin sugar substitute
sac•cha•rine sweet; sentimental
sac•er•do•tal
sac•er•do•tal•ism
sa•chet small packet; *cf* sashay
sack bag; to plunder, etc.; *cf* sac
sack•but
sack•cloth
sack•er
sack•ful (*pl* •fuls)
sack•ing
sa•cra *pl of* sacrum
sa•cral
sac•ra•ment
sac•ra•men•tal
sa•cred
sa•cred•ness
sac•ri•fice
sac•ri•fi•cial
sac•ri•fi•cial•ly
sac•ri•lege
sac•ri•legious
sac•ri•legious•ly
sac•ris•tan
sac•ris•ty (*pl* •ties)
sac•ro•sanct
sac•ro•sanc•tity
sa•crum (*pl* •cra)
sad (sad•der, sad•dest)
sad•den

sad•den•ing
sad•der
sad•dest
sad•dle
saddle•back
saddle•bag
saddle•cloth
sad•dler
sad•dlery (pl
•dleries)
Sad•du•cee
sad•ism
sad•ist
sa•dis•tic
sa•dis•ti•cal•ly
sad•ly
sad•ness
sado•maso•chism
sado•maso•chist
sado•maso•chis•tic
sa•fa•ri (pl •ris)
safe
safe-conduct
safe•crack•er
safe-deposit box
(or safety-)
safe•guard
safe•keeping
safe•ly
safe•ness
safe•ty (pl •ties)
saf•flow•er
saf•fron
sag (sag•ging,
sagged)
saga
sa•ga•cious
sa•gac•ity
saga•more

sage
sage•brush
sagged
sag•ging
sago (pl sagos)
sa•gua•ro (or
•hua•; pl •ros)
Sa•hap•tian (or
Sha•)
said
sail cruise; part of
boat, etc.; cf sale
sail•able
sail•board
sail•boat
sail•cloth
sail•er sailing
vessel; cf sailor
sail•fish (pl •fish or
•fishes)
sail•ing
sail•or seaman; cf
sailer
sail•plane
saint
Saint Ber•nard
saint•ed
saint•hood
saint•li•ly
saint•li•ness
saint•ly
saint•pau•lia
St. Vitus's dance
sake benefit
sake (or saké, saki)
Japanese liquor
sal•abil•ity (or
•able•ness)
sal•able (or sale•)

sal•ably
sa•la•cious
sa•la•cious•ly
sa•la•cious•ness (or
sa•lac•ity)
sal•ad
sala•man•der
sa•la•mi
sala•ry (n, pl •ries;
vb •ries, •ry•ing,
•ried)
sale selling, etc.; cf
sail
sale•able variant
spelling of salable
sales•clerk
sales•man (pl
•men)
sales•man•ship
sales•person
sales•room
sales•woman (pl
•women)
sali•cyl•ic acid
sa•li•ence (or
•en•cy)
sa•li•ent
sa•li•ent•ly
sa•line
sa•lin•ity
sa•li•va
sali•vary
sali•vate
sali•va•tion
sal•low
sal•low•ness
sal•ly (n, pl •lies; vb
•lies, •ly•ing, •lied)

salm•on (pl •on or
•ons)
salmon•berry (pl
•berries)
sal•mo•nel•la (pl
•las, •la, or •lae)
sal•mo•nel•lo•sis
sa•lon reception
room; beauty
establishment,
etc.
sa•loon large
room; bar
sal•sa
salt
salt•box
salt•bush
salt•cellar
salt•ed
salt•er
salti•ly
salti•ness
salt•pan
salt•pe•ter (Brit
•tre)
salt•water (adj)
salt•works
salt•wort
salty (salti•er,
salti•est)
sa•lu•bri•ous
sa•lu•bri•ous•ly
sa•lu•bri•ous•ness
sa•lu•bri•ous•ness
(or •bri•ty)
sa•lu•ki
salu•tari•ly
salu•tari•ness
salu•tary

beneficial; cf
salutatory
salu•ta•tion
sa•lu•ta•to•ry
welcoming; cf
salutary
sa•lute
sa•lut•er
salv•able
sal•vage rescue; cf
selvage
sal•vage•able
sal•vag•er
sal•va•tion
sal•va•tion•al
salve
sal•ver tray; cf
salvor
sal•via
sal•vo (pl •vos or
•voes)
sal vola•ti•le
sal•vor one who
salvages; cf salver
Sa•mari•tan
sam•ba (pl •bas)
same
same•ness
Sa•mo•an
samo•var
sam•pan
sam•ple
sam•pler
sam•pling
samu•rai (pl •rai)
sana•to•rium (or
sani•, •ta•; pl
•riums or •ria)
sanc•ti•fi•ca•tion

sanc•ti•fi•er
sanc•ti•fy (•fies,
•fy•ing, •fied)
sanc•ti•mo•ni•ous
sanc•ti•mo•ni•
ous•ly
sanc•ti•mo•ni•ous•
ness
sanc•ti•mo•ny
sanc•tion
sanc•tion•able
sanc•ti•tude
sanc•tity (pl •tities)
sanc•tu•ary (pl
•aries)
sanc•tum (pl •tums
or •ta)
sand
san•dal
san•daled (Brit
•dalled)
sandal•wood
sand•bag (vb
•bag•ging,
•bagged)
sand•bag•ger
sand•bank
sand•blast
sand•blast•er
sand-blind
sand-blindness
sand•box
sand•er
sand•er•ling
sand•grouse
sand•hog
sandi•ness
sand•lot
sand•paper

sand•piper
sand•pit
sand•soap
sand•stone
sand•storm
sand•wich
sand•worm
sand•wort
sandy (sandi•er, sandi•est)
sane
sane•ly
sane•ness
sang
sang•froid
san•gria
san•gui•nary
san•guine
san•guine•ly
san•guine•ness (or •guin•ity)
sani•cle
san•itari•ly
sani•tari•ness
sani•ta•rium
variant spelling of sanatorium
sani•tary
sani•ta•tion
sani•tize
sani•to•rium
variant spelling of sanatorium
san•ity
sank
san•se•vieria
San•skrit
San•ta Claus

sap (sap•ping, sapped)
*saphire *incorrect spelling of* sapphire
sa•pi•ence (or •en•cy)
sa•pi•ent
sap•ling
sapo•dil•la
sa•po•ta
sapped
sap•per
Sap•phic
sap•phire (*NOT* saphire)
sap•ping
sap•py (•pi•er, •pi•est)
sap•ro•phyte
sap•ro•phyt•ic
sap•sucker
sap•wood
sar•casm
sar•cas•tic
sar•cas•ti•cal•ly
sar•co•ma (*pl* •mas or •ma•ta)
sar•copha•gus (*pl* •gi or •guses)
sar•dine (*pl* •dines or •dine)
sar•don•ic
sar•doni•cal•ly
sar•doni•cism
sar•don•yx
sar•gas•so (or •sum; *pl* •sos or •sums)

sari (*or* saree; *pl* saris *or* sarees)
sa•rong
sar•sa•pa•ril•la (*NOT* sarsparilla)
sar•to•rial
sar•to•rial•ly
sash
sash•ay strut; stroll; *cf* sachet
sas•ka•toon
*sarsparilla *incorrect spelling of* sarsaparilla
sass
sas•sa•fras
sas•si•ly
sas•si•ness
sas•sy (•si•er, •si•est)
sat
Satan
sa•tan•ic (or •tani•cal)
sa•tani•cal•ly
Sa•tan•ism
Sa•tan•ist
satch•el
sate
sat•el•lite
sa•ti•abil•ity (or •able•ness)
sa•ti•able
sa•ti•ably
sa•ti•ate
sa•tia•tion
sa•ti•ety
sat•in
satin•wood

sat•iny

sat•ire parody; *cf*
satyr

sa•tiri•cal (*or*
•tir•ic)

sa•tiri•cal•ly

sati•rist

sati•ri•za•tion

sati•rize

sati•riz•er

sat•is•fac•tion

sat•is•fac•to•ri•ly

sat•is•fac•to•ri•ness

sat•is•fac•tory

sat•is•fi•able

sat•is•fy (•fies,
•fy•ing, •fied)

sat•is•fy•ing•ly

sat•su•ma

satu•rabil•ity

satu•rable

satu•rate

satu•rat•ed

satu•ra•tion

satu•ra•tor

Sat•ur•day

sat•ur•nine

sat•ur•nine•ness (*or*
•nin•ity)

sa•tyr goatlike
deity; lustful man;
cf satire

saty•ria•sis

sauce relish;
impudence; *cf*
source

sauce•pan

sau•cer

sau•cer•ful (*pl*
•fuls)

sau•ci•ly

sau•ci•ness

saucy (•ci•er,
•ci•est)

Sau•di (*or* Sau•di
Ara•bian)

sau•er•kraut

sau•ger

sau•na

saun•ter

saun•ter•er

sau•rian

sau•ry (*pl* •ries)

sau•sage

sau•té (•té•ing,
•téed *or* •téd)

sav•able (*or* save•)

sav•age

sav•age•ly

sav•age•ness

sav•age•ry (*pl*
•ries)

sa•van•na (*or* •nah)

sa•vant

save

save•able *variant
spelling of* savable

sav•er

sav•ing

sav•ings

sav•ior (*Brit* •iour)

sa•voir faire

sa•vor (*Brit* •vour)

sa•vori•ness (*Brit*
•vouri•)

sa•vory (*Brit*
•voury; *pl* •vories;

Brit •vouries) not
sweet; appetizing;
appetizer

sa•vory (*pl* •vories)
plant

sa•voy

sav•vy (•vies,
•vy•ing, •vied)

saw (saw•ing,
sawed, sawed *or*
sawn)

saw•bill

saw•buck

saw•dust

sawed

sawed-off (*Brit*
sawn-)

saw•fish (*pl* •fish
or •fishes)

saw•fly (*pl* •flies)

saw•horse

saw•ing

saw•mill

sawn

saw•tooth

saw•yer

saxi•frage

saxo•phone

saxo•phon•ic

sax•opho•nist

say (say•ing, said)

say•er

say•ing

say-so (*pl* -sos)

scab (scab•bing,
scabbed)

scab•bard

scab•bi•ness

scab•by (•bi•er,
•bi•est)
sca•bies
sca•bi•ous scabby;
plant
sca•brous scaly;
salacious
scad (pl scad or
scads) fish
scads large
quantity
scaf•fold
scaf•fold•ing
scal•able
scal•age
sca•lar math term;
cf scaler
scala•wag (or
scal•ly•)
scald
scald•fish (pl •fish
or •fishes)
scale
scal•er one that
scales; cf scalar
scales
scali•ness
scall
scal•lion
scal•lop (or scol•)
scal•lop•er
scal•ly•wag variant
spelling of
scalawag
scalp
scal•pel
scalp•er
scalp•ing

scaly (scali•er,
scali•est)
scamp
scamp•er
scam•pi (pl •pi)
scamp•ish
scan (scan•ning,
scanned)
scan•dal
scan•dali•za•tion
scan•dal•ize
scan•dal•iz•er
scandal•monger
scan•dal•ous
scan•dal•ous•ly
scan•dal•ous•ness
Scan•di•na•vian
scan•ner
scan•sion
scant
scanti•ly
scanti•ness
scant•ly
scant•ness
scanty (scanti•er,
scanti•est)
scape•goat
scapu•la (pl •lae or
•las)
scar (scar•ring,
scarred)
scar•ab
scarce
scarce•ly
scarce•ness
scar•city (pl •cities)
scare
scare•crow
scare•monger

scar•er
scarf (pl scarfs or
scarves)
scari•fi•ca•tion
scari•fi•er
scari•fy (•fies,
•fy•ing, •fied)
scar•la•ti•na
scar•let
scarp
scary (scari•er,
scari•est)
scat (scat•ting,
scat•ted)
scathe
scath•ing
scath•ing•ly
scato•logi•cal
scat•ter
scatter•brain
scatter•brained
scat•ter•er
scat•ter•ing
scat•ti•ly
scat•ti•ness
scat•ty (•ti•er,
•ti•est)
scaup (pl scaup or
scaups)
scav•enge
scav•en•ger
sce•nario (pl
•narios)
sce•nar•ist
scene setting; view;
cf seen
scen•ery (pl •eries)
sce•nic
sce•ni•cal•ly

scent odor; *cf* sent
scent•ed
scent•less
scep•ter (*Brit* •tre)
scep•tered (*Brit* •tred)
scep•tic *Brit spelling of* skeptic; *cf* septic
sched•ule
sche•ma (*pl* •ma•ta or •mas)
sche•mat•ic
sche•mati•cal•ly
sche•ma•ti•za•tion
sche•ma•tize
scheme
schem•er
schem•ing
schem•ing•ly
scher•zo (*pl* •zos or •zi)
schism
schis•mat•ic (*or* •mati•cal)
schis•mati•cal•ly
schist
schizo (*pl* schizos)
schiz•oid
schizo•phre•nia
schizo•phren•ic
schle•miel
schlep (*or* schlepp, shlep; schlep•ping, schlepped *or* shlep•ping, shlepped)
schlock

schmaltz (*or* schmalz)
schmaltzy
schmooze (*or* schmoose)
schnapps (*or* schnaps)
schnecke (*pl* schneck•en)
schnit•zel
schnook
schnor•rer
schnoz•zle
schol•ar
schol•ar•li•ness
schol•ar•ly
schol•ar•ship
scho•las•tic
scho•las•ti•cal•ly
scho•las•ti•cism
school
school•book
school•boy
school•child (*pl* •children)
school•girl
school•house
school•ing
school•marm (*or* •ma'am)
school•master
school•mate
school•mistress
school•room
school•teacher
school•yard
schoon•er
sci•at•ic
sci•ati•ca

sci•ence
sci•en•tif•ic
sci•en•tifi•cal•ly
sci•en•tist
sci-fi
scil•la
scimi•tar
scin•til•la
scin•til•late
scin•til•lat•ing•ly
scin•til•la•tion
sci•on
scis•sion
scis•sor (*vb*)
scis•sors (*pl n*)
scle•ro•sis (*pl* •ses)
scle•rot•ic
scle•rous
scoff
scoff•er
scoff•ing•ly
scoff•law
scold
scold•er
scold•ing
scold•ing•ly
scol•lop *variant spelling of* scallop
scom•broid
sconce
scone
scoop
scoop•er
scoot
scoot•er
scope
scorch
scorch•er
scorch•ing

score
score•board
score•card
scor•er
scorn
scorn•er
scorn•ful
scorn•ful•ly
scorn•ful•ness
scor•pi•on
Scot a Scottish
person; cf Scots
Scotch of
Scotland; whisky
scotch thwart;
wedge
sco•ter (pl •ters or
•ter)
scot-free
Scots Scottish;
Scottish people;
cf Scot
Scots•man (pl
•men)
Scots•woman (pl
•women)
Scot•tish
scoun•drel
scoun•drel•ly
scour
scour•er
scourge
scourg•er
scout
scout•er
scout•master
scow
scowl
scowl•er

Scrab•ble (*Trade-
mark*) game
scrab•ble fumble;
grope
scrab•bler
scrag (scrag•ging,
scragged)
scrag•gi•ly
scrag•gi•ness
scrag•gly (•gli•er,
•gli•est) untidy
scrag•gy (•gi•er,
•gi•est) scrawny
scram
(scram•ming,
scrammed)
scram•ble
scram•bler
scrap (scrap•ping,
scrapped)
scrap•book
scrape
scrap•er
scrap•er•board
scrap•pi•ly
scrap•pi•ness
scrap•py (•pi•er,
•pi•est)
scratch
scratch•board
scratch•er
scratchi•ly
scratchi•ness
scratch•proof
scratchy
(scratchi•er,
scratchi•est)
scrawl
scrawl•er

scrawly
scrawni•ly
scrawni•ness
scrawny
(scrawni•er,
scrawni•est)
scream
scream•er
scree
screech
screech•er
screechy
screed
screen
screen•able
screen•er
screen•play
screen-test (*vb*)
screen•writer
screw
screw•ball
screw•driv•er
screw•er
screw•worm
screwy (screwi•er,
screwi•est)
scrib•ble
scrib•bler
scrib•bly
scribe
scrim•mage
scrim•mag•er
scrimp
scrimpy
(scrimpi•er,
scrimpi•est)
scrim•shaw
scrip
script

scrip•tur•al
Scrip•ture Bible
scrip•ture sacred writings
script•writer
script•writing
scrive•ner
scrod
scrofu•la
scrofu•lous
scroll
scroll•work
scro•tal
scro•tum (pl •ta or •tums)
scrounge
scroung•er
scrub (scrub•bing, scrubbed)
scrub•ber
scrub•bi•ness
scrub•by (•bi•er, •bi•est)
scrub•land
scruff
scruffi•ly
scruffi•ness
scruffy (scruffi•er, scruffi•est)
scrump•tious
scrump•tious•ly
scrump•tious•ness
scrunch
scru•ple
scru•pu•lous
scru•pu•lous•ly
scru•pu•lous•ness
scru•ti•neer
scru•ti•nize

scru•ti•niz•er
scru•ti•ny (pl •nies)
scu•ba
scud (scud•ding, scud•ded)
scuff
scuf•fle
scull oar; cf skull
scull•er
scull•ery (pl •leries)
scul•pin (pl •pins or •pin)
sculpt
sculp•tor
sculp•tur•al
sculp•tur•al•ly
sculp•ture
scum (scum•ming, scummed)
scum•mer
scum•my (•mi•er, •mi•est)
scup (pl scup or scups)
scup•per•nong
scurf
scurfy
scur•ril•ity (pl •ities)
scur•ril•ous
scur•ril•ous•ly
scur•ri•lous•ness
scur•ry (vb •ries, •ry•ing, •ried; n, pl •ries)
scur•vy (•vi•er, •vi•est)
scut•ter
scut•tle

scythe
sea expanse of water; cf see
sea•bed
sea•bird
sea•board
sea•borne
sea•farer
sea•faring
sea•food
sea•front
sea•going
sea•gull
seal
seal•able
sea-lane
seal•ant
seal•er
seal•skin
seam join; stratum; cf seem
sea•man (pl •men) sailor; cf semen
sea•man•ly
sea•man•ship
seam•er
seami•ness
seam•less
seam•stress (or semp•)
seamy (seami•er, seami•est)
sé•ance (Brit se•)
sea•plane
sea•port
sear scorch; cf seer; sere
search
search•able

search•er
search•ing
search•ing•ly
search•light
sear•ing
sea•scape
sea•shell
sea•shore
sea•sick
sea•sick•ness
sea•side
sea•son
sea•son•able
sea•son•able•ness
sea•son•ably
sea•son•al
sea•son•al•ly
sea•soned
sea•son•er
sea•son•ing
seat
seat•ed
seat•er
seat•ing
sea•ward (*adj*)
sea•ward (*Brit*
•wards; *adv*)
sea•water
sea•way
sea•weed
sea•worthi•ness
sea•worthy
se•ba•ceous
se•bum
se•cant
seca•teurs
se•cede
se•ces•sion
se•ces•sion•ism

se•ces•sion•ist
se•clude
se•clud•ed
  sheltered; *cf*
  seclusive
se•clud•ed•ness
se•clu•sion
se•clu•sive
  reclusive; *cf*
  secluded
se•clu•sive•ness
sec•ond
sec•ond•ari•ly
sec•ond•ary (*pl*
  •aries)
second-best (*adj*)
second-class (*adj*)
sec•ond•er
second-floor (*adj*)
second-guess (*vb*)
second•hand (*adj*,
  adv)
sec•ond•ly
se•cond•ment
second-rate
second-rater
second-sighted
se•cre•cy (*pl* •cies)
se•cret hidden;
  something
  hidden; *cf* secrete
sec•re•tar•ial
sec•re•tari•at
sec•re•tary (*pl*
  •taries)
secretary-general
  (*pl* secretaries-
  general)
sec•re•tary•ship

se•crete conceal;
  exude; *cf* secret
se•cre•tion
se•cre•tive
se•cre•tive•ly
se•cre•tive•ness
se•cret•ly
se•cre•tory
sect
sec•tar•ian
sec•tari•an•ism
sec•tion
sec•tion•al
sec•tion•al•ism
sec•tion•al•ist
sec•tion•ali•za•tion
sec•tion•al•ize
sec•tion•al•ly
sec•tor
secu•lar
secu•lar•ism
secu•lar•ist
secu•lar•is•tic
secu•lar•ity (*pl*
  •ities)
secu•lari•za•tion
secu•lar•ize
se•cur•able
se•cure
se•cure•ly
se•cure•ment
se•cure•ness
se•cur•er
se•cu•rity (*pl*
  •rities)
se•dan
se•date
se•date•ly
se•date•ness

se•da•tion
seda•tive
sed•en•tari•ly
sed•en•tari•ness
sed•en•tary
sedge
sedgy
sedi•ment
sedi•men•tary
sedi•men•ta•tion
se•di•tion
se•di•tion•ary (pl
•aries)
se•di•tious
se•di•tious•ly
se•duce
se•duc•er
se•duc•ible
se•duc•tion
se•duc•tive
se•duc•tive•ly
se•duc•tive•ness
se•duc•tress
se•du•lity
sedu•lous
sedu•lous•ly
sedu•lous•ness
se•dum
see (see•ing, saw,
seen) perceive;
understand;
diocese; cf sea
seed (pl seed or
seeds) embryo
plant; cf cede
seed•bed
seed•cake
seed•er
seedi•ly

seedi•ness
seed•less
seed•ling
seedy (seedi•er,
seedi•est)
see•ing
seek (seek•ing,
sought)
seek•er
seem appear; cf
seam
seem•ing
seem•ing•ly
seem•li•ness
seem•ly (•li•er,
•li•est)
seen past participle
of see; cf scene
seep
seep•age
seer prophet; cf
sear; sere
seer•suck•er
see•saw
seethe
seeth•ing•ly
see-through
seg•ment
seg•men•tal
seg•men•tary
seg•men•ta•tion
seg•re•gate
seg•re•ga•tion
seg•re•ga•tion•al
seg•re•ga•tion•ist
seg•re•ga•tive
seg•re•ga•tor
*seige incorrect
spelling of siege

seise legal term; cf
seize
seis•mic (or •mal,
•mi•cal)
seis•mi•cal•ly
seis•mo•graph
seis•mog•ra•pher
seis•mo•graph•ic
seis•mog•ra•phy
seis•mo•log•ic (or
•logi•cal)
seis•molo•gist
seis•mol•ogy
*seive incorrect
spelling of sieve
seiz•able
seize (NOT sieze)
grasp; cf seise
seiz•er
sei•zure
sel•dom
se•lect
se•lec•tion
se•lec•tive
se•lec•tive•ly
se•lec•tive•ness
se•lec•tiv•ity
se•lect•ness
se•lec•tor
self (pl selves)
self-absorbed
self-absorption
self-abuse
self-addressed
self-
aggrandizement
self-analysis
self-appointed
self-assertion

self-assertive
self-assurance
self-assured
self-aware
self-awareness
self-centered (*Brit* -centred)
self-centeredness (*Brit* -centredness)
self-confessed
self-confidence
self-confident
self-confidently
self-conscious
self-consciously
self-consciousness
self-contained
self-control
self-controlled
self-deception (*or* -deceit)
self-defeating
self-defense (*Brit* -defence)
self-denial
self-denying
self-destruct
self-determination
self-discipline
self-disciplined
self-educated
self-effacement
self-effacing
self-employed
self-employment
self-esteem
self-evidence
self-evident
self-explanatory

self-expression
self-government
self-help
self-image
self-importance
self-important
self-importantly
self-imposed
self-improvement
self-indulgence
self-indulgent
self-indulgently
self-inflicted
self-interest
self•ish
self•ish•ly
self•ish•ness
self-justification
self-justifying
self-knowledge
self•less
self•less•ly
self•less•ness
self-loading
self-made
self-opinionated (*or* -opinioned)
self-pity
self-pitying
self-portrait
self-possessed
self-possession
self-preservation
self-propelled
self-protection
self-reliance
self-reliant
self-respect
self-respecting

self-restraint
self-righteous
self-righteously
self-righteousness
self-rule
self-sacrifice
self-sacrificing
self•same
self-satisfaction
self-satisfied
self-sealing
self-seeker
self-seeking
self-service
self-starter
self-styled
self-sufficiency
self-sufficient (*or* -sufficing)
self-supporting
self-taught
self-willed
self-winding
sell (**sell•ing, sold**) exchange for money; *cf* **cell**
sell•er one who sells; *cf* **cellar**
sell•out
sel•vage (*or* •**vedge**) edge of fabric; *cf* **salvage**
selves *pl of* **self**
se•man•tic
se•man•ti•cal•ly
se•man•tics
sema•phore
sem•blance

se•men ejaculated
fluid; *cf* **seaman**
se•mes•ter
se•mes•tral
semi (*pl* semis)
semi•auto•mat•ic
semi•breve
semi•cir•cle
semi•cir•cu•lar
semi•co•lon
semi•con•scious
semi•con•scious•
ness
semi•de•tached
semi•fi•nal
semi•fi•nal•ist
semi•nal
semi•nal•ly
semi•nar
semi•nary (*pl*
•naries)
Semi•nole (*pl*
•noles or •nole)
semi•per•meable
semi•pre•cious
semi•pro•fes•
sion•al
semi•qua•ver
semi•re•tired
semi•skilled
Se•mite (*or*
Shem•ite)
Se•mit•ic (*or* She•)
semi•tone
semi•tropi•cal
semo•li•na
semp•stress *variant
spelling of*
seamstress

Sen•ate senate of
USA, etc.
sen•ate legislative
body
sena•tor
sena•to•rial
send (send•ing,
sent)
send•able
send•er
send-off (*n*)
send-up (*n*)
Sen•eca (*pl* •eca or
•ecas)
sen•ega (*or* •eca)
se•nes•cence
se•nes•cent
se•nile
se•nil•ity
sen•ior
sen•ior•ity (*pl*
•ities)
sen•na
se•ñor (*or* •nor; *pl*
•ñores or •nors)
se•ño•ra (*or* •no•)
se•ño•ri•ta (*or*
•no•)
sen•sate
sen•sa•tion
sen•sa•tion•al
sen•sa•tion•al•ly
sen•sa•tion•al•ism
sen•sa•tion•al•ist
sen•sa•tion•al•is•tic
sen•sa•tion•al•ize
sense
sense•less
sense•less•ly

sense•less•ness
sen•sibil•ity (*pl*
•ities)
sen•sible
sen•sible•ness
sen•sibly
sen•si•tive
sen•si•tive•ly
sen•si•tive•ness
sen•si•tiv•ity (*pl*
•ities)
sen•si•ti•za•tion
sen•si•tize
sen•si•tiz•er
sen•sor sensing
device; *cf* **censor**
sen•so•ry (*or* •rial)
sen•sual gratifying
the senses; *cf*
censual; sensuous
sen•su•al•ism
sen•su•al•ist
sen•su•al•ity (*pl*
•ities)
sen•su•al•ly
sen•su•ous pleasing
to the senses; *cf*
sensual
sen•su•ous•ly
sen•su•ous•ness
sent transmitted; *cf*
scent
sen•tence
sen•ten•tial
sen•ten•tious
sen•ten•tious•ly
sen•ten•tious•ness
sen•tience (*or*
•tien•cy)

sen•ti•ent
sen•ti•ment
sen•ti•ment•al
sen•ti•men•tal•ism
sen•ti•men•tal•ist
sen•ti•men•tal•ity
(pl •ities)
sen•ti•men•tali•za•
tion
sen•ti•men•tal•ize
sen•ti•men•tal•ly
sen•ti•nel
sen•try (pl •tries)
se•pal
sepa•rabil•ity (or
•rable•ness)
sepa•rable
sepa•rate
sepa•rate•ly
sepa•rate•ness
sepa•ra•tion
sepa•ra•tism
sepa•ra•tist (or
•ra•tion•ist)
sepa•ra•tor
Se•phar•di (pl
•dim)
Se•phar•dic
se•pia
sep•sis
Sep•tem•ber
sep•tet (or •tette)
sep•tic putrefying;
cf sceptic; skeptic
sep•ti•cemia (Brit
•cae•mia)
sep•ti•cemic (Brit
•cae•mic)
sep•ti•cal•ly

sep•tic•ity
sep•tua•genar•ian
sep•tup•let
sep•ul•cher (Brit
•chre)
se•pul•chral
se•pul•chral•ly
se•quel
se•quence
se•quent
se•quen•tial
se•quen•ti•al•ity
se•quen•tial•ly
se•ques•ter
se•ques•trant
se•ques•trate
se•ques•tra•tion
se•ques•tra•tor
se•quin
se•quined
se•quoia
sera pl of serum
ser•aph (pl •aphs
or •aphim)
se•raph•ic
Serb
Ser•bian
sere (or sear)
withered; cf sear;
seer
ser•enade
ser•enad•er
ser•en•dip•ity
se•rene
se•rene•ly
se•rene•ness
se•ren•ity (pl •ities)
serf medieval
peasant; cf surf

serf•dom (or •hood)
serge fabric; cf
surge
ser•geant (Brit also
•jeant)
se•rial story in
installments; in
series; cf cereal
se•rial•ism
se•riali•za•tion
se•rial•ize
se•rial•ly
se•ri•ate
se•ries (pl •ries)
se•rin•ga rubber
tree; cf syringa
se•rio•com•ic (or
•comi•cal)
se•rio•comi•cal•ly
se•ri•ous grave; cf
serous
se•ri•ous•ly
se•ri•ous•ness
ser•jeant variant
Brit spelling of
sergeant
ser•mon
ser•mon•ize
ser•mon•iz•er
se•rous of serum;
cf serious
ser•pent
ser•pen•tine
ser•rate
ser•rat•ed
ser•ra•tion (or
•ture)
ser•ried

se•rum (*pl* •rums
or •ra)
serv•able (or
serve•)
ser•val (*pl* •vals or
•val)
serv•ant
serve
serv•er
ser•vice
ser•vice•abil•ity (or
•able•ness)
ser•vice•able
ser•vice•ably
ser•vice•berry (*pl*
•berries)
ser•vice•man (*pl*
•men)
ser•vice•woman (*pl*
•women)
ser•vile
ser•vil•ity (or
•vile•ness)
serv•ing
ser•vi•tor
ser•vi•tude
ser•vo (*pl* •vos)
sesa•me
ses•sion meeting; *cf*
cession
ses•sion•al
ses•tet six-line
verse; *cf* sextet
set (set•ting, set)
place; harden;
firm; group; etc.;
cf sett
set-aside (n)
set•back

sett (or set) paving
stone; *cf* set
set•tee
set•ter
set•ting
set•tle
set•tle•ment
set•tler colonist
set•tlor one who
makes a legal
settlement
set-to (*pl* -tos)
set•up (n)
sev•en
sev•en•fold
sev•en•teen
sev•en•teenth
sev•enth
sev•en•ti•eth
sev•en•ty (*pl* •ties)
sev•er
sev•er•able
sev•er•al
sev•er•al•ly
sev•er•ance
se•vere
se•vere•ly
se•vere•ness
se•ver•ity (*pl* •ities)
sew (sew•ing,
sewed, sewn or
sewed) to stitch; *cf*
so; sow
sew•age waste
matter; *cf*
sewerage
sew•er sewage
drain; *cf* suer

sew•er one who
sews; *cf* sower
sew•er•age system
of sewers; *cf*
sewage
sew•ing
sewn
sex
sexa•genar•ian
sex•ag•enary (*pl*
•enaries)
sexi•ly
sexi•ness
sex•ism
sex•ist
sex•less
sex•less•ness
sex•olo•gist
sex•ol•ogy
sex•tant
sex•tet (or •tette)
group of six; *cf*
sestet
sex•ton
sex•tup•let
sex•ual
sexu•al•ity
sex•ual•ly
sexy (sexi•er,
sexi•est)
shab•bi•ly
shab•bi•ness
shab•by (•bi•er,
•bi•est)
shack
shack•le
shad (*pl* shad or
shads)
shad•bush

shade
shadi•ly
shadi•ness
shad•ing
shad•ow
shadow•box
shadow•boxing
shad•ow•er
shad•owi•ness
shad•owy (•owi•er,
 •owi•est)
shady (shadi•er,
 shadi•est)
shaft
shag (shag•ging,
 shagged)
shag•bark (or
 shell•bark)
shag•gi•ly
shag•gi•ness
shag•gy (•gi•er,
 •gi•est)
shah
Sha•hap•tian
 variant spelling of
 Sahaptian
shah•dom
shak•able (or
 shake•)
shake (shak•ing,
 shook, shak•en)
shake•down (n)
shak•er
Shake•spear•ean
 (or •ian, •sper•,
 Shak•)
shake-up (n)
shaki•ly
shaki•ness

shaky (shaki•er,
 shaki•est)
shale
shall (should)
shal•lot
shal•low
shal•low•ly
shal•low•ness
sha•lom Jewish
 greeting; *cf* slalom
shaly
sham (sham•ming,
 shammed)
sham•an
sham•an•ism
sham•ble walk
 awkwardly
sham•bles mess
sham•bol•ic
shame
shame•faced
shame•faced•ly
shame•faced•ness
shame•ful
shame•ful•ly
shame•ful•ness
shame•less
shame•less•ly
shame•less•ness
sham•mer
sham•poo (n, pl
 •poos; vb •poos,
 •poo•ing, •pooed)
sham•poo•er
sham•rock
shan•dy (pl •dies)
shan•dy•gaff
shang•hai (•hais,
 •hai•ing, •haied)

shank
shan•tung
shan•ty (pl •ties)
 hut
shan•ty (or
 shan•tey) *variant*
 spellings of
 chantey
shanty•town
shap•able (or
 shape•)
shape
shape•less
shape•less•ness
shape•li•ness
shape•ly (•li•er,
 •li•est)
shap•er
shar•able (or
 share•)
shard (or sherd)
share
share•crop
 (•crop•ping,
 •cropped)
share•crop•per
share•holder
share-out (n)
shar•er
share•ware
shark
shark•skin
sharp
sharp•en
sharp•en•er
sharp•er
sharp-eyed
sharp•ish
sharp•ly

sharp•ness
sharp-set (*adj*)
sharp•shooter
sharp-sighted
sharp-sighted•ness
sharp-tongued
sharp-witted
sharp-witted•ness
shat•ter
shat•ter•ing•ly
shatter•proof
shave (shav•ing,
 shaved, shaved *or*
 shav•en)
shav•er
shav•ing
shawl
Shaw•nee (*pl* •nees
 or •nee)
she
sheaf (*pl* sheaves)
shear (shear•ing,
 sheared, sheared
 or shorn) cut;
 deformation; *cf*
 sheer
shear•er
shear•ling
shears
shear•water
sheath (*n, pl*
 sheaths)
sheathe (*vb*)
sheath•ing
sheave
shed (shed•ding,
 shed)
sheen
sheeny

sheep (*pl* sheep)
sheep-dip
sheep•dog
sheep•fold
sheep•ish
sheep•ish•ly
sheep•ish•ness
sheep•shank
sheeps•head (*pl*
 •head *or* •heads)
sheep•shearer
sheep•shearing
sheep•skin
sheer steep;
 transparent;
 absolute; deviate;
 cf shear
sheer•ly
sheer•ness
sheet
sheet•ing
sheik (*or* sheikh)
sheik•dom (*or*
 sheikh•)
shek•el
shelf (*pl* shelves)
shell
shel•lac (•lack•ing,
 •lacked)
shell•bark *variant*
 of shag•bark
shell•fire
shell•fish (*pl* •fish
 or •fishes)
shell•proof
shell-shocked
shel•ter
shel•ter•er
shelve (*vb*)

shelv•er
shelves *pl of* shelf
shelv•ing
Shem•ite *variant*
 spelling of Semite
She•mit•ic *variant*
 spelling of Semitic
shep•herd
shep•herd•ess
sher•bet
sherd *variant of*
 shard
sher•iff
sher•ry (*pl* •ries)
shes more than
 one female
she's she is; she has
shi•at•su
shib•bo•leth
shied
shield
shi•er (*adj*) *variant*
 spelling of shyer
shi•er (*or* shy•; *n*)
shi•est *variant*
 spelling of shyest
shift
shift•er
shifti•ly
shifti•ness
shift•ing•ly
shift•less
shift•less•ly
shift•less•ness
shifty (shifti•er,
 shifti•est)
Shi•ite
shi•ly *less common*
 spelling of shyly

shim•mer
shim•mer•ing•ly
shim•mery
shim•my (*n, pl*
•mies; *vb* •mies,
•my•ing, •mied)
shin (shin•ning,
shinned)
shin•bone
shin•dig (*or* •dy; *pl*
•digs, •dys, *or*
•dies)
shine (shin•ing,
shone)
shin•er
shin•gle
shin•gles
shin•gly
shini•ness
shin•ny (*Brit* •ty; *pl*
•nies; *Brit* •ties)
Shin•to
Shin•to•ism
shiny (shini•er,
shini•est)
ship (ship•ping,
shipped)
ship•board
ship•builder
ship•building
ship•load
ship•mate
ship•ment
ship•owner
ship•per
ship•ping
ship•shape
ship•way
ship•wreck

ship•wright
ship•yard
shire
shirk
shirk•er
shirr
shirr•ing
shirt
shirti•ly
shirti•ness
shirt•ing
shirt•sleeve
shirt•tail
shirty (shirti•er,
shirti•est)
shit (shit•ting,
shit•ted *or* shit)
shit•ty
shiv•er
shiv•er•er
shiv•er•ing•ly
shiv•ery
shlep *variant*
spelling of schlep
shoal
shoaly
shock
shock•abil•ity
shock•able
shock•er
shock•ing
shock•ing•ly
shock•ing•ness
shock•proof
shod
shod•di•ly
shod•di•ness
shod•dy (•di•er,
•di•est)

shoe (shoe•ing,
shod *or* shoed)
footwear; *cf*
choux; shoo
shoe•horn
shoe•lace
shoe•maker
shoe•making
shoe•string
shone
shoo (shoos,
shoo•ing, shooed)
chase off; *cf*
choux; shoe
shook
shoot (shoot•ing,
shot) to fire; plant
growth; *cf* chute
shoot•er
shoot-out (*n*)
shop (shop•ping,
shopped)
shop•keeper
shop•keeping
shop•lifter
shop•lifting
shop•per
shop•ping
shop•talk
shop•worn (*Brit*
•soiled)
shore
shore•front
shore•less
shore•line
shore•ward (*adj*)
shore•ward (*Brit*
•wards; *adv*)
shor•ing

shorn

short

short•age

short•bread

short•cake

short•change

short-circuit (*vb*)

short•coming

short•cut

short•en

short•en•er

short•en•ing

short•fall

short•hand

short•handed

short•ish

short-list (*vb*)

short-lived

short•ly

short•ness

short-range (*adj*)

shorts

short•sighted

short•sighted•ly

short•sighted•ness

short•stop

short-tempered

short-term (*adj*)

short•wave

Sho•sho•ne (or •ni; *pl* •nes, •ne or •nis, •ni)

Sho•sho•nean (or •nian)

shot

shot•gun (•gun•ning, •gunned)

shot-putter

should

shoul•der

shout

shout•er

shove

shov•el (•el•ing, •eled; *Brit* •el•ling, •elled)

shov•el•er duck

shov•el•er (*Brit* •el•ler) one who shovels

shovel•ful (*pl* •fuls or shovels•ful)

shovel•head

shovel•nose

shov•er

show (show•ing, showed, shown or showed)

show•biz

show•boat

show•case

show•down

show•er

shower•proof

show•ery

show•girl

showi•ly

showi•ness

show•ing

show•man (*pl* •men)

show•man•ship

shown

show-off (*n*)

show•piece

show•room

showy (showi•er, showi•est)

shrank

shrap•nel

shred (shred•ding, shred•ded or shred)

shred•der

shrew

shrewd

shrewd•ly

shrewd•ness

shrew•ish

shrew•ish•ness

shriek

shriek•er

shrift

shrike

shrill

shrill•ness

shrilly

shrimp

shrimp•er

shrine

shrink (shrink•ing, shrank or shrunk, shrunk or shrunk•en)

shrink•able

shrink•age

shrink•er

shrink•ing•ly

shrink-wrap (-wrapping, -wrapped)

shriv•el (•el•ing, •eled; *Brit* •el•ling, •elled)

shroud

shrub

shrub•bery (*pl* •beries)

shrub•by (•bi•er, •bi•est)

shrug (shrug•ging, shrugged)

shrunk

shrunk•en

shuck

shuck•er

shud•der

shud•der•ing•ly

shud•dery

shuf•fle

shuf•fler

shun (shun•ning, shunned)

shun•ner

shunt

shunt•er

shush

shut (shut•ting, shut)

shut•down

shut-eye

shut•off

shut•out

shut•ter

shut•ter•ing

shut•tle

shuttle•cock

shy (*adj* shy•er, shy•est *or* shi•er, shi•est; *vb* shies, shy•ing, shied; *n*, *pl* shies)

shy•er (*n*) *variant spelling of* shier

shy•ly

shy•ness

shy•ster

Sia•mese (*pl* •mese)

Si•berian

sibi•lance

sibi•lant

sibi•late

sibi•la•tion

sib•ling

sib•yl (*NOT* sybil)

sib•yl•line (*or* si• byl•ic, si•byl•lic)

sic (*Latin*) thus; *cf* sick

Si•cil•ian

sick ill; *cf* sic

sick•bay

sick•bed

sick•en

sick•en•ing

sick•en•ing•ly

sick•le

sickle•bill

sick•li•ness

sick•ly (•li•er, •li•est)

sick•ness

sick-out (*n*)

sick•room

side

side•board

side•burns (*Brit* •boards)

side•car

side•kick

side•light

side•line

side•long

si•dereal

side•saddle

side•show

side•slip (•slip•ping, •slipped)

sides•man (*pl* •men)

side•splitting

side•step (•step•ping, •stepped)

side•stepper

side•track

side•walk

side•ward (*adj*)

side•ward (*Brit* •wards; *adv*)

side•ways

side•winder

sid•ing

si•dle

siege (*NOT* seige)

si•en•na

si•er•ra

si•es•ta

sieve (*NOT* seive)

*sieze *incorrect spelling of* seize

sift

sift•er

sift•ings

sigh

sigh•er

sight vision; *cf* cite; site

sight•ed

sight•er

sight•less
sight•less•ness
sight•li•ness
sight•ly (•li•er,
•li•est)
sight-read
(-reading, -read)
sight read•er
sight•see (•see•ing,
•saw, •seen)
sight•seer
sig•ma
sign indicator; etc.;
write one's name;
cf sine
sig•nal (•nal•ing,
•naled; Brit
•nal•ling, •nalled)
sig•nal•er (Brit
•nal•ler)
sig•nal•ize
sig•nal•ly
signal•man (pl
•men)
sig•na•tory (pl
•tories)
sig•na•ture
sign•board
sign•er
sig•net seal on
ring; cf cygnet
sig•nifi•cance
sig•nifi•cant
sig•nifi•cant•ly
sig•ni•fi•ca•tion
sig•nifi•ca•tive
sig•ni•fi•er
sig•ni•fy (•fies,
•fy•ing, •fied)

si•gnor (or •gnior;
pl •gnors, •gnori,
or •gniors)
si•gno•ra (pl •ras
or •re)
si•gnori•na (pl
•nas or •ne)
sign•post
Sikh
Sikh•ism
si•lage
si•lence
si•lenc•er
si•lent
si•lent•ly
sil•hou•ette
sili•ca mineral; cf
silicon; silicone
sili•cate
si•li•ceous (or
•cious)
sili•con chemical
element; cf silica;
silicone
sili•cone polymer;
cf silica; silicon
silk
silk•en
silki•ly
silki•ness
silk•worm
silky (silki•er,
silki•est)
sill
sil•la•bub variant
spelling of
syllabub
sil•li•ly
sil•li•ness

sil•ly (adj •li•er,
•li•est)
silo (pl silos)
silt
sil•ta•tion
silty
sil•ver
silver•fish (pl •fish
or •fishes)
sil•veri•ness
sil•ver•ing
silver•smith
silver-tongued
silver•ware
sil•very
sim•ian
simi•lar
simi•lar•ity (pl
•ities)
simi•lar•ly
simi•le (pl •les)
si•mili•tude
sim•mer
sim•pa•ti•co
sim•per
sim•per•er
sim•per•ing•ly
sim•ple
simple•minded
simple•minded•ly
simple•minded•ness
sim•ple•ness
sim•ple•ton
sim•plex
sim•plic•ity (pl
•ities)
sim•pli•fi•ca•tion
sim•pli•fi•er

sim•pli•fy (•fies,
•fy•ing, •fied)
sim•plis•tic
sim•plis•ti•cal•ly
simp•ly
simu•la•crum (*pl*
•cra)
simu•late
simu•lated
simu•la•tion
simu•la•tive
simu•la•tor
si•mul•cast
si•mul•ta•neous
si•mul•ta•neous•ly
si•mul•ta•neous•
ness (*or* •ta•neity)
sin (sin•ning,
sinned)
since
sin•cere
sin•cere•ly
sin•cer•ity (*or*
•cere•ness)
sine trigonometry
term; (*Latin*)
without; *cf* sign
si•ne•cure
sine qua non
sin•ew
sin•ewy
sin•ful
sin•ful•ly
sin•ful•ness
sing (sing•ing,
sang, sung)
sing•able
singe (singe•ing,
singed)

sing•er
Sin•gha•lese (*or*
•ha•; *pl* •lese)
sin•gle
single-action (*adj*)
single-breasted
single-handed
single-handed•ly
single-minded
single-minded•ly
single-minded•ness
sin•gle•ness
sin•glet
sin•gle•ton
single-track (*adj*)
sin•gly
sing•song
sin•gu•lar
sin•gu•lar•ity (*pl*
•ities)
sin•gu•lari•za•tion
sin•gu•lar•ize
sin•gu•lar•ly
sin•gu•lar•ness
Sin•ha•lese *variant
spelling of*
Singhalese
sin•is•ter
sin•is•ter•ly
sin•is•ter•ness
sink (sink•ing, sank
or sunk, sunk *or*
sunk•en)
sink•able
sink•er
sink•hole
sink•ing
sin•less
sin•less•ness

sinned
sin•ner
Sinn Féin
sin•ning
sinu•os•ity (*pl*
•ities)
sinu•ous
sinu•ous•ly
sinu•ous•ness
si•nus (*pl* •nuses)
si•nusi•tis
Siouan (*pl* Siouan
or Siouans)
Sioux (*pl* Sioux)
sip (sip•ping,
sipped)
si•phon (*or* sy•)
si•phon•age
si•phon•al (*or* •ic)
sipped
sip•per
sip•ping
sir
sire
si•ren
sir•loin
sir•ree (*or* siree)
sir•up *variant
spelling of* syrup
sis
si•sal
sis•sy (*pl* •sies)
sis•ter
sis•ter•hood
sister-in-law (*pl*
sisters-)
sis•ter•li•ness
sis•ter•ly
sit (sit•ting, sat)

si•tar
si•tar•ist
sit•com
sit-down (*n*, *adj*)
site place; *cf* cite;
  sight
sit-in (*n*)
sit•ter
sit•ting
situ•ate
situa•tion
situa•tion•al
six
six•fold
six-footer
six•teen
six•teenth
sixth
six•ti•eth
six•ty (*pl* •ties)
siz•able (*or* size•)
siz•able•ness (*or*
  size•)
siz•ably (*or* size•)
size
sized
siz•er
siz•zle
siz•zler
siz•zling
skate (*n*, *vb*) sport
skate (*pl* skate *or*
  skates) fish
skate•board
skate•board•er
skate•board•ing
skat•er
skat•ing
skein

skel•etal
skel•etal•ly
skel•eton
skep•tic (*Brit*
  scep•) doubter; *cf*
  septic
skep•ti•cal (*Brit*
  scep•)
skep•ti•cal•ly (*Brit*
  scep•)
skep•ti•cism (*Brit*
  scep•)
sker•rick
sketch
sketch•able
sketch•book
sketch•er
sketchi•ly
sketchi•ness
sketchy (sketchi•er,
  sketchi•est)
skew
skew•bald
skew•er long pin;
  cf skua
ski (*vb* skis,
  ski•ing, skied;
  n, *pl* skis *or* ski)
ski•able
skid (skid•ding,
  skid•ded)
skid•proof
skid•way
skied
ski•er
skiff
skif•fle
ski•ing

skil•ful *Brit*
  spelling of skillful
skill
skilled
skil•let
skill•ful (*Brit* skil•)
skill•ful•ly (*Brit*
  skil•)
skill•ful•ness (*Brit*
  skil•)
skim (skim•ming,
  skimmed)
skim•mer
skimp
skimpi•ly
skimpi•ness
skimpy (skimpi•er,
  skimpi•est)
skin (skin•ning,
  skinned)
skin-deep
skin•flint
skin•ful
skink
skinned
skin•ner
skin•ni•ness
skin•ning
skin•ny (•ni•er,
  •ni•est)
skin•tight
skip (skip•ping,
  skipped)
skip•jack (*pl*
  •jacks *or* •jack)
ski-plane
skip•per
skip•ping
skir•mish

skir•mish•er
skirt
skirt•ing
skit
skit•ter
skit•tish
skit•tish•ly
skit•tish•ness
skit•tle
skive
skiv•er
skiv•vy (*pl* •vies)
skua bird; *cf*
  skewer
skul•dug•gery *Brit*
  spelling of
  skullduggery
skulk
skulk•er
skull head bones;
  cf scull
skull•cap
skull•dug•gery
  (*Brit* skul•)
skunk (*pl* skunks
  or skunk)
sky (*n, pl* skies; *vb*
  skies, sky•ing,
  skied)
sky•dive (•div•ing,
  •dived *or* •dove)
sky•div•er
sky-high
sky•jack
sky•jack•er
sky•lark
sky•light
sky•line
sky•rocket

sky•scrap•er
sky•ward (*Brit*
  •wards)
sky•writer
sky•writing
slab (slab•bing,
  slabbed)
slack
slack•en
slack•er
slack•ly
slack•ness
slacks
slag (slag•ging,
  slagged)
slag•gy
slain
slake
sla•lom skiing race;
  cf shalom
slam (slam•ming,
  slammed)
slan•der
slan•der•er
slan•der•ous
slan•der•ous•ly
slang
slangi•ly
slangi•ness
slangy
slant
slant•ing
slant•ing•ly
slant•wise (*or*
  •ways)
slap (slap•ping,
  slapped)
slap•dash
slap•per

slap•stick
slash
slash•er
slat (slat•ting,
  slat•ted)
slate
slat•er
slat•ing
slat•tern
slat•tern•ly
slaty (slati•er,
  slati•est)
slaugh•ter
slaugh•ter•er
slaughter•house
slaugh•ter•ous
Slav
slave
slave-drive
  (-driving, -drove,
  -driven)
slave driv•er
slav•er
slav•er•er
slav•ery
Slav•ic *variant of*
  Slavonic
slav•ish
slav•ish•ly
slav•ish•ness
Sla•von•ic (*or*
  Slav•ic)
slay (slay•ing, slew,
  slain) kill; *cf*
  sleigh
slay•er
sleaze
slea•zi•ly
slea•zi•ness

slea•zy (•zi•er,
•zi•est)
sled (sled•ding,
sled•ded)
sled•der
sledge
sledge•hammer
sleek
sleek•ly
sleek•ness
sleep (sleep•ing,
slept)
sleep•er
sleepi•ly
sleepi•ness
sleep•ing
sleep•less
sleep•less•ly
sleep•less•ness
sleep•walk
sleep•walker
sleep•walking
sleepy (sleepi•er,
sleepi•est)
sleet
sleety
sleeve
sleeve•less
sleigh sled; cf slay
sleight trick; cf
slight
slen•der
slen•der•ize
slen•der•ly
slen•der•ness
slept
sleuth
slew past tense of
slay

slew (or slue) large
number; cf
slough; slue
slice
slice•able
slic•er
slick
slick•er
slick•ly
slick•ness
slid
slid•able
slide (slid•ing, slid)
slid•er
slid•ing
sli•er variant
spelling of slyer
sli•est variant
spelling of slyest
slight small; snub;
cf sleight
slight•ing•ly
slight•ly
slight•ness
sli•ly variant
spelling of slyly
slim (adj slim•mer,
slim•mest; vb
slim•ming,
slimmed)
slime
slimi•ly
slimi•ness
slim•line
slim•mer
slim•ming
slim•ness
slim•sy (or slimp•)

slimy (slimi•er,
slimi•est)
sling (sling•ing,
slung)
sling•er
sling•shot
slink (slink•ing,
slunk)
slinki•ly
slinki•ness
slinky (slinki•er,
slinki•est)
slip (slip•ping,
slipped)
slip•knot
slip-on (n)
slip•page
slip•per
slip•pered
slip•peri•ness
slip•pery (•peri•er,
•peri•est)
slip•pi•ness
slip•py (•pi•er,
•pi•est)
slip•shod
slip•stream
slip•up
slip•way
slit (slit•ting, slit)
slith•er
slith•ery
sliv•er
slob
slob•ber
slob•ber•er
slob•bery
sloe fruit; cf slow
sloe-eyed

slog (slog•ging,
 slogged)
slo•gan
slog•ger
sloop
slop (slop•ping,
 slopped)
slope
slop•ing
slop•ing•ly
slop•pi•ly
slop•pi•ness
slop•py (•pi•er,
 •pi•est)
slot (slot•ting,
 slot•ted)
sloth
sloth•ful
sloth•ful•ly
sloth•ful•ness
slouch
slouch•er
slouchy
slough (or slew)
 bog; cf slew; slue
slough to shed;
 shed skin, etc.
slov•en
slov•en•li•ness
slov•en•ly
slow not fast, etc.;
 cf sloe
slow•ly
slow•ness
slow•poke
slow-witted
slow•worm
slub (slub•bing,
 slubbed)

sludge
sludgy
slue (or slew;
 slu•ing, slued or
 slew•ing, slewed)
 to twist; cf slew;
 slough
slug (slug•ging,
 slugged)
slug•gard
slug•gard•ly
slug•gish
slug•gish•ly
slug•gish•ness
sluice
slum (slum•ming,
 slummed)
slum•ber
slum•ber•er
slum•ber•ous (or
 slum•brous)
slum•my (•mi•er,
 •mi•est)
slump
slung
slunk
slur (slur•ring,
 slurred)
slurp
slur•ry (pl •ries)
slush
slushi•ness
slushy (slushi•er,
 slushi•est)
slut
slut•tish
slut•tish•ness
sly (sly•er, sly•est
 or sli•er, sli•est)

sly•ly (or sli•)
sly•ness
smack
smack•er
small
small•ish
small-minded
small-minded•ly
small-minded•ness
small•ness
small•pox
small-scale
small-time (adj)
smarmy
 (smarmi•er,
 smarmi•est)
smart
smart•en
smart•ly
smart•ness
smash
smash•er
smash•ing
smash•up
smat•ter
smat•ter•ing
smaze
smear
smear•er
smeari•ness
smeary (smeari•er,
 smeari•est)
smell (smell•ing,
 smelled or smelt)
smelli•ness
smelly (smelli•er,
 smelli•est)
smelt (pl smelts or
 smelt)

smel•ter
smid•gen (or •geon, •gin)
smile
smil•er
smil•ing•ly
smirch
smirk
smirk•er
smirk•ing•ly
smith
smith•er•eens
smithy (pl smithies)
smit•ten
smock
smock•ing
smog
smog•gy
smok•able (or smoke•)
smoke
smoke•less
smok•er
smoke•stack
smoki•ly
smoki•ness
smok•ing
smoky (smoki•er, smoki•est)
smol•der (Brit smoul•)
smooth
smooth•able
smooth•er
smooth-faced
smooth•ly
smooth•ness
smooth-tongued
smor•gas•bord

smoth•er
smoul•der Brit spelling of smolder
smudge
smudgi•ly
smudgi•ness
smudgy (smudgi•er, smudgi•est)
smug (smug•ger, smug•gest)
smug•gle
smug•gler
smug•gling
smug•ly
smug•ness
smut (smut•ting, smut•ted)
smut•ti•ly
smut•ti•ness
smut•ty (•ti•er, •ti•est)
snack
sna•fu (•fues, •fu•ing, •fued)
snag (snag•ging, snagged)
snag•gy
snail
snake
snake•bite
snake•root
snake•skin
snaki•ly
snaki•ness
snaky (snaki•er, snaki•est)
snap (snap•ping, snapped)
snap•dragon

snap•pable
snap•per
snap•pi•ly
snap•pi•ness
snap•pish
snap•pish•ly
snap•pish•ness
snap•py (•pi•er, •pi•est)
snap•shot
snare
snar•er
snarl
snarl•er
snarl•ing•ly
snarl-up (n)
snarly
snatch
snatch•er
snaz•zi•ly
snaz•zi•ness
snaz•zy (•zi•er, •zi•est)
sneak
sneak•ers
sneaki•ly
sneaki•ness
sneak•ing
sneak•ing•ly
sneaky (sneaki•er, sneaki•est)
sneer
sneer•er
sneer•ing
sneer•ing•ly
sneeze
sneez•er
sneezy

snick•er (*or* snig•ger)
snide
snide•ly
snide•ness
sniff
sniff•er
sniffi•ly
sniffi•ness
snif•fle
snif•fler
snif•fly
snif•fy (•fi•er, •fi•est)
snif•ter
snig•ger *variant of* snicker
snip (snip•ping, snipped)
snipe (*pl* snipe *or* snipes)
snipe•fish (*pl* •fish *or* •fishes)
snip•er
snip•pet
sniv•el (•el•ing, •eled; *Brit* •el•ling, •elled)
sniv•el•er (*Brit* •el•ler)
sniv•el•ly
snob
snob•bery (*pl* •beries)
snob•bish
snob•bish•ly
snob•bish•ness (*or* snob•bism)
snook rude gesture

snook (*pl* snook *or* snooks) fish
snook•er
snoop
snoop•er
snoopy (snoopi•er, snoopi•est)
snooti•ly
snooti•ness
snooty (snooti•er, snooti•est)
snooze
snooz•er
snore
snor•er
snor•kel (•kel•ing, •keled; *Brit* •kel•ling, •kelled)
snort
snort•er
snot
snot•ti•ly
snot•ti•ness
snot•ty (•ti•er, •ti•est)
snout
snow
snow•ball
snow•berry (*pl* •berries)
snow•bird
snow-blind (*or* -blinded)
snow blind•ness
snow•bound
snow•cap
snow•capped
snow•drift
snow•drop

snow•fall
snow•flake
snowi•ly
snowi•ness
snow•man (*pl* •men)
snow•mo•bile
snow•plow (*Brit* •plough)
snow•shoe (•shoe•ing, •shoed)
snow•storm
snow•suit
snowy (snowi•er, snowi•est)
snub (snub•bing, snubbed)
snub-nosed
snuff
snuff•box
snuf•fle
snuf•fler '
snuf•fly
snug (*adj* snug•ger, snug•gest; *vb* snug•ging, snugged)
snug•gle
snug•ly
snug•ness
so thus; *cf* sew; sow
soak
soak•ing
soap
soap•bark
soap•berry (*pl* •berries)
soap•box
soap•stone

soap•wort

soapy (soapi•er, soapi•est)

soar to fly; cf sore

sob (sob•bing, sobbed)

so•ber

so•ber•ly

so•ber•ness

so•bri•ety

so•bri•quet (or sou•)

so-called

soc•cer

so•cia•bil•ity (or •ble•ness)

so•cia•ble

so•cia•bly

so•cial

so•cial•ism

so•cial•ist

so•cial•is•tic

so•cial•ite

so•ci•al•ity (pl •ities)

so•ciali•za•tion

so•cial•ize

so•cial•iz•er

so•cial•ly

so•ci•etal

so•ci•ety (pl •eties)

so•cio•eco•nom•ic

so•cio•logi•cal

so•ci•olo•gist

so•ci•ol•ogy

sock

sock•dolo•ger (or •dola•)

sock•et

sock•eye

sod (sod•ding, sod•ded)

soda

sod•den

sod•den•ness

*sodder incorrect spelling of solder

so•dium

sodo•mite

sodo•mize

sodo•my

sofa

soft

soft•ball

soft-boiled

soft-core (adj)

sof•ten

sof•ten•er

soft•headed

soft•hearted

soft•hearted•ly

soft•hearted•ness

soft•ly

soft•ness

soft-pedal (-pedaling, -pedaled; Brit -pedalling, -pedalled)

soft-shoe (adj)

soft-soap (vb)

soft-spoken

soft•ware

soft•wood

sog•gi•ly

sog•gi•ness

sog•gy (•gi•er, •gi•est)

soi•gné (fem •gnée)

soil

soi•ree (or •rée)

so•journ

sol•ace

so•la•num

so•lar

so•lar•ium (pl •laria or •lar•iums)

sold

sol•der (NOT sodder)

sol•der•able

sol•der•er

sol•dier

sol•dier•ly

sol•diery (pl •dieries)

sole only; underside of foot or shoe; cf soul

sole (pl sole or soles) fish; cf soul

sol•ecism

sol•ecis•tic

sole•ly

sol•emn

sol•em•ness variant spelling of solemnness

so•lem•ni•fi•ca•tion

so•lem•ni•fy (•fies, •fy•ing, •fied)

so•lem•ni•ty (pl •nities)

sol•em•ni•za•tion

sol•em•nize

sol•em•niz•er

sol•emn•ly
sol•emn•ness (*or* •em•ness)
so•lenoid
so•lic•it
so•lici•ta•tion
so•lici•tor
so•lici•tous
so•lici•tous•ly
so•lici•tous•ness
so•lici•tude
sol•id
soli•da•go (*pl* •gos)
soli•dar•ity (*pl* •ities)
so•lidi•fi•ca•tion
so•lidi•fi•er
so•lidi•fy (•fies, •fy•ing, •fied)
so•lid•ity (*pl* •ities)
sol•id•ly
sol•id•ness
solid-state (*adj*)
soli•dus (*pl* •di)
so•lilo•quize
so•lilo•quy (*pl* •quies)
sol•ip•sism
sol•ip•sist
sol•ip•sis•tic
soli•taire
soli•tari•ly
soli•tari•ness
soli•tary (*pl* •taries)
soli•tude
solo (*pl* solos)
so•lo•ist
sol•stice

sol•ubil•ity (*pl* •ities)
sol•uble
sol•uble•ness
sol•ubly
so•lu•tion
solv•abil•ity (*or* •able•ness)
solv•able
solve
sol•ven•cy
sol•vent
solv•er
So•ma•li (*pl* •li *or* •lis)
som•ber (*Brit* •bre)
som•ber•ly (*Brit* •bre•)
som•ber•ness (*Brit* •bre•)
som•brero (*pl* •breros)
some•body (*pl* •bodies)
some•day
some•how
some•one
some•place
som•er•sault (*or* sum•mer•)
some•thing
some•time (*adv*, *adj*)
some•times
some•way (*or* •ways)
some•what
some•where

som•melier
som•nam•bu•lant
som•nam•bu•late
som•nam•bu•la• tion
som•nam•bu•la•tor
som•nam•bu•lism
som•nam•bu•list
som•no•lence
som•no•lent
son male child; *cf* sun
so•nar
so•na•ta
song
song•bird
song•writer
son•ic
son-in-law (*pl* sons-)
son•net
son•net•eer
son•ny (*pl* •nies) boy; *cf* Sunni; sunny
so•nor•ity (*pl* •ities)
so•no•rous
so•no•rous•ly
so•no•rous•ness
soon
soon•er
soot
soothe
sooth•er
sooth•ing
sooth•ing•ly
sooth•say•er
sooti•ly

sooti•ness
sooty (sooti•er,
  sooti•est)
sop (sop•ping,
  sopped)
soph•ism
soph•ist
so•phis•tic (or
  •ti•cal)
so•phis•ti•cal•ly
so•phis•ti•cate
so•phis•ti•cat•ed
so•phis•ti•ca•tion
soph•ist•ry (pl
  •ries)
sopho•more
sopo•rif•ic
sopo•rifi•cal•ly
sopped
sop•pi•ly
sop•pi•ness
sop•ping
sop•py (•pi•er,
  •pi•est)
so•pra•no (pl •nos
  or •ni)
sor•bet
sor•cer•er (fem
  •ess)
sor•cery (pl •ceries)
sor•did
sor•did•ly
sor•did•ness
sore painful; a
  wound; cf soar
sore•head
sore•ly
sore•ness
sor•ghum

so•ror•ity (pl •ities)
sor•rel
sor•ri•ly
sor•ri•ness
sor•row
sor•row•er
sor•row•ful
sor•row•ful•ly
sor•row•ful•ness
sor•ry (•ri•er,
  •ri•est)
sort type; class; cf
  sought
sort•able
sort•er
sor•tie (•tie•ing,
  •tied)
so-so
sou•bri•quet
  variant spelling of
  sobriquet
souf•fle medical
  term
souf•flé (n) light
  baked dish
souf•flé (or •fléed;
  adj)
sough
sought past tense of
  seek; cf sort
soul spirit; cf sole
soul-destroying
soul•ful
soul•ful•ly
soul•ful•ness
soul•less
soul•less•ly
soul•less•ness
soul-searching

sound
sound•er
sound•ing
sound•less
sound•less•ly
sound•less•ness
sound•ly
sound•ness
sound•proof
soup
soup•çon
soupy (soupi•er,
  soupi•est)
sour
source origin;
  spring; cf sauce
sour•dough
sour•ly
sour•ness
sour•sop
souse
south
south•bound
south•east
south•easter
south•easter•ly (pl
  •lies)
south•eastern
south•er•ly (pl
  •lies)
south•ern
south•ern•er
south•ern•most
south•paw
South Pole
south-southeast
south-southwest
south•ward (adj)

south•ward (*Brit* •wards; *adv*)

south•west

south•wester wind; *cf* sou'wester

south•wester•ly (*pl* •lies)

south•western

sou•venir

sou'•west•er hat; *cf* southwester

sov•er•eign

sov•er•eign•ty (*or* sov•ran•ty; *pl* •ties)

So•vi•et of the former USSR

so•vi•et a Soviet council

sow female pig

sow (sow•ing, sowed, sown *or* sowed) plant seed; *cf* so; sew

sow•er one who sows; *cf* sewer (one who sews)

sow•ing

sown

soy

soy•bean (*or* soya bean)

spa mineral spring; *cf* spar

space

space-age (*adj*)

space•craft

space•man (*pl* •men)

spac•er

space•ship

space•walk (*vb*)

space•woman (*pl* •women)

spa•cial *variant spelling of* spatial

spac•ing

spa•cious roomy; *cf* specious

spa•cious•ly

spa•cious•ness

spade

spade•fish (*pl* •fish *or* •fishes)

spade•ful (*pl* •fuls)

spade•work

spa•ghet•ti

span (span•ning, spanned)

spang

span•gle

span•gly

Span•iard

span•iel

Span•ish

Spanish-American

spank

spank•er

spank•ing

span•ner

spar (spar•ring, sparred) fight; nautical gear; mineral; *cf* spa

spare

spare•ly

spare•ness

spar•er

spare•rib

spar•ing frugal; *cf* sparring

spar•ing•ly

spark

spar•kle

spar•kler

spar•kling

spar•ling (*pl* •lings *or* •ling)

spar•ring fighting; *cf* sparing

spar•row

sparse

sparse•ly

sparse•ness (*or* spar•sity)

Spar•tan

spasm

spas•mod•ic (*or* •modi•cal)

spas•modi•cal•ly

spas•tic

spat

spate

spa•tial (*or* •cial)

spa•tial•ly

spat•ter

spatu•la

spawn

spay

speak (speak•ing, spoke, spo•ken)

speak•able

speak•easy (*pl* •easies)

speak•er

speak•ing

spear

spear•er
spear•head
spear•mint
spec (spec•cing, specced *or* spec'd) speculation; specification; provide specifications; *cf* speck
spe•cial
spe•cial•ism
spe•cial•ist
spe•ci•al•ity *Brit spelling of* specialty
spe•ciali•za•tion
spe•cial•ize
spe•cial•ly
spe•cial•ness
spe•cial•ty (*Brit* •ity; *pl* •ties; *Brit* •ities)
spe•cies (*pl* •cies)
speci•fi•able
spe•cif•ic
spe•cifi•cal•ly
speci•fi•ca•tion
speci•fi•er
speci•fy (•fies, •fy•ing, •fied)
speci•men
spe•cious deceptively plausible; *cf* spacious
spe•cious•ly
spe•cious•ness
speck mark; *cf* spec
speck•le

spec•ta•cle
spec•ta•cled
spec•ta•cles
spec•tacu•lar
spec•tacu•lar•ly
spec•tate
spec•ta•tor
spec•ter (*Brit* •tre)
spec•tra *pl of* spectrum
spec•tral
spec•trom•eter
spec•tro•met•ric
spec•trom•etry
spec•tro•scope
spec•tro•scop•ic (*or* •scopi•cal)
spec•tros•co•py
spec•trum (*pl* •tra *or* •trums)
specu•late
specu•la•tion
specu•la•tive
specu•la•tive•ly
specu•la•tor
specu•lum (*pl* •la *or* •lums)
sped
speech
speechi•fy (•fies, •fy•ing, •fied)
speech•less
speech•less•ly
speech•less•ness
speech•maker
speech•making
speech•writer
speed (speed•ing, sped *or* speed•ed)

speed•boat
speed•er
speedi•ly
speedi•ness
speed•om•eter
speed•way
speed•well
speedy (speedi•er, speedi•est)
spe•leo•logi•cal
spe•leolo•gist
spe•leol•ogy
spell (spell•ing, spelled *or* spelt)
spell•able
spell•bind (•bind•ing, •bound)
spell•er
spell•ing
spelt
spend (spend•ing, spent)
spend•able
spend•er
spend•thrift
spent
sperm (*pl* sperm *or* sperms)
sper•mat•ic
sper•ma•to•zo•on (*or* •an; *pl* •zoa *or* •ans)
sper•mi•ci•dal
sper•mi•cide
spew
sphag•num
sphere

spheri•cal (*or* spher•ic)
spheri•cal•ly
sphe•ric•ity
sphinc•ter
sphinx (*pl* sphinxes *or* sphin•ges)
spice
spice•berry (*pl* •berries)
spice•bush
spic•er
spici•ly
spici•ness
spick-and-span (*or* spic-)
spicy (spici•er, spici•est)
spi•der
spider•wort
spi•dery
spied
spiel
spif•fy (•fi•er, •fi•est)
spig•ot
spike
spike•nard
spiki•ly
spiki•ness
spiky (spiki•er, spiki•est)
spill (spill•ing, spilled *or* spilt)
spill•age
spill•er
spill•over
spilt

spin (spin•ning, spun)
spi•na bi•fi•da
spin•ach
spi•nal
spi•nal•ly
spin•dle
spin•dly (•dli•er, •dli•est)
spin-dry (-dries, -drying, -dried)
spin-dryer
spine
spine-chiller
spine-chilling
spine•less
spine•less•ly
spine•less•ness
spin•et
spini•ness
spin•na•ker
spin•ner
spin•ning
spin-off
spin•ster
spin•ster•hood
spin•ster•ish
spiny (spini•er, spini•est)
spi•ral (•ral•ing, •raled; *Brit* •ral•ling, •ralled)
spi•ral•ly
spire
spi•rea (*Brit* •raea)
spir•it
spir•it•ed
spir•it•ed•ly
spir•it•ed•ness

spir•it•less
spir•it•less•ly
spir•it•less•ness
spir•itu•al
spir•itu•al•ism
spir•itu•al•ist
spir•itu•al•ity (*pl* •ities)
spir•itu•al•ly
spirt *variant spelling of* spurt
spit (spit•ting, spat *or* spit) expectorate
spit (spit•ting, spit•ted) pointed rod; pierce
spite
spite•ful
spite•ful•ly
spite•ful•ness
spit•fire
spit•ter
spit•tle
spit•toon
spitz
splash
splash•board
splash•down
splash•er
splashy (splashi•er, splashi•est)
splat
splat•ter
splay
splay•foot
spleen
splen•did
splen•did•ly

splen•dif•er•ous
splen•dor (*Brit* •dour)
splen•dor•ous (*or* •drous)
sple•net•ic (*or* •neti•cal)
splice
splic•er
splint
splin•ter
splin•tery
split (split•ting, split)
split-level
split-second (*adj*)
split•ter
split•ting
splotch
splotchy
splurge
splut•ter
spoil (spoil•ing, spoiled *or* spoilt)
spoil•age
spoil•er
spoils
spoil•sport
spoke
spo•ken
spoke•shave
spokes•man (*pl* •men)
spokes•person (*pl* •persons *or* •people)
spokes•woman (*pl* •women)
spo•lia•tion

spo•lia•tory
spon•dee
sponge
sponge•able
spong•er
spon•gi•ly
spon•gi•ness
spon•gy (•gi•er, •gi•est)
spon•sor
spon•sor•ship
spon•ta•neity (*pl* •neities)
spon•ta•neous
spon•ta•neous•ly
spon•ta•neous•ness
spoof
spook
spooki•ly
spooki•ness
spooky (spooki•er, spooki•est)
spool
spoon
spoon•bill
spoon•er•ism
spoon-feed (-feeding, -fed)
spoon•ful (*pl* •fuls *or* spoons•ful)
spoor (*pl* spoor *or* spoors) animal trail; *cf* spore
spo•rad•ic (*or* •radi•cal)
spo•radi•cal•ly
spore reproductive body; *cf* spoor
sport

sport•er
sporti•ly
sporti•ness
sport•ing
sport•ing•ly
spor•tive
spor•tive•ly
spor•tive•ness
sports•cast
sports•cast•er
sports•man (*pl* •men)
sports•man•ly
sports•man•ship
sports•wear
sports•woman (*pl* •women)
sporty (sporti•er, sporti•est)
spot (spot•ting, spot•ted)
spot-check (*vb*)
spot•less
spot•less•ly
spot•less•ness
spot•light (•light•ing, •light•ed *or* •lit)
spot•ted
spot•ter
spot•ti•ly
spot•ti•ness
spot•ty (•ti•er, •ti•est)
spot-weld
spot-welder
spouse
spout
spout•er

sprain
sprang
sprat
sprawl
sprawl•ing
spray
spray•er
spread (spread•ing, spread)
spread•able
spread-eagle
spread•er
spread•sheet
spree
sprig (sprig•ging, sprigged)
spright•li•ness
spright•ly (•li•er, •li•est)
spring (spring•ing, sprang or sprung, sprung)
spring•board
spring•bok (pl •bok or •boks)
spring-clean
spring-cleaning
springi•ly
springi•ness
spring•time
springy (springi•er, springi•est)
sprin•kle
sprin•kler
sprin•kling
sprint
sprint•er
sprite
spritz•er

sprock•et
sprout
spruce
spruce•ly
spruce•ness
sprung
spry (spri•er, spri•est)
spry•ly
spry•ness
spun
spunk
spunki•ly
spunki•ness
spunky (spunki•er, spunki•est)
spur (spur•ring, spurred)
spurge
spu•ri•ous
spu•ri•ous•ly
spu•ri•ous•ness
spurn
spurn•er
spurt (or spirt)
sput•nik
sput•ter
spu•tum (pl •ta)
spy (n, pl spies; vb spies, spy•ing, spied)
spy•ing
squab (pl squabs or squab)
squab•ble
squab•bler
squad
squad•ron
squal•id

squal•id•ly
squal•id•ness
squall
squal•ly
squal•or
squan•der
squan•der•er
square
square•ly
square•ness
squar•ish
squash
squash•er
squashi•ness
squashy (squashi•er, squashi•est)
squat (squat•ting, squat•ted)
squat•ness
squat•ter
squaw
squawk
squawk•er
squeak
squeak•er
squeaki•ly
squeaki•ness
squeaky
squeaky-clean
squeal
squeal•er
squeam•ish
squeam•ish•ly
squeam•ish•ness
squee•gee (•gee•ing, •geed)
squeez•able
squeeze

squeez•er

squelch

squelchy

sque•teague (pl •teague)

squib (squib•bing, squibbed)

squid (pl squid or squids)

squig•gle

squig•gly

squil•la (pl •las or •lae)

squint

squint•er

squinty

squire

squirm

squirmy

squir•rel

squirrel•fish (pl •fish or •fishes)

squirt

squirt•er

squishy (squishi•er, squishi•est)

stab (stab•bing, stabbed)

stab•ber

sta•bil•ity (pl •ities)

sta•bi•li•za•tion

sta•bi•lize

sta•bi•li•zer

sta•ble

stable•boy

sta•ble•ness

sta•bling

sta•bly

stac•ca•to

stack

stack•er

sta•dium (pl •diums or •dia)

staff (pl staffs) personnel

staff (pl staffs or staves) pole

staff (or stave; pl staffs or staves) musical term

stag

stage

stage•coach

stage•craft

stage•hand

stage-manage

stag•er

stage•struck

stag•ger

stagger•bush

stag•ger•er

stag•ger•ing

stag•ger•ing•ly

stagi•ly

stagi•ness

stag•ing

stag•nan•cy

stag•nant

stag•nate

stag•na•tion

stagy (stagi•er, stagi•est)

staid sedate; cf stayed

staid•ly

staid•ness

stain

stain•able

stain•er

stain•less

stair step; cf stare

stair•case

stairs

stair•way

stair•well

stake stick; money; cf steak

stake•out

stal•ac•tite downward projection in cave

stal•ag•mite upward projection in cave

stale

stale•ly

stale•mate

stale•ness

stalk stem; pursue; stride; cf stork

stalk•er

stalking-horse

stalky (stalki•er, stalki•est)

stall

stal•lion

stal•wart

stal•wart•ly

stal•wart•ness

sta•men (pl sta•mens or stami•na)

stami•na

stam•mer

stam•mer•er

stam•mer•ing•ly

stamp
stam•pede
stam•ped•er
stamp•er
stance
stanch (*or* staunch)
 check blood flow;
 variant spelling of
 staunch
stan•chion
stand (stand•ing,
 stood)
stand•ard
standard-bearer
stand•ard•i•za•tion
stand•ard•ize
stand•ard•iz•er
stand•by
stand•er
stand-in (*n*)
stand•ing
stand•off•ish
stand•pipe
stand•point
stand•still
stand-up (*adj, n*)
stank
stan•za
staphy•lo•coc•cal
staphy•lo•coc•cus
 (*pl* •ci)
sta•ple
sta•pler
star (star•ring,
 starred)
star•board
starch
starch•er
starchi•ly

starchi•ness
starchy (starchi•er,
 starchi•est)
star-crossed
star•dom
star•dust
stare look at; *cf*
 stair
star•er
star•fish (*pl* •fish
 or •fishes)
star•flower
star•gazer
star•gazing
stark
stark•ly
stark•ness
star•less
star•let
star•light
star•ling
star•lit
star-of-Bethlehem
starred
star•ri•ness
star•ring
star•ry (•ri•er,
 •ri•est)
starry-eyed
star-spangled
star-studded
start
start•er
star•tle
star•tling
star•tling•ly
star•va•tion
starve
starv•er

starv•ing
star•wort
stash
stat•able (*or* state•)
state
state•craft
state•hood
state•less
state•less•ness
state•li•ness
state•ly (•li•er,
 •li•est)
state•ment
state-of-the-art
 (*adj*)
state•room
state•side
states•man (*pl*
 •men)
states•man•like
states•man•ly
states•man•ship
states•woman (*pl*
 •women)
stat•ic
stati•cal•ly
stat•ice
stat•ics
sta•tion
sta•tion•ari•ness
sta•tion•ary not
 moving; *cf*
 stationery
sta•tion•er
sta•tion•ery
 writing materials;
 cf stationary
station•master
sta•tis•tic

sta•tis•ti•cal
sta•tis•ti•cal•ly
stat•is•ti•cian
sta•tis•tics
statu•ary (pl •aries)
statue
statu•esque
statu•esque•ly
statu•esque•ness
statu•ette
stat•ure
sta•tus (pl •tuses)
sta•tus quo
stat•ute
statu•to•ri•ly
statu•tory
staunch (or stanch) loyal; *variant spelling of* stanch
staunch•ly
staunch•ness
stave (stav•ing, staved *or* stove) wooden strip; to crush; *variant of* staff
staves *pl of* staff (pole; musical term) *or* stave
stay
stayed *past tense of* stay; *cf* staid
stay•er
stead
stead•fast (or sted•)
stead•fast•ly (or sted•)

stead•fast•ness (or sted•)
steadi•ly
steadi•ness
steady (adj steadi•er, steadi•est; vb stead•ies, steady•ing, stead•ied)
steak meat; *cf* stake
steak•house
steal (steal•ing, stole, sto•len) take without permission; *cf* steel
steal•er
stealth
stealthi•ly
stealthi•ness
stealthy (stealthi•er, stealthi•est)
steam
steam•boat
steam•er
steami•ly
steami•ness
steam•roller
steam•ship
steamy (steami•er, steami•est)
sted•fast *variant spelling of* steadfast
steed
steel alloy; *cf* steal

steel•head (pl •heads *or* •head)
steeli•ness
steel•work
steel•worker
steel•working
steel•works
steely (steeli•er, steeli•est)
steel•yard
steep
steep•en
steep•ish
stee•ple
steeple•chase
steeple•chas•er
steeple•jack
steep•ly
steep•ness
steer
steer•able
steer•age
steer•er
steer•ing
stel•lar
stel•late (or •lat•ed)
stem (stem•ming, stemmed)
stench
sten•cil (•cil•ing, •ciled; *Brit* •cil•ling, •cilled)
sten•cil•er (*Brit* •cil•ler)
Sten gun
ste•nog•ra•pher
steno•graph•ic (or •graphi•cal)
ste•nog•ra•phy

sten•to•rian
step (step•ping, stepped) pace; stage; etc.; *cf*
steppe
step•brother
step•child (*pl* •children)
step•daughter
step•father
stepha•no•tis
step•ladder
step•mother
step•parent
steppe grassy plain; *cf* step
step•per
step•sister
step•son
step-up (*n*)
ste•reo (*pl* •reos)
ste•reo•phon•ic
ste•reo•phoni•cal•ly
ste•reo•scope
ste•reo•scop•lc (*or* •scopi•cal)
ste•reo•scopi•cal•ly
ste•reo•type
ste•reo•typ•ic (*or* •typi•cal)
ster•ile
ste•ril•ity
steri•liz•able
steri•li•za•tion
steri•lize
steri•liz•er
ster•ling
stern

stern•ly
stern•ness
ster•num (*pl* •na *or* •nums)
ster•oid
ster•oidal
ster•to•rous
stetho•scope
stet•son
ste•vedore
stew
stew•ard
stew•ard•ess
stew•ard•ship
stewed
stich line of poetry; *cf* stitch
stick (stick•ing, stuck)
stick•er
sticki•ly
sticki•ness
stickle•back
stick•ler
stick•up
sticky (sticki•er, sticki•est)
stiff
stiff•en
stiff•en•er
stiff•ly
stiff•ness
sti•fle
sti•fler
sti•fling
sti•fling•ly
stig•ma (*pl* •mas) mark; flower part

stig•ma (*pl* •ma•ta) Crucifixion mark
stig•mat•ic
stig•ma•ti•za•tion
stig•ma•tize
stile steps over fence; *cf* style
sti•let•to (*pl* •tos *or* •toes)
still
still•birth
still•born
still life (*pl* still lifes)
still•ness
stilt
stilt•ed
stilt•ed•ly
stilt•ed•ness
stimu•lant
stimu•late
stimu•la•tion
stimu•la•tive
stimu•la•tor (*or* •lat•er)
stimu•lus (*pl* •li)
sting (sting•ing, stung)
sting•er
stin•gi•ly
stin•gi•ness
sting•ray
stin•gy (•gi•er, •gi•est)
stink (stink•ing, stank *or* stunk)
stink•er
stink•horn
stink•ing•ly

stint (*pl* stints *or* stint)
stint•er
sti•pend
sti•pen•di•ary (*pl* •aries)
stip•ple
stip•pler
stip•pling
stipu•late
stipu•la•tion
stipu•la•tor
stipu•la•tory
stir (stir•ring, stirred)
stir-fry (-fries, -frying. -fried)
stir•rable
stir•rer
stir•ring
stir•ring•ly
stir•rup
stitch needlework link; *cf* stich
stitch•er
stitch•ing
stitch•wort
stoat (*pl* stoats *or* stoat)
stock
stock•ade
stock•breeder
stock•breeding
stock•broker
stock•brokerage (*or* •broking)
stock•er
stock•holder
stock•holding

stocki•ly
stocki•ness
stock•ing
stock•inged
stock•ist
stock•man (*pl* •men)
stock•pile
stock•piler
stock•pot
stock•room
stock-still
stock•taking
stocky (stocki•er, stocki•est)
stock•yard
stodge
stodgy (stodgi•er, stodgi•est)
sto•gy (*or* •gie, •gey; *pl* •gies)
Sto•ic philosopher
sto•ic self-controlled person
stoi•cal
stoi•cal•ly
stoi•cism
stoke
stok•er
stole
stol•en
stol•id
sto•lid•ity (*or* stol•id•ness)
sto•lid•ly
sto•ma (*pl* •ma•ta *or* •mas)
stom•ach
stomach•ache

sto•mach•ic
stomp
ston•able (*or* stone•)
stone
stone-blind
stone•crop
stone•cutter
stone•cutting
stoned
stone-deaf
stone-ground
stone•less
stone•mason
stone•masonry
ston•er
stone•wall (*vb*)
stone•ware
stone•washed
stone•work
stone•worker
stoni•ly
stoni•ness
stony (*or* stoney; stoni•er, stoni•est)
stony-hearted
stony-hearted•ness
stood
stooge
stook
stool
stoop
stop (stop•ping, stopped)
stop•cock
stop•gap
stop•light
stop•over
stop•pable

stop•page
stop•per
stop•ping
stop•watch
stor•able
stor•age
sto•rax
store
store•house
store•keeper
store•keeping
store•room
sto•rey *Brit spelling of* story (level)
sto•ried recorded
sto•ried (*Brit* •reyed) multileveled
stork bird; *cf* stalk
storks•bill
storm
storm•bound
stormi•ly
stormi•ness
storm•proof
stormy (stormi•er, stormi•est)
sto•ry (*pl* •ries) tale
sto•ry (*Brit* •rey; *pl* •ries; *Brit* •reys or •ries) level
story•book
story•teller
story•telling
stout
stout•hearted
stout•hearted•ly
stout•hearted•ness

stout•ly
stout•ness
stove
stove•pipe
stov•er
stow
stow•age
stow•away
stra•bis•mus
strad•dle
strad•dler
strafe
strag•gle
strag•gler
strag•gly (•gli•er, •gli•est)
straight not curved; directly; *cf* strait
straight•away
straight•en put straight; *cf* straiten
straight•en•er
straight-faced
straight•forward
straight•forward•ly
straight•forward• ness
straight•jacket *variant spelling of* straitjacket
straight-laced *variant spelling of* strait-laced
straight•ly
straight•ness
strain
strained

strain•er
strait sea channel; difficulty; *cf* straight
strait•en embarrass financially; *cf* straighten
strait•jacket (*or* straight•)
strait-laced (*or* straight-)
strand
strand•ed
strange
strange•ly
strange•ness
stran•ger
stran•gle
strangle•hold
stran•gler
stran•gu•late
stran•gu•la•tion
strap (strap•ping, strapped)
strap•hanger
strap•less
strap•per
strap•ping
stra•ta *pl of* stratum
strata•gem
stra•tegic (*or* •tegi•cal)
stra•tegi•cal•ly
strat•egist
strat•egy (*pl* •egies)
strati•fi•ca•tion
strati•fy (•fies, •fy•ing, •fied)

strato•cu•mu•lus
(pl •li)
strato•sphere
strato•spher•ic
stra•tum (pl •ta or
•tums) layer
stra•tus (pl •ti)
cloud
straw
straw•berry (pl
•berries)
strawy
stray
stray•er
streak
streaked
streak•er
streaki•ly
streaki•ness
streak•ing
streaky (streaki•er,
streaki•est)
stream
stream•er
stream•line
stream•lined
street
street•car
street•light
street•walker
street•walking
street•wise
strength
strength•en
strength•en•er
strenu•os•ity (or
•ous•ness)
strenu•ous
strenu•ous•ly

strep•to•coc•cal (or
•cic)
strep•to•coc•cus
(pl •ci)
stress
stress•ful
stress•ful•ly
stretch
stretch•able
stretch•er
stretcher-bearer
stretchi•ness
stretchy
(stretchi•er,
stretchi•est)
strew (strew•ing,
strewed, strewed
or strewn)
strew•er
stri•ate (or •at•ed)
stria•tion
strick•en
strict
strict•ly
strict•ness
stric•ture
stride (strid•ing,
strode, strid•den)
stri•dence (or
•den•cy)
stri•dent
stri•dent•ly
strife
strik•able
strike (strik•ing,
struck, struck or
strick•en)
strike•bound
strike•breaker

strike•breaking
strik•er
strik•ing
strik•ing•ly
string (string•ing,
strung)
stringed
strin•gen•cy
strin•gent
strin•gent•ly
string•er
stringi•ly
stringi•ness
stringy (stringi•er,
stringi•est)
strip (strip•ping,
stripped)
stripe
strip•per
strip•tease
stripy (stripi•er
stripi•est)
strive (striv•ing,
strove or strived,
striv•en)
striv•er
strobe
stro•bo•scope
stro•bo•scop•ic (or
•scopi•cal)
strode
stroke
stroll
stroll•er
strong
strong-arm (adj,
vb)
strong•box
strong•hold

strong•ly
strong-minded
strong-mindedness
strong-willed
strove
struck
struc•tur•al
struc•tur•al•ism
struc•tur•al•ist
struc•tur•al•ly
struc•ture
struc•ture•less
stru•del
strug•gle
strug•gler
strum (strum•ming, strummed)
strum•mer
strung
strut (strut•ting, strut•ted)
strut•ter
strych•nine
stub (stub•bing, stubbed)
stub•bi•ly
stub•bi•ness
stub•ble
stub•bly
stub•born
stub•born•ly
stub•born•ness
stub•by (•bi•er, •bi•est)
stuc•co (n, pl •coes or •cos; vb •coes or •cos, •co•ing, •coed)
stuck

stuck-up
stud (stud•ding, stud•ded)
stu•dent
stu•dent•ship
stud•ied
stu•dio (pl •dios)
stu•di•ous
stu•di•ous•ly
stu•di•ous•ness
study (n, pl studies; vb stud•ies, study•ing, stud•ied)
stuff
stuffed
stuff•er
stuf•fi•ly
stuffi•ness
stuff•ing
stuffy (stuffi•er, stuffi•est)
stul•ti•fi•ca•tion
stul•ti•fy (•fies, •fy•ing, •fied)
stum•ble
stum•bler
stum•bling•ly
stump
stump•er
stumpi•ness
stumpy (stumpi•er, stumpi•est)
stun (stun•ning, stunned)
stung
stunk
stun•ner
stun•ning

stun•ning•ly
stunt
stunt•ed
stunt•ed•ness
stu•pefac•tion
stu•pefy (•pefies, •pefy•ing, •pefied)
stu•pen•dous
stu•pen•dous•ly
stu•pen•dous•ness
stu•pid
stu•pid•ity (pl •ities)
stu•pid•ly
stu•pid•ness
stu•por
stur•di•ly
stur•di•ness
stur•dy (•di•er, •di•est)
stur•geon
stut•ter
stut•ter•er
stut•ter•ing•ly
sty (sties, sty•ing, stied) to pen pigs
sty (or stye; pl sties or styes) pig's pen; inflamed eye spot
style form; elegance; flower part; cf stile
styl•er
styl•ing
styl•ish
styl•ish•ly
styl•ish•ness
styl•ist

sty•lis•tic
sty•lis•ti•cal•ly
styli•za•tion
styl•ize
sty•lus (*pl* •li *or* •luses)
sty•mie (*or* •my; *vb* •mies, •mie•ing *or* •my•ing, •mied; *n*, *pl* •mies)
styp•tic
su•able (*NOT* sueable)
suave
suave•ly
suav•ity (*or* suave•ness)
sub (sub•bing, subbed)
sub•aquat•ic
sub•arc•tic
sub•atom•ic
sub•com•mit•tee
sub•con•scious
sub•con•scious•ly
sub•con•scious•ness
sub•con•ti•nent
sub•con•ti•nen•tal
sub•con•tract
sub•con•trac•tor
sub•cul•tur•al
sub•cul•ture
sub•cu•ta•neous
sub•di•vide
sub•di•vi•sion
sub•du•able
sub•du•al
sub•due (•du•ing, •dued)

sub•dued•ness
sub•equa•to•rial
sub•group
sub•head•ing (*or* sub•head)
sub•hu•man
sub•ject
sub•ject•able
sub•jec•tion
sub•jec•tive
sub•jec•tive•ly
sub•jec•tiv•ism
sub•jec•tiv•ist
sub•jec•tiv•ity (*or* •tive•ness)
sub ju•di•ce
sub•ju•gate
sub•ju•ga•tion
sub•ju•ga•tor
sub•junc•tive
sub•lease
sub•les•see
sub•les•sor
sub•let (•let•ting, •let)
sub•li•mate
sub•li•ma•tion
sub•lime
sub•lime•ly
sub•limi•nal
sub•limi•nal•ly
sub•lim•ity (*pl* •ities)
sub•ma•chine gun
sub•ma•rine
sub•ma•rin•er
sub•merge (*or* •merse)

sub•mers•ibil•ity (*or* •merg•)
sub•mers•ible (*or* •merg•)
sub•mer•sion (*or* •merg•ence)
sub•mis•sion
sub•mis•sive
sub•mis•sive•ly
sub•mis•sive•ness
sub•mit (•mit•ting, •mit•ted)
sub•mit•table (*or* •mis•sible)
sub•mit•tal
sub•mit•ter
sub•nor•mal
sub•nor•mal•ity
sub•nor•mal•ly
sub•or•di•nate
sub•or•di•nate•ly
sub•or•di•nate•ness
sub•or•di•na•tion
sub•orn
sub•or•na•tion
sub•plot
sub•poe•na (•na•ing, •naed)
sub•rou•tine
sub•scribe
sub•scrib•er
sub•script
sub•scrip•tion
sub•scrip•tive
sub•sec•tion
sub•se•quent
sub•ser•vience (*or* •vi•en•cy)
sub•ser•vi•ent

sub•ser•vi•ent•ly
sub•set
sub•side
sub•sid•ence
sub•sid•er
sub•sidi•ar•ity
sub•sidi•ary (*pl*
•aries)
sub•si•diz•able
sub•si•di•za•tion
sub•si•dize
sub•si•diz•er
sub•si•dy (*pl* •dies)
sub•sist
sub•sist•ence
sub•sist•ent
sub•sist•er
sub•soil
sub•spe•cies (*pl*
•cies)
sub•stance
sub•stand•ard
sub•stan•tial
sub•stan•ti•al•ity
(*or* •tial•ness)
sub•stan•tial•ly
sub•stan•ti•ate
sub•stan•tia•tion
sub•stan•tive
sub•stan•tive•ly
sub•sta•tion
sub•sti•tuta•bil•ity
sub•sti•tut•able
sub•sti•tute
sub•sti•tu•tion
sub•stra•tum (*pl*
•ta)
sub•struc•tur•al (*or*
•tion•al)

sub•struc•ture (*or*
•tion)
sub•sum•able
sub•sume
sub•sump•tion
sub•ten•ant
sub•ter•fuge
sub•ter•ra•nean
sub•ti•tle
sub•tle
sub•tle•ness
sub•tle•ty (*pl* •ties)
sub•tly
sub•to•tal (•tal•ing,
•taled; *Brit* •tal•
ling, •talled)
sub•tract
sub•tract•er
sub•trac•tion
sub•trac•tive
sub•tropi•cal
sub•trop•ics
sub•urb
sub•ur•ban
sub•ur•ban•ite
sub•ur•bani•za•tion
sub•ur•ban•ize
sub•ur•bia
sub•ver•sion
sub•ver•sive
sub•ver•sive•ly
sub•ver•sive•ness
sub•vert
sub•vert•er
sub•way
sub-zero
suc•ceed
suc•ceed•er
suc•cess

suc•cess•ful
suc•cess•ful•ly
suc•cess•ful•ness
suc•ces•sion
suc•ces•sion•al
suc•ces•sive
suc•ces•sive•ly
suc•ces•sive•ness
suc•ces•sor
suc•cinct
suc•cinct•ly
suc•cinct•ness
suc•cor (*Brit* •cour)
aid; *cf* sucker
suc•co•tash
suc•cu•lence (*or*
•len•cy)
suc•cu•lent
suc•cu•lent•ly
suc•cumb
such
such•like
suck
suck•er one that
sucks; dupe; *cf*
succor
suck•le
suck•ler
suck•ling
suc•tion
sud•den
sud•den•ly
sud•den•ness
suds
sudsy
sue (su•ing, sued)
*sueable *incorrect
spelling of* suable
suede (*or* suède)

suer one who sues;
cf sewer (sewage
drain)
suet
su•ety
suf•fer
suf•fer•able
suf•fer•ance
suf•fer•er
suf•fer•ing
suf•fice
suf•fi•cien•cy (*pl*
•cies)
suf•fi•cient
suf•fi•cient•ly
suf•fix
suf•fo•cate
suf•fo•cat•ing•ly
suf•fo•ca•tion
suf•frage
suf•fra•gette
suf•fra•gism
suf•fra•gist
suf•fuse
suf•fu•sion
suf•fu•sive
Sufi (*pl* Sufis)
Su•fism
sug•ar
sugar•coat (*vb*)
sug•ari•ness
sug•ary
sug•gest
sug•gest•er
sug•gest•ibil•ity
sug•gest•ible
sug•ges•tion
sug•ges•tive
sug•ges•tive•ly

sug•ges•tive•ness
sui•ci•dal
sui•ci•dal•ly
sui•cide
suit clothes; set of
cards; petition; to
be appropriate; *cf*
suite
suit•abil•ity (*or*
•able•ness)
suit•able
suit•ably
suit•case
suite set of rooms;
furniture; musical
piece; *cf* suit;
sweet
suit•ing
suit•or
sul•fa (*Brit* •pha)
class of drugs; *cf*
sulfur
sul•fate (*Brit*
•phate)
sul•fide (*Brit*
•phide)
sul•fite (*Brit* •phite)
sul•fit•ic (*Brit*
•phit•)
sul•fona•mide (*Brit*
•phona•)
sul•fur (*Brit* •phur)
chemical element;
cf sulfa
sul•fur•ate (*Brit*
•phur•)
sul•fu•ra•tion (*Brit*
•phu•)

sul•fu•reous (*Brit*
•phu•)
sul•fu•ric (*Brit*
•phu•)
sul•fu•ri•za•tion
(*Brit* •phu•)
sul•fu•rize (*Brit*
•phu•)
sul•fu•rous (*Brit*
•phu•)
sulk
sulk•er
sulki•ly
sulki•ness
sulky (sulki•er,
sulki•est)
sul•len
sul•len•ly
sul•len•ness
sul•ly (•lies, •ly•ing,
•lied)
sul•pha *Brit
spelling of* sulfa
sul•phate *Brit
spelling of* sulfate
sul•phide *Brit
spelling of* sulfide
sul•phite *Brit
spelling of* sulfite
sul•phona•mide
Brit spelling of
sulfonamide
sul•phur *Brit
spelling of* sulfur
sul•tan
sul•tana
sul•tan•ate
sul•tri•ly
sul•tri•ness

sul•try (•tri•er, •tri•est)

sum (sum•ming, summed) total; add up; cf some

su•mac (or •mach)

sum•ma cum lau•de

sum•ma•ri•ly

sum•mari•ness

sum•ma•riz•able

sum•ma•ri•za•tion

sum•ma•rize

sum•mary (pl •maries) brief account; cf summery

sum•ma•tion

sum•mer

summer•house

sum•meri•ness

sum•mer•sault variant spelling of somersault

summer•time

sum•mery like summer; cf summary

summing-up (pl summings-)

sum•mit

sum•mit•ry

sum•mon (vb)

sum•mon•able

sum•mons (pl •monses)

sumo

sump

sump•tu•ous

sump•tu•ous•ly

sump•tu•ous•ness (or •tu•os•ity)

sun (sun•ning, sunned) luminous body; to bask; cf son

sun•baked

sun•bathe

sun•bather

sun•bathing

sun•beam

sun•burn

sun•burned (or •burnt)

sun•dae dessert

Sun•day day

sun•der

sun•dew

sun•dial

sun•down

sun•dress

sun-dried

sun•dry (pl •dries)

sun•fish (pl •fish or •fishes)

sun•flower

sung

sun•glasses

sunk

sunk•en

sun•less

sun•light

sun•lit

sunned

Sun•ni (pl •nis) Muslim sect; cf sonny; sunny

sun•ni•ly

sun•ni•ness

sun•ning

sun•ny (•ni•er, •ni•est) sunlit; cf sonny; Sunni

sun•rise

sun•roof

sun•set

sun•shade

sun•shine

sun•shiny

sun•spot

sun•stroke

sun•tan

sun•tanned

sun-trap

sun•up

sun•ward (Brit •wards)

sun•wise

sup (sup•ping, supped)

su•per

super•able

super•ably

super•abound

super•abun•dance

supera•bun•dant

super•an•nu•ate

super•an•nu•at•ed

super•an•nua•tion

su•perb

su•perb•ly

su•perb•ness

super•cede variant spelling of super-sede

super•charge

super•char•ger

super•cili•ous

super•cili•ous•ly
super•cili•ous•ness
super•fi•cial
super•fi•ci•al•ity
(or •cial•ness)
super•fi•cial•ly
super•fine
super•flu•ity
super•flu•ous
super•flu•ous•ly
super•flu•ous•ness
super•glue
super•he•ro (pl
•roes)
super•high•way
super•hu•man
super•im•pose
super•im•po•si•tion
super•in•tend
super•in•tend•ence
super•in•tend•en•cy
(pl •cies)
super•in•ten•dent
su•peri•or
su•peri•or•ity
super•la•tive
super•la•tive•ly
super•la•tive•ness
super•man (pl
•men)
super•mar•ket
super•natu•ral
super•natu•ral•ism
super•natu•ral•ly
super•no•va (pl
•vae or •vas)
super•nu•mer•ary
(pl •aries)
super•pow•er

super•scribe
super•script
super•scrip•tion
super•sede (or
•cede)
super•son•ic
super•soni•cal•ly
super•son•ics
super•star
super•sti•tion
super•sti•tious
super•sti•tious•ly
super•sti•tious•ness
super•store
super•struc•tur•al
super•struc•ture
super•tank•er
super•vene
super•ven•tion
super•vise
super•vi•sion
super•vi•sor
super•vi•sory
su•pine
su•pine•ly
su•pine•ness
supped
sup•per
sup•ping
sup•plant
sup•plan•ta•tion
sup•plant•er
sup•ple
supple•jack
sup•ple•ly variant
spelling of supply
(adv)
sup•plement
sup•plemen•tal

sup•plemen•ta•ry
(pl •ries)
sup•plemen•ta•tion
sup•ple•ness
sup•pli•able
sup•pli•ance
sup•pli•ant
sup•pli•cant (or
•pli•ant)
sup•pli•cate
sup•pli•ca•tion
sup•pli•ca•tory
sup•pli•er
sup•ply (n, pl •plies;
vb •plies, •ply•ing,
•plied) provision;
provide
sup•ply (or
sup•ple•ly)
pliantly
sup•port
sup•port•abil•ity
sup•port•ably
sup•port•able
sup•port•er
sup•port•ing
sup•port•ive
sup•port•ive•ly
sup•pos•able
sup•pose
sup•posed
sup•pos•ed•ly
sup•pos•er
sup•pos•ing
sup•po•si•tion
sup•po•si•tion•al
sup•po•si•tious (or
•posi•ti•tious)

sup•posi•tory (*pl* •tories)
sup•press
sup•pres•sant
sup•press•ible
sup•pres•sion
sup•pres•sive
sup•pres•sor (*or* •press•er)
sup•pu•rate
sup•pu•ra•tion
sup•pu•ra•tive
su•prema•cy
su•preme
su•preme•ly
sur•charge
sure
sure•fire
sure•footed
sure•footed•ly
sure•footed•ness
sure•ly
sure•ness
sure•ty (*pl* •ties)
surf breaking waves; *cf* serf
sur•face
sur•fac•er
sur•fac•tant
surf•bird
surf•board
surf•boat
sur•feit
surf•er
surf•ing
surf•perch
surfy
surge rush; *cf* serge
sur•geon

surgeon•fish (*pl* •fish *or* •fishes)
sur•gery (*pl* •geries)
sur•gi•cal
sur•gi•cal•ly
sur•li•ly
sur•li•ness
sur•ly (•li•er, •li•est)
sur•mis•able
sur•mise
sur•mis•er
sur•mount
sur•mount•able
sur•mount•er
sur•name
sur•pass
sur•pass•able
sur•pas•sing
sur•pass•ing•ly
sur•plice vestment
sur•plus (*pl* •pluses) excess
sur•prise (*or* •prize)
sur•pris•ing
sur•pris•ing•ly
sur•prize *variant spelling of* surprise
sur•re•al
sur•re•al•ism
sur•re•al•ist
sur•re•al•is•tic
sur•re•al•is•ti•cal•ly
sur•re•al•ly
sur•ren•der
sur•rep•ti•tious

sur•rep•ti•tious•ly
sur•rep•ti•tious•ness
sur•ro•ga•cy
sur•ro•gate
sur•round
sur•round•ing
sur•round•ings
sur•tax
sur•veil•lance
sur•veil•lant
sur•vey
sur•vey•able
sur•vey•ing
sur•vey•or
sur•viv•able
sur•viv•al
sur•vive
sur•vi•vor
sus•cep•tibil•ity (*pl* •ities)
sus•cep•tible
sus•cep•tibly
sus•cep•tible•ness
sus•cep•tive
su•shi
sus•pect
sus•pect•er
sus•pend
sus•pend•er
sus•pense
sus•pense•ful
sus•pen•sion
sus•pen•sive
sus•pen•sive•ness
sus•pen•so•ry (*pl* •ries)
sus•pi•cion
sus•pi•cious

sus•pi•cious•ly
sus•pi•cious•ness
sus•tain
sus•tain•able
sus•tain•ed•ly
sus•tain•er
sus•te•nance
su•ture
svelte
swab (swab•bing, swabbed)
swab•ber
swad•dle
swag (swag•ging, swagged)
swag•ger
swag•ger•er
swag•ger•ing•ly
Swa•hi•li (*pl* •li or •lis)
swal•low
swal•low•able
swal•low•er
swallow•tail
swam
swa•mi (*pl* •mis)
swamp
swamp•land
swampy (swampi•er, swampi•est)
swan (swan•ning, swanned)
swank
swanki•ly
swanki•ness
swanky (swanki•er, swanki•est)

swan's-down (*or* swans•)
swap (*or* swop; swap•ping, swapped *or* swop•ping, swopped)
swap•per (*or* swop•)
sward turf; *cf* sword
swarm
swarthi•ly
swarthi•ness
swarthy (swarthi•er, swarthi•est)
swash•buck•ler
swash•buck•ling
swas•ti•ka
swat (swat•ting, swat•ted)
swatch
swath (*or* swathe; *n*)
swathe (*vb*)
swat•ter
sway
sway•able
sway•er
swear (swear•ing, swore, sworn)
swear•er
swear•word
sweat (sweat•ing, sweat *or* sweat•ed)
sweat•band
sweat•er
sweati•ly

sweati•ness
sweat•shirt
sweat•shop
sweaty (sweati•er, sweati•est)
Swede native of Sweden
swede (*Brit*) rutabaga
Swe•dish
sweep (sweep•ing, swept)
sweep•er
sweep•ing
sweep•ing•ly
sweep•ing•ness
sweep•ings
sweep•stakes (*Brit* •stake)
sweet sugary; pleasant; *cf* suite
sweet-and-sour
sweet•bread
sweet•en
sweet•en•er
sweet•en•ing
sweet•heart
sweetie
sweet•ly
sweet•meat
sweet•ness
sweet•sop
sweet-talk (*vb*)
swell (swell•ing, swelled, swelled *or* swol•len)
swell•fish (*pl* •fish *or* •fishes)
swell•ing

swel•ter
swel•ter•ing
swel•ter•ing•ly
swept
swerve
swerv•er
swift
swift•ly
swift•ness
swig (swig•ging,
swigged)
swig•ger
swill
swill•er
swim (swim•ming,
swam, swum)
swim•mable
swim•mer
swim•ming•ly
swim•suit
swin•dle
swin•dler
swine (pl swine)
swing (swing•ing,
swung)
swing•er
swing•ing
swingy (swingi•er,
swingi•est)
swin•ish
swin•ish•ly
swin•ish•ness
swipe
swirl
swirly
swish
swishy
Swiss
switch

switch•back
switch•blade
switch•board
switch•er
switch•eroo
switch•over
swiv•el (•el•ing,
•eled; *Brit* •el•ling,
•elled)
swiz•zle
swol•len
swol•len•ness
swoon
swoop
swoosh
swop *variant
spelling of* swap
sword *weapon; cf*
sward
sword•bill
sword•fish (pl •fish
or •fishes)
sword•play
swords•man (pl
•men)
swords•man•ship
sword•tail
swore
sworn
swum
swung
syba•rit•ic
*sybil *incorrect
spelling of* sibyl
syca•more
syco•phan•cy (pl
•cies)
syco•phant
syco•phan•tic

syco•phan•ti•cal•ly
syl•lab•ic
syl•labi•cal•ly
syl•labi•fi•ca•tion
syl•labi•fy (•fies,
•fy•ing, •fied)
syl•la•ble
syl•la•bub (or sil•)
syl•la•bus (pl
•buses or •bi)
syl•lo•gism
syl•lo•gis•tic
syl•lo•gis•ti•cal•ly
syl•lo•gize
sylph
sylph•like
sym•bio•sis (pl
•ses)
sym•bi•ot•ic (or
•oti•cal)
sym•bi•oti•cal•ly
sym•bol (•bol•ing,
•boled; *Brit*
•bol•ling, •bolled)
sign; symbolize; *cf*
cymbal
sym•bol•ic (or
•boli•cal)
sym•boli•cal•ly
sym•bol•ism
sym•bol•ist
sym•bol•is•tic
sym•boli•za•tion
sym•bol•ize
sym•met•ri•cal
sym•met•ri•cal•ly
sym•me•try (pl
•tries)
sym•pa•thet•ic

sym•pa•theti•cal•ly
sym•pa•thize
sym•pa•thiz•er
sym•pa•thy (*pl* •thies)
sym•phon•ic
sym•phoni•cal•ly
sym•pho•nist
sym•pho•ny (*pl* •nies)
sym•po•sium (*pl* •siums *or* •sia)
symp•tom
symp•to•mat•ic
symp•to•mati•cal•ly
symp•toma•tol•ogy
syna•gogue (*or* •gog)
syn•apse
sync (*or* synch)
syn•chro•mesh
syn•chro•nism
syn•chro•nis•tic (*or* •ti•cal)
syn•chro•nis•ti•cal•ly
syn•chro•ni•za•tion
syn•chro•nize
syn•chro•niz•er
syn•chro•nous
syn•chro•nous•ly
syn•chrony
syn•co•pate
syn•co•pa•tion
syn•co•pa•tor
syn•di•cate
syn•di•ca•tion
syn•drome

syn•drom•ic
syn•er•get•ic (*or* •gis•tic)
syn•er•gic
syn•er•gism
syn•er•gy (*pl* •gies)
syn•od
syn•od•al (*or* •odi•cal)
syn•od•ic
syno•nym
syno•nym•ic (*or* •nymi•cal)
syno•nym•ity
syn•ony•mize
syn•ony•mous
syn•ony•mous•ly
syn•ony•mous•ness
syn•ony•my (*pl* •mies)
syn•op•sis (*pl* •ses)
syn•op•size
syn•op•tic
syn•op•ti•cal•ly
syn•tac•tic (*or* •ti•cal)
syn•tac•ti•cal•ly
syn•tax
syn•the•sis (*pl* •ses)
syn•the•sist
syn•the•si•za•tion
syn•the•size
syn•the•siz•er
syn•thet•ic
syn•theti•cal
syn•theti•cal•ly
syphi•lis
syphi•lit•ic

sy•phon *variant spelling of* siphon
Syr•ian
sy•rin•ga orna-mental shrub; *cf* seringa
sy•ringe
sy•rin•geal
syr•up (*or* sir•)
syr•upy (*or* sir•)
sys•tem
sys•tem•at•ic methodical; *cf* systemic
sys•tem•ati•cal•ly
sys•tema•tism
sys•tema•tist
sys•tema•ti•za•tion
sys•tema•tize
sys•tem•ic affecting whole body; *cf* systematic
sys•temi•cal•ly
sys•temi•za•tion
sys•tem•ize
sys•to•le
sys•tol•ic

T

tab (tab•bing, tabbed)
Ta•bas•co (*Trademark*)
tab•bou•leh
tab•by (*pl* •bies)
tab•er•nac•le

ta•ble
tab•leau (*pl* •leaux
  or •leaus)
table•cloth
ta•ble d'hôte (*pl*
  ta•bles d'hôte)
table-hop
  (-hopping,
  -hopped)
table-hopper
table•spoon
table•spoon•ful
  (*pl* •fuls *or*
  •spoons•ful)
tab•let
table•ware
tab•loid
ta•boo (*or* tabu; *pl*
  •boos *or* tabus)
ta•bor (*or* •bour)
tabu•lar
tabu•late
tabu•la•tion
tabu•la•tor
tacho•graph
  speed-recording
  device
ta•chom•eter
  speed-measuring
  device; *cf*
  tachymeter
tacho•met•ric
ta•chym•eter
  surveying
  instrument; *cf*
  tachometer
tac•it
tac•it•ly
taci•turn

taci•tur•nity
tack
tack•er
tacki•ly
tacki•ness
tack•le
tack•ler
tacky (tacki•er,
  tacki•est)
taco (*pl* tacos)
tact
tact•ful
tact•ful•ly
tact•ful•ness
tac•tic
tac•ti•cal
tac•ti•cal•ly
tac•ti•cian
tac•tics
tac•tile
tac•til•ity
tact•less
tact•less•ness
tac•tual
tad
tad•pole
taf•fe•ta
taf•fy (*pl* •fies)
tag (tag•ging,
  tagged)
ta•glia•tel•le
ta•hi•ni
Ta•hi•tian
tail appendage;
  follow; *cf* tale
tail•back
tail•board
tail•gate
tail•ing

tail•less
tail•light (*or* •lamp)
tai•lor
tailor-made
tail•piece
tail•pipe
tail•plane
tail•spin
tail•wind
taint
take (tak•ing, took,
  tak•en)
take•down
tak•en
take•off
take•out (*Brit*
  •away)
take•over
tak•er
tak•ing
tak•ings
talc (talck•ing,
  talcked *or*
  talc•ing, talced)
tal•cum
tale story, *cf* tail
tale•bearer
tal•ent
tal•ent•ed
tale-teller
tal•is•man (*pl*
  •mans)
tal•is•man•ic
talk
talka•tive
talka•tive•ly
talka•tive•ness
talk-back (*n*)
talk•er

talkie film; *cf* talky
talking-to (*pl* -tos)
talky (talki•er,
  talki•est)
  talkative; *cf* talkie
tall
tall•boy
tall•ish
tall•ness
tal•low
tal•ly (*vb* •lies,
  •ly•ing, •lied; *n, pl*
  •lies)
Tal•mud
Tal•mud•ic (*or*
  •mudi•cal)
Tal•mud•ist
tal•on
tal•oned
tam•able (*or* tame•)
ta•ma•le
ta•man•dua
tama•rack
tama•rin monkey
tama•rind tree,
  fruit
tama•risk tree
tam•bour
tam•bou•rine
tam•bou•rin•ist
tame
tame•able *variant
  spelling of
  tamable*
tame•ly
tame•ness
tam•er
tamp
tam•per

tam•per•er
tam•pon
tan (tan•ning,
  tanned)
tana•ger
tan•dem
tan•doori
tang
tan•gen•cy
tan•gent
tan•gen•tial
tan•gen•tial•ly
tan•ge•rine
tan•gibil•ity (*or*
  •gible•ness)
tan•gible
tan•gibly
tangi•ness
tan•gle
tan•gler
tan•gly
tan•go (*n, pl* •gos;
  vb •gos, •go•ing,
  •goed)
tangy (tangi•er,
  tangi•est)
tank
tank•age
tank•ard
tank•er
tank•ful (*pl* •fuls)
tanned
tan•ner
tan•nery (*pl*
  •neries)
tan•nic
tan•nin
tan•ning
tan•sy (*pl* •sies)

tan•ta•li•za•tion
tan•ta•lize
tan•ta•liz•er
tan•ta•liz•ing•ly
tan•ta•mount
tan•trum
Tan•za•nian
Tao•ism
Tao•ist
tap (tap•ping,
  tapped)
tap•as
tap-dance (*vb*)
tap danc•er
tape
tap•er one who
  tapes; *cf* tapir
ta•per become
  narrower; candle;
  cf tapir
tape-record
tap•es•tried
tap•es•try (*pl*
  •tries)
tape•worm
tapio•ca
ta•pir (*pl* •pir *or*
  •pirs) animal; *cf*
  taper
tap•pable
tapped
tap•per
tap•pet
tap•ping
tap•root
tar (tar•ring,
  tarred)
ta•ra•ma•sa•la•ta
tar•an•tel•la dance

ta•ran•tu•la (*pl* •las *or* •lae) spider

tar•di•ly

tar•di•ness

tar•dy (•di•er, •di•est)

tare plant; receptacle weight; *cf* tear

tar•get

tar•iff

Tar•mac (*Trademark*) road-surfacing material

tar•mac road, runway, etc., paved with Tarmac

tar•na•tion

tar•nish

tar•nish•able

taro (*pl* taros) plant

ta•rot card

tar•pau•lin

tar•pon (*pl* •pon *or* •pons)

tar•ra•gon

tarred

tar•ri•ness

tar•ring

tar•ry (*vb* •ries, •ry•ing, •ried; *adj* •ri•er, •ri•est)

tar•sal

tar•sus (*pl* •si)

tart

tar•tan

Tar•tar *variant spelling of* Tatar

tar•tar deposit on teeth; fearsome person; chemical substance; *cf* Tatar

tar•tar (*or* •tare) sauce

tar•tar•ic

tar•tar•ous

tart•let

tart•ly

tart•ness

tar•trate

tarty (tarti•er, tarti•est)

task

task•master (*fem* •mistress)

tas•sel (•sel•ing, •seled; *Brit* •sel•ling, •selled)

tas•sel•ly

tast•able

taste

taste•ful

taste•ful•ly

taste•ful•ness

taste•less

taste•less•ly

taste•less•ness

tast•er

tasti•ly

tasti•ness

tasty (tasti•er, tasti•est)

tat (tat•ting, tat•ted)

Ta•tar (*or* Tar•)

Mongoloid people; *cf* tartar

tat•ted *past tense of* tat; *cf* tattered

tat•ter

tat•tered ragged; *cf* tatted

tat•ting

tat•tle

tat•tler

tattle•tale

tat•too (*n, pl* •toos; *vb* toos, •too•ing, •tooed)

tat•too•ist (*or* •er)

tat•ty (•ti•er, •ti•est)

tau Greek letter; *cf* tor; tore

taught *past tense of* teach; *cf* taut

taunt

taunt•er

taunt•ing•ly

taupe brownish gray, *cf* tope

taut tight; *cf* taught

taut•en

taut•ly

taut•ness

tau•tog (*or* •taug)

tau•to•logi•cal (*or* •log•ic, tau•tolo•gous)

tau•to•logi•cal•ly

tau•tolo•gize

tau•tol•ogy (*pl* •gies)

tav•ern

taw•dri•ly
taw•dri•ness
taw•dry (•dri•er,
　•dri•est)
taw•ny
tax
tax•abil•ity (or
　•able•ness)
tax•able
taxa•tion
tax-deductible
tax•er
tax-exempt
taxi (n, pl taxis or
　taxies; vb taxis or
　taxies, taxi•ing or
　taxy•ing, tax•ied)
taxi•cab
taxi•der•mal (or
　•mic)
taxi•der•mist
taxi•der•my
taxi•meter
tax•ing
taxi•plane
taxi•way
tax•man (pl •men)
tax•on (pl taxa or
　•ons)
taxo•nom•ic (or
　•nomi•cal)
taxo•nomi•cal•ly
tax•ono•mist
tax•ono•my
tax•payer
tax•paying
tay•ra
T-bone
tea beverage; cf tee

teach (teach•es,
　teach•ing, taught)
teach•able
teach•er
teach-in
teach•ing
tea•cup
tea•cup•ful (pl
　•fuls)
teak
tea•kettle
teal (pl teal or
　teals)
team group; cf
　teem
team•mate
team•ster
team•work
tea•pot
tear (tear•ing, tore,
　torn) rip; cf tare
tear drop from
　eye; cf tier
tear•able
tear•er
tear•ful
tear•ful•ly
tear•ful•ness
tear•ing
tear•jerker
tear•less
tear-stained
teary-eyed
tease
tea•sel
teas•er
teas•ing•ly
tea•spoon

tea•spoon•ful (pl
　•fuls)
teat
tea•time
techi•ly variant
　spelling of tetchily
techi•ness variant
　spelling of tetchi-
　ness
tech•nic variant
　spelling of tech-
　nique
tech•ni•cal
tech•ni•cal•ity (pl
　•ities)
tech•ni•cal•ly
tech•ni•cian
Tech•ni•col•or
　(Trademark)
tech•nics
tech•nique (or •nic)
tech•noc•ra•cy (pl
　•cies)
tech•no•crat
tech•no•crat•ic
tech•no•logi•cal
tech•no•logi•cal•ly
tech•nolo•gist
tech•nol•ogy (pl
　•ogies)
tech•no•struc•ture
techy variant
　spelling of tetchy
tec•ton•ic
tec•toni•cal•ly
tec•ton•ics
ted•dy (pl •dies)
te•di•ous
te•di•ous•ly

te•di•ous•ness
te•dium
tee (tee•ing, teed)
  golf term; T-
  shaped part; *cf*
  tea
teem abound; *cf*
  team
teem•ing
teen
teen•age
teen•aged
teen•ager
tee•ny (•ni•er,
  •ni•est)
teeny•bopper
tee•pee *variant*
  spelling of tepee
tee shirt *variant*
  spelling of T-shirt
tee•ter
teeth *pl of* tooth
teethe (*vb*)
teeth•ing
tee•to•tal
tee•to•tal•er (*Brit*
  •tal•ler)
tee•to•tal•ism
Tef•lon
  (*Trademark*)
tele•cam•era
tele•cast (•cast•ing,
  •cast *or* •cast•ed)
tele•cast•er
tele•com•mu•ni•ca•
  tion
tele•com•mu•ni•ca•
  tions
tele•com•mut•ing

tele•con•fer•ence
tele•dra•ma
tele•gen•ic
tele•gram
  (•gram•ming,
  •grammed)
tele•graph
te•leg•ra•pher (*or*
  •phist)
tele•graph•ic
tele•graphi•cal•ly
te•leg•ra•phy
tele•ki•ne•sis
tele•ki•net•ic
teleo•logi•cal (*or*
  •log•ic)
tele•ol•ogy
tele•mar•ket•ing
tele•path•ic
tele•pathi•cal•ly
te•lepa•thist
te•lepa•thize
te•lepa•thy
tele•phone
tele•phon•er
tele•phon•ic
te•lepho•nist
te•lepho•ny
tele•photo (*pl*
  •photos)
tele•play
tele•print•er
Tele•Promp•Ter
  (*Trademark*)
tele•scope
tele•scop•ic
tele•scopi•cal•ly
te•les•co•py
tele•text

tele•thon
Tele•type
  (*Trademark*)
tele•van•gel•ist
tele•vise (*NOT*
  televize)
tele•vi•sion
tele•vis•ual
tele•writ•er
tel•ex
tell (tell•ing, told)
tell•able
tell•er
tell•ing
tell•ing•ly
tell•tale
tel•ly (*pl* •lies)
te•mer•ity
temp
tem•per
tem•pera painting
  medium; *cf*
  tempura
tem•pera•ment
tem•pera•men•tal
tem•pera•men•
  tal•ly
tem•per•ance
tem•per•ate
tem•per•ate•ly
tem•per•ate•ness
tem•pera•ture
tem•pest
tem•pes•tu•ous
tem•pes•tu•ous•ly
tem•pes•tu•ous•
  ness
tem•plate (*or* •plet)
tem•ple

tem•po (*pl* •pos *or* •pi)
tem•po•ral
tem•po•ral•ly of time
tem•po•rari•ly not permanently
tem•po•rari•ness
tem•po•rary (*pl* •raries)
tem•po•ri•za•tion
tem•po•rize
tem•po•riz•er
tempt
tempt•able
temp•ta•tion
tempt•er
tempt•ing
tempt•ing•ly
tempt•ress
tem•pu•ra
  Japanese food; *cf* tempera
ten
ten•abil•ity (*or* •able•ness)
ten•able
ten•ably
te•na•cious
te•na•cious•ly
te•nac•ity (*or* •na•cious•ness)
ten•an•cy (*pl* •cies)
ten•ant
ten•ant•able
ten•ant•ry (*pl* •ries)
tend
ten•den•cy (*pl* •cies)

ten•den•tious (*or* •cious)
ten•den•tious•ness
ten•der
ten•der•er
tender•foot (*pl* •foots *or* •feet)
tender•hearted
tender•hearted•ly
tender•hearted•ness
ten•deri•za•tion
ten•der•ize
ten•der•iz•er
ten•der•loin
ten•der•ly
ten•der•ness
ten•don
ten•dril
ten•ebrous (*or* te•neb•ri•ous)
ten•ement
ten•et
ten•fold
ten•ner 10-dollar bill; *cf* tenor
ten•nis
ten•on
ten•or singer; general drift; *cf* tenner
ten•pin bowling pin
ten•pins game
tense
tense•ly
tense•ness
ten•sile
ten•sil•ity
ten•sion

ten•sion•al
ten•sor
tent
ten•ta•cle
ten•ta•cled
ten•tacu•lar
tent•age
ten•ta•tive
ten•ta•tive•ly
ten•ta•tive•ness
tent•ed
ten•ter
tenter•hook
tenth
tenu•ity
tenu•ous
tenu•ous•ly
tenu•ous•ness
ten•ure
tenu•rial
te•pee (*or* tee•)
tep•id
tep•id•ly
te•pid•ity (*or* tep•id•ness)
te•qui•la
ter•cen•te•nary (*or* •ten•nial; *pl* •naries *or* •nials)
ter•gi•ver•sate
ter•gi•ver•sa•tion
ter•gi•ver•sa•tor
teri•ya•ki
term
ter•ma•gant
ter•mi•nable
ter•mi•nal
ter•mi•nal•ly
ter•mi•nate

ter•mi•na•tion
ter•mi•na•tor
ter•mi•na•tory
ter•mi•no•logi•cal
ter•mi•nolo•gist
ter•mi•nol•ogy (*pl* •ogies)
ter•mi•nus (*pl* •ni or •nuses)
ter•mite
term•less
tern bird; *cf* turn
ter•na•ry (*pl* •ries)
ter•race
terra-cotta
ter•ra fir•ma
ter•rain
ter•ra•pin
ter•raz•zo
ter•rene earthly; *cf* terrine; tureen
ter•res•trial
ter•res•tri•al•ly
ter•ri•ble
ter•ri•ble•ness
ter•ri•bly
ter•ri•er
ter•rif•ic
ter•rifi•cal•ly
ter•ri•fi•er
ter•ri•fy (•fies, •fy•ing, •fied)
ter•ri•fy•ing•ly
ter•rine dish; pâté; *cf* terrene; tureen
ter•ri•to•rial
ter•ri•to•ri•al•ism
ter•ri•to•ri•al•ist
ter•ri•to•ri•al•ity

ter•ri•to•ri•ali•za•tion
ter•ri•to•ri•al•ize
ter•ri•to•rial•ly
ter•ri•tory (*pl* •tories)
ter•ror
ter•ror•ism
ter•ror•ist
ter•rori•za•tion
ter•ror•ize
ter•ror•iz•er
terror-stricken (*or* -struck)
terse
terse•ly
terse•ness
ter•tiary (*pl* •tiaries)
ter•va•lent *variant of* trivalent
tes•sel•latc
tes•sel•la•tion
test
test•abil•ity
test•able
tes•ta•cy
tes•ta•ment
tes•ta•men•tal
tes•ta•men•tary
tes•tate
tes•ta•tor
tes•ta•trix (*pl* •ta•tri•ces)
test-drive (*vb*; -driving, -drove, -driven)
test•er
tes•tes *pl of* testis

tes•ti•cle
tes•ticu•lar
tes•ti•fi•ca•tion
tes•ti•fi•er
tes•ti•fy (•fies, •fy•ing, •fied)
testi•ly
tes•ti•mo•nial
tes•ti•mo•ny (*pl* •nies)
testi•ness
test•ing
test•ing•ly
tes•tis (*pl* •tes)
tes•tos•ter•one
test-tube (*adj*)
tes•ty (•ti•er, •ti•est)
teta•nus
tetchi•ly (*or* techi•)
tetchi•ness (*or* techi•)
tetchy (*or* techy; tetchi•er, tetchi•est *or* techi•er, techi•est)
tête-à-tête (*pl* -têtes *or* -tête)
teth•er
tether•ball
tet•ra (*pl* •ra *or* •ras)
tetra•chlo•ride
tet•rad
tetra•gon
te•trago•nal
tetra•he•dral
tetra•he•dron (*pl* •drons *or* •dra)

te•tral•ogy (*pl* •ogies)
tetra•pod
te•trarch
Teu•ton•ic
text
text•book
tex•tile
tex•tu•al of text; *cf* textural
tex•tu•al•ly
tex•tur•al of texture; *cf* textual
tex•tur•al•ly
tex•ture
Thai (*pl* Thai *or* Thais)
tha•lido•mide
thal•lium
than
thank
thank•ful
thank•ful•ly
thank•ful•ness
thank•less
thank•less•ness
Thanks•giving holiday
thanks•giving giving thanks
that
thatch
thatch•er
thatch•ing
thaw
the definite article; *cf* thee
thea•ter (*Brit* •tre)

theater•goer (*Brit* theatre•)
the•at•ri•cal
the•at•ri•cal•ity (*or* •cal•ness)
the•at•ri•cal•ly
the•at•ri•cals dramatic entertainments
the•at•rics exaggerated mannerisms
thee pronoun; *cf* the
theft
their of them; *cf* there; they're
theirs
the•ism
the•ist
the•is•tic (*or* •ti•cal)
the•is•ti•cal•ly
them
the•mat•ic
the•mati•cal•ly
theme
them•selves
then
thence
thence•forth
thence•forward
the•oc•ra•cy (*pl* •cies)
theo•crat•ic (*or* •crati•cal)
the•odo•lite
theo•lo•gian
theo•logi•cal

theo•logi•cal•ly
the•olo•gist
the•olo•gize
the•ol•ogy (*pl* •ogies)
theo•rem
theo•reti•cal (*or* •ret•ic)
theo•reti•cal•ly
theo•reti•cian
theo•ret•ics
theo•rist
theo•ri•za•tion
theo•rize
theo•riz•er
theo•ry (*pl* •ries)
theo•soph•ic (*or* •sophi•cal)
theo•sophi•cal•ly
the•oso•phist
the•oso•phy
thera•peu•tic
thera•peu•ti•cal•ly
thera•peu•tics
thera•pist
thera•py (*pl* •pies)
there in that place; *cf* their; they're
there•about (*or* •abouts)
there•after
there•at
there•by
there•fore
there•in
there•of
there•to
there•upon
ther•mal

ther•mal•ly
ther•mal•ize
ther•mic
ther•mo•cou•ple
ther•mo•dy•nam•ic
(or •nami•cal)
ther•mo•dy•nami•cal•ly
ther•mo•dy•nam•ics
ther•mo•elec•tric
(or •tri•cal)
ther•mo•elec•tri•cal•ly
ther•mo•elec•tric•ity
ther•mom•eter
ther•mo•nu•clear
ther•mo•plas•tic
Ther•mos
(Trademark)
ther•mo•set•ting
ther•mo•stat
ther•mo•stat•ic
ther•mo•stati•cal•ly
the•sau•rus (pl •ri
or •ruses)
these
the•sis (pl •ses)
Thes•pian (or thes•)
the•ta
they
they're they are; cf
their; there
thia•min (or •mine)
thick
thick•en

thick•en•er
thick•en•ing
thick•et
thick•head
thick•headed
thick•ly
thick•ness
thick•set
thick-skinned
thick-witted
thick-witted•ness
thief (pl thieves)
thieve
thiev•ery (pl •eries)
thiev•ing
thiev•ish
thiev•ish•ly
thiev•ish•ness
thigh
thigh•bone
thim•ble
thim•ble•ful (pl •fuls)
thimble•weed
thimble•wit
thin (adj thin•ner,
thin•nest; vb thin•ning, thinned)
thine
thing
thinga•ma•bob
thinga•ma•jig (or thingu•)
think (think•ing, thought)
think•able
think•er
think•ing
thin•ly

thin•ner
thin•ness
thin-skinned
thio•sul•fate (Brit •phate)
third
third-class (adj)
third•ly
third-party (adj)
third-rate
thirst
thirsti•ly
thirsti•ness
thirsty (thirsti•er, thirsti•est)
thir•teen
thir•teenth
thir•ti•eth
thir•ty (pl •ties)
this
this•tle
thistle•down
this•tly
thong
tho•rac•ic
thor•ax (pl thor•axes or tho•ra•ces)
thorn
thorn•bill
thorni•ly
thorni•ness
thorny (thorni•er, thorni•est)
thor•ough
Thorough•bred
horse
thorough•bred
purebred

thorough•fare
thorough•going
thor•ough•ly
thor•ough•ness
those
thou
though
thought
thought•ful
thought•ful•ly
thought•ful•ness
thought•less
thought•less•ly
thought•less•ness
thought-out
thou•sand
thou•sandth
thrall
thrall•dom (or
 thral•)
thrash
thrash•er
thrash•ing
thread
thread•bare
thread•er
threadi•ness
thread•worm
thready (threadi•er,
 threadi•est)
threat
threat•en
threat•en•er
threat•en•ing•ly
three
three-decker
three-dimensional
three-
 dimensional•ly

three•fold
three-legged
three-piece
three-ply
three-quarter (adj)
three•score
three•some
three-wheeler
thresh
thresh•er
thresh•old
threw *past tense of*
 throw; *cf* through
thrice
thrift
thrifti•ly
thrifti•ness
thrift•less
thrift•less•ly
thrift•less•ness
thrifty (thrifti•er,
 thrifti•est)
thrill
thrill•er
thrill•ing
thrips (*pl* thrips)
thrive (thriv•ing,
 throve *or* thrived,
 thrived *or*
 thriv•en)
throat
throati•ly
throati•ness
throaty (throati•er,
 throati•est)
throb (throb•bing,
 throbbed)
throe *violent pang;*
 cf throw

throm•bose (*vb*)
throm•bo•sis (*pl*
 •ses)
throm•bot•ic
throne *ceremonial*
 seat; cf thrown
throng
throt•tle
throt•tler
through (*or* thru)
 by way or means
 of; up to and in-
 cluding; cf threw
through•out
through•put
through•way
 variant spelling of
 thruway
throve
throw (throw•ing,
 threw, thrown)
 cast; cf throe
throw-away (*adj, n*)
throw•back
throw•er
thrown *past tense*
 of throw; *cf* throne
thru *variant*
 spelling of through
thrum
 (thrum•ming,
 thrummed)
thrum•mer
thrush
thrust
thrust•er
thru•way (*or*
 through•)

thud (thud•ding, thud•ded)

thug

thug•gery

thug•gish

thu•ja

thumb

thumb•nail

thumb•nut

thumb•print

thumb•screw

thumb•stall

thumb•tack

thump

thump•er

thump•ing

thun•der

thunder•bird

thunder•bolt

thunder•clap

thunder•cloud

thun•der•er

thunder•head

thun•der•ing

thun•der•ous

thunder•shower

thunder•storm

thunder•struck (or •stricken)

thun•dery

Thurs•day

thus

thwack

thwart

thy

thyme herb; cf time

thy•mus (pl •muses or •mi)

thymy (or thym•ey)

thy•roid

thy•self

ti

ti•ara

ti•ar•aed

Ti•bet•an

tibia (pl tibiae or tibias)

tib•ial

tic twitch

tick parasite; mark; click; mattress case

tick•er

tick•et

tick•ing

tick•le

tick•ler

tick•lish

tick•lish•ness

tick•ly

tick•tack (or tic•tac)

tick•tack•toe (or tic-tac-toe)

tick•tock

tid•al

tid•al•ly

tid•bit (Brit tit•)

tiddly•winks

tide rise and fall of sea level; cf tied

tide•mark

tide•water

tide•way

ti•di•ly

ti•di•ness

tid•ings

tidy (adj tidi•er, tidi•est; vb ti•dies, tidy•ing, ti•died; n, pl ti•dies)

tie (ty•ing, tied)

tie•back

tie•breaker (or •break)

tied past tense of tie; cf tide

tie-dye (-dyeing, -dyed)

tie-in (n)

tie•pin

tier layer; cf tear

tiered

tiff

ti•ger

tiger•eye (or tiger's-eye)

ti•ger•ish

tight

tight•en

tight•en•er

tight-fisted

tight-knit

tight-lipped

tight•ly

tight•ness

tight•rope

tights

tight•wad

ti•gon (or tig•lon)

ti•gress

tike variant spelling of tyke

til•de

tile

tile•fish (pl •fish or •fishes)

til•er
til•ing
till
till•able
till•age
till•er
tilt
tilt•er
tilth
tim•ber wood; *cf* timbre
tim•bered
tim•ber•ing
timber•land
timber•work
tim•bre tone quality; *cf* timber
time duration; to regulate; *cf* thyme
time•card
time-consuming
time-honored (*Brit* -honoured)
time•keeper
time•keeping
time-lapse (*adj*)
time•less
time•less•ly
time•less•ness
time•li•ness
time•ly (•li•er, •li•est)
time-out (*n*)
time•piece
tim•er
time•saver
time•saving
time•server
time•serving

time•table
time•work
time•worker
time•worn
tim•id
ti•mid•ity (*or* tim•id•ness)
tim•id•ly
tim•ing
tim•or•ous
tim•or•ous•ly
tim•or•ous•ness
tim•pa•ni (*or* tym•; *pl n*) kettledrums; *cf* tympanum
tim•pa•nist (*or* tym•)
tin (tin•ning, tinned)
tina•mou
tinc•ture
tin•der
tinder•box
tin•dery
tine
tin•foil
ting
tinge (tinge•ing *or* ting•ing, tinged)
tin•gle
tin•gly
tin•horn
ti•ni•ly
ti•ni•ness
tink•er
tink•er•er
tin•kle
tin•kly
tinned

tin•ni•ly
tin•ni•ness
tin•ning
tin•ni•tus
tin•ny (•ni•er, •ni•est)
tin-plate (*vb*)
tin•sel (•sel•ing, •seled; *Brit* •sel•ling, •selled)
tin•smith
tint
tint•ed
tint•er
tin•tin•nabu•la•tion
tin•ware
tin•work work in tin
tin•works smelting establishment
tiny (tini•er, tini•est)
tip (tip•ping, tipped)
tip-off (*n*)
tip•per
tip•ping
tip•ple
tip•pler
tip•si•ly
tip•si•ness
tip•ster
tip•sy (•si•er, •si•est)
tip•toe (•toe•ing, •toed)
tip-top
ti•rade
tire exhaust

tire (*Brit* tyre)
 wheel ring
tired
tire•less
tire•less•ly
tire•less•ness
tire•some
tire•some•ly
tire•some•ness
tir•ing
tiro *variant Brit spelling of* tyro
ti•sane
tis•sue
tit
ti•tan•ic
ti•ta•nium
tit•bit *Brit spelling of* tidbit
ti•ter (*Brit* •tre)
tithe
tit•il•late
tit•il•la•tion
titi•vate (*or* tit•ti•)
titi•va•tion (*or* tit•ti•)
ti•tle
ti•tled
title•holder
tit•mouse (*pl* •mice)
ti•trate
ti•tra•tion
ti•tre *Brit spelling of* titer
tit•ter
tit•ter•er
tit•ti•vate *variant spelling of* titivate

tit•tle
tittle-tattle
tittle-tattler
titu•lar (*or* •lary; *pl* •lars *or* •laries)
tiz•zy (*pl* •zies)
Tlin•git (*pl* •git *or* •gits)
to toward; *cf* too; two
toad
toad•fish (*pl* •fish *or* •fishes)
toad•flax
toad•stool
toady (*n, pl* toad•ies; *vb* toad•ies, toady•ing, toad•ied)
toady•ism
to-and-fro (*adj*)
toast
toast•er
toast•master (*fem* •mistress)
to•bac•co (*pl* •cos *or* •coes)
to•bac•co•nist
to•bog•gan
to•bog•gan•er (*or* •ist)
toby (*pl* tobies)
toc•ca•ta
toc•sin alarm bell; *cf* toxin
to•day
tod•dle
tod•dler
tod•dy (*pl* •dies)

to-do (*pl* -dos)
tody (*pl* todies)
toe (toe•ing, toed) digit of the foot; *cf* tow
toe•cap
toed
toe•hold
toe•ing
toe•nail
tof•fee (*or* •fy; *pl* •fees *or* •fies)
tofu
toga
to•geth•er
to•geth•er•ness
tog•gle
toil
toil•er
toi•let bathroom apparatus
toi•let (*or* •lette) act of dressing
toi•let•ry (*pl* •ries)
toil•some
To•kay
to•ken
to•ken•ism
tol•booth *variant spelling of* tollbooth
told
tol•er•able
tol•er•able•ness (*or* •abil•ity)
tol•er•ably
tol•er•ance
tol•er•ant
tol•er•ant•ly

tol•er•ate
tol•era•tion
tol•era•tor
toll
toll•booth (*or* tol•)
toll•gate
toll•house
Tol•tec (*pl* •tecs *or* •tec)
tolu•ene
tom
toma•hawk
tom•al•ley
to•ma•to (*pl* •toes)
tomb
tom•boy
tom•boy•ish
tomb•stone
tom•cat
tom•cod (*pl* •cod *or* •cods)
tome
tom•fool
tom•fool•ery (*pl* •eries)
tommy•rot
to•mor•row
tom•tit
tom-tom
ton imperial weight; *cf* tonne; tun
ton•al
to•nal•ity (*pl* •ities)
ton•al•ly
tone
tone-deaf
tone•less
tone•less•ly

tone•less•ness
ton•er
tongs
tongue (tongu•ing, tongued)
tongue-in-cheek
tongue-lash
tongue-lashing
tongue-tie
tongue-tied
ton•ic
toni•cal•ly
to•nic•ity
to•night
ton•ing
ton•ka bean
ton•nage
tonne metric weight; *cf* ton; tun
ton•sil
ton•sil•lar (*or* •lary)
ton•sil•lec•to•my (*pl* •mies)
ton•sil•li•tis
ton•so•rial
ton•sure
too also; excessively; *cf* to; two
took
tool implement; *cf* tulle
tool•box
tool•er
tool•ing
tool•less
tool•maker
tool•making
toot

toot•er
tooth (*pl* teeth)
tooth•ache
tooth•brush
toothed
toothi•ly
toothi•ness
tooth•less
tooth•paste
tooth•pick
tooth•powder
tooth•some
tooth•wort
toothy (tooth•ier, toothi•est)
too•tle
toot•sy (*or* •sie; *pl* •sies)
top (top•ping, topped)
to•paz
top•coat
top-drawer (*adj*)
top-dress (*vb*)
tope to drink; *cf* taupe
to•pee (*or* topi; *pl* •pees *or* topis) tropical helmet; *cf* toupee
top-flight (*adj*)
top-heavy
to•pia•rist
to•pi•ary (*pl* •aries)
top•ic
topi•cal
topi•cal•ity
topi•cal•ly
top•knot

top•less
top•less•ness
top-level (*adj*)
top•min•now (*pl*
•nows *or* •now)
top•most
top•notch
to•pog•ra•pher
topo•graph•ic (*or*
•graphi•cal)
topo•graphi•cal•ly
to•pog•ra•phy (*pl*
•phies) mapping;
cf topology
topo•log•ic (*or*
•logi•cal)
topo•logi•cal•ly
to•polo•gist
to•pol•ogy branch
of geometry; *cf*
topography
topped
top•per
top•ping
top•ple
top•sail
top-secret (*adj*)
top•side
top•soil
top•spin
topsy-turvy
tor hill; *cf* tau; tore
To•rah
torch
torch•bearer
torch•light
torch•wood
tore *past tense of*
tear; *cf* tau; tor

torea•dor
tor•ment
tor•ment•ing•ly
tor•men•tor (*or*
•ment•er)
torn
tor•nad•ic
tor•na•do (*pl* •does
or •dos) storm; *cf*
tournedos
tor•pe•do (*n, pl*
•does; *vb* •does,
•do•ing, •doed)
tor•pid
tor•pid•ity (*or*
•ness)
tor•pid•ly
tor•por
tor•rent
tor•ren•tial
tor•ren•tial•ly
tor•rid
tor•rid•ity (*or*
•ness)
tor•rid•ly
tor•sion
tor•sion•al
tor•so (*pl* •sos *or*
•si)
tort legal term
torte (*pl* tor•ten *or*
tortes) cake
tor•tel•li•ni
tor•til•la
tor•toise
tortoise•shell
tor•tu•os•ity (*pl*
•ities)
tor•tu•ous twisting;

devious; *cf*
torturous
tor•tu•ous•ly
tor•tu•ous•ness
tor•ture
tor•tur•er
tor•tur•ous causing
pain; *cf* tortuous
Tory (*pl* Tories)
tosh
toss
toss•er
toss•up
tos•ta•da (*or* •do)
tot (tot•ting,
tot•ted)
to•tal (•tal•ing,
•taled; *Brit*
•tal•ling, •talled)
to•tali•tar•ian
to•tali•tar•ian•ism
to•tal•ity (*pl* •ities)
to•tal•ize
to•tal•iz•er
to•tal•ly
tote
to•tem
to•tem•ic
to•tem•ism
tot•er
tot•ted
tot•ter
tot•ter•er
tot•tery
tot•ting
tou•can
touch
touch•able
touch-and-go (*adj*)

touch•back
touch•down
tou•ché
touch•er
touchi•ly
touchi•ness
touch•ing
touch•ing•ly
touch•line
touch•mark
touch-me-not
touch•stone
touch-type
touch-typist
touch•up
touch•wood
touchy (touchi•er, touchi•est)
tough
tough•en
tough•en•er
tough•ly
tough-minded
tough•ness
tou•pee hairpiece; cf topee
tour
tour de force (pl tours de force)
tour•er
tour•ism
tour•ist
tour•is•tic
tour•isty
tour•ma•line (or tur•, •lin)
tour•na•ment
tour•nedos (pl

•nedos) steak; cf tornado
tour•ni•quet
tou•sle
tout
tow pull; fibers; cf toe
tow•age
to•ward (or •wards)
tow•bar
tow•boat
tow•el (•el•ing, •eled; Brit •el•ling, •elled)
tow•er
tow•er•ing
tow•head
tow•headed
tow•hee
tow•line
town
townie (or towny; pl townies)
town•scape
towns•folk
town•ship
towns•man (pl •men)
towns•people
towns•woman (pl •women)
towny variant spelling of townie
tow•path
tow•rope
tox•emia (Brit •aemia)
tox•ic
toxi•cal•ly

tox•ic•ity
toxi•co•logi•cal (or •log•ic)
toxi•colo•gist
toxi•col•ogy
toxi•co•sis
tox•in poison; cf tocsin
tox•ophi•lite
tox•ophi•ly
toy
trace
trace•abil•ity (or •able•ness)
trace•able
trace•less
trac•er
trac•ery (pl •eries)
tra•chea (pl •cheae or •cheas)
tra•cheal
tra•che•oto•my (pl •mies)
trac•ing
track
track•able
track•er
track•less
tract
trac•tabil•ity (or •table•ness)
trac•table
trac•tably
trac•tion
trac•tion•al
trac•tive
trac•tor
trad•able (or trade•)

trade
trade-in (*n*)
trade-last (*n*)
trade•mark
trade-off (*n*)
trad•er
trad•es•can•tia
trades•man (*pl* •men)
trades•people
trades•woman (*pl* •women)
trad•ing
tra•di•tion
tra•di•tion•al
tra•di•tion•al•ism
tra•di•tion•al•ist
tra•di•tion•al•is•tic
tra•di•tion•al•ly
tra•di•tion•ist
tra•duce
tra•duce•ment
tra•duc•er
traf•fic (•fick•ing, •ficked)
traf•fick•er
traga•canth
tra•gedian (*fem* •gedi•enne)
trag•edy (*pl* •edies)
trag•ic (*or* tragi•cal)
tragi•cal•ly
tragi•com•edy (*pl* •edies)
tragi•com•ic (*or* •comi•cal)
trail
trail•blazer

trail•blazing
trail•er
train
train•able
train•bearer
trainee
train•er
train•ing
train•load
traipse
trait
trai•tor (*fem* •tress *or* •tor•ess)
trai•tor•ous
tra•jec•tory (*pl* •tories)
tram (tram•ming, trammed)
tram•mel (•el•ing, •eled; *Brit* •el•ling, •elled)
tram•mel•er (*Brit* •mel•ler)
tramp
tramp•er
tram•ple
tram•pler
tram•po•line
tram•po•lin•er (*or* •ist)
tram•way
trance
tranche
tran•quil
tran•quili•za•tion (*Brit* •quil•li•za•tion)
tran•quil•ize (*Brit* •quil•lize)

tran•quil•iz•er (*Brit* •quil•lizer)
tran•quil•lity (*or* •quil•ity)
tran•quil•ly
trans•act
trans•ac•tion
trans•ac•tion•al
trans•ac•tor
trans•at•lan•tic
trans•ceiv•er
trans•cend
tran•scend•ence (*or* •en•cy)
trans•cend•ent
tran•scen•den•tal
tran•scen•den•tal•ism
tran•scen•den•tal•ist
tran•scen•den•tal•ly
tran•scend•ent•ly
trans•con•ti•nen•tal
trans•con•tl•nen•tal•ly
tran•scribe
tran•scrib•er
tran•script
tran•scrip•tion
tran•scrip•tion•al
trans•duc•er
trans•duc•tion
tran•sect
tran•sec•tion
tran•sept
trans•fer (•fer•ring, •ferred)

trans•fer•abil•ity
trans•fer•able (*or* •fer•rable)
trans•fer•al (*or* •fer•ral)
trans•feree
trans•fer•ence
trans•fer•or one who makes a legal transfer
trans•fer•rer (*or* •fer•er) one who transfers
trans•fig•u•ra•tion
trans•fig•ure
trans•fix
trans•form
trans•form•able
trans•for•ma•tion
trans•for•ma•tion•al
trans•forma•tive
trans•form•er
trans•fuse
trans•fus•er
trans•fus•ible (*or* •able)
trans•fu•sion
trans•gress
trans•gres•sion
trans•gres•sive
trans•gres•sor
tran•ship *variant spelling of* transship
tran•si•ence (*or* •en•cy, •ent•ness)
tran•si•ent
tran•si•ent•ly

tran•sis•tor
tran•sis•tori•za•tion
tran•sis•tor•ize
trans•it
tran•si•tion
tran•si•tion•al (*or* •ary)
tran•si•tion•al•ly
tran•si•tive
tran•si•to•ri•ly
tran•si•to•ri•ness
tran•si•tory
trans•lat•abil•ity (*or* •able•ness)
trans•lat•able
trans•late
trans•la•tion
trans•la•tion•al
trans•la•tor
trans•lit•er•ate
trans•lit•era•tion
trans•lit•era•tor
trans•lo•cate
trans•lo•ca•tion
trans•lu•cence (*or* •cen•cy)
trans•lu•cent
trans•mi•grant
trans•mi•grate
trans•mi•gra•tion
trans•mi•gra•tor
trans•mi•gra•tory
trans•mis•sibil•ity
trans•mis•sible
trans•mis•sion
trans•mis•sive
trans•mit (•mit•ting, •mit•ted)

trans•mit•table (*or* •tible)
trans•mit•tal
trans•mit•ter
trans•mog•ri•fi•ca•tion
trans•mog•ri•fy (•fies, •fy•ing, •fied)
trans•mut•able
trans•mu•ta•tion
trans•mute
trans•mut•er
trans•ocean•ic
tran•som
trans•par•ence
trans•par•en•cy (*pl* •cies)
trans•par•ent
trans•par•ent•ly
trans•par•ent•ness
tran•spi•ra•tion
tran•spire
trans•plant
trans•plant•able
trans•plan•ta•tion
trans•plant•er
trans•port
trans•port•abil•ity
trans•port•able
trans•por•ta•tion
trans•port•er
trans•pos•able
trans•pos•al
trans•pose
trans•pos•er
trans•po•si•tion
trans•po•si•tion•al (*or* trans•posi•tive)

trans•put•er
trans•sexu•al
trans•sex•ual•ism
trans•ship (*or* tran•ship; •ship•ping, •shipped)
trans•ship•ment (*or* tran•ship•)
tran•sub•stan•tia•tion
trans•ver•sal
trans•verse
trans•verse•ly
trans•ves•tism (*or* •ves•ti•tism)
trans•ves•tite
trap (trap•ping, trapped)
trap•door
tra•peze
tra•pezium (*pl* •peziums *or* •pezia)
trap•ezoid
trap•per
trap•pings
Trap•pist
trash
trashi•ly
trashi•ness
trashy (trashi•er, trashi•est)
trat•to•ria
trau•ma (*pl* •mas *or* •ma•ta)
trau•mat•ic
trau•mati•cal•ly
trau•ma•tism

trau•ma•ti•za•tion
trau•ma•tize
trav•ail
trav•el (•el•ing, •eled; *Brit* •el•ling, •elled)
trav•el•er (*Brit* •el•ler)
trav•elogue (*or* •elog)
tra•vers•able
tra•vers•al
trav•erse
tra•vers•er
trav•es•ty (*n, pl* •ties; *vb* •ties, •ty•ing, •tied)
tra•vois (*pl* •vois *or* •voises)
trawl
trawl•er
tray
treach•er•ous
treach•er•ous•ly
treach•er•ous•ness
treach•ery (*pl* •eries)
trea•cle
trea•cli•ness
trea•cly
tread (tread•ing, trod, trod•den *or* trod)
tread•er
trea•dle
tread•mill
trea•son
trea•son•able (*or* •ous)

trea•son•able•ness
trea•son•ably
treas•ure
treas•ur•er
treas•ur•er•ship
treasure-trove
Treas•ury government department
treas•ury (*pl* •uries) treasure store
treat
treat•able
treat•er
trea•tise
treat•ment
trea•ty (*pl* •ties)
tre•ble
tre•bly
tree (tree•ing, treed)
tree•hopper
tree•less
tre•en
tree•nail (*or* tre•, trun•nel)
treen•ware
tre•foil
trek (trek•king, trekked)
trek•ker
trel•lis
trellis•work
trema•tode
trem•ble
trem•bler
trem•bling•ly
trem•bly
tre•men•dous
tre•men•dous•ly

tre•men•dous•ness
tremo•lo (*pl* •los)
trem•or
tremu•lous
tremu•lous•ly
tremu•lous•ness
tre•nail *variant spelling of* treenail
trench
trench•an•cy
trench•ant
trench•ant•ly
trench•er
trend
trendi•ly
trendi•ness
trend•setter
trendy (trendi•er, trendi•est)
tre•pan (•pan•ning, •panned) rock-boring tool; bore with a trepan
trepa•na•tion
tre•pang sea cucumber
tre•phine surgical instrument
trepi•da•tion
tres•pass
tres•pass•er
tress
tres•tle (*or* •sel)
tri•able
Tri•ad Chinese secret society
tri•ad group of three
tri•age

tri•al
tri•an•gle
tri•an•gu•lar
tri•an•gu•late
tri•an•gu•la•tion
tri•ath•lon
trib•al
trib•al•ism
trib•al•ist
trib•al•ly
tribe
tribes•man (*pl* •men)
tribu•la•tion
tri•bu•nal
trib•une
tribu•tary (*pl* •taries)
trib•ute
trice
tri•cen•ten•ary (*or* •ten•nial; *pl* •aries *or* •nials)
tri•ceps (*pl* •cepses *or* •ceps)
tri•cera•tops
tri•cho•lo•gist
tri•chol•ogy
tri•chro•mat•ic (*or* •chro•mic)
trick
trick•er
trick•ery (*pl* •eries)
tricki•ly
tricki•ness
trick•le
trick-or-treat (*vb*)
trick•si•ness
trick•ster

trick•sy (•si•er, •si•est)
tricky (tricki•er, tricki•est)
tri•col•or (*Brit* •our)
tri•col•ored (*Brit* •oured)
tri•cy•cle
tri•cy•clist
tri•dent
tried
tri•en•nial
tri•en•nial•ly
tri•er (*NOT* tryer)
tri•fle
tri•fler
tri•fling
tri•fo•cal
tri•fur•cate (*or* •cat•ed)
tri•fur•ca•tion
trig•ger
trigger•fish (*pl* •fish *or* •fishes)
trigger-happy
trigo•no•met•ric (*or* •ri•cal)
trigo•nom•etry
tri•lat•er•al
tri•lat•er•al•ly
tri•lin•gual
trill
tril•lion
tril•lionth
tril•lium
tri•lo•bite
tril•ogy (*pl* •gies)
trim (*adj* trim•mer,

trim•mest; *vb*
trim•ming,
   trimmed)
tri•ma•ran
tri•mes•ter
tri•mes•tral (*or*
   •trial)
trim•ly
trim•mer
trim•ming
trim•ness
Trin•ity God
trini•ty (*pl* •ities)
   group of three
trin•ket
trin•ket•ry
trio (*pl* trios)
trip (trip•ping,
   tripped)
tri•par•tite
tripe
tri•plane
tri•ple
tri•plet
trip•li•cate
trip•li•ca•tion
tri•plic•ity (*pl*
   •ities)
triply
tri•pod
tripo•dal
tripped
trip•per
trip•ping
trip•tych
tri•reme
tri•sect
tri•sec•tion

tri•sec•tor
tri•syl•lab•ic (*or*
   •labi•cal)
tri•syl•la•ble
trite
trite•ly
trite•ness
trit•ium
tri•umph
tri•um•phal
tri•um•phal•ly
tri•um•phant
tri•um•phant•ly
tri•umph•er
tri•um•vir (*pl* •virs
   or •vi•ri)
tri•um•vi•rate
tri•va•lence (*or*
   •len•cy)
tri•va•lent (*or* ter•)
triv•et
trivia
triv•ial
trivi•al•ity (*pl*
   •ities)
trivi•ali•za•tion
trivi•al•ize
trivi•al•ly
trivi•al•ness
tri•week•ly (*pl*
   •lies)
trod
trod•den
trog•lo•dyte
trog•lo•dyt•ic (*or*
   •dyti•cal)
tro•gon
troi•ka
Tro•jan

troll
trol•ley (*or* •ly; *n,*
   pl •leys *or* •lies; *vb*
   •leys, •ley•ing,
   •leyed *or* •lies,
   •ly•ing, •lied)
trol•lop
trom•bone
trom•bon•ist
trompe l'oeil (*pl*
   trompe l'oeils)
troop large group;
   move in group; *cf*
   troupe
troop•er soldier;
   policeman; *cf*
   trouper
troops
troop•ship
tro•phy (*pl* •phies)
trop•ic
tropi•cal
tropi•cal•ly
trop•ics
tropo•sphere
trot (trot•ting,
   trot•ted)
trot•ter
trou•ba•dour
trou•ble
trouble•maker
trouble•making
trou•bler
trouble•shoot•er
trouble•shoot•ing
trou•ble•some
trou•ble•some•ly
trou•ble•some•ness
trou•bling•ly

trou•blous

trough

trounce

troupe group of performers; *cf* troop

troup•er performer; *cf* trooper

trou•pial

trou•sered

trou•sers

trous•seau (*pl* •seaux *or* •seaus)

trout (*pl* trout *or* trouts)

trove

trow•el (•el•ing, •eled; *Brit* •el•ling, •elled)

troy (*or* troy weight)

tru•an•cy (*pl* •cies)

tru•ant

truce

truck

truck•age

truck•er

truck•ing

truck•le

truck•ler

truck•load

trucu•lence (*or* •len•cy)

trucu•lent

trucu•lent•ly

trudge

trudg•er

true (*adj* tru•er,

tru•est; *vb* tru•ing, trued)

true-blue (*adj*)

true•born

true-life (*adj*)

true•love

true•ness

truf•fle

tru•ism

tru•is•tic (*or* •ti•cal)

tru•ly

trump

trump•ery (*pl* •eries)

trum•pet

trum•pet•er

trun•cate

trun•cat•ed

trun•ca•tion

trun•cheon

trun•dle

trunk

trunk•fish (*pl* •fish *or* •fishes)

trunk•ful (*pl* •fuls)

trunks

trun•nel variant of treenail

truss

trust

trust•able

trust•bust•er

trus•tee (•tee•ing, •teed) controller of legal trust; *cf* trusty

trus•tee•ship

trust•er

trust•ful (*or* •ing)

trust•ful•ly (*or* •ing•)

trust•ful•ness (*or* •ing•)

trusti•ly

trusti•ness

trust•ing

trust•worthi•ness

trust•worthy

trusty (trusti•er, trusti•est) reliable; *cf* trustee

truth

truth•ful

truth•ful•ly

truth•ful•ness

try (*vb* tries, try•ing, tried; *n, pl* tries)

*tryer incorrect spelling of trier

try•ing•ly

try•out

trypa•no•some

trypa•no•so•mia•sis

tryst

tsar variant spelling of czar

tset•se (*or* tzet•ze)

T-shirt (*or* tee shirt)

tsu•na•mi (*pl* •mis *or* •mi)

tua•ta•ra

tub (tub•bing, tubbed)

tuba (*pl* tubas *or* tubae) musical

instrument; *cf*
 tuber
tu•bal
tubbed
tub•bi•ness
tub•bing
tub•by (•bi•er,
 •bi•est)
tube
tube•less
tu•ber under-
 ground plant
 stem; *cf* tuba
tu•ber•cle
tu•ber•cu•lar
tu•ber•cu•lin
tu•ber•cu•lo•sis
tu•ber•cu•lous
tub•ing
tub-thumper
tub-thumping
tubu•lar
tu•bule
tuck
tuck•er
Tues•day
tuft
tuft•ed
tufty
tug (tug•ging,
 tugged)
tug•boat
tug•ger
tui•tion
tui•tion•al (*or* •ary)
tu•lip
tulip•wood
tulle fabric; *cf* tool
tum•ble

tumble-down
tum•bler
tum•bler•ful (*pl*
 •fuls)
tumble•weed
tum•brel (*or* •bril)
tu•mefac•tion
tu•mefy (•mefies,
 •mefy•ing,
 •mefied)
tu•mes•cence
tu•mes•cent
tu•mid
tu•mid•ity (*or*
 •ness)
tum•my (*pl* •mies)
tu•mor (*Brit*
 •mour)
tu•mor•ous (*or*
 •mor•al)
tu•mult
tu•mul•tu•ous
tu•mul•tu•ous•ly
tu•mul•tu•ous•ness
tu•mu•lus (*pl* •li)
tun (tun•ning,
 tunned) cask; *cf*
 ton; tonne
tuna (*pl* tuna *or*
 tunas)
tun•able (*or* tune•)
tun•dra
tune
tune•ful
tune•ful•ly
tune•ful•ness
tune•less
tun•less•ly
tune•less•ness

tun•er
tune-up
tung•sten
tu•nic
tun•ing
Tu•ni•sian
tun•nel (•nel•ing,
 •neled; *Brit*
 •nel•ling, •nelled)
tun•nel•er (*Brit*
 •nel•ler)
tun•ny (*pl* •nies *or*
 •ny)
tu•pelo (*pl* •pelos)
Tupi (*pl* •pis *or* •pi)
tur•ban
tur•baned (*or*
 •banned)
tur•bid opaque;
 muddy; *cf* turgid
tur•bid•ity (*or*
 •ness)
tur•bine
tur•bo•charg•er
tur•bo•elec•tric
tur•bo•fan
tur•bo•gen•era•tor
tur•bo•jet
tur•bo•prop
tur•bo•super•
 charg•er
tur•bot (*pl* •bot *or*
 •bots)
tur•bu•lence (*or*
 •len•cy)
tur•bu•lent
tur•bu•lent•ly
turd

tu•reen soup dish;
  cf terrene; terrine
turf (*pl* turfs *or*
  turves)
turfy (turfi•er,
  turfi•est)
tur•ges•cence (*or*
  •cen•cy)
tur•ges•cent
tur•gid swollen;
  pompous; *cf*
  turbid
tur•gid•ity (*or*
  •ness)
Turk
tur•key (*pl* •keys
  or •key)
Turk•ish
tur•ma•line *variant*
  spelling of
  tourmaline
tur•mer•ic
tur•moil
turn move around;
  cf tern
turn•able
turn•about
turn•around
turn•coat
turn•er
turn•ing
tur•nip
turn•key
turn•off
turn-on (*n*)
turn•out
turn•over
turn•pike
turn•stile

turn•table
turn•up
tur•pen•tine
tur•pi•tude
tur•quoise (*or*
  •quois)
tur•ret
tur•ret•ed
tur•tle
turtle•dove
turtle•neck
Tus•ca•ro•ra (*pl*
  •ras *or* •ra)
tusk
tusk•er
tus•sle
tus•sock
tus•socky
tut (tut•ting,
  tut•ted)
tu•tee
tu•te•lage
tu•te•lary (*or* •telar;
  pl •telaries *or*
  •telars)
tu•tor
tu•tor•age (*or*
  •ship)
tu•to•ri•al
tu•to•ri•al•ly
tutti-frutti
tutu (*pl* tutus)
tux•edo (*pl* •edos
  or •edoes)
twad•dle
twad•dler
twain
twang
twangy

tweak
tweed
tweedy (tweedi•er,
  tweedi•est)
tweet
tweet•er
tweeze
twee•zers
twelfth
twelve
twen•ti•eth
twen•ty (*pl* •ties)
twice
twid•dle
twid•dler
twig (twig•ging,
  twigged)
twig•gy (•gi•er,
  •gi•est)
twi•light
twill
twin (twin•ning,
  twinned)
twine
twin•er
twin•flower
twinge
twin•jet
twin•kle
twin•kler
twin•kling
twin•kly
twin-screw (*adj*)
twirl
twirl•er
twist
twist•able
twist•er

twisty (twisti•er, twisti•est)
twit (twit•ting, twit•ted)
twitch
twitch•er
twitchi•ly
twitchi•ness
twitchy (twitchi•er, twitchi•est)
twit•ter
twit•ter•er
twit•tery
two (pl twos) number; cf to; too
two-bit
two-by-four (adj, n)
two-cycle
two-dimensional
two-dimensional•ly
two-edged
two-faced
two-fisted
two•fold
two-handed
two-handed•ly
two-phase
two-piece
two-ply (pl -plies)
two-seater
two-sided
two•some
two-step
two-time (adj, vb)
two-timer
two-tone (or -toned)
two-way
ty•coon

ty•ing
tyke (or tike)
tym•pa•ni variant spelling of timpani
tym•pa•nist variant spelling of timpanist
tym•pa•num (pl •na or •nums) part of ear; architectural term; cf timpani
type
type•cast (•cast•ing, •cast)
type•face
type•script
type•set (•set•ting, •set)
type•set•ter
type•write (•writ•ing, •wrote, •writ•ten)
type•writ•er
ty•phoid
ty•phoon
ty•phus
typi•cal (or typ•ic)
typi•cal•ly
typi•cal•ness (or •ity)
typi•fi•ca•tion
typi•fi•er
typi•fy (•fies, •fy•ing, •fied)
typ•ing
typ•ist
typo (pl typos)
ty•pog•ra•pher

ty•po•graphi•cal (or •graph•ic)
ty•po•graphi•cal•ly
ty•pog•ra•phy
ty•ran•ni•cal (or •ran•nic)
ty•ran•ni•cal•ly
tyr•an•nize
ty•ran•no•saur (or •saur•us)
tyr•an•nous
tyr•an•nous•ly
tyr•an•ny (pl •nies)
ty•rant
tyre Brit spelling of tire (wheel ring)
tyro (Brit also tiro; pl tyros or Brit tiros)
tzet•ze variant spelling of tsetse

U

ubiqui•tous
ubiquity (or ubiqui•tous•ness)
U-boat
ud•der
UFO (pl UFOs)
ufol•ogy
Ugan•dan
ugli (pl uglis or uglies)
ug•li•fi•ca•tion
ug•li•fy (•fies, •fy•ing, •fied)
ug•li•ly

ug•li•ness
ugly (ug•li•er, ug•li•est)
uke•lele *variant spelling of* ukulele
Ukrain•ian
uku•lele (*or* uke•)
ul•cer
ul•cer•ate
ul•cera•tion
ul•cera•tive
ul•cer•ous
ulna (*pl* ulnae *or* ulnas)
ul•nar
ul•ster
ul•te•ri•or
ul•ti•mate
ul•ti•mate•ly
ul•ti•ma•tum (*pl* •tums *or* •ta)
ul•tra
ultra•con•ser•va• tive
ultra•high
ultra•light
ultra•ma•rine
ultra•mod•ern
ultra•mod•ern•ism
ultra•mod•ern•ist
ultra•mon•tane
ultra•pas•teur•ize
ultra•son•ic
ultra•soni•cal•ly
ultra•son•ics
ultra•sound
ultra•vio•let
ultra•vi•rus
ulu•lant

ulu•late
ulu•la•tion
um•bel•lif•er•ous
um•ber
um•bili•cal
um•bili•cus (*pl* •ci *or* •cuses)
um•bra (*pl* •bras *or* •brae)
um•brage
um•bral
um•brel•la
um•laut
um•pire
ump•teen
ump•teenth
un•abashed
un•abat•ed
un•able
un•abridged
un•ab•sorbed
un•ac•cent•ed
un•ac•cep•table
un•ac•claimed
un•ac•com•mo•dat• ing
un•ac•com•pa•nied
un•ac•com•plished
un•ac•count•able
un•ac•count•ably
un•ac•count•ed
unaccounted-for
un•ac•cus•tomed
un•ack•nowl•edged
un•ac•quaint•ed
un•ad•mit•ted
un•adorned
un•adul•ter•at•ed
un•ad•ven•tur•ous

un•ad•vised
un•ad•vis•ed•ly
un•af•fect•ed
un•af•fect•ed•ly
un•af•fili•at•ed
un•af•ford•able
un•afraid
un•aid•ed
un•al•loyed
un•al•ter•able
un•al•ter•ably
un•al•tered
un•am•bigu•ous
un•am•bigu•ous•ly
un•am•bi•tious
un-Ameri•can
una•nim•ity (*or* unani•mous•ness)
unani•mous
unani•mous•ly
un•an•nounced
un•an•swer•able
un•an•swered
un•an•tici•pat•ed
un•ap•peal•ing
un•ap•pe•tiz•ing
un•ap•pre•ciat•ed
un•ap•pre•cia•tive
un•ap•proach•able
un•ap•proved
un•argu•ably
un•armed
un•ashamed
un•asham•ed•ly
un•asked
un•as•sail•able
un•as•sist•ed
un•as•sumed
un•as•sum•ing

un•at•tached
un•at•tain•able
un•at•tend•ed
un•at•trac•tive
un•at•trac•tive•ly
un•authen•ti•cat•ed
un•author•ized
un•avail•able
un•avail•ing
un•avoid•abil•ity
(or •able•ness)
un•avoid•able
un•avoid•ably
un•aware
un•aware•ness
un•awares (adv)
un•bal•anced
un•ban (•ban•ning, •banned)
un•bar (•bar•ring, •barred)
un•bear•able
un•bear•able•ness
un•bear•ably
un•beat•able
un•beat•en
un•be•com•ing
un•be•com•ing•ly
un•be•fit•ting
un•be•known (or •knownst)
un•be•lief
un•be•liev•abil•ity
(or •able•ness)
un•be•liev•able
un•be•liev•ably
un•be•liev•er
un•be•liev•ing
un•be•liev•ing•ly

un•bend (•bend•ing, •bent)
un•bend•able
un•bi•ased (or •assed)
un•bid•den
un•bind (•bind•ing, •bound)
un•blem•ished
un•blink•ing
un•blink•ing•ly
un•block
un•blush•ing
un•bolt
un•born
un•bound released; not bound
un•bound•ed unlimited
un•break•able
un•bri•dled
un•bro•ken
un•buck•le
un•bur•den
un•business•like
un•but•ton
uncalled-for
un•can•ni•ly
un•can•ny (•ni•er, •ni•est)
uncared-for
un•car•ing
un•ceas•ing
un•ceas•ing•ly
un•cen•sored not banned or cut
un•cen•sured not criticized
un•cer•emo•ni•ous

un•cer•emo•ni•ous•ly
un•cer•emo•ni•ous•ness
un•cer•tain
un•cer•tain•ly
un•cer•tain•ty (pl •ties)
un•chal•lenge•able
un•chal•lenged
un•change•able
un•changed
un•chang•ing
un•chap•er•oned
un•char•ac•ter•is•tic
un•chari•table
un•chari•tably
un•chari•table•ness
un•chart•ed not mapped
un•char•tered not authorized
un•checked
un•chris•tian
un•cir•cum•cised
un•civ•il
un•civi•lized
un•civil•ly
un•civ•il•ness
un•claimed
un•clas•si•fied
un•cle
un•clean
un•clean•li•ness
un•clean•ly
un•clean•ness
un•clear

un•clip (•clip•ping,
•clipped)
un•clothe
(•cloth•ing,
•clothed *or* •clad)
un•cloud•ed
un•clut•tered
un•coil
un•com•fort•able
un•com•fort•ably
un•com•mer•cial
un•com•mit•ted
un•com•mon
un•com•mon•ly
un•com•mon•ness
un•com•mu•ni•ca•
tive
un•com•peti•tive
un•com•plain•ing
un•com•plain•
ing•ly
un•com•plet•ed
un•com•pli•cat•ed
un•com•pli•men•
ta•ry
un•com•pre•hend•
ing
un•com•pro•mis•
ing
un•com•pro•mis•
ing•ly
un•con•cealed
un•con•cerned
un•con•cern•ed•ly
un•con•di•tion•al
un•con•di•tion•al•ly
un•con•di•tioned
un•con•firmed
un•con•ge•nial

un•con•ge•nial•ly
un•con•nect•ed
un•con•quer•able
un•con•quered
un•con•scion•able
un•con•scious
un•con•scious•ly
un•con•scious•ness
un•con•sent•ing
un•con•sid•ered
un•con•soli•dat•ed
un•con•sti•tu•
tion•al
un•con•sti•tu•
tion•al•ly
un•con•strained
un•con•tami•nat•ed
un•con•test•ed
un•con•trol•lable
un•con•trol•lably
un•con•ven•tion•al
un•con•ven•tion•
al•ly
un•con•vert•ed
un•con•vinced
un•con•vinc•ing
un•con•vinc•ing•ly
un•cooked
un•cool
un•co•opera•tive
un•co•ordi•nat•ed
un•cork
un•cor•robo•rat•ed
un•couth
un•cov•er
un•criti•cal
un•criti•cal•ly
un•cross
un•crowned

unc•tion
unc•tu•os•ity (*or*
•tu•ous•ness)
unc•tu•ous
unc•tu•ous•ly
un•cul•ti•vat•ed
un•cured
un•curl
un•cut
un•dam•aged
un•dat•ed
un•daunt•ed
un•de•cid•ed
un•de•clared
un•de•feat•ed
un•de•fend•ed
un•de•filed
un•de•mand•ing
un•demo•crat•ic
un•demo•crati•
cal•ly
un•de•mon•stra•
tive
un•de•ni•able
un•de•ni•ably
un•der
under•achieve
under•achieve•ment
under•achiev•er
under•age
under•arm
under•belly (*pl*
•bellies)
under•bid
(•bid•ding, •bid)
under•brush
under•carriage
under•charge
under•class

under•clothes (*or* •clothing)
under•coat
under•cook
under•cover
under•current
under•cut (•cut•ting, •cut)
under•de•vel•op
under•de•vel•op•ment
under•dog
under•done
under•dressed
under•edu•cat•ed
under•es•ti•mate
under•es•ti•ma•tion
under•ex•pose
under•ex•po•sure
under•feed (•feed•ing, •fed)
under•floor
under•foot
under•fund•ed
under•garment
under•go (•goes, •go•ing, •went, •gone)
under•graduate
under•ground
under•growth
under•hand
under•hand•ed (*or* •hand)
under•hand•ed•ly
under•hand•ed•ness
under•in•sured
under•lay (•lay•ing, •laid) to place under

under•lie (•ly•ing, •lay, •lain) to lie under
under•line
under•ling
under•ly•ing
under•manned
under•mine
under•neath
under•nour•ished
under•nour•ish•ment
under•paid
under•pants
under•pass
under•pay (•pay•ing, •paid)
under•pay•ment
under•pin (•pin•ning, •pinned)
under•play
under•price
under•privi•leged
under•rate
under•ripe
under•score
under•seal
under•secretary (*pl* •secretaries)
under•sell (•sel•ling, •sold)
under•sexed
under•shirt
under•side
under•signed
under•sized (*or* •size)

under•skirt
under•sold
under•spend (•spend•ing, •spent)
under•staffed
under•stand (•stand•ing, •stood)
under•stand•able
under•stand•ably
under•stand•ing
under•stand•ing•ly
under•state
under•state•ment
under•stood
under•study (*n, pl* •stud•ies; *vb* •stud•ies, •study•ing, •stud•ied)
under•take (•tak•ing, •took, •tak•en)
under•tak•er
under•tak•ing
under-the-counter (*adj*)
under•tone
under•took
under•tow
under•valu•ation
under•value (•valu•ing, •val•ued)
under•water
under•wear
under•weight
under•went
under•whelm
under•world

under•write
 (•writ•ing, •wrote,
 •writ•ten)
under•writ•er
un•de•served
un•de•serv•ed•ly
un•de•serv•ing
un•de•sir•abil•ity
 (*or* •able•ness)
un•de•sir•able
un•de•sir•ably
un•de•tect•ed
un•de•ter•mined
un•de•terred
un•de•vel•oped
un•di•ag•nosed
un•did
un•dif•fer•en•ti•
 at•ed
un•di•gest•ed
un•dig•ni•fied
un•di•lut•ed
un•dim•in•ished
un•dimmed
un•dis•cern•ing
un•dis•ci•plined
un•dis•closed
un•dis•cov•ered
un•dis•crimi•nat•
 ing
un•dis•guised
un•dis•mayed
un•dis•put•ed
un•dis•tin•guished
un•dis•turbed
un•di•vid•ed
undo (un•does,
 un•do•ing, un•did,
 un•done)

un•docu•ment•ed
un•doubt•ed
un•doubt•ed•ly
un•dress
un•drink•able
un•due
un•du•lant
un•du•late
un•du•la•tion
un•du•la•tory
un•du•ly
un•dy•ing
un•earned
un•earth
un•earth•li•ness
un•earth•ly
un•ease
un•easi•ly
un•easi•ness
un•easy
un•eat•able
un•eat•en
un•eco•nom•ic
un•eco•nomi•cal
un•eco•nomi•cal•ly
un•ed•it•ed
un•edu•cat•ed
un•elect•able
un•em•bar•rassed
un•emo•tion•al
un•emo•tion•al•ly
un•em•ploy•abil•ity
un•em•ploy•able
un•em•ployed
un•em•ploy•ment
un•en•cum•bered
un•end•ing
un•en•light•ened
un•en•ter•pris•ing

un•en•thu•si•as•tic
un•en•thu•si•asti•
 cal•ly
un•en•vi•able
un•equal
un•equaled (*Brit*
 •equalled)
un•equal•ly
un•equivo•cal
un•equivo•cal•ly
un•equivo•cal•ness
un•err•ing
un•err•ing•ly
un•ethi•cal
un•ethi•cal•ly
un•even
un•even•ly
un•even•ness
un•event•ful
un•event•ful•ly
un•ex•cep•tion•able
 beyond criticism
un•ex•cep•tion•
 ably
un•ex•cep•tion•al
 ordinary
un•ex•cep•tion•
 al•ly
un•ex•cit•ing
un•ex•pec•ted
un•ex•pec•ted•ly
un•ex•pect•ed•ness
un•ex•plained
un•ex•plod•ed
un•ex•plored
un•ex•posed
un•ex•pressed
un•ex•pur•gat•ed
un•fad•ing

un•fail•ing
un•fail•ing•ly
un•fair
un•fair•ly
un•fair•ness
un•faith•ful
un•faith•ful•ly
un•faith•ful•ness
un•fa•mil•iar
un•fa•mili•ar•ity
un•fash•ion•able
un•fash•ion•ably
un•fas•ten
un•fath•om•able
un•fa•vor•able
  (Brit •vour•)
un•fa•vor•ably
  (Brit •vour•)
un•fazed
un•feel•ing
un•feigned
un•fet•tered
un•filled
un•fin•ished
un•fit
un•fit•ness
un•flag•ging
un•flap•pable
un•flat•ter•ing
un•flinch•ing
un•fold
un•forced
un•fore•see•able
un•fore•seen
un•for•get•table
un•for•giv•able
un•for•giv•en
un•for•giv•ing
un•for•got•ten

un•for•tu•nate
un•for•tu•nate•ly
un•found•ed
un•framed
un•freeze (•freez•
  ing, •froze,
  •fro•zen)
un•fre•quent•ed
un•friend•li•ness
un•friend•ly (•li•er,
  •li•est)
un•frock
un•fruit•ful
un•ful•filled
un•furl
un•fur•nished
un•gain•li•ness
un•gain•ly (•li•er,
  •li•est)
un•gen•er•ous
un•gen•er•ous•ly
un•glued
un•god•li•ness
un•god•ly (•li•er,
  •li•est)
un•gov•ern•able
un•gra•cious
un•gra•cious•ly
un•gram•mati•cal
un•grate•ful
un•grate•ful•ly
un•grate•ful•ness
un•grudg•ing
un•guard•ed
un•guard•ed•ly
un•guent
un•gu•late
un•hal•lowed
un•hap•pi•ly

un•hap•pi•ness
un•hap•py (•pi•er,
  •pi•est)
un•harmed
un•healthi•ly
un•healthi•ness
un•healthy
  (•healthi•er,
  •healthi•est)
un•heard
unheard-of
un•heed•ed
un•heed•ing
un•help•ful
un•help•ful•ly
un•her•ald•ed
un•hesi•tat•ing
un•hesi•tat•ing•ly
un•hinge
un•ho•ly (•li•er,
  •li•est)
un•hook
unhoped-for
un•hur•ried
un•hurt
un•hy•glen•ic
un•hy•gieni•cal•ly
uni•cam•er•al
uni•cel•lu•lar
uni•corn
uni•cy•cle
uni•cy•clist
un•iden•ti•fi•able
un•iden•ti•fied
uni•fi•able
uni•fi•ca•tion
uni•fied
uni•form

uni•form•ity (*pl*
•ities)
uni•form•ly
uni•fy (•fies,
•fy•ing, •fied)
uni•lat•er•al
uni•lat•er•al•ism
(*or* •ity)
uni•lat•er•al•ly
un•im•agi•nable
un•im•agi•nably
un•im•agi•na•tive
un•im•agi•na•
tive•ly
un•im•ag•ined
un•im•paired
un•im•peach•able
un•im•ped•ed
un•im•por•tant
un•im•pressed
un•im•pres•sive
un•im•proved
un•in•formed
un•in•hab•it•able
un•in•hab•it•ed
un•in•hib•it•ed
un•in•jured
un•in•spired
un•in•spir•ing
un•in•sured
un•in•tel•li•gent
un•in•tel•li•gent•ly
un•in•tel•li•gible
un•in•tel•li•gibly
un•in•tend•ed
un•in•ten•tion•al
un•in•ten•tion•al•ly
un•in•ter•est•ed not

interested; *cf*
disinterested
un•in•ter•est•ing
un•in•ter•rupt•ed
un•in•vit•ed
un•in•vit•ing
un•ion
un•ion•ism
un•ion•ist
un•ioni•za•tion
un•ion•ize
unique
unique•ly
unique•ness
un•ironed
uni•sex
uni•son
unit
Uni•tar•ian
Uni•tari•an•ism
uni•tary
unite
unit•ed•ly
unity (*pl* unities)
uni•va•lent
uni•ver•sal
uni•ver•sal•ity (*pl*
•ities)
uni•ver•sal•ly
uni•verse
uni•ver•si•ty (*pl*
•sities)
un•just
un•jus•ti•fi•able
un•jus•ti•fi•ably
un•jus•ti•fied
un•just•ly
un•just•ness
un•kempt

un•kempt•ness
un•kind
un•kind•li•ness
un•kind•ly
un•kind•ness
un•know•able
un•know•ing
un•know•ing•ly
un•known
un•known•ness
un•la•beled (*Brit*
•belled)
un•lace
un•la•den
un•lady•like
un•lam•ent•ed
un•latch
un•law•ful
un•law•ful•ly
un•law•ful•ness
un•lead•ed
un•leash
un•leav•ened
un•less
un•let•tered
un•li•censed
un•light•ed
un•like
un•like•li•ness (*or*
•hood)
un•like•ly
un•like•ness
un•lim•it•ed
un•lined
un•list•ed
un•lived-in
un•load
un•lock
unlooked-for

un•lov•able
un•loved
un•love•ly
un•lov•ing
un•lucki•ly
un•lucki•ness
un•lucky (•lucki•er,
•lucki•est)
un•made
un•make
(•mak•ing, •made)
un•man (•man•
ning, •manned)
un•man•age•able
un•man•ly
un•manned
un•man•ner•ly
un•marked
un•mar•ried
un•mask
un•matched
un•mean•ing
un•meant
un•meas•ur•able
unable to be
measured, *cf*
immeasurable
un•meas•ured
un•men•tion•able
un•mer•ci•ful
un•mer•ci•ful•ly
un•mis•tak•able
un•mis•tak•ably
un•miti•gat•ed
un•mo•ti•vat•ed
un•moved
un•mu•si•cal
un•named
un•natu•ral

un•natu•ral•ly
un•natu•ral•ness
un•navi•gable
un•nec•es•sari•ly
un•nec•es•sary
un•neigh•bor•ly
(*Brit* •bour•)
un•nerve
un•nerv•ing
un•no•ticed
un•num•bered
un•ob•jec•tion•able
un•ob•ser•vant
un•ob•served
un•ob•tain•able
un•ob•tru•sive
un•ob•tru•sive•ly
un•oc•cu•pied
un•of•fi•cial
un•of•fi•cial•ly
un•opened
un•op•posed
un•or•gan•ized
un•origi•nal
un•ortho•dox
un•pack
un•pack•er
un•paid
un•paint•ed
un•pal•at•able
un•par•al•leled
un•par•don•able
un•par•don•ably
un•pas•teur•ized
un•pat•ri•ot•ic
un•per•son
un•per•turbed
un•pick

un•pin (•pin•ning,
•pinned)
un•pity•ing
un•planned
un•play•able
un•pleas•ant
un•pleas•ant•ly
un•pleas•ant•ness
un•pleas•ing
un•plug (•plug•
ging, •plugged)
un•plumbed
un•pol•lut•ed
un•popu•lar
un•popu•lar•ity
un•prac•ticed (*Brit*
•tised)
un•prec•edent•ed
un•pre•dict•abil•ity
(*or* •able•ness)
un•pre•dict•able
un•pre•dict•ably
un•preju•diced
un•pre•medi•tat•ed
un•pre•pared
un•pre•pos•sess•ing
un•pre•sent•able
un•pre•ten•tious
un•pre•ten•tious•
ness
un•prin•ci•pled
un•print•able
un•pro•duc•tive
un•pro•fes•sion•al
un•pro•fes•sion•
al•ly
un•prof•it•able
un•prof•it•ably
un•prom•is•ing

un•prompt•ed
un•pro•nounce•able
un•pro•tect•ed
un•prov•able
un•proved
un•prov•en
un•pro•voked
un•pub•lished
un•punc•tual
un•pun•ished
un•quali•fied
un•quench•able
un•ques•tion•able
un•ques•tion•ably
un•ques•tioned
un•ques•tion•ing
un•ques•tion•ing•ly
un•quote
un•rav•el (•el•ing,
•eled; *Brit* •el•ling,
•elled)
un•reach•able
un•read
un•read•able
un•real
un•re•al•is•tic
un•re•al•isti•cal•ly
un•re•al•ity
un•re•al•ized
un•rea•son•able
un•rea•son•able•
ness
un•rea•son•ably
un•rec•og•niz•able
un•rec•og•nized
un•re•cord•ed
un•re•deemed
un•re•fined
un•re•hearsed

un•re•lat•ed
un•re•lent•ing
un•re•li•abil•ity (*or*
•able•ness)
un•re•li•able
un•re•mark•able
un•re•mit•ting
un•re•mit•ting•ly
un•re•peat•able
un•re•pent•ant
un•re•pent•ant•ly
un•rep•re•senta•
tive
un•re•quit•ed
un•re•served
un•re•serv•ed•ly
un•re•sist•ing
un•re•solved
un•re•spon•sive
un•rest
un•re•strained
un•re•strict•ed
un•re•ward•ed
un•re•ward•ing
un•right•eous
un•ripe (*or*
•rip•ened)
un•ri•valed (*Brit*
•valled)
un•roll
un•ruf•fled
un•ru•li•ness
un•ru•ly (•li•er,
•li•est)
un•safe
un•said
un•sal•able (*Brit*
•sale•)
un•salt•ed

un•sat•is•fac•
tori•ly
un•sat•is•fac•tory
un•sat•is•fied
un•sat•is•fy•ing
un•satu•rat•ed
un•sa•vori•ly (*Brit*
•vouri•)
un•sa•vori•ness
(*Brit* •vouri•)
un•sa•vory (*Brit*
•voury)
un•say (•say•ing,
•said)
un•scarred
un•scathed
un•scent•ed
un•sched•uled
un•schooled
un•sci•en•tif•ic
un•sci•en•tifi•cal•ly
un•scram•ble
un•scram•bler
un•screened
un•screw
un•script•ed
un•scru•pu•lous
un•scru•pu•lous•ly
un•scru•pu•lous•
ness
un•seal
un•sea•son•able
un•sea•son•ably
un•sea•soned
un•seat
un•sea•wor•thy
un•secured
un•seed•ed
un•seem•li•ness

un•seem•ly
un•seen
un•self•con•scious
un•self•con•
 scious•ly
un•self•ish
un•self•ish•ly
un•self•ish•ness
un•set•tle
un•set•tled
un•shack•le
un•shak•able (or
 •shake•)
un•shak•en
un•shav•en
un•sheathe
un•shed
un•shock•able
un•shod
un•shrink•able
un•sight•li•ness
un•sight•ly
un•signed
un•sink•able
un•skilled
un•skill•ful (Brit
 •skil•ful)
un•smil•ing
un•smil•ing•ly
un•so•ciabil•ity (or
 •ciable•ness)
un•so•ciable
un•so•ciably
un•sold
un•so•lic•it•ed
un•solved
un•so•phis•ti•cat•ed
un•sought
un•sound

un•spar•ing
un•speak•able
un•speak•ably
un•speci•fied
un•spoiled (or
 •spoilt)
un•spo•ken
un•sports•man•like
un•sta•ble
un•steadi•ly
un•steadi•ness
un•steady (adj
 •steadi•er, •steadi•
 est; vb •stead•ies,
 •steady•ing,
 •stead•ied)
un•stick (•stick•
 ing, •stuck)
un•stint•ing
un•stop•pable
un•stressed
un•struc•tured
un•stuck
un•sub•stan•tial
un•sub•stan•ti•
 at•ed
un•suc•cess•ful
un•suc•cess•ful•ly
un•suit•abil•ity (or
 •able•ness)
un•suit•able
un•suit•ably
un•suit•ed
un•sul•lied
un•sung
un•sure
un•sur•passed
un•sus•pect•ed
un•sus•pect•ing

un•sweet•ened
un•swerv•ing
un•swerv•ing•ly
un•sym•pa•thet•ic
un•sym•pa•theti•
 cal•ly
un•sys•tem•at•ic
un•sys•tem•ati•
 cal•ly
un•taint•ed
un•tame•able
un•tamed
un•tan•gle
un•tapped
un•tast•ed
un•taught
un•taxed
un•teach•able
un•ten•able
un•test•ed
un•think•able
un•think•ably
un•think•ing
un•think•ing•ly
un•ti•di•ly
un•ti•di•ness
un•ti•dy (adj •di•er,
 •di•est; vb •dies,
 •dy•ing, •died)
un•tie (•ty•ing or
 •tie•ing, •tied)
un•til
un•time•ly
un•tir•ing
un•ti•tled
unto
un•told
un•touch•abil•ity
un•touch•able

un•touched
un•to•ward
un•trained
un•tram•eled
  (*Brit* •melled)
un•trans•lat•able
un•treat•able
un•treat•ed
un•tried
un•trod•den
un•trou•bled
un•true
un•trust•wor•thy
un•truth
un•truth•ful
un•truth•ful•ly
un•truth•ful•ness
un•tuck
un•turned
un•tu•tored
un•twist
un•us•able
un•used
un•usual
un•usu•al•ly
un•ut•ter•able
un•ut•ter•ably
un•var•ied
un•vary•ing
un•vary•ing•ly
un•veil
un•veil•ing
un•want•ed
un•war•rant•able
un•war•rant•ed
un•wari•ly
un•wari•ness
un•wary
un•washed

un•wa•ver•ing
un•weary•ing
un•wel•come
un•well
un•whole•some
un•whole•some•ly
un•whole•some•
  ness
un•wieldi•ly
un•wieldi•ness
un•wieldy
un•will•ing
un•will•ing•ly
un•will•ing•ness
un•wind (•wind•ing,
  •wound)
un•wise
un•wise•ly
un•wit•ting
un•wit•ting•ly
un•wont•ed
un•work•able
un•world•li•ness
un•world•ly
un•worn
un•worthi•ly
un•worthi•ness
un•wor•thy (•thi•er,
  •thi•est)
un•wound
un•wrap (•wrap•
  ping, •wrapped)
un•writ•ten
un•yield•ing
un•zip (•zip•ping,
  •zipped)
up (up•ping, upped)
up-and-coming
up•beat

up•braid
up•bringing
up•country
up•date
up•end
up•front
up•grade
up•heav•al
up•held
up•hill
up•hold (•hold•ing,
  •held)
up•hold•er
up•hol•ster
up•hol•ster•er
up•hol•stery (*pl*
  •steries)
up•keep
up•land
up•lift
up•lift•er
up•lift•ing
up•market
up•most *variant of*
  uppermost
upon
up•per
upper-case (*adj, vb*)
upper-class (*adj*)
upper•class•man
  (*pl* •men)
upper•most (*or*
  up•most)
up•pi•ty
up•right
up•right•ness
up•ris•ing
up•river
up•roar

up•roari•ous
up•roari•ous•ly
up•root
up•scale
up•set (•set•ting, •set)
up•set•ter
up•set•ting
up•shot
up•side
upside-down
up•si•lon
up•stage
up•stairs
up•stand•ing
up•start
up•state
up•stream
up•stroke
up•surge
up•swept
up•take
up•tight
up-to-date
up-to-date•ness
up•town
up•trend
up•turn
up•ward (*adj*)
up•ward (*Brit* •wards; *adv*)
up•ward•ly
up•wind
urae•mia *Brit spelling of* **uremia**
ura•nium
urate
ur•ban of cities

ur•bane sophisticated
ur•bane•ly
ur•bane•ness
ur•ban•ism
ur•ban•ity (*pl* •ities)
ur•bani•za•tion
ur•ban•ize
ur•chin
Urdu
urea
ure•mia (*Brit* urae•)
ure•mic (*Brit* urae•)
ureter
ureter•al (*or* •ic)
ure•thra (*pl* •thras *or* •thrae)
ure•thral
urethri•tis
uret•ic
urge
ur•gen•cy (•cies)
ur•gent
ur•gent•ly
urg•er
uric
uri•nal
uri•naly•sis (*pl* •ses)
uri•nary (*pl* •naries)
uri•nate
uri•na•tion
urine
uri•no•geni•tal

variant of **urogenital**
uri•nous (*or* •nose)
urn
uro•geni•tal (*or* uri•no•)
uro•log•ic (*or* •logi•cal)
urolo•gist
urol•ogy
ur•sine
ur•ti•caria
ur•ti•car•ial
Uru•guay•an
us
us•abil•ity (*or* •able•ness, use•)
us•able (*or* use•)
us•age
use
use•abil•ity (*or* •able•ness)
variants of **usability**
use•able *variant spelling of* **usable**
used
use•ful
use•ful•ly
use•ful•ness
use•less
use•less•ly
use•less•ness
user
user-friendly
ush•er
ush•er•ette
usu•al
usu•al•ly

usu•al•ness
usu•rer
usu•ri•ous
usurp
usurp•a•tion
usurp•a•tive (*or* •tory)
usurp•er
usu•ry (*pl* •ries)
Ute (*pl* Utes *or* Ute)
uten•sil
uter•ine
uter•us (*pl* uteri)
utili•tar•ian
utili•tari•an•ism
util•ity (*pl* •ities)
uti•liz•able
uti•li•za•tion
uti•lize
uti•liz•er
ut•most (*or* utter•)
Uto•pia
Uto•pian (*or* uto•)
ut•ter
ut•ter•able
ut•ter•ance
ut•ter•er
ut•ter•ly
utter•most *variant of* utmost
U-turn
uvu•la (*pl* •las *or* •lae)
uvu•lar
uxo•rial wifely
uxo•ri•ous wifeloving

V

va•can•cy (*pl* •cies)
va•cant
va•cant•ly
va•cat•able
va•cate
va•ca•tion
va•ca•tion•er (*or* •ist)
vac•ci•nate
vac•ci•na•tion
vac•ci•na•tor
vac•cine
vac•il•late
vac•il•la•tion
vac•il•la•tor
vacua *pl of* vacuum
va•cu•ity (*pl* •ities)
vacu•ole
vacu•ous
vacu•ous•ly
vacu•um (*pl* •ums *or* vacua)
vacuum-packed
vaga•bond
vaga•bond•age (*or* •ism)
va•gary (*pl* •garies)
va•gi•na (*pl* •nas *or* •nae)
vagi•nal
va•gran•cy (*pl* •cies)
va•grant
vague
vague•ly
vague•ness
vain conceited;

unsuccessful; *cf* vane; vein
vain•glo•ri•ous
vain•glo•ry
vain•ly
vain•ness
val•ance drapery; *cf* valence
val•anced
vale valley; *cf* veil
val•edic•tion
val•edic•tory (*pl* •tories)
va•lence (*Brit also* •len•cy; *pl* •lences *or* •cies) chemistry term; *cf* valance
val•en•tine
val•et
val•etu•di•nar•ian (*or* •di•nary; *pl* •ians *or* •naries)
val•etu•di•nar•ian•ism
val•iance (*or* •ian•cy, •iant•ness)
val•iant
val•iant•ly
val•id
vali•date
vali•da•tion
vali•da•tory
va•lid•ity
va•lid•ly
va•lise
Val•ium (*Trademark*)
val•ley
val•or (*Brit* •our)

val•or•ous
valu•able
valu•able•ness
valu•ably
valu•ate
valua•tion
valua•tor
value (valu•ing, valued)
value-added tax
value•less
valu•er
valve
val•vu•lar
va•moose
vamp
vam•pire
vam•pir•ic (*or* •ish)
vam•pir•ism
van
va•na•dium
van•dal
van•dal•ism
van•dal•is•tic (*or* •dal•ish)
van•dal•ize
vane thin blade; *cf* vain; vein
van•guard
va•nil•la
van•ish
van•ish•er
van•ish•ing•ly
van•ity (*pl* •ities)
van•quish
van•quish•able
van•quish•er
van•quish•ment
van•tage

vap•id
va•pid•ity
vap•id•ly
vap•id•ness
va•por (*Brit* •pour)
va•por•if•ic
va•por•im•eter
va•por•iz•able
va•pori•za•tion
va•por•ize
va•por•iz•er
va•por•ous
va•por•ous•ly
va•por•ous•ness (*or* •os•ity)
va•pour *Brit spelling of* vapor
va•que•ro (*pl* •ros)
vari•abil•ity (*or* •able•ness)
vari•able
vari•ably
vari•ance
vari•ant
vari•ation
vari•ation•al (*or* vari•ative)
vari•cel•la
vari•col•ored (*Brit* •oured)
vari•cose
vari•cos•ity (*pl* •ities)
var•ied
var•ied•ness
varie•gate
varie•gat•ed
varie•ga•tion
va•ri•ety (*pl* •eties)

vari•form
vari•ous
vari•ous•ly
vari•ous•ness
var•nish
var•nish•er
var•sity (*pl* •sities)
vary (varies, vary•ing, var•ied)
vary•ing•ly
vas•cu•lar
vas•cu•lar•ity
vas de•fe•rens (*pl* vasa de•fe•ren•tia)
vase
vas•ec•to•mize
vas•ec•to•my (*pl* •mies)
Vas•eline (*Trademark*)
vas•sal
vast
vast•ly
vast•ness
vat (vat•ting, vat•ted)
Vati•can
vaude•ville
vaude•vil•lian
vault
vault•ed
vault•er
vault•ing
vaunt
vaunt•er
vaunt•ing•ly
veal
vec•tor
vec•to•rial

veer
veery (*pl* veeries)
ve•gan
vege•bur•ger
veg•eta•ble
veg•etal
veg•etar•ian
veg•etari•an•ism
veg•etate
veg•eta•tion
veg•eta•tive
veg•eta•tive•ness
ve•he•mence
ve•he•ment
ve•he•ment•ly
ve•hi•cle
ve•hicu•lar
veil head covering;
  cf vale
veiled
veil•ing
vein blood vessel;
  cf vain; vane
vein•ing
veiny (veini•er,
  veini•est)
Vel•cro (*Trade-
mark*)
veld (*or* veldt)
vel•lum parch-
  ment; *cf* velum
ve•loc•ity (*pl* •ities)
ve•lours (*or* •lour;
  pl •lours)
ve•lum (*pl* vela)
  biological mem-
  brane; *cf* vellum
vel•vet
vel•vet•een

vel•vety
vena cava (*pl*
  ve•nae ca•vae)
ve•nal open to
  bribery; *cf* venial
ve•nal•ity
ve•nal•ly
vend
vend•able *variant
  spelling of
  vendible*
ven•dee
vend•er *variant
  spelling of* vendor
ven•det•ta
vend•ible (*or* •able)
vend•ing
ven•dor (*or*
  vend•er)
ven•due
ve•neer
ve•neer•er
ve•neer•ing
ven•er•abil•ity (*or*
  •able•ness)
ven•er•able
ven•er•ably
ven•er•ate
ven•era•tion
ven•era•tor
ve•nereal
ve•nere•olo•gist
ve•nere•ol•ogy
Ve•ne•tian
Ven•ezue•lan
venge•ance
venge•ful
venge•ful•ly
venge•ful•ness

ve•nial easily
  forgiven; *cf* venal
ve•ni•al•ity (*or*
  ve•nial•ness)
ve•nial•ly
veni•son
ven•om
ven•om•ous
ven•om•ous•ly
ve•nous
vent
ven•ti•late
ven•ti•la•tion
ven•ti•la•tor
ven•tral
ven•tral•ly
ven•tri•cle
ven•tricu•lar
ven•tri•lo•quial (*or*
  •qual)
ven•trilo•quism (*or*
  •quy)
ven•trilo•quist
ven•trilo•quize
ven•trilo•quy
  *variant of
  ventriloquism*
ven•ture
ven•tur•er
ven•ture•some (*or*
  •tu•rous)
venue
Venus's-flytrap (*or*
  Venus fly•trap)
ve•ra•cious
  truthful; *cf*
  voracious
ve•ra•cious•ly
ve•ra•cious•ness

ve•rac•ity (*pl* •ities)
ve•ran•dah (*or* •da)
ve•ran•dahed (*or* •daed)
verb
ver•bal
ver•bal•ism
ver•bal•ist
ver•bali•za•tion
ver•bal•ize
ver•bal•iz•er
ver•bal•ly
ver•ba•tim
ver•be•na
ver•bi•age
ver•bose
ver•bose•ly
ver•bos•ity (*or* •bose•ness)
ver•dan•cy
ver•dant
ver•dict
ver•di•gris
ver•din
ver•dure
ver•dur•ous
verge
verg•er
veri•fi•able
veri•fi•ca•tion
veri•fi•er
veri•fy (•fies, •fy•ing, •fied)
veri•si•mili•tude
veri•table
veri•tably
ver•ity (*pl* •ities)
ver•mi•cel•li
ver•mi•cid•al

ver•mi•cide
ver•micu•lite
ver•mi•form
ver•mi•fuge
ver•mil•ion (*or* •mil•lion)
ver•min
ver•mi•nous
ver•mouth
ver•nacu•lar
ver•nacu•lar•ism
ver•nal
ver•nal•ly
ver•ni•er
ve•roni•ca
ver•ru•ca (*pl* •cae *or* •cas; *NOT* verucca)
ver•ru•cose
ver•sa•tile
ver•sa•til•ity (*or* •tile•ness)
verse
versed
ver•si•cle
ver•si•fi•ca•tion
ver•si•fi•er
ver•si•fy (•fies, •fy•ing, •fied)
ver•sion
ver•sion•al
ver•so (*pl* •sos) left-hand page
ver•sus against
ver•te•bra (*pl* •brae *or* •bras)
ver•te•bral
ver•te•brate
ver•tex (*pl* •texes

or •ti•ces) apex; *cf* vortex
ver•ti•cal
ver•ti•cal•ity (*or* •ness)
ver•ti•cal•ly
ver•ti•ces *pl of* vertex
ver•tigi•nous
ver•tigi•nous•ly
ver•ti•go (*pl* •ti• goes *or* •tigi•nes)
*verucca *incorrect spelling of* verruca
ver•vain
verve
ver•vet
very
Very light
vesi•cal of the bladder
vesi•cle small cavity
ves•pers
ves•sel
vest
ves•tal
vest•ed
ves•ti•bule
ves•tige
ves•tig•ial
vest•ment
vest-pocket (*adj*)
ves•try (*pl* •tries)
vet (vet•ting, vet•ted)
vetch
vetch•ling
vet•er•an

vet•eri•nar•ian
vet•eri•nary (*pl* •naries)
veti•ver
veto (*n, pl* ve•toes; *vb* ve•toes, ve•to•ing, ve•toed)
ve•to•er
vet•ted
vet•ting
vex
vexa•tion
vexa•tious
vexa•tious•ly
vexa•tious•ness
vexed
vex•er
vex•ing•ly
via
vi•abil•ity
vi•able
vi•ably
via•duct
vial *variant spelling of* phial; *cf* vile; viol
vi•ati•cum (*pl* •ca *or* •cums)
vibes
vi•bran•cy
vi•brant
vi•brant•ly
vi•bra•phone
vi•bra•phon•ist
vi•brate
vi•bra•tion
vi•bra•tion•al
vi•bra•tive
vi•bra•to (*pl* •tos)

vi•bra•tor
vi•bra•tory
vi•bur•num
vic•ar
vic•ar•age
vi•cari•ous
vi•cari•ous•ly
vi•cari•ous•ness
vice sin; deputy; in place of; *cf* vise
vice ad•mi•ral
vice-chairman (*pl* -chairmen)
vice-chancellor
vice-consul
vice-presidency (*pl* -presidencies)
vice president
vice-presidential
vice•roy
vice ver•sa
vi•chy•ssoise
vi•cin•ity (*pl* •ities)
vi•cious
vi•cious•ly
vi•cious•ness
vi•cis•si•tude
vic•tim
vic•tim•iza•tion
vic•tim•ize
vic•tim•iz•er
vic•tor
Vic•to•rian
vic•to•ri•ous
vic•to•ri•ous•ly
vic•to•ri•ous•ness
vic•to•ry (*pl* •ries)
vict•ual (•ual•ing,

•ualed; *Brit* •ual•ling, •ualled)
vict•ual•ler (*or* •ual•er)
vict•uals
vi•cu•ña (or •na)
video (*n, pl* videos; *vb* videos, video•ing, videoed)
vide•og•ra•phy
video•phile
video•phone
video•phon•ic
video•tape
video•tex (*or* •text)
vie (vying, vied)
Vi•en•nese (*pl* •nese)
Vi•et•cong (or Viet Cong; *pl* •cong *or* Viet Cong)
Vi•et•nam•ese (*pl* •ese)
view
view•able
view•er
view•er•ship
view•finder
view•ing
view•point
vig•il
vigi•lance
vigi•lant
vigi•lan•te
vigi•lan•tism
vigi•lant•ly
vi•gnette
vig•or (*Brit* •our)
vig•or•ous

vig•or•ous•ly
vig•or•ous•ness
vig•our *Brit spelling of* vigor
Vi•king
vile evil; unpleasant; *cf* vial; viol
vile•ly
vile•ness
vili•fi•ca•tion
vili•fi•er
vili•fy (•fies, •fy•ing, •fied)
vil•la
vil•lage
vil•lag•er
vil•lain (*fem* •lain•ess) wicked person; *cf* villein
vll•lain•ous
vil•lain•ous•ly
vil•lain•ous•ness
vil•lainy (*pl* •lainies)
vil•lein serf; *cf* villain
vil•li *pl of* villus
vil•li•form
vil•lous (*or* •lose)
vil•lus (*pl* •li)
vim
vinai•grette
vin•cibil•ity
vin•cible
vin•di•cable
vin•di•cate
vin•di•ca•tion
vin•di•ca•tor

vin•di•ca•tory
vin•dic•tive
vin•dic•tive•ly
vin•dic•tive•ness
vine
vine•dresser
vin•egar
vin•egary
vine•yard (*NOT* vinyard)
vini•cul•ture
vini•cul•tur•ist
vi•nifi•ca•tion
vino (*pl* vinos)
vin or•di•naire (*pl* vins or•di•naires)
vi•nos•ity (*pl* •ities)
vi•nous
vin•tage
vint•ner
viny (vini•er, vini•est)
vinyard incorrect spelling of vine-yard
vi•nyl
viol musical instrument; *cf* vial; vile
vi•ola
vio•lable
vio•late
vio•la•tion
vio•la•tor (*or* •lat•er)
vio•lence
vio•lent
vio•lent•ly
vio•let

vio•lin
vio•lin•ist
vi•ol•ist
vio•lon•cel•lo (*pl* •los)
vi•per
vi•ra•go (*pl* •goes *or* •gos)
vi•ral
vireo (*pl* vireos)
vir•gin
vir•gin•al
vir•gin•al•ly
vir•gin•ity
virgin's-bower
viri•des•cence
viri•des•cent
vir•ile
vi•ril•ity
vi•ro•logi•cal
vi•rolo•gist
vi•rol•ogy
vir•tual
vir•tu•al•ity (*pl* •ities)
vir•tu•al•ly
vir•tue
vir•tu•os•ity (*pl* •ities)
vir•tuo•so (*pl* •sos *or* •si)
vir•tu•ous
vir•tu•ous•ly
vir•tu•ous•ness
viru•lence
viru•lent
viru•lent•ly
vi•rus (*pl* •ruses)

visa (vi•sa•ing, vi•saed)

vis•age

vis-à-vis (*pl* -vis)

vis•ca•cha (*or* viz•)

vis•cera *pl of* viscus

vis•cer•al

vis•cid

vis•cid•ity (*or* •ness)

vis•cose

vis•cos•ity (*pl* •ities)

vis•count

vis•count•cy (*or* •county; *pl* •cies *or* •counties)

vis•count•ess

vis•cous thick; *cf* viscus

vis•cous•ness

vis•cus (*pl* •cera) internal organ; *cf* viscous

vise (*Brit* vice) tool; *cf* vice

vis•ibil•ity (*pl* •ities)

vis•ible

vis•ible•ness

vis•ibly

vi•sion

vi•sion•al

vi•sion•ary (*pl* •aries)

vis•it

vis•it•able

visi•tant

vis•ita•tion

visi•tor

visi•to•rial

vi•sor (*or* •zor)

vi•sored (*or* •zored)

vis•ta

vis•taed

vis•ual

visu•ali•za•tion

visu•al•ize

visu•al•iz•er

visu•al•ly

vi•tal

vi•tal•ism

vi•tal•ist

vi•tal•ity (*pl* •ities)

vi•tali•za•tion

vi•tal•ize

vi•tal•iz•er

vi•tal•ly

vi•tals

vita•min

vi•ti•ate

vi•tia•tion

vi•tia•tor

viti•cul•ture

viti•cul•tur•er (*or* •ist)

vit•re•ous

vit•re•ous•ness (*or* •os•ity)

vi•tres•cence

vi•tres•cent

vit•ri•fi•ca•tion

vit•ri•fy (•fies, •fy•ing, •fied)

vit•ri•ol (•ol•ing, •oled *or* •ol•ling, •olled)

vit•ri•ol•ic

vi•tu•per•ate

vi•tu•pera•tion

vi•tu•pera•tive

vi•tu•pera•tor

vi•va•cious

vi•va•cious•ly

vi•va•cious•ness

vi•vac•ity (*pl* •ities)

vi•var•ium (*pl* •varia *or* •iums)

viva voce

viv•id

viv•id•ly

viv•id•ness

vivi•fi•ca•tion

vivi•fy (•fies, •fy•ing, •fied)

vivi•par•ity (*or* vi•vipa•rism, vi•vipa•rous•ness)

vi•vip•ar•ous

vivi•sect

vivi•sec•tion

vivi•sec•tion•al

vivi•sec•tion•ist

vivi•sec•tor

vix•en

vix•en•ish

viz•ca•cha *variant spelling of* viscacha

vi•zier

vi•zor *variant spelling of* visor

V-necked

vo•cabu•lary (*pl* •laries)

vo•cal

vo•cal•ism

vo•cal•ist
vo•cal•ity (*or* •ness)
vo•cali•za•tion
vo•cal•ize
vo•cal•iz•er
vo•cal•ly
vo•ca•tion
vo•ca•tion•al
vo•ca•tion•al•ly
voca•tive
vo•cif•er•ate
vo•cif•era•tion
vo•cif•era•tor
vo•cif•er•ous
vo•cif•er•ous•ly
vo•cif•er•ous•ness
vod•ka
vogue
voguish
voice
voiced
voice•less
voice•less•ness
voice-over
voice•print
voic•er
void
void•able
void•ness
voile
vola•tile
vola•til•ity
vo•lati•liza•tion
vo•lati•lize
vol-au-vent
vol•can•ic
vol•cani•cal•ly
vol•ca•no (*pl* •noes *or* •nos)

vol•can•olo•gist (*or* vul•)
vol•can•ol•ogy (*or* vul•)
vole
vo•li•tion
vo•li•tion•al
vol•ley
volley•ball
vol•ley•er
volt
volt•age
vol•ta•ic
vol•ta•ism
vol•tam•eter
	instrument
	measuring electric
	charge; *cf*
	voltmeter
volte-face (*pl*
	volte-face)
volt•meter instru-
	ment measuring
	volts; *cf*
	voltameter
vol•ubil•ity (*or*
	•uble•ness)
vol•uble
vol•ubly
vol•ume
volu•met•ric
vo•lu•mi•nos•ity (*or*
	•nous•ness)
vo•lu•mi•nous
vo•lu•mi•nous•ly
vol•un•tar•ily
vol•un•tari•ness
vol•un•tary (*pl*
	•aries)

vol•un•teer
vo•lup•tu•ary (*pl*
	•aries)
vo•lup•tu•ous
vo•lup•tu•ous•ly
vo•lup•tu•ous•ness
	(*or* •os•ity)
vom•it
vomi•tory (*pl*
	•tories)
voo•doo (*n, pl*
	•doos; *vb* •doos,
	•doo•ing, •dooed)
voo•doo•ism
voo•doo•ist
voo•doo•is•tic
vo•ra•cious greedy;
	cf veracious
vo•ra•cious•ly
vo•rac•ity (*or*
	•ra•cious•ness)
vor•tex (*pl* •texes
	or •ti•ces)
	whirling mass; *cf*
	vertex
vor•ti•cal
vor•ti•ces *pl of*
	vortex
vor•ti•cism
vor•ti•cist
vot•able (*or* vote•)
vo•ta•ry (*pl* •ries)
vote
vote•able *variant
	spelling of* votable
vot•er
vo•tive
vouch
vouch•er

vouch•safe
vow
vow•el
vow•er
vox po•pu•li
voy•age
voy•ag•er traveler
vo•ya•geur
  transporter; guide
vo•yeur
vo•yeur•ism
vo•yeur•is•tic
vo•yeur•is•ti•cal•ly
vul•can•ite
vul•can•iz•able
vul•cani•za•tion
vul•can•ize
vul•can•iz•er
vul•can•ol•ogy
  variant spelling of
  volcanology
vul•gar
vul•gar•ian
vul•gar•ism
vul•gar•ity (*pl*
  •ities)
vul•gari•za•tion
vul•gar•ize
vul•gar•iz•er
vul•gar•ly
vul•gar•ness
Vul•gate Latin
  Bible
vul•gate commonly
  accepted text;
  vernacular
vul•ner•abil•ity (*or*
  •able•ness)
vul•ner•able

vul•ner•ably
vul•pine
vul•ture
vul•tur•ine (*or*
  •ous)
vul•va (*pl* •vae *or*
  •vas)
vul•val (*or* •var,
  •vate)
vy•ing

W

wab•ble *variant*
  spelling of wobble
wacky (wacki•er,
  wacki•est)
wad (wad•ding,
  wad•ded)
wad•able (*or*
  wade•)
wad•ding
wad•dle
wad•dler
wade
wade•able *variant*
  spelling of
  wadable
wad•er one who
  wades; bird
wad•ers (*pl n*)
  boots
wadi (*pl* wadis)
wa•fer
wa•fery
waf•fle
waft
waft•er

wag (wag•ging,
  wagged)
wage
wa•ger
wages
wagged
wag•gery (*pl*
  •geries)
wag•ging
wag•gish
wag•gish•ly
wag•gish•ness
wag•gle
wag•gly
Wag•ne•rian
wag•on (*Brit also*
  wag•gon)
wag•on•er
wagon•load
wag•tail
wa•hoo (*pl* •hoos)
waif
wail cry; *cf* whale
wail•er
wail•ful
wail•ing•ly
wain•scot
wain•scot•ed (*or*
  •scot•ted)
wain•scot•ing (*or*
  •scot•ting)
wain•wright
waist
waist•band
waist•coat (*Brit*)
  vest
waist•ed
waist•line

wait pause; *cf*
  weight
wait•er
wait•ress
waive relinquish; *cf*
  wave
waiv•er
  relinquishment; *cf*
  waver
Wa•kash•an
wake (wak•ing,
  woke, wok•en)
wake•ful
wake•ful•ly
wake•ful•ness
wak•en
wak•er
wake-robin
wak•ing
Wal•dorf sal•ad
walk
walk•able
walk•er
walkie-talkie (*or*
  walky-talky; *pl*
  -talkies)
walk-in (*adj, n*)
walk•ing
Walk•man
  (*Trademark*)
walk-on (*n*)
walk•out (*n*)
walk•over (*n*)
walk-through (*n*)
walk•up (*or* -up)
walk•way
walky-talky
  variant spelling of
  walkie-talkie

wall
wal•la•by (*pl* •bies
  or •by)
wall•board
walled
wal•let
wall•eye (*pl* •eyes
  or •eye)
wall•eyed
wall•flower
wal•lop
wal•lop•er
wal•lop•ing
wal•low
wal•low•er
wall•paper
wall-to-wall
wal•nut
wal•rus (*pl* •ruses
  or •rus)
waltz
waltz•er
wam•pum
wan (wan•ner,
  wan•nest)
wand
wan•der
wan•der•er
wan•der•ing
wan•der•lust
wane
wan•gle
wan•gler
wan•ly
wanna-be
wan•ner
wan•ness
wan•nest

want need; lack; *cf*
  wont
want•er
want•ing
wan•ton
wan•ton•ly
wan•ton•ness
wapi•ti (*pl* •ti *or*
  •tis)
war (war•ring,
  warred) battle; *cf*
  wore
war•ble
war•bler
ward
war•den
ward•er (*fem* •ress)
ward•robe
ward•room
ward•ship
ware•house
wares
war•fare
war•fa•rin
war•head
war•horse
wari•ly
wari•ness
war•like
war•lock
war•lord
warm
warm-blooded
warm-blooded•ness
warm•er
warm•hearted
warm•hearted•ly
warm•hearted•ness
warm•ish

warm•ly
warm•ness
war•monger
warmth
warm-up (*n*)
warn
warn•er
warn•ing
warn•ing•ly
warp
war•path
warp•er
war•plane
war•rant
war•rant•abil•ity
war•rant•able
war•rant•ably
war•ran•tee
war•rant•er one
 who warrants
war•ran•tor
 warranty giver
war•ran•ty (*pl*
 •ties)
warred
war•ren
war•ring
war•ri•or
war•ship
wart
wart•hog
war•time
warty (warti•er,
 warti•est)
wary (wari•er,
 wari•est)
was
wash
wash•abil•ity

wash•able
wash-and-wear
wash•basin
wash•board
wash•bowl
wash•cloth
washed-out
washed-up
wash•er
washer•man (*pl*
 •men)
washer•woman (*or*
 wash•; *pl* •women)
wash•ery (*pl* •eries)
wash•ing
wash•out
wash•rag
wash•room
wash•stand
wash•tub
wash•up
wash•woman
 variant of
 washerwoman
washy (washi•er,
 washi•est)
wasn't
WASP (*or* Wasp)
 White Anglo-
 Saxon Protestant
wasp insect
wasp•ish
wasp•ish•ly
wasp•ish•ness
waspy
wast•able
wast•age
waste
waste•basket

waste•ful
waste•ful•ly
waste•ful•ness
waste•land
waste•paper
wast•er
wast•rel
wa•tap (*or* •ta•pe)
watch
watch•able
watch•band (*Brit*
 •strap)
watch•dog
watch•er
watch•ful
watch•ful•ly
watch•ful•ness
watch•maker
watch•making
watch•man (*pl*
 •men)
watch•strap (*Brit*)
 watchband
watch•tower
watch•word
wa•ter
water•borne
water•color (*Brit*
 •colour)
water•color•ist
 (*Brit* •colour•)
water-cooled
water•course
water•cress
watered-down
wa•ter•er
water•fall
water•fowl
water•front

wa•teri•ness
wa•ter•less
water•logged
water•mark
water•melon
water•power
water•proof
water-repellent
water-resistant
water•shed
water•side
water-ski (*n, pl* -skis *or* -ski; *vb* -skis, -skiing, -skied)
water-skier
water•spout
water•tight
water•tight•ness
water•way
water•weed
water•works
wa•tery
watt unit; *cf* what
watt•age
watt-hour
wat•tle
watt•meter
wave undulation, etc.; move to and fro; *cf* waive
wave•length
wav•er hesitate; one who waves; *cf* waiver
wa•ver•er
wa•ver•ing•ly
wavi•ly
wavi•ness

wavy (wavi•er, wavi•est)
wax
wax•berry (*pl* •berries)
wax•bill
wax•en
waxi•ness
wax•wing
wax•work object
wax•works exhibition
waxy (waxi•er, waxi•est)
way direction; method; *cf* weigh; whey
way•far•er
way•far•ing
way•lay (•lay•ing, •laid)
way•lay•er
way-out (*adj*)
way•side
way•ward
way•ward•ly
way•ward•ness
we pronoun; *cf* wee
weak feeble; diluted; *cf* week
weak•en
weak•fish (*pl* •fish *or* •fishes)
weak-kneed
weak•ling
weak•ly (•li•er, •li•est) sickly; in a

weak manner; *cf* weekly
weak-minded
weak-minded•ness
weak•ness
weak-willed
weal (*or* wheal) mark on skin; *cf* we'll; wheel
wealth
wealthi•ly
wealthi•ness
wealthy (wealthi•er, wealthi•est)
wean
wean•er
wean•ling
weap•on
wea•pon•ry
wear (wear•ing, wore, worn) to have on; erode; deterioration; *cf* were; where; whir
wear•abil•ity
wear•able
wear•er
wea•ri•ly
wea•ri•ness
wear•ing
wea•ri•some
wea•ri•some•ly
wea•ry (*adj* •ri•er, •ri•est; *vb* •ries, ry•ing, •ried)
wea•ry•ing•ly
wea•sel (*pl* •sels *or* •sel)

wea•sel•ly

weath•er climatic conditions; *cf* wether; whether

weather-beaten (*or* -beat)

weather•board

weather•boarding

weather-bound

weather•cock

weath•ered

weath•er•ing

weather•man (*pl* •men)

weather•proof

weather-wise

weave (weav•ing, wove *or* weaved, wo•ven *or* weaved) to intertwine; *cf* we've

weav•er one who weaves; *cf* weever

weaver•bird

web (web•bing, webbed)

web•bing

web•by (•bi•er, •bi•est)

web•foot

web-footed

wed (wed•ding, wed•ded *or* wed)

we'd we had; we would; we should; *cf* weed

wed•ding

wedge

Wedg•wood (*Trademark*)

wedgy (wedgi•er, wedgi•est)

wed•lock

Wednes•day

wee tiny; *cf* we

weed plant; *cf* we'd

weed•er

weedi•ly

weedi•ness

weed•killer

weedy (weedi•er, weedi•est)

week seven days; *cf* weak

week•day

week•end

week•end•er

week•ly (*pl* •lies) once a week; publication; *cf* weakly

week•night

wee•ny (*or* ween•sy; •ni•er, •ni•est *or* •si•er, •si•est)

weep (weep•ing, wept)

weep•er

weepi•ly

weepi•ness

weepy (weepi•er, weepi•est)

wee•ver fish; *cf* weaver

wee•vil

wee•vily (*or* •vil•ly)

weft

wei•ge•la

weigh measure heaviness; *cf* way; whey

weigh•able

weigh•bridge

weigh•er

weigh-in (*n*)

weight heaviness; *cf* wait

weighti•ly

weighti•ness

weight•less

weight•less•ness

weighty (weighti•er, weighti•est)

weir (*NOT* wier) low dam; *cf* we're

weird (*NOT* wierd)

weird•ly

weird•ness

weir•do (*or* •die, •dy; *pl* •dos *or* •dies)

welch *variant spelling of* welsh

wel•come

wel•com•er

weld

weld•able

weld•er (*or* wel•dor)

wel•fare

*welk *incorrect spelling of* whelk

well (bet•ter, best)

we'll we will; we

shall; cf weal;
wheel
well-acquainted
well-adapted
well-adjusted
well-advised
well-appointed
well-argued
well-attended
well-aware
well-balanced
well-behaved
well•being
well-bred
well-built
well-chosen
well-connected
well-defined
well-deserved
well-developed
well-disposed
well-documented
well-done
well-dressed
well-earned
well-educated
well-endowed
well-equipped
well-established
well-favored (Brit
 -favoured)
well-fed
well-founded
well-groomed
well-grounded
well•head
well-heeled
well-informed
well-intentioned

well-judged
well-kept
well-knit
well-known
well-liked
well-loved
well-made
well-mannered
well-matched
well-meaning
well-nigh
well-off
well-oiled
well-organized
well-paid
well-pleased
well-preserved
well-proportioned
well-provided
well-qualified
well-read
well-received
well-respected
well-rounded
well-spent
well-spoken
well•spring
well-thought-of
well-timed
well-to-do
well-trained
well-tried
well-trodden
well-turned
well-used
well-wisher
well-wishing
well-worn
well-written

Welsh of Wales
welsh (or welch)
 fail in obligation
Welsh•man (pl
 •men)
Welsh rab•bit (or
 rare•bit)
welt
wel•ter
welter•weight
wench
wend
went
wept
were past tense of
 be; cf wear; where;
 whir
we're we are; cf
 weir
weren't
were•wolf (pl
 •wolves)
west
west•bound
west•er•li•ness
west•er•ly (pl •lies)
west•ern
west•ern•er
west•erni•za•tion
west•ern•ize
west•ern•most
West In•dian
west-northwest
west-southwest
west•ward (adj)
west•ward (Brit
 •wards; adv)
wet (adj wet•ter,
 wet•test; vb

wet•ting, wet *or*
wet•ted) not dry;
make wet; *cf* whet

weth•er male
sheep; *cf* weather;
whether

wet•lands

wet•ly

wet•ness

wet-nurse (*vb*)

wet•table

wet•ted

wet•ter

wet•test

wet•ting

wet•tish

we've we have; *cf*
weave

whack

whack•er

whack•ing

whale (*pl* whales
or whale) animal;
cf wail

whale•boat

whale•bone

whal•er

whal•ing

wham (wham•
ming, whammed)

wham•my (*pl*
•mies)

wharf (*pl* wharves
or wharfs)

wharf•age

what which thing;
that which; *cf*
watt

what•ever

what•not

what•so•ever

wheal *variant
spelling of* weal

wheat

wheat•ear

wheat•en

whee•dle

whee•dler

whee•dling•ly

wheel disk; *cf* weal;
we'll

wheel•barrow

wheel•base

wheel•chair

wheel•er

wheeler-dealer

wheelie

wheel•less

wheel•wright

wheeze

wheezi•ly

wheezi•ness

wheezy (wheezi•er,
wheezi•est)

whelk (*NOT* welk)

whelp

when

when•ever

where at what
place; *cf* wear;
were; whir

where•abouts

where•as

where•by

where•upon

wher•ever

where•with•al

whet (whet•ting,
whet•ted) sharp-
en; stimulate; *cf*
wet

wheth•er if; either;
cf weather; wether

whet•stone

whet•ter

whey watery
liquid; *cf* way;
weigh

whey•face

whey•faced

which pronoun;
adjective; *cf* witch

which•ever

whiff

while during the
time that; *cf* wile

whilst

whim

whim•per

whim•per•er

whim•per•ing•ly

whim•si•cal

whim•si•cal•ity (*pl*
•ities)

whim•si•cal•ly

whim•sy (*or* •sey;
n, pl •sies *or* •seys)

whine moan; *cf*
wine

whin•er

whin•ing•ly

whin•ny (*vb* •nies,
•ny•ing, •nied; *n,
pl* •nies)

whiny (whini•er,
whini•est) peevish;
cf winy

whip (whip•ping,
  whipped)
whip•cord
whip•lash
whip•per
whip•per•snap•per
whip•pet
whip•ping
whip•poor•will
whip•py (•pi•er,
  •pi•est)
whip•saw
whir (or whirr;
  whir•ring,
  whirred) buzz; cf
  wear; were; where
whirl spin;
  confusion; cf
  whorl
whirl•about
whirl•er
whirli•gig
whirl•pool
whirl•wind
whirly•bird
whirr variant
  spelling of whir
whisk
whisk•er
whisk•ered
whisk•ers
whisk•ery
whis•key US or
  Irish spirit
whis•ky (pl •kies)
  Scottish or
  Canadian spirit
whis•per
whis•per•er

whist
whis•tle
whistle-blower
whis•tler
whistle-stop
  (-stop•ping,
  -stopped)
whis•tling
Whit Christian
  festival
whit iota; cf wit
white
white•bait
white•beam
white•cap
white-collar (adj)
whit•ed sep•ul•cher
  (Brit •chre)
white•fish (pl •fish
  or •fishes)
white•fly (pl •flies)
white-hot
white-knuckle (or
  -knuckled; adj)
white•ly
whit•en
whit•en•er
white•ness
whit•en•ing
white•out
whites
white•wall
white•wash
white•wash•er
white•wood
whith•er where; cf
  wither
whit•ing (pl •ing or
  •ings) fish

whit•ing (or
  •en•ing) ground
  chalk
whit•ish
whit•low
Whit•sun
Whit•sun•tide
whit•tle
whit•tler
whiz (or whizz;
  whiz•zing,
  whizzed)
whiz•zer
who
who•dun•it (or
  •dun•nit)
who•ever
whole entire; cf
  hole
whole•hearted
whole•hearted•ly
whole•hearted•ness
whole•ness
whole•sale
whole•sal•er
whole•some
whole•some•ly
whole•some•ness
whole-wheat (adj)
who'll
whol•ly entirely; cf
  holey; holy
whom
whom•ever
whoop shout; cf
  hoop
whoo•pee
whoop•ing cough
whoops

whoosh
whop (whop•ping,
  whopped)
whop•per
whop•ping
whore
whor•ish
whorl spiral
  pattern or
  arrangement; cf
  whirl
whorled
who's who is; who
  has
whose of whom
why
wick
wick•ed
wick•ed•ly
wick•ed•ness
wick•er
wicker•work
wick•et
wick•ing
wicki•up (or wiki•)
wico•py (pl •pies)
wide
wide-angle (adj)
wide-awake (adj, n)
wide-eyed
wide•ly
wid•en
wid•en•er
wide•ness
wide-open
wide-ranging
wide-screen (adj)
wide•spread
widg•et

wid•ow
wid•ow•er
wid•ow•hood
width
width•wise (or
  •ways)
wield
wield•able
wield•er
wieldy (wieldi•er,
  wieldi•est)
wie•ner (or •nie,
  wiener•wurst)
Wie•ner schnit•zel
*wier incorrect
  spelling of weir
*wierd incorrect
  spelling of weird
wife (pl wives)
wife•li•ness
wife•ly
wig (wig•ging,
  wigged)
wig•gle
wig•gler
wig•gly
wig•wag
  (•wag•ging,
  •wagged)
wig•wam
wiki•up variant
  spelling of wickiup
wild
wild•cat
wil•de•beest (pl
  •beests or •beest)
wil•der•ness
wild-eyed
wild•fire

wild•fowl
wild-goose chase
wild•life
wild•ly
wild•ness
wile craftiness;
  trick; cf while
wil•ful Brit spelling
  of willful
wili•ly
wili•ness
will
wil•let (pl •let)
will•ful (Brit wil•)
will•ful•ly (Brit
  wil•)
will•ful•ness (Brit
  wil•)
wil•lies
will•ing
will•ing•ly
will•ing•ness
wil•li•waw
will-o'-the-wisp
wil•low
wil•lowy
will•power
willy-nilly
wilt
wily (wili•er,
  wili•est)
wimp
wimp•ish (or
  wimpy)
wim•ple
win (win•ning, won)
wince
winc•er
winch

winch•er
wind (wind•ing, wound) coil
wind (wind•ing, wind•ed) air current, etc.
wind•able
wind•bag
wind•blown
wind•borne
wind•break
wind•burn
wind•burned (or •burnt)
wind•cheater
wind•chill
wind•ed
wind•er
wind•fall
wind•flower
windi•ly
windi•ness
wind•ing
wind•lass
wind•mill
win•dow
window-dresser
window-dressing
window•pane
window-shop (-shopping, -shopped)
window-shopper
window•sill
wind•pipe
wind•shield
wind•sock
wind•storm
wind•surfer

wind•surfing
wind•swept
wind•up
wind•ward
windy (windi•er, windi•est)
wine fermented grape juice; cf whine
wine•glass
wine•glass•ful (pl •fuls)
wine•press
win•ery (pl •eries)
win•ey variant spelling of winy
wing
wing•ding
winged
wing•er
wing•less
wing•span (or •spread)
wink
wink•er
win•kle
win•nable
Win•ne•ba•go (pl •go, •gos, or •goes)
win•ner
win•ning
win•ning•ly
win•nings
win•now
win•now•er
wino (pl winos)
win•some
win•some•ly

win•some•ness
win•ter
winter•green
winter•time
win•tri•ness (or •teri•)
win•try (or •tery; •tri•er, •tri•est)
winy (or win•ey; wini•er, wini•est) like wine; cf whiny
wipe
wipe•out
wip•er
wire
wire•haired
wire•man (pl •men)
wir•er
wire•puller
wire•pulling
wire•tap (•tap•ping, •tapped)
wire•worm
wiri•ly
wiri•ness
wir•ing
wiry (wiri•er, wiri•est)
wis•dom
wise
wise•acre
wise•crack
wise•crack•er
wise•ly
wise•ness
wish
wish•bone
wish•er
wish•ful

wish•ful•ly
wish•ful•ness
wishy-washy
wisp
wispi•ly
wispi•ness
wispy (wispi•er,
 wispi•est)
wis•teria (or •taria)
wist•ful
wist•ful•ly
wist•ful•ness
wit humor;
 intelligence; cf
 whit
witch sorceress; cf
 which
witch•craft
witch elm variant
 spelling of wych
 elm
witch•ery (pl
 •eries)
witch ha•zel (or
 wych ha•zel)
witch-hunt
witch-hunter
witch-hunting
witch•ing
with
with•draw (•draw•
 ing, •drew,
 •drawn)
with•draw•able
with•draw•al
with•draw•er
with•er shrivel; cf
 whither
with•er•ing

with•er•ing•ly
with•ers
with•hold (•hold•
 ing, •held)
with•hold•er
with•in
with•out
with•stand
 (•stand•ing,
 •stood)
wit•less
wit•less•ly
wit•less•ness
wit•ness
wits
wit•ti•cism
wit•ti•ly
wit•ti•ness
wit•ting•ly
wit•ty (•ti•er,
 •ti•est)
wives pl of wife
wiz•ard
wiz•ard•ry (pl
 •ries)
wiz•en
wiz•ened
woad
wob•ble (or wab•)
wob•bler (or wab•)
wob•bli•ness (or
 wab•)
wob•bly (or wab•;
 •bli•er, •bli•est)
woe
woe•be•gone
woe•ful
woe•ful•ly
woe•ful•ness

wog•gle
wok
woke
wok•en
wolf (pl wolves)
wolf•fish (pl •fish
 or •fishes)
wolf•hound
wolf•ish
wolf•ish•ly
wolf•ish•ness
wolf-whistle (vb)
wol•ver•ine
wolves pl of wolf
wom•an (pl •en)
wom•an•hood
wom•an•ish
wom•an•ize
wom•an•iz•er
wom•an•kind
wom•an•li•ness
wom•an•ly
womb
wom•bat
wom•en pl of
 woman
women•folk (or
 •folks)
won past tense of
 win; cf one
won•der
won•der•er
won•der•ful
won•der•ful•ly
wonder•land
won•der•ment
wonder-worker
wonder-working
 (adj)

won•drous
won•drous•ly
wont habit; *cf* want
won't will not
wont•ed
woo (woos,
  woo•ing, wooed)
wood timber; *cf*
  would
wood•bine (*or*
  •bind)
wood•borer
wood•carver
wood•carving
wood•chuck
wood•cock (*pl*
  •cocks *or* •cock)
wood•craft
wood•cut
wood•cutter
wood•cutting
wood•ed
wood•en
wooden•head
wood•en•ly
wood•en•ness
woodi•ness
wood•land
wood•land•er
wood•lark
wood•man (*pl*
  •men)
wood•pecker
wood•pile
wood•shed
  (•shed•ding,
  •shed•ded)
woods•man (*pl*
  •men)

wood•wind
wood•work
wood•worker
wood•working
wood•worm
woody (woodi•er,
  woodi•est)
wooed
woo•er
woof
woo•ing
wool
wool•en (*Brit*
  wool•len)
wool•gatherer
wool•gathering
wool•li•ness
wool•ly (*or* wooly;
  adj wool•li•er,
  wool•li•est *or*
  wooli•er,
  wooli•est; *n, pl*
  wool•lies *or*
  woolies)
woozi•ly
woozi•ness
woozy (woozi•er,
  woozi•est)
word
word-blind
word•book
wordi•ly
wordi•ness
word•ing
word•less
word•less•ly
word•less•ness
word-perfect (*Brit*
  letter-perfect

word•play
word•smith
wordy (wordi•er,
  wordi•est)
wore *past tense of*
  wear; *cf* war
work
work•abil•ity (*or*
  •able•ness)
work•able
work•aday
work•ahol•ic
work•bag
work•bench
work•book
work•box
work•day
work•er
work•fare
work•force
work•horse
work•house
work•ing
working-class (*adj*)
work•load
work•man (*pl*
  •men)
work•man•like (*or*
  •ly)
work•man•ship
work•mate
work•out
work•room
works
work•shop
work-shy
work•table
work-to-rule (*n*)
work•week

world
world-beater
world-class (*adj*)
world•li•ness
world•ling
world•ly (•li•er,
•li•est)
worldly-wise
world-shaking
world-weariness
world-weary
world•wide
worm
worm•cast
worm-eaten
worm•er
worm•hole
worm•seed
worm•wood
wormy (wormi•er,
wormi•est)
worn
worn-out
wor•ried•ly
wor•ri•er
wor•ri•ment
wor•ri•some
wor•ry (*vb* •ries,
•ry•ing, •ried; *n, pl*
•ries)
wor•ry•ing•ly
worse
wors•en
wor•ship (•ship•ing,
•shiped; *Brit*
•ship•ping,
•shipped)
wor•ship•er (*Brit*
•ship•per)

wor•ship•ful
wor•ship•ful•ly
wor•ship•ful•ness
worst most bad; *cf*
wurst
wor•sted fabric
worst•ed defeated
worth
wor•thi•ly
wor•thi•ness
worth•less
worth•less•ly
worth•less•ness
worth•while
wor•thy (*adj*
•thi•er, •thi•est; *n,
pl* •thies)
would auxiliary
verb; *cf* wood
would-be (*adj, n*)
wouldn't
wound
wound•able
wound•er
wound•ing•ly
wove
wo•ven
wow
wrack seaweed;
variant spelling of
rack (destruction)
wraith
wran•gle
wran•gler
wrap (wrap•ping,
wrapped) enfold;
garment; *cf* rap
wrap•around
wrapped covered,

enclosed, etc.; *cf*
rapped; rapt
wrap•per covering;
robe; *cf* rapper
wrap•ping
wrath
wrath•ful
wrath•ful•ly
wrath•ful•ness
wreak cause;
inflict; *cf* reek
wreak•er
wreath (*n, pl*
wreaths)
wreathe (*vb*)
wreck
wreck•age
wreck•er
wren
wrench
wrest seize; *cf* rest
wres•tle
wres•tler
wres•tling
wretch miserable
person; *cf* retch
wretch•ed
wretch•ed•ly
wretch•ed•ness
wri•er *variant
spelling of* wryer
wri•est *variant
spelling of* wryest
wrig•gle
wrig•gler
wrig•gly (•gli•er,
•gli•est)
wring (wring•ing,

wrung) squeeze; *cf*
ring
wring•er
wrin•kle
wrin•kly (•kli•er,
•kli•est)
wrist
wrist•band
wrist•watch
writ
writ•able
write (writ•ing,
wrote, writ•ten)
inscribe; *cf* right;
rite
write-off (*n*)
writ•er
write-up (*n*)
writhe
writ•ing
writ•ten
wrong
wrong•doer
wrong•doing
wrong-foot (*vb*)
wrong•ful
wrong•ful•ly
wrong•ful•ness
wrong-headed
wrong-headed•ly
wrong-headed•ness
wrong•ly
wrong•ness
wrote
wrought
wrung
wry (wry•er,
wry•est or wri•er,

wri•est) askew;
droll; *cf* rye
wry•ly
wry•neck
wry•ness
wun•der•kind (*pl*
•kinds *or* •kind•er)
wurst German
sausage; *cf* worst
wych elm (*or* witch
elm)
wych ha•zel *variant
spelling of* witch
hazel

X

x-axis (*pl* -axes)
X-chromosome
xe•non
xeno•phile
xeno•phobe
xeno•pho•bia
xeno•pho•bic
xc•rog•ra•phcr
xe•ro•graph•ic
xe•ro•graphi•cal•ly
xe•rog•ra•phy
Xer•ox (*Trade-
mark*)
xi (*pl* xis)
Xmas
X-radiation
X-rated
X-ray (*or* x-ray)
xy•lem
xy•lo•graph
xy•log•ra•phy

xy•lo•phone
xy•lopho•nist

Y

yacht
yacht•ing
yachts•man (*pl*
•men)
yachts•woman (*pl*
•women)
ya•hoo (*pl* •hoos)
yak animal
yak (*or* yack;
yak•king, yakked
or yack•ing,
yacked) chatter
yam
yam•mer
yam•mer•er
yang
yank
Yan•kee (*or* Yank)
yap (yap•ping,
yapped)
yap•per
yap•py
yard•age
yard•arm
yard•stick
yar•mul•ke (*or*
•mel•)
yarn
yar•row
yash•mak (*or* •mac)
yaup *variant
spelling of* yawp
yau•pon

yaw

yawl

yawn

yawn•er

yawn•ing•ly

yawp (*or* yaup)

yaws

y-axis (*pl* -axes)

Y-chromosome

yea

year

year•book

year•ling

year•long

year•ly

yearn

yearn•ing

yearn•ing•ly

year-round (*adj*)

yeast

yeasty (yeasti•er,
   yeasti•est)

yell

yell•er

yel•low

yellow-belly (*pl*
   -bellies)

yellow•hammer

yel•low•ish

yellow•legs

yellow•tail (*pl* •tail
   or •tails)

yellow•wood

yel•lowy

yelp

yelp•er

yen (yen•ning,
   yenned) longing;
   to yearn

yen (*pl* yen)
   Japanese currency

yeo•man (*pl* •men)

yer•ba

yes

ye•shi•va (*or* •vah;
   pl •vahs *or* •voth)

yes-man (*pl* -men)

yes•ter•day

yes•ter•year

yeti

yew tree; *cf* ewe;
   you

Yid•dish

yield

yield•er

yield•ing

yin

yip•pee

ylang-ylang (*or*
   ilang-ilang)

yo•del (•del•ing,
   •deled; *Brit*
   •del•ling, •delled)

yo•del•er (*Brit*
   •del•ler)

yoga

yo•ghurt *variant
   spelling of* yogurt

yogi (*or* yo•gin; *pl*
   yogis *or* •gins)

yo•gic

yo•gism

yo•gurt (*or* •ghurt)

yoke frame;
   burden; link; part
   of garment; *cf*
   yolk

yo•kel

yolk part of egg; *cf*
   yoke

yolky

Yom Kip•pur

yon•der

yoo-hoo

yore

you pronoun; *cf*
   ewe; yew

you'd

you'll you will; you
   shall; *cf* yule

young

young•berry (*pl*
   •berries)

young•ish

young•ster

your of you

you're you are

yours

your•self (*pl*
   •selves)

youth

youth•ful

youth•ful•ly

youth•ful•ness

you've

yowl

yo-yo (*pl* -yos)

yuc•ca

Yu•go•sla•vian

yuk (*or* yuck)

yuk•ky (*or* yucky)

yule Christmas; *cf*
   you'll

yule•tide

yum•my (•mi•er,
   •mi•est)

yup•pie (*or* •py)

Z

za•ba•glio•ne
Za•ïr•ian (or •ese)
Zam•bian
za•mia
za•ni•ly
za•ni•ness
zany (adj zani•er,
 zani•est; n, pl
 zanies)
zap (zap•ping,
 zapped)
Za•po•tec (pl •tecs
 or •tec)
zap•py (•pi•er,
 •pi•est)
z-axis (pl -axes)
zeal
zeal•ot
zeal•ot•ry
zeal•ous
zeal•ous•ly
zeal•ous•ness
ze•bra (pl •bras or
 •bra)
zebra•wood
zebu
zee (Brit zed)
Zeit•geist
Zen
ze•nith
zeph•yr
zep•pe•lin (or Zep•)
zero (n, pl zeros or
 zeroes; vb zeroes,
 ze•ro•ing, ze•roed)
zero-rated
ze•roth

zest
zest•ful
zest•ful•ly
zest•ful•ness
zesty
zeta
zig•gu•rat (or
 zik•ku•rat,
 ziku•rat)
zig•zag (•zag•ging,
 •zagged)
zig•zag•ger
zilch
zil•lion (pl •lions
 or •lion)
Zim•ba•bwe•an (or
 •bwi•)
zinc (zinc•ing,
 zinced or
 zinck•ing,
 zincked)
zin•fan•del
zing
zingy (zingi•er,
 zingi•est)
zin•nia
Zi•on•ism
Zi•on•ist
zip (zip•ping,
 zipped)
zip code (or ZIP
 code)
zip•per
zip•pered
zip•py (•pi•er,
 •pi•est)
zir•con
zir•co•nium
zit

zith•er
zith•er•ist
zlo•ty (pl •tys or
 •ty)
zo•di•ac
zo•dia•cal
zom•bie (or •bi; pl
 •bies or •bis)
zom•bi•ism
zon•al (or zona•ry)
zo•na•tion
zone
zone•time
zon•ing
zonked
zoo (pl zoos)
zoo•keeper
zoo•logi•cal
zo•olo•gist
zo•ol•ogy (pl
 •ogies)
zoom
zoo•mor•phic
zoo•mor•phism
zoo•plank•ton
zoo•spore
zoot suit
Zo•ro•as•trian
Zo•ro•as•tri•an•
 ism
zos•ter
zuc•chi•ni (pl •ni
 or •nis)
Zulu (pl Zulus or
 Zulu)
zwie•back
zy•gote

SPELLING RULES

Inflections

NOUNS

1 Regular plurals are formed by adding -s to the singular (**cat, cats**), or, for nouns ending in -s, -x, -z, -ch, or -sh, by adding -es (**pass, passes; branch, branches**).

2 Nouns ending in -y preceded by a vowel form their plurals by adding -s (**guy, guys**).
Nouns ending in -y preceded by a consonant change -y to -i before adding -es (**family, families**).
NB All proper nouns ending in -y simply add˝ -s (the **Kellys**).

3 Most nouns ending in -i form their plurals by adding -s (**rabbi, rabbis**).
NB A few nouns ending in -i can add either -s or -es (**taxi, taxis** or **taxies**).

4 Most nouns ending in -o form their plurals either by adding -s (**piano, pianos**) or by adding -es (**tomato, tomatoes**).

5 Most nouns ending in -f or -fe form their plurals by adding -s (**chief, chiefs; safe, safes**).

Some nouns ending in -f or -fe change -f or -fe to -v or -ve before adding -s (**calf, calves; knife, knives**).
NB A few nouns ending in f have two plural forms (**hoof, hooves** or **hoofs**).

6 Some nouns derived from foreign languages retain their foreign plural forms.

a Some Latin-derived nouns ending in -us change -us to -i (**alumnus, alumni**). A few Latin-derived nouns ending in -us can change -us to -era or have a regular plural (**genus, genera** or **genuses**).
Some Latin-derived nouns ending in -a change -a to -ae (**alga, algae**).
Some Latin-derived nouns ending in -um change -um to -a (**bacterium, bacteria**).
Some Latin-derived nouns ending in -ies have the same form in both singular and plural (**series, series**).

b Some Greek-derived nouns ending in -on can change -on to -a or have a regular plural (**criterion, criteria** or **criterions**).
Some Greek-derived nouns

ending in -*is* change -*is* to -*es* (**oasis, oases**).

c Some Italian-derived nouns ending in -*o* change -*o* to -*i* (**graffito, graffiti**)

7 A few nouns form their plurals by changing the middle vowel or vowels (**man, men; foot, feet**).

8 A few nouns, mostly names of animals, have the same form in both singular and plural (**sheep, sheep**).

Some such nouns have two plural forms (**fish, fish** or **fishes**).

9 In most compound nouns, it is the final element that is changed to form the plural (**drive-in, drive-ins**).

In some compound nouns, where the first element is a noun, the noun element is changed (**runner-up, runners-up**).

NB A few compound nouns have two plural forms (**spoonful, spoonfuls** or **spoonsful**).

10 A very small number of nouns form their plurals by adding -*en* or -*ren* (**ox, oxen; child, children**).

11 Letters, numerals, and sometimes abbreviations usually form their plurals

by adding -'*s* or -*s* (**the 1990's** or **the 1990s; I's**).

VERBS

1 In regular verbs, the third person singular of the present tense is formed by adding -*s* to the verb stem (**jump, jumps**) or, for verbs ending in -*s*, -*x*, -*z*, -*ch*, or -*sh*, by adding -*es* (**wish, wishes**).

The present participle is formed by adding -*ing* to the verb stem (**ask, asking**).

The present tense and past participle are formed by adding -*ed* to the verb stem (**pull, pulled**).

2 In verbs ending in -*e* preceded by a consonant, the -*e* is dropped before -*ing* or -*ed* is added (**hate, hating, hated**).

NB A few such verbs retain the -*e* before -*ing* to avoid confusion with similar words (**singe, singeing**).

3 In verbs ending in -*e* preceded by any vowel other than *i*, the -*e* is dropped before -*ed* is added but retained before -*ing* (**hoe, hoeing, hoed**)

4 Verbs ending in -*ie* form the present participle by changing -*ie* to -*y* before adding -*ing* (**die, dying**).

5 Verbs ending in -*y* preceded by a consonant form the third person singular of the present tense by changing -*y* to -*i* before adding -*es*, and the past tense and past participle by changing -*y* to -*i* before adding -*ed* (**worry, worries, worried**).

6 Verbs of one syllable ending in a consonant preceded by a single vowel form the present participle, past tense, and past participle by doubling the final consonant before adding -*ing* or -*ed* (**dip, dipping, dipped**).

NB A few such verbs can have either a single or a double consonant before -*ing* or -*ed* (**bus, busing** or **bussing, bused** or **bussed**).

7 In verbs of more than one syllable ending in a consonant preceded by a vowel, if the accent is on the final syllable, the final consonant is doubled before -*ing* or -*ed* is added (**refer, referring, referred**).

If the accent is on any syllable other than the final one, the final consonant is not doubled before -*ing* or -*ed* is added (**marvel, marveling, marveled**; **sadden, saddening, saddened**).

NB In British English, if the final consonant is -*l*, this consonant is doubled before adding -*ing* or -*ed* irrespective of which syllable is stressed (**travel, travelling, travelled**).

8 Verbs ending in -*c* usually add -*k* before -*ing* or -*ed* (**panic, panicking, panicked**).

ADJECTIVES

1 The comparative and superlative of most adjectives containing one or two syllables are formed by adding -*er* and -*est* respectively (**tight, tighter, tightest**).

2 Adjectives ending in -*e* drop the -*e* before adding -*er* or -*est* (**fine, finer, finest**).

3 Adjectives ending in -*y* preceded by a consonant form the comparative and superlative by changing -*y* to -*i* before adding -*er* or -*est* (**pretty, prettier, prettiest**).

4 Adjectives that contain one syllable ending in a consonant preceded by a single vowel form the comparative and superlative by doubling the final consonant before adding -*er* or -*est* (**big, bigger, biggest**).

5 Adjectives that contain three or more syllables are preceded by *more* and *most* to form the comparative and superlative (**beautiful, more beautiful, most beautiful**).

Suffixes

1 Words consisting of one syllable ending in a consonant preceded by a single vowel double the final consonant before a suffix, such as *-age* or *-er* (**bag, baggage**; **bat, batter**).

2 Words of more than one syllable ending in a consonant preceded by a single vowel usually double the final consonant before a suffix, such as *-er* or *-able*, if the accent is on the final syllable (**control, controller, controllable**).

NB There are some exceptions to this rule, especially where the addition of the suffix changes the accent to the first syllable (**preferable**).

3 Words ending in *-e* usually drop the *-e* before a suffix beginning with a vowel (**note, notable**).

NB There are some exceptions to this rule, especially words ending in *-ce* or *-ge* (**notice, noticeable**).

4 Words ending in *-e* usually retain the *-e* before a suffix beginning with a consonant (**pure, purely**; **arrange, arrangement**).

NB There are some exceptions to this rule (**true, truly**; **judge, judgment**).

5 Most words ending in *-y* change *-y* to *-i* before a suffix (**happy, happily, happiness**).

6 Words ending in *-y* preceded by a vowel usually retain the *-y* before a suffix (**joy, joyful, joyous**).

NB There are some exceptions to this rule (**gay, gaily, gaiety**).

Spelling Problems

1 Generally, the rule "i before e except after c" applies where the two letters combined are pronounced "ee" (**siege**; **receive**).

NB There are exceptions to this rule (**seize**).

2 Where these two letters combined are pronounced in any way other than "ee," the order is usually "ei" (**neighbor, height**).

NB There are exceptions to this rule (**friend, sieve**).

3 Most verbs whose final syllable is pronounced "seed"

are spelt -*cede* (**precede**).

NB Exceptions are **exceed**, **proceed**, **succeed**, and **supersede**.

4 In both British and American English -*ize* is preferred to the variant -*ise* for verbs (and their derivatives) ending in this suffix (**criticize**, **specialize**).

NB There are exceptions to this rule, including **advertise**, **advise**, **comprise**, **compromise**, **devise**, **improvise**, **supervise**, **surmise**, **televise**.

5 A few words that often cause spelling problems: a**cc**o**mm**odate, co**mm**emorate, co**mm**i**tt**ee, desi**cc**ate, ecstasy, emba**rr**a**ss**, ga**u**ge, ha**r**a**ss**, in**o**culate, mille**nn**ium, ne**c**e**ss**ary, separate, thre**sh**old, wi**thh**old

PUNCTUATION GUIDE

Period

A period is used:

1 at the end of a sentence that is neither a question nor an exclamation:

She went to school.

2 within or after some abbreviations:

M.D.
Calif.

3 after a person's initials:

O. J. Simpson
Franklin D. Roosevelt

Question mark

A question mark is used:

1 at the end of a question:

Is it raining?
"Are you sure?" he asked.

2 to indicate doubt.

Sitting Bull, ?1831–90
Next meeting July 8 at 10:30?
(to be confirmed)

Exclamation point

An exclamation point is used:

1 at the end of an exclamation:

Wow!
How gross!

2 at the end of a command:

Get out!

3 to indicate disagreement or disbelief:

They claim to make the best pizza in town (!).
He says he will pay me back (!).

Comma

A comma is used:

1 after a dependent clause that comes before a main clause:

When I got home, he was out.
Although I am older, she is taller.

2 after a phrase that comes before a statement:

In my opinion, this is her best movie yet.
Nevertheless, I still like him.

3 to mark off a nonrestrictive relative clause from the rest of a sentence:

The boy, who was hungry, asked for a cookie.

NB Commas are not used to punctuate restrictive relative clauses:

The boy who won the race was given a prize.

4 to mark off an explanatory or qualifying phrase from the rest of a sentence:

My sister, a teacher, is very fond of children.

5 to separate a series of short, related statements:
Boy meets girl, boy loses girl, boy finds girl again.
I laughed, I cried, I yelled.

6 to separate elements in a list or series:
I need milk, eggs, and bread.
He got up, showered, dressed, and had breakfast.

7 to separate two or more adjectives qualifying the same noun:
He is a cruel, arrogant man.
She was a precocious, independent child.

8 to mark off a name or other form of address from the rest of the sentence:
Hi, Bill, how are you?
Come on, kids, be quiet.

9 to mark off a related question added on after a statement:
You're John, aren't you?
He did look up, didn't he?

10 when quoting someone's exact words, to mark off these words from the rest of the sentence:
"I'm cold," she said.
He asked, "Is it raining?"

11 to separate the elements of a date or address:
The party is on Saturday, November 5.
They live at 77 Gilbert Road, Sayville, New York.

12 after the opening greeting in an informal letter and the closing greeting in any letter:
Dear Carlo,
Sincerely yours, Jane Green

13 to separate a last name and a first name or initials, for example in a list or catalog:
Heller, Joseph
Shaw, G. B.

14 to separate thousands and millions in large numbers:
17,123
5,000,000

Semicolon

A semicolon is used:

1 to separate phrases or clauses in a series or list:
Refer to the sections marked: Verbal test; Verbal analysis; and Guide to Spelling.
This leaflet introduces each part of the program; gives an idea of what to expect; provides hints on preparation.

2 to separate two short related statements:
I need money; therefore, I must find a job.
She goes out to work; he looks after the children.

Colon

A colon is used:

1 to introduce a piece of information, often a list or series:
Language: French. Currency: franc. Capital: Paris.
There were four Beatles: John, Paul, George, and Ringo.

2 to introduce a direct quotation or other material that forms a complete sentence:
A police spokesman said: "Sarah is no longer regarded by us as a missing person."

3 after the opening greeting in a formal letter:
Dear Sir or Madam:

4 to separate the title and subtitle of a book, movie, etc.:
Bird: The Legend of Charlie Parker
2001: A Space Odyssey

5 to express time or ratio:
Swimming class begins at 5:30.
The ratio of boys to girls is 3:1.

Parentheses

Parentheses are used:

1 to mark off an explanatory or qualifying phrase or sentence from the rest of a sentence or paragraph:
She was born way out west (in Montana).
Make sure you know how to get there (plan beforehand).

2 around numbers or letters in a list or series:
There are two types of fat: (1) saturated fats and (2) unsaturated fats.
Are you (a) married, (b) divorced or separated, (c) widowed, or (d) single?

Brackets

Brackets are used:

1 to mark off an explanatory word or phrase from the surrounding text, for example to indicate a word or phrase that is not a direct quotation within a direct quotation:
He [Mr. Nelson] intends to sue his former employers.

2 to enclose a piece of information, for example in a dictionary:
[from Old French]

Dashes

An en dash (short dash) is used:

to mean "to" in a range, for example of pages or dates:
For further information, see pages 55–58.
John Fitzgerald Kennedy (1917–63).

An em dash (medium-length dash) is used:

1 to mark off a digression or a piece of explanatory information from the rest of a sentence:

The boy said—and I believe him—that he didn't steal the money.

2 between a quotation and the name of its author or source:

"I have a dream."—Martin Luther King

A two-em dash (long dash) is used:

to represent a name or word, or part of a name or word:

My father was a farmer in —— County.

"Oh s——!" he said.

Apostrophe

An apostrophe is used:

1 to indicate possession:

Sue borrowed Maria's coat.
He is staying at his parents' home.

2 to indicate that part of a word or number is omitted:

He's my brother.
My daughter was born in '89.

3 to form the plural of letters, numerals, and (sometimes) abbreviations:

He was born in the 1950's.
Dot the i's and cross the t's.

Quotation marks

Double quotation marks are used:

1 when quoting someone's exact words, to mark these words off from the rest of a sentence:

"Come on," she said.
"Dad," said Mike, "can I borrow your car?"

2 to mark off the title of a song, short poem, article, short story, or chapter of a book from the rest of the sentence:

Frank Sinatra recorded "My Way" in 1969.

Single quotation marks are used:

to mark off a quotation when it occurs within double quotation marks:

"His exact words were 'I shall see you later,'" she said.